Letters from a Life:
The Selected Letters of Benjamin Britten 1913–1976

Previous volumes in this series, published by Faber and Faber Limited:

LETTERS FROM A LIFE:

THE SELECTED LETTERS AND DIARIES OF BENJAMIN BRITTEN
VOLUME ONE: 1923–1939

THE SELECTED LETTERS AND DIARIES OF BENJAMIN BRITTEN
VOLUME TWO: 1939–1945

THE SELECTED LETTERS OF BENJAMIN BRITTEN
VOLUME THREE: 1946–1951

EDITOR-IN-CHIEF: PHILIP REED
CO-ORDINATING EDITOR: JILL BURROWS

Letters from a Life: The Selected Letters of Benjamin Britten 1913–1976

VOLUME FOUR
1952–1957

EDITED BY
PHILIP REED
MERVYN COOKE
AND DONALD MITCHELL

THE BOYDELL PRESS
in association with
THE BRITTEN–PEARS FOUNDATION

© The Britten–Pears Foundation, 2008

All Rights Reserved. Except as permitted under current legislation
no part of this work may be photocopied, stored in a retrieval system,
published, performed in public, adapted, broadcast, transmitted,
recorded or reproduced in any form or by any means, without
the prior permission of the copyright owner.

First published 2008
The Boydell Press, Woodbridge
in association with
The Britten–Pears Foundation
ISBN 978-1-84383-382-6

The Boydell Press is an imprint of Boydell & Brewer Ltd
PO Box 9, Woodbridge, Suffolk IP12 3DF, UK
and of Boydell & Brewer inc.
668 Mt Hope Avenue, Rochester, NY 14620, USA
website: www.boydellandbrewer.com

The letters and all other writings by Benjamin Britten and by Peter Pears,
all quotations from Britten's unpublished music and reproductions of
the composer's original manuscripts, and all editorial matter and annotations
are © The Britten–Pears Foundation, 2008.

A catalogue record for this book is available
from the British Library.

This publication is printed on acid-free paper.

Phototypset by Agnesi Text, Hadleigh, Suffolk
Printed and bound in Great Britain by
CPI Antony Rowe Ltd, Chippenham, Wiltshire

To the memory of
Imogen Holst 1907–1984

CONTENTS

Index of Correspondents ix
List of Illustrations xi
Editorial Method xix
Acknowledgements xxi
Key to Bibliographical Abbreviations xxv

Introduction 1
Philip Reed

LETTERS

I   Fit for a Queen: The Writing of *Gloriana* 15
    January 1952–July 1953

II Absolute Singleness, Clearness and Roundness: *The Turn of the Screw* 169
    August 1953–September 1954

III On the Threshold of a New Musical World:
    Towards *The Prince of the Pagodas* 285
    October 1954–October 1955

IV As Complicated as Schoenberg: Eastern Encounters 339
    October 1955–March 1956

V   Beyond Bali: The Completion of *The Prince of the Pagodas* 431
    March 1956–January 1957

VI In the Naive Medieval Style: *Noye's Fludde* 491
    January–December 1957

Bibliography 587
Index of Britten's Works 601
Index of Other Composers 606
General Index 609

INDEX OF CORRESPONDENTS

ERNEST ANSERMET   *Letter* 862

LESLEY BEDFORD   726
GEORGE BEHREND   866
MARY BEHREND   781, 793
LENNOX BERKELEY   738, 752, 772, 809
JAMES BLADES   853
JOY BOWESMAN   796
HENRY BOYS   727
DENNIS BRAIN   885
OWEN BRANNIGAN   912
BENJAMIN BRITTEN *from Peter Pears*   757, 836

BASIL COLEMAN   723, 743, 744, 806, 829, 886, 899, 907
JOHN CRANKO   837
JOAN CROSS   808
ERIC CROZIER   736
from Jeremy Cullum   795

NORMAN DEL MAR   827, 889
CARL DOLMETSCH   785
BASIL DOUGLAS   846, 908
RALPH DOWNES   782
ROGER DUNCAN   815, 834, 840, 845, 848, 852, 855, 856, 857, 865, 901
RONALD DUNCAN   776, 832, 833, 838, 859, 871, 876, 887

NANCY EVANS   881

JAMES FISHER   888
E. M. FORSTER   778, 894

ANTHONY GISHFORD   724, 787, 824, 841, 843, 861, 870, 877, 878, 879, 891, 892

THE EARL OF HAREWOOD   731
JONATHAN HARVEY   864
TREVOR HARVEY   830

PRINCE LUDWIG OF HESSE AND THE RHINE 906
PRINCESS MARGARET OF HESSE AND THE RHINE 813, 817, 858, 902, 903, 904
from The Prince and Princess of Hesse and the Rhine 894
IMOGEN HOLST 739, 755, 842, 844, 849, 850, 854, 893

JOHN IRELAND 814

HANS KELLER 760
FRIEDRICH KREBS 900

JAMES LAWRIE 884

ELIZABETH MAYER 728, 777, 779, 883, 895 905, 911
TONY MAYER 788
YEHUDI MENUHIN 753
DONALD MITCHELL 760

PETER PEARS 756, 758, 762, 765, 766, 805, 872, 873, 874, 880, 890, 898
from Peter Pears 757, 817, 836, 842, 863, 894, 902, 903, 904
LESLIE PERITON 839
MYFANWY PIPER 784, 789, 791, 792, 794, 795, 797, 798, 800, 801, 802, 803, 807, 810, 812
WILLIAM PLOMER 729, 730, 733, 734, 735, 740, 742, 745, 747, 749, 750, 751, 754, 759, 763, 764, 767, 769, 774, 775, 790, 799, 820, 823, 828, 868, 897
MARY POTTER 847
FRANCIS POULENC 786, 811, 896

PAUL ROGERSON 737

PAUL SACHER 860
EDWARD SACKVILLE-WEST 819
DESMOND SHAWE-TAYLOR 822
EDITH SITWELL 818, 831, 835, 867, 875, 913
ERWIN STEIN 783, 826, 910

BARRY TILL 771
THE TIMES 863
MICHAEL TIPPETT 825

NINETTE DE VALOIS 851

DAVID WEBSTER 732, 746, 748, 761, 768, 770, 816, 869, 882
ERIC WALTER WHITE 741, 773, 780, 804, 821

GRETL ZANDER 725
OLIVE ZORIAN 909

LIST OF ILLUSTRATIONS

PLATE SECTION I
between pages 166 and 167

1 Benjamin Britten in his vintage Rolls-Royce, early 1950s
   Joan Cross Collection; courtesy of The Britten–Pears Library
2 Britten and Peter Pears in Canada, August 1957
   Photo Herb Nott & Co.; courtesy of The Britten–Pears Library
3 In the garden of Crag House, Aldeburgh: Imogen Holst, Pears, Sally and Sebastian Welford, Paul Rogerson, Maria Curcio, Britten and Roguey Welford
4 Britten with his miniature dachshunds, Clytie and Jove
5 Nellie Hudson, Britten's housekeeper, with her cat Bang
6 Jeremy Cullum, Britten's secretary and driver
7 London 1953: Lord Harewood, Erwin Stein and William Plomer
   Photo Roger Wood, © The Royal Opera House Collections
8 Ski-ing holiday at Gargellen, March 1952: Pears, the Harewoods and Britten
9 *Gloriana*, Royal Opera House, Covent Garden, May 1953: Britten and John Pritchard
   Photo Roger Wood, © The Royal Opera House Collections
10 *Gloriana*: piano rehearsal in the Crush Bar, with Pears (Earl of Essex), Basil Coleman and Joan Cross (Elizabeth I)
   Photo Roger Wood, © The Royal Opera House Collections
11 *Gloriana*: Elizabeth I (Joan Cross)
   Photo Helga Sharland; courtesy of the Britten–Pears Library
12 *Gloriana*, Act III scene 1: Essex (Peter Pears) and Elizabeth I (Joan Cross)
   Photo Helga Sharland; courtesy of The Britten–Pears Library
13 *Gloriana*, Act II scene 1: Queen Elizabeth's progress to Norwich – the masque presented in the sovereign's honour
   Photo Roger Wood, © The Royal Opera House Collections
14 *Gloriana*, Act I scene 1, 'Happy were he': Essex (Peter Pears sings his Second Lute Song to the Queen (Joan Cross)
   Photo Roger Wood, © The Royal Opera House Collections

15 *Gloriana*, Act II scene 3: Elizabeth I (Joan Cross) humiliates Lady Essex (Monica Sinclair)
   Photo Roger Wood, © The Royal Opera House Collections
16 *Gloriana*, Act III scene 3: Lady Essex (Monica Sinclair) pleads with the Queen (Joan Cross) for Essex's life
   Photo Roger Wood, © The Royal Opera House Collections
17 *The Turn of the Screw*, La Fenice, Venice, September 1954: Act I scene 5: the Governess (Jennifer Vyvyan) and Peter Quint (Peter Pears)
   Photo Denis de Marney © Getty Images
18 *The Turn of the Screw*, Act II scene 1, 'The ceremony of innocence is drowned': Quint (Peter Pears) and Miss Jessel (Arda Mandikian)
   Photo Herb Nott & Co.; courtesy of The Britten–Pears Library
19 *The Turn of the Screw*, Act II scene 2: Flora (Olive Dyer), Miles (David Hemmings), Mrs Grose (Joan Cross) and the Governess (Jennifer Vyvyan)
   Photo Denis de Marney © Getty Images
20 *The Turn of the Screw*, Act II scene 5: Quint (Peter Pears) and Miles (David Hemmings)
   Photo Denis de Marney © Getty Images
21 *The Turn of the Screw*, Act II scene 3: Miss Jessel (Arda Mandikian) and the Governess (Jennifer Vyvyan)
   Photo Denis de Marney © Getty Images
22 *The Turn of the Screw*, Act II scene 8: Miles (David Hemmings) and the Governess (Jennifer Vyvyan)
   Photo Henk Jonker © MAI
23 La Fenice, Venice, 14 September 1954, curtain call after the premiere of *The Turn of the Screw*: David Hemmings (Miles), Jennifer Vyvyan (Governess), Benjamin Britten, Myfanwy Piper and Basil Coleman
   Photo Erich Auerbach © Getty Images
24 Street picnic in Venice during rehearsals for *The Turn of the Screw*: John Piper, Benjamin Britten, Peter Pears, Myfanwy Piper, and Edward and Clarissa Piper
   Photo Erich Auerbach © Getty Images
25 Venetian gondola ride: Erwin Stein, Benjamin Britten, Sophie Stein, Basil Coleman and Peter Pears

PLATE SECTION II
between pages 358 and 359

26 Benjamin Britten, Ronald Duncan and Peter Pears on their way to Aldeburgh's public tennis courts
   Photo Kurt Hutton; courtesy of The Britten–Pears Library
27 Britten marking out the grass tennis court at the Red House, Aldeburgh
   Joan Cross Collection; courtesy of The Britten–Pears Library
28 The Red House, 1950s. Britten, partnered by Mary Potter, playing tennis
29 Journey East, 1955–56: Peter Pears and Benjamin Britten

LIST OF ILLUSTRATIONS xiii

30 20 January 1956, Ubud, Bali: Peter Pears, the Hesses and Benjamin Britten in traditional Balinese costume
31 Benjamin Britten in Tenganan, a village in the hills to the east of Bali
32 Bali, 1956: a young girl is given a dancing lesson to the accompaniment of the gamelan
33 Benjamin Britten playing the *shō*, with encouragement from Kei-ichi Kurosawa, Tokyo, February 1956
    Courtesy of Hiroshi (Peter) Kurosawa
34 8 February 1956, Tokyo: Peter Pears and Benjamin Britten arrive in Japan
35 Prince Ludwig of Hesse and the Rhine and Peter Pears mimic the playing of Japanese drums, using wastepaper baskets
36 Peter Pears and Benjamin Britten join the Tokyo Madrigal Singers, conducted by Kei-ichi Kurosawa
    Courtesy of Hiroshi (Peter) Kurosawa
37 Benjamin Britten playing the piano for a televised recital for NHK
    Photo Nippon Hoso Kyokai; courtesy of The Britten–Pears Library
38 Peter Pears performing for the NHK televised recital
    Photo Nippon Hoso Kyokai; courtesy of The Britten–Pears Library
39 The Artistic Directors of the 1956 Aldeburgh Festival – Imogen Holst, Benjamin Britten and Peter Pears – meet in the garden of Crag House
    Photo Kurt Hutton; courtesy of The Britten–Pears Library
40 A meeting of the Aldeburgh Music Club at Crag House: the recorder quartet of Julian Potter, Imogen Holst, Benjamin Britten and Mary Potter
41 Britten rehearsing for an Aldeburgh Festival concert with Imogen Holst turning the pages
    Photo Ian Graham; courtesy of The Britten–Pears Library
42 Imogen Holst and Basil Douglas
    Photo Kurt Hutton; courtesy of The Britten–Pears Library
43 Noel Mewton-Wood
44 Dennis Brain
45 Birmingham, 22 January 1952: Peter Pears, Kathleen Ferrier and Benjamin Britten on a tour in aid of the English Opera Group
    Photo Birmingham Evening Despatch; courtesy of The Britten–Pears Library
46 Benjamin Britten in rehearsal
    Photo Hans Wild; courtesy of The Britten–Pears Library
47 Julian Bream and Peter Pears, mid-1950s
    Photo Lotte Meitner-Graf; courtesy of The Britten–Pears Library
48 Benjamin Britten and Francis Poulenc
49 Royal Opera House, Covent Garden, January 1957, *The Prince of the Pagodas*, Act II, scene 2: the appearance of the Prince (David Blair) as a salamander
    Photo Snowdon, © Camera Press, London
50 John Cranko
    Photo Robert Belton, © Fact Photograph

51 *The Prince of the Pagodas*, Act II scene 2: the Prince (David Blair) and Belle Rose (Svetlana Beriosova)
   Photo Snowdon, © Camera Press, London
52 David Webster
53 Roger Duncan, a snapshot probably taken by Benjamin Britten
54 Roger Duncan and Benjamin Britten, *c.* 1955
55 Paul Rogerson on Aldeburgh beach
56 David Hemmings and Clytie, Aldeburgh, August 1954
57 Benjamin Britten and David Hemmings playing marbles, Aldeburgh, August 1954
   Joan Cross Collection, The Britten–Pears Library

ILLUSTRATIONS IN THE TEXT

page 16 Britten to William Plomer, 21 January 1953: Letter 759
   © The Britten–Pears Foundation; courtesy of Durham University Library and Duff Hart-Davis
20 Cartoon by David Low, *Manchester Guardian*, 2 June 1953
25 *Canticle II: 'Abraham and Isaac'*: the opening page of Britten's composition draft; BL Add. MS. 60601
   © Boosey & Hawkes, used by courtesy of The British Library and The Britten–Pears Library
26–7 Britten's annotated copy of the Chester miracle play *Histories of Lot and Abraham*, from Pollard's edition of *English Miracle Plays, Moralities and Interludes*, showing the composer's adaptation of the text for his setting of *Canticle II*
40 Programme for a performance of Schubert's song-cycle *Die schöne Müllerin*, Victoria & Albert Museum, London, 17 February 1952
51 The duet for Marcus and Rose from Plomer's libretto for *Tyco the Vegan*, in the librettist's hand
   Courtesy of Duff Hart-Davis
59 A note in Lord Harewood's hand showing his lineage traced from Robert Devereux, 2nd Earl of Essex
   Courtesy of Lord Harewood
61 An early draft cast list for *Gloriana* from a back page in Britten's 1952 diary
   © The Britten–Pears Foundation
65 Programme for the Covent Garden Opera Company's production of *Billy Budd*, Paris, May 1952
75 Programme for a recital at Copenhagen's Tivoli Gardens, 3 July 1952
77 Programme for a recital at the Aix-en-Provence Festival, 24 July 1952
79 Britten's draft scenario for *Gloriana*, early July 1952
   © The Britten–Pears Foundation
80 The opening of Essex's Second Lute Song, 'Happy were he', from Act I scene 2 of *Gloriana*, in Britten's composition draft
   © Boosey & Hawkes; courtesy of The Britten–Pears Library

LIST OF ILLUSTRATIONS

84–5 Two pages from William Plomer's first draft libretto of *Gloriana*, Act I scene 2, with annotations, revisions and corrections by Plomer and Britten
© Boosey & Hawkes; courtesy of The Britten–Pears Library and Duff Hart-Davis

89 Programme for a recital at St Matthew's, Northampton, 27 September 1952

105 Programme for a recital by Peter Pears and Noel Mewton-Wood, King's Lynn, 28 November 1952

107 Programme note from the 1953 Aldeburgh Festival Programme Book for the first performance of *Variations on an Elizabethan Theme*

127 Advertisement for the 'concert reading' of Lennox Berkeley's *Nelson*, Wigmore Hall, London, 14 February 1953

146 Oliver Messel's decorative front and back programme covers for the Gala premiere of *Gloriana*, Royal Opera House, Covent Garden, London, 8 June 1953

148–9 Programme for the Gala premiere of *Gloriana*, Royal Opera House, Covent Garden, London, 8 June 1953

162 Programme for the sixth of a series of eight concerts marking the Coronation, presented at the Royal Festival Hall, London, 3 June 1953

167 Cover of the *Gloriana* vocal score, designed by John Piper
© Boosey & Hawkes; courtesy of Clarissa Lewis

167 Advertisement for the first edition of the vocal score of *Gloriana*

170 Britten to Myfanwy Piper, 1 August 1954: Letter 812
© The Britten–Pears Foundation; courtesy of Clarissa Lewis

183 Programme for the first performance of *Winter Words*, on this occasion entitled 'Hardy Songs', Harewood House, Leeds, 8 October 1953

184 Britten's list of possible poems for *Winter Words*, drawn up by the composer in the back of his copy of Hardy's *Collected Poems*

185 Britten's composition draft of 'Proud Songsters', the sixth song from *Winter Words*, composed 5 September 1953
© Boosey & Hawkes; courtesy of The Britten–Pears Foundation

191 Mary Potter's lithograph for 'June', 1954 Aldeburgh Festival calendar
Courtesy of Julian Potter

205 Britten's handwritten list of characters for *The Turn of the Screw*, which he inscribed in his copy of Henry James's novella

208 Kennedy's *Shorter Latin Primer*, with a list of nouns marked by Britten, for Miles in Act I scene 6 of *The Turn of the Screw*

215 The second, canonic version of *Am Stram Gram* sent by Britten to Tony Mayer, 31 January 1954, for André Roussin's 'comédie-farce'

222 Myfanwy Piper's anotated copy of the audition list of children for *The Turn of the Screw*, 12 December 1953

225 Britten's earliest version of Miles's 'Malo' song for David Hemmings to try out, composed March 1954; BL Add. MS. 60602
© Boosey & Hawkes, used by courtesy of The British Library and The Britten–Pears Library

229 Programme for a Pears–Britten recital at Dorchester, 10 February 1954
231 A page of Britten's sketches for *The Turn of the Screw* showing his working out of the twelve-note theme on which the sequence of variation-interludes is based. BL Add. MS. 60602
© Boosey & Hawkes, used by courtesy of The British Library and The Britten–Pears Library
250 Britten's working copy of the draft libretto for *The Turn of the Screw*, Act II scene 1, 'Colloquy and Soliloquy'
© Boosey & Hawkes; courtesy of The Britten–Pears Library
253 Leaflet publicizing the proposed Aldeburgh Festival Theatre, 1954
255 Programme for an English Opera Group concert at York, 3 July 1954
259 A page from John Cranko's draft scenario for *The Prince of the Pagodas*, entitled 'General Shape The Green Serpent'
262–3 The opening of the discarded version of the Prologue from the composition draft of *The Turn of the Screw*, BL Add. MS. 60602
© Boosey & Hawkes, used by courtesy of The British Library and The Britten–Pears Library
273 La Fenice, Venice, 14 September 1954: the programme book for the first performance of *The Turn of the Screw*
286 Britten to Basil Coleman, 3 February 1955: Letter 829
© The Britten–Pears Foundation; courtesy of Basil Coleman
292–3 Britten's fair-copy manuscript of *Canticle III*: variation v and verse vi
© Boosey & Hawkes; courtesy of The Britten–Pears Library
295 Programme for Lord Harewood's introductory talk on *The Turn of the Screw*, Wigmore Hall, London, 30 September 1954
297 Advertisement for the English Opera Group's 1954 London season
317 Programme for the memorial concert for Noel Mewton-Wood, Wigmore Hall, London, 4 December 1954
325 Britten's new ending for 'Calypso', revised in May 1955 for the *Punch Revue*
© Faber Music; courtesy of The Britten–Pears Library
340 Britten to Imogen Holst, 17 January 1956: Letter 850
© The Britten–Pears Foundation
344 Pears's expenses notebook for the world trip: opening entry
© The Britten–Pears Foundation
355 Pears's expenses notebook: Belgrade and Istanbul entries
© The Britten–Pears Foundation
358 Programme for a Pears–Britten recital at Maribor, 22 November 1955
362–5 Britten's fair copy of *Timpani Piece for Jimmy*, composed 8/9 December 1955, Istanbul
© Boosey & Hawkes; courtesy of The Britten–Pears Library
412 Cards accompanying bouquets of flowers for Britten and Pears, following their concert with the NHK Orchestra, Tokyo, 18 February 1956
415 Kei-ichi Kurosawa's instructions to Britten on how to play the *shō*
419 The programme for the performance of *Sumidagawa* Britten attended on 19 February 1956

LIST OF ILLUSTRATIONS   xvii

- 428 Invitation to the final recital of the world tour, Madras, 11 March 1956
- 432 Britten to Peter Pears, 4 December 1956: Letter 880
- 442–3 'The Pagodas revolve like merry-go-rounds': Britten's evocation of Balinese gamelan in Act II scene 2 of *The Prince of the Pagodas*, in the composition draft
  © Boosey & Hawkes; courtesy of The Britten–Pears Library
- 451 Britten's composition draft of his arrangement of the folk song 'The Shooting of his Dear', for voice and guitar
  © Boosey & Hawkes; courtesy of The Britten–Pears Library
- 460 Programme for *The Heart of the Matter*, Aldeburgh Parish Church, 21 June 1956
- 463 The pedigree certificate for Clytie II
- 480–81 Programme for the first performance of *The Prince of the Pagodas*, Royal Opera House, Covent Garden, London, 1 January 1957
- 492 Britten to Elizabeth Mayer, 13 January 1957: Letter 883
  © The Britten–Pears Foundation
- 530 Britten's copy of the vocal of Poulenc's *Les Mamelles de Tirésias*, annotated by Britten to correspond to the second piano part
- 563 Britten's annotated copy of the Chester miracle play *Noah's Flood*
- 576 Britten's composition draft of 'The Herd-Boy' from *Songs from the Chinese*
  © Boosey & Hawkes; courtesy of The Britten–Pears Library
- 582 Mary Potter's woodblock illustration of the Red House used by Britten and Pears as their 1957 Christmas card
  Courtesy of Julian Potter
- 585 The final page of Britten's composition draft of *Noye's Fludde*
  © Boosey & Hawkes; courtesy of The Britten–Pears Library

end papers
Bali, 1956: dancing lesson to gamelan accompaniment

EDITORIAL METHOD

THE TEXTS OF THE LETTERS

Britten's spelling, as he was himself aware, could be uncertain. Throughout the text that follows there are examples of him questioning himself, even when he had a spelling correct; these self-doubts we reproduce as they appear in his letters. However, we have silently corrected the majority of his mistakes; it seemed needlessly pedantic and distracting not only to reproduce every one of his errors but also to identify it as such, lest, as could all too easily be the case, the mistake might be read as a printing error. We have occasionally retained a mis-spelling but only when it adds something to the character and flavour of what Britten was writing or provokes a smile. (We have found nothing to match the classic entry in one of Britten's diaries when he refers to a 'Bach sweet'.) Likewise, in the case of his sometimes idiosyncratic punctuation, we have adjusted it in order to clarify his intended meaning. While generally more reliable than Britten's, Pears's spelling and punctuation have received similar editorial attention in this volume. In Britten's and Pears's letters, the writers' use of ampersands, 's'-spellings (e.g. 'realise' rather than 'realize') and underscoring have been retained; deletions of text are shown only when meaningful. In letters and documents by other hands, obvious mistakes have been silently corrected and the presentation of the text conforms to current publishing practice.

In the case of one correspondent, we have acceded to the recipient's request that his letters from the composer should not be published in their entirety. The omissions in these letters are indicated using the [. . .] convention.

FORMAT

The diverse layout of addresses in the original letters has been rationalized, and small capitals employed to indicate a printed letterhead. Dates appear in the format given in the original document. Where addresses or dates have been conjectured, this information appears within square brackets, as does editorial information about the medium of communication, e.g. postcard or telegram. We indicate where letters are typed (as distinct from handwritten) and where handwritten interpolations have been made; typed file copies and carbon copies of typed letters are also indicated. All postscripts are placed after the signature, although Britten, having finished the main text of a letter, would often add an afterthought at the top of the first page, above the date and address (see, for example, p. 492).

Opus numbers for Britten's works are not used in the annotations but are included in the Index of Britten's Works (pp. 601–5). Full bibliographical information for published material cited in the annotations is included in the Bibliography (pp. 587–98).

The abbreviation IC1/2/3 refers to the Index of Correspondents for volumes 1, 2 and 3.

ACKNOWLEDGEMENTS

We owe a special debt to The Britten–Pears Foundation, owner of the copyright in Benjamin Britten's letters, diaries and other writings, and his unpublished music, and in the copyright in Peter Pears's letters and other writings. We thank the Trustees of the Britten–Pears Foundation and the Directors of the Britten Estate Limited for their continued support of *Letters from a Life*.

We are grateful to the Arts and Humanities Research Council (AHRC) for funding a period of research leave for Mervyn Cooke devoted to the project.

We warmly acknowledge the following individuals and institutions for their invaluable co-operation in placing at our disposal their correspondence from Benjamin Britten and Peter Pears: the late Sir Lennox Berkeley; the late James Blades; Boosey & Hawkes Music Publishers Ltd (Leslie Boosey; Anthony Gishford); Joy Bowesman; the late Henry Boys; The Britten–Pears Library, Aldeburgh (George Behrend, Mary Behrend, the Britten–Pears correspondence, John Barbirolli, T. C. Bean, Dennis Brain, Owen Brannigan, John Cranko, Carl Dolmetsch, Roger Duncan, James Fisher, Boris Ford, Anthony Gishford, Friedrich Krebs, James Lawrie, Frank Lee, Elizabeth Mayer, G. F. Mitchell; Trinity College, Dublin; Ursula Nettleship, Lady Salisbury, Neil Saunders, Michael Tippett, Olive Zorian); the late Barbara Britten; Basil Coleman; the late Eric Crozier; the late Norman Del Mar; the late Peter Diamand; the late Ralph Downes; the late Basil Douglas; the late Ronald Duncan; Durham University Library (William Plomer Archive); the late Nancy Evans; Geneva Conservatoire (Ernest Ansermet); the late Sir Reginald Goodall; The Earl of Harewood; Professor Jonathan Harvey; the late Trevor Harvey; the Hessisches Staatsarchiv, Darmstadt (Prince and Princess of Hesse and the Rhine); the late Imogen Holst; The Humanities Research Centre, Texas (Edith Sitwell); the late Hans Keller; the Library of King's College, Cambridge (E. M. Forster); the late Tony Mayer; the late Lord Menuhin; Paul Sacher Stiftung, Basel (Paul Sacher); the late Leslie Periton; the late John Piper; the late Myfanwny Piper; Julian Potter (Mary Potter); the late Alec Robertson; Paul Rogerson; Royal Opera House Collections (Ninette de Valois; David Webster); the late

Humphrey Searle; Mme Rosine Seringe (Francis Poulenc); the late Desmond Shawe-Taylor; Rosamund Strode; Marion Thorpe (Erwin Stein); Barry Till; the late Patrick Trevor-Roper (Edward Sackville-West); the late Eric Walter White; and Benjamin Zander (Gretl and Walter Zander). The names of the correspondents are listed on pp. ix–x.

We acknowledge with pleasure the co-operation of all the staff (past and present) of the Britten–Pears Library, Aldeburgh, but especially Dr Christopher Grogan (Librarian), Dr Andrew Plant, Dr Nicholas Clark and Jude Brimmer. Particular thanks are owed to Pamela Wheeler and Anne Surfling for their meticulous checking of the texts of all letters and other quoted matter. To one member of the team at the Red House – Andrew Plant – we extend a special vote of thanks for his indefatigable assistance and encouragement.

Our publishers Boydell & Brewer have rendered invaluable support throughout the preparation of this volume and we are pleased to thank Peter Clifford, Michael Richards and Mike Webb. Readers of *Letters from a Life* will recall that earlier volumes in the series were published by Faber and Faber, and we salute Belinda Matthews and her colleagues for their continued interest in the project.

We are especially pleased to acknowledge the following copyright holders of previously unpublished letters to Britten, Pears and others included in our annotations; we are grateful for their generous collaboration: Boosey & Hawkes Ltd (Anthony Gishford; Ernst Roth); The Britten–Pears Foundation (Joan Cross); Jonathan Del Mar (Norman Del Mar); Roger Duncan; Muki Fairchild (Elizabeth Mayer); The Earl of Harewood; Duff Hart-Davis (William Plomer); David Higham Associates (Boris Ford; Edith Sitwell); G. & I. Holst Ltd, © The Estate of Imogen Holst (Imogen Holst); Clarissa Lewis (Myfanwy Piper); Marina Mahler (Alma Mahler-Werfel); Gerard Menuhin (Yehudi Menuhin); Donald Mitchell (Ann Instone and Julian Herbage); Royal Opera House Collections (Ninette de Valois; David Webster); Mme Rosine Seringe (Francis Poulenc); Marion Thorpe (Erwin Stein), and Miranda Weston-Smith (Ronald Duncan).

The extracts from Imogen Holst's diary (1952–54) are reprinted by kind permission of G. & I. Holst Ltd and are © The Estate of Imogen Holst. The extracts from *Ausflug Ost*, Prince Ludwig of Hesse and the Rhine's privately published diary, translated by Richard Stokes, are © The Britten–Pears Foundation and appear by kind permission.

Copyright material from the following newspapers, journals and magazines has been reproduced with permission: *Birmingham Post*; *Daily Express*; *Daily Mail*; *Daily Telegraph*; *Evening Standard*; *Guardian*; *Manchester Guardian*; *Manchester Guardian Weekly*; *Musical Times*; *News Chronicle*; *New Statesman and Nation*; *New York Herald Tribune*; *New York Times*; *Nottingham Guardian*; *Opera*; *Observer*; *Spectator*; *The Sunday Times*; *The Times*, and *Yorkshire Post*.

Publication details of copyright material from published sources may be found in the Bibliography, pp. 587–98.

The details of all photographic credits and copyrights are given in the List of Illustrations, pp. xi–xvii, along with all copyright acknowledgements for printed and manuscript music reproduced here.

Every reasonable effort to trace copyright owners has been made. We would be pleased to hear from those whom we have been unable to locate or have inadvertently omitted, to whom we extend our apologies.

PR, MC, DM
March 2008

Arts & Humanities Research Council

The AHRC funds postgraduate training and research in the arts and humanities, from archaeology and English literature to design and dance. The quality and range of research supported not only provides social and cultural benefits but also contributes to the economic success of the UK. For further information on the AHRC, please visit www.ahrc.ac.uk.

KEY TO BIBLIOGRAPHICAL ABBREVIATIONS

BBMCPR	Mervyn Cooke and Philip Reed, *Benjamin Britten: 'Billy Budd'*
CHPP	Christopher Headington, *Peter Pears: A Biography*
CPBC	Christopher Palmer (ed.), *The Britten Companion*
DHOBB	David Herbert (ed.), *The Operas of Benjamin Britten*
DMCN	Donald Mitchell, *Cradles of the New: Writings on Music 1951–1991*, selected by Christopher Palmer, edited by Mervyn Cooke
DMDV	Donald Mitchell (comp. and ed.), *Benjamin Britten: 'Death in Venice'*
DMHK	Donald Mitchell and Hans Keller (eds.), *Benjamin Britten: A Commentary on His Works from a Group of Specialists*
EWW	Eric Walter White, *Benjamin Britten: His Life and Operas*, 2nd edn, edited by John Evans
HCBB	Humphrey Carpenter, *Benjamin Britten*
IHD	Imogen Holst, 'Aldeburgh Diary 1952–54', in Christopher Grogan (ed.), *Imogen Holst: A Life in Music*, pp. 129–91
JBBC	John Bridcut, *Britten's Children*
LHAO	Prince Ludwig of Hesse and the Rhine, *Ausflug Ost*
MCBFE	Mervyn Cooke, *Britten and the Far East*
MCCCBB	Mervyn Cooke (ed.), *The Cambridge Companion to Benjamin Britten*
MKBMM	Michael Kennedy, *Britten*
PBBG	Paul Banks (ed.), *Britten's 'Gloriana': Essays and Sources*
PBCPW	Paul Banks (comp. and ed.), *Benjamin Britten: A Catalogue of Published Works*
PFL	Donald Mitchell and John Evans, *Pictures from a Life: Benjamin Britten 1913–1976*
PHTS	Patricia Howard (ed.), *Benjamin Britten: 'The Turn of the Screw'*
PKBM	Paul Kildea (ed.), *Britten on Music*
PKSB	Paul Kildea, *Selling Britten: Music and the Market Place*
PPT	Marion Thorpe (ed.), *Peter Pears: A Tribute on his 75th Birthday*

PRIM	Philip Reed, *The Incidental Music of Benjamin Britten: A Study and Catalogue of His Music for Film, Theatre and Radio*
PROMB	Philip Reed (ed.), *On Mahler and Britten*
PRPP	Philip Reed (ed.), *The Travel Diaries of Peter Pears 1936–1978*
RDWB	Ronald Duncan, *Working with Britten: A Personal Memoir*
TBB	Anthony Gishford (ed.), *Tribute to Benjamin Britten on His Fiftieth Birthday*
WRMC	Mervyn Cooke, *Benjamin Britten: 'War Requiem'*

The abbreviation BPL is used to indicate the Britten–Pears Library, Aldeburgh, and its collections of printed and manuscript music, books, art and ephemera. Details of the work of the Britten–Pears Library may be accessed on the website www.brittenpears.org

INTRODUCTION

Philip Reed

With the fourth volume of *Letters from a Life: The Selected Letters of Benjamin Britten*, we reach not only the mid-point of the series but also the central decade of Britten's creative life. As in earlier volumes of the series, the pattern of the composer's creative output has been mirrored in the structure of the book. Therefore the present volume, which spans the years 1952–57, has been subdivided into six parts, each of which has a central musical focus: the Coronation opera *Gloriana*, first performed in 1953, the year Britten turned forty; *The Turn of the Screw*, based on Henry James's celebrated novella; the full-length ballet, *The Prince of the Pagodas*; the trip to the Far East Britten and Pears made during the winter of 1955–56; the completion of *Pagodas* and its premiere, and, finally, the setting of the Chester miracle play *Noye's Fludde*.

From the correspondence with his librettists during this period, William Plomer (*Gloriana*) and Myfanwy Piper (*The Turn of the Screw*), emerges an extraordinarily vivid picture of exactly how Britten functioned as an opera composer. No less significant in this context are the composer's letters to Basil Coleman, the director responsible for the first productions of these operas. The writing and staging of Britten's earlier operas was a notable topic of volumes 2 and 3 of *Letters from a Life*; but Plomer's and Piper's geographical remoteness from the composer – Plomer resided in Sussex, Myfanwy Piper in rural Oxfordshire – has resulted in an extensive and richly detailed sequence of letters charting the progress of their respective operas. The surviving correspondence with Britten's earlier librettists – W. H. Auden (*Paul Bunyan*), Montagu Slater (*Peter Grimes*), Ronald Duncan (*The Rape of Lucretia*), Eric Crozier (*Albert Herring, The Little Sweep, Billy Budd*) and E. M. Forster (*Billy Budd*) – reveals far less of the minutiae of creative exchange that we find in the correspondence with Plomer and Piper.[1] Indeed, it would not be too great an exaggeration to draw a comparison here (though it is one Britten himself would have loathed) with Verdi's

---

1 Comparable exchange between Britten and his previous librettists would most certainly have taken place: either many letters have not survived, or the dialogue was conducted by other means. For example, when Crozier was writing the libretto of *Albert Herring*, Britten kept him close at hand: see Letter 538 n. 5.

correspondence with Arrigo Boito, the librettist of *Otello* and *Falstaff*.[2] Like Verdi before him, Britten is revealed in his letters to Plomer and Piper to be testing his librettists' words against his own musical and dramaturgical demands, suggesting revisions, often ruthlessly tightening passages, and occasionally offering his own solutions for their approval. It remains a curious fact that some of the most memorable phrases in Britten's operas use words fashioned by the composer rather than his librettist.

With *Gloriana* and *The Turn of the Screw*, both Plomer and Piper were embarking on new creative journeys; neither had previously written librettos (it remains a very distinct and difficult genre), and the correspondence discloses the value they placed on Britten's support, patience, and clear and practical advice (see, for example, Piper to Britten following a complete play-through of *The Turn of the Screw*, Letter 812 n. 3). Their inexperience as librettists may actually have made them more attractive to Britten as collaborators, and it is noteworthy that, unlike all of his previous librettists (with the exception of Ronald Duncan), Britten was to maintain close professional and personal links with them both. Plomer and Piper went on to write further texts for the composer: Plomer the three Church Parables in the 1960s, and Piper *Owen Wingrave* (Britten's second Jamesian opera) and *Death in Venice*.[3] The somewhat hesitant trajectory of Plomer's career as librettist, which began in volume 3 with *The Tale of Mr Tod*, the aborted 1951 children's opera after Beatrix Potter, continues in the present volume with *Gloriana* and at least two further projects for children, *Tyco the Vegan* (1952) and an opera based on Greek myth (1954), both of which were abandoned. The congenial working relationship between Britten and Plomer was cemented by their collaboration on *Gloriana*: 'reasonable & skilful' was how the composer described his librettist to Basil Coleman at an early stage in their work on the text for *Gloriana* (Letter 743); 'so easy to work with, & always stimulating' was his later assessment when writing to Elizabeth Mayer (Letter 777). Despite the critical drubbing the opera received – one might argue that the impossible circumstances of its premiere, a gala performance before the newly crowned Queen, the royal families of Europe, members of the diplomatic corps and assorted politicians, doomed it to critical failure from the outset – Britten himself was delighted with Plomer's contribution: 'I've loved working with you [. . .] you've produced a most wonderful libretto [. . .] it is impossible for me adequately to express my gratitude' (Letter 774). But for his ambivalent attitude towards Henry James's novella, Plomer would surely have been an obvious candidate as librettist of *The Turn of the Screw*. At the close of the present volume, it is

2   Marcello Conati and Mario Medici (eds.), *The Verdi–Boito Correspondence*, English-language edition prepared by William Weaver (Chicago: University of Chicago Press, 1994).
3   In addition, Myfanwy Piper provided a 'Prologue' for *A Midsummer Night's Dream* in 1959, which remained unset except for a four-bar sketch: see MCCCBB, pp. 135–6. At Britten's request, Plomer advised Colin Graham in the mid-1960s about the latter's libretto for *Anna Karenina*, after Tolstoy's novel: see Colin Graham, 'Staging First Productions 3', in DHOBB, pp. 51–3. It was a project the composer eventually abandoned.

with Plomer that Britten is soon to embark on a fresh collaboration, prompted by the composer's encounter with Japanese Nō theatre in Tokyo in 1956: a musical adaptation of *Sumidagawa*, the realization of which would be refined and revised over several years, and despite several postponements, until it emerged in 1964 as *Curlew River*, the first of the Church Parables.

As Britten was to discover, the compositional processes involved in the writing of a ballet were of an altogether different magnitude from those required for writing operas; with the three-act ballet *The Prince of the Pagodas*, the first evening-length score commissioned by the Sadler's Wells Ballet, Britten found himself in distinctly uncharted territory. The collaboration between the composer and the choreographer John Cranko was of a very different order from that experienced by Britten while working with Plomer or Piper. Having devised his scenario and provided the composer with a list of individual dances indicating their approximate durations, Cranko would appear to have more or less abandoned Britten to his own devices. One wonders if the situation Britten found himself in – i.e. with Cranko's 'shooting script' (the choreographer's term obviously borrowed from cinema) – did not bring to mind his days, twenty years earlier, writing music to the stopwatch for the documentary film movement. Certainly, this document acted as a valuable stimulus to the composer. There were, of course, occasional meetings and discussion of the ballet with Cranko, as well as with Ninette de Valois and others (see, for example, Letter 859 n. 2 and Letter 873, when the choreographer was holidaying in Aldeburgh while Britten was desperately trying to finish Act III); Cranko's close involvement with the project would only recommence with the fashioning of the choreography, which could occur only after Britten had completed his composition draft and a piano score was made available for dance rehearsals.[4] Unlike in opera, where Britten had been accustomed to undertaking close scrutiny and refinement of the draft text in collaboration with his librettists, the wordless medium of ballet, in which movement and gesture convey the narrative and motivation of the characters, proved a challenge for the composer. To a creative artist of Britten's sensibilities, which throughout his career thrived on collaborating with artists from complementary disciplines, Cranko's attitude must have seemed puzzling and frustrating, the more so as the composer had plunged into, for him, an entirely new genre,[5] for which he most certainly would have welcomed advice from a seasoned practitioner. Musical assistance was on hand in the

[4] In his article 'Making a Ballet – 2', *The Sunday Times* (20 January 1957), Cranko mentions that the 'entire choreography had to be revisualized' after he heard Britten's music: see Letter 882 n. 4. In his interview with Michael Oliver (London, January 1992), Sir John Tooley offers an insightful account of the working relationship between Britten and Cranko: see Letter 882 n. 4.

[5] While still a student, Britten composed in 1931 a one-act ballet entitled *Plymouth Town*, to a scenario by Violet Alford. The ballet was submitted to the Camargo Society; the Society rejected it and *Plymouth Town* remained unperformed during Britten's lifetime. See also Letter VII n. 1 (vol. 3, pp. 69–70).

masterly ballet scores of Tchaikovsky, Prokofiev and Stravinsky, several of which we know Britten consulted and to which he made allusion in *The Prince of the Pagodas*. It remains an aspect of *Pagodas* that is too often overlooked, so dazzled are we by the gamelan inspirations of Act II and their significance to Britten's future development; *Pagodas* stands as Britten's conscious homage to the great Russian ballet masterpieces of the past and the dance tradition from which they sprang.[6] But the challenges Britten faced were immense, even by his own exacting standards; as his correspondence reveals, he seriously miscalculated the amount of time needed to write the ballet (an extremely rare occurrence in Britten's career) and experienced 'writer's block' during its composition (an even rarer symptom for the composer). The composition of *The Prince of the Pagodas* left Britten scarred: his reporting to Prince Ludwig of Hesse and the Rhine of the completion of the full score on 7 November 1956 – 'That b. Ballet is <u>FINISHED</u>, & I feel as if I've been just let out of prison after 18 months hard labour' – says it all. In later years Britten could barely bring himself to open the pages of the score of what proved to be by far his most sustained purely orchestral composition (it is of almost two hours' duration).

Throughout his career Britten counterpointed the writing of major works with shorter – though by no means less significant – pieces. This pattern began to emerge in the mid-1940s, when *Peter Grimes* was immediately succeeded by *The Holy Sonnets of John Donne*, and *Albert Herring* by *Canticle I: 'My Beloved is Mine'*, and was to continue most conspicuously in the 1950s, with *Canticle II*, the Thomas Hardy settings, *Winter Words*, and *Canticle III* following in the wake of *Billy Budd*, *Gloriana* and *The Turn of the Screw*. In the examples of the second and third Canticles there are also musical and dramatic links to their immediately preceding operas.

From a compositional point of view, it would appear that Britten found this practice almost a form of relaxation after the sustained focus over many months necessitated by his writing large-scale stage works. The first of the Hardy songs, 'Wagtail and Baby', was sketched, characteristically, during the well-deserved vacation Britten took immediately after completing the full score of *Gloriana* at the end of March 1953. It comes as something of a surprise that in spite of enduring over six months' concentrated work on the opera, for which the composer was forced to adhere to one of the most exacting schedules of his entire career, Britten could not stem the creative flow. It is also surprising to find that *Winter Words*, generally acknowledged to be one of Britten's most masterly settings of words by a great English poet, began its life as a one-off, independent setting with no apparent sense of that song's eventual destiny. However, several of Britten's song-cycles, particularly those centred on a single poet, began in this seemingly haphazard manner, with the composer assembling several settings over a period

---

6   In the context of Britten's interest in contributing to long-established genres by making allusion to existing models, the example of *War Requiem* and its relationship to the *Messa di Requiem* of Verdi is central. See MCBBWR, pp. 49–52.

INTRODUCTION

of time from which he would subsequently make his final selection.[7] A comparable process would have also occurred in respect of the choice of texts, with Britten drawing up a long-list of potential poems. (See p. 184 for the list of poems Britten drew up and inscribed in his copy of Hardy's *Collected Poems*.) The genesis of these songs is not to be found in Britten's correspondence (he barely mentions them) but rather in Imogen Holst's diary (IHD), probably the most valuable documentary source about the composer after his own diaries and letters; it is a crucial text for our understanding of Britten in the early 1950s, offering countless insights into his complex creative personality. The downbeat manner in which *Winter Words* emerged is echoed by other Britten song-cycles: one is immediately reminded of the *Serenade* for tenor, horn and strings from a decade earlier. The *Serenade* remains one of the composer's key works, notably for its exploration of the expressive possibilities of Peter Pears's voice and its Brittenesque subject-matter – night, sleep and dreams. Yet when Britten mentions its composition in one of his letters, it is remarkably offhand and without any pretension: 'It is not important stuff, but quite pleasant, I think.'[8]

There is, of course, absolutely nothing casual or relaxed about the compositional techniques Britten brought to *Winter Words*; it further explores issues of structural and motivic organization in the context of the genre of the song-cycle that became of increasing significance to Britten as the 1950s progressed. In the aftermath of the premiere of *Billy Budd*, the writing of which had preoccupied the composer throughout 1950 and 1951, Britten followed the opera with his *Canticle II*, a setting of the story of Abraham and Isaac using the text of the Chester miracle play which Britten himself adapted (see pp. 26–7). The impetus for this jewel of a work was a series of fund-raising concerts for the English Opera Group, which Britten, Pears and Kathleen Ferrier were to give in January and February 1952. Yet emerging from what might so easily be dismissed as a rather low-key occasion, especially in comparison to the prestigious circumstances of the first performance of *Billy Budd* at the Royal Opera House a month or so earlier, is one of Britten's most strikingly moving and 'perfect' vocal works. The touching naivety of the setting was evidently not easily won: as Britten writes to Lesley Bedford on 12 February 1953 (Letter 726), *Canticle II* 'gave me great trouble in coming into the world!'; and Britten's composition draft reveals the usual evidence of the struggle with the notes (crossed through bars and rubbed-out passages: see p. 25 for the opening page of Britten's draft). As we mention in Letter 723 n. 4, *Canticle II* discloses

---

7   A consequence of this process is the existence of discarded complete songs. For example, there are two Hardy settings that failed to reach the cycle: 'If it's ever Spring again' and 'The children and Sir Nameless'; see Letter 777 n. 11. Interestingly, at the first performance of *Winter Words* Britten was at pains not to have the piece described as a song-cycle, either in the programme or by Pears in his spoken introduction (see Letter 777 n. 11).
8   See Letter 425, Britten to Elizabeth Mayer, 6 April 1943.

Britten's exploring to the utmost the potential of his fundamental musical materials. This had already been a notable characteristic of another, earlier 'small' work, his *Lachrymae* for viola and piano, subtitled 'Reflections on a Song of John Dowland', composed in May 1950 while Britten was immersed in *Billy Budd*. In the sequence of variations that comprises *Lachrymae*, virtually each phrase, each motivic cell, each harmonic progression, can be traced back to Dowland's song 'If my complaints could passions move', on which Britten's piece is based and which emerges in its original tranquil clarity only at the work's conclusion.[9]

The critics of *The Times* (traditionally anonymous, but often Frank Howes at this period) and of the *New Statesman and Nation* (Desmond Shawe-Taylor, in the 1950s one of the more sympathetic and perceptive critics of Britten's work) recognized in *Lachrymae* early signs of Britten's striking out in a new direction.[10] As the 1950s progressed, it becomes apparent that the close motivic working of these works – *Lachrymae*, *Canticle II* and *Winter Words* – did indeed herald a new direction for the composer, reaching its apogee in *The Turn of the Screw* and *Canticle III*: '*Still falls the Rain – The Raids, 1940, Night and Dawn*, a setting of Edith Sitwell's poem. The subject matter of these last two compositions drew from Britten an economy of musical organization and intensity of emotional expression not hitherto to be found to such a degree in his output. It was in fact something that Britten, rarely given to making portentous pronouncements about his compositional ambitions and aspirations in his correspondence (or, for that matter, anywhere else), articulated in a letter to Edith Sitwell of 28 April 1955 (Letter 831):

[...] writing this work [*Canticle III*] has helped me so much in my development as a composer. I feel with this work & the Turn of the Screw [...] that I am on the threshold of a new musical world (for me, I am not pretentious about it!) I am worried by the problems which arise, & that is one reason that I am taking off next winter to do some deep thinking. But your great poem has dragged something from me that was latent there, & shown me what lies before.

---

9   In the sixth variation, marked 'Appassionato', Britten quotes another Dowland song, 'Flow my tears', which was published in 1604 as *Lachrimae Antiquae*. For pages from Britten's composition draft, see vol. 3, pp. 592–3. Britten was to follow a similar structural plan in his later Dowland-inspired work, the *Nocturnal after John Dowland*, for solo guitar, composed in 1963 for Julian Bream and also subtitled 'Reflections', in which Dowland's song 'Come, heavy sleep' forms the basis of a sequence of eight variations but is itself revealed in its entirety only at the end of the piece.
10   See Letter 663 n. 3. Writing in the *Manchester Guardian Weekly* (15 October 1953), Colin Mason advanced the possibility that *Winter Words* demonstrated a 'greater austerity of their language' than previous Britten song-cycles, with Britten 'now seeking to do more subtly what he knows he has the facility to do obviously'. Mason concluded: 'Perhaps the set marks a new stage in the evolution of his style.' See also Letter 777 n. 11. Britten himself observed to Mary Behrend (Letter 793): 'I am afraid many people find them difficult or elusive.'

We note that even when making this declaration to Sitwell – and it is of no little interest that he makes this disclosure to a non-musician – Britten immediately undercuts his remark with a self-deprecating aside. But having found his way to the 'threshold of a new musical world', Britten needed time for proper consideration of the compositional possibilities open to him. In short, what was he to do, faced with a musical language that had distilled to such a degree? By 1955 Britten was in his early forties; he had already enjoyed a career of more than twenty years' standing and had emerged in the mid-1940s as the most successful British composer of his generation, with a surprisingly strong international following. But the quantity of works from the decade that began with *Peter Grimes* and ended with *The Turn of the Screw* could not realistically be sustained, even for a composer of Britten's prodigious gifts. Turning the pages of his catalogue of compositions between 1944 and 1954 leaves one dizzy in admiration not only for the sheer amount of notes composed but also for the range of his compositions. It will surely come to be recognized as one of the most sustained compositional feats of twentieth-century music; the achievement is all the more remarkable when one recalls just how frantically busy Britten was throughout this period as performer, conductor, festival organizer and administrator. No doubt if Britten had not possessed the specific creative personality he did, he might have continued, perhaps at a slightly less frenetic pace, on the path he had already marked out as his own. But his aim for achieving maximum communication articulated through the most concentrated musical material – the 'easier/simpler' and 'difficult' allusion that Britten made to Donald Mitchell in 1953 or 1954 (see Letter 783 n. 12) – led the composer to a point in 1955 where he wanted to stand back and take stock of the situation. As Part IV of the present volume reveals, the timing of the world trip he and Pears made in 1955–56 coincidentally came at the very moment when Britten was contemplating which direction his music should take. Through his first-hand encounter with Far Eastern music at this key juncture, Britten alighted on techniques with which he could identify and assimilate into his own music language. The effects of his identification with the techniques of the music he heard in Indonesia, Japan and India in 1956 would permeate Britten's music thereafter.

*

A prominent subtheme of the present volume is Britten's increased status within the international musical community. His and Pears's numerous recitals in the most important European concert halls and festivals bestowed on them an enviable international following among the public that was sustained to the very end of their partnership. Britten's description of the duo's reception in Vienna in November 1955 (see Letter 840) – they were giving concerts as part of the celebrations to mark the re-opening of the Vienna State Opera after the war – is not untypical of the kind of excitement they created both on and off the platform. Britten's reputation as the leading British composer of his generation had steadily grown in the 1940s, not least because of the success of *Peter Grimes* in 1945, which spawned further productions in the United States and throughout Europe: Eric Walter White lists more than twenty stagings, concert performances and radio broadcasts of the opera between 1946 and 1949.[11] The founding of the English Opera Group as a small-scale touring company in 1946–47 gave Britten a platform to promote his own chamber operas, often in performances under his own baton, both in the UK and Europe. The EOG was an early visitor to the incipient Holland Festival in the late 1940s; as the company's reputation grew, invitations were made for it to appear at other prestigious venues across Europe. The activities of the EOG continue to be a major theme of the present volume of *Letter from a Life*, which concludes with the Group's first North American tour, to Canada in August and September 1957 for performances of *The Turn of the Screw* at Stratford, Ontario (see Letters 901–5); the end of Volume 4 also marks a reduction in the EOG's activities and the acrimonious 'redundancy' of its General Manager Basil Douglas and his assistant Maureen Garnham (see Letter 908), and the dismissal of Olive Zorian as Leader of the EOG Orchestra (see Letter 909). Having established in the late 1940s a core repertory for the company with *The Rape of Lucretia*, *Albert Herring*, *The Beggar's Opera*, *The Little Sweep* and an edition of Purcell's *Dido and Aeneas*, Britten encouraged others to write for the Group (for example, Lennox Berkeley,[12] Brian Easdale and Arthur Oldham), as well as exploring suitable existing repertoire such as Holst's *Sāvitri* and *The Wandering Scholar*. The climax of the EOG's international reputation, and Britten's status as one of the world's leading opera composers, was the invitation to give the first performance of *The Turn of the Screw* at Venice's historic La Fenice theatre in 1954. In a career hardly lacking high-profile first nights, the premiere of *The Turn of the Screw* was one of the most significant public occasions in Britten's career to date (*Gloriana* not excepted). The premiere was attended by a large press corps of leading UK and European music critics, and broadcast live by Radio Italia, the BBC Third Programme and several other European stations. Britten was conscious of the honour being paid to him personally; but he would have taken greater pleasure in the honour being paid to the EOG, and to British music in general. (In this context, it is worth recalling that exactly three years previously, on 11 September 1951, La Fenice had hosted the premiere of Stravinsky's *The Rake's Progress*.[13]) The critical success of *The Turn of the Screw* (see Letter 817 nn. 1 and 3) must have provided considerable consolation to the composer after the critical debacle of *Gloriana* fifteen months earlier.

11 See Eric Walter White, *Benjamin Britten: A Sketch of his Life and Works*, second edition, revised and enlarged (London: Boosey & Hawkes, 1954), pp. 197–8.
12 As Letter 809 reveals, Britten could not help himself from offering Berkeley friendly advice about *A Dinner Engagement* following its premiere at the 1954 Aldeburgh Festival.
13 For Britten's largely negative views on Stravinsky's opera, the libretto of which was by W. H. Auden, see Letter 712 n. 4 and Letter 717.

Britten's profile in the UK in the 1950s rose markedly, partly through the ongoing success of the Aldeburgh Festival, but also because the composer secured three major premieres at the Royal Opera House – *Billy Budd* in 1951, *Gloriana* two years later, and *The Prince of the Pagodas* in 1957 – though none of these works was particularly well received by the musical press. The General Administrator at the Opera House throughout this period was David Webster, who was evidently astute enough to recognize the broader cultural significance of Britten to the nation's musical life and wanted to use it to enhance Covent Garden's own standing both within the UK and the wider international sphere. (We should recall that the Covent Garden Opera Company was a post-war creation and in the period under discussion in the present volume remained a fledgling organization, despite some early notable successes. It was competing with major European opera houses that, in the late 1940s and 1950s, were re-opening after the war.) Dismissing petty criticisms of favouritism from some members of his board, Webster entertained an ambition in 1952 to secure Britten as the company's new Musical Director, in succession to Karl Rankl. He had been encouraged in this initiative by Britten's close friend, Lord Harewood, himself then working at Covent Garden. To have the leading British opera composer–conductor at the helm must have seemed an extremely attractive proposition, one virtually guaranteed to enhance Covent Garden's reputation. Britten ultimately rejected Webster's proposal and was wise to do so: he was not the figure Covent Garden needed, despite Webster himself failing at first to realize this.

By the early 1950s Britten was regarded in some quarters as a figure of the Establishment: the high-profile circumstances surrounding *Gloriana*, his close friendship with minor royalty such as the Harewoods (Lord Harewood was the Queen's first cousin; his mother, the Princess Royal) and the Prince and Princess of Hesse and the Rhine, his appointment as a Companion of Honour at the age of thirty-nine, his lunching with the Queen (see Letter 898 n. 11), etc., all contributed to this impression.[14] Moreover, he was regularly featured in popular weekly magazines such as *Picture Post* as well as the daily broadsheets, and his life and music had been the subject of not one but two books published in quick succession.[15] Inevitably,

---

14 Britten's reaction to Pears's CBE is telling: 'it delighted his friends & admirers, & also put heart into those few who try & do serious things without show off & senseless glamour & publicity' (Letter 895).

15 Of these two publications, the symposium edited by Hans Keller and Donald Mitchell (DMHK) was by far the more controversial, and sprang from their advocacy of the composer in *Music Survey*, the journal they jointly edited from 1949 to 1952. Britten was to express to the editors his pleasure at the book's publication, though he explained he was not 'pleased with every contribution' (see Letter 760); in private, he and Imogen Holst (one of the contributors) exchanged less guarded views about some of the contributions (see Letter 760 n. 3). Ironically, the appearance of this volume and the seriousness of purpose that lay at its roots might actually have fuelled the critical backlash made towards Britten in this period, which culminated a few months after the book's appearance in the reception of *Gloriana*. The indignant, if not downright hostile, tones adopted by several of the book's reviewers suggest that these two

jealousies and intrigues, real or imagined, of and about Britten were rife. The irony here is that while outwardly the composer appeared to conform (and to some extent, his conventional middle-class upbringing meant that he could hardly do otherwise), below the surface Britten made for a somewhat unconventional public figure. He was discreetly homosexual (though his and Pears's sexual orientation was tacitly acknowledged in the music profession and elsewhere); he was a well-known pacifist who had registered as a conscientious objector during the Second World War, and, despite the outward trappings of his success, he had never completely abandoned socialist principles forged in the 1930s. For example, he was impressed by what he witnessed of society in the former Yugoslavia in 1955: 'I'd honestly rather have a country like that, where everyone is working together, and not where there are terribly rich & terribly poor side-by-side. I know they are communist, but it is really as far as I can see a kind of socialism – a genuine attempt to work things out'; however, he was not completely naive about Tito's regime, adding 'all of this is only a foreigner's superficial idea, but certainly we liked it so much that we are planning to come back'.[16]

Traces of his non-Establishment views surface occasionally in the present volume: for example, he is a signatory to a letter to *The Times* (Letter 733 n. 1) requesting that there be a pacifist element to the Coronation ceremonies of 1953, in addition to the conventional military display; and an attempt to visit Greece with the Harewoods is thwarted following advice from the British Foreign Office and the Queen's private secretary (who was presumably involved as Lord Harewood was related to the Queen) because Britten and Pears had been signatories to a document petitioning for a fair trial for some prisoners in the country (see Letter 766 n. 11). And not surprisingly, he is quick to condemn the first-night audience at *Gloriana* as 'stuck pigs' (Letter 771). During the period of the anti-gay purge initiated under the supervision of Conservative Home Secretary David Maxwell-Fyffe, Scotland Yard officers interviewed the composer, though details of their precise line of questioning have never emerged into the public domain.[17] From the perspective of the more enlightened socio-sexual climate of the present day, it makes for distinctly uncomfortable reading to discover Britten's casually suggesting to Imogen Holst the possibility that Pears might marry (no prospective wife is identified) as a decoy to protect the relationship between the two men. (The episode is reported by Imogen Holst in her diary: see Letter 769 n. 3.) As we discuss in our annotations

---

young editors thoroughly irritated their more senior colleagues by their support for a living composer. For a time, it would be Britten who would suffer.

16 Britten to Roger Duncan, 3 December 1955, quoted in Letter 842 n. 3.
17 The source of this information is to be found in Kathleen Tynan's biography of her husband, Kenneth Tynan, in 1954 the newly appointed drama critic of the *Observer*. 'In a letter to Lord Beaverbrook, the *Evening Standard*'s editor wrote that Scotland Yard was stepping up its action against homosexuals, that Benjamin Britten had been interviewed, and that Cecil Beaton was on the list' (Kathleen Tynan, *The Life of Kenneth Tynan* (London: Methuen, 1988), p. 110).

concerning *The Turn of the Screw*, at least one distinguished commentator has argued recently that the Latin tags in the opera can be decoded to reveal a hitherto hidden response on Britten's part to the homophobia of British society during the early 1950s (see Letter 784 n. 4).

One unexpected yardstick with which to measure Britten's position as a public figure during the period under scrutiny is to uncover just how far he had infiltrated popular culture of the time. We quote the text of Flanders's and Swann's affectionate 'Guide to Britten' (see Letter 832 n. 3) and the *New Statesman and Nation*'s resident satirical poet 'Sagittarius' (see Letter 734 n. 2); and we recall David Low's marvellous cartoon portraits of the composer, also from this period (see PFL, plates 267 and 274),[18] as well as Low's inclusion of Britten and Pears (mischievously captioned as 'Donald Peers', a popular singer of the day) as one of the prominent new Elizabethans in his 'Cultural addition to the procession' for the Coronation (see p. 20), a caricature published in the *Manchester Guardian* (2 June 1953).[19] How far attitudes towards culture have shifted in the intervening years! One cannot imagine for a moment the activities or output of comparable figures from today's contemporary classical-music scene finding their way into the popular imagination.

*

The range of Britten's correspondents in the present volume remains as wide and varied as in all previous volumes of the series, though it is true to say that we have found the increased abundance of available material (there are thousands upon thousands of items of correspondence at BPL) has necessitated our making some difficult choices in respect of what to include and what to exclude. A glance at the Index of Correspondents (pp. ix–x) will immediately reveal the composer's significant correspondents from this period. William Plomer, Myfanwy Piper, Basil Coleman and David Webster have already been mentioned earlier in this Introduction; others include Erwin Stein and Anthony Gishford of Boosey & Hawkes, Britten's publishers; the French composer Francis Poulenc, the writers Edith Sitwell and Ronald Duncan, and Duncan's son, Roger. To the latter Britten sent a

---

18 Philip Reed has in his possession a mass-produced copy of one of Low's cartoon drawings of the composer (reproduced as PFL, plate 267) which is accompanied by an anonymous poem (by Low?) entitled 'Benjamin Britten', of which the final two stanzas read:

He can't help his sure way with cantatas
   With a song he can never go wrong,
For the words are as near to his heart as
   The notes of a song.

No labour, no critic he fears,
   No challenge, orchestral or choric.
His place like a star in the spheres,
   His course meteoric.

19 See also Heather Wiebe, '"Now and England": Britten's *Gloriana* and the "New Elizabethans"', *Cambridge Opera Journal* 17/2 (2005), pp. 147–8.

fascinating, 'autobiographical' account of his and Pears's world trip in the form of a sequence of letters, which we have included virtually in its entirety in addition to a representative sample of the many letters the composer sent to the schoolboy, beginning in 1954. As the warmth of this correspondence reveals, the relationship with Roger Duncan was of paramount significance to Britten over many years (see Letter 815 n. 1). Other important friendships with teenage boys from these years include those with Paul Rogerson (see Letter 737 n. 1) and David Hemmings, the first Miles in *The Turn of the Screw* (see Letter 792 n. 6). While our understanding of Britten's relationship with Hemmings has been greatly enriched by the work of the film-maker and writer John Bridcut, as well as by the posthumous publication of Hemmings's autobiography,[20] it remains a grievous loss that none of Britten's letters to him, either during the period he was performing with the EOG or later, has survived.

The closeness of the relationship between Britten and Pears – intimate, tender, loving, supportive and creatively inspiring – continues as before, in a correspondence that remains unique to the series (see, for example, Letter 880). To Pears, one realizes, Britten could confide his deepest thoughts and concerns, not least about the difficulties and frustrations of work in progress. This is especially true of the many compositions that were to involve the tenor, and there are occasional references in Britten's letters to his partner about the nature of the role or the quality of the music he was writing for him, and of how he could hear Pears's voice in his mind's ear. One role from these years – the Earl of Essex in *Gloriana* – appears to have been greeted with less than enthusiasm by the tenor, despite the pleasure he evidently derived from singing the pair of Lute Songs in the first act; but he remained never fully reconciled to the part, the more so after the hostile press reception (see Letter 740 n. 3). The writing of *Gloriana* not only placed an enormous physical strain on Britten: it also proved a trial for Pears, for its composition deprived him of working with his established accompanist for the best part of a year; and the situation was exacerbated by the composer's bursitis almost immediately after the opera's premiere, a condition that caused him to cancel the majority of his concerts for a further six months.

One correspondent from earlier volumes of *Letters from a Life* was to play a central role in Britten's creative life for over a decade from 1952. This was Imogen Holst, daughter of the composer Gustav Holst, and a musician of exceptional and wide-ranging gifts in her own right, which have been hitherto too little appreciated. She first met Britten and Pears at Dartington in 1943 (see Letter 436) when the composer had been moved by her response to a recital he and Pears had given there. Both men remained in close touch with her through their many visits to Dartington (where she was Director of Music in the Arts Department from 1943 until 1951) and her occasional trips to Aldeburgh. In 1951 she undertook some freelance copying work for

---

20   See JBBC, pp. 194–210, and David Hemmings, *Blow-Up and Other Exaggerations* (London: Robson Books, 2004), pp. 51–8.

the composer on *Billy Budd*, and the following year orchestrated *Rejoice in the Lamb* for the Aldeburgh Festival at his request, as well as assisting in practical ways during the Festival. Out of the success of her involvement in 1951 and 1952 came a request from the composer that she assist 'on a really professional basis' at future festivals (see Letter 739); her arrival at Aldeburgh in September 1952 coincided with the beginning of Britten's work on the writing of *Gloriana* and she was soon employed in helping the composer with the laborious task of preparing the vocal and full scores of the opera, as well as relieving him of many of the mundane administrative duties associated with the running of the Aldeburgh Festival.[21]

The closeness of the friendship can be judged by the fascinating journal she kept from her first day in Aldeburgh until March 1954, when she was forced to abandon it because of pressures of work. (Oddly, the final entry – 22 March 1954 – stops in mid-sentence.) The diary's great strength, apart from the obvious one of being a rich documentary resource for Britten during this period, is her decision to write down, without comment or criticism, what Britten said or did. She is nearly always non-judgemental and remarkably self-effacing in these entries, and we can be confident that the conversations she records therein are very close to what was actually said at the time. The text is exceptional for its total focus on the composer and his activities; as Christopher Grogan has observed, this in itself is as revealing of her personality and the nature of her relationship with Britten.[22]

Without a shadow of doubt, it was music that lay at the heart and the genuine success of their relationship, and it was only when musical values were placed in jeopardy that she would appear to have spoken her mind and risked censuring Britten. As she told Donald Mitchell, 'The most difficult thing [in working for Britten] was *judging* whether I could *risk* criticizing details that I felt passionately were wrong [. . .] to risk it without interrupting the flow of his ideas; and because of this marvellous thing that music matters most, I had the courage to do it.'[23] After working alongside her as his music assistant for three months, Britten warmly acknowledged her

---

[21] During a visit to Dartington in March 1951, Pears had been deeply impressed by her gifts. He wrote to Britten, prophetically as it turned out: 'I am quite sure that somehow we have got to use Imo in the biggest way – as editor, as trainer, as teacher, etc. – she is most impressive' (Letter 703).

[22] Imogen Holst's diary forms the centrepiece of Christopher Grogan (ed.), *Imogen Holst: A Life in Music* (Woodbridge: The Boydell Press, 2007), pp. 141–291; for a full discussion of the relationship between Britten and Imogen Holst, see Dr Grogan's introduction to the diary, ibid., pp. 130–40. This volume, which also contains contributions from Colin Matthews, Rosamund Strode and Christopher Tinker, has been generally recognized as offering a significant (and long-overdue) reassessment of Imogen Holst.

[23] Interview with Donald Mitchell, Aldeburgh, January 1980; transcript at BPL. In an earlier interview with Mitchell (Aldeburgh, 22 June 1977), following comments about Pears's indifferent attitude to *The Prince of the Pagodas* and the difficulties Britten experienced during final rehearsals at Covent Garden, she remarked, 'It wasn't my job to encourage Ben, because I didn't do that side. I did it through the music, but nothing else' (see Letter 880 n. 1).

contribution: 'Over & over again you have saved my sanity in so many different ways, by your energy, intelligence, infinite skill & affection' (Letter 755). Without her unflinching practical support, notably in the making of piano reductions, Britten quite simply would not have been able to achieve the three major stage compositions of these years.

Because she and Britten were so often working together in Aldeburgh, there are far fewer letters than one might expect to so trusted and valued a colleague. But it is striking that when Britten is away on his world trip in 1955–56, it is to Imogen Holst that he writes, with the exception of Roger Duncan, the most regularly (we include five examples: Letters 842, 844, 849, 850 and 854). And it is to her, whose musicianship he admired and respected, that he discloses the excitement of his discovery and growing understanding of Balinese gamelan (see Letter 850), which on his return he would emulate in the second act of *The Prince of the Pagodas*.

Unfortunately we have no diary from Imogen Holst to allow us to follow the daily vicissitudes of Britten's progress on *Pagodas*, but it is clear from the correspondence that she provided rock-like support for the composer throughout the project, both in Aldeburgh during composition (he even took her with him for a working holiday in Switzerland during August 1956, when he needed to make progress on the full score) and at Covent Garden during rehearsals (see Letter 880 n. 1). Her understanding of ballet – throughout her childhood she had trained as a dancer – must have lent her involvement in *Pagodas* special significance, which Britten signalled by making her a co-dedicatee of the ballet (the other dedicatee was Ninette de Valois, but this was surely a matter of obligation for the composer), and by presenting her with the composition draft of the work on the occasion of her fiftieth birthday in April 1957 (see Letter 893). We very much hope that our dedicating the fourth volume of *Letters from a Life* to her memory not only echoes Britten's own dedication to her of *The Prince of the Pagodas*, but that it would be one in which he would wholeheartedly concur.

Orford, Suffolk
Easter 2008

I FIT FOR A QUEEN: THE WRITING OF *GLORIANA*

JANUARY 1952–JULY 1953

4·CRABBE ST·ALDEBURGH·SUFFOLK Jan 21ᶜᵗ 1953

My dear William,

Only a brief note to thank you so much for your very warm & welcome letter. Writing Gloriana with you has been the greatest pleasure; more even than I expected, & I was pretty greedy in anticipation too! I think, apart from your wonderful gifts, that you have shown the greatest possible good-temper & amenability, which can't always have been easy considering

Britten to William Plomer, 21 January 1953: Letter 759

CHRONOLOGY 1952–1953

YEAR	EVENTS AND COMPOSITIONS
1952	
January	COMPOSITION *Canticle II: 'Abraham and Isaac'*
21 January	Nottingham: first performance of *Canticle II* by Kathleen Ferrier, Pears and Britten, with further performances during January and February in Birmingham, Liverpool, Manchester, London, Bristol and Rhyl
February	Begins collaboration with William Plomer on projected children's opera, *Tyco the Vegan*; this project is abandoned in favour of *Gloriana*
6 February	Death of King George VI
1 and 3 March	Recitals with Pears in Salzburg and Vienna
March	Ski-ing holiday in Austria with Pears and the Harewoods, during which the idea of an opera about Queen Elizabeth I to celebrate Queen Elizabeth II's Coronation is first discussed
22 March	Wiesbaden: attends performance of *Billy Budd*, while staying for the first time at Schloss Wolfsgarten, the home of the Prince and Princess of Hesse and the Rhine
4 April	Conducts *Billy Budd* with the Covent Garden Opera Company in Birmingham, with further performances at the Royal Opera House, Covent Garden, during April and May
May	Britten and Plomer first discuss *Gloriana*; the plan for the Coronation opera is made public on 28 May
26–27 May	Paris: conducts two performances of *Billy Budd* with the Covent Garden Opera Company at the Théâtre des Champs-Elysées
14–22 June	Fifth Aldeburgh Festival, which includes a new work by Lennox Berkeley, an arrangement by Imogen Holst of Britten's *Rejoice in the Lamb* and a visit from the Copenhagen Boys' Choir

1–6 July	Recitals with Pears in Copenhagen
16 July– 21 August	Motoring holiday in France with Pears and the Harewoods; reading first draft libretto of *Gloriana*
24 and 26 July	Recitals with Pears in the South of France
5 August	Conducts concert of English music at Menton
18 August	Recital with Pears at Salzburg
September	Begins composition draft of *Gloriana*
29 September	Imogen Holst commences work in Aldeburgh as Britten's music assistant
18 October	New York: 'Scenes from *Billy Budd*', with Theodor Uppman as Billy, televised in the United States by NBC
December	Publication of *Benjamin Britten: A Commentary on His Works by a Group of Specialists*, edited by Donald Mitchell and Hans Keller
Christmas	Plomer stays with Britten and Pears in Aldeburgh; Britten spends New Year with the Harewoods in Yorkshire, returning to Aldeburgh on 12 January

1953

January	COMPOSITION Variation 4 of *Variations on an Elizabethan Theme*, a composite work by Oldham, Tippett, Lennox Berkeley, Britten, Searle and Walton
31 January	East Coast storms and floods; Britten's home damaged by flood water
c. 11 February	Completes composition draft of *Gloriana*
14 February	Plays through *Gloriana* to Covent Garden staff
15 February	Begins scoring *Gloriana*
13 March	COMPOSITION *Gloriana*
16–29 March	Holiday in Ireland with Pears and the Harewoods
28 March	Composes Hardy setting, 'Wagtail and Baby' (*Winter Words*)
9–10 May	Wiesbaden: conducts two performances of *Albert Herring* with the EOG
16 May	Moves into new London home at 5 Chester Gate, NW1
18 May	Joan Cross, Pears and Britten perform extracts from *Gloriana* to the Queen and Prince Philip at a dinner party at the Harewoods' London home; Plomer also attends
1 June	Created a Companion of Honour (CH) in the Coronation Honours List

2 June	Westminster Abbey, London: Coronation of Queen Elizabeth II
8 June	Royal Opera House, Covent Garden, London: first performance of *Gloriana*, with Joan Cross (Elizabeth I) and Pears (Earl of Essex), conducted by John Pritchard
16 June	BBC Third Programme: first performance of *Variations on an Elizabethan Theme*, Aldeburgh Festival Orchestra, conducted by Britten
20–28 June	Sixth Aldeburgh Festival, which includes the first public performance of *Variations on an Elizabethan Theme*, a revival of *Albert Herring* and a lecture by W. H. Auden
10–19 July	Performs at the inaugural Taw and Torridge Festival, Devon

A Coronation cartoon by David Low, *Manchester Guardian*, 2 June 1953

723 To Basil Coleman[1]

4 CRABBE STREET, ALDEBURGH, SUFFOLK
Jan 8th 1952

My dear Basil,

I have owed you a letter for so long – but what with the piece of music for Kath[2] & Peter[3] to write,[4] & with the Southend concert[5] & its rehearsals there simply hasn't been a moment. Please forgive –

The book, the books[6] are lovely – we haven't got either of them (surprisingly!) & they are lovely, both to look at & to read. Thank you so very much, & for your patience in changing them. I do regret that we'd got the Michelangelo already because it would have been lovely to have it given to us by you. But I shan't forget that you did once give it us!

Thank you also for your letter.[7] I hope in the meantime to have spoken to you about your visit here. I am slightly alarmed by the prospect of an EOG descent on me that week – what with Periton[8] (accountant), Imogen Holst,[9] yourself & Plomer[10] (because I am expecting you with him on 17th) already booked. However it'll be easier to talk this on the phone, & how important it is to dispel Anne's[11] gloom immediately!

I was glad to have better news musically & publicly about 'Let's Make' from Basil D.[12] It's been a worry I know, but I'm sure it is worth your trouble & skill – if only for the sake of the young company. It is excellent the way Gladys Whitred's[13] come on, for instance.

You've probably already bought yourself Bevis[14] – if so give it away – if not here it is, with my love.

And finally – many, many thanks, my dear for all you've done for me in every way in 1951 – your achievement, especially in 'Budd', has been really remarkable – & I can't begin to express my thanks. I only hope your health will now recover 100% from the terrifying strain.

With much love, & admiration,

BEN

1 British director of opera, theatre and television (b. 1916), who worked extensively with the English Opera Group during the 1940s and 1950s, and collaborated with Britten on the first stagings of *The Little Sweep*, *Billy Budd*, *Gloriana* and *The Turn of the Screw*. See also Letter 632 n. 6 and William Kerley's interviews with Basil Coleman (London, May/June 2004), a transcript of which is available at BPL.

2 Kathleen Ferrier (1912–1953), British contralto, who with Nancy Evans created the role of Lucretia in *The Rape of Lucretia* at Glyndebourne in 1946 (her first stage appearances), and for whom Britten wrote the contralto parts in his *Spring Symphony* and *Canticle II: 'Abraham and Isaac'*. See also Letters 462 n. 5 and 517 n. 5; the BBC *Omnibus* film *Blow the Wind Southerly*

(6 October 1968), written, narrated and directed by John Drummond, and to which both Britten and Pears made memorable contributions; the LP *Kathleen Ferrier: The Singer and the Person*, introduced by Pears (BBC Artium, 1979), based on the radio programme *A Voice is a Person*, broadcast on 4 October 1978 to mark the twenty-fifth anniversary of Ferrier's death, which included spoken contributions from Britten (taken from Drummond's 1968 film) and an excerpt from Act II of *The Rape of Lucretia*, taken from the first broadcast performance of the opera (BBC Third Programme, 4 October 1946), sourced from a private recording owned by Lord Harewood; Suzanne Phillips's documentary film *Kathleen Ferrier: An Ordinary Diva* (Forget About Film and TV for BBC Wales, 2003); and Paul Campion, *Ferrier: A Career Recorded*, 2nd edn.

Britten's contribution to Drummond's film is close in spirit to part of his 1954 essay 'Three Premieres', first published in *Kathleen Ferrier: A Memoir*, edited by Neville Cardus (reprinted in PKBM, pp. 123–7). In the interview he begins by recalling the first occasion he heard Ferrier, in a Westminster Abbey performance of *Messiah*:

Here was a voice that could sing this *extremely* awkward music without any effort. I mean, just in the part of the voice which is usually the weakest, Kathleen's voice was the strongest. And so the music sailed across the vast spaces with a confidence and a beauty which I think I'd never heard before.

Almost before, I think, although it's difficult to remember exactly, almost before I wrote the music [of *The Rape of Lucretia*], we were discussing who was to sing it, and I think it was Peter Pears who, in fact I'm sure it was, who said, 'Well, what about Kathleen Ferrier?' and, of course, having heard that performance in Westminster Abbey I realized that, well, anyhow there was, that was an idea, and that the voice could inspire me, and then I remembered that there was this very *grand* personality.

It was only slowly, I think, that Kathleen developed the right kind of confidence for the later scenes. The beginning was always marvellous. I mean she sang it beautifully. She didn't find the music as difficult as I think she felt she was going to find it, and her natural beauty, sitting there on the stage, as soon as the curtain went up – one realized that – this was Lucretia.

She always had a natural feeling for phrase and she wanted to make sense of the music, and one could talk in a quite elaborate way about this, this – not about the words, but the phrase of music must have its rise and fall. And that Kathleen always understood, and that one could work really very seriously with her.

We did it first of all – *Lucretia* – in Glyndebourne for a couple of weeks and then we went to Holland and round the place and round England in a, not a very easy tour at all with very, very bad houses, as you probably know. And, of course, nerves got on edge, and there was one very serious quarrel which I myself was involved with, with one of my closest friends in the company. And I can remember Kathleen taking me aside one day and saying, 'Look, do try and be nice.' And so I tried to be nice – and it worked.

Recalling Ferrier in Mahler's *Das Lied von der Erde*, which she performed with Pears and Bruno Walter at the Edinburgh Festival in 1947 (see Letter 554 n. 7), Britten remarked:

The *Das Lied von der Erde* was simply extraordinary. Again, you see, this voice in the – at the end. No singer I've ever heard can equal Kathleen's ease in those very difficult registers – and you see also her voice, not being a very long one, being a rather short voice – it had real tension at the top. I know she had difficulty with that, but that gave the music an intensely moving quality.

In considering the link between Ferrier's personality and her voice, Britten commented:

That was something that [...] touched me the first time I heard her in Westminster Abbey, and it's a thing that *always* moves me, rather, the *only* thing which moves me about singers, and that is that the voice is something which comes naturally from their personality and is a vocal expression of their personality. I *loathe* what is normally called 'a beautiful voice' because to me it's like an over-ripe peach which says nothing, and Kathleen never had that.

Even if she made mistakes, even if one could criticize her, her voice was always Kathleen and the weaknesses in the voice were the weaknesses in Kathleen; and the glories in the voice, which were, I've no need to say, which were many, were the glories of Kathleen.

For an account of Britten's and Pears's involvement in Drummond's project, including Britten's demands that he would agree to participate only if neither Nancy Evans nor Eric Crozier appeared in the film, see John Drummond, *Tainted by Experience: A Life in the Arts*, pp. 168–9.

3 Peter Pears (1910–1986), British tenor, Britten's partner and musical collaborator for nearly forty years; creator of numerous operatic roles and first performer of many concert works written for his voice by Britten and others. See also Letter 113 n. 1; IC1/2/3; CHPP, PPT and PRPP. For an assessment of Pears's achievements as a recording artist, see Alan Blyth, 'Reputations: Peter Pears', *Gramophone* (January 2005), pp. 30–33.

4 Britten was composing his *Canticle II: 'Abraham and Isaac'*, for alto, tenor and piano, a setting of part of the medieval Chester Miracle Play *Histories of Lot and Abraham*, the text of which had been given to him by Eric Crozier in Alfred Pollard's edition of *English Miracle Plays, Moralities and Interludes: Specimens of the Pre-Elizabethan Drama*. This same volume was later to provide the text for *Noye's Fludde*. See also Letter 726 n. 2.

In his tribute to Kathleen Ferrier, 'Three Premieres', Britten recalled:

The third and last close artistic association I had with Kathleen Ferrier [after *The Rape of Lucretia* and *Spring Symphony*] was perhaps the loveliest of all, a kind of Indian summer. It was in the early days of 1952, the period after her first serious operation, and when we dared to hope that the miracle had happened, that she might possibly be getting well. It was a series of concerts organized for the funds of the English Opera Group – which, after all, she helped to launch by her wonderful Lucretia performances in 1946 and 1947 – to be given in London and the provinces by her, Peter Pears, and myself. It was a programme which we all could enjoy: early English songs, including some of Morley's canzonets, ravishingly sung, some big Schubert *Lieder*, some folk songs, grave and gay, ending up with the comic duet

'The Deaf Woman's Courtship', which Kathleen sang in a feeble, cracked voice, the perfect reply to Peter's magisterial roar. A masterpiece of humour, which had the audience rocking, but never broke the style of the rest of the concert.

To complete the programme I wrote a Canticle for the three of us, a setting of a part of one of the Chester Miracle Plays – *Abraham and Isaac*. It was principally a dialogue for contralto (the boy) and tenor (the father), although on occasions the voices joined together to sing the words of God, and there was a little *Envoi* in canon.

We performed this programme in Nottingham, Birmingham, Manchester, Bristol, and Liverpool, a broadcast, and at the Victoria and Albert Museum in London, the happiest of concerts. Everything seemed to go well, with big friendly audiences. *Abraham and Isaac*, when performed with such sincerity and charm, pleased the public. Only in Nottingham was there a cloud, but we did not realize the size of it. Kathleen seemed to trip and slightly wrench her back walking off the platform and she was in pain for some of the time. It turned out to be a recurrence of her terrible illness [cancer], but no one suspected anything – or perhaps she did and said nothing.

We all determined to repeat the concerts the next year, to write a companion piece to *Abraham and Isaac*, but operations and long and painful convalescences intervened and we had to give them up. But there was one more performance of the Canticle. Kathleen spent some days in Aldeburgh in June 1952, while the Festival was going on. She was convalescing but managed to go to quite a few concerts, lectures, and operas. Each morning my sister [Barbara Britten] would walk along to the Wentworth Hotel, where she was staying, would go through the programmes with her, and she would make her choice for the day. She became a familiar and much loved figure in the town. Finally, towards the end of the week [on 19 June], she joined Peter and me in our yearly recital in a touching performance of *Abraham and Isaac*. Many people have said they will never forget the occasion: the beautiful church, her beauty and incredible courage, and the wonderful characterization of her performance, including every changing emotion of the boy Isaac – the boyish nonchalance of the walk up to the fatal hill, his bewilderment, his sudden terror, his touching resignation to his fate – the simplicity of the *Envoi*, but, above all, combining with the other voice, the remote and ethereal sounds as 'God speaketh'. In the short run-through before the concert Kathleen failed to make her entry in one passage. Apologizing and laughing, she said she was fascinated by Peter's skill in eliding an 'l' and an 'm' in a perfect *legato* – 'Farewell, my dear son'. She really must practise that, she said, she never could do it as well.

For Britten's recollection of the unsuccessful attempt to record *Canticle II* with the original performers, see Letter 779 n. 14.

Abraham and Isaac sets part of the Chester Miracle Play to a sectionalized scheme similar to that of *Canticle I: 'My beloved is mine'*, now rationalized by the more rigorous motivic working that becomes an increasingly prominent feature of Britten's music in the 1950s. The Miracle Play text suggests an obvious parallel with the later treatment of *Noye's Fludde*, a connection made explicit by Britten's handling in *Canticle II* of the transition from God's instructions at the opening to Abraham's decisive course of action. There is a parallel too with *Billy Budd* (completed shortly before the Canticle): both Isaac and Billy receive their sentences of death to sequences of common

Canticle II: 'Abraham and Isaac': the opening page of Britten's composition draft;
BL Add. MS. 60601

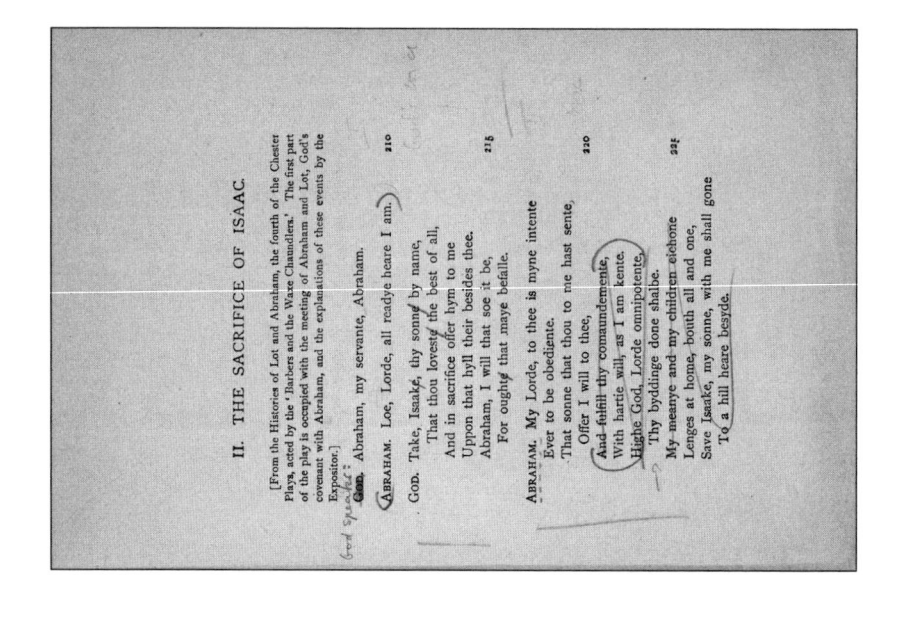

II. THE SACRIFICE OF ISAAC.

[From the Histories of Lot and Abraham, the fourth of the Chester Plays, acted by the 'Barbers and the Waxe Chaundlers.' The first part of the play is occupied with the meeting of Abraham and Lot, God's covenant with Abraham, and the explanations of these events by the Expositor.]

GOD. Abraham, my servante, Abraham.
ABRAHAM. Loe, Lorde, all readye heare I am.   210
GOD. Take, Isaake, thy sonne by name,
   That thou lovest the best of all,
   And in sacrifice offer hym to me
   Uppon that hyll their besides thee.
   Abraham, I will that soe it be,   215
   For oughte that maye befalle.
ABRAHAM. My Lorde, to thee is myne intente
   Ever to be obediente.
   That sonne that thou to me hast sente,
   Offer I will to thee,   220
   And fulfill thy comaundemente,
   With hartie will, as I am kente.
   Highe God, Lorde omnipotente,
   Thy byddinge done shalbe.
   My meanye and my children eichone   225
   Longes at home, bouth all and one,
   Save Isaake, my sonne, with me shall gone
   To a hill heare besyde.

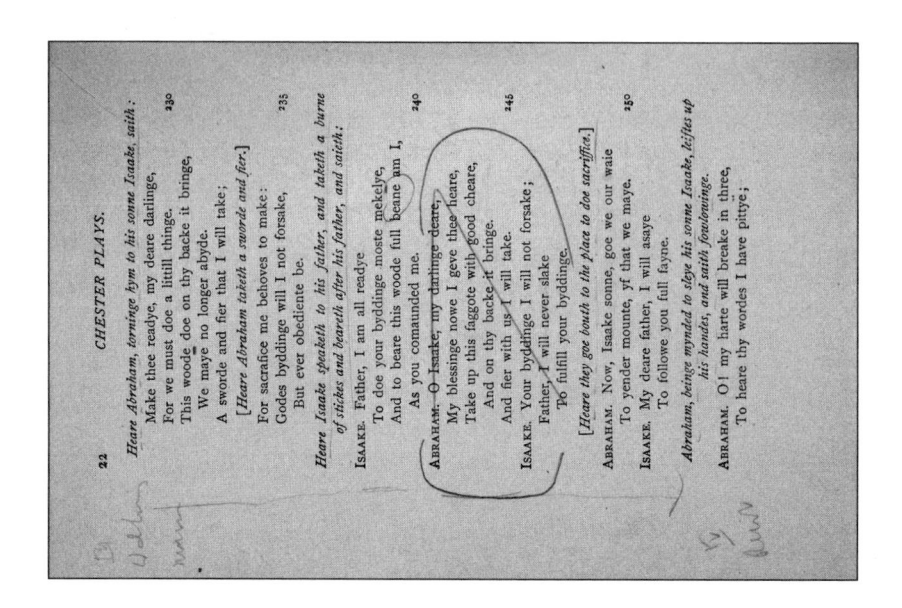

CHESTER PLAYS.

Heare Abraham, torninge hym to his sonne Isaake, saith:
   Make thee readye, my deare darlinge,
   For we must doe a litill thinge.   230
   This woode doe on thy backe it bringe,
   We maye no longer abyde.
   A sworde and fier that I will take;
   [Heare Abraham taketh a sworde and fier.]
   For sacrafice me behoves to make:
   Godes byddinges will I not forsake,   235
   But ever obediente be.
Heare Isaake speaketh to his father, and taketh a burne of stickes and beareth after his father, and saith:
ISAAKE. Father, I am all readye
   To doe your byddinge moste mekelye,
   And to beare this woode full beane am I,
   As you comaunded me.   240
ABRAHAM. O Isaake, my darlinge deare,
   My blessinge nowe I geve thee heare,
   Take up this faggote with good cheare,
   And on thy backe it bringe.
   And fier with us I will take.   245
ISAAKE. Your byddinge I will not forsake;
   Father, I will never slake
   Po fulfill your byddinge.
   [Heare they goe bouth to the place to doe sacrifiice.]
ABRAHAM. Now, Isaake sonne, goe we our waie
   To yender mountte, yf that we maye,   250
ISAAKE. My deare father, I will asaye
   To followe you full fayne.
Abraham, beinge mynded to sleye his sonne Isaake, liftes up his handes, and saith fowloeinge.
ABRAHAM. O! my harte will breake in three,
   To heare thy wordes I have pittye;

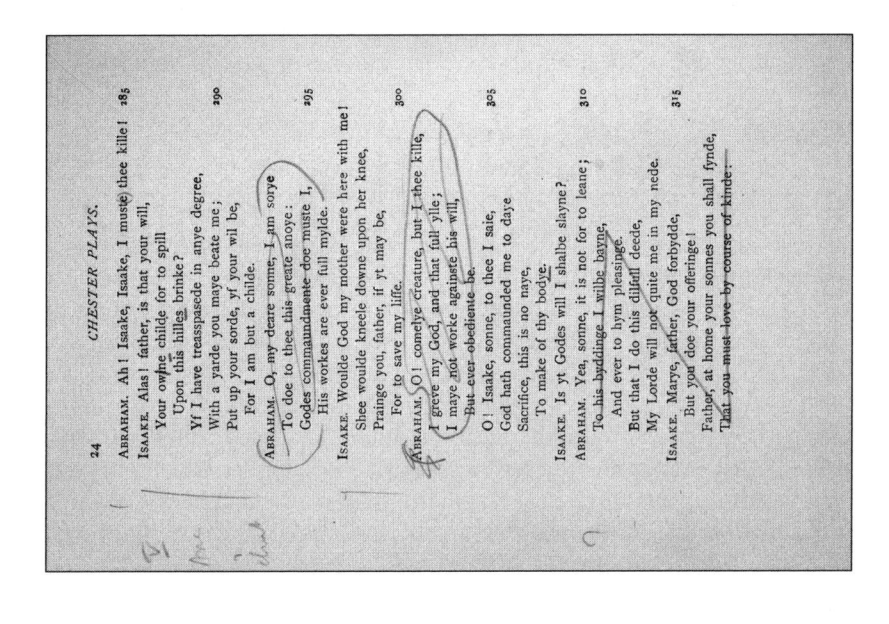

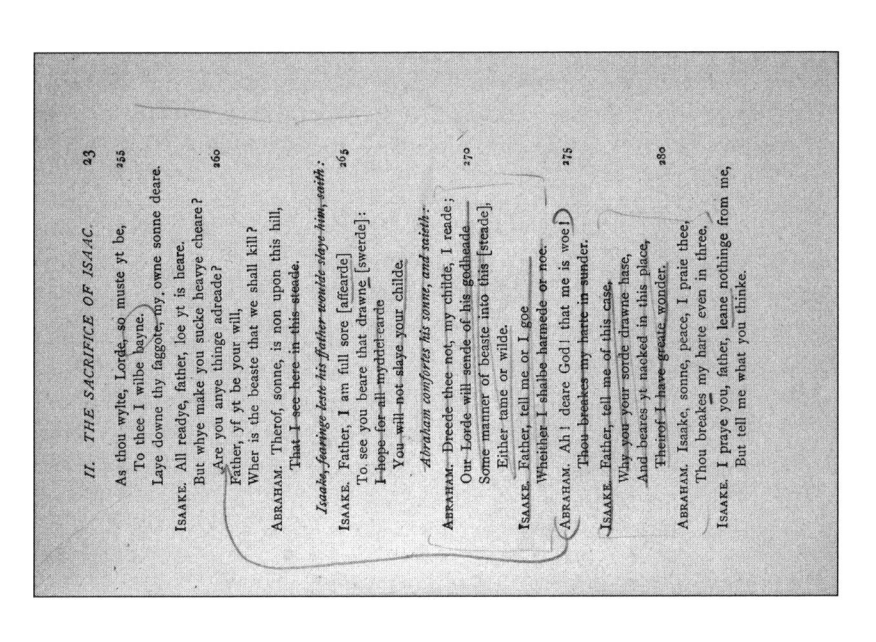

Britten's annotated copy of the Chester miracle play *Histories of Lot and Abraham*, from Pollard's edition of *English Miracle Plays, Moralities and Interludes*, showing the composer's adaptation of the text for his setting of *Canticle II*

triads. In 1961, the year in which Britten recorded *Canticle II* with Pears and alto John Hahessy (later to become the tenor John Elwes), the composer borrowed extensively from *Abraham and Isaac* in his *War Requiem*, where material from the Canticle is ironically distorted to accompany Wilfred Owen's inversion of the biblical story, 'The Parable of the Old Man and the Young', which concludes:

> Offer the Ram of Pride instead of him.
> But the old man would not so, but slew his son,
> And half the seed of Europe, one by one.

See also Eric Roseberry, '"Abraham and Isaac" Revisited: Reflections on a Theme and its Inversion', in PROMB, pp. 253–66, and WRMC, pp. 67–70.

Around 1970 Britten expressed interest in making a string-orchestra version of *Canticle II* for the mezzo-soprano Janet Baker and Pears to perform. This project, which remained unrealized, was in response to an unauthorized orchestration of the work that had been brought to his attention by Boosey & Hawkes; the idea might also have been connected with Britten's first thoughts about writing a work especially for Baker. This was achieved during the summer of 1975 in the dramatic cantata *Phaedra*, which is dedicated to Baker, who gave the first performance at the 1976 Aldeburgh Festival.

5 On 6 January 1952 the Southend-on-Sea Music Club presented the English Opera Group in an 'Operatic Concert', with singers Joan Cross, Peter Pears and Otakar Kraus, and Britten at the piano. The programme, introduced by the Earl of Harewood, comprised arias, duets and trios by Mozart, Verdi, Tchaikovsky and Britten (including Vere's Epilogue from *Billy Budd*). The printed programme for this event includes a review of the EOG season by Basil Douglas.

6 There are two copies at BPL of Ludwig Goldscheider's *Michelangelo Drawings*, first published in 1951. It is likely that this was the 'Michelangelo' book given to Britten and Pears by Coleman, presumably as a Christmas present. The other volume remains unidentified.

7 Coleman's letter to Britten has not survived at BPL. Britten's diary for the week of Coleman's proposed visit indicates that the composer received visits from Leslie Periton (12–15 January), Imogen Holst (15th–16th), Ethel Bridge (16th) and William Plomer (17th–19th). The deletion of 'Group [i.e. EOG] to Aldeburgh' on 14–15 January suggests that the visit by Coleman and members of the EOG management was cancelled.

8 Leslie Periton (1908–1983), Britten's accountant, close friend and adviser, and an Executor of the composer's Will. See Letter 636 n. 2. In an undated lettercard to Periton, Britten wrote, 'you are so helpful & wise about so many things that we always feel better for your visits!'; and, in another card, from the 1960s, 'As ever an evening with you puts my mind at ease over 100 things, & is a great pleasure into the bargain.'

9   British composer, conductor, teacher and writer (1907–1984), daughter of the composer Gustav Holst. In September 1952 she came to live in Aldeburgh to work as Britten's music assistant, a role that included making manuscript fair copies and vocal scores, and preparing full scores: see Holst's contribution to Alan Blyth (ed.), *Remembering Britten*, pp. 54–61, and her 'Working for Benjamin Britten (I)' in CPBC, pp. 46–50, both of which incorporate material from her 'Working for Benjamin Britten', *Musical Times* 118 (March 1977), pp. 202–6. During her first eighteen months as the composer's assistant, Holst kept a diary (IHD) that provides a detailed and insightful account of Britten's activities during this period. See also Letters 436 n. 1 and XXVI n. 1 (vol. 3, p. 107), IC1/2/3, Christopher Grogan (ed.), *Imogen Holst: A Life in Music* and Donald Mitchell's interview with Imogen Holst (Aldeburgh, 22 June 1977) at BPL.

In her interview with Mitchell, Imogen Holst spoke revealingly about aspects of the relationship between Britten and Pears. For example, recollecting an occasion at Long Melford in the 1960s when she was conducting Pears in a Bach cantata, she remarked:

There was that thing, that Peter is always right about everything [. . .] A great deal must have gone on that none of us saw in the way of Ben criticizing him. We were rehearsing an aria of Peter's, and we were going along and then Peter suddenly stopped and said, 'Why are you too slow, Imo? You're nearly half as slow as you should be.' And I knew I wasn't, so I went back on exactly the same thing hoping that he'd realize as he was doing it, and he said, 'No – you're much too slow!' And at that moment Ben [who was listening to the rehearsal] came to my rescue, and drew him aside; and we didn't hear what he said, but he [Pears] came back and we did it again with exactly the same tempo [as before].

In discussing Britten's and Pears's work as Artistic Directors of the Aldeburgh Festival, Holst recognized Britten's strengths as an administrator and criticized Pears's shortcomings: 'He can't put himself in the place of anyone who is organizing.' On working for Britten, she remarked, 'One nearly died of the strain of trying to keep up to what he wanted'. Her coming to Aldeburgh in 1952 was not only to act as his music assistant but also to take on some of the Festival organization with Elizabeth Sweeting, who, as Holst remarked, saw her as 'a rival [. . .] another female, knowing more about music'. See also HCBB, pp. 310–11.

10 William Plomer (1903–1973), South African-born poet, novelist and librettist, who wrote the librettos for *Gloriana* and the three Church Parables: *Curlew River*, *The Burning Fiery Furnace* and *The Prodigal Son*. See Letter 711 n. 1 and IC3, and, for a personal memoir of Plomer, James Lees-Milne, *Fourteen Friends*, pp. 88–102. In 1952 Plomer and Britten were working on a children's opera, subsequently abandoned, entitled *Tyco the Vegan*: see Letter 729 n. 1.

11 Anne Wood (1907–1998), British contralto, who was General Manager of the English Opera Group, 1947–48, and an Artistic Director from 1949. See

Letter 545 n. 2. 'Anne's gloom' concerned an EOG financial crisis, which was discussed at a weekend meeting of the Artistic Directors (with Pears, Basil Douglas and Myfanwy Piper also attending) held on 18–19 January 1952 at the Pipers' home.

12 Basil Douglas (1914–1992), British music administrator and agent, General Manager of the English Opera Group, 1951–57. See also Letter 600 n. 3.

13 The soprano Gladys Whitred had sung Alison in the EOG production of Gustav Holst's *The Wandering Scholar* at the 1951 Cheltenham Festival (see Letter 592 n. 4; she had auditioned for the EOG in January 1951) and was performing Rowan in the 1952 revival of Britten's *Let's Make an Opera*. She subsequently sang songs in the original BBC Television *Watch with Mother* series of *Andy Pandy* and *The Flowerpot Men* (in which she was also the voice of the character Little Weed).

14 Richard Jeffries's *Bevis: The Story of a Boy* (1882), a novel that played a large part in the tradition on which Arthur Ransome drew in his *Swallows and Amazons* series. Both Jeffries's and Ransome's child characters possess unexpected practical skills – for example, sailing boats and building shelters – and are allowed considerable freedom by their parents. Britten was clearly as much an enthusiast for Jeffries's book as he was for those by Ransome. Britten's copy of *Bevis*, a 1948 imprint with an introduction by C. Henry Warren, is at BPL.

Britten's identification with a particular kind of literature for boys was long-standing and not confined solely to English-language authors: for example, Erich Kästner's *Emil und die Detektive* and Jules Renard's *Poil de Carotte*, both made into films also admired by Britten, were great favourites in the early 1930s, and, particularly in the case of *Emil*, exerted a powerful hold on his creative imagination. See also Letter 40 n. 7, JBBC, pp. 26–35, and John Bridcut's film, *Britten's Children*. This aspect of Britten's personality was also surely responsible for his continuous use, from the early 1950s until his death in 1976, of Letts Schoolboy Diaries as his pocket engagement diary.

Arthur Ransome lectured at the 1949 Aldeburgh Festival, in the Baptist Chapel on 14 June, on the subject of 'Sailing in East Anglia'.

724 To Anthony Gishford[1]

4 CRABBE STREET, ALDEBURGH, SUFFOLK

Jan. 15th 1952

My dear Tony,

Thanks for indulging me in some critics[2] – slightly offsetting the Berlin weekend news,[3] which made me sick! Interesting that Waterhouse[4] (not usually bright) saw so much – but then he's a <u>literary</u> ~~block~~ bloke(!) &

obviously knows the book. I understand about ½ dear Willi Schuh[5] says – my subconscious refuses to let me understand the bad bits, so I'm happy with it. He's one of the few who take trouble. The enclosed effusion about 'Rejoice in the Lamb' has been sent to me by some well-meaning Yank – & asks me to send it to you for use (if that's ever likely) – written by a Professor of Religion & Philosophy at Carleton College – & according to his wife (who sent it) immensely distinguished.[6] I'm glad to see that my Theology is so acceptable; a pity my music isn't always quite so . . . !

Hope you're well. How's that gay little Critics' Circle?[7]

Many thanks,
Yours ever,
BEN

1 British music publisher (1908–1975), a director of Boosey & Hawkes. Gishford was a supportive and sympathetic friend to Britten and was appointed an Executor of Britten's Will. (He was to predecease the composer.) See Letter 556 n. 3.

2 Gishford had sent Britten a selection of reviews of *Billy Budd*.

3 On 2 January 1952 the East German government had rejected a request by the United Nations to supervise free national elections. On 11 January, the former Reich Chancellor Dr Joseph Wirth had held a press conference in Berlin in which he criticized the West German government, praised that of the East, and urged for negotiations to take place between the two sides of the divided nation. West Berlin was at this time isolated from the remainder of West Germany by Communist-controlled East Germany.

4 John Waterhouse (1904–1989), British music critic of the *Birmingham Post*, had been Reader in English at the University of Birmingham before the Second World War. See also Letter IX n. 1 (vol. 3, p. 75). For his review of *Billy Budd* in the *Birmingham Post* (17 December 1951), see Letter 718 n. 2.

5 Swiss musicologist (1900–1986), who was music editor of the *Neue Zürcher Zeitung*, 1944–65; see also Letter 556 n. 4. He contributed a review of *Billy Budd* to Zurich's *Schweitzerische Musikzeitung* (1 January 1952), pp. 15–18.

6 *Rejoice in the Lamb*, Britten's cantata for soloists, chorus and organ, composed in 1943, in which he set words by Christopher Smart (1722–1771). The enclosure from the unidentified professor at Carleton College, Minnesota, USA, has not survived.

7 The professional association of critics of drama, music, cinema and dance, founded in 1913, and superseding the Society of Drama Critics established in 1907.

725 To Gretl Zander[1]

4 CRABBE STREET, ALDEBURGH, SUFFOLK
Jan. 31st 1952

Dear Mrs Zander,

I feel I must write you a note to thank you for your really heroic work on behalf of 'Let's Make an Opera'![2] You really have worked splendidly – & it is encouraging to all of us that the people you persuaded to come to the Lyric enjoyed the work & production so much. I only hope that the production at Gerrards Cross goes well; I must somehow get down to see it.

I wish I'd known that the children would have liked to go to the Lyric with me – but actually I was only able to go very rarely – & once completely surrounded & sat on by all the powder monkeys, midshipmen & cabin boys of 'Billy Budd'.[3] I hope I can manage to suggest a day when you & Mr Zander[4] could have luncheon with me in London & talk over Benji's schooling.[5] But I am in London so very rarely nowadays – & when I am I am so overwhelmed with business matters! But I hope it can be managed. What chance is there of him getting a scholarship? – What do his present masters say? I should suggest offhand Lancing, Sherborne, Radley – or, if his classics are really brilliant, Eton.[6] I'm not so convinced about the ordinary run of public schools for a boy like him; however we can discuss it.[7]

Please forgive the scribble, but this is written in great haste.

Yours with gratitude,
BENJAMIN BRITTEN

1 The mother (1905–1968) of Benjamin ('Benji') Zander (b. 1939), who was to become a well-known British conductor. Britten had been in occasional correspondence with the Zander family since 1950 about Benjamin's musical education. See also Letter 666 n. 1. Gretl Zander was the prime instigator of a production of *Let's Make an Opera* at High Wycombe Grammar School in July 1952, which she invited Britten to conduct; he declined.

Benjamin Zander has written about his early association with Britten, Imogen Holst and Aldeburgh:

I began to compose at nine and wrote a number of compositions of modest pretensions, three of which my mother entered into the local Arts Festival in the village of Gerrards Cross in Buckinghamshire where we lived. The Adjudicator, the composer Michael Head, down from London to judge the competition, decided that the compositions were unworthy of consideration and actually said out loud in front of the large crowd gathered that afternoon in the Village Hall, that 'this young man should be discouraged from ever composing again'. It seems now, in retrospect, a most peculiar thing to say about a nine-year-old, but my mother's response, in the absence of my much more knowledgeable father in India, was even more peculiar.

Instead of comforting me, complaining to the organizers or boxing Mr Head's ears, my mother gathered my compositions together in an envelope, together with a note she had written and the comments of Mr Head and sent them to Benjamin Britten, England's leading composer. Four days later the telephone rang. It was Ben Britten. He reassured my mother that the compositions were perfectly appropriate for a kid of my age, and that if the family would like to spend the summer holidays in Aldeburgh [. . .] he would be delighted to keep an eye on my musical development.

So for three summers the entire Zander family went to Aldeburgh for the holidays. To say I studied with Britten would be an exaggeration. I met with him frequently at his house on 4, Crab Lane [sic], usually around tea-time, and after tea, he would look at my compositions and make comments, especially about the songs. He was always fascinated by the words. When I played and sang to him my highly dramatic rendition of the tale of Casey Jones, he called in his partner, the great tenor Peter Pears, to hear it. They took down various books of folk poetry and showed me different versions. I remember asking anxiously if I had set the wrong version, which they greeted with peals of kindly laughter.

It was at this time that Ben Britten suggested that my father should ask Imogen Holst to teach me. At first she turned down the idea. It was too far to travel for her and she had too much to do for Ben. One morning, as we were in the rowing boat on the sea, we told Britten that she had refused. 'Do you think it might help if I asked her?' Britten inquired ingenuously. 'Yes,' said my father. He did and this time she agreed. Imo, as she was known, was a peerless teacher. She travelled from Aldeburgh to my home in Gerrards Cross in Buckinghamshire by train once a week and gave me what I remember as lessons in the dance. Not that I actually danced! But she did. She would waft around the room as I played my harmony and counterpoint exercises. It was from Imo that I learned that music is a kinetic art – essentially about the dance.

'It doesn't flow,' she would say, 'I can't dance to it.'

('If it doesn't flow, I can't dance to it', from Benjamin Zander's website, accessed in 2007: www.benjaminzander.com/journal.)

2 Gretl Zander had encouraged over one hundred people from Gerrards Cross to attend performances of *Let's Make an Opera* during its run at the Lyric Theatre, Hammersmith, which ended on 26 January. In these performances the piano-duet part was performed by Robert Keys and Marion Harewood, with the latter replaced for the final run of performances by Sheila Randell (the mother of Mervyn Cooke).

3 The date of this performance was probably 19 January, on which day a note in Britten's pocket diary reads 'Boys to Let's Make'. The 'Boys', from Kingsland Central School, were members of the chorus, i.e. the ship's crew, in the original Covent Garden production of *Billy Budd*.

4 Dr Walter Zander (1898–1993), German-born Jewish lawyer and scholar. Following military service in the First World War, during which he was decorated with the Iron Cross, Zander established a legal practice in Berlin; however, the rise of Nazism in the 1930s impelled him and his family to emigrate to the UK, where they settled in Buckinghamshire, Zander founding a

printing business in Slough. Like other 'enemy aliens', he was interned on the Isle of Man for a period following the outbreak of the Second World War. In 1944 he was appointed Secretary to the British Friends of the Hebrew University in Jerusalem, a post he held until 1971. In 1948 he published *Is This The Way?*, an influential pamphlet exploring Zionism's attitude to the Arabs. See also the obituary by Sir James Craig, *Independent* (18 April 1993) and Daniel Snowman, *The Hitler Emigrés: The Cultural Impact on Britain of Refugees from Nazism*, p. 110.

5   On 6 April, Britten wrote to Walter Zander to thank him for the present of a 'magnificent book'. He continued, 'It has been a great pleasure & excitement for me to meet young Benji: I am full of hope for his future, & I shall do whatever I can to help him in whatever way his talent develops. I am always interested to see young and talented children growing up, & one, as brilliant as Benji is, is really exciting.'

6   Lancing College, Sussex, where Pears had been a pupil; Sherborne School, Sherborne, Dorset; Radley College, Abingdon, Oxfordshire; and Eton College, near Windsor, Berkshire.

7   On 15 May, Britten wrote again to Walter Zander to apologize for his 'long silence', and revealed that he had written on Benjamin's behalf to the music master at Oundle School (at which he had performed with Pears on 10 February). He described Oundle to Zander as

a conventional, but not hide-bound public-school – with plenty of music & generally a civilised artistic policy. I think the firm discipline which this school will have will be good for Benji (I am always an advocate of it!).

Zander eventually attended Uppingham School, Rutland, from September 1952.

Britten's relationships with the Zanders came under some strain early in 1953, when the composer's private comments on Benjamin were misrepresented to Gretl Zander by a mutual acquaintance. As a result, Britten felt it necessary to write to Mrs Zander on 6 February that year, explaining that his remarks had concerned the danger of the boy becoming 'spoiled', and of the need for him to find a 'specialisation' for his musical talents. Benjamin himself had written to the composer. Britten told his mother:

The letter he wrote to me is entirely unimportant, and I will not mention it to him when I write for the simple reason that I wish him to write to me always exactly as he feels without any sense of restraint – I certainly hope you will not mention it to him either. When I see him I will talk to him about the larger matter of which the letter is but a symptom.

Please do not worry about the matter nor think that I have in any way retracted from my opinions or affection for the boy. I will continue to help him in any way that I can, and I feel certain that our high hopes of his future will be justified.

726 To Lesley Bedford[1]

4 CRABBE STREET, ALDEBURGH, SUFFOLK
Feb. 12th 1952

My dearest Lesley,

Your letter about Abraham & Isaac gave me great pleasure.[2] You are sweet to have written, & you need never worry that I shall be bored to hear from you! I love your warm praise – for, seriously, if you & your friends are pleased with my music, that's what I write it for. I'm naturally glad that you like my youngest child, because – as is so often the case – he gave me great trouble in coming into the world!

I hope you have good news of all your dear ones. I hope to be able to drive down to Lancing with Peter later this term, so I hope to see Dave[3] in all his glory!

Lots of love & thanks,
Yours ever,
BEN

1 Née Duff (1907–1987), British soprano, mother of the composer David Bedford (see n. 3 below) and the conductor and pianist Steuart Bedford. She was a member of the English Opera Group from its inception and created the roles of Lucia in *The Rape of Lucretia*, Emmie in *Albert Herring* and Mrs Vixen in Britten's realization of Gay's *The Beggar's Opera*. Britten was close to the whole family. See also Letter 555 n. 2 and 1C3.

2 Britten's *Canticle II: 'Abraham and Isaac'* had been given its first performance in the Albert Hall, Nottingham, on 21 January by Kathleen Ferrier, Pears and Britten. The work was repeated on a brief tour to Birmingham (22 January; broadcast on the BBC Midland Home Service on 18 February); Liverpool (24 January), and Manchester (25 January), and further performances followed at London's Victoria and Albert Museum (3 February), for the BBC (4 February, for transmission on the Third Programme on the 6th; this broadcast, however, was postponed until 13 May because of King George VI's death), and at Bristol (5 February) and Rhyl (6 February). These performances had been planned in order to raise money for the English Opera Group. Britten's pocket engagement diary indicates that he and Pears planned a second short recital tour with Ferrier in April 1953: however, the return of Ferrier's cancer – she gave her last performance on 6 February that year – meant the tour was cancelled.

On 14 October 1952, Britten wrote to Gretl Zander:

> I am very happy that you and your husband enjoyed "Abraham & Isaac" at the V. & A. Certainly it can never be sung better than by those two artists – miraculous singing. I wish I'd heard it.

The pianist at this Victoria and Albert Museum recital on 5 October was

Gerald Moore, who was standing in for the composer (then at work on *Gloriana*).

During the tour, Ferrier wrote to John Newmark (28 January 1952; Christopher Fifield (ed.), *Letters and Diaries of Kathleen Ferrier*, p. 173):

Ben wrote a new Canticle for the two of us [i.e. Ferrier and Pears] on the Biblical story of Abraham and Isaac – the ink was still wet for the 1st performance! But it's a sweet piece – simple and very moving.

When *Canticle II* was published in March 1953, Britten sent Ferrier an inscribed copy: 'For my dear Kath / the 1st copy – and who / could deserve it more! / with all my love / & deepest admiration / Ben / March 3rd 1953 / Aldeburgh'. (The score is now part of the Ferrier Collection at Blackburn Museum.)

An anonymous review of the first performance appeared in the *Nottingham Guardian* (22 January 1952; an edited version of the same review appeared in the *Nottingham Journal* of the same date):

The vocal interpreters of the work [. . .] brought to bear their considerable powers and sense of artistic perception with moving result. Mr Britten said afterwards how impressed he was by the way Nottingham received his new work. It is interesting to note that this work is now being performed only in cities where Mr Britten hopes to bring his operas.

The reviewer was evidently granted an interview with the composer, who declared that he hoped to have a 'new children's opera ready for production this year' and that 'he is now collaborating with the novelist, William Plomer, on a children's opera on a contemporary theme. In 1953 he plans a full-scale opera, a successor to his current Covent Garden triumph, *Billy Budd*.'

John W. Waterhouse contributed a review of the performance given in Birmingham Town Hall to the *Birmingham Post* (23 January 1952):

As surely as *Billy Budd*, [*Canticle II*] demonstrates its composer's musical-emotional maturity. It must strike even through the thickest ears that 'profounder note' which some people have for so long been demanding of Mr Britten. The lovely movement beginning with Isaac's plea 'Father, do with me as you will' comes out of the same box, so to say, as the execution-ballad of the handcuffed Billy, but I incline to like it even better. The entire setting, from its Schütz-like opening device of giving God to two singers, builds and completes a wholly satisfying musical entity, with a climax magnificently approached and achieved. Mr Britten has written no more strikingly original vocal concert-piece since *Les Illuminations*; and he is a greater composer than he was then.

Following the Manchester performance, Colin Mason contributed a review to the *Manchester Guardian* (26 January 1952):

This slightly disappointing piece seemed little more than a sketch for a more considerable work. The characteristic features of Britten's vocal melody are scarcely discernible, nor is there any great interest in the texture, except when God speaks and contralto and tenor sing together in two parts which converge and diverge with fascinating effect. Elsewhere there is little real two-part writing, and the simplicity of the vocal writing, against the slenderest of accompaniments, borders on monotony. There is no doubt that this extreme technical simplicity and tranquil, unemotional expression were deliberately sought, probably to convey a sense of naive devotion, and it may well be that what was ineffective on the concert platform would be very moving in a suitable religious setting – as is to some extent true, for instance, of Haydn's *Seven Last Words*.

Following the Canticle's London premiere, the critic of *The Times* (5 February 1952) was altogether more approving:

Dignified and simple in style, as befits the restrained pathos of the old text, it strikes the imagination at once, as the piano gravely rolls major thirds in E flat up the keyboard and the voice of God is heard calling 'Abraham!' to a haunting phrase on the same interval. The spirit of Purcell is evoked in the flowing interchange of recitative, arioso, and duet; most effective is the dovetailing of solo passages, when one voice takes over from another – the refined singing of Miss Kathleen Ferrier and Mr Peter Pears here, especially, realized the composer's intentions with powerful beauty. In one duo a higher norm of dissonance is employed, but the texture at this point is in two parts; for the most part solemn mystery is represented in spare dramatic terms, with emphasis on elegant vocal line and clear communication.

3 David Bedford (b. 1937), British composer; see also Letter 586 n. 1 and 1C3. Bedford was a pupil at Lancing College, which Britten and Pears were to visit on 29 March.

727 To Henry Boys[1]

4 CRABBE STREET, ALDEBURGH, SUFFOLK
Feb. 12th 1952

My dear Henry,

How nice to hear from you – even tho' your letter had business colourings! You don't, alas, say a word of how things are going with you. I'm always hoping that you'll turn up somewhere somehow, but (apart from Cheltenham) it never seems to happen. I shall be around London a lot after Easter (doing Budds)[2] – <u>please</u> materialise then.

I'm afraid I can't do anything at the moment about a ballet for Belgium.[3] I am very much committed for sometime, & anyhow, I've always promised that my first original ballet will be with Freddy Ashton.[4] But the last seems to be growing more & more remote, as he gets more & more difficult to know, & is so elusive anyhow. He seems to have lost so much spirit & courage these days. Could you thank Mde Huysmans for me, & say how flattered I was by her invitation?

Yes, that young girl was a hell of a bore – but I think I frightened her off the last time – & there's been a month or two's silence, thank God![5]

Peter joins me in sending love to both of you. Although we so seldom seem to meet, we talk of you with great affection & admiration constantly.

Love from

BEN

1 British critic, composer and teacher (1910–1992), dedicatee of Britten's Violin Concerto, and a contemporary of Britten at the Royal College of Music. He had written perceptively of Britten's early music and was responsible for preparing the vocal scores of *The Rape of Lucretia* and *Albert Herring*. See also Letter 74 n. 2; IC1/2, and Letter 560 n. 1.

2 Britten travelled to Birmingham on 3 April and conducted *Billy Budd* there on the following day. Back in London, he rehearsed the opera at Covent Garden on 15 April, prior to performances on 18 and 21 April, and 1 and 13 May. Performances on 26 April and 8 May were conducted by Peter Gellhorn, Head of Music Staff at Covent Garden. For further information on the tensions surrounding Gellhorn's involvement in these early performances, see BBMCPR, pp. 163–4, n. 32.

3 No information has come to light about this proposed ballet, which may have been for the company of La Monnaie, Brussels. Nor has it been possible to identify Madame Huysmans, who apparently initiated the invitation.

4 Frederick Ashton (1904–1988), British dancer and choreographer, founder–choreographer of the Royal Ballet, of which he was Director, 1963–70. He directed the first production of *Albert Herring* in 1947 and was to choreograph the movement and dance sequences for *Death in Venice* in 1973. See also Letters 138 n. 3 and 627 n. 8, and Julie Kavanagh, *Secret Muses: The Life of Sir Frederick Ashton*, pp. 336–40 and 535–9.

In the event, Britten's first full-length ballet was to be choreographed by John Cranko. Ashton was considered a possible choreographer for the dance elements in *Gloriana* (although this task was assigned to Cranko when Ashton's services were required for the Sadler's Wells Ballet's contribution to the Coronation celebrations: see Letter 746) and he did not work on another original Britten stage work until *Death in Venice* in 1973. When Cranko proved to be an unreliable director during the first staging of *A Midsummer Night's Dream* in 1960, Britten was to contemplate calling in Ashton to save the production (HCBB, p. 392).

Prior to *Albert Herring*, contact between Britten and Ashton had been intermittent. In 1938 Ashton had expressed interest in choreographing Britten's *Variations on a Theme of Frank Bridge* (see Letter 138 and Kavanagh, *Secret Muses*, pp. 236–7); that same year there had been the possibility of a ballet commission for Britten from Sadler's Wells, in which Ashton was to have been involved (see Letter 120 n. 2); and in 1939 Ashton was proposed as the principal dancer in an interpretation of Bunyan's *The Pilgrim's Progress*, for which Britten was invited to write the music (see

Letter 164 n. 3). After Britten's return from the United States, Ashton had wanted to create his own ballet using Britten's *Soirées Musicales* and *Matinées Musicales* (see Letters 413 and 415), though no details of any such Ashton ballet have been traced. Julie Kavanagh reports (p. 304) that Ashton intended to work with the composer on *Peter Grimes*, in which, according to Edmund Burra, he was to make a silent appearance. This came to nothing; but perhaps Ashton saw himself as a contender for the silent role of Dr Crabbe, which was taken by the Czech dancer and director Sasa Machov in the first performance.

Post-*Herring*, and despite the frictions that occurred during the rehearsal period at Glyndebourne in 1947 (for an account of Ashton's growing antipathy to Britten during *Herring*, see HCBB, pp. 251–2), Ashton was considered, in 1950, as director for the English Opera Group staging of Britten's and Imogen Holst's edition of Purcell's *Dido and Aeneas* (see Letter 670 n. 5) and, as late as February 1951, for the premiere production of *Billy Budd* (see Letters 672 and 694).

Ashton's early interest in the *Bridge Variations* came to fruition in his ballet *Le Rêve de Léonor*, first produced by the Ballets de Paris, at the Prince's Theatre, London, in April 1949, for which Arthur Oldham rearranged Britten's score, conceived originally for strings, for full orchestra (see Kavanagh, pp. 359–60, and David Vaughan, *Frederick Ashton and His Ballets*, 2nd edn, pp. 237 and 495). Ashton created two other ballets using Britten's music: *Illuminations*, based on the song-cycle *Les Illuminations*, with scenery and costumes by Cecil Beaton, for the New York City Ballet in March 1950 (see Kavanagh, pp. 375–80, who reports that Ashton first heard the cycle at a BBC Promenade Concert in September 1945, sung by Pears and conducted by Britten, and 'had promised Britten that a ballet to the score would soon follow' (p. 375), and Vaughan, pp. 238–44 and 495–6); and *Variations on a Theme of Purcell*, based on *The Young Person's Guide to the Orchestra*, first performed by the Sadler's Wells Ballet at the Royal Opera House, Covent Garden, in January 1955 (see Kavanagh, p. 413; Vaughan pp. 274–7 and 500; and Letter 826 n. 5).

5 This reference remains obscure and it is not the only instance of Britten's discomfort at being the target of unsolicited advances from female admirers. Ronald Duncan vividly recounts the case of a woman who claimed to be the composer's wife in the mid-1950s. She began by sending him over a dozen 'amorous postcards' from Huddersfield, then wrote to him from a false address in Bayswater before embarrassing the composer in person at a performance of *The Turn of the Screw*: see Letter 861 n. 5 and RDWB, pp. 134–5.

For a further example of Britten's being harassed by a psychologically troubled woman, see Maureen Garnham, *As I Saw It*, pp. 18–19.

VICTORIA & ALBERT MUSEUM
South Kensington

By kind permission of the Director, Sir Leigh Ashton

MUSEUM GALLERY CONCERTS

English Opera Group

present

PETER PEARS
BENJAMIN BRITTEN

IN

"DIE SCHÖNE MÜLLERIN"

SCHUBERT

SUNDAY, FEBRUARY 17th, 1952

PROGRAMME
ONE SHILLING

Management:
IBBS & TILLETT LTD.
124 Wigmore Street, W.1

---

728 To Elizabeth Mayer[1]

HOTEL VERGALDEN, GARGELLEN [Austria][2]
March 14th 1952

My dearest Elizabeth,

Months & months have gone by since I wrote to you. I am so sorry that it has been so long, & actually so much has happened that it is even longer than the calendar says! But I think you must have picked up the main items of news about us, one way or another, & so I needn't bore you too much with facts, but talk more about the things which interest us.

Your parcels have given us all great joy; Peter, Miss Hudson,[3] & the many friends who visit us (so many now friends of yours) have all shared in my birthday & Christmas packages. You are an angel to send them, to choose them with such care, & to wrap them so beautifully. As you will guess life domestically remains, & is increasingly, difficult. Miss Hudson manages excellently, & of course we travel a great deal which eases the tension, but all the same the parcels such as you, dear Elizabeth, so generously send have helped so much. But please don't do it if it is a financial embarrassment to you. I know life cannot always be too easy for you, how terribly expensive things are becoming – & besides you must save up for the visit over here which we are all hoping you & William will make this summer!! I hope that before long that Elizabeth Sweeting[4] will be sending you the prospectus of the Festival. I hope it will whet your appetite. It is perhaps a little more modest this year than previously, because money is so tight, but I think many things will tempt you both. Do come.

You will be surprised at this address. We are in the middle of a really glorious holiday. Peter, Marion & George[5] & I have promised ourselves this present for ages, as a reward for what has been for all of us a very hectic winter. We had some concerts in Austria, one in Salzburg, & two in Vienna[6] – & came up here to the mountains in the middle of last week to ski & generally energetically relax. We are all dark brown, burnt by the lovely snowy sun, & feeling new people. Our ski-ing is wild & eccentric,[7] but we go on long tours with a charming local Führer – & even plan to do an overnight one this weekend. We must, alas, leave next week – Peter has to be back in England to sing, & the Harewoods & I are going to Wiesbaden to hear Billy Budd in German. It had its German Erstaufführung there 2 or 3 weeks ago, & in such a good performance, we hear, that it is worthwhile making a little detour to see it.[8] It is now on tour in England but without Peter or me – except for one performance in April in Birmingham where we will join the Covent Garden Company. It comes back to London in May for some performances. Dear Elizabeth – I long for you to see it. I think you will like it, it has a lot of Forster[9] & me in it – & the performance is good too. Lovely settings by Piper,[10] & a good production by Basil Coleman (did you meet him?) – and an outstanding, haunting performance by our Peter. The American boy did very well – we were most lucky to find him.[11] He looks the part & has a charming voice – between ourselves we shall hear the part better sung, but perhaps not for some time. The reaction from the public has been quite overwhelming – they have taken the work to their hearts – surprisingly because it cannot be obviously everyone's meat. Next season Grimes joins Budd in the Covent Garden repertory, & I will be conducting both.[12] That is surprising, & not really to my taste, because you know how I dislike conducting. But because of Krips'[13] sudden defaulting I had to take on Budd, & it has gone so well that it was difficult to refuse to do some other works. Whether I ever will do my precious Mozart or Verdi there remains to be seen – I will give no promises yet.[14] My life is already so full, that I hesitate to pack it even fuller. I won't willingly either give up any of my other activities – my writing becomes more & more important to me (I am in the middle of planning another opera, a Children's one, with William Plomer,[15] an excellent novelist & poet, great friend of Morgan Forster), my concerts with Peter are too precious (we are at the Salzburg, Aix, & Menton festivals this summer),[16] the Opera Group which must go on, the Aldeburgh Festival takes a lot of care – so how to add conducting regularly to all these? Well. Time will show.

Beth & her family[17] were well when I saw them last – but then, she writes much more regularly than I do, so you know all her news. She tells me, by the way, that you would like a Billy Budd première programme. I will send one when I get back. Barbara[18] is also well – & terribly happy freelancing. You know she gave up her job? – largely at my instigation, & is going to live in the country, when she looks for a house! At the moment she is far too happy doing all the things around & in London she has never, all these years, had time to do. She is helping Peter & me find a flat somewhere, because reluctantly we have all, mutually, decided that Melbury Road[19] is not satisfactory anymore. Sophie[20] is getting a little tired, & if we are in London much, finds it a great strain – & honestly we find it a bit small. So we shall find somewhere more central, but shall see a lot of them both, to whom we are still naturally devoted. Sophie of course has the time of her life with her little grandson, who is really very sweet. Peter & I had some concerts up North[21] before we came up here & we did them from Harewood, & so saw a lot of David,[22] who is a sweet kid, very good-tempered & gay.

How is Beata, & her little ones? And Michael & Christopher?[23] Do give them lots of love from us both, & every good wish. It seems ages since we saw you all, & it will certainly be ages before we come to America again.[24] We often get asked if we will cross the Ocean again, but time is so short & big journeys get more & more remote. Anyhow the thought that you & William may be coming this summer is very exciting – please try & manage it!

This rather rambly, dull note (written in the middle of a snow & sun-drunk holiday!) comes with lots of love from Peter & your devoted

BEN

Love also
from George & Marion

1 The wife (1884–1970) of Dr William Mayer (1887–1956), who was formerly Medical Director at the Long Island Home, a psychiatric institution. The Mayer family had provided generous hospitality and profound emotional support for Britten and Pears throughout their stay in the United States, 1939–42. See also Letter 194 n. 1 and 1c1/2/3. Elizabeth Mayer had made the German translation of the libretto of *The Rape of Lucretia*, and was the dedicatee of *Hymn to St Cecilia*.

2 Britten and Pears were enjoying a ski-ing holiday at Gargellen, having given recitals in Salzburg and Vienna. As Britten explains, they spent the vacation in the company of George and Marion Harewood, and during it the party first discussed the topic of Elizabeth I as a potential operatic subject.

3 Elizabeth (Nellie) Hudson (1898–1982), Britten's housekeeper from 1948 to 1973. See plate 5 and Letter 682 n. 10.

4 British arts administrator (1914–1999), General Manager of the Aldeburgh Festival, 1948–55. See Letter 576 n. 2.

5 George Lascelles, 7th Earl of Harewood (b. 1923), British opera administrator and writer, a first cousin of Queen Elizabeth II; see Letter 614 n. 9 and 1c3. In 1949 he had married Marion Stein (b. 1926), the daughter of Britten's publisher at Boosey & Hawkes, Erwin Stein, and an intimate friend of both Britten and Pears since 1942; see Letter 418 n. 7, Letter 525 n. 21 and 1c1/2/3, Harewood's autobiography, *The Tongs and the Bones* (especially pp. 129–49) and Donald Mitchell's filmed interview with Harewood (2006) at BPL. The Harewoods were joint dedicatees of *Billy Budd*, and of *A Wedding Anthem (Amo Ergo Sum)*, which Britten composed for their marriage ceremony.

6 The recital in Salzburg took place in the Konzertsaal of the Mozarteum on 1 March and included the *Michelangelo Sonnets*. M. Kaindl-Hönig's notice in the *Salzburg Nachtrichten* (3 March 1952) concluded with a slightly idiosyncratic postscript in English:

A notice for Benjamin Britten and Peter Pears: It was perhaps the finest concert of two soloists I ever heard. However, I couldn't write it [in German in the review] as too many people who missed always here best chances – wouldn't believe it.

On 3 March in the Mozartsaal of the Vienna Konzerthaus, Britten and Pears gave a recital that included the *Donne Sonnets* and Schubert *Lieder*. No programme survives at BPL for the other Vienna concert Britten mentions in this letter, though Christopher Headington (CHPP, p. 179) notes that Britten and Pears gave a recital at the Palais Pallavicini, Vienna, on 4 March.

7 Christopher Headington writes: 'In these earlyish days before ski-lifts they struggled up slopes on wooden skis with skins, only to slide down again with much laughter, Pears being quite good though no expert' (CHPP, p. 179).

8 Britten attended a performance of the first production of *Billy Budd* sung in German, at the Staatsoper, Wiesbaden, on 22 March 1952, with the Harewoods. The production, which had opened on 3 March, was directed by Heinrich Köhler-Helffrich, designed by Wilhelm Reinking and conducted by Josef Zosel, with Karl Liebl (Vere), Georg Stern (Claggart) and August Gschwend (Budd). See Letter 731 n. 2 for Harewood's *Opera* review of the production and for further information on the Wiesbaden production.

From Gargellen, Britten and his companions travelled to Zurich, where (after Pears's return to the United Kingdom) Britten enjoyed a performance of Tchaikovsky's *Eugene Onegin*: according to Lord Harewood (*The Tongs and the Bones*, p. 135),

> We buzzed with shared pleasure throughout dinner afterwards, and Ben commented on the touching and striking dramatic effect made by the disappearance of Olga after her disastrous provocation of Lensky in the first scene of Act II, which he compared acutely and accurately with the unexplained but equally convincing removal of the Fool from *King Lear*.

(Britten was to give serious consideration to adapting Shakespeare's *King Lear* as an opera in the early 1960s.)

One scene in *Onegin* – Tatyana's letter scene from Act I – exerted its own powerful influence on Britten. According to Ronald Duncan, it was a scene the composer admired (see RDWB, p. 92) and was to emulate in *The Turn of the Screw* when the Governess writes to Miles's and Flora's guardian (Act II scene 3).

9 E. M. (Edward Morgan) Forster (1879–1970), British novelist and man of letters, who, with Eric Crozier, wrote the libretto for *Billy Budd*. See Letter 571 n. 9 and IC3.

10 John Piper (1903–1992), British painter, stained-glass and stage designer, who, from *The Rape of Lucretia* onwards, was to be one of Britten's most frequent and long-serving artistic collaborators, designing the majority of the composer's stage works. See also Letter 523 n. 1.

11 Theodor (Ted) Uppman (1920–2005), American baritone who created the title role in *Billy Budd* at Covent Garden in 1951, a part originally intended for Geraint Evans; Uppman continued to perform the role until the 1970s, singing it at the US stage premiere of the opera at Chicago in 1970. Born in California, Uppman studied at the Curtis Institute (1939–41) and was involved in opera workshops at Stanford University (1941–42) and the University of Southern California (1948–50). In 1947 he sang Pelléas in concert at San Francisco with Maggie Teyte as Mélisande, a performance conducted by Pierre Monteux, and subsequently sang the role in 1948 at the New York City Opera and at his Metropolitan Opera debut in 1953. His career at the Met continued every year until 1978 in roles including Guglielmo, Masetto, Papageno (the latter conducted by Bruno Walter), Eisenstein (*Die Fledermaus*), Kothner (*Die Meistersinger*), Sharpless (*Madama Butterfly*) and

Harlequin (*Ariadne auf Naxos*). In 1983 he sang the seven baritone roles in Britten's *Death in Venice* in Geneva. Following his retirement Uppman taught in New York at Mannes College and the Manhattan School of Music, and at the Britten–Pears School at Snape where he was an honorary director.

An off-air recording of the BBC Third Programme broadcast of the premiere of *Billy Budd* was issued on CD in 1993, and Uppman took part in the much abridged NBC Television production broadcast in 1952 (see Letter 899 n. 3 and BBMCPR, pp. 152–3), a copy of which is available at BPL. Also at BPL is a recording of Uppman's appearance at the 1975 Aldeburgh Festival when, on 19 June, he performed Budd's aria, 'Billy in the Darbies', with the English Chamber Orchestra conducted by Steuart Bedford.

See also vol. 3, plates 45–7, and Letters 688 n. 1, and 718 n. 2; BBMCPR, p. 55; Gary Schmidgall, 'The Natural: Theodor Uppman is Billy Budd', *Opera News* (28 March 1992), pp. 13–16; and obituaries in the *Daily Telegraph* (19 March 2005); by Anthony Tommasini, *New York Times* (19 March 2005); Alan Blyth, *Guardian* (22 March 2005); Elizabeth Forbes, *Independent* (22 March 2005); in *The Times* (23 March 2005); and by Alan Blyth, *Opera* (May 2005). In 1999 VAI Audio issued a CD, *The Art of Theodor Uppman*, comprising a selection of operatic arias, *Lieder* and songs from Broadway musicals, first broadcast between 1954 and 1957.

Blyth's *Guardian* obituary recalled how Uppman was chosen for the role of Billy Budd:

> Uppman, whose career seemed to have stalled after a promising start, had worked with Alfred Drake on a Broadway musical. When it became known that David Webster, General Administrator at Covent Garden, was in New York auditioning for a Billy Budd, [Drake] persuaded Uppman to enter the fray.
>
> Turning up at the audition, tanned and blond, Uppman seemed ideal material. His voice was taped and the results taken back to Britten with a strong recommendation from Webster. He got the job, and Britten was delighted. His ideal for the role – a baritone who was youthful, enthusiastic and innocent-looking – had been completely fulfilled.
>
> [...] I recall how fresh and spontaneous an interpreter he proved to be. His looks and mellow, yet virile, tone, allied to a seemingly natural gift for portraying a strong, yet still boyish sailor were unforgettable attributes, and he made his solo, when condemned to death ['Billy in the Darbies'], as eloquent as it should be.

12 In the event *Billy Budd* was not revived at Covent Garden in the 1952–53 season. *Peter Grimes*, however, was revived in 1953, when it was conducted not by the composer, who was suffering from bursitis, but by Reginald Goodall.

13 Josef Krips (1902–1974), Austrian conductor, who had been engaged to conduct the premiere of *Billy Budd* and whose withdrawal meant that Britten had to step in at short notice as his replacement. See Letter 705 n. 2 and Harriett Krips, *Ohne Liebe kann man keine Musik machen: Erinnerungen*.

14 The only operas Britten conducted at Covent Garden were his own, but this remark reveals his enthusiasm for the operas of Mozart and Verdi. Of

Mozart's operas, Britten conducted only *Idomeneo* (Aldeburgh Festivals 1969–70, and BBC2 Television, broadcast 10 May 1970), though there were plans for a production of *Don Giovanni* (presumably with Pears as Don Ottavio) at Aldeburgh in 1973, which remained unfulfilled because of the illness that ended Britten's performing activities. Both Hans Keller and Donald Mitchell tried on occasion to persuade Britten to conduct *Così fan tutte* at Aldeburgh.

Much as he admired them and was influenced by them, Britten never conducted any of Verdi's operas.

In November 1952 Britten was invited to become Musical Director of Covent Garden in succession to Karl Rankl, an offer he declined (see Letter 748 n. 5).

15 Plomer and Britten had been discussing various subjects for this opera, and the composer had asked Plomer to send him the first part of the draft libretto of *Tyco the Vegan* to Gargellen. Britten wrote to Plomer about the project on the same day that he wrote to Elizabeth Mayer (see Letter 729).

16 Pears and Britten gave recitals at Aix-en-Provence (Cour de l'Hôtel de Ville, 24 July) and Salzburg (Grossen Saal of the Mozarteum, 18 August), the programmes of which included songs by Dowland, Purcell, Handel and Arne, Schubert *Lieder*, and Britten's *Michelangelo Sonnets* and folk-song arrangements. On 5 August, as part of the 3rd Festival de Musique de Menton, Pears was the soloist in a 'Soirée Anglaise' given by the Hamburg Chamber Orchestra (NWDR) conducted by Britten; the programme comprised Purcell's Chacony in G minor, Britten's Suite for tenor and orchestra arranged from Purcell's *Orpheus Britannicus*, 'Two Pieces' for orchestra by Dowland, possibly arranged by Britten whose interest in Dowland was strong at this period (see, for example, his *Lachrymae* (1951) for viola and piano, subtitled 'Reflections on a Song of John Dowland': see Letter 663 n. 3 and vol. 3, plate 24) and Britten's *Variations on a Theme of Frank Bridge* and *Les Illuminations*.

17 Charlotte Elizabeth (Beth) Britten (1909–1989), Britten's sister, had married Christopher (Kit) Welford (1911–1973) in 1938. The Welfords had three children: Thomas Sebastian, known as Sebastian (b. 1939); Sarah Charlotte, known as Sally (b. 1943), and Elizabeth Ellen Rosemary, known as Roguey (b. 1945). The family was living at Hasketon, near Woodbridge, in Suffolk, where Kit Welford was a doctor in general practice. See IC1/2/3 and Donald Mitchell's and Philip Reed's interview (London, 21 July 2005) with Sally Schweitzer (née Welford) at BPL.

18 Edith Barbara Britten (1902–1982), the elder of Britten's two sisters, was a qualified social worker. See IC1/2/3.

19 From spring 1948, as a London *pied-à-terre*, Britten and Pears had rented

20 Sophie Stein (1882–1965), the wife of Erwin Stein and mother of Marion Harewood.

21 Britten and Pears gave recitals in Hull (23 February), Skipton (24th) and Leeds (26th).

22 David Lascelles (b. 1950), the Harewoods' first child.

23 The Mayer family included four children: Beata (1912–2000), Elizabeth's daughter by a previous marriage; Michael (b. 1916), Ulrica (b. 1918) and Christopher (b. 1924). In 1942 Beata had married Max Wachstein (1905–1965), a doctor. The Wachsteins had two children: Margaret Anne, known as Muki (b. 1947), and Monica Elizabeth Marie (b. 1950). See also Letter 194 n. 1.

24 Britten and Pears were not to revisit North America until 1957 when the English Opera Group toured to Stratford, Ontario, Canada; see Letters 902–5. Elizabeth Mayer met up with them again at Stratford.

729 To William Plomer

HOTEL VERGALDEN, GARGELLEN
March 14th 1952

My dear William,

I have been meaning to write to you for several weeks, since I left in fact, to ask you to send the first bit of Tyco the Vegan out here.[1] Actually I was so weary, & the first part of the tour so hectic, that I decided I couldn't really read the draft with intelligence, & that it would be better to wait till I got back. That will be now on 24th,[2] I think, & I shall go straight to Aldeburgh for about a week. Could you be an angel & send it there for me to read, & when I come to London again we can meet & discuss it?

In the intervals of concerts & falling down in the snow (I am yet a very inadequate skier) I've been thinking a lot about the piece, with, I must say, increasing pleasure. I've also been considering the continuation of it – how, for instance, to get the children back to Earth again. I don't remember if you've seen Let's Make an Opera; but whatever you think of the quality of the piece (& I'm sure you'll have reservations about the first part), the Audience participation has been everywhere, in every country, an unqualified success, & has given the piece a very friendly atmosphere. Now, altho' there isn't the same obvious reason for the audience to start singing in Tyco as in Let's Make, I believe that we could evolve one. It might be something like this: the children are doubtful about whether to return to Earth or not. Either the audience is directly appealed to (Tinkerbell like!), & sings a song about missing them, or (as Peter suggests) as part of the Television idea[3] the audience is watched & listened to singing a similar song. We could make the song serious & un-whimsy, that I'm sure of, but it might make an effective turning point in the story. It could be rehearsed, quite straight, in the interval. We might also add one for the Finale to the whole work like the Coaching Song[4] in 'Let's Make' – but I'm forgetting, you've probably not seen the piece. If, incidentally, you want to have a taste of this piece – I believe it's on in Wimbledon this week.[5] Basil Douglas (the general manager of E.O.G. – Langham 3146) could tell you details if you cared to go.

We're having a lovely, exhausting holiday. A very quiet place, in heavenly mountain scenery; very few people, & good not alarming ski-ing. Is it a thing you do, at all? I can recommend it.

Peter joins me in sending love.

Hope to see you soon,
Yours ever,
BEN

1 Britten refers to a Prologue to the projected children's opera, the subject-matter of which tapped into the growing public fascination for outer space and the possibilities of space travel prevalent in the early 1950s, and reflected by, for example, the seminal science-fiction film *Destination Moon* (1950). Plomer's seven-page draft of the Prologue, all that has apparently survived of the project, is at BPL (see p. 51). *Tyco the Vegan* had replaced an earlier scheme to base a children's opera on Beatrix Potter's *The Tale of Mr Tod*, which had recently fallen through owing to copyright difficulties; see also Letter 711 n. 2. Britten had written to Plomer on 22 February, 'I am delighted that you have got on so well with the libretto. I long to see it & talk it over with you.' In the same letter Britten suggested that he and Plomer should meet on 27 February to discuss the new opera. Plomer's biographer, Peter F. Alexander, draws attention to an error in EWW that gives the date of *Tyco* as 'about 1954' (*William Plomer*, p. 374, n. 5). See also Andrew Plant, *Rumours and Visions*, exhibition catalogue, pp. 30–31.

Also of interest is a little-known 'play for children in four scenes' by Eric Walter White entitled *Men in the Moon*, which was privately published in 1952, the same year Britten and Plomer were working on *Tyco the Vegan*; Britten's copy, presumably sent to him by the author, is at BPL. Like Britten's and Plomer's proposed opera, White's play was conceived for a small cast of three adults and four children. Set in East Anglia, a space rocket (called 'The Flying East Anglian') transports the children to the moon where they encounter what they take to be two 'moonmen' conversing in 'moon language'; in fact, the 'moonmen' are a Soviet scientist and his apprentice speaking in Russian. The Anglo-Soviet dimension to White's play, though naively expressed, touches on aspects of the ensuing Cold War between the West and the Soviet Union, as well as the space race that would preoccupy the United States and Soviet governments during the 1950s and 1960s; both were to become potent subtexts in the boom of Hollywood science-fiction films in the later 1950s.

It is possible, though the suggestion is not substantiated by documentary evidence, that Britten's thoughts were already turning towards Japanese Nō drama in connection with the libretto for *Tyco*. According to Ronald Duncan (RDWB, p. 112), the children's opera was 'based on the theme of a journey to the moon, and Britten had talked to me about its structure because he thought my association with Ezra Pound gave me some knowledge of the Japanese Nō plays, which Pound had translated and which Britten had found fascinating'. Lord Harewood also suggests that the opera Britten intended to write for the 1952 Aldeburgh Festival was to have a libretto by Plomer 'based on a Nō play ... If William Plomer refused to be diverted from the Nō play, then the only man to write the libretto [for *Gloriana*] quickly enough would be Ronald Duncan' (*The Tongs and the Bones*, pp. 134–5).

The link between Duncan, Britten and the Nō theatre extended back to 1938, when Duncan had founded the *Townsman*, to which Pound contributed several articles on musical criticism. Noel Stock (*The Life of Ezra Pound*, p. 370) recalls a meeting between Pound and Duncan in London during 1938 which shows that Britten became involved in a rather eccentric attempt to reconstruct the atmosphere of a Nō play:

[Pound] wanted badly to see a Nō play performed in a theatre and to this end Ronald Duncan persuaded Ashley Dukes to lend them the Mercury Theatre. Benjamin Britten produced a musician who could play gongs and another of Duncan's friends, Henry Boys, suggested a female dancer by the name of Suria Magito. One afternoon, with Duncan as audience, Pound recited one of his own Nō translations while the girl danced.

This bizarre staging was scarcely authentic, since neither female dancers nor multiple gongs figure in the genuine Nō theatre. In 1916 Pound had published translations of fifteen Nō plays, but Britten did not obtain a copy of Pound's edition until 1953 when his thoughts began to turn more positively towards the Japanese theatrical arts. This was approximately one year after the timing suggested by Duncan and Harewood here, and it seems likely that their recollection of the chronology is confused: see MCBFE, pp. 24–5 and 117–18, and Letter 153 n. 3.

Rather than the unlikely topic of space travel, it was the lost innocence so hauntingly treated in the Nō play *Sumidagawa* that caught Britten's imagination when he visited Japan himself in 1956, having decided to attend the Nō theatre in person on the strong recommendation of Plomer. This experience was to lead to the creation of the first Church Parable, *Curlew*

River, with a libretto by Plomer, completed in 1964.

2 According to Britten's diary, the journey home took place on 20 March.

3 The precise nature of the 'Television idea' remains unclear, although the children were to watch a broadcast of the audience. The introduction of television into the scenario was entirely in keeping with the contemporary concept of the subject-matter. In 1952, television in the UK was still a rare phenomenon; its popularity would begin to gain significant momentum only in 1953 with the televising of the Coronation.

4 'The horses are champing, eagerly stamping', the last of the audience songs in *The Little Sweep*, which functions as the opera's finale.

5 *Let's Make an Opera* played at the Wimbledon Theatre, 17–22 March 1952, in performances conducted by Edward Renton and Boyd Neel.

730 To William Plomer

4 CRABBE STREET, ALDEBURGH, SUFFOLK
April 2nd 1952

My dear William,

So sorry not to have answered you before, or written about the Prologue before, but since I got back from abroad I've been terribly busy.[1]

Anyhow – I think it's enchanting. Very gay & full of excellent points. I love the Marcus–Rose duet, & the Plato aria.[2] I very much want to discuss with you the form of the whole – whether it should all be set to music (in which case some of the dialogue would have to be slightly stylised) or with spoken bits. I incline to the former, since it is a Prologue & essentially an atmospheric one. Could we discuss this some time? I don't want to nag, but of course I feel we talk more easily & fully here, rather than at a casual meeting in London. I am here till after Easter, & then for about a month spending the odd days in London while Billy Budd is on. I will leave it to you entirely – if you can face a trek into the wilds, please do – ring (Aldeburgh 323) or wire your arrival – or otherwise we can lunch or whatever in London.

We must also discuss continuation of plot. I am very glad you approve of 'audience participation' – it is very valuable in this kind of piece, especially in the possible schools' performances (which judging by Let's Make, are very likely to occur). We must find the right way of introducing it.[3]

My love to you, & many thanks for the most exciting start to our collaboration. Music leapt to the mind when I read your sketch. (I'm clinging on to it – hope you don't mind.)

Yours ever,
BEN

LETTER 730: APRIL 1952

③

SPIKE: Jim!
JIM: I don't want to rob no kids.
SPIKE: 'Oo asked yer? 'ark—

When the kids is snugly sleepin'
All tucked up in "Dolly Lodge,"
I'll be waitin', you'll be creepin',
I'm the window — that's the dodge.
You'll be findin' where she's keepin'
What's worth pinchin' — don't pinch 'er!
You'll be creepin', quietly peepin',
Mind you make no sound or stir —

[JIM at this moment inadvertently
kicks an empty watering-can which
rolls over with a loud clatter. He
and SPIKE instantly switch off
their flashlights and hide.]

MARCUS [appearing on balcony and
    looking down]:
Who's there?
Anybody there?
ROSE [appearing beside him]:
What's up?
Anything the matter?
MARCUS: Don't know:
Heard a bang and a clatter.
A bang and a clatter.

④

ROSE: Down there?
MARCUS: Down there.
    Clatter and a bang
    Like a tin can.
ROSE: May have been a dog—
MARCUS: May have been a cat—
ROSE } May have been a hedgehog,
MARCUS} May have been a rat.
ROSE: May have been a poltergeist—
MARCUS: May have been a spook—
ROSE } May have been a burglar,
MARCUS} May have been a crook.
MARCUS: May have been a bunch of crooks
    Out a bit late—oh—
ROSE: Planning how to rob or kill
MARCUS} Miss Madge Plato!
ROSE }

[They laugh merrily, but stop
abruptly when Miss Plato herself
steps out on to the balcony. Her
hair is short. Broad in the beam,
she is wearing tight trousers and a
high-necked sweater, and is smoking
a cigarette in a long holder.]

The duet for Marcus and Rose from Plomer's libretto for *Tyco the Vegan*, in the librettist's hand

1 Plomer had evidently sent Britten 'the first bit of Tyco the Vegan' (see Letter 729 above).

2 See p. 51 for a facsimile of the text of the duet. The aria for Miss Madge Plato runs as follows:

> Unlike you, Marcus,
> Unlike you, Rose,
> I never catch a cold
> Or have a runny nose:
> We Platos are a hardy race,
> We're tough and fit and spry,
> We never cough, we never sneeze
> And we hardly *ever* die!

3 Plomer had recently seen *Let's Make an Opera* at Hammersmith, and commented in his letter of 22 March:

> I thought it a most remarkable proceeding, with great freshness, vitality, and charm, & the 'audience participation' was wonderfully spontaneous and – for an English audience – unselfconscious. I think it an excellent idea to make the audience participate in Tycho [*sic*], on the lines you suggest.

731 To the Earl of Harewood

4 CRABBE STREET, ALDEBURGH, SUFFOLK

April 6th 1952

My dear George,

Just back from Birmingham[1] I find Marion's letter (please thank her for it) & your article[2] waiting for me, & so I hasten to post the latter back to you –

I think it's very good. I don't see how one can sugar the pill more about Wiesbaden,[3] although they probably won't like it – neither may Boosey & Hawkes! But it strengthens my case against them,[4] which incidentally they rather fail to take seriously, & anyhow it raises points which simply must be raised, & I think you do it tactfully & well.

I've made one or two notes. It might be worth exonerating some of the singers for lack of characterisation (& Vere in Act II Sc. I), because at the dotty tempi they couldn't do much! But if there is room (& time) I'd like you to lam into the singers for not singing more. Notes do matter, as I had to point out to some of the cast in Birmingham. That performance, by the way, was interesting. Scenically it suffered less on a small stage & from a small chorus than one might have expected. Of course it has, musically & histrionically, slipped a bit from being done on tour & under-rehearsed. But it keeps its freshness & obviously (this is strange) is an easy piece for audiences, provincial ones, to take. Why, do you think? Is the story a more sympathetic one than one thought? Words are clearer? The performance went with a great swing, & in many ways I was very pleased. Uppman has come on greatly; Dalberg,[5] alas, sings less & less, although acting with phenomenal energy![6] Chorus was good.

My love to you all. Peter tells me the news of Nanny – I hope the new one will be a success; so glad she's Austrian; I'm sure that'll make her warmer & friendlier than the others.

See you soon – Happy Easter.

Yours ever,
BEN

1 Britten had conducted *Billy Budd* at the Theatre Royal, Birmingham, on 4 April: see Letter 732.

2 Lord Harewood had sent Britten a draft of his review of the first German-language production of *Billy Budd*, given at the Staatsoper, Wiesbaden, in March 1952. (At this time the opera was still in its original four-act version; when it was revised in 1960 Britten adopted a two-act structure.) Harewood's review was published as part of 'Foreign Diary' in the 'Britten issue' of *Opera* 2/6 (May 1952), pp. 268 and 307:

Naturally the first Continental production of Britten's work had a peculiar fascination, particularly for someone who had seen *Billy Budd* in England. The opera had been prepared entirely with local resources, and neither conductor nor producer had seen or heard the Covent Garden performances, nor had they called in any adviser who had. It is important to say at the outset that this performance has been an unqualified public success (additional performances had been arranged, and this was the sixth within three weeks of the first night), each house has been packed, and the audience's enthusiasm at the end was something I cannot remember ever having seen excelled elsewhere. And yet, it is not easy to find anything to praise in the musical side of the performances – except the music itself. The score was drastically cut, with the intention, one is forced to conclude, of eliminating the tenderness and understanding which reconcile the listener to acceptance of the background of brutality. Half the novice's lament in Act I had gone, almost all the *scherzando* quartet which follows, a large part of Vere's address to the crew in the finale of the Act. 'Don't like the French' was begun at the reprise, part of the second shanty went, and some of the fight between Billy and Squeak. In Act III, the cuts were even more serious: the crew's prayer for victory and a favourable breeze was mostly omitted, as were the quartet for Vere and the officers at the end of the scene, and the lyrical duet for Vere and Billy at the beginning of the next one; part of the officers' trio had gone as well. Hardly a tempo was within reach of those the composer had specified in the score and which he followed at Covent Garden; and the quite excessive speed at which most of the music was taken frequently made a very curious effect. The Prologue and the first scene of Act II were hardly recognizable (the latter taken throughout at fast recitative pace) and the tempo for the funeral march (Act IV, scene 2) turned into something nearer a gallop. The wonder is that the piece still impressed the audience [...]

Much of the production (by the Intendant, [Heinrich] Köhler-Helffrich) was excellent and had obviously been studied with great care. It was a pity that the curtains for the second scenes of Acts II and III rose bars earlier than indicated, but the battle scene for example had enormous excitement (Billy's descent from the foretop was a splendidly athletic moment). Karl Liebl sang Vere, at the same time the most difficult role and the one for which comparison was with a performance which came near to perfection. He was more a man of action than a thinker, and hindered by tempi, failed in the Prologue and Act II, scene 2; but the duet with Claggart was better and the monologue after the trial scene had considerable authority, although the rest of the characterization had done little to prepare for this side of Vere. August Gschwend's voice seemed to lie rather low for Billy, and, though his personality and lyrical singing were well suited to the role, he lacked the top notes for 'Billy Budd, king of the birds'. Georg Stern (Claggart) was far the best member of the cast, though his baritone voice sounded odd in this bass role, and his slight physique took one aback at first. He sang with real authority, so much so that the musical performance came to life for the first time at the beginning of his Act II monologue ['O beauty, o handsomeness goodness'], from which point it never quite lost the impetus he had given it. There was disappointingly little characterization in the rest of the cast: the Novice (Erwin Euller) realized some of the pathos of his role, particularly at the end of Act II, but the officers were three unindividualized toughs. Probably, the very fast tempi made characterization a difficult matter, but something would have been achieved if everyone had concentrated on singing; too often we had neither accuracy nor line from Wiesbaden's singers.

What did the performance show? (1) How the composer is always at the mercy of the performer, and, conversely, (2) how much of a work of genius comes through to an audience in spite of performance; (3) how little translation need affect the musical side of a work – 'Doch ich hätte ihn retten können' for 'But I could have saved him' was the one seriously disturbing moment.

3   Britten and the Harewoods saw *Billy Budd* at Wiesbaden while staying with the Prince and Princess of Hesse and the Rhine near Darmstadt. Christopher Headington notes that this was the first time Britten stayed at the Hesses' home, Schloss Wolfsgarten: see CHPP, p. 179. He had been introduced to Prince Ludwig and Princess Margaret by Lord Harewood, and they were soon to become firm friends. As Harewood relates, the performance 'wasn't very good, with a clumsy translation and hefty cuts; when we got home Ben had a lot to drink at supper and then gave a hilarious performance of the opening of the Tchaikovsky concerto [Piano Concerto No. 1] as rendered by an inebriated pianist' (*The Tongs and the Bones*, p. 135). For further comment on the production of *Billy Budd* in Wiesbaden, see Letter 732.

4   Britten's disagreement with his publishers – one of the first of several over the ensuing decade that culminated in his leaving Boosey & Hawkes for Faber Music – must surely have centred on their allowing *Billy Budd* to be

performed at Wiesbaden with cuts, as mentioned by Harewood in his *Opera* notice; the cuts were not sanctioned by the composer. A letter from Ernst Roth of Boosey & Hawkes to Britten (31 March 1952) indicates that he was aware of Britten's displeasure at what had occurred and that the composer's views had been passed on to the Intendant at Wiesbaden.

The warning bells must have sounded for Britten when Roth wrote to him on 11 July 1952 about a proposal from La Scala, Milan, to stage *Budd* in a cut version. In his memoir, *The Business of Music: Reflections of a Music Publisher* (p. 229), Roth recounts a meeting between Britten and Victor de Sabata, then Principal Conductor at La Scala:

De Sabata began in his most Italian manner. Making use of great gestures to fill the gaps in his English vocabulary he declared that for him *Billy Budd* was the most important dramatic work since *Tristan* (which was an unwise thing to say because Britten hates all Wagner). Unperturbed by Britten's apparent discomfort, de Sabata continued to explain the difference between the English and the Italian public, the latter being much more experienced and much quicker, and tending to become impatient when told the same thing twice. All of which Britten disliked no less than the comparison with *Tristan*.

As de Sabata did not seem to be coming to the point I reminded him that he wanted to make certain suggestions. 'Oh yes,' he said and opened the vocal score, 'this aria comes too late.' 'You mean,' I asked, 'that it should come earlier on?' 'No, no,' de Sabata replied, 'it must be left out.' That was enough for Britten and he departed somewhat abruptly. I had to release the Scala from its contract, and it substituted *Gloriana* for *Billy Budd*. But *Gloriana*, then no more than an idea in Britten's mind, also failed eventually to find favour with de Sabata, and was never performed in Milan.

While the proposal for *Billy Budd* foundered, it is of interest to note that the conductor suggested by La Scala's management was Carlo Maria Giulini, who was later to enjoy a successful collaboration with Britten on several occasions in the 1960s, notably for *War Requiem*. See Philip Reed's CD liner notes – 'An Historic Partnership' – to the BBC Legends recording issued in 2000 of *War Requiem*, conducted by Giulini and Britten at the Royal Albert Hall, Easter Day 1969.

Unauthorized cuts, as described by Harewood, were regularly introduced into Britten's operas during his lifetime. His publishers too, at least until the time Faber Music was established, were sometimes all too ready to go along with current practice, the principal ambition of which was the securing of a further performance. That practice had its roots in the opera houses of the nineteenth century, when operatic works, particularly those by Verdi and, later, Puccini, were often cut. Even today the stage works of Richard Strauss, especially his operas of extended duration such as *Der Rosenkavalier* or *Die Frau ohne Schatten*, are performed in the world's opera houses with cuts that have become, through long practice, traditional. Britten's protests to his publishers about the introduction of cuts in his operatic works effectively nipped in the bud any possible establishment of an undesirable performing custom.

5 Frederick Dalberg (1908–1988), British bass, leading singer at Covent Garden from 1951 to 1957 where he sang many of the principal bass roles, especially in Wagner, and, in addition to Claggart, created roles in Britten's *Gloriana* (Raleigh) in 1953 and Walton's *Troilus and Cressida* (Calkas) in 1954. See also the obituary in *The Times* (9 May 1988).

6 Theodor Uppman and Frederick Dalberg had repeated their roles, as Billy and Claggart respectively, in the Birmingham performance of *Billy Budd*.

732 To David Webster[1]

4 CRABBE STREET, ALDEBURGH, SUFFOLK
April 7th 1952

My dear David,

I went to Birmingham & did Billy Budd, & was pretty pleased with it. Lot[2] did as well as he could with 1st Lieutenant – but he is no great shakes, I'm afraid! It has slipped musically & histrionically, but considering conditions rather little. I am in touch with Miss Kerr[3] about rehearsals for next week to get it back into shape again.

One thing I want to bother you with . . .

I saw the work in Wiesbaden – a ghastly experience, except for a few details – but one thing they did which I have always wanted to do, & would like to try in these performances: they did it in two parts with only one, admittedly big, interval. Can we try that next week? I am certain (& Basil [Coleman] agrees) that the intensity of the work would be quite enormously increased. You see – it was planned that way, the music of Act I leads to Act II, & similarly that of Act III to Act IV.[4] I had a word with the stage staff, & they can get the sets changed quickly I think, only a minute or so for the audience to wait – & Basil is confirming this with Justin.[5] I am coming up on 14th or 15th & can discuss it with you fully, but I thought I'd like to put the idea into your head first. I don't think the <u>bar</u> can object if we give them a nice <u>long</u> interval!

Happy Easter to you,
Yours ever,
BEN

P.S. Many congratulations on the smashing success of Bonne Bouche[6] – I'm as pleased as if I had written it myself!

1 British arts administrator (1903–1971), General Administrator of Sadler's

Wells (subsequently Royal) Ballet and of Covent Garden (subsequently Royal) Opera companies, 1945–70; knighted in 1961. See also Letter 549 n. 1.

2 Lawrence Lot, who sang the role of Lieutenant Ratcliffe.

3 Muriel Kerr, Webster's personal assistant.

4 Following performances in Cardiff (7 March), Manchester (14 March), Glasgow (28 March) and Birmingham (4 April), *Billy Budd* returned to the Royal Opera House, Covent Garden, for six performances between 18 April and 13 May, the conducting shared between the composer and Peter Gellhorn. A programme for the performance on 21 April 1952 indicates that Webster met Britten halfway in the matter of the intervals: there were breaks after Acts I and II, while Acts III and IV were performed without an interval. A revised, two-act version of *Billy Budd* was broadcast by the BBC Third Programme in November 1960, and first performed on stage at the Royal Opera House in January 1964. For full details of the revisionary process, which Britten clearly had in mind at this early stage, see BBMCPR, pp. 74–84.

5 A member of the opera-house staff.

6 *Bonne-Bouche*, a 1920s comedy, was John Cranko's first ballet to be presented by the Sadler's Wells Ballet at Covent Garden, on 4 April 1952. The music was by Arthur Oldham and the designs, judged by the critics to have been the most successful aspect of the venture, by Osbert Lancaster. Oldham recalled (*Living with Voices: An Autobiography*, p. 35) that 'the story had, as its heroine, a young lady missionary in the Salvation Army who gets eaten by a black man whilst pursuing her vocation in Africa – hence the ballet's title: *Bonne-Bouche*'. See also John Percival, *Theatre in My Blood: A Biography of John Cranko*, pp. 88–90.

   Britten's diary indicates that he attended a performance of the ballet on 6 May.

733 To William Plomer

4 CRABBE STREET, ALDEBURGH, SUFFOLK
April 27th 1952

My dear William,

I have been meaning to write to you for ages, but my plans these last weeks have been so topsy-turvy that I haven't known what to say. It now transpires I have to conduct Billy Budd on May 1st so that means that those days I have alas to be in London – but all the same it is imperative that I see you; about what I can only explain, when I see you.[1] Could you spare me some time on May 1st or 2nd – perhaps luncheon on either of these days?[2] I will keep both free, if you could let me have a card to

Melbury Road (22A) (W14); and please bring your diary along too!

So very sorry to be so vague & hectic (an unhappy combination, but not alas rare with me), but I think I can explain it if & when we meet.

In haste, with infinite apologies,
with love,
Yours,
BEN

1 Britten refers to initial plans for the opera *Gloriana*, written to celebrate the Coronation of Elizabeth II in 1953. According to Lord Harewood, it was a discussion about operatic nationalism at Gargellen that sparked the idea for the Coronation project. Harewood's interest in the subject of Elizabeth I's relationship with Robert Devereux, Earl of Essex, was no doubt intensified by the fact that he was himself a distant descendant of Essex (see illustration facing, and PBBG, p. 21).

Britten would contemplate committing himself to the project only if it were to be 'made in some way official, not quite commanded but at least accepted as part of the celebrations' (Lord Harewood, *The Tongs and the Bones*, p. 135). Harewood's cousin, Alan 'Tommy' Lascelles, was the Queen's Private Secretary, and it was at a meeting between the two relatives at Buckingham Palace on 23 April that the Queen's official approval was discussed. When its status was confirmed, Britten 'had to give up the section of the Coronation service which had been commissioned from him, a March to go with the Entry of the Princesses. He had decided this should be for my mother [Princess Mary, the Princess Royal] and was planning to introduce the note of her much-used dog whistle, which he said he associated inevitably with her!' (*The Tongs and the Bones*, p. 137). The completed score of *Gloriana* was to be dedicated 'by gracious permission to HER MAJESTY QUEEN ELIZABETH II in honour of whose Coronation it was composed'; Britten could not resist giving the opera the opus number 53 (corresponding to the year of the Coronation) even though his Op. 52, *Winter Words*, was composed after the opera had been completed.

Clearly *Gloriana* was uppermost in Britten's mind at the end of April, and had now entirely supplanted *Tyco the Vegan*. The date of Plomer's meeting with Britten is unknown (see n. 2 below), but after it the librettist evidently delayed somewhat before committing himself to the project: see Letter 734 n. 3.

One wonders if the discussion on 23 April might have made mention of a letter to *The Times*, published on 16 April 1952, of which Britten – along with the writers Leslie Baily, Philip Gibbs, Laurence Housman and J. W. Robertson Scott, and the actor Sybil Thorndike – was a signatory. Referring to the funeral of the Queen's father, George VI, the letter draws attention to the sizeable military presence at the ceremony and proposes that 'as the Sovereign represents all the people of this nation, it is equally

A note in Lord Harewood's hand showing his lineage traced from Robert Devereux, 2nd Earl of Essex. It was found inserted in Britten's copy of Strachey's Elizabeth and Essex.

right [...] that a pacific show should be presented to the world, as well as a military one [...] We believe that a good external effect would be made on world opinion if Britain led the way in this new symbolism.' The letter suggests that Elizabeth II's forthcoming Coronation would provide an opportunity for 'dignified civil participation', and concludes:

> There is a widespread aspiration that we now go forward into a new Elizabethan age. Under the first Elizabeth the artists and scientists and craftsmen made England great, sharing honour at court with the soldiers and sailors. May we hope that in the second Elizabethan age the outward expression of our monarchy may be brought into line with that modern conception of democratic sovereignty which is held nowadays by millions of the Queen's subjects, a people who should be mirrored in State pageantry as both a civilian and a military nation.

2 There is no reference in Britten's diary to a meeting with Plomer on either of these dates. The first entry for Plomer after these dates is on the evening of 21 May.

734 To William Plomer

BOOSEY & HAWKES, 295 REGENT STREET, W1
As from 22A Melbury Road, W14
[7 May 1952][1]

My dear William,

The Queen has graciously given her OK to the scheme I told you about[2] – there is a slight money difficulty, but I've had a word with David Webster (of Covent Garden) who says that that is no obstacle as far as they are concerned (i.e. If the Treasury does not fork out direct, Cov. Gard. will find the money). Everything seems set, therefore; only with the librettist, there is a doubt still ... ?[3] I hope not, & that these days' silence means an agreement. I want to go to my agent today or tomorrow to cancel everything for the year (till April), so could I possibly see you for a moment today; or if not any time tomorrow. Could you, if you are in, send a message back with this boy who brings this, let me call on you at 5.00 or 5.30 today; or if not any time tomorrow, save the evening (from 5.00 p.m.), I am free. If you are not in, could you be an angel & ring me as early as possible (Western 6390) saying if & when we can meet.

Sorry to bother – but the matter is now really urgent, & also, I feel very exciting too.

With love
BEN

1 This date is conjectured by Peter F. Alexander (*William Plomer*, pp. 271 and 374 n. 7).

An early draft cast list for Gloriana *– headed 'E & E' ('Elizabeth and Essex') – from a back page in Britten's 1952 diary. The list includes some characters, for example Mary, Queen of Scots, who do not appear in the opera.*

2 The parodist Olga Katzin (1896–1987), under her pseudonym 'Sagittarius', responded to the proposed Coronation opera in the *New Statesman and Nation* (7 June 1952), p. 665, with 'The Elizabethans', a nod to Ben Jonson:

> Hee who the death of Culture doth lament
> In this, oure new Elizabethan Age,
>   Shoulde now ask pardon,
> For Poet and Musician will present
> A goodly Royalle Masque upon the stage
>   Of Covent Garden.
>
> What though society bee levelled downe,
> By levelling some uppe, to make one class?

> Future historians
> May name these names to bee of such renowne,
> They Georgians and Edwardians doe surpass—
>   Even Victorians!
>
> Lette none then judge beforehand and disdain
> Elizabethan opera not yet writ.
>   These tuneful revels
> (Passed by the ancient Lord Great Chamberlayne)
> May elevate the groundlings of the pit
>   To higher levels.
>
> This Age hath genius too of high report,
> And now, conjoined with some artistic Earls,
>   Arts Council gallants
> Doe cheer them on to bow before the Court,
> As Shakespeare once, and Spenser, Tudor churls,
>   Displayed their talents.
>
> It may well bee that judges yet unborn,
> Will finde these wordes and musick are as fine
>   As any written,
> And say of oure Elizabethan morne,
> 'O, dulcet ayres! O, Plomer's mighty line!
>   O, rare Ben Britten!'

Katzin's *jeu d'esprit* clearly reveals that within a few months of the start of the new Queen's reign the notion of a dawning of a second Elizabethan Age was very much part of the national mood.

3 Peter F. Alexander (*William Plomer*, p. 271) has explained Plomer's initial hesitancy in agreeing to Britten's invitation to write the libretto for the Coronation opera:

> It is clear that, having worked with Plomer on two different operas [*The Tale of Mr Tod* and *Tyco the Vegan*], even though neither had come to fruition, Britten had complete confidence in his abilities. Characteristically, it was Plomer who seems to have hesitated, probably because he feared the inevitable publicity, and because the very tight schedule to which they would have to work would mean putting off many other tasks.

Pears, too, apparently shared Plomer's discomfort about the need to postpone pressing engagements, which included Britten's commission from the Venice Biennale Festival to compose *The Turn of the Screw* (see Letter 768 n. 6 and PBBG, p. 18). Lord Harewood recalls that Noel Mewton-Wood was proposed as a substitute accompanist for Pears during Britten's work on the new opera (*The Tongs and the Bones*, p. 135).

Plomer replied to this letter promptly on 8 May, enclosing for Britten's interest a copy of the 1950 edition of J. E. Neale's *Queen Elizabeth*, which had been first published in 1934 (see Letter 735). Plomer described this book as 'a sort of corrective' to Lytton Strachey's *Elizabeth & Essex, A Tragic History*, which had stimulated Harewood to propose the subject in the first place. Harewood had already marked up a copy of Strachey's historical novel with a view to his possible collaboration with Ronald Duncan on the new libretto, Britten having initially been unsure whether Plomer would agree to participate. For further on the genesis of *Gloriana*, see PBBG, pp. 18–19.

Surviving at BPL is Britten's copy of Strachey's *Elizabeth & Essex*, which is unmarked but for one short passage on p. 4 against a paragraph describing conflicting aspects of Essex's personality. (The paucity of annotations suggests Britten had another copy that is now missing.) For discussion of the significance of this passage, see PBBG, pp. 20–21 and 74–5. Also surviving at BPL is Britten's copy of J. E. Neale's *Elizabeth I and Her Parliaments, 1584–1601*, published in 1957.

735 To William Plomer

4 CRABBE STREET, ALDEBURGH, SUFFOLK
May 11th 1952

My dear William,

Neale's Q.E. has arrived & I am deep in it, & enjoying it thoroughly. I haven't got on to the later bits, so I haven't yet felt the 'corrective' to Strachey; but I am learning a lot about the extraordinary woman & times.

I long to start planning with you. My feelings at the moment are that I want the opera to be crystal clear, with lovely pageantry (however you spell it) but linked by a strong story about the Queen & Essex – strong & simple. A tall order, but I think we can do it![1]

In haste, with many thanks for the book & for all you're going to do for the opera!

With love,
BEN

1 Britten's intention to compose an opera that was 'crystal clear, with lovely pageantry [. . .] but linked by a strong story about the Queen & Essex' was precisely borne out by the format adopted for the work, which alternates scenes of an exterior and interior nature: see MCCCBB, pp. 117–18. Britten told Lord Harewood: 'It's got to be serious. I don't want to do just folk dances and village green stuff' (quoted in PBBG, p. 13), and would later tell David Webster at Covent Garden, 'The work is a serious one and has never been planned as a hotch-potch' (see Letter 761).

The first press release concerning *Gloriana* was issued on 28 May: see PBBG, pp. 20 and 173–4. Plomer visited Britten at Aldeburgh two days later to discuss the project further, just one day after Britten returned home from the Paris performances of *Billy Budd* (see Letter 736 n. 2). On 3 June, Pears wrote to Mary Behrend, 'Now Ben's back & hard at work discussing "Elizabeth (& ? Essex)" with William Plomer!!' On 4 June, Plomer wrote to Britten, 'I am very happy to think that we have made such a hopeful beginning with our great proceeding.' He scribbled in the margin the following lines, which were later to be adapted into the opera's memorable refrain:

> The rose is red, the leaves are green:
> Long live Elizabeth, our noble Queen!

See Plomer, 'Notes on the Libretto of *Gloriana*', *Tempo* 28 (summer 1953), pp. 5–7, in which the librettist admitted these lines were 'written by an Elizabethan boy in one of his school-books'.

736 To Eric Crozier[1]
From Benjamin Britten and Peter Pears
[*Postcard*: The Seine, Paris]

[Postmarked Paris, 28 May 1952]

Budd was most warmly received last night, & the insults to the French taken in good humour.[2] It was a wonderful performance, our best so far. Paris is full of exciting chefs-oeuvres, but very hot & tiring, & full of Americans!

Love to you & Nancy,[3]

BEN

The shop windows are more alluring than ever – what clothes & silks & art books! Nice for a short time!

Love from

PETER

1 British director, librettist and translator (1914–1994). Crozier directed the first productions of *Peter Grimes* and *The Rape of Lucretia* and provided the texts for *The Young Person's Guide to the Orchestra*, *Albert Herring*, *Saint Nicolas*, *Let's Make an Opera* and, with E. M. Forster, *Billy Budd*. He was a co-founder of the English Opera Group and the Aldeburgh Festival. He had married Nancy Evans in 1949. See also Letters 496 n. 3 and 529 n. 2, and 1/C3. A significant collection of Crozier's and Evans's papers, including correspondence and unpublished items, is held at BPL.

2 The Covent Garden production of *Billy Budd* was performed twice in Paris, with the composer conducting, at the Théâtre des Champs-Elysées on 26 and 27 May 1952 as part of the Oeuvre du XXième Siècle festival, given under the auspices of the Congress of Cultural Freedom; Britten had conducted rehearsals in London on 20–21 May before travelling to Paris on the 22nd for a final rehearsal on the 25th. The 'insults to the French' mentioned

THEATRE DES CHAMPS-ELYSEES   LUNDI 26 ET MARDI 27 MAI 1952

EXPOSITION INTERNATIONALE DES ARTS
L'ŒUVRE DU XXᵉ SIÈCLE
SOUS LES AUSPICES DU CONGRES POUR LA LIBERTE DE LA CULTURE

THE ROYAL OPERA HOUSE
COVENT GARDEN LTD
Administrateur Général : DAVID L. WEBSTER

présente

"BILLY BUDD"
OPERA EN QUATRE ACTES

Livret de E. M. Forster et Eric Crozier

d'après Herman Melville

Musique de Benjamin Britten

Décors et Costumes de John Piper

Mise en scène de Basil Coleman

ORCHESTRE DU ROYAL OPERA HOUSE
Premier violon : THOMAS MATTHEWS
sous la direction de
BENJAMIN BRITTEN

Programme for the Covent Garden Opera Company's production of *Billy Budd*, Paris, May 1952. The orchestra was led by Thomas Matthews, the uncle of Paul Rogerson: see Letter 737 n. 1.

by Britten occur in Act II scene 1 (four-act version), when Redburn and Flint sing a duet containing the prominently repeated lines, 'Don't like the French. Don't like their frenchified ways.' In spite of Britten's positive remarks here, the critical reception was tinged with a trace of chauvinism on the part of the French critics: see BBMCPR, p. 141. Pears wrote to Mary Behrend on 3 June to say of the Parisians:

> I fancy 'Billy Budd' was not really their cup of tea at all, although the audiences took it very well, but that curious cold sophisticated lot which goes everywhere did not convince one. They are really very provincial in many ways, musically certainly [...] Anyway we had a good time & did very good performances!

On 29 May Britten wrote to Ronald Duncan to express regret that he had missed seeing him in Paris, and commented:

> We were so worn out by the end of the week by parties & performances (which didn't end till nearly 1 am!) that I feel that a visit to Montmartre would have wrecked us – if only with excitement! Poor Sophie [Stein] hasn't quite got over the disappointment of missing the indecencies!
>
> Budd went very well, & was greatly appreciated as far as one can tell – even 'Don't like the French' was passed over with a good-natured giggle! But I'm no Paris, or Paris-society, fan. I look forward to removing my French-apathy by a visit to Provence this Summer.

Britten and Pears were to sail for France from Folkestone on 15 July. Their summer trip to Provence included concerts and sight-seeing in Aix (24 July), Orange (26 July) and Menton (5 August); see Letter 740 n. 1.

Among the audience in Paris for *Billy Budd* was W. H. Auden, who told William Walton, then at work on *Troilus and Cressida*, about it. In a letter of 10 June 1952 to Christopher Hassall, the librettist of *Troilus*, Walton wrote: 'Auden's just returned from Paris where he'd seen both B.B's [i.e. *Billy Budd* and Benjamin Britten]; & said he thought the opera absolutely the end & hadn't gone down too well.' See Malcolm Hayes (ed.), *The Selected Letters of William Walton*, p. 219, and Addenda to vol. 2 (Letter 397 n. 2), pp. 1338–40.

The performances of *Billy Budd* were well covered in the French press, with reviews in, among others, *Le Figaro* (28 May 1952) and *Le Monde* (28 May 1952). In her *Sunday Times* column, 'Paris' (22 June 1952), Nancy Mitford pronounced both *Billy Budd* and Virgil Thomson's *Four Saints in Three Acts* as 'outstanding failures' of the festival:

> *Billy Budd* was pronounced too long and too dull but 'honourable'; the American opera was considered unworthy of a place in such a festival.
>
> As all is grist to the Parisian mill, *Billy Budd* has provided various catchwords now in current use at the Canasta tables. 'Wretched boy, what have you done?' 'We have no choice!' and 'Save me, Captain Vere!' are chanted at appropriate moments; and the fancy-dress parties are full of characters from *Four Saints in Three Acts*.

3 Nancy Evans (1915–2000), British mezzo-soprano, who created the roles of Lucretia (with Kathleen Ferrier), Nancy (*Albert Herring*), Polly Peachum

and Dido (in Britten's realizations of *The Beggar's Opera* and *Dido and Aeneas* respectively), and for whom Britten wrote *A Charm of Lullabies*. After her retirement from singing, she was much involved with the Britten–Pears School for Advanced Musical Studies. See also Letters 496 n. 3 and 517 n. 7, and 1/c3.

737 To Paul Rogerson[1]

4 CRABBE STREET, ALDEBURGH, SUFFOLK
June 3rd 1952

My dear old Paul,

Sorry not to have answered your letter before, but since I've been back from Paris (only three or four days ago) I have been hard at work here, & not had time to write a single letter. It was a most interesting letter, thank you very much for it. I was glad that the debate on Apartheid was so serious; it is something we all must think seriously about these days, whether we agree or not. I was naturally pleased with the result! Why did you not take part yourself – or is that a matter of previous selection, or tossing-up? I should like to hear you make a speech one day!

We had a good, interesting, but fearfully tiring time in Paris. It was madly festive, thousands of people from every country, & lots of parties (most of which we managed to avoid), & we saw lots of exhibitions, concerts & theatre shows. Billy Budd went well – the French didn't get up & throw things at 'Don't like the French', which we'd rather expected, though some of the audience felt a bit sore about it! There were some whistles at one point (which means they didn't approve) but that made the cheers only louder, as it usually does.

We've had a pretty wet Whitsun here – I expect you have too – with some strong winds, so Billy[2] & the others haven't brought us any lobsters. But I'm writing this now before breakfast in the garden, in the hot sun, & I've seen lots of fishermen go by the gate so they've been out alright today.

Glad you're playing golf so well (or was your opponent rather dim that you got a bottle of Cydrax[3] off him?) – but don't forget your cricket & tennis . . . You must be good when you come here next holidays! I've not got much time to play at the moment what with preparations for the Festival (starts next week) & plans for the new opera (did you read about that in the papers?) . . . The man who's writing the libretto's staying here now, & we're working & talking like mad.

Sorry about the photo difficulties in your cubicle – shall I not remind Peter to send his?

Lots of love to you, be good,
BB

1 British arts administrator (b. 1935), whose parents – Mamie and Haydn Rogerson – were both musicians well known to Britten. Rogerson's father was for many years principal cello of the Hallé Orchestra, and his uncle, Thomas Matthews, was leader of the London Philharmonic Orchestra and the Covent Garden Orchestra, and gave the first UK performance of Britten's Violin Concerto in April 1941 (see PFL, plate 137, and Letter 312 n. 4). It was through these family and musical connections with Britten that the sixteen-year-old Paul Rogerson was first invited to stay with the composer at Aldeburgh in April 1952. It is clear from an entry in Imogen Holst's diary (8 February 1953; IHD, pp. 199–200), that on first seeing Paul, Britten had been powerfully attracted to him:

> [Britten] began telling me about Paul – 'Do you know, Paul & I fell in love with each other, if that is how you can describe it, a whole year before we met.' It was at a concert when Peter was singing the *Serenade*, & they just looked at each other. Then a year later Paul went to the first night of *Budd* [1 December 1951] & they met & Paul said, 'Do you remember going to that concert?'

The chronology of events was slightly more compressed than Britten remembered: the performance of the *Serenade*, with the Hallé Orchestra conducted by Paul Kletzki, and Pears and Dennis Brain as soloists, took place on 2 February 1951 in Sheffield (a few miles from Rogerson's Derbyshire school), with the premiere of *Billy Budd* following ten months later. According to Rogerson, 'Britten lent me his dinner suit [. . .] when I went to the first performance of *Billy Budd*' (interview with Donald Mitchell, London, 27 July 2005; BPL).

Of Britten's remark, 'Paul & I fell in love', Rogerson commented in his interview with Mitchell:

> I find that, looking back, it was a special relationship. He was exceedingly thoughtful and very kind and he used to write to me at school. I can't think of too many other people who wrote [. . .] He used to write very fond and loving letters.

The powerful attraction Britten felt towards this young man is unquestionable, but Rogerson insisted there was nothing sexual in their relationship:

> He would come upstairs. I'd have gone to bed and he'd come upstairs and give me a kiss and say good night and sleep well and all that. He was like a godfather. He was a dear. It was an honour and a privilege, thinking back now.

Nor did Rogerson's parents have any concerns about the friendship, despite warnings from friends; but Mrs Rogerson 'paid no attention [. . .] They [Britten and Pears] were very devoted to my mother and father.'

The friendship continued throughout 1952 and 1953, with Rogerson coming to Aldeburgh in the school holidays and Britten writing to him during the school term, much as he had done with, for example, Humphrey Maud (see Letter 598 n. 6 and vol. 3, pp. 11–29 *passim*), and was later to do with Roger Duncan (see Letter 815 n. 1). Rogerson had also attended the premiere of *Gloriana*, for which occasion Britten this time lent him a set of tails.

Rogerson recalls:

We used to go out bird watching, brass rubbing, on the beach, go out with Billy Burrell, playing, marvellous playing in the evening in front of the fire, Chenka, that sort of thing.

Like Humphrey Maud, Rogerson was a cellist:

I took my cello down and – God Almighty! – probably one of the finest pianists in the world, certainly one of the greatest accompanists. He was so patient. I remember this Sammartini sonata. He was very patient, but so encouraging too. 'Come on, let's get your cello out, see what you make of this, what we can make of it together.' Really, a privilege.

Rogerson also has warm memories of Pears:

He was always lovely, absolutely. A real gentleman, a lovely man, Peter. My mother was very, very fond of Peter. She fancied him – I think a lot of people did. He was a very handsome fellow.

But the friendship with Rogerson was abruptly halted not by parental intervention, as in the case of Maud, but by the young man's decision in 1953 to enter a Jesuit order. Imogen Holst records in her diary (22 July 1953; IHD, p. 233): 'Ben very depressed because he'd just heard that Paul was going to be a Jesuit – 15 years away from everyone.' Rogerson came down to Aldeburgh for one last weekend in August before going on retreat preparatory to becoming a novice, when he would be separated from his family, friends and possessions. Holst notes the events of that weekend (IHD, pp. 245–8):

14 AUGUST 1953 [Friday]
I went round at 12 & found them just going to have a bathe – Ben, Peter, Paul, Mary [Potter] and a v. nice schoolboy called Richard [Kihl].

16 AUGUST 1953 [Sunday]
Went to Crag House after breakfast to give Miss Hudson my rations. She told me that Ben had sprained his ankle the evening before, playing tennis. So I went out into the garden and there he was sitting with it bandaged & propped up, while Peter was in his bathing things. Ben said, 'This is a judgement, isn't it!' He was obviously in pain and feeling wretched: – Paul's last day & he was out in Father Jolly's boat, and Ben had meant to go with them [...]
   I went back later at 12.30. Mary Potter was there: – Ben was saying that he could never remember that he was older than some of the very mature young men who seemed so much more assured than he was [...] Then Ben began to talk about Paul and how he'd asked him about the 15 years the night before. Ben hated the very word 'Jesuit', and was appalled to think that Paul mustn't take *any* possessions away to his novitiate. Then we went out into the garden and sat in the sun [where Pears was cataloguing his programmes] [...] But he [Pears] stopped sorting, and a deep gloom descended on them both and an utter silence [...] Then Ben asked Peter if the wind was too much for him and he said no. Then Ben said, 'What's the matter with you?' and Peter didn't answer and for the very first time I felt really uncomfortable in their

presence, apart from the few moments when I've heard Ben swearing at Peter in times of extreme exhaustion [...]

That evening, at the Music Club rehearsal, I asked Peter what time Paul was leaving – he said 9.

17 AUGUST 1953 [Monday]
Got to Miss Hudson's door at 9 but Peter leaned through the hatch & said he was catching the 10.30 after all [...] At 10 I waited outside the front door: Paul came out to fetch me in. All three were in tears, Ben being the calmest & most matter-of-fact. He hobbled to the front door to see them off and I waved from the middle of the road till the car had turned the corner.

A week after Rogerson's departure, Holst notes that 'Ben talked a lot: – said he'd talked to Father Jolly [the Roman Catholic priest in Aldeburgh, and a friend of the composer] who'd been very reassuring about Paul' (26 August 1953; IHD, p. 250), and on 6 September (IHD, p. 254): 'He asked me if he could send my love to Paul, who was going in tomorrow. He'd decided not to go & see him off.' Rogerson had been accepted as a novice at the monastery at Harlaxton Manor, in Lincolnshire. On the eve of his departure, Britten wrote him a letter exceptional for its overt affection:

My dearest Paul,
As your mother may have hinted to you I am afraid I shall not be able to get to London tomorrow to see you off to Harlaxton. In many ways I should have loved to have been there, in spite of the fact that I'm not at all good at 'farewells', but I'm hard at work again and, as usual very behindhand! So although I shan't be there, my thoughts will be, and not only at the station, but on the journey, & in your first days – and in the many months to come! In fact, my dear, my thoughts are with you more often than you would imagine. You have meant a great deal to me these last two years, a great comfort, & a great pleasure. And, although I shan't see you much for the next few years – I won't trouble you by making frequent calls at the Manor – the clear memory of our many times together will be also a great comfort & pleasure.

I am sure that you are clear in your mind about what you are doing. I know you will be always true to the real 'Paul'. Always know that whatever you do, and however, there is a great deal of love awaiting you in your

devoted
BEN

Britten continued to have news via the boy's mother, to whom he wrote on 29 November 1953:

Thank you for all your little scraps of news of Paul – they are precious. I will write him a note, & hope he gets it, & also, if I can manage it try & call in one of these days, & pray for a chance of seeing him. Every sign of a high tide we think of him, & of his stirling [sic] work clearing up the house after the Great Flood [in February]!

And when two years later Rogerson was about to take his vows, Britten wrote to him (6 September 1955):

My dear Paul,

I believe that the 8th is a big day for you, & this is a message to say I shall be thinking of you – being with you in Spirit, & praying that you will be happy.

I also hear that there is a chance of seeing you when you are in London on 18th – I will do everything in my power to get to London for that opportunity, you may be sure, because I long to see you –

With a great deal of love,
Yours,
BEN

Rogerson was to leave the Jesuits in 1959:

I tried it for six years and came out. I came out because I ploughed an examination for the third time [...] I was very pleased I came out because I wasn't enjoying it there.

He and Britten were immediately in touch with each other and Britten invited him to Aldeburgh for a fortnight; he visited again in 1964. After undertaking some teaching and administrative work, Rogerson joined Wilfred Van Wyck's artists agency where he met his future wife. He subsequently spent some thirty-five years managing the Chichester Festival Theatre.

For more on Britten's relationship with Paul Rogerson, see JBBC, pp. 160–70 and George Behrend, *An Unexpected Life*, pp. 594–6.

2 Billy Burrell (1925–1999), an Aldeburgh fisherman and friend of Britten from 1947; see also Letter 688 n. 4.

3 Brand name for a non-alcoholic version of cider.

738 To Lennox Berkeley[1]

4 CRABBE STREET, ALDEBURGH, SUFFOLK
June 27th 1952

My dear Lennox,

Thank you so much for your nice letter.

I am so sorry you had so much worry over the new work[2] – that the choir wasn't, well, sophisticated enough to make you feel easier in the performance. But I assure you that a great deal came across – & a great deal of enjoyment was felt by many people I have talked to. Thank you so very much for writing such a lovely piece for us. Apart from the pleasure, it was a great honour for the little Aldeburgh Festival to have a new piece from your pen. Please don't feel in any way discouraged from writing something again for us – either slightly easier (!) for the chorus, or just chamber music, or anything which strikes your fancy. It is so lovely for us all to have these musical expressions of your connections with & feelings for Suffolk!

I do hope that you & Freda³ (& even perhaps my godchild⁴ too) can & will come here to stay this Autumn. I will write & suggest a weekend sometime, or will you suggest yourselves ... perhaps both methods is safest!

With love & thanks to you all,
Yours ever,
BEN

1 British composer (1903–1989). Britten's and Berkeley's close friendship dated from 1936, a relationship that was consolidated by their joint composition, *Mont Juic*, and their shared occupancy of the Old Mill at Snape. Britten dedicated his Piano Concerto to Berkeley. See also Letter 86 n. 2, and 1/C1, 2 and 3.

2 Berkeley's *Variations on a Hymn-tune of Orlando Gibbons*, Op. 35, for tenor, chorus, organ and orchestra, which had been commissioned by the English Opera Group for the 5th Aldeburgh Festival. It was given its first performance at an Aldeburgh Festival concert in Aldeburgh Parish Church on 21 June 1952 by Pears, the Aldeburgh Festival Choir and Orchestra, and Ralph Downes (organ), conducted by Leslie Woodgate.

3 Berkeley's wife (b. 1923), whom he met while he was working as an orchestral programme planner at the BBC (1942–45). They married in 1946.

4 The Berkeleys' eldest child, Michael (b. 1949), British composer. He has been a Trustee of the Britten–Pears Foundation since 1996 and was Director of the Cheltenham Festival for a decade, retiring in 2004. As a boy chorister at Westminster Cathedral, Michael Berkeley took part in the first performance of Britten's *Missa Brevis* in 1959. When Michael began to compose seriously, Britten offered the young adult encouragement and practical advice. In the mid-1970s, Berkeley composed a Thomas Hardy song-cycle, *Wessex Graves*, for Peter Pears and the harpist Osian Ellis. Dismayed by the lack of a scheduled performance, he learned from the composer Nicholas Maw that his choice of one of Britten's favourite poets, set by him in *Winter Words*, was probably an error of tact. See JBBC, pp. 261–2.

739 To Imogen Holst

4 CRABBE STREET, ALDEBURGH, SUFFOLK
July 9th 1952

My dear Imo,

Please forgive the lateness of this note; but after the effects of the Festival wore off, I had so many rather automatic letters of thanks & acknowledgement to write – & yours is far from being an 'automatic' letter – that I didn't have time to write to you, & tell you how immensely grateful & moved Peter & I were by your contributions to the Festival – both <u>behind</u>

the scenes & very much on them!¹ It has been an indescribable comfort to us to have you with us, working so closely. It has been wonderful to know there was someone one could trust, not only to do the things, but to do them with a skill & efficiency which amounts to genius. We are both grateful – & so is everyone connected with the Festival. I have heard paeans of praise from organisers, singers, players & audience – & that just about covers everyone!

Now the next thing is – next year! Alas, Elizabeth [Sweeting] is still away, & so before we go off on our trip around the Continent, we cannot make the right formula for tying you down for that! But, always supposing you would like to come in & help us, & in future on a really professional basis, will you count yourself as definitely engaged – in the preparations, & running of Aldeburgh Festival nos. 6, 7, 8, 9 . . . ? Please say yes!

Peter & I get back at the end of August, & then we must settle down to plans. Could you come & stay some days with us – to post mortem, & in the light of experience (some bitter) map out next year?

We have just come back from an adorable four or five days in Copenhagen.² A ravishing town with ravishing people. It was lovely to see some of the boys again. They obviously adored their stay here.³

I hope you'll enjoy Bryanston.⁴ Don't work too hard.

And with much love, infinite thanks, & great anticipation for next year –

Your devoted

BEN

1 For the 1952 Festival, Holst's commitments included arranging Britten's *Rejoice in the Lamb* for a performance on 21 June, and auditioning and rehearsing the Aldeburgh Festival Choir, though according to Humphrey Carpenter she was reluctant to reject any applicant for the Choir on the grounds that music-making should be free to all (HCBB, p. 310). She also ran the smaller Purcell Singers (a professional group), and was subsequently made a Festival Director in 1956.

  While working with Imogen Holst at Dartington in February 1951 Pears had drawn her formidable qualities to Britten's attention (see Letter 701 n. 1; HCBB, p. 309, and CHPP, p. 171).

2 Britten and Pears flew to Denmark on the afternoon of 1 July, rehearsed there on the following day and gave concerts in Copenhagen on the 3rd (Tivoli Gardens: see p. 75), 4th and 5th.

3 The Copenhagen Boys' Choir, under its director, Mogens Wöldike, had performed at the 1952 Aldeburgh Festival: on 14 June in Aldeburgh Parish Church, with the Aldeburgh Festival Orchestra, the Choir had participated in a programme of music by Jeppesen, Buxtehude and Pergolesi, and performed Britten's *A Ceremony of Carols* (with Enid Simon (harp), conducted

by the composer); and on the 15th, in the Jubilee Hall, it contributed mainly Danish part-songs to a 'Serenade Concert'. The 1952 Aldeburgh Festival Programme Book included an article about the Choir and a message from the Danish Ambassador. In September 1953 the Choir was to record *A Ceremony of Carols* for Decca (LW 5070), again with Enid Simon, under the composer's direction: see Letter 777 n. 4.

4 Bryanston Summer School of Music, established in 1948 at Bryanston School, Dorset, by William Glock: see Letter 585 n. 1. Holst had presumably been invited to teach at the Summer School, where she first taught in the year of its foundation (see Christopher Grogan (ed.), *Imogen Holst: A Life in Music*, p. 117).

740 To William Plomer

Aix-en-Provence
July 24th 1952

My dear William,

Here we are – after a lovely (if hot) motor across the country, seeing many lovely things, & eating much scrumptious food.[1] We were for three or four days in the country about 30 miles from here staying with friends, which was nice & peaceful after all the hotels & packing. Now we have a concert tonight, which is a horrid thought coming in the middle of a holiday![2] However – in spite of travelling, I've done a lot of reading & thinking about Gloriana,[3] & here are some random remarks about the new version of Act I.

Terribly good. I am delighted with it & ideas come fast & furious. I'd like to start the tournament earlier, so, in fact that practically the whole of it could be described by Cuffe. Could Essex have some more asides – such as 'Heavens' – 'I can't bear it' kind of thing? Which leads to one general worry ... I think that metre & rhyme (especially the latter) may make the recitatives very square, & unconversational. Can we take out a word here & there to break them up?

Could Essex (& Mountjoy perhaps) have a reaction (an aside even) to Raleigh's little song[4] in the 1st scene – it will pave the way for the later outbursts. Similarly there could be generally more reactions from the crowd, through this scene.

Could Essex, in the final ensemble have a more personal couplet? I don't think this need be regarded as realistic – just his thoughts.

I am thrilled with Act I Scene II. It is a lovely, a really lovely scene. One comment – wasn't Essex called Robin, by the Queen? It would be nice & tender I think, & also prevent confusion with Cecil.

One or two general remarks on future scenes. I still don't like the

LETTER 740: JULY 1952

KONCERTSALEN

Kl. 19.30
Bror Kalles Kapel underholder
Gratis entré

1. Københavner march .... Th. Poulsen
2. Pilagårdspolka .... Karl Severin
3. Bondevals .... Theo Pinét
4. De lystige clarinetter .... Bøhling Petersen
   Solister: Willy Hansen og Helge Sørensen
5. Fynsk polka .... arr. Bror Kalle
6. Sørens hopsa .... arr. Bror Kalle
7. Kuk-kuk valsen .... J. E. Jonasson
8. De to trompeter .... Hans Peter Nielsen
   Solister: Harald Huess og Erhardt Hansen
9. Nordisk polka .... Karl Severin
10. Scottish-potpourri .... arr. Robert Kaas
11. Prinsesse Toben .... arr. Bror Kalle
12. Champagne polka .... Lawrence Welk
13. Rheinländer-potpourri .... arr. Robert Kaas
14. Skæve Thorvald .... ***

Kl. 21
BENJAMIN BRITTEN - PETER PEARS

Billetter à 1 og 2 kr. fås i billetsalget ved Tivolis hovedindgang kl. 10—20, samt koncertaftenen ved koncertsalens billetkontor fra kl. 20.15

1. Thanks be to God .... C. F. Händel
2. Under the greenwood tree .... Thomas Arne
3. Recitativ og arie »Col partir la bella Clori«.. C. F. Händel
4. a) Man is for the woman made. ...... Henry Purcell
   b) Alleluia.
5. a) Auf der Bruck. b) Fischermädchen. ...... Schubert
   c) Im Frühling.
6. a) Provenzalisches Lied. b) Aufträge. ...... Schumann
   c) Frühlingsnacht.
7. Folkesange i arrangement. .... Britten
   a) The Ploughboy. b) The water is wide.
   c) The King is gone a-hunting. b) Heigh ho! Heigh hi!

Flygel: Hornung & Møller

TIVOLI

Program

TORSDAG DEN 3. JULI 1952

25 ØRE

reference to Lady E's dress in Act 2 Scene 2 – it seems quite against the mood of the moment, & anyhow she wouldn't be wearing her glamorous ball-gown in the garden, would she? Couldn't she come in in it at the beginning of the Ballroom scene, & then when the grand ladies retire to 'change their linen', Elizabeth could swap the dress & come back in it. It would be more fun to have it more closely in the audience's mind.

And I've had a big idea about the end of the opera, which I'll hint at, only, now. After the great discussion, & the deputations about Essex' execution, & the signing of the warrant – could we make a quite unrealistic slow fade out of the Queen? Like this. Signing of warrant. Take lights down except for a spot on Elizabeth. Then, so as to suggest her mind is on Essex, play an orchestral version of the 'Brambleberry' song,[5] while people come & hand her documents to sign, consult her on matters – to which she replies automatically or not at all. Then finally, perhaps one might suggest she's dying; some doctor tells her to go to bed – she won't, but continues to stand there gauntly, like some majestic fowl, & slow fade of all lights to show the end. Could you think about this?[6]

Excuse scribble – but I must be off to a rehearsal. Nice as it is exploring the Continent I long to be back at Aldeburgh & at work on Gloriana!

Love to you & Charles,[7] & from Peter,

BEN

1 Britten and Pears had sailed to France from Folkestone on an overnight car ferry on the evening of 15 July, taking with them Britten's Rolls-Royce. They were accompanied by the Harewoods and their Austin Princess (PBBG, p. 24). On the day of their departure, Britten sent a postcard to Plomer to thank him for their lunch on the previous day (see n. 3 below) and to inform him that between 19 and 30 July they would be staying at Ménerbes with Tony Mayer, the French Cultural Attaché in London. During the trip, Lord Harewood read Henry James's *The Turn of the Screw* and found it 'so suggestive and creepy that, when I discovered the room Marion and I were to occupy was separate from the main house [at Ménerbes], I could only read it by day' (*The Tongs and the Bones*, p. 139).

On 24 July, Britten and Pears gave a recital at the Festival in nearby Aix-en-Provence. Tony Mayer (in PPT, p. 63) recalled:

Tapestries hung from the ancient walls. There were flowers everywhere. And Peter and Ben performed one of those programmes in which they have always been unique. Song after song filled the air with poetic sound. (Even after all these years I cannot enter the Cour de l'Hôtel de Ville without hearing Peter's soft voice, his impeccable phrasing, conjuring up the distant past.) The audience was bewitched.

Britten wrote to the Hesses from Aix on the following day:

We are having a glorious trip across France with George & Marion. Their car

> # Jeudi 24 Juillet 1952 à 21 heures
> ## COUR DE L'HOTEL DE VILLE
>
> # RÉCITAL
> # PETER PEARS
> # BENJAMIN BRITTEN
>
> | | |
> |---|---|
> | Have you seen but a whyte lilie grown | Anonyme |
> | In darkness let me dwell | DOWLAND |
> | Man is for the Woman made | PURCELL |
> | Récit et Air : Col partir | HAENDEL |
> | Under the Greenwood Tree | ARNE |
> | Auf der Brück | SCHUBERT |
> | Grabe an Silmos | SCHUBERT |
> | Im Frühling | SCHUBERT |
> | Nacht und Traüme | SCHUBERT |
> | Der Müsensohn | SCHUBERT |
> | The Seven Sonnets of Michelangelo XVI, XXXI, XXX, LV, XXXVIII, XXXII, XXIV | BENJAMIN BRITTEN |
> | Down by the the Sally Gardens
Ca' the Yowes
La Belle est au jardin d'amour
Le Roi s'en va-t-en chasse | Anonymes
Arrangements de BENJAMIN BRITTEN |

doesn't like the heat, & ours didn't for one moment – but really neither do we, terribly. Still there's lots to see (Chartres & Vezelay to say nothing of Pont du Gard & Avignon which I expect you know backwards) & glorious bathing in the sun, & lots of nice people.

On 1 August they moved on to Menton. Having taken in the sights of Monte Carlo, Pears and Britten gave a concert with the Hamburg Chamber Orchestra at Menton on 5 August during their nine-day stay at the Riviera Palace Hotel. Moving on to Salzburg on 14 August, Britten and Pears performed there on the 18th before a leisurely return trip to Aldeburgh, sailing back to the UK from the Hook of Holland on 21 August.

2 Britten and Pears sent a postcard to Mary Potter on 2 August. Britten declares: 'We're enjoying the holiday but rather resent having to give concerts occasionally!' (As Harewood recalls, however, these recitals 'were planned in effect to provide and to finance [the] holiday': see *The Tongs and the Bones*, p. 136.)

3 Plomer had attended the Aldeburgh Festival, at which he gave a talk on his eighteenth-century forebears, Martin Folkes and Martin Rishton, on 17 June. Britten wrote to him on 29 June to thank him for his lecture ('a disconcertingly charming & gay one, but one that sticks most clearly in the mind') and to arrange a second visit in between his trip to Copenhagen (1–6 July) and his five-week spell in France and Austria (15 July–21 August). Plomer duly visited Aldeburgh during the period specified by Britten (7–11 July) to make further progress with the libretto drafts (see PBBG, p. 24). The visit had evidently concluded by 10 July, when Plomer wrote to thank Britten for his hospitality ('I feel, & I hope you do, that that was a fruitful visit'). The earliest extant scenario for the opera, in Britten's hand, is preserved on headed notepaper of the United Steamship Company in Copenhagen and therefore presumably dates from this time: it is reproduced in facsimile opposite. Plomer's letter of 10 July indicates that he thoroughly revised the first scene after their meeting. Britten had lunch with Plomer in London on 14 July, on which occasion both men visited the National Portrait Gallery in order to absorb the period flavour of Elizabethan England, its characters and costumes. They purchased at least five postcards there: reproductions of portraits representing Elizabeth I, the Earl of Essex, Sir Robert Cecil, Sir Walter Raleigh and Sir Philip Sidney (see PBBG, p. 24). Britten had commented in his letter of 29 June that he hoped 'to be able to carry something of Elizabeth in my head abroad, to cogitate on, & perhaps even to start sketching'. The postcards survive at BPL among Britten's libretto materials for *Gloriana*.

According to Lord Harewood, discussions of the opera on the French trip were blighted by the composer's pathological fear of falling ill during the process of composition, and by Pears's growing antipathy to the project – sufficiently strong to inspire Britten at one point to consider alternative singers for the role of Essex when Pears expressed the wish to take on the minor role of Cecil (*The Tongs and the Bones*, p. 136). However, by September Pears seemed to be reconciled to singing Essex; in a letter of 5 September 1952, Erwin Stein told Tony Mayer, 'There is much to tell but I do not know where to begin: with Ben's "Gloriana" which he is just beginning to write after Peter has given in.' See also Letter 750. Julian Bream recalled that during the 1952 Festival he and Pears gave an impromptu performance of Elizabethan lute songs at a party held at 4 Crabbe Street, noting that Pears's passion for such music was considerable (CHPP, p. 173). Pears told John Evans in 1983 (Nicholas John (ed.), *Peter Grimes/Gloriana*, p. 68):

I adored the lute songs [in *Gloriana*], of course, and there are two wonderful duets

Britten's draft scenario for *Gloriana*, early July 1952. At this early stage in the opera's creation, Britten is already at pains to fashion an alternating pattern of public and private scenes. Also of interest are '(Song?)' in Act I scene 2, a reference to what eventually became Essex's two contrasting lute songs; and the use of the term 'Diversion' for the Queen's progress to Norwich (eventually to become Act II scene 1) and the parallel 'Diversion?' in Act III (eventually Act III scene 2, although at this stage the idea of the blind Ballad Singer had evidently not been mooted; see Letter 745 n. 1).

with Elizabeth [. . .] I think that in many ways in the rest of the part I was wrongly cast. I'm not sure but I think somebody else should have done it rather than me.

In her diary entry for 23 November 1952 (IHD, p. 167) Imogen Holst shed interesting light on Pears's sometimes critical attitude to the score, noting that he was 'very insistent that Scene II isn't right for the beginning of the act' (referring to Britten's reluctance to write the Masque scene that introduces Act II), but continuing, 'Peter very much moved by the Second Lute Song, and obviously longing to begin work on his part, and Ben terribly happy that he should be so thrilled by it.'

4 'Both lords are younglings', Act I scene 1, No. 7.

5 The 'Brambleberry' song was Britten's working label for what later became known as the Second Lute Song, sung by Essex to the Queen in Act I scene 2 and containing a reference to 'hips and haws and brambleberry'. The opening phrase of this song, modelled on John Wilbye's 'Happy, O Happy He'

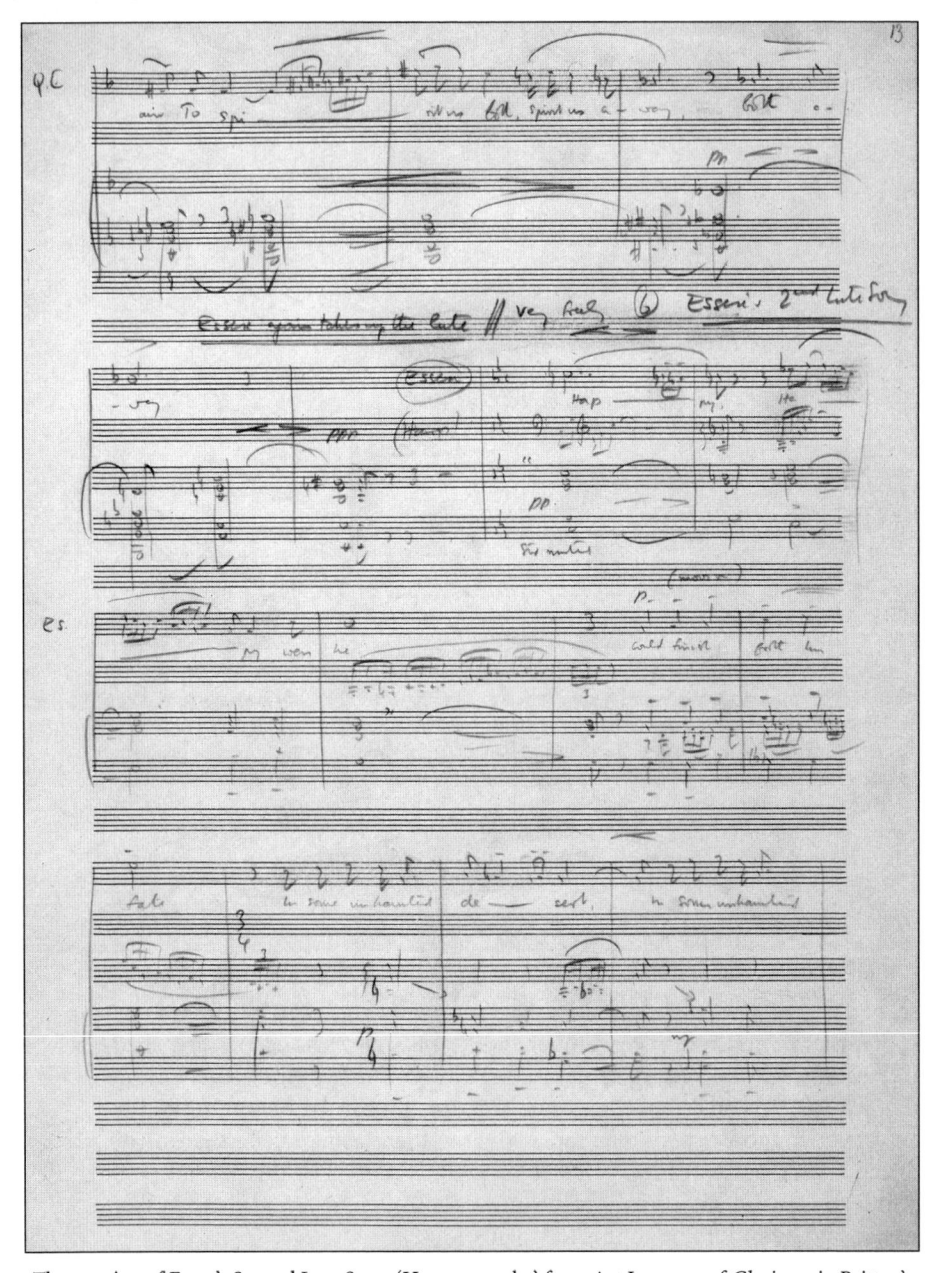

The opening of Essex's Second Lute Song, 'Happy were he', from Act I scene 2 of *Gloriana*, in Britten's composition draft (see comparative music examples in MCCCBB, pp. 126–7), was indeed to receive a powerful and hauntingly fragmented recapitulation throughout the opera's Epilogue.

6 Plomer replied on 2 August:

> I was very glad to get your letter from Aix and to see in the paper on the same day a good account of your concert and of your and Peter's accomplishments. I am not less glad to know that you have not been prevented from thinking about *Gloriana*. It is a great comfort to me to feel that you're pleased with the way Act I is shaping. I am sure the first scene can be improved on the lines you suggest, and the recitative *throughout* can easily be loosened up and freed from the harness of metre and rhyme, as seems best. I will see what I can do and will confer with you as soon as we meet.
>
> Yes, I like the idea of the Q. [Queen] calling Essex 'Robin' in Act I scene 2.
>
> I've been working on Act II scene 2. I am still inclined to think that Lady Essex *ought* to stroll in the garden in her 'too fine' dress. I will explain why when we meet, but I won't be obstinate about the point. We must simply search out always what is most effective and appropriate to our purpose.
>
> I like *very much* your suggestions about the final scene of the opera.

Plomer also reported that he had met with the opera's designer, John Piper, and that he had discussed the opera and the prospect of a 'new Elizabethan Age' with the Queen Mother at Houghton (see PBBG, pp. 26–7). For a detailed analysis of how the libretto drafts were shaped during this period, see PBBG, pp. 28–33; see also Peter F. Alexander, *William Plomer*, pp. 272–8.

The opera's unorthodox ending was further discussed in later letters from Plomer to Britten. On 3 November, for instance, the librettist wrote:

> I am much occupied with Act III scene 3, and shall soon I hope be able to send or show you a rough first draft for it. It is of course the end or last part that presents the most problems. I rather want to have the Archbishop kneeling about a bit – and Cecil, fussing about a bit – but not processions of phantoms, or dissolving portraits, or flashbacks: and most of all a sense of Queen Elizabeth's solitude, of her facing death, and of a sort of golden timelessness radiating from the glorious old fowl.

Two days later he sent Britten the draft in question: 'It contains a good many of Gloriana's own utterances on various occasions. The end will evidently be the chief problem.'

7 Charles Erdmann (1909–?), a German refugee (he had been born in London to German–Polish parents but the family returned to Germany when Erdmann was a child), whom Plomer first met in 1944, and who became what Peter F. Alexander describes as 'an ideal combination of factotum and companion' soon after, remaining with Plomer until the latter's death in 1973. See Alexander, *William Plomer*, pp. 247–8, and facing p. 239 for a portrait photograph of Erdmann. Many of Plomer's friends were surprised that the relationship lasted but, as Alexander observes, Erdmann 'suited Plomer precisely because he was not highly educated, witty, or talkative' (p. 262).

Erdmann was invited by Britten and Pears to join Plomer at Aldeburgh for Christmas 1952, but as Imogen Holst writes in her diary for 23 December (IHD, p. 187): 'It was quite a strain having five people in the house over Christmas and things had already begun badly because Charles had been too shy to come downstairs and William was looking drawn & worried.'

741 To Eric Walter White[1]

4 CRABBE STREET, ALDEBURGH, SUFFOLK
Sept. 8th 1952

My dear Eric,

Thank you for your two nice letters – taking the second first, I was much amused by the Essex poem[2] (especially the refrain) & will show it to Plomer. The libretto is going very well, & (hush!) I have already penned – no pencilled – the first notes!

Apropos the first, & documented, letter, you will all, I have no doubt, have considered whether it'll be a good idea to have another book about me coming out so soon – after all the market must be very small, for even the most chatty books about serious composers! You don't think it would be best to wait? Of course I am very pleased that you've got John P. to agree to such a generous lot of illustrations (it'll be lovely to have new East Anglian Pipers!) and I am very flattered that you want to re-open the Britten subject – although I should have thought you'd have had your fill of it three or four years ago![3] I will help all I can if you feel sure you want to go ahead with it – although if you would come here some time during the winter the help will be easier – but my own feelings quite seriously are that the moment is a little too early as yet. The scheme, by-the-way, looks all right – but I always feel that in writing about such as I, the background is more important than the foreground, & should be dwelt on & emphasised as much as poss. (Why who became what & how.)

Hope you're all enjoying your holiday & aren't getting swamped.

Love to you all,
BEN

1 British writer on music, arts administrator and poet (1905–1985). At this period White was Assistant Secretary to the Arts Council, where he was to remain until 1971, ultimately as Literature Director. See also Letter 574 n. 1 and I/c3.

2 This has not survived at BPL.

3 White's *Benjamin Britten: A Sketch of His Life and Works* had been published by Boosey & Hawkes in 1948 (see Letter 574 n. 2), and was to be issued

in a revised edition in 1954. White's proposal for a further book on the composer would have followed quickly on from the publication of DMHK. In the event, White's new book, which was to have been published by John Lehmann Ltd, foundered when Lehmann retired from his publishing house. The revised edition of White's 1948 book did not include any illustrations by Piper or, indeed, by anyone else. It is possible that White's securing of Piper's involvement in the cancelled volume had been prompted by the illustrations by Milein Cosman reproduced in DMHK. A considerably more expansive treatment of Britten's work appeared in White's *Benjamin Britten: His Life and Operas* (1970), which was revised by John Evans in 1983 (EWW).

742 To William Plomer

4 CRABBE STREET, ALDEBURGH, SUFFOLK
Sept 14th 1952

Dear William,

Your letter & the very nice little song for Essex is days' old, but we've had the house full of Harewoods & what little spare time has been at work on Gloriana.[1] I think it is <u>excellent</u>, & it'll go in very well. Thank you so much.

I've written the first section – the tournament & got Mountjoy on to the stage. But I await your next visit here with impatience, because I have had to make drastic changes in the form of this part (I have been searching for ages for the correct form for the music for it, & <u>think</u> I've got it at last), & I hope & pray you'll approve. When do you think this will be?[2] Literally any time does, except for Sat. & Sunday week (27 & 28) – the sooner the better. Will you write & suggest yourself? In the meantime I'll go ahead & hope we can sort out any difficulties later. (This weekend isn't possible I suppose?)

This can't be a long note, but I can't end without saying what a great experience it has been to read 'Museum Pieces'.[3] Both Peter & I found it hauntingly tender & touching & although I wasn't aware of it while reading, because the touch is so light, it leaves a powerful impression. I do congratulate you, my dear.

No more now – hope to have a note soon from you saying you'll be coming.

With love, & to Charles, & from Peter,
Yours ever,
BEN

P.S. George & Marion (H.) have recently met & been charmed by Lord Salisbury & they (& he) are keen for us to pay a visit one day to Hatfield. I'd love to go – would you?[4]

A stir at the door.
PAGE: My lord of Essex!
Essex enters, kneels, and rises.
QUEEN: Welcome, my lord. Sir Robert here,
So wise in counsel, will return anon.
Cecil bows himself out.

QUEEN: Cousin, I greet ~~and bless this~~ you.
ESSEX: ~~But cares of State oppress me~~
ESSEX: Your liege-man ~~would relieve you~~.
QUEEN: ~~You fetters, I believe you~~.
ESSEX: Cares most in lonely hours belong,
And Majesty perforce alone
Raised high and dazzling as a throne;
Pray let me speak in song.
QUEEN: ~~Albert~~ Robert One with a song

QUEEN: Queen of my life!

QUEEN: Cares of State eat up my days,
There lies my lute;
Take it and play.

ESSEX: (song) (entered thus)

QUEEN: Too light, too gay;
A song for careless hearts,
Turn to the lute again,
Evoke some far-off place or time,
A dream, a mood, an air
To spirit us both away.

LETTER 742: SEPTEMBER 1952　　　　　　　　　　　　　　　　85

Essex:

Quick music heals
When the heart is distressed,
Then one moment reveals
~~That~~ quick music's best:
　　　　Hallaloo, hallallay.

Quick music's best
For the pipe or the strings
When the heart after rest
Upriseth and sings:
　　　　Hallaloo, hallallay.

Two pages from Plomer's first draft libretto of *Gloriana*, Act I scene 2, with annotations, revisions and corrections by Plomer and Britten. It is evident from Britten's annotations that he felt the transition into the lute song 'Happy were he' (there was originally only one song) to be too abrupt: Britten's faint annotation 'Another song/gay' indicates that he wanted to preface 'Happy were he' with an additional lute song for Essex. This text, beginning 'Quick music heals', Plomer supplied on a separate folio by post on

1 Following Britten's return from his tour of France and Austria, Plomer had spent several days with him in Aldeburgh (between 28 August and 1 September). The 'very nice little song for Essex' to which Britten refers is the First Lute Song ('Quick music is best') in Act I scene 2. Plomer had sent this to the composer on 4 September (see p. 85), and commented in his covering letter:

> Here is a little song for Essex to sing before the Brambleberry Song. It is intended to be light and slight, and relevant to his immediate purpose of cheering and diverting the Queen, and I hope it may lend itself to a lively tempo before the elegiac mood of the Brambleberry. The phrase 'Quick music's best' comes from John Hilton (d. 1657), from a rather suggestive little madrigal by him: the rest from my noddle.

For details of work on the libretto undertaken by the collaborators when Plomer made a return visit to Aldeburgh in the following week, see PBBG, p. 33. Plomer replied to Britten's letter on 15 September, reporting that he had completed the libretto drafts for Act II scene 3 and Act III scene 1.

2 At some point over the next ten days Britten evidently played part of the music to Plomer, for the librettist wrote to him on 25 September to say, 'The Prelude is ringing most spiritedly and excitingly in my ear and bosom.' It seems likely that Britten's comment in the present letter that he had been 'searching for ages for the correct form of music' for the opening of Act I ('& think I've got it at last') refers to the ritornello scheme arising from this preludial music. Such ritornello structures were to be a notable feature of his later scores: prominent examples are to be found in the *Nocturne*, *A Midsummer Night's Dream* and *Cantata Misericordium*.

3 Plomer's fifth and final novel, *Museum Pieces*, had recently met with considerable critical acclaim; it was described by Edith Sitwell (quoted in Peter F. Alexander, *William Plomer*, p. 267) as 'a tragic, wise, humane, and, so often, wildly funny, book!' Plomer had completed the novel in November 1951 at the same time as planning *The Tale of Mr Tod* with Britten. Britten's and Pears's copy of *Museum Pieces* is at BPL, inscribed: 'for Ben & Peter with love from William Augt. 1952'.

4 Lord Harewood recalls (*The Tongs and the Bones*, p. 136), 'We arranged with the Salisburys [the 5th Marquis of Salisbury (1893–1977) and his wife; Lord Salisbury was the direct descendant of Sir Robert Cecil, Queen Elizabeth I's chief minister] to take Ben down to Hatfield [House] to absorb Cecil and Elizabethan atmosphere.' Britten's pocket diary notes 'Lord Salisbury' on Sunday 26 October. Plomer joined them on the excursion, although he was already beginning to suffer from the medical condition that would overtake him in November (see Letters 747 and 749–51). In a letter to Britten following the visit to Hatfield House (31 October 1952), Plomer comments:

> I expect you've heard about an absurd person called I think Lord Calverley who opened his mouth in the House of Lords on the subject of the Coronation opera and said something about 'either Wagner or *Merrie England*'. I looked him up in

Who's Who. His name is George Duff & he used to be a 'textile worker'. Where the looms clacked, there clacked he, merrily, merrily. [Plomer alludes to the song from *The Tempest*, 'Where the bee sucks, there suck I'.] I expect he likes nice woollen music, in gaudy colours, suitable for trades union festivities.

Lord Calverley (1877–1955) was, as George Duff, the former Labour MP for Hull East, 1935–45. He was created 1st Baron Calverley in 1945.

Britten thanked Lady Salisbury on 30 October 1952:

It was completely fascinating to see the wonderful house, and the marvels it contains, & it was most kind of you and Lord Salisbury to take so much trouble & thought in showing it to us [. . .] It is hard to exaggerate how inspiring these beautiful contemporary objects are. I hope you won't be too shocked when you finally see the opera (as I hope you will)!

Among the artefacts that Britten and Plomer saw at Hatfield House was a letter in Queen Elizabeth I's hand, which, as Imogen Holst records (IHD, p. 158), 'Ben was thrilled with'.

743 To Basil Coleman

4 CRABBE STREET, ALDEBURGH, SUFFOLK

Sept. 25th 1952

My dear Basil,

Thank you for your sweet letter. It comforted me a great deal – troubled as I have been by this wretched EOG v. Gloriana situation.[1] However largely owing to Basil D's [Douglas's] acceptance of the decision (in very good part), I am feeling better about it now. Nor do I see that the EOG season will be seriously harmed, providing we plan carefully & prevail on the Wiesbadens & Venices to make up their minds in time.

It is unnecessary, & even dangerous, to tell me to be selfish! I am that naturally, I fear – for now the problem of writing a good opera is more in my mind than anything else – other problems seem remoter every day! It is going well, especially from the libretto problem.[2] William's been here again, & we have sketched out fully all the work except the last two scenes – & very satisfactorily sketched too. He is a great sweet, & fine to work with; reasonable & skilful. John P. (with Myfanwy)[3] is coming here next weekend to talk about it, & also, I expect The Turn of the Screw.[4] Soon, I hope to be able to send you a copy of the [*Gloriana*] libretto to think about. I haven't seen [David] Webster at all – so, nothing further is achieved over casting matters, but that's no urgent matter, as long as Joan[5] & Peter are settled.

I am so glad Bristol seems so good, & that you're enjoying the work so much.[6] When is your first first night? All my love & best wishes for it. We will remember Eddison.[7] He sounds most interesting. Festival matters are a bit upside-down here – Elizabeth S. [Sweeting] being particularly hopeless, & worrying. However dear Imo Holst is taking up residence next week to help straighten things out.[8]

Well – back to Gloriana, & her problems. It's lovely to think you'll be in on it with us all – our team is now complete!

Lots of love & thanks – yours ever,
BEN

1 The situation concerned difficulties in resolving Britten's commitments to the English Opera Group because he needed to be free to compose *Gloriana*, in particular the immediate need to postpone the premiere of *The Turn of the Screw*, at La Fenice, Venice, by a year. The reference to Wiesbaden at the end of the paragraph concerns an unresolved proposal for the EOG to perform there. The EOG were to give two well-received performances of *Albert Herring* at the Wiesbaden Festival on 9 and 10 May 1953.

2 Probably a slip of the pen: Britten surely intended 'point of view' or 'aspect' rather than 'problem'.

3 Myfanwy Piper (1911–1997), British writer, John Piper's second wife; she was editing *AXIS*, 'a Quarterly Review of Contemporary "Abstract" Painting and Sculpture', when Britten first met her in 1937 at the Group Theatre conference at the Pipers' home (see Letter 89 n. 2). She was to write the librettos for *The Turn of the Screw*, *Owen Wingrave* and *Death in Venice*. See also Letter 523 n. 1.

4 In an interview with Humphrey Carpenter (quoted in HCBB, p. 331), Eric Crozier recalled that *The Turn of the Screw* arose from the possibility that the EOG might be involved in an opera film, in which the producer Michael Balcon was interested. Myfanwy Piper recalled in an interview with Elizabeth Sweeting (September 1986; quoted in HCBB, p. 331) that it was she who first suggested Henry James's novella to Pears as a possible subject for the opera film. In the event, the opera film was abandoned, but 'some time later Ben was casting about for something to do, and Peter said he'd just re-read *The Turn of the Screw*, and he remembered that I'd suggested it'. Mrs Piper recalled that the collaboration began on a casual basis:

> Ben said to me, 'Would you try and think of a way it [*The Turn of the Screw*] might be done and then we might get someone in to write it.' [...] So I worked out a possible way, and then we began to work on it together, and there seemed no reason to ask anyone else.

See also HCBB, pp. 331–2.

5 Joan Cross (1900–1993), British soprano, and of the first importance to Britten as artist, colleague, collaborator and friend. She created the roles of Ellen Orford (*Peter Grimes*), Female Chorus (*The Rape of Lucretia*), Lady

CHURCH OF S. MATTHEW, NORTHAMPTON

MUSIC RECITAL

BY

BENJAMIN BRITTEN Piano
PETER PEARS Tenor

SATURDAY 27 SEPTEMBER 1952 AT 3 P.M.

Alleluia
Morning Hymn   *Henry Purcell*
Evening Hymn   *1659-1695*

Three Arias from JEPHTHA   *Handel 1685-1759*

   1   Open thy marble jaws.

   2 (*a*) Deeper and deeper still.
     (*b*) Waft her, angels.

   3   For ever blessed.

Three Songs   *Schubert 1797-1828*
Der Einsame (The Solitary One)
Du bist dei Ruh' (Thou art my Rest)
Der Musensohn (The Poet)

Eia Mater   *Lennox Berkeley (b. 1903)*

Two Lyrics by Richard Rolle
                         Arthur Oldham (b. 1926)

Thou hast made me   Donne   *Benjamin Britten*
Death, be not proud   *(b. 1913)*

Folk Songs and Carols

Programme for a recital at St Matthew's, Northampton, 27 September 1952. It was for this church's first St Matthew's Day Festival in 1943 that the incumbent, the Reverend Walter Hussey, had commissioned Britten's *Rejoice in the Lamb*. The 1952 programme includes an excerpt from Lennox Berkeley's *Stabat Mater* and two songs from Arthur Oldham's cycle *The Commandment of Love*, which was first performed by Pears and Britten at the 1951 Aldeburgh Festival.

Billows (*Albert Herring*), Elizabeth I (*Gloriana*) and Mrs Grose (*The Turn of the Screw*). See also Letter 515 n. 4, 1/C3, and the Joan Cross Archive at BPL, which includes her unpublished autobiography, scrapbooks and several photograph albums.

6 Coleman was in rehearsals for his production of Shakespeare's *Measure for Measure*, which opened at the Bristol Old Vic on 30 September 1952. The following month he directed Goldsmith's *She Stoops to Conquer*, which opened on 21 October.

7 Robert Eddison (1908–1991), British actor and a noted Shakespearean who played Angelo in Coleman's production of *Measure for Measure*.

8 As the first entry in IHD reveals (p. 142), Holst's first day in Aldeburgh was 29 September 1952.

744 To Basil Coleman

4 CRABBE STREET, ALDEBURGH, SUFFOLK
October 6th 1952

My dear Basil,

Just a scribble (with a horrid Biro to boot!) to give you latest report on the Gloriana situation! – I rushed up to London to try & help cope with the Arthur[1] – Boosey & Hawkes – E.O.G. crisis a little, & took the opportunity of seeing [David] Webster about Gloriana & casts etc.[2] Talked about you, & he was perfectly happy about it. So that's a good thing! Also discussed choreography a bit – which at the moment is a little tricky . . . you see the Ballet is up in arms because they aren't doing the Coronation Gala. They forget that if we'd not had the idea of the new Opera & George H. [Harewood] hadn't bullied the Queen there wouldn't have been a gala at all – & they forget that they've had the other two galas there have been since the war. But still, there it is, & they are jealous. I've said that if they want there are the two little ballets in the opera where they can hop around & make their little bows . . . further than that I can't go. When the situation calms, we can possibly discuss with them & you who should collaborate in the ballets. It must be someone you like, respect & can work with. Freddy Ashton???[3]

The opera itself progresses.[4] I've done the first scene, am well on with the 2nd. The libretto is doing fine – all except the last two scenes written, & in excellent shape. William is a treasure. Myfanwy & John & he are all going to be here next weekend – what a pity the party will be incomplete without you! No hope I suppose? – but I suspect that first nights will be looming up at you now.

Do let's know how all is with you & if you are still as happy with the company.

I will send you a libretto as soon as I can – as soon as it is typed & corrected. I hope you'll like it.

When we meet you must remind me to tell you a funny story about the Martello tower[5] – too long, & perhaps too indiscreet to write.

Lots of love, my dear – <u>very</u> happy that Webster was so amenable about your doing Gloriana – now with you, Joan, Peter & John & William I feel the party is complete!

BEN

1 Arthur Oldham (1926–2003), British composer, pianist and chorus master. He was one of Britten's very few composition pupils and made the vocal scores of a number of Britten's works. See Letter 590 n. 5. The crisis to which Britten refers was perhaps connected with Oldham's ballad opera, *Love in a Village*.

2 Britten met Oldham on 1 October, then travelled to London the next day for meetings with Basil Douglas (2 October) and William Plomer (3 October).

3 In the event, the balletic elements in *Gloriana* were to be the responsibility of the South African choreographer John Cranko: see Letter 746. Friction concerning the desire of the Sadler's Wells Ballet (then resident at Covent Garden) to make its own contribution to the Coronation celebrations came to a head in January 1953: see Letters 759 and 761. John Percival (*Theatre in My Blood*, p. 96) writes:

There was a good deal of ill-feeling between the opera and ballet companies at Covent Garden over the fact that an opera had been chosen for the Coronation Gala (and David Webster, General Administrator of the Opera House, made clear his belief that the kind of audience present on such an occasion would not appreciate the work). Consequently, there was some foot-dragging by the ballet company over the arrangements: first, in agreeing that John [Cranko] should stage the dances, and even after that it took repeated requests on his part (accompanied, finally, by the director, Basil Coleman, for an interview that lasted almost an hour) before [Ninette] de Valois agreed to allow [Svetlana] Beriosova to dance in the ballet.

Beriosova was later to dance the role of Belle Rose in *The Prince of the Pagodas*: see Letter 886 n. 3.

4 Imogen Holst (CPBC, p. 47), recalled:

It was astonishing to see how strictly [Britten] could keep to his time schedule of work. He was able to say in the middle of October 1952, when he was at the beginning of Act I of *Gloriana*, that he would have finished the second act before the end of January.

5 The most northerly of the series of fortified towers built on the east and south coasts between 1805 and 1812 to resist a potential invasion by Napoleon. (The name is either a corruption of Mortella, a Corsican tower attacked by the British in 1793, or taken from *torre di martello*, literally 'hammer towers', in which a bell was struck by a hammer to warn of imminent assault.) The one at Aldeburgh – lying to the south of the town between the river and the sea – has a unique quadruple tower design. In the 1930s it became a private residence; it has been in the ownership of the Landmark Trust since the 1970s.

745 To William Plomer
[*Postcard*]

[Postmarked Aldeburgh, 17 October 1952]

What an excellent idea – let the ballad-singer be blind; that also makes sense of the little urchin![1] Mountjoy surely took the night plane from Ireland to come & plead for his friend??[2] I've today finished (roughly) Act I – & am starting on Act II Scene II. Looking forward to your coming.[3]

Love from

BEN

1 On an undated postcard to Britten, Plomer had written, 'I wonder whether the ballad-singer in Act 3 Sc 2 might not be *blind*.' Britten was characteristically keen for *Gloriana* to include a part for at least one child performer, and had felt a boy's role might be included in the second scene of Act III, which features a ballad-singer in a London street. On 7 November, he wrote to Plomer again to propose a 'small boy' for the projected Tumbler, who was to appear in the courtly dances of Act II scene 3 (see Letter 747).

2 The inclusion of the scene for the ballad-singer also allowed the passage of time in the opera to be implied, thus allowing the pleading for Essex's life by Mountjoy, Lady Essex and Lady Rich to occur after a suitable pause.

3 Plomer accompanied Britten on a research trip to Hatfield House on 26 October, and may have visited Aldeburgh two days earlier since Britten's entry in his pocket diary for that date reads, 'William? arr Ald. 6.14.' When spending the weekend with Britten, Plomer habitually caught the 3.33 train from Liverpool Street to Saxmundham on a Friday afternoon.

746 To David Webster
[*Typed*]

4 CRABBE STREET, ALDEBURGH
5th November, 1952

My dear David,

    Thank you for sending the prospectus of the current operas. I hope very much, if Gloriana's progress allows, to be able to go next week (12th and 13th) to Ballo and Norma.[1] I will let you know definitely about this towards the end of the week.

    I am now about halfway through the second act, and am fairly pleased with the way things are going.[2] There is, however, one thing which holds me up considerably, and that is the choice of choreographer. I have had to omit the first scene of the second act (the mask [*sic*] scene) because before writing it I must be able to discuss in detail the shapes and styles of the dances. If the idea of having a ballet in the programme on the Gala night still holds, it would seem that Freddy Ashton will be all-absorbed in it. In which case I should be only too happy if I could work with John Cranko.[3] Being young and enterprising, he will not feel that collaborating in an opera with a producer is a rather dull job (as I feel his seniors might). One would, therefore, get his utmost enthusiasm and skill. He will also have by then worked with Basil Coleman at Sadler's Wells and they will know each other well.[4] I know he is sympathetic to my music, and so would make a very strong plea for having him join in what I am certain is going to be a very happy "working party". Only, dear David, I must ask for a decision on this immediately, because this gaping void of the Progress Scene is awkward to say the least.

    I have been studying the Elizabethan dances for which I am now writing the music (in Act 2, Scene 3).[5] It seems to me fairly clear that we shall need a corps de ballet to dance these dances. However simplified they may be, I do not feel that any <u>chorus</u> could cope with them. I hope you will not mind this.

    I discussed with George Harewood the other day the idea of his driving you down here some time soon so that I could play you more of the music, and we could discuss some of these points. But perhaps I shall see you at the Garden before that.

With best wishes,
Yours ever,
BEN

[*Handwritten:*] P.S. Robert Keys[6] (the coach I mentioned to you) is wondering whether you'll want him before Christmas – as he's been offered a tour? But I expect you are in touch with him.

1 Lord Harewood recalls (*The Tongs and the Bones*, pp. 136–7):

> We took Ben to see [Maria] Callas and [Ebe] Stignani in *Norma* at Covent Garden. (He was quite smitten with Callas and the magnitude of her performance and wanted her for the projected Scala performance of *Gloriana* next season; it never materialized, as [Victor] de Sabata got cold feet after reading the notices.)

Britten's pocket diary confirms the dates on which he attended Verdi's *Un ballo in maschera* (12 November) and Bellini's *Norma* (13 November) at Covent Garden. The visit to Covent Garden also allowed Britten to assess John Pritchard's conducting. He was in search of a conductor for *Gloriana*, and Pritchard had been commended to him by Anthony Gishford. On 17 November 1952, Imogen Holst noted in her diary (IHD, p. 165), that Britten

> thought he'd found the right conductor, because he was really impressed with the way Pritchard had done *Norma*. 'So I'll be able to sit in the stalls and listen!' I said, 'But you'll conduct the first night?', and he said no, very firmly.

2 Britten wrote to Anthony Gishford on the next day, 6 November, 'Gloriana is being a bit troublesome at the moment, but I suppose one must expect truculent periods from such a strong character!'

3 South African dancer and choreographer (1927–1973) who was to collaborate with Britten on several projects, most significantly the full-length ballet *The Prince of the Pagodas*. Cranko had been introduced to Britten by John Piper, with whom the choreographer had collaborated on *Sea Change*, performed at Dublin's Gaiety Theatre in July 1949 (see John Percival, *Theatre in My Blood*, p. 72, where the author suggests that *Peter Grimes* might have been an influence on the 1949 venture). Cranko and Piper also collaborated for Sadler's Wells Ballet on *The Shadow* (based on Dohnányi's Suite in F sharp minor), which opened on 3 March 1953. Cranko's most popular venture to date had undoubtedly been *Pineapple Poll*, a ballet based on the music of Arthur Sullivan and devised by Charles Mackerras, which had proved enormously successful in 1951. Cranko's later collaborations with Britten were to include a revival of *Peter Grimes* in November 1953 (see Letter 779 n. 3) and the first staging of the opera *A Midsummer Night's Dream* at Aldeburgh in 1960. He also directed the English Opera Group production of Poulenc's *Les Mamelles de Tirésias* at the 1958 Aldeburgh Festival (see Letter 896 n. 1).

Following prosecution for homosexuality, Cranko relocated to Stuttgart, where, at the age of thirty-three, he became Director of the city's ballet company, which he developed into a world-class ensemble.

See also Myfanwy Piper, 'Portrait of a Choreographer', *Tempo* 32 (summer 1954), pp. 14–23; Horst Kögler et al., *John Cranko und das Stuttgarter Ballett*, and John Percival, *Theatre in My Blood*.

4 Coleman and Cranko had collaborated on the English Opera Group production of Oldham's *Love in a Village* (see Letter 637 n. 2).

5   On 8 October, Imogen Holst wrote in her diary of the courtly dances in Act II scene 3 (IHD, p. 148): 'When I said he'd got the right Elizabethan flavour with contemporary materials he said I was to swear to tell him directly it began to turn into a pastiche.' She undertook to visit Oxford to research the character and techniques of certain dances – pavane, galliard, coranto and la volta – with the help of a friend who was well versed in their mysteries, and demonstrated the dance steps to Britten, with Pears assisting, on her return (p. 160). On 4 November, a play-through of work-in-progress on the courtly dances resulted in the decision to include a tumbler performing a morris dance (PBBG, p. 35): see Letter 747 n. 3. The dances were one element of several in the score extracted by Britten for concert use after the opera's disastrous critical reception.

6   Robert Keys had recently performed the piano-duet part in the Lyric Theatre, Hammersmith, production of *Let's Make an Opera*: see Letter 712 n. 10.

747   To William Plomer

4 CRABBE STREET, ALDEBURGH, SUFFOLK
November 7th 1952

My dear William,

I was very grieved to hear your medical news on the telephone this morning.[1] What a horrid nuisance for you! I do hope that your doctor is a good one, & very cautious. Please don't let him do anything rash to you – I didn't at all like the idea of not knowing 'until they'd unstitched you' what was wrong. After all there are x-rays & things (& lots of magic too) these days to tell you everything about yourself – it's difficult to have any secrets about oneself. Have you thought of second opinions? Sorry to be fussy & old-henny, but I don't want you to have more trouble than you've absolutely got to have.

Please don't worry about Gloriana. I've got lots to do for ages without bothering you. I can also easily write my problems & you can reply at your leisure.[2]

Do you mind if instead of 'Tumbler' (which reference books & Imogen Holst suggest was slightly lower-class) we have a small boy (with a blackened face) doing a Morris dance? Arbeau (in Orchesography) has a good description of one (in 'fashionable circles') & the music is excellent and a complete contrast to what's gone before.[3] Besides a little creature hopping around the place would look lovely after the La Volta swirlings. Please let me sometime have a p.c. with your reactions.

Do hope you're not too discomfortable, my dear. You're in my thoughts a lot.[4]

Much love from
BEN

1 Plomer suffered from chronic haemorrhoids.

2 It is interesting to compare Britten's relaxed and solicitous attitude here to his insistent pressure on Plomer later in the month when beginning to grow anxious about impending deadlines: see Letter 751 n. 2.

3 Imogen Holst's diary entry for 4 November (IHD, p. 161) records the circumstances in which this idea was born, during Britten's play-through of work-in-progress on the courtly dances:

> He asked about the tumbler, and in the same breath talked about the morris, so I leapt at it, and he showed me a paragraph in Arbeau which mentioned a small boy dancing a morris jig in aristocratic circles! So I showed him some steps and told him why they painted their faces black.

Holst had lent Britten her copy of the sixteenth-century cleric and author Thoinot Arbeau's celebrated dance manual, *Orchésographie, et tracte en forme de dialogue, par lequel toutes personnes peuvent facilement apprendre & practiquer l'honneste exercice des dances* (1588), in the translation by C. W. Beaumont (1925).

4 On 17 November Britten wrote to Pears, who was staying with the Harewoods in London, to say, 'I heard via Erwin [Stein] via George [Harewood] that there's no definite news of William yet. Let me know when there is.'
   On the next day, Britten wrote anxiously to Plomer:

> You probably won't feel like reading letters at the moment – but this doesn't contain anything important or alarming; just to send my love & ardent hopes that the op. has gone well, that things are not out-of-the-way uncomfortable for you, & that convalescence is only just around the corner. Peter, I think, will have more definite news, if he has been able to ring Charles as we planned. If there's anything I can do, however major, you will let me know, won't you? (Such as sending the car up to fetch you down here?) All I can do otherwise is to feel sympathetically ill, as I have done for the last four days. Today I'm feeling fine, & so I hope that means the worst is over with you!
> Gloriana proceeds apace. The end of this scene is in sight, & I am aching to get on to the Maidies scene. There'll be lots to show & play to you when you come down.

This letter reveals that he was approaching the end of Act II scene 3 and about to commence work on the first scene of Act III, which features a chorus of Maids of Honour in the Queen's ante-room at Nonesuch. (See also Letter 750.)

When Pears received Britten's letter of 17 November, he evidently paid Plomer a personal visit and then relayed news of his recuperation to Britten in a telephone call on 19 November: see Letter 749. Pears continued to pursue his recital engagements at this time – with Noel Mewton-Wood (piano) and Julian Bream (lute/guitar) – in spite of Britten's enforced sabbatical from accompanying duties, the composer writing to Mary Behrend on 25 November,

Peter managed to get here for last weekend, in between concerts and journeys (he's now in Holland again). He is well, but working terribly hard. I must say we both miss our concerts together this year – but we shall go back to them next Autumn with renewed energy & enthusiasm.

748 To David Webster

4 CRABBE STREET, ALDEBURGH, SUFFOLK
Nov. 20th 1952

O David – dear David –

Can nothing be done to stop K. Clark's[1] silly mouth? I have, five minutes ago, received yet <u>another</u> second-hand message from my Lord of Upper Terrace[2] about the Ballet v. Gloriana situation (it was thro' the 'usual channels' of course). I am now informed that there is going to be a short ballet on June 8th – <u>before</u> poor old Glory Anna. Just like that. Now if anything fresh was settled at your last Board meeting – please can <u>you</u> tell me direct and not have just any-old trustee sending messages. Anyhow you know that only over my dead body, & dead opera too, will there be a ballet before Gloriana that night. Let them prance on their points as much as anyone wants <u>after</u> – but <u>not</u> before. Anyhow, if it matters, that's the traditional way round.[3]

Are you coming down next week? Hope so – then we can plot & plan! Any news of Cranko? Plomer is over his operation O.K. so I hope to resume work with him soon.[4] Excuse scribble please – but I'm still shaking with temper![5]

Love –
BEN

1 Kenneth ('Kay') Clark (1903–1983), British art historian, who was Director of the National Gallery, 1934–45, and Chairman of the Arts Council, 1953–60. He was one of the first board members of the English Opera Group and frequently lectured at the Aldeburgh Festival. He had been knighted in 1938 and was to be awarded a life peerage in 1969. See also Letter 432 n. 2.

2 Clark's address was Upper Terrace House, Hampstead, London.

3 See Letters 759 and 761 n. 5.

4 Plomer was recovering from his operation at St Vincent's nursing home, London.

5 Given the angry tone of certain of Britten's letters to David Webster in this period (cf. Letter 770), it is important to note that Covent Garden's respect for the composer was sufficient for him to be invited to succeed Karl Rankl as Musical Director. Britten confided to Imogen Holst on 27 November 1952

(IHD, p. 169) that he had informed Webster he would contemplate accepting the post only if Covent Garden would accommodate the entire English Opera Group:

> Webster said he wouldn't do that because people would say it was turning into a clique. Ben furious, and said that everything that ever got done in music was done by a clique – that that was the word that was used when people disapproved, and that when they approved they called it a 'group' or something else.

David Webster and Lord Harewood were in Aldeburgh on 26 November to discuss the proposal, on which occasion Britten played them Act I of *Gloriana* on the piano (see PBBG, p. 43).

In *The Tongs and the Bones* (pp. 133–4), Harewood recalls the proposal that Britten should become Musical Director at Covent Garden. The plan had originated with Erwin Stein and Harewood himself, who believed that Britten need only 'conduct his own works, a Mozart opera every year and perhaps one other that he really loved – *Traviata* or Gluck's *Iphigénie en Tauride* or Tchaikovsky's *Eugene Onegin*'. When Webster eventually put the proposal to the Board of Covent Garden, there was dissension from two board members, William Walton and Leslie Boosey. When Walton asked if Britten would conduct his own *Troilus and Cressida*, then due for performance – an unlikely conducting engagement for Britten – Harewood replied in the affirmative. Boosey, Britten's publisher, argued that Britten was first a composer and a performer second, and was obviously concerned that such a public role in an international opera house would take up too much of his time.

In 1958 Webster was still entertaining the possibility of Britten becoming Musical Director at Covent Garden, or at the very least having some formal connection with the company: see Norman Lebrecht, *Covent Garden – The Untold Story: Dispatches from the English Culture War, 1945–2001*, p. 145. In the light of Imogen Holst's diary entry of 27 November 1952, it is of interest to note that the EOG did eventually come under the management of the Royal Opera House in 1961.

A revealing character sketch of Webster is provided by Harewood, who worked at Covent Garden from 1953 until 1960 (*The Tongs and the Bones*, pp. 150–53). Harewood concludes (p. 153) that Webster was

> a remarkable chief to work for, easy to criticize because he wore his faults on his sleeve, more difficult to praise as his greatest virtues were plainly visible only to those who worked with him. His reluctance to commit himself made people think he was indecisive. I once told him, 'People say you won't make up your mind', and he replied: 'You should never have to *take* a decision. The right course should be obvious. If it isn't, you may be committing yourself the wrong way.' Himself scrupulously loyal to his subordinates, he had little trouble in inspiring a reciprocal loyalty, even devotion – rare emotion! – inside the company.

749 To William Plomer

4 CRABBE STREET, ALDEBURGH, SUFFOLK
November 20th 1952

My dear William,

Peter rang last night saying he'd been round & seen you – & that you were feeling more comfortable & cheerful.[1] That's excellent news. I hope today's Doctors' verdict will be equally excellent & that it won't be long before you're convalescent & on the way to the old Plomer health again.

I'm having quite a struggle with the end of the Act, which won't go right. But I have had an idea today which may improve matters; & which – if you're feeling up to it – I will tentatively suggest now.

Essex, & rightly, takes no part in the great 'ensemble' after the Queen's proclamation of his Ireland job. Could he have a shortish heroic reply to all the exhortations "Go into Ireland" saying he'll have a smash at them etc. etc.?? It'll round off the scene well, & should I think have a somewhat characteristic & ironic flavour considering what's just gone before & what's coming next. You write 'too overcome to speak' but although dramatically that is right, operatically (espec. this kind of opera) I think those rules of realism don't apply (think of the asides, the 'fortissimo' silences one knows, & they aren't just comic opera nonsense either). Do you agree? If so, please just scribble a sentence or two (as much as you feel inclined) on a p.c. It can be in prose if you wish – to balance the Queen's speech.[2]

I long to know what you feel – but of course don't bother if you don't feel up to it – it can wait.

Please forgive me for trespassing on the quiet of the Nursing home – how are the Nuns? All Boy Scouts, as I suspected?

Do you want anything?

Love to Charles,
& lots from me to you –
BEN

1 This letter crossed with one from Plomer to Britten, written on the same day, in which Plomer declared that Pears had 'arrived & listened so patiently to my patter that I almost stopped him getting away to his dinner'.

2 Plomer replied on 21 November:

I am sorry you are having a struggle with the end of that act, but have no doubt that you will wring an excellent result from the struggle. It had occurred to me that Essex was 'acting dumb' to an excessive degree, and I thoroughly concur with your proposal that he should open his mouth. Out of it should issue, I think, a short and rather rhetorical prose speech – if that will fit with your intentions.

Plomer then gave an example of the kind of speech he had in mind for Essex at the end of Act II scene 3, which in the final version of the libretto begins: 'Armed with the favour of our gracious Empress, I am armed like a god.' The speech of Elizabeth's that it is intended to balance is her proclamation that Essex is to be Lord Deputy in Ireland ('My lord of Essex, Knight of our most noble Order of the Garter . . .').

750 To William Plomer

4 CRABBE STREET, ALDEBURGH, SUFFOLK
Nov. 23rd 1952

My dear William,

Two lovely presents from you.[1] The Fitz book looks quite delicious & I look forward a great deal to reading it, & will treasure it greatly for what it is & where it comes from . . .[2] The other the lovely Essex speech which fits what I'd planned (& even sketched in!) like a glove.[3] A lovely case of thought transference! The other bits are fine also although I haven't actually fitted them in yet.

I wish there had been a third present, a message that the Doctor had pronounced you absolutely free & that you were soon coming down here. But I'm hoping that it's only a postponement & that in a day or so I will get that best of all presents.

I had a nice birthday – Peter got here (& with two lovely Gaudier drawings[4]), & we had a nice dinner with the Potters[5] & sister Beth. Imogen came in after & we had a nice gay time.[6] (A pity you weren't here too – but that's only a matter of time.)

I finished Act II (except the Masque scene) last week, & tomorrow start Act III which I look forward to greatly.[7] I played the whole of what I've done through to Peter this morning & we were both pleased – remarkably so for this uncomfortable middle stage of the work. (He's beginning to like his part.)

Lots of love & many thanks again for the lovely presents & thoughts. Get better & better & better.

love to Charles,
& a load to you, & from Peter,
Yours ever
[BEN]

1 Britten had celebrated his thirty-ninth birthday on 22 November.

2 A first edition (1895) of *Two Suffolk Friends*, Francis Hindes Groome's account of the friendship between his father, Robert Hindes Groome, Archdeacon of Suffolk, and Edward FitzGerald. On the flyleaf Plomer inscribed:

LETTER 750: NOVEMBER 1952

I have always thought this a book of great charm, and not having seen a copy of it on your shelves, I send it to you with love from William on your birthday, and with his best wishes for the greatest possible number of happy returns.

3 A reference to the specimen speech included by Plomer in his letter of 21 November.

4 Pears had purchased *Boy's Head* and *Children with Kite and Duck* by the French sculptor and painter Henri Gaudier-Brzeska (1891–1915), who was killed in the First World War (the titles of the drawings are taken from Pears's own handwritten record of his art collection at BPL). Pears admired Gaudier-Brzeska's work and purchased several examples of it around this period, including a bronze *Torso* and two further pen-and-ink drawings. It would seem that he sold these items at a later date. The only Gaudier-Brzeska remaining in the collection at his death was a crayon portrait of Horace Brodsky.

5 Stephen Potter (1900–1969), British writer and radio producer, and his wife, the artist Mary Potter (1900–1981), who came to live at the Red House, Aldeburgh, in 1951, and soon became friends of Britten and Pears. Stephen and Mary Potter were divorced in 1955; she continued to live in the Red House until 1957, when she and Britten exchanged homes (see Letter 890 n. 13).

Stephen Potter joined the BBC in 1938 as a writer–producer in the Features Department, where among his first programmes were two in a four-part series entitled *Lines on the Map* for which Britten composed incidental music (see PRIM, pp. 581–2). Among the most celebrated of his contributions during his long career at the BBC were the twenty-nine 'How' programmes, written with Joyce Grenfell, in which commonplace subjects were treated in a satirical manner. These included *How to Listen to the Radio*, which was the first programme broadcast on the Third Programme, in September 1946. Post-war, Potter wrote his humorous book *The Theory and Practice of Gamesmanship, or The Art of Winning Games Without Actually Cheating* (1947), the first in a series of '–manship' volumes which became immensely popular. See also Alan Jenkins, *Stephen Potter: Inventor of Gamesmanship* and Julian Potter, *Stephen Potter at the BBC: 'Features' in War and Peace*.

Mary Potter was one of Britten's closest Aldeburgh friends for over twenty years. She studied at the Slade School of Fine Art in the 1920s, had her first solo exhibition in 1932 in London, and despite the difficulties of domestic family life, especially in wartime, managed to continue painting and regularly exhibiting throughout the 1940s and the early 1950s. Once at Aldeburgh, she became much involved with the Aldeburgh Music Club and the Aldeburgh Festival, and apart from evocative landscapes capturing the East Anglian light, painted several portraits, her subjects including Pears (1953), Imogen Holst (1954; see PFL, plate 287) and Britten (*c.* 1959, though there are earlier and later examples; see PFL, plate 229). The BPL collection includes many examples of her work, including watercolour portraits of Miss Hudson (Britten's housekeeper; see PFL, plate 230) and Roger Duncan. For a full account of her life and work, see Julian Potter, *Mary Potter: A Life of Painting*.

In the catalogue to accompany a 1989 exhibition of Mary Potter's work, Donald Mitchell contributed a memoir of her relationship with Britten and Pears (*Mary Potter: 1900–1981 – A Selective Retrospective*, pp. 16–18). He recalled Mary Potter as 'very self-contained, self-sufficient and a very non-metropolitan, non-fashionable person', which, in Mitchell's view, made her rather like Britten:

I think that's why Ben and Mary got on so well, actually. They were both people who were profoundly content in getting on with their work in an environment where they felt happy and untouched by glamour which so many people strive to achieve [...]

That's why they were such awfully good neighbours – because she was so self-contained. But on the other hand when Ben was working or when Peter was away, he was always very happy for Mary to come in. They'd share lunch. Because they were both working artists and they could meet either on his side of the fence or her side of the fence and simply enjoy each other's company, there was this empathy that worked most successfully for all of them. That must have been very much the case in agreeing to build Red Studio, which Ben and Peter did for her in order to enable her to make the Red House available for them.

Instead of paying rent Mary used to pay them in pictures and that's why the Red House has a terrific collection of Mary's paintings – because of Ben and Peter choosing what pictures they'd like whenever the time came for some sort of transaction of that kind [...]

I think most of the windows on the world of painting would have been opened for Britten by Pears really. But modern painting – things like Cubism and Picasso's later development and so on – I wouldn't think that meant much to either of them honestly. On the other hand, a lot of Mary's later painting substantially teetered on the brink of abstraction, but I would have thought that there was a kind of human scale with Mary that they liked very much [...]

I think Mary's interest in music was certainly a genuine interest but it wasn't a particularly sophisticated one. But that would have suited Ben very well: he just liked the natural instinctive reaction and they enjoyed each other's work.

But to have very warm, intimate, undemanding friendships in the immediate vicinity was very important to Ben, and I think that's why Mary was such an ideal person – a fine creator in her own right and a marvellous friend. There was no friction ever, no competing interests. It was an ideal relationship really.

Mary Potter occasionally accompanied Britten and Pears abroad. For example, in 1955, following her divorce, she went with them to Zermatt for a ski-ing holiday; when injury forced her to abandon the slopes, Britten composed his *Alpine Suite* for recorders to keep her amused. She also accompanied them to Venice in 1968 when Britten was writing *The Prodigal Son*.

6 Imogen Holst writes in her diary (IHD, p. 166) for 22 November 1952:

Got back from London at 10 pm & went into Crag House for the last bit of Ben's birthday party. It had already been going on for some time – champagne & lots of other drinks including Drambuie which was just right after a cold bus journey. Peter in good form looking younger & very beautiful. Tony Gishford was there, also the Potters. Everyone quite absurd:– Stephen whistling God Save the King and humming the bass – Ben doing flutter-tongue whistled trills: on late 19th-century waltzes.

7 On the same date as this letter Imogen Holst recorded in her diary (IHD, p. 167),

He said he'd give anything *not* to have to write the Mask for Scene I – and he thought Scenes II and III would make a complete act in themselves. But obviously this is because he's still weary with the effort of having written the dances in Scene III, and dreads having to do it all over again. Peter very insistent that Scene II isn't right for the beginning of the act.

For the 1954 revival of *Gloriana*, the masque scene (Act II scene 1) was omitted: see Letter 790 n. 1.

751 To William Plomer

4 CRABBE STREET, ALDEBURGH, SUFFOLK
Nov. 27th 1952

My dearest William,

I hope that this letter will not have had to be taken 'round the corner' by Charles, & that it'll welcome you home.[1] It is good news that you're feeling so much better. I can't wait to get you here, you know – & not only for work's sake too. I'll write or ring later in the week to see how you feel – but if you'd in any way like it, or feel relieved by it – the car can easily be driven up to fetch you. That's what cars are for.[2] If you want to come earlier or later – do – just say. And if Charles would like to come – please bring him. And stay a nice long time; really enjoy your convalescence! What a lot of motherly hen cluckings! But I've felt very worried about you, & this is the relief that things are looking up!

Gloriana proceeds: I'm well into Act III & it takes lots of time – hence this scribble – but I know you'll forgive me, or at any rate understand. John Piper is away, as you'll find out. But he proposes coming down here in December with the choreographer (J. Cranko) & it is most important that you be here – please. No more cluckings – into the post with it –

lots of love,
BEN

1 Plomer had been discharged from the nursing home.

2 Britten had sent Plomer a postcard the previous day (26 November) to say that he had a few queries about Act III – 'but they can wait till you come here. Any idea when that'll be?' As Peter F. Alexander points out (*William Plomer*, p. 277), Plomer must by this stage in their collaboration have felt that Britten was 'breathing down his neck' in his anxiety to make progress with the opera in spite of his librettist's indisposition. Plomer's response, written the next day, shows that he was nevertheless willing to arrange a meeting with John Piper to discuss the progress of the opera's design at this time in spite of his need to 'spend a few quiet days [...] and get going again'. (As it turned out, Piper was himself taking a 'natural cure' in Warwickshire and was not available, and Britten too had several bouts of illness during these frantic months.) Britten's offer to drive Plomer down to Aldeburgh was repeated in his letter of 30 November. Working at phenomenal speed, Britten had already started to write music for portions of the opera that as yet had no libretto.

In his letter of 27 November, Plomer politely but firmly reiterated his need for a period of rest, and proposed visiting Britten on 5 December 'for 2 or 3 days'. Britten wrote again on 30 November in even more insistent terms:

> I was a little distressed by your letter. Don't you think it would really be more sensible to come here for longer? Apart entirely from work (& there's quite a bit of that to do!) I think it's crazy, whatever the doctor says next Thursday, to think of going back to London & work so soon. I don't want to bully, but I always feel you're so sensitive about 'putting' on me on these occasions. You would be really no trouble, could be coddled (both Miss Hudson & I are expert at that) & really recover from the beastly operation. And if you're worried about Charles, bring him too. I think, unless you show reason about this, I'll come up on Thursday to see you & the doctor & drive you down – dreadful threat! Work is going well – well on with big duet between Eliz. & Ess.
>
> lots of love – & please be sensible,
BEN

Britten's preoccupation with making headway with *Gloriana* has blinded him to the inconsistency of insisting that Plomer come to Aldeburgh for 'work' in spite of the danger to his friend's health if he were to go back 'to London & work so soon'.

752 To Lennox Berkeley

4 CRABBE STREET, ALDEBURGH, SUFFOLK
November 28th 1952

My dear Lennox,

I gather that Peter mentioned to you the proposed Variations on Sellinger's Round – for the Coronation Concert in Aldeburgh next June.[1] Here is the version by Byrd which we propose to take as the Statement; & set it for a small string orchestra (4, 2, 2, 2, 1).[2] I do hope, my dear, that you

KING'S LYNN LUNCHTIME CONCERT SOCIETY

The Guildhall of Saint George Friday 28 November 1952
at 1 o'clock

LUNCHTIME CONCERT

Organised by Lady Fermoy

and given with the support of the

ARTS COUNCIL OF GREAT BRITAIN

PETER PEARS (Tenor)
MEWTON-WOOD (Piano)

PROGRAMME

I

CANTATA, K. 619 : Die ihr des unermesslichen .... *Mozart*
      Weltalls Schöpser ehrt

II

AN DIE FERNE GELIEBTE, Op. 98   .... *Beethoven*
    Auf den Hügel sitz'ich spahend
    Wo die Berge so blau
    Leichte Segler in den Höhen
    Diese Wolken in den Höhen
    Es kehret der Waien, es blühet die Au
    Nimm sie hin denn, diese Lieder

III

THREE IMPROMPTUS, Op. 90   ....   *Schubert*

IV

FOLK SONGS FROM NORFOLK   ....   arr. *E. J. Moeran*
    Down by the Riverside
    The Press Gang
    The Shooting of his Dear
    The Oxford Sporting Blade

During the 1952–53 season, when Britten was preoccupied with *Gloriana*, Noel Mewton-Wood took over from the composer as Pears's accompanist. As this King's Lynn programme reveals, Pears used this opportunity to explore repertory – for example Beethoven's *An die ferne Geliebte* and folk-song arrangements by Moeran – that might not usually be available to him when working with his regular partner. Beethoven was a composer for whom Britten had little empathy at this period.

can do it for us. It would be such an honour & pleasure if you'll contribute a nice typical bit of Berkeley! I'm writing to Willy,[3] Alan Rawsthorne[4] & Michael[5] – & I'll do whatever Variation is necessary to fit in – so you can do whatever you like, fast or slow, long or short! The date is June 20th – so please keep it, & come to hear the masterpiece! I don't know if Peter told you, but the Six variations on a Provençale theme which we heard last July, by Auric,[6] Honegger,[7] Poulenc[8] etc. etc. were most amusing and interesting – but I think we can make ours just as good!

My love to all of you – especially to Michael[9] whom I haven't seen for ages, & miss greatly. When you come for the long promised weekend will you bring him, or would it be more of a change for you to leave him behind? I leave it to you. I think Peter suggested a date after Christmas, didn't he?

I was furious to hear about stupid, from every point of view, Sadler's Wells. I'm certain that when people hear the 'run-through' that they will realise what fools they have been, & I hope do something to remedy it.[10]

I hope you're well. Is the Finale scene done yet?

Yours ever,
BEN

1 Although the *Variations on an Elizabethan Theme* were to be given their first public performance at the Coronation Choral Concert at the Aldeburgh Festival on 20 June 1953, Britten conducted a broadcast performance for the BBC Third Programme four days earlier. The Aldeburgh Festival performance was recorded live by Decca (see Letter 765 n. 10).

The idea for commissioning a set of variations on a single theme from several different composers had been suggested to Britten by *La Guirlande de Campra* (which featured contributions from Honegger, Lesur, Roland-Manuel, Tailleferre, Poulenc, Sauguet and Auric), of which he had heard the first performance in Aix-en-Provence on 31 July 1952 (see also PBCPW, p. 98). Britten contributed Variation 4 himself, quoting the 'Green leaves' motif from *Gloriana* in honour of the new monarch; the remaining variations were composed by Oldham, Tippett, Lennox Berkeley, Searle and Walton, with the initial statement of the theme 'Sellinger's Round' arranged by Imogen Holst from the keyboard version by Byrd. Both Alan Rawsthorne and Edmund Rubbra had also been approached to contribute, but had declined the invitation. As Imogen Holst notes in her diary (19 April 1953; IHD, p. 219), it was only when Rubbra withdrew 'at the *very* last minute' that Britten suggested Oldham and Searle. According to Michael Kennedy (*Portrait of Walton*, p. 167), it was Walton's idea that each composer might introduce a brief quotation from one of his own works, and that the authorship of the individual variations was not to be revealed at the initial performances of the work, with the audience at Aldeburgh being

> 5. *VARIATIONS ON AN ELIZABETHAN THEME*
> For String Orchestra
>
> The first performance of this work, which has been specially written for the occasion by LENNOX BERKELEY, BENJAMIN BRITTEN, ARTHUR OLDHAM, HUMPHREY SEARLE, MICHAEL TIPPETT, WILLIAM WALTON. These variations are written on the tune of *Sellenger's Round*, or *The Beginning of the World*. This dance tune was already well known when Byrd set it for the Virginals. It remained a popular country dance throughout the seventeenth and eighteenth centuries, appearing in Playford's "Dancing Master". Today we shall hear the theme with Byrd's harmonies, as an introduction to the new variations.
>
> The names of the composers of the Variations are given here in alphabetical order. Festival visitors are invited to fit these names to the right Variations as a competition. The forms for this purpose are to be obtained from the Festival Office, the Festival Club, and from ushers outside the Church at both performances (second performance— Saturday, 27 June, 2.30 p.m.). The entrance fee, 2s. 6d. for each entry submitted, will go to the Festival funds. The completed forms and the entrance fees can be accepted *at the Festival Office only*. The closing date for this competition is Monday, 29 June, by which date all forms should be handed in or sent by post. Valuable prizes will be announced at the beginning of the Festival.

Programme note from the 1953 Aldeburgh Festival Programme Book for the first performance of *Variations on an Elizabethan Theme*.

invited to guess their identities. Tippett's contribution later had a life of its own as part of his *Divertimento on 'Sellenger's Round'*, for chamber orchestra, which was featured in the 1955 Aldeburgh Festival: see also Letter 825 n. 3.

2 Four first violins, two second violins, two violas, two cellos and one double-bass.

3 William Walton (1902–1983), British composer; see also Diary for 9 September 1931, n. 1, and Letter 528 n. 7.

Walton told David Webster (22 January 1953) that he had temporarily to abandon work on *Troilus and Cressida*, 'while I indulge in an orgy of Coronation music – a superb Te Deum, a spanking March [*Orb and Sceptre*] & a piece for Aldeburgh. Quite a feat for me to have got it over so quickly!'

To Christopher Hassall, librettist of *Troilus and Cressida*, Walton expressed his jealousy about *Gloriana* and what he considered to be Britten's preferential treatment:

Owing to Harewood's royal connections he has wangled that the Queen has commanded an opera for the Coronation season. It is, I need hardly say, not T&C, but a new one 'Elizabeth & Essex' by Billy Britten. How he is going to get it done in 9 months (it must go into rehearsal at the end of March) I don't know. But genius will out [...]. B.B. has to give up all his engagements and Cov. Gar, which is already broke, has to compensate him. But there it is, we've no friends at Court so we must put on a smiling face and pretend we like it.

See Malcolm Hayes (ed.), *The Selected Letters of William Walton*, pp. 219 and 222.

4 British composer (1905–1971).

5 Michael Tippett (1905–1998), British composer, a close friend and colleague of Pears and Britten. He composed two song-cycles for Pears and he and Britten dedicated works to each other. See Letters 430 n. 4 and 572 n. 10.

Among the most significant of recent biographical publications about Tippett is the edition of *Selected Letters of Michael Tippett*, prepared by Thomas Schuttenhelm, published in 2005. Although occasionally wayward in chronology and in the transcription of the original letters, this volume presents a substantial selection of Tippett's correspondence with Britten, covering a period from 1942 to 1965. The letters are exceptionally revealing of the closeness of the relationship between the two composers. (The originals are at BPL.) The publication of these letters is all the more significant to our understanding of the Britten–Tippett relationship because of the paucity of surviving correspondence from Britten to Tippett: we know of only two examples, the earliest of which is Letter 825, and a brief acknowledgement card from 1975. Studying, for example, Tippett's letters to Britten following the premieres of *The Midsummer Marriage* (see Letter 825 n. 6) and the Second Symphony makes the reader curious to know just what it was that Britten had said or written to his colleague. It was not only about music that the two corresponded: it is evident that Tippett appreciated Britten's advice on his often difficult personal relationships and turned to him as a confidant on several occasions. Elsewhere in Schuttenhelm's edition, there are many references to Britten in Tippett's letters to other correspondents. Schuttenhelm did not select any of Tippett's letters to Peter Pears (also at BPL), many of which are concerned with *Boyhood's End* and *The Heart's Assurance*.

6 Georges Auric (1899–1983), French composer, who had composed the music to Gabriel Pascal's film of George Bernard Shaw's *Caesar and Cleopatra* after Britten had declined the commission (see Letter 415 n. 2). According to John Huntley (*British Film Music*, p. 132), Auric came to England in 1945 for discussions with Pascal and Shaw and 'was introduced to the British Press by Benjamin Britten'. Auric was one of the contributors to DMHK ('The Piano Music: I. Its Place in Britten's Development', pp. 266–8).

7 Arthur Honegger (1892–1955), Swiss-French composer; see also Letter 525.

8 Francis Poulenc (1899–1963), French composer and pianist. Britten and Poulenc had first met in London in 1945 as soloists in Poulenc's Two-Piano Concerto and remained friends until Poulenc's death. The English Opera Group was to give the first UK performance of Poulenc's *Les Mamelles de Tirésias* at the 1958 Aldeburgh Festival. See also Letter 500 n. 1.

9 Lennox's son. By 1952 Britten's godchildren, of whom Michael was one, had grown so numerous that he noted all their names in the back of his pocket diary for this year: the list also includes Humphrey Gyde (which the com-

poser misspells as 'Gide'), Jeremy Rudney, Sebastian Welford, 'Nicholas?', David Lascelles, Suzanna Piper and Matthew Roberton.

10 There was a 'concert reading' of Berkeley's opera *Nelson* at the Wigmore Hall on 14 February 1953, under the aegis of the English Opera Group; see Letter 763 n. 1 and the advertisement reproduced on p. 127. *Nelson* finally received its Sadler's Wells premiere in November 1954.

753 To Yehudi Menuhin[1]
[*Typed*]

4 Crabbe Street, Aldeburgh, Suffolk
1st December, 1952

My dear Yehudi,

I was delighted to hear from you after all these years, and thrilled with the news your letter contained.[2]

It is true, I did make some small revisions in my Violin Concerto[3] about two years ago, and it will give me great pleasure to send you the "authorised version".

Yes, Gimpel[4] has been playing the concerto in Europe this last season, but apart from a few performances in England, I am not certain in what countries he played it. However, I sincerely hope this will not deter you from playing it here which would give so many of us great pleasure.

I shall be in London most of April, May and the first weeks of June next year preparing my new opera for its performance, and it would give me great pleasure to meet you. Perhaps we could discuss the concerto, but certainly talk over the old days, especially our German trip which was so memorable.[5]

My best wishes to you and your wife. Hoping to see you in London in the summer.

Yours ever,
BEN

1 American-born, British-naturalized violinist and conductor (1916–1999). Menuhin had a long friendship with Britten and Pears and was a frequent performer at the Aldeburgh Festival. See also Letter 504 n. 4.

2 Menuhin had written to Britten on 19 November 1952 from New York, indicating that he was intending to play Britten's Violin Concerto with Dimitri Mitropoulos and the New York Philharmonic Orchestra in New York the following season. The letter was the first contact between the violinist and the composer since 1945 (see n. 5 below). Although in his letter Menuhin suggested playing through the Concerto with Britten some time

in April or June 1953, when he would be in London, there is no record of their having done so.

Menuhin played the Concerto at the 1968 Edinburgh Festival when Britten was (with Schubert) the featured composer. Kathleen Mitchell writes in her 'Edinburgh Diary 1968' (see PROMB, p. 196):

> Ben had been very nervous about the Violin Concerto. In fact, listening to a performance is as much agony as performing or conducting – perhaps more. In the event Yehudi managed quite well & looked as if he loved the music [. . .] At the interval Ben told us the sad story of the man for whom it was written [Antonio Brosa]. He seems to have fallen on to stony times.

It was around this period that Menuhin wanted to record the Violin Concerto with Britten conducting; as both artists had long-standing exclusive contracts with rival recording companies – Britten with Decca, and Menuhin with EMI – the proposal foundered. During the 1960s, and following on from Menuhin's appearances at the Aldeburgh Festival, there was discussion of Britten writing a piece for the violinist. This idea was never realized.

3 See Letter 681, in which Britten sets out the nature of these revisions.

4 Bronislaw Gimpel (1911–1979), Polish-born violinist. He had performed Britten's Violin Concerto, conducted by Thomas Beecham, in December 1951 in the presence of the composer (see PFL, plate 248).

5 Britten and Menuhin had performed together on a recital tour of the recently liberated German concentration camps, including two performances at Belsen, in July 1945. See Letters 504 n. 4, 505 n. 5, and 524 n. 5. In his letter of 19 November 1952 to Britten, Menuhin had written:

> I often recall the days of our joint trip to Germany and the wonderful way in which you fell into the spirit of the concerts, as well as the musical satisfaction that your playing brought me.

754 To William Plomer

4 CRABBE STREET, ALDEBURGH, SUFFOLK
December 10th 1952

My dear William,

Here is the typed first part of Act III Sc. III. I think it reads nicely, don't you?

It was lovely having you here & I am only sorry you didn't stay longer – but we won't go into that again![1] But do take care of yourself, my dear – the shock & discomfort of an operation pull you down more than you think, & you can easily overdo things.

I've finished Sc. I & now have started sc. II, but not very happy about it.[2]

However, that may be because I've now landed with a filthy cold which is a horrid depressant.

Excuse inky scribble, but my pen is weeping – keeping my nose company of course.

Lots of love & BE CAREFUL,
(And to Charles),
BEN

1 Britten and Plomer had worked on the libretto draft of the final scene of *Gloriana* in Aldeburgh between 7 and 9 December (see PBBG, p. 43). In a letter to Britten dated 14 December, Plomer sent the composer 'gratitude for your maternal "bullying"' – a remark echoing Britten's reference to his (mother-hen) 'clucking' in Letter 751. Plomer returned to Aldeburgh later in the month, writing on 29 December to thank the composer for 'a wonderful Christmas [. . .] looking back I see it like a brilliant picture in a dark frame'.

2 Imogen Holst notes in her diary for 9 December 1952 (IHD, pp. 179–80):

> He asked my advice for ballads in Act III scene II and I didn't know a tune of the rhythm he wanted, and I didn't know what acc. [accompaniment] if any they'd have had in Elizabethan England so was no use. He wants a fiddle to embroider round the straight tune of the song. His first idea for the tune had a falling major 6th, submediant to tonic, which he thinks too 'hill-billy'. He doesn't know the Appalachian ballads.

Britten wrote to Princess Margaret of Hesse and the Rhine (11 December 1952):

> The Opera goes on ahead – in a way I'm so rushed & exhausted that I don't know whether it's wonderful or dreadful. Probably it's neither, just, as usual, somewhere in between.

755 To Imogen Holst

4 CRABBE STREET, ALDEBURGH, SUFFOLK
Dec. 23rd 1952

My dear Imo,

It is quite impossible to thank you for what you have done for me & meant to me these last months[1] – nor for what you've done for or meant to so many of our dear friends in Aldeburgh. Everywhere one goes one hears praise & affection for you, it is heartily echoed in my own heart. Over & over again you have saved my sanity in so many different ways, by your energy, intelligence, infinite skill & affection. My great worry is that it may be sapping your own strength – but I have far too much respect for your own wisdom & judgement not to trust you in that respect, as in all the others. And so I won't bother you with misplaced avuncular advice! I haven't got a real Xmas present for you, but I send you the enclosed with my love (I haven't got a proper copy of Budd which you want).[2]

BEN

1 For a concise summary of Holst's involvement in the preparation of the *Gloriana* vocal and full scores, see PBBG, pp. 110–14, nn. 28–31. A full listing of the opera's source material is to be found in PBBG, pp. 102–70.

2 Britten gave Holst the composition draft of *Billy Budd* as a Christmas present, a manuscript she subsequently presented to BPL in 1983. In her diary for 23 December 1952 (IHD, p. 187), she writes:

> Ben gave me a large untidy parcel for a Christmas present, with a letter 'explaining it', and said he'd pick me up at the end of my drive at a quarter to seven as he'd got to go to Sax. [Saxmundham] to meet the 7.10 [train]. When I got home & opened the parcel I found that it was the original M.S. of *Billy Budd*, so I *nearly* died, and when I'd read the letter I still more nearly died.

A facsimile of Britten's inscription on the manuscript is to be found in Christopher Grogan (ed.) *Imogen Holst: A Life in Music*, plate 19.

756 To Peter Pears

HAREWOOD HOUSE, LEEDS
[before 6 January 1953]

My darling –

One or two letters which I've opened for you – mostly nice, nothing urgent. Others I have forwarded to you direct. I hope Glasgow wasn't too dreary & that (in spite of the silly Ibbs & T.[1] mistake!) you found a hotel.[2] We all thought of you a great deal & wished you the happiest of New Years. I do hope it will be for you, my dearest – all the things you love, & none of those you hate. (I hope 'Essex' will be in the first category!).[3]

All goes well & easily here. I've started work – work quietly all the mornings & then walk & talk for rest of day. The Spenders[4] came on New Year's Eve which was surprisingly nice – Stephen very amiable, but he's a poor confused, rather silly creature I'm afraid.

How nice about Morgan – we sent a wire to him & Kath from us all, including you. I'm pleased about Kath too.[5]

Well – my poppage – I must go on with Act III Sc. III – & put these in the post for you.

I do hope you manage to get down to Aldeburgh for a night.

Bon Voyage – enjoy Switzerland[6] & come quick home;

I'll be waiting for you!

All my love,
B

N.B.!!! Have you written to Yvonne Lefébure?[7]

1 Ibbs & Tillett, the artists' agents representing Britten and Pears at this time.

2 Pears had been in Glasgow for a performance of Handel's *Messiah* on 31 December 1952, with Jennifer Vyvyan (soprano), Nancy Thomas (contralto), Marian Nowakowski (bass), the Glasgow Choral Union and the Scottish National Orchestra, conducted by Karl Rankl. Britten's diary records that Pears had returned to their London address at 22A Melbury Road on 2 January.

3 The role of Robert Devereux, Earl of Essex, was to be taken by Pears in the first production of *Gloriana*. Britten alludes here to Pears's antipathy to the part: see Letter 740 n. 3. As this letter reveals, Britten had reached Act III scene 3, and was making the most of a quiet stay at Harewood House, where he worked in his own room each morning before joining his hosts for lunch (PBBG, p. 44). Lord Harewood (*The Tongs and the Bones*, p. 137) recalls:

> We had some gloriously sunny, frosty weather and went over to Plompton Rocks not far from Harewood. Plompton has an echo, and to try it out we found ourselves, hopefully alone, yelling with less than total conviction 'Henry James!' to the answering rocks.
>
> Ben was writing the title role [of *Gloriana*] for Joan Cross in almost mezzo range, but after he had left Harewood I listened to a broadcast of Bartók's *Bluebeard* and heard so pure, so easy a top C from Joan that I was tempted to ring Ben and tell him that he need not worry about at least an occasional top note for her.

It subsequently transpired that the top C on the recording was faked, Cross's highest note (the B flat below) having been recorded and artificially raised a tone for the purposes of the broadcast.

4 Stephen Spender (1909–1985), British poet and critic, and his wife, the pianist Natasha Litvin (b. 1919). See also Letter VIII n. 1 (vol. 3, p. 72).

5 E. M. Forster was created a CH (Companion of Honour) and Kathleen Ferrier a CBE (Commander of the British Empire) in the New Year's Honours List.

6 Pears was due to fly to Switzerland on 6 January: see Letter 757. No details of his Swiss concerts survive at BPL, though Letter 758 indicates that he performed Britten's *Serenade* for tenor, horn and strings.

7 French pianist (1898–1986) and wife of the critic Frederick Goldbeck; she was to play at the 1958 Aldeburgh Festival. See Letter 553 n. 6.

757 To Benjamin Britten
From Peter Pears

[London]
Tuesday morning [6 January 1953][1]

My darling –

I'm just off to Der Schweiz and it's snowing here – or only just stopped – so it's as well that I'm not flying like John & Jessie [Blackwell][2] are at this moment. I shall almost certainly come back on Saturday night to London, & must stay up here for some days I think – Flat business,[3] another treatment from Dr McCready (had one very good one yesterday – he is nice)[4] etc., so I will probably stay until the 15th up here.

How are you? Your ears must have burned a lot of yesterday. First of all Imo & Leonard Isaacs[5] & I seemed to talk a good deal about you, & arranged for you to conduct the Aldeburgh Variations & Holst Concerto in a Preview Programme of the Festival, in the Studio on June 16th or so (programme to include Bartók Sonata & Trumpet Sonata (Addison?) & possibly songs by me – a mixed lot but designed as a preview of the Festival & helpful to rehearsals etc. Hope you agree to this.[6]

Then last night I was up with Paul Hamburger[7] for supper – Keller[8] should have come but has 'flu or something, so Donald Mitchell[9] came instead – very sweet, young, dotty & enthusiastic – you were of course the main topic of con. [conversation].[10] Why not? You're my main topic of thought – honey- bunch –

I do hope you're getting on all right & are happy. Please give lots of love to everyone. I look forward very much to seeing you again, my own Bee –

much love
ever your P

1 Date deduced from Britten's diary entry for 6 January, which notes the name of the Swiss hotel in which Pears was due to stay: 'PP Hotel Pecht St Gallen'.

2 Pears's second surviving sister and her husband.

3 Britten and Pears were flat-hunting in London, having resolved to move from 22A Melbury Road. As Letter 765 reveals, the possibility of securing a residence in Harley Street appears to have fallen through, and they eventually moved to 5 Chester Gate, Regent's Park, in May. Pears told his friend Oliver Holt (CHPP, p. 172), 'Having spent 6 months dithering [...] we have suddenly grown impatient, & having found a charming house in Chester Gate and are now making an offer for it.' On 29 October, Britten commented in a letter to Plomer, 'Peter's new house is getting along nicely. We get a fresh room furnished almost every week.' For a photograph of 5 Chester

LETTER 757: JANUARY 1953

Gate, see PFL, plate 165. Britten and Pears were to use this address until 1958, when they moved their London base to 59 Marlborough Place, NW8.

4 Dr Michael McCready was Britten's and Pears's London-based physician. He was one of several doctors Britten consulted when suffering from bursitis in the right arm during the second half of 1953. See also IHD, p. 261.

5 British (naturalized Canadian from 1973) administrator and musician (1909–1997), who had studied at the Royal College of Music and subsequently in Paris (with Alfred Cortot) and Berlin (with Egon Petri). He held various production and senior administrative posts in the BBC (1936–63); in 1953 he was Third Programme Music Organizer. On moving to Canada in 1963 he served as Director of the School of Music, University of Manitoba (1963–74), and taught at the University of Calgary and at Banff. His arrangement (1952) for chamber orchestra of Bach's *Art of Fugue* was recorded by George Malcolm and the Philomusica of London. See also Leonard Isaacs, *Five Lives in One: Selected Memoirs*.

6 The preview concert for the 1953 Aldeburgh Festival was broadcast by the Third Programme on 16 June. The final programme comprised Holst's *Fugal Concerto* for flute, oboe and strings (John Francis (flute); Joy Boughton (oboe)); the first performance of Priaulx Rainier's *Declamation* for unaccompanied tenor (Pears); Bartók's Sonata for two pianos and percussion (Noel Mewton-Wood and Noel Lee (pianos); William Bradshaw and James Blades (percussion)), and the first performance of *Variations on an Elizabethan Theme*. Pears's reference to a 'Trumpet Sonata (Addison?)' is puzzling: it seems likely that the Aldeburgh Festival had commissioned, or thought of commissioning, such a work from the British composer John Addison (1920–1998), later to achieve recognition for his theatre and film music. No trumpet sonata was included in the 1953 Festival, although Addison's *Serenade* for wind and harp and his *Divertimento* for brass were included in the 1958 and 1962 Festivals respectively.

7 Austrian-born pianist, writer and teacher (1920–2004), whose Jewish descent forced him to leave his native Vienna following the *Anschluss* in 1938. He arrived in England in 1939 and, after the outbreak of war in September that year, was interned on the Isle of Man where he found himself in the company of musicians such as Norbert Brainin and Sigmund Nissel (future members of the Amadeus Quartet), Erwin Stein and Hans Keller. On his release, he entered the Royal College of Music where he studied with Vaughan Williams and the pianist Frank Merrick.

In the late 1940s and early 1950s he was especially active as a writer on music, and made several notable contributions to *Music Survey* as well as two chapters – 'The Chamber Music' and 'The Pianist' – to DMHK. The originality and seriousness of Hamburger's analysis of Britten's chamber-music output was of an entirely different order from what was then common in

British musical writing; and his performer's comprehension of Britten's consummate abilities at the keyboard informed his no less original article on Britten as pianist.

He joined the English Opera Group in 1952 as a coach and accompanist, leaving in 1956 to become a member of the music staff at Glyndebourne. In 1962 he became a BBC staff accompanist, giving frequent broadcasts with a wide range of artists, both singers and instrumentalists; from 1976 until 1981 he was a music producer with BBC Radio 3. His final years were spent teaching at the Guildhall School of Music and Drama and at the Royal College of Music. Throughout his career, he worked as a freelance accompanist and coach, partnering singers such as Heather Harper, Elisabeth Söderström, Janet Baker, Helen Watts, Thomas Hemsley, Philip Langridge and Geraint Evans.

See also the obituaries by Leo Black, with an afterword by Roger Vignoles, *Independent* (21 April 2004); in *The Times* (22 April 2004) and *Daily Telegraph* (29 April 2004), and by Donald Mitchell, with an afterword by Thomas Hemsley, *Guardian* (29 April 2004).

8 Hans Keller (1919–1985), Viennese-born writer, editor, critic, teacher, translator, analyst and senior member of the BBC's Music Department from 1959 to 1979. He was one of the few intellectuals to whose views Britten was generally prepared to give serious consideration. He made translations into German of the texts of a number of Britten works, and was the dedicatee of the Third String Quartet. See also Letter 709 n. 2.

9 British musicologist, critic and publisher (b. 1925). In 1964, following a suggestion from Britten, who was at the time disillusioned with his publishers, Boosey & Hawkes, Mitchell founded Faber Music. He was appointed founding Professor of Music at the University of Sussex in 1971. A close adviser and friend of Britten, Mitchell was, with his wife Kathleen, a dedicatee of *The Burning Fiery Furnace*. As one of Britten's four Executors, a senior Trustee of the Britten–Pears Foundation and Chairman of the Britten Estate Ltd, he has played a significant role in promoting Britten's music worldwide through performances, recordings, lectures and publications. See also Letter 709 n. 3.

10 Mitchell and Keller had been joint editors of *Music Survey* since 1949, Mitchell having been founder editor in 1947. Mitchell's and Keller's passionate commitment to Britten's music, which they featured regularly in the pages of their journal, led them to edit a symposium entitled *Benjamin Britten: A Commentary on his Works from a Group of Specialists* (DMHK). As Mitchell commented in an interview with Humphrey Carpenter (HCBB, p. 315) some forty years later, they regarded the book as

> a necessary corrective to critical attitudes to Britten at that time. These were often prejudiced or ignorant; and even when they weren't, it seemed to us that the positive comment was almost as ill-informed as the negative [...] It opened up the

possibility of a radical change in critical approach to Britten and his music [...] Its critics of course tried to rubbish it. But who remembers them now? As for the music, it's won its (and our) case, hasn't it?

For the critics' and Britten's own reactions to this venture, see Letter 760.

758 To Peter Pears

HAREWOOD HOUSE, LEEDS
Jan. 9th 1953

My darling P.,

Your letters have made me very happy. Thank you so much for them. I have been thinking so very much about you, thanking God you haven't been flying in this weather, wondering how it is all going. I hope the horn player wasn't quite so panicky as the Birmingham one![1]

Here, all goes the same. I work hard – am getting on quite well, nearing the end of the last scene now – we walk (slowly!) & talk (a little!) but it is good to be quiet & relaxed! Tony Gishford was here last night, & dear William comes this afternoon which will be lovely.[2] George [Harewood] went to London for the night, & is generally rather moody with Ma'am[3] – but otherwise sweet & intelligent.

I shall go back on Monday or Tuesday, I think. And expect you on Thursday or so? I hope all goes well with the Flat arrangements. It'll be lovely to have something of our own – I look forward to that a lot. I'll be able to come up, these next weeks, quite a bit to help you I think – to give you my expert advice!

I was thrilled that you were asked to do 'Vere' in Berlin.[4] Please do it, if you can. It means so much to all of us if you will – it is so very valuable for the work to have you doing it. Please!!

Just out for a walk with Ma'am & David [Lascelles] so I must stop this. It is only a Welcome Home to bring all my love,

my dearest P.,

B

1 Pears had given a performance of Britten's *Serenade* with James Kirby (horn) and the City of Birmingham Symphony Orchestra, conducted by Rudolf Schwarz, at Birmingham Town Hall on 28 December 1952.

2 Britten had written to Plomer from Harewood House two days earlier to confirm the arrangements for the librettist's visit, adding in a mischievous postscript: 'H.R.H. will be in residence – so plumage, please!'

3 HRH Princess Mary (1897–1965), the Princess Royal, daughter of George V; Lord Harewood's mother.

4 The proposed Berlin production of *Billy Budd* did not take place. The first German production of the opera had been mounted at the Wiesbaden Staatsoper in March 1952 (see Letters 728 and 731); Britten's poor view of that staging must have made him anxious to secure a better production in Germany. Later German productions in Britten's lifetime took place in Cologne (January 1966, conducted by István Kertész, whose work Britten admired) – described in an undated letter from Britten to Forster as 'an excellent performance' that 'deeply touched the audience' – and in Hamburg (May 1972, conducted by Gary Bertini). Pears never sang the role of Vere in Germany, his only foreign appearances in the part taking place in Paris (May 1952) and New York (September 1978): see BBMCPR, pp. 150–51.

759 To William Plomer

4 CRABBE STREET, ALDEBURGH, SUFFOLK
Jan 21st 1953

My dear William,

Only a brief note to thank you so much for your very warm & welcome letter.[1] Writing Gloriana with you has been the greatest pleasure; more even than I expected, & I was pretty greedy in anticipation too! I think, apart from your wonderful gifts, that you have shown the greatest possible good-temper & amenability, which can't always have been easy considering the conditions and not over-precision of your colleague on the job!

It seems that all after all may be well about the Ballet.[2] There was a meeting yesterday at which the thing was thrashed out again, & I gather that if all proceeds to plan & if the Ballet people don't tear the place down, that there will be no ballet that evening. Thank God for that anyhow!

Will you by any happy chance be free the weekend of Feb. 1st? I am planning to spend it at Henley with the Pipers.[3] Basil Coleman can come too, & we could have the urgently needed preliminary discussions on the settings & production.[4] If you can't manage the whole time, perhaps a long day then – but much more preferable would be the whole weekend, because we could discuss & then sleep on the discussions, if need be!

I haven't, quite frankly, made much progress since I got back. I've been up to my eyes in the yearly tax figures, in Festival business, & in trying to get Act III Sc. II into shape. There's not much success in the latter to be reported, alas; I am quite addlepated at the moment. I've started the Progress, though.[5]

Lots of love, my dear; I hope you continue well, & without discomfort.

Love to Charles,
Yours ever,
BEN

1 Plomer had written to Britten on 13 January, thanking the composer for driving him home after his recent visit to Harewood House. Plomer commented:

> What a heavenly time that was at Harewood and how thankful I am to have been able to contribute to your progress with *Gloriana* during these last few days – and indeed all along. When obstacles have arisen, you have always charmed or reasoned them away, and it has been above all a *happiness* to be working with you and to be with you. I look forward not only to being able to help as much as I can to get *Gloriana*, so to speak, into her farthingale, but to the possibility of being able to be helpful to you in the future.
>
> I haven't really said plainly enough how excited I am by the music or how much I admire your imagination and your resourcefulness. I think I see *Gloriana* rising like a planet (I don't mean in any Holstian sense!) in the musical sky.

2 See Letters 744, 746 and 748, and IHD, p. 193.

3 Britten's diary reveals that Plomer duly visited Henley on 1 February.

4 Discussions concerning production details for *Gloriana* were already well under way, Britten having met Basil Coleman for this purpose on 17 January.

5 Britten refers to Queen Elizabeth's progress to Norwich, Act II scene 1, the composition of which he had postponed from the autumn of 1952 while issues about the choreographic element of this masque scene were being resolved. Britten's confidence was somewhat misplaced: see Letter 761.

760 To Hans Keller and Donald Mitchell

4 CRABBE STREET, ALDEBURGH, SUFFOLK

Jan. 21st 1953

Dear Hans Keller & Donald Mitchell,

I am so sorry not to have answered your letter & enclosures before this, but I have been wildly busy, & letter-writing has been entirely neglected.[1] I expect by now that the matter of the telegram has settled itself – after your very strong message it certainly ought to have done! Anyhow I entirely agree with your attitude. The telegram was a private one of thanks (& regrets for absence) & not for public consumption.[2] Anyhow the book was not published with my authority – one of its strongest virtues! – because at no point was I consulted (& didn't want to be!). It would be idle for me to write a blurb for the book, if it were needed, because it is obvious that I am pleased & flattered by its appearing; a fool wouldn't be.

Of course you wouldn't believe me if I said I was equally pleased with every contribution. But what I <u>am</u> delighted with, is the seriousness of it, the thoroughness of its planning & editing, its excellent get-up, & the admirable quality of a great deal of the contents, in which I would like to include both of your contributions.³ I haven't time to write fully about it, but I don't see why we should continue to please our detractors by remaining strangers – can't we really meet & have a good talk, someday when this opera is finished & we can all be in London?

Excuse haste & scribble, & with sincere thanks for your skill, sympathy & hard work.

Yours sincerely,
BENJAMIN BRITTEN

1 The letter and enclosures have not survived at BPL, but were presumably connected with the publication of DMHK: see also n. 3 below. The enclosures may have been related to a complaint from Mitchell and Keller following John Amis's broadcast review of DMHK during the BBC Home Service radio programme *Music Magazine*, on 8 February 1953, in the course of which Amis mentioned that, as editors, Mitchell and Keller, 'one presumes, chose their contributors and briefed them as to what they might say and what they might not say'. Mitchell wrote to the editors of *Music Magazine*, Anna Instone and Julian Herbage, on 17 February, concerned that Amis's

> little phrase [...] is arousing exceptional interest. Both of us now have had numerous enquiries [...] and last night when I was giving a talk on Britten at Hendon Technical College(!) almost the first question asked by someone after the meeting referred to Amis's statement. As Amis's statement is without any foundation in fact and seems to be doing quite a bit of damage do you think you could possibly oblige us by disclaiming it on our behalf in the next *Music Magazine*? We should be most grateful and it might do a bit of good, though I think we should have taken action earlier. But at the time we didn't believe that anybody would be taken in by Amis's 'disclosure' [...] We're not especially impressed by review by rumour but since others evidently are we feel obliged to do something about it.

Herbage responded on 22 February:

> I confess I am a little surprised at [your letter's] contents, because I am sure you will recollect that Amis's remark [...] was a presumption only on his part, although one for which he seems to have had some foundation. It was in no way a statement of fact, as you suggest.

The disclaimer Mitchell and Keller sought was refused. (The transcript of Amis's review and the exchange of correspondence is at BPL, Donald Mitchell Papers.)

2 Britten had sent a telegram to Rockliff, the publishers of DMHK, on 8 December 1952:

MUCH REGRET GLORIANA PREVENTS MY BEING PRESENT THIS AFTERNOON [at the launch party for the book]. PLEASE CONVEY KELLER MITCHELL AND OTHER CONTRIBUTORS PRESENT MY GREAT GRATITUDE FOR AND PLEASURE IN MAGNIFICENT BOOK.

LETTER 760: JANUARY 1953   121

Presumably the publishers had made use of this telegram in marketing the book until receiving protests from the editors.

3 The editors' contributions were 'The Musical Atmosphere' (Mitchell) and '*Peter Grimes*: The Story; The Music not Excluded' and 'The Musical Character' (Keller). On at least two occasions Britten discussed the volume with Imogen Holst, conversations that she recorded in her diary. On 4 December 1952 (IHD, p. 177), she notes that Britten

> showed me the copy of the book about him & laughed a lot at the v. elaborate analysis of his early oboe quartet [by Paul Hamburger, pp. 212–18], and read out a terrible sentence about 'sado-masochism' [see Keller's 'The Musical Character', p. 350]: – he said they must have noticed in my chapter ['Britten and the Young', pp. 276–86] that his favourite instrument was the whip! On the whole he was pleased with the book: – said he liked George Malcolm's chapters v. much ['The Purcell Realizations', pp. 74–82; '*Dido and Aeneas*', pp. 186–97]. But the analysis diagrams in Paul Hamburger's made him think of one of Bill [Burrell]'s nets. He said he'd no idea he was a clever as that: – 'I've come to the conclusion I must have a very clever subconscious.'

And on 19 December (IHD, pp. 183–4), at the end of 'one of the worst weeks he'd ever known':

> We talked about the book about him: – he said it made him feel like a small and harmless rabbit being cut up by a lot of grubby schoolboys when he'd *much* rather be frisking about in the fields. I quoted one or two of Keller's inaccurate generalizations, and he said that it was distressing when people made arrogant statements – that he'd almost rather have the English 'perhaps' or 'possibly' [. . .] He said what a relief it was after wading through Keller on him [. . .] to go back to William [Plomer] – he'd not been able to sleep a couple of nights ago (this was the evening he'd worked till 9 o'clock) and he'd read a whole volume of William's poems at 3 in the morning, and had enjoyed it.

Critical reaction to the Mitchell–Keller symposium was distinctly barbed in several quarters, with some reviewers using the appearance of the volume as an excuse to attack Britten himself. Ernest Newman, who had already shown himself to be out of sympathy with the composer's style in his inept review of *Billy Budd* (see Letter 718 n. 2), wrote in *The Sunday Times* (4 January 1953) that the book was 'frankly of the adoring order' and that Britten himself suffered from an 'impatience of hostile criticism'. (Newman was to return to the Mitchell–Keller symposium in his *Sunday Times* column on 18 January 1953.) Most savage of all was Peter Tranchell's review, 'Britten and Brittenites', in *Music & Letters* 34/3 (April 1953), pp. 124–32. Tranchell took several of the symposium's contributors to task for their modish use of 'musicological jargon', the author barely disguising his resentment that here was a book daring to consider a living composer 'great' in spite of his objection that 'the serious appraisal of a creative artist's work must be left to posterity'. Tranchell concluded by extending 'to the subject of this hero worship my condolences that the book should not have been better written and that he should have been the victim of so inopportune an outburst of noble intentions'. For other hostile criticisms, see HCBB, p. 316.

A complete set of reviews of DMHK is held at BPL, Donald Mitchell Papers. The extent of the coverage – over a hundred individual items, far more than might be expected today – speaks eloquently for the change in attitudes that has occurred towards serious music and books about serious music in the daily and weekly press in the UK since 1953.

761 To David Webster
[*Typed file copy*]

4 Crabbe Street, Aldeburgh, Suffolk
27th January, 1953

My dear David,

I hope you had a pleasant trip to Copenhagen with amicable talks on the way.[1]

I have, in the meantime, had a long letter from Dame Ninette[2] which puts her demands, and the reasons for them, very clearly.[3] She reiterates in her letter her telephone request to me of having a private meeting before our general meeting on Friday afternoon. But in the light of her letter I do not think that after all this is necessary – especially as since I returned from London on Saturday I have been laid low with the 'flu germ and am still in bed. I am very hopeful that this will not prevent me coming to London on Friday but it does mean that the visit will have to be a short one.

I saw William Plomer on Saturday morning, and discussed the ballet situation in Act 2 Scene 1 with him. We will go as far as we can towards meeting the ballet's demands, but as the opera is planned (and the rest of it completely written) we cannot enlarge this scene out of proportion and wreck the work, nor can we do something out of the period and style. The work is a serious one and has never been planned as a hotch-potch.[4]

About the Freddie [Ashton] v. Johnnie [Cranko] battle: I do not see why, if Johnnie were originally good enough to do the work in the opera (and I have Dame Ninette's blessing on his collaboration in it in writing)[5] he should now be inadequate! Anyhow, we can discuss this on Friday afternoon. I have suggested to William Plomer that he should come with me to meet you at four o'clock. Perhaps you would let me know if this is not convenient.[6]

Yours ever,
[BEN]

1 Britten had met Webster for lunch in London on 23 January, attending a performance of Tchaikovsky's *Pique Dame* at Covent Garden that same evening.

2 Ninette de Valois (1898–2001), Irish-born British ballerina, teacher and administrator. She toured with Sergey Diaghilev and partnered Anton Dolin before becoming Director of Ballet at the Abbey Theatre, Dublin. In 1931 she founded the Sadler's Wells Ballet School and was Artistic Director of the company, which became the Royal Ballet in 1956, until 1963. She was created a DBE in 1951, a CH in 1982 and an OM in 1992. See also obituaries in the *Daily Telegraph*; by Mary Clarke and James Monahan, *Guardian*, and by Peter Brinson, *Independent* (all 9 March 2001).

Britten jointly dedicated *The Prince of the Pagodas* to de Valois and Imogen Holst.

3 On 23 January, de Valois wrote to Britten to inform him that the Sadler's Wells Ballet still wished to give an independent performance. She also indicated her wish to replace Cranko with Ashton as choreographer.

4 Two days before Britten wrote this letter, Imogen Holst noted in her diary (IHD, p. 195): '[Britten] said that the ballet situation was pretty bad, I asked if they wanted to introduce some Delibes into Act II scene 1 and he said, "Well, very nearly."'

5 Britten had retained a letter from de Valois, sent from the Royal Opera House on 6 December 1952, in which she had written, 'How nice of you to send me the first version of the libretto for the Masque Scene of *Gloriana*. I am so happy that John Cranko is going to do this work and I feel sure that he will do well.' Two days after writing Letter 761, the composer wrote to de Valois:

I must immediately say that at this stage of writing a work, any considerable extension to the ballet scene is inconceivable. It might have been possible when I sent you the libretto last year, but now the rest of the work is written and in the process of being prepared for study, you will understand that the form of the work is now fixed.

I am also extremely loath to give up Cranko. We have discussed his participation in the work generally, and we have discussed in detail together this ballet scene. I need not say that this is not a reflection on Fred, to whom, as you know, I am devoted. And I understood he would have other things to do, and anyhow you will remember that in your other letter to me you were happy that Cranko would collaborate in the work with us.

As he indicated to Webster, Britten declined de Valois's suggestion that they meet privately before the Friday afternoon general meeting to discuss the situation.

6 Britten wrote to Plomer in a letter postmarked 29 January:

Sorry not to have written before but I've still not heard whether 4.0 tomorrow afternoon (Friday) is all right for Webster at Covent Garden. However I've today sent him a wire saying we'll turn up unless we hear to the contrary. So could you be an angel & pick me up at 2 Orme Square [Lord Harewood's London address] about 3 p.m.? We can then discuss what we're going to say, & I can show you some letters I've written to them.

Britten was due to attend on the next day, 30 January, a concert reading of Lennox Berkeley's opera *Nelson* (see Letter 763 n. 1), although this was postponed until 14 February. On 31 January Britten and Plomer travelled down to Henley to visit the Pipers.

762 To Peter Pears

4 CRABBE STREET, ALDEBURGH, SUFFOLK

[before 7 February 1953]

My sweet P.,

Just one or two notes that have arrived –

We're getting on, the cellar is nearly clear, & so we expect to feel less damp tomorrow.[1]

I think we're going to try sleeping here tonight.

Hope Bournemouth isn't too horrible. I'll try & listen on Sunday.[2] Love to Szymon.[3]

It was heaven, a real ray of sun to have you here. Please come back soon & let the sun shine again.

All my love

BEN

1 The storm along the East Coast on the night of 31 January had resulted in severe flooding at 4 Crabbe Street. In Britten's absence from the house, Elizabeth Sweeting retrieved his manuscripts from the downstairs sitting room (HCBB, p. 315). Elizabeth Mayer wrote to Britten on 3 February to express her anxiety at 'hearing and reading all those news about the ghastly storms and floods in England and beyond the sea. How are you, alright? and dear Crag House, and dear Aldeburgh alright. Please, please, let me know – two lines only [. . .]' Two letters written by Britten, one to Barbara Britten on 7 February and the other to Pears (undated), reveal that a quantity of mud needed to be cleared from the house. Britten informed his sister, 'It is all rather horrid but people are being splendid.' Pears was at the time away on a recital tour in the West Country, performing in Bideford on 1 February and Burford on 3 February, and staying with Mary Behrend. On 6 February he wrote to his hostess to thank her for her hospitality, and added:

I got back to Aldeburgh to find the flood subsided from the drawing room but still

LETTER 762: FEBRUARY 1953 125

a little in the cellar; however it gets better all the time – Miss Hudson had a horrid time, so did Elizabeth Sweeting, but it might have been much worse [...]

On 4 February, Imogen Holst had written (IHD, p. 197):

Everything still in a state, and Miss Hudson looking weary. Ben had spent most of Tuesday trying to clean out the cellar. He said that after dark (the electricity was off) he went up to the Potters [at the Red House] and Mary gave him an extra stiff drink and he managed to write Concord's song [in the *Gloriana* masque scene, Act II scene 1], 'All concords – that's the sort of joke one can make, I think.'

On 25 February, Britten wrote to Pears (who was much occupied giving concerts elsewhere during this period), 'The house is upside-down with electricians re-wiring us. The damp is still coming up, downstairs. We shan't be able to use that room for ages, I'm a bit afraid.' Ronald Duncan remembered (RDWB, p. 116) how Britten's collection of gramophone records was affected, this being one reason why the composer subsequently spent little time listening to recorded music: 'As a result of the flood most of the labels floated off the discs. He dried them out. But complained that later when he put a record of Bartók on his hi-fi, it turned out to be a piece by Bach or Beethoven'. As Rosamund Strode recalled (in a talk on *The Turn of the Screw* given at a Britten–Pears Library study weekend on 20–21 October 2000), Britten later habitually stored belongings of lesser value 'below the flood-line', i.e. in the cellar, where he had formerly stored his gramophone records. Plans for the forthcoming Aldeburgh Festival were also affected, Britten writing to Henry Boys on 14 March to lament that a projected performance of Stravinsky's *The Soldier's Tale* had had to be cancelled, 'owing to the flood and consequent drastic economy'. For more on these floods, see Letter 777.

2 In an undated note to Pears, evidently written after a telephone conversation, Britten refers to Bournemouth '& the V. & A. tomorrow. I'll listen if I can.' Pears and Mewton-Wood gave a recital at St Peter's Hall, Bournemouth, on 7 February (Mozart, Beethoven, Tippett's *The Heart's Assurance*, Grieg and folksong arrangements by Grace Williams, Vaughan Williams, Copland and Warlock). On 8 February at the Victoria and Albert Museum, Pears performed two Bach cantatas (Nos. 160 and 189) as part of an all-Bach programme with Szymon Goldberg (violin), John Francis (flute), Joy Boughton (oboe), Terence Weil (cello) and George Malcolm (harpsichord); the concert was broadcast.

3 Szymon Goldberg (1909–1993), American violinist and conductor of Polish birth, who studied first in Warsaw before further studies in Berlin with Carl Flesch. In the years before the Second World War Goldberg appeared as a soloist in concertos and recitals as well as playing chamber music (with Paul Hindemith and Emanuel Feuermann), and was appointed leader of the Berlin Philharmonic Orchestra by Furtwängler. He was captured as a prisoner-of-war by the Japanese in Java in 1942, but resumed his career post-war.

Between 1951 and 1965 he was a member of the Festival Piano Quartet at Aspen, Colorado, in which William Primrose was the violist, and in 1955 Goldberg became Musical Director of the newly formed Netherlands Chamber Orchestra with which he toured internationally. Goldberg appeared in recital with Britten, Pears and Terence Weil (cello) at the 1956 Aldeburgh Festival (Telemann, J. C. Bach and J. S. Bach), and at the 1960 Festival with the Netherlands Chamber Orchestra, which he directed in two concerts (an all-Bach programme; and Haydn, Mozart, Schubert, Henk Badings and Stravinsky). See also obituary by Margaret Campbell, *Independent* (23 July 1993).

763 To William Plomer

4 CRABBE STREET, ALDEBURGH, SUFFOLK

Feb. 11th 1953

My dearest William,

– A briefest note & in great haste, please forgive the scribble. Yes, if you don't mind a late luncheon – on Saturday.[1] I don't get up for the play-through of Gloriana until 11.0, & so I don't think we shall be through until about 1.30. You don't say if you will be coming to it? If you're not, could you possibly pick me up at the Garden at 1.30, & we can have a meal before Nelson in that vicinity (there won't be time for me to go to Bayswater I'm afraid)? Unless I hear, then, you'll either be at the play-through (interesting, because I hope some of the cast will be there), or at the stage door about 1.30.

Could you read the enclosed & give me your reactions when we meet?

The sea gets higher & higher, as the wind gets stronger* – please pray for us – !!

lots of love

BEN

* Crag house was flooded in January.

1 Britten had written to Plomer on a postcard postmarked 9 February to say:

I am 'motoring' up for the day on Saturday (between the two high tides!) (a) to play Gloriana to the Covent Garden staff in morning, & to hear Nelson in the afternoon. Could you come with me for that? Perhaps we could lunch together first & discuss some points of Act II Sc. I?

On 14 February 1953 at the Wigmore Hall, the English Opera Group presented what was billed as 'a concert reading' of Berkeley's *Nelson*, an event that had been postponed owing to illness. The cast was led by Pears (Nelson) and Arda Mandikian (Emma, Lady Hamilton), with Thomas Hemsley (Sir William Hamilton), Nancy Evans (Lady Nelson), Catherine

Lawson (Mrs Cadogan) and Trevor Anthony (Hardy), with Robert Keys (piano). The programme carried a disclaimer: 'Two other characters in the opera, the Fortune Teller and Lord Minto, are not presented in this reading, nor is the chorus of guests, townspeople and sailors.'

On 20 February Pears, who was then staying in Dundee during a concert tour of Scotland, wrote to Britten: 'The local amateur opera coy [...] is seriously considering investigating the possibilities of doing *Nelson* sometime on the strength of its notices!! Bless them.'

WIGMORE HALL
- WIGMORE STREET, W.1 -

SATURDAY, FEBRUARY 14th at 3 p.m.

THE ENGLISH OPERA GROUP ASSOCIATION

presents

A Concert Reading of a new Opera

"NELSON"

the music by **LENNOX BERKELEY**

the libretto by **ALAN PRYCE-JONES**

Introduced by the librettist and directed by the composer

CAST in order of appearance :—

Mrs. Cadogan	CATHERINE LAWSON
Emma, Lady Hamilton	ARDA MANDIKIAN
Sir William Hamilton	THOMAS HEMSLEY
Horatio, Lord Nelson	PETER PEARS
Lady Nelson	NANCY EVANS
Hardy	TREVOR ANTHONY

Two other characters in the opera, the Fortune Teller and Lord Minto, are not presented in this reading, nor is the chorus of guests, townspeople and sailors.

At the piano : **ROBERT KEYS**

NO SMOKING

Advertisement for the 1953 'concert reading' of Berkeley's *Nelson*

764 To William Plomer

4 CRABBE STREET, ALDEBURGH, SUFFOLK
Feb. 15th 1953

My dearest William,
 – Still feeling a bit guilty at having chivvied you around so much yesterday[1] – but I do feel you may understand how one gets a little out of control after an early start and a long journey, three hours nervous playing & then seeing lots of people one doesn't quite know & getting embarrassed – However . . .
In haste; my suggestion for the amended dance of Time is thus:

Yes, he is Time,
   Lusty and blithe!
Time is at his apogee!
   Altho' you thought to see
A bearded ancient with a scythe.

No reaper he
   That cries 'Take heed!'
Time is at his apogee!

???   Here he comes,   at his prime
       Here he is,   in his prime

Behold the sower of the seed.

This is anyhow the rhythm I'd like ($-\smile-, -\smile-$). Any suggestions?[2]
The only other urgency (i.e. that can't really wait until next weekend) is – do you mind a lot of repetitions at the end of the Dance of the Rustics & Fishermen? i.e.

      . . . . .
      Yearling fleeces
×   Woven, woven, woven blankets,
      With cream & junkets
⊕   With cream & junkets
      And rustic Trinkets
⊕   And rustic Trinkets
        rustic Trinkets
      The best they know!

I don't mind ×, but I feel the others, especially ⊕ may be a bit much. What d'you think?[3]
Excuse the 'midnight black' ink – only my pen has now to be filled with it since the score of Gloriana (on which I am now embarking) has to be written in a photographable colour.[4]

LETTER 764: FEBRUARY 1953

May I say again, my dear, what a permanent comfort & inspiration it is to have you around on such occasions as yesterday?

Excuse hopeless scribble, but after our long (& extremely cold) drive down last night, we are a bit behindhand this morning!

lots of love,
BEN

1 Plomer had attended Britten's play-through of the score of *Gloriana* to the staff at the Royal Opera House on the previous day. Plomer replied to this letter on 16 February: 'Not at all! You weren't a bit "out of control" and I wasn't a bit "chivvied". It was a memorable day – you played with great vitality in the morning and *Gloriana* all came freshly to one, as she does every time, the old evergreen.' He added, 'It was a strange step from her to *Nelson*', referring to the concert read-through of Berkeley's opera they had attended together that same afternoon. Plomer's letter concluded with several paragraphs of comment on the libretto lines here quoted by Britten.

On 10 February, during a visit to Aldeburgh by Leslie Boosey and his wife, Britten was asked to play excerpts from *Gloriana*. Imogen Holst notes in her diary (IHD, p. 200):

They didn't know the story so Ben began telling them & then Peter rang up so I had to go on with the story [...] – Boosey yawned openly and *jingled the coins* in his pocket during the 2nd Lute Song, and when it was over he said, '*Very* effective. You've managed to get away from your usual style, haven't you? But I suppose when we hear the orchestration it will sound more like the usual Britten.' (!) I *nearly* hit him. But Ben behaved *beautifully* throughout [...]

The following morning, prior to his departure, Boosey and Britten held a private meeting. Holst reports Britten saying (IHD, p. 201),

Well, I've had my talking to, and that's over. I've been told I'm *very* expensive to the firm [...] Oh well, it's worth it if they're going to keep Erwin [Stein] on, & I think they are.

2 The line supplied by Plomer in the final version of the libretto reads, 'Young and strong, in his prime'.

3 Britten's concern about excessive repetition in the part of the text marked ⊕ is interesting, since this was one of the few aspects of his vocal setting to receive occasional criticism. However, Plomer's final version of this text did provide Britten with two additional lines in order to avoid having quite so much repetition:

Yearling fleeces,
Woven blankets;
New cream and junkets,
And rustic trinkets

On wicker falskets,
   Their country largess –
   The best they know!

4 At this period Britten normally used pencil for his composition drafts and ink for his manuscript full scores. He later preferred to use pencil for both drafts and full scores. On the day he wrote this letter, Imogen Holst wrote in her diary (IHD, p. 203) that she realized 'I shall *never* be able to keep up with him. He writes it [i.e. the opera's full score] quicker than one could ever believe would be possible.' And on the next day (16 February; ibid.): 'The hardest day's work I've ever done [...] Ben had written *28* pages of full score in one day.'

765 To Peter Pears

4 CRABBE STREET, ALDEBURGH, SUFFOLK

Feb. 22nd 1953

My darling Pyje,

– Excuse the black ink, not mourning, only what I use for scoring, therefore my pen is filled with it.

Thank you for your sweet note; terribly happy to have it this morning, & to know you are well & happy. I hope Glasgow was also good, & that you'll enjoy Edinburgh & Karl R.[1] Give him my regards. I did actually try to telephone you twice while you were in Dundee, but you were out each time. I thought maybe that you'd tried to 'phone me on Wednesday evening. You see I heard the telephone ring in the evening – over the roar of the sea – rushed to it, & the operator said that 'they'd cleared' as it had been ringing sometime (It is a curse, this not hearing it ring; but we've now applied for it to be moved). I had expected you to ring about the flat. How is that situation now? Do let me know, because if it (the Harley St) has fallen through,[2] then I've got a plan of flat-hunting which I can set in motion, (friends of Imo's – as you might imagine!).

All goes along here. I score & score – in the middle of Act. I Sc. II now, so it's going quite fast. I played Badminton (very badly!) last night, & enjoyed it. William [Plomer] comes this evening (Saturday). I've seen Billy [Burrell] several times – <u>very</u> low, bored with river walls & crises, so I'm taking him in ten minutes for a drive away from Sea & Aldeburgh. Barbara [Burrell, Billy's wife] is coming too.

We've got a Friends meeting tomorrow night. Hope it'll go all right. They'll need pushing a bit I think, but Stephen[3] is quite keen & energetic. Saw Fidelity[4] yesterday – she's very happy with the programme changes. Just had a note from Mable[5] saying she can't sing Miss Wordsworth – blast her! Who can we get now – E. Morrison?[6] – Gwen Catley?[7] – Lovely Dyer?[8]

What you think?[9]

I've fixed an earlyish luncheon with Decca on March 3rd.[10] O.K.? O.K. about the Greece arrangements (visas just come!!)[11] End of News Bulletin –

but not end of my love, which goes on for ever –

BEN

1 Karl Rankl (1898–1968), British conductor and composer of Austrian birth; see also Letter 547 n. 6. He directed the Scottish National Orchestra from 1952 (following his resignation from the Covent Garden Opera Company) until 1957. Britten had in November 1952 been invited to succeed Rankl as Musical Director at Covent Garden: see Letter 748 n. 5.

Pears was staying at the Royal British Hotel, Dundee, where he gave a recital with Mewton-Wood on 19 February, followed by appearances in Milngavie (20 February) and the Freemasons' Hall, Edinburgh (23 February). Pears appeared with the Scottish National Orchestra and Rankl at St Andrew's Hall, Glasgow, on 28 February, performing operatic arias by Mozart and Bach's Cantata No. 55.

2 See Letter 757 n. 3.

3 Stephen Potter was Chairman of the Aldeburgh Festival Friends.

4 Fidelity Cranbrook, the Dowager Countess of Cranbrook (b. 1912), who was the first Chairman of the Aldeburgh Festival, 1948–1981; see also Letter 576 n. 4.

5 Margaret (Mabel) Ritchie (1903–1969), British soprano, who created the roles of Lucia in *The Rape of Lucretia* and Miss Wordsworth in *Albert Herring*; see also Letter 553 n. 4.

6 Elsie Morison (b. 1924), Australian soprano, who appeared as Anne Trulove in the first UK staging of Stravinsky's *The Rake's Progress* in 1953 and as Blanche in the British premiere of Poulenc's *Dialogues des Carmélites* in 1958. She was married to the conductor Rafael Kubelík.

7 British soprano (1906–1996).

8 Olive Dyer, British soprano who created the role of Flora in the premiere production of *The Turn of the Screw* in 1954 (see Letter 817 n. 1). In *As I Saw It*, p. 14, Maureen Garnham writes:

Olive Dyer, tiny in stature and though a mature woman a marvellous impersonator of a little girl, sang Flora with enormous character and conviction. Olive had a husband and a schoolgirl daughter, to both of whom she was devoted. Somehow I never really got to know her, nor learned anything about her previous career though I believe she had done some fine work. She came to the rehearsal or the performance, did her job admirably, and went home; she was a pleasant but self-effacing colleague.

9 Britten refers to casting arrangements for the forthcoming English Opera Group revival of *Albert Herring*, which he conducted. Two performances were given in Wiesbaden (Hessisches Staatstheater, 9 and 10 May 1953), with a further performance at the Aldeburgh Festival (20 June). At Wiesbaden April Cantelo played Miss Wordsworth; at Aldeburgh Margaret Ritchie sang the role.

10 Arrangements were being made for Decca to make a series of live recordings at the forthcoming Aldeburgh Festival. In 1953 the company recorded the *Variations on an Elizabethan Theme*, and in 1956 live performances of Britten conducting two Haydn symphonies, Nos. 45 and 55, and as soloist in Mozart's A major Piano Concerto, K. 414. The Haydn and Mozart recordings were reissued on CD by Decca as part of their 'Britten at Aldeburgh' series in 2000. In an undated letter to Decca's Artists' Manager, Frank Lee, evidently written after the 1953 Festival, Britten comments:

> The tests [test pressings] have now arrived and sound very good in the respects that they were excellent when we heard them at your studios.

He goes on to point out that because of various minor problems, including a number of 'slips' and technical glitches,

> I think we are all agreed that even if it means a slight delay in the issuing of the record, it would be a thousand pities to spoil the chances of the success of the series by issuing records which are obviously faulty.

11 Britten's diary reveals that he and Pears had been hoping to leave for Greece on 16 March for a stay of several weeks, the trip serving (in a pattern that was by then firmly established in their working lives) as both holiday and concert tour. In his letter from Dundee on 20 February, Pears wrote:

> Rang Seymour [Whinyates, of the British Council] on Wednesday & she is trying to get all our jobs in the last 2 or 3 days of Greece. Their Sunday concerts take place in the morning, & if we were performing in the 1st half of the concert on the 29th we could still catch a BEA [British European Airways] plane at 1.15. Anyway that's *my* last plane – it goes to Rome where I'd change for Amsterdam. You all could stay longer perhaps.

In a postscript, he notes that they could travel to Athens via Zurich on 16 March in order to avoid spending a night in Rome *en route*. In his next letter to Britten, written in Edinburgh on 21 February, Pears reported that he had booked the flight via Zurich and reiterated that he was bound to return on the 29th and that 'We still could do the orch. concert that morning, if we did our stuff in the first half. You could come back later if you wanted to!'

The planned trip to Greece fell through for political reasons, largely as a result of Britten's and Pears's support of the League for Democracy in Greece. According to Imogen Holst (26 February 1953; IHD, p. 209), Britten had 'signed a petition about the prisoners who'd not had a fair trial'. The

League for Democracy in Greece, launched in October 1945 under the presidency of Sir Compton Mackenzie and with the support of some Labour MPs, aimed to rebuild and strengthen the traditional friendship between the peoples of Greece and Britain on the basis of the establishment and development of democracy in Greece. Influencing parliamentary action was a major part of its work, and involved supplying information to MPs for questions in the House and briefing them to take up cases with the Foreign Office.

Britten wrote to Pears on 24 February:

George [Harewood] was here last night, & we talked a great deal about this & that, all nice & sympathetic & a good deal useful as well. One thing did however transpire which makes the Greek tour a little doubtful – He's been summoned to see Alan Lascelles [the Queen's Private Secretary] to inquire into this thing we're sponsors of (League for Democracy in Greece) – as the Foreign Office take a dim view of it, & the Greeks (in spite of the fact they've given us Visas) are angry. However I gave him the letter I received (with names of Presidents etc.) & he's taken that along, & we can only wait & see what happens. I've rung Seymour & told her to hang on for a day or so. But this, coupled with the fact that the fares each cost the horrifying amo[unt] of £112 (which I think almost puts George & Marion off), may put the scheme off??

He wrote again on the next day:

If you are free on Monday evening I wish you'd keep it so, & be able to discuss the Greek question with us [i.e. Britten and the Harewoods]. It is rather worrying – & I think we may be forced to think of going somewhere else. The Greeks are obviously fed up about us signing that thing – & I don't want to have our precious 2 weeks ruined by nastiness. Isn't there a nearer British Colony we could go to – or even Sicily? (Morocco?)

Britten concluded this letter with a cheerful declaration that he was halfway through the process of preparing the full orchestral score for *Gloriana*.

Pears wrote to Britten from Edinburgh (on *c.* 25 February):

Was afraid Greece might go that way – v. sorry that Geo. sh'd be fussed into it. Dreary old F.O. [Foreign Office]. Anyway it is fearfully dear – so let's stay at home instead or go motoring somewhere.

In the event, they went to Ireland: see Letter 767.

766 To Peter Pears

4 CRABBE STREET, ALDEBURGH, SUFFOLK
Feb. 23rd 1953

My darling P.,

Thank you for your sweet letter – just arrived. Don't worry about the concerts, I am sure they are fine – anything you do will always be that.[1] But however good Noel[2] is, I am certain that you & I together have something very special, & it won't be long before that happens again! I'm getting on well with the score, Act I nearly done, so Gloriana is nearly behind us – !

William [Plomer] went off this morning after a busy weekend of work, & walks. It was a glorious spring day yesterday, & in spite of the depressing look of the Floods everywhere the countryside looked lovely when we went for a bit of a drive after tea. I'm soon off to Ipswich to meet George [Harewood] so I'll see some more of it – can't see too much of Spring! How I wish you were coming too, my darling – but it isn't so long now. I hope you'll enjoy some of the concerts this week. My greetings to Karl Rankl.

I'll ring up Seymour[3] about her letter. Yes I suppose we'd better do the King & Queen – only if it can be done in the last 3 days tho'.[4] I'll talk a little to George this evening about it, & the plans generally.

The enclosed note from Kathleen – rather pathetic & brave, isn't it? But I hope she really is getting better.[5]

I see I didn't put the full address on your letter on Saturday – & so I do hope it reached you & that I don't get a rather doubtful letter returned to me "to the writer of a letter to darling P." – !

Nice joke from William – the Queen Mum & Princess Margaret[6] who often go around together are frequently referred to as 'Ma'am & super-ma'am' – nice?

Lots of love, my dearest. Take care. See you very soon.

Love to Noel too.

Your devoted

B

1 Pears had written to Britten from Edinburgh on 21 February:

Another concert over (at Milngavie this time) – and a day nearer to seeing you. The concert was all right. I'm not sure how good a programme it is. The first half is very tense, & the 2nd half rather too light.

The programme for this Scottish tour with Noel Mewton-Wood comprised: Mozart's Masonic Cantata, K. 619, Beethoven's *An die ferne Geliebte*, Schubert's G flat and A flat Impromptus, Tippett's *The Heart's Assurance*; after the interval, they performed four songs by Grieg; two piano solos by Debussy ('Reflets dans l'eau' and 'Poissons d'or'); and folksong arrangements by Grace Williams, Vaughan Williams, Copland and Warlock.

2 Noel Mewton-Wood (1922–1953), Australian pianist (see also Letter 518 n. 5), who was serving as Pears's accompanist while Britten devoted all his energies to *Gloriana*. In this year, Pears and Mewton-Wood recorded together Tippett's two song-cycles, *Boyhood's End* and *The Heart's Assurance*.

3 Seymour Whinyates, Director of the Music Department of the British Council, 1943–59.

4 Britten refers to a proposed party at the end of the planned visit to Greece. The party was to be hosted by the UK's Ambassador in Athens, to which Britten, Pears, the Harewoods and the King and Queen of Greece were to have been invited.

5 Kathleen Ferrier was gravely ill with cancer; see Letter 779 n. 14.

6 HM Queen Elizabeth, The Queen Mother (1900–2002), Patron of the Aldeburgh Festival from 1974 onwards, and her younger daughter HRH Princess Margaret (1930–2002).

767 To William Plomer

4 CRABBE STREET, ALDEBURGH, SUFFOLK

March 8th 1953

My dear William,

So sorry to have neglected you for so long, – but (apart from one very rushed & exceedingly foggy jaunt to London) I've been sitting at the score of Gloriana all day & almost every night since you left. She's well on the way to being finished now, & will be, I hope, before we leave for . . . Ireland next Monday week![1] Why 'Ireland' is a long, & sad story, which can wait till we meet, which I hope can be next Sunday.[2] On our way abroad I promised John Piper & Basil C. [Coleman] to meet them & have a final & big session on the scenery, with models & all. This is happening next Sunday. Will you by any chance be free? I'll let you know place & time later. I expect to be motoring up in the morning & perhaps could collect you.

Excuse haste – but the scribble brings a lot of my love, & to Charles too.

Yours ever,

BEN

1 Britten and Plomer were doubtless aware of an irony inherent in this unexpected departure for Ireland, where the Earl of Essex fails to prove his military mettle in *Gloriana*. This is evident from Plomer's response to this letter, dated 9 March: 'I know you'll bring back victory & peace from the rainy west – which I hope won't be rainy at all.' (In the opera's libretto, Essex declares to his Queen, 'With God's help I will have victory, and you shall have peace.') In the same reply, Plomer reports that the 'clear-cut' libretto of *Gloriana* is being typed ('I hope with fitting clarity') prior to delivery to Ernst Roth at Boosey & Hawkes.

Pears wrote to Mary Behrend, also on 9 March,

> We are alas! not going to Greece after all – various reasons, distance, expense, & some dreary political echoes – and instead decided to go to Ireland! We take the car next Monday [16 March] – Dublin for a few days then South and West.

Their travelling companions were to be George and Marion Harewood, who had been due to accompany them on the aborted trip to Greece; their itinerary included Parknasilla and Ross Castle, Killarney (both County Kerry) and Bantry Bay (County Cork). Harewood's grandmother, Queen Mary, died on 24 March (*The Tongs and the Bones*, p. 137):

> and we had to cut everything short to get back for the funeral [on 31 March]. It was said that my grandmother had expressed great concern in case the Coronation might be postponed on her account – the papers were full of it – so that particular worry over *Gloriana* was laid quickly to rest.

Coincidentally, Britten had two weeks before declined an invitation to accept an honorary degree from Trinity College, Dublin. He wrote to the College's Registrar, G. F. Mitchell, on 21 February:

> Please convey to the Board of Trinity College my deepest thanks for the honour they pay me in suggesting my name for the degree of Doctor in Music Honoris Causa.
> Would you please explain to the Board that although I am very aware of this honour, I must, I am afraid, very reluctantly decline it. I have visited Dublin in the past, but I have, alas, no connection with the City, and I feel that such a distinction as the Board has suggested must be founded on some kind of contact [. . .]

On 18 February, Britten had told Imogen Holst 'how glad he was that he'd refused [i.e., decided to decline] that Dr of music the day before' (IHD, p. 204).

2 15 March, the day before Britten's departure for Ireland. In his reply dated 9 March, Plomer declared, 'Next Sunday, the 8th [*sic*], is carefully reserved for a grand session on the scenery.' Plomer subsequently met John Piper for further discussions during Britten's absence in Ireland, and a further meeting between Britten, Plomer, Piper and Coleman took place in Aldeburgh on 30 March, the day after the composer's return to Aldeburgh (on which date Pears departed for Amsterdam to fulfil further performing engagements).

768 To David Webster
[*Typed*]

4 Crabbe Street, Aldeburgh, Suffolk
9th March, 1953

My dear David,

I do not know if you are back yet from America, but I am having a brief holiday at the end of this week and thought I ought to write even if the letter has to wait till your return. The score of Gloriana is getting on well, and (excepting the Progress Scene) I hope to reach the end before I leave.¹ Imogen Holst will still have some bar lines to draw and some voices to fill in, but that will not take more than a week or so. I think, however, that in this respect we are well up to time.

I wrote to Jennifer Vyvyan² as you asked me and had a nice but firm letter back. It is a great pity she cannot come to Rhodesia but this seems already fixed.³ Shall you then ask Leigh⁴ to do Lady Rich in Rhodesia and the Lady-in-waiting here, or would you rather give the Lady-in-waiting entirely to Dunne⁵ (whom I am afraid I have not heard.)? If Leigh would do it I feel the former is probably the best suggestion.

I have been thinking a great deal about myself going to Rhodesia. As you know I have been tempted for Covent Garden's and my own sakes, but when I consider how much time I shall want to give you in the autumn (which I gather you discussed with George Harewood) I feel I must have a clear August and September for work. I am seriously behindhand with my own commitments, many of which were postponed by Gloriana. Not least among them is my opera for Venice next year.⁶ There is also a considerable matter of rehearsal which alarmed me. Not being a regular conductor I could not take over performances without rehearsal and I do not see how I [could] arrange any either in July or before the first performance in Rhodesia. What I suggest is that we get a conductor to assist Pritchard⁷ in the preparation and London performances and that the same person goes to Rhodesia and takes over when Pritchard has to return to Edinburgh.⁸ Who do you think this person should be? Someone on your staff? As you know I was not very happy with Gellhorn⁹ last season and I gather that Gellhorn is doing none too well at the moment.¹⁰ If we go outside the Company I expect we shall have to be rather modest in our ambitions since it will only be a second conductor that is wanted. What [about] Tausky,¹¹ or Susskind,¹² or even Del Mar?¹³ I will go on thinking and send you postcards from time to time as ideas occur.

How was your trip to America? I hope you enjoyed it. Did you hear any good conductors?!

[*Handwritten:*] Hope you are well,
Yours ever,
BEN

1 Britten wrote to Henry Boys on 14 March to say that he had 'quarter of an hour ago written the last notes of Gloriana'. Imogen Holst recorded (IHD, p. 214) that he completed the score at 3 p.m. on 13 March. Britten left for Ireland on 16 March.

2 British soprano (1925–1974), a leading member of the English Opera Group.

She created the roles of the Governess in *The Turn of the Screw* and Tytania in *A Midsummer Night's Dream*. See also Letter 592 n. 7.

3 The Covent Garden Company had been invited to Southern Rhodesia (now Zimbabwe) to take part in the Rhodes Centenary celebrations, which also marked the fiftieth anniversary of the country's founding. A government-sponsored exhibition included a specially built Theatre Royal, a single-storey, hangar-like structure, situated on the outskirts of Bulawayo, where, during a four-week stay, the Covent Garden Opera Company presented performances of *Aida*, *Le nozze di Figaro*, *La Bohème* and *Gloriana*. Other visiting companies participating in the celebrations included the Sadler's Wells Ballet, the Hallé Orchestra, and a company of actors led by John Gielgud in Shakespeare's *Richard II*.

Members of the company flew out on 12 July, the day after the final performance of *Gloriana* in the Coronation season. The visit was described by the *Daily Herald* (16 July 1953) as the 'biggest airlift ever in the world of entertainment', with the journey taking days rather than hours. Reginald Goodall had taken over the conducting of the last two performances of *Gloriana* in London, and was to conduct eight performances of the opera in Bulawayo, with Joan Cross as Elizabeth I and John Lannigan as Essex. Gielgud told his mother (24 July 1953; Richard Mangan (ed.), *Gielgud's Letters*, p. 168):

Poor David [Webster] has 200 people to cope with – opera singers, orchestra and chorus and four operas to present, including *Gloriana*, which I should think they will hate. Also he has to stay two or three weeks – and he is far more of a sybarite than I am!

On his return to London, Webster wrote to Britten on 4 September 1953 (quoted in John Lucas, *Reggie: The Life of Reginald Goodall*, pp. 129–30):

I did send you a telegram from Bulawayo saying how fine Goodall was with *Gloriana*, very much better than our other gentleman [i.e. John Pritchard, see n. 7 below] and the performance itself was very striking. We had a very good house for the first, I gather not quite so good for the others, but I am told that the enthusiasm of the people who went was very considerable indeed, particularly the younger generation. I can't wait to do it here. Personally I'm awfully happy about having Goodall do *Grimes*, and if necessary *Budd* before the end of the season. Equally when we come to revive *Gloriana* again and if you don't do it yourself I think he should.

Britten responded on 6 September:

I am so glad to hear about Reggie Goodhall [*sic*] in *Gloriana*. I had already heard golden things from Cranko & Joan Cross about him (stupidly, no telegram ever arrived from you about it). It is in more than one way a relief, because I am afraid my arm is no better in spite of rest & medical treatment. So it looks as if he might have to do *Grimes* too.

Because of the composer's persistent bursitis, the re-staging of *Grimes* at Covent Garden, directed by Cranko, was indeed conducted by Goodall, as was the revival of *Gloriana* at Covent Garden and on tour in 1954. Britten sent Goodall a first-night telegram before *Grimes* on 14 November 1953:

NO NEED FOR GOOD WISHES HAVE UTMOST CONFIDENCE IN YOUR GREAT MUSICALITY AND GIFTS BEN

4 Adèle Leigh (1928–2004), British soprano, who was a resident soprano at Covent Garden from 1948 until 1956. She sang the role of the Lady-in-Waiting in the premiere of *Gloriana*, and created the role of Bella in Tippett's *The Midsummer Marriage* at Covent Garden in 1955. She achieved notable success in operetta and musicals, and pursued a career in variety, appearing with Geraldo and his Orchestra, Harry Secombe and Bruce Forsyth. See also obituaries in the *Daily Telegraph* (26 May 2004), *The Times* (29 May 2004) and *Guardian* (18 June 2004).

Helen Conway (*Sir John Pritchard: His Life in Music*, p. 109) reports an anecdote – possibly apocryphal – about Leigh and the role of the Lady-in-Waiting in *Gloriana*. While rehearsing for another opera at Covent Garden Leigh would occasionally go to the Crush Bar to watch rehearsals of *Gloriana*:

I went to Ben Britten who was conducting the rehearsal and asked, 'Why aren't I in this?' He replied, 'There isn't a part for you.' 'But I want to be in it. It's an opera that you've done for the Coronation and I want to be in it. Can't you write me something, even the part of the maid?' So he went away and wrote the role of the Lady-in-Waiting for me.

5 Veronica Dunne (b. 1927), Irish soprano and singing teacher, whom Webster had recently signed to Covent Garden where she sang many roles, including Sophie (*Der Rosenkavalier*), Mimì (*La Bohème*), Susanna (*Le nozze di Figaro*) and Euridice in Gluck's *Orfeo ed Euridice* opposite Kathleen Ferrier. Dunne later appeared with almost all the other UK opera companies, and since her retirement has become Ireland's leading singing teacher.

6 This is the earliest reference in Britten's letters to *The Turn of the Screw*, the chamber opera based on Henry James's novella that he was to compose in 1954. The work was already under consideration in May 1951 as a potential new Britten opera for the English Opera Group, and a schedule from a year later indicates that the premiere was planned for September 1953 at the Edinburgh Festival. By July 1952, however, the Venice Biennale had expressed interest in presenting the first performance as part of the 1953 Biennale, and the Edinburgh scheme was dropped. However, Britten's decision to write *Gloriana* for the Coronation celebrations in June 1953, as well as the acute bursitis in his right arm, delayed the composition of *The Turn of the Screw* until 1954, a year in which the Biennale was not held. *The Turn of the Screw* was premiered, therefore, at Venice's twenty-seventh International Festival of Contemporary Music, an event presented under the aegis of the Biennale. See also Letter 817 n. 1.

7   John Pritchard (1921–1989), British conductor, who studied privately and in Italy before joining Glyndebourne in 1947 as a repetiteur; in 1948 he became chorus master and assistant to Fritz Busch, whose sudden indisposition during a performance in 1951 led to Pritchard's conducting debut at Glyndebourne in mid-performance. He remained associated with Glyndebourne for the remainder of his career, acting as Music Director from 1969 until 1978. His career burgeoned in the 1950s with appearances at the Vienna Staatsoper and his Covent Garden debut in the autumn of 1952 (Verdi's *Un ballo in maschera*). His many appointments included Musical Director of the Royal Liverpool Philharmonic Orchestra, 1957–63, and of the London Philharmonic Orchestra, 1962–66; the Cologne Opera, from 1978; the Théâtre de la Monnaie, Brussels, from 1981; the BBC Symphony Orchestra, 1982–89, and the San Francisco Opera, from 1986. Pritchard championed new music, particularly in the 1950s and 1960s, conducting the first performances of *Gloriana*, and Tippett's *The Midsummer Marriage* and *King Priam* for Covent Garden, and the UK premiere of Henze's *Elegy for Young Lovers* at Glyndebourne. He was created a CBE in 1962 and knighted in 1983. Throughout his career he was often criticized for slackness of preparation: see, for example, n. 8 below. See also Helen Conway, *Sir John Pritchard: His Life in Music*, pp. 108–11.

8   For an account of Britten's – and others' – disapproval of Pritchard's conducting during the rehearsals for *Gloriana*, see HCBB, p. 318. In an undated diary entry (late May/early June 1953; IHD, p. 225), Imogen Holst noted Britten's anxiety about Pritchard:

> At the second orch. rehearsal Ben said he was going to conduct the 1st ½ hr and as we were alone in the passage I said, 'Oh, now it will be *right!*' and he blew up in an absolute fury, the first time he's ever lost his temper with me [. . .] I was so shattered that I could hardly listen [. . .] In the pub, over a meal, while correcting the newest batch of proofs, I realized that he'd been angry because I'd said what was in his own mind, which he didn't want to think. He said, 'Everyone will have to help me to think that Pritchard is going to be all right.'

According to Lord Harewood (Conway, *Sir John Pritchard: His Life in Music*, pp. 109–10), the main reason for Britten's irritation with Pritchard was his lateness in arriving at rehearsals (Pritchard was driving up from Sussex each morning as he was rehearsing and performing at Glyndebourne):

> I think that often he was about an hour late and other people would have to start the rehearsal. He certainly didn't satisfy the composer as he would otherwise have done, because of this circumstance. It might sound incompetent but he achieved. He had an 'easy' nerve and didn't mind risking being late, very late.

Joan Cross later complained that she suffered discomfort during the first performance because the work was 'under-rehearsed musically' (Nicholas John (ed.), *Peter Grimes/Gloriana*, p. 66).

9   Peter Gellhorn (1912–2004), German-born conductor, composer, pianist and teacher. Gellhorn's pre-war career had been curtailed by having to flee Nazi Germany. Having moved to London, he was Musical Director of Toynbee Hall from 1935, but was, like his fellow émigrés, interned for a time as an enemy alien at the outbreak of the Second World War. He was appointed Assistant Conductor with the Sadler's Wells Opera in 1941, but his career was once again interrupted by factory war work from 1943. After a spell as Conductor with the Carl Rosa Company (1945–46), Gellhorn joined Covent Garden as Conductor (later Head of Music Staff) in 1947. He was Conductor and Chorus Master at Glyndebourne from 1954, and held a similar position with the BBC Chorus (1961–72) as well as undertaking many freelance engagements. He also taught at the London Opera Centre and the Guildhall School of Music and Drama. He collaborated with many of the leading composers of the day, including Britten, Messiaen and Boulez. His many pupils included the composer George Benjamin. See also obituaries by John Calder and George Benjamin, *Guardian*, and in *The Times* (both 16 February 2004), by Martin Anderson, *Independent* (21 February 2004) and in the *Daily Telegraph* (26 February 2004).

10 For further information on Britten's sometimes strained relationship with Gellhorn, see Letter 768.

11 Vilem Tausky (1910–2004), Moravian-born conductor. Tausky's pre-war career in his native land included a spell at the Brno Opera, where he was the vocal coach for the premiere of Janáček's last opera, *From the House of the Dead*. Arriving in the UK in the late 1930s, he took every opportunity to conduct, and by the early 1950s was Music Director of Welsh National Opera (1951–56); he also conducted for the EOG during this period, his commitments including Berkeley's *A Dinner Engagement* (1954). He had made his Covent Garden debut in 1951 and was also associated with the Sadler's Wells Opera. For a decade from 1956, he was Music Director of the BBC Concert Orchestra. He published his autobiography, *Vilem Tausky Tells His Story*, in 1979. See also obituaries in the *Daily Telegraph* and *The Times* (both 18 March 2004); by Meirion Bowen, *Guardian* (19 March 2004) and by Graham Melville-Mason, *Independent* (20 March 2004).

12 Walter Susskind (1918–1980), British conductor of Czech birth; see also Letter 593 n. 7.

13 Norman Del Mar (1919–1994), British conductor, composer and writer on music, Principal Conductor of the English Opera Group from 1949 to 1954. See also Letter 617 n. 8.

769 To William Plomer

4 CRABBE STREET, ALDEBURGH, SUFFOLK
April 8th 1953

My dearest William,

Thank you so very much for doing the Clodd piece.[1] It is excellent. Just what we wanted – a specialised piece but with general overtones. Thank you so much. We shan't, of course, cut a word. You will get a proof, naturally.

I have just had a most exciting morning's work with Joan Cross. Judging by a performance in a small room & with her only just getting it into her voice & personality, it is going to be a great performance. It suits her down to the ground. Most of the time I was too excited to play the piano properly. When Peter joins her this weekend I expect I shall burst. (Longing for you to hear it come to life.)[2]

I have a horrid request. You know all these photos & bothers with press & films we've had. I've had finally to come to an arrangement with them & have said I will see them next Tuesday afternoon for not more than an hour. They, of course, want you. Can you possibly manage it? Please say yes, because apart from the obvious fact that it is as much your work as it is mine, it'll make it so much less painful if you are there with me! (I'll let you know time & place in a day or so.)

Morgan [Forster] is here with me, & seems in excellent form. He sends his love. Thank you & Charles for the Easter card. Lovely to get it. Apart from a gay Easter service at Lancing Chapel[3] Easter has rather passed us by this year.

Lots of love, & many thanks indeed for the Clodd.

and love to Charles too,
BEN

1 Plomer contributed an essay, 'The Quest for Clodd', to the 1953 Aldeburgh Festival Programme Book. Edward Clodd (1840–1930), the English banker and popular anthropologist, had grown up in Aldeburgh (his father was born in the town). From 1878 Clodd used his Aldeburgh home – Strafford House, on Crag Path – as a gathering place for the leading intellectuals and writers of his day, notably Thomas Hardy, who visited Clodd at Aldeburgh on several occasions.

2 Among Britten's many commitments related to the intensive preparations for the forthcoming premiere of *Gloriana* in this period were several meetings with John Cranko and David Webster in late April and early May, interrupted by his conducting two performances of *Albert Herring* (with Pears in the title role) at Wiesbaden, during which period he and Pears stayed with the Hesses.

On 18 May, the laconic entry 'Q.E. Harewoods' in Britten's appointment diary relates to a dinner party at the Harewoods' London home in Orme Square at which Britten met the Queen and Prince Philip. Pears and Joan Cross were also present, and sang their parts in the new opera to the royal guests, with Britten at the piano. Plomer and Harewood's mother, the Princess Royal, were also present. According to Lord Harewood (*The Tongs and the Bones*, p. 137), 'This seemed to go well, with what felt like an appreciative audience; the right seeds, we felt, were sown.' But Joan Cross (CHPP, p. 166) recalled that the evening was heavy going: 'I don't think *they* enjoyed the evening any more than we did.' Plomer amused the Queen and Prince Philip by relating how the Lord Chamberlain had felt obliged to censor the moment in Act III scene 2 when Cuffe is showered with the contents of a chamber pot: 'There just happens to be a rule of long standing, and the Lord Chamberlain has had *to set his face against chamber pots*' (Peter F. Alexander, *William Plomer*, p. 278).

Rehearsals for the opera began in earnest on 26 May, with the dress rehearsal scheduled for 6 June.

3 Britten had driven to Lancing College (where he stayed with Esther Neville-Smith over Easter) on 4 April, dropping off Imogen Holst at her mother's home in Dunmow, Essex, *en route*. He collected her on his way back on the 6th. Britten had presumably attended a concert at Glyndebourne on Easter Sunday (5 April) in which Pears was one of the soloists in Bach's Cantata No. 145, with the Royal Philharmonic Orchestra conducted by John Pritchard.

During the drive back to Suffolk, Britten revealed to Imogen Holst (IHD, p. 217) something wholly unexpected:

Just near Snape he became more confidential than ever before & talked about Peter & how if he [Peter] found the right girl to marry he supposed he'd have 'to lump it' and that nothing would ever interfere with their relationship.

Perhaps the reference to nothing interfering with 'their relationship' here means the professional relationship between Pears and Britten as singer and accompanist/composer, should Pears, as Britten speculates, ever marry. But it could equally be interpreted differently: that Pears, who, it should be remembered, had several long-standing female admirers, might indeed be prepared to marry from a desire to protect his and Britten's homosexual relationship, which, in the UK in 1953, was illegal. The socio-political climate in which Britten's remark was made should be borne in mind. It was in October 1953 that a virulent anti-homosexual campaign was instigated by the then Home Secretary, Sir David Maxwell-Fyffe; and that autumn Britten was one of several gay men who were interviewed by police officers from Scotland Yard (see Letter 670 n. 1; Donald Mitchell's 'Introduction: Happy Families?', vol. 3, pp. 7–9; and HCBB, pp. 334–5). In April 1953, was Britten, who in public was always so circumspect about his relationship with Pears, anxious that he or Pears might be subjected to close scrutiny and possibly criminal prosecution? Their reputations and careers would have been dealt a devasting blow had a case been brought.

This was a very real fear, one that the celebrated actor John Gielgud, a friend of Britten and Pears, himself experienced in 1953. Gielgud, who was knighted in this year for services to the theatre, was arrested for soliciting and fined in October. Swift admission of his culpability plus the sympathetic support of friends and the general public allowed him to recover his career without lasting damage, though he was evidently scarred by the experience. Thanking Cecil Beaton (28 October 1953) for his support, Gielgud remarked, 'Things would not have been so twenty years ago (though I don't think either the press would have been so cruelly open).'

It says much for the closeness of Britten's friendship with Imogen Holst that he felt able to raise this matter with her.

770 To David Webster
[*Handwritten draft*]

5 Chester Gate, N.W.1.[1]
June 1st, 1953

My dear David,

That is <u>exactly</u> what I thought would happen, & what I anticipated in my letter to you the other day.[2] It comes, I fear, like so many things at the Opera House, from your not making up your mind in time, or if you have decided something imagining that other people are thought-readers. Often people help you out at considerable wear & strain to themselves, but this time I cannot help you (as I made clear in my letter). Perhaps if the musical side of the House were better organised I might be able to – but the wear of the last weeks, coping with hopeless arrangements has been too great. Besides <u>IT IS TOO LATE</u>. To recapitulate (& I am keeping a copy of this letter) – on May 13th I asked you to ask other composers (not only Walton [was] mentioned) to compose the Fanfare & God Save the Queen. You demurred, but agreed to think it over. (The idea of using the Gloriana Fanfare wasn't mentioned – it had been casually suggested weeks before, but dropped at once.)[3] I heard nothing till Whit-Saturday when Walton told me he was doing (b). I wrote to protest about not being told of the situation & to say that I didn't want suddenly to be saddled with (a) at the last moment & anyhow there are reasons why I didn't want to be called on to do (a), & the opera & not the 'Queen'. Now you come back innocently, with just the request I feared. And it isn't any good. If you'd let me know <u>as you agreed</u> soon after your meeting – but there's no point in going round & round. I know you are too busy – well then, <u>delegate</u>

some of your power. And don't, David, go round saying I've let you down, because it isn't true.

                                                                    Yours ever,
                                                                    BEN

P.S. Piper was not too busy to do sketches for the Vocal Score cover, 'weeks ago', & one of those could perhaps have been used – at least in place of Messel's[4] idea of Gloriana on the back. But what about my other suggestion – of using the magnificent inside title page?[5]

1 In her diary entry for 16 May 1953 (IHD, p. 223), Imogen Holst notes that 'Miss Hudson was wanted in London to help move into Chester Gate'.

2 Webster's well-known inability to make decisions had evidently led to confusions and misunderstandings. He asked Britten in a letter of 30 May – too late, as the composer complains – to provide the fanfare to herald the arrival of the royal party at the first performance of *Gloriana*. As he believed the original plan to use a fanfare from *Gloriana* (see n. 3 below) had been discarded, he thought Britten was writing a new one and repeated the invitation for Britten to do so, adding that he wanted to know by 1 June if Britten would be able to comply.

  Webster had commissioned an arrangement of the National Anthem from Walton, and this was played before and after the performance. As Michael Kennedy notes (*Portrait of Walton*, p. 167), the rendering of the National Anthem was not without incident:

  The performance on the Queen's entry into the royal box was disastrous, half the orchestra waiting (correctly) until all the royal party had taken their places before beginning to play. Such was the atmosphere of professional partisanship and hostility in regard to *Gloriana* that some people believed Walton had planned some sort of sabotage and these false accusations caused him intense distress.

  See also Helen Conway, *Sir John Pritchard: His Life in Music*, p. 110–11, for Pritchard's letter to Webster in which he defends himself from accusations from both Walton and Buckingham Palace that he 'caused the Anthem to appear in an unfavourable light [...] a slight mistake was made in one note by a double-bass player but any suggestion that the rendering travestied the composer's intention is hereby refuted by me'.

3 The fanfares in Act I scene 1, which involve no fewer than twelve trumpeters, were later used (in an arrangement prepared by Rosamund Strode under the composer's supervision) at the opening ceremonies of the 1967 Aldeburgh Festival, when Queen Elizabeth II opened the Snape Maltings Concert Hall on 2 June. See PBBG, pp. 166–7.

4 Oliver Messel (1904–1978), theatre, ballet and film designer, known for his frequently sumptuous and romantic approach. Messel was responsible

for the special decoration of the theatre, Entrance Hall and Crush Bar – 'gorgeously dressed with flags and flowers' (Philip Hope-Wallace, *Manchester Guardian Weekly*, 11 June 1953) – at the gala performance of *Gloriana*, as well as providing a decorative cover for the gala programme. Britten evidently disapproved of Messel's programme design, the back cover of which was a portrait of Elizabeth I by Messel (see below), and he would have preferred something by John Piper to have been used instead. The 'inside title page' refers to the calligraphic rather than typeset title page of the vocal score.

Webster explained to Britten on 30 May that Messel's involvement in the programme cover was considered to be part of his responsibility for the front-of-house decorations.

5 Piper's design for the cover of the vocal score of *Gloriana* incorporated one of his costume designs for Elizabeth I.

Oliver Messel's decorative front and back programme covers for the Gala premiere of *Gloriana*

771 To Barry Till[1]

Aldeburgh, Suffolk
11th June, 1953

Dear Barry,

Thank you for your nice letter of congrats & good wishes. It was good of you to write. You didn't miss much on Monday night because the Gala was a shocking occasion – an audience of stuck pigs – but I hope you'll see her later under more auspicious circumstances.[2]

Love from
BEN

1 Barry Till (b. 1923), a friend of Lord Harewood, was ordained in 1950 and later served as Chaplain and Dean of Jesus College, Cambridge, and as Dean of Hong Kong (1960–64) before becoming Principal of Morley College (1965–86).

2 The Gala premiere of *Gloriana* took place at the Royal Opera House, Covent Garden, on Monday, 8 June 1953. Further performances followed on 11, 13, 18 and 30 June, and 2, 4, 7, 9 and 11 July. The performances on 8 June and 2 July were broadcast by the BBC Third Programme. On the day after the first performance, Plomer wrote to the composer, '*Gloriana* is *transcendently* beautiful – as to the music. Last night was a tremendous culmination of the great happiness you have given me by letting me "march along" with you.' Interestingly, this letter makes no reference to any negative aspect of the occasion: for further on Plomer's subsequent views, see his article 'Let's crab an opera', *London Magazine* 3/7 (October 1964), pp. 101–4. Plomer had been impressed that Prince Philip had studied the libretto in detail in advance of the performance. He wrote to his brother James on 12 June (quoted in Peter F. Alexander, *William Plomer*, pp. 278–9):

It went quite well, but the audience was so largely official that it was afraid the stuffing might run out of its stuffed shirts, and was not as demonstrative as a musical audience. The Royal Family turned up in force and splendour, and I had some conversation with them in the 1st interval. [. . .] They seemed to enjoy themselves and said very nice things. He took great trouble to read the libretto and I think he now knows it better than I do. [. . .] It was all rather fun.

In an undated letter to Ursula Nettleship from this period, Britten wrote, 'I am so very glad that you liked Gloriana. Rather like a naughty child, I am most jealous for her!' Britten's fullest expression of his feelings after the debacle of the first performance are to be found in Letter 777 (written to Elizabeth Mayer on 30 August), in which he describes the work as 'the best I have yet done'.

Lord Harewood recalls the atmosphere of what has since become the most infamous of Britten's operatic premieres, which he describes as 'one of the great disasters of operatic history' (*The Tongs and the Bones*, p. 138):

THE ROYAL OPERA HOUSE, COVENT GARDEN LTD.

General Administrator - David L. Webster
Deputy General Administrator - Sir Steuart Wilson

GALA PERFORMANCE

ON THE OCCASION OF
THE CORONATION OF
HER MAJESTY
QUEEN ELIZABETH II

MONDAY, 8TH JUNE, 1953
at 8 p.m.

God Save The Queen
Arranged by SIR WILLIAM WALTON

THE COVENT GARDEN OPERA

in the first performance of

GLORIANA

OPERA IN THREE ACTS

Music by BENJAMIN BRITTEN *Libretto by* WILLIAM PLOMER

Producer - BASIL COLEMAN *Scenery and Costumes by* JOHN PIPER
Choreography by JOHN CRANKO *Lighting by* JOHN SULLIVAN
Conductor - JOHN PRITCHARD

THE COVENT GARDEN OPERA CHORUS
Chorus Master - DOUGLAS ROBINSON

THE COVENT GARDEN ORCHESTRA
Leader - CHARLES TAYLOR

Characters in Order of Appearance

Robert Devereux, Earl of Essex	PETER PEARS
Henry Cuffe, a satellite of Essex	RONALD LEWIS
Charles Blount, Lord Mountjoy	GERAINT EVANS
Queen Elizabeth the First	JOAN CROSS
Sir Walter Raleigh, Captain of the Guard	FREDERICK DALBERG
Sir Robert Cecil, Secretary of the Council	ARNOLD MATTERS
The Recorder of Norwich	MICHAEL LANGDON
The Spirit of the Masque	WILLIAM McALPINE
Penelope (Lady Rich), sister to Essex	JENNIFER VYVYAN
Frances, Countess of Essex	MONICA SINCLAIR
A Lady-in-Waiting	ADELE LEIGH
The Master of Ceremonies	DAVID TREE
A Blind Ballad-Singer	INIA TE WIATA
A Housewife	EDITH COATES
The City Crier	RHYDDERCH DAVIES
Sir John Harington	LEONARD LAW
The French Ambassador	RONALD FIRMAGER
Solo Dancers	
Concord	SVETLANA BERIOSOVA
Time	DESMOND DOYLE
Morris Dancer	JOHAAR MOSEVAAL

Citizens, Maids of Honour, Ladies and Gentlemen of the Household, Courtiers, Masquers, Old Men, Men and Boys of Essex's Following, Councillors, Country Girls, Rustics and Fishermen, Pages.

Dancers from the Sadler's Wells Ballet School
Ballet Master - HAROLD TURNER

The Children are members of the Kingsland Central School and have been trained by MR. GEORGE HURREN

ACT I.	Scene 1:	Outside a tilting-ground
	Scene 2:	A private apartment at Nonesuch
ACT II.	Scene 1:	The Guildhall at Norwich
	Scene 2:	The garden of Essex House in the Strand
	Scene 3:	A great room in the Palace of Whitehall
ACT III.	Scene 1:	An anteroom at Nonesuch
	Scene 2:	A street in the City of London
	Scene 3:	A room in the Palace of Whitehall

God Save The Queen

The audience, so far from being a gathering of artistic Britain to honour the Queen (as we had naively hoped) consisted of Cabinet, Diplomatic Corps and official London first and foremost, and the rest apparently nowhere. They applauded if at all with their kid gloves on and the press, critics as well as journalists, gathered next day to castigate composer, performance, and choice. Ben was criticized for his music, I was criticized for pushing such an obviously poor choice for such an occasion; it was clear that some sort of simple-minded glorification was what had been expected, not the passionate, tender drama inside the public pageantry that Ben had contrived. [. . .]

Ben was clearly mortified by the whole fiasco, and a few weeks later, when we were changing before an opera recital at the Devon Festival [the Taw and Torridge Festival], confided to me that he had received a broadside from Peter – did not the reception confirm his worst fears? Should they not in future stick to the public that wanted them, the loyal Aldeburgh friends, and not get mixed up with something that was none of their concern?

Lord Drogheda recalled (*Double Harness*, pp. 240) that

'Boriana' was on everyone's lips. Most distressing was that in one scene the elderly Queen Elizabeth I removed her wig from her head and was revealed as almost bald: and this was taken, for no good reason at all, as being in bad taste.

In an interview with John Evans, '*Peter Grimes* and *Gloriana*', in Nicholas John (ed.), *Peter Grimes/Gloriana*, pp. 66–8, Pears and Cross shared their memories of *Gloriana*:

PEARS: It was absolutely fatal, of course, to have made a royal gala out of the first night. Quite fatal! That was really the trouble.
CROSS: What I remember about the first night was an uncomfortable feeling that the piece was under-rehearsed musically.
PEARS: You may be quite right about that, because something intensified the first-night nerves, not only because of the artificiality of the occasion [. . .] What was hoped for by many was a kind of superior *Merrie England*. This story about an ageing monarch was considered quite unsuitable for the young Queen at the start of her reign.

Of the first-night audience, Pears and Cross recalled:

PEARS: It was such an unusual relationship with the audience. It was almost like performing to an empty house.
CROSS: It really was quite an experience to sing to such an audience! At most, 15 per cent were musical and able to appreciate the work. It was a relief to find that the reaction to the first public performance at Covent Garden contradicted the impression that the command performance had been a disaster.

Cross remembered preparing for the role:

I stayed in Aldeburgh for some weeks in order to work with Ben whenever he had time. [The pianist] Viola Tunnard came and stayed and was very, very helpful. She bullied me. I had begun to find it very difficult, at that stage of my life, to memorize new music. [Britten] was after a *musical* performance, but, as always, he was deeply interested in the characterization and the theatrical dimension of the role. His remarkable understanding of the stage made him immensely stimulating. The historical period is so well documented it was only necessary to read what had been written about Elizabeth and integrate it with Ben's score.

She especially enjoyed the challenge of the final scene in which the character of Elizabeth I not only sings but also speaks:

I well remember, when rehearsing this piece, that Basil Coleman took immense trouble persuading me to use enough voice. When I came to rehearse this scene with him, we went through it and he said to me, 'That won't do, you know', and I was shattered. He said, 'You've really got to make a big speaking sound.' So we worked at it: he went to one end of a huge rehearsal room while I stood yelling at him from the other. Those speeches are remarkable in that they're *echt*, you know, they are historically recorded and accurately transcribed in the libretto.

It was a scene that Britten and Plomer revised in 1966, considerably sharpening the melodrama.

Befitting such a high-profile Coronation event, the first performance of *Gloriana* received considerable attention in the press, in the shape of both first-night notices and news stories. It is not possible to give full coverage here, but included below is a representative cross-section of the available press.

Reporting for the *Daily Mail* ('*Gloriana* brings a night of Coronation glory', 9 June 1953), Stephen Bayliss described the scenes outside the theatre:

Standing on dining-room chairs and lining the narrow pavements outside Bow Street Police Court five deep, 3,500 people welcomed the Queen and the Duke of Edinburgh when they arrived at Covent Garden last night for Benjamin Britten's new opera *Gloriana*.

Three hundred police lined Bow Street, Long Acre, and surrounding streets.

The people of the gaily decorated Fletcher Buildings, Covent Garden, crowded on to their concrete balconies to look down at the Opera House through the narrow alleyway of Martlett Court.

Covent Garden porters stood on public-bar benches, raised their glasses and caps, and cheered as the Queen drove by.

A barrow boy was ordered to 'move on' with his barrowload of children.

Other children, who were allowed to stay up long past their bedtime, cheered and waved flags in the narrow streets by Peabody Buildings, which, for one night, had become the Queen's Way.

When the Queen disappeared inside the doorways of the Doric façade the crowds broke through the police cordons and stood cheering for several minutes.

A detailed report in the *Daily Telegraph* ('The Queen goes to see new Britten opera', 9 June 1953) noted that:

The audience, many of whom had been in the theatre nearly an hour and a half, rose to their feet as the Queen took her seat. There was a fanfare by six State trumpeters before the audience stood for the new arrangement of the National Anthem by Sir William Walton [...]

When the performance ended nearly half an hour behind the scheduled time the

Queen applauded vigorously for eight minutes as the company, the composer, and the librettist between them took 10 curtain calls.

The Walton arrangement of the National Anthem was played again. The audience joined the Covent Garden company in the singing and after a short silence began to cheer. The Queen waved four or five times in acknowledgement and the Duke of Edinburgh bowed before the Royal party left their box.

James Thomas, *News Chronicle* ('But the glitter was cold', 9 June 1953), was less circumspect than the *Telegraph* about the audience's reaction to the opera:

The opera's reception was no more than polite from the most unusual audience at the Opera House for years.

A few of the regulars up in the gallery raised a cheer for the composer when he walked on the stage after flowers had been handed to all the principal women.

'The stickiest audience we have ever known,' was how some of the singers described it.

Following *Gloriana*'s second performance, the *Daily Express* ('Bow for Britten', 12 June 1953) reported that Britten himself took six out of eleven curtain calls, whereas at the first night

the applause was scarcely strong enough to get the curtain up for the third time. Last night there were 11 curtains, six of them specially for Britten.

Few in the full house were in evening dress. There was not a tiara in sight. Why this difference between Monday and last night's enthusiasm? Said a doorkeeper, 'Ah, you see, these are lovers of opera. And, of course, they have paid for their seats.'

The music critics of the daily press responded overnight. *The Times* (9 June 1953) considered that:

In the music Britten has dealt with a wider range of emotion than hitherto and has put on one side his predilection for persecution and compassion, though the most moving passage in the score was the plea for mercy in the final scene. The librettist has provided him with opportunity for gay, excited, capricious, and ceremonious music, upon which he has brought to bear his astonishingly fertile resource and invention. What he has not quite commanded is the full-blooded vigour of the age he set out to depict. And the root cause of that is partly technical – a curious reluctance to wed the sound of violins with that of voices, so that he voluntarily forgoes the lifting power of that alliance. The opera went well, grew in intensity dramatically, was prodigal of passing beauties, but did not quite make the strong direct impact that it ought to do.

Miss Joan Cross as the Queen looked the part, bore herself with regal authority and feminine feeling, made her words audible but had not the sheer vocal power and singing resonance to make a complete operatic portrait. Mr Peter Pears also made a vivid portrait of Essex, but again hardly filled out a role that would profit by heroic vocal quality. There were many small parts, of which Misses Jennifer Vyvyan, Adèle Leigh, and Monica Sinclair as Ladies at Court contributed to the vocal pleasures of the evening.

Mr John Pritchard conducted and kept the opera moving at the right tempo, though a firmer hand would have made it more taut. The dancing devised by John

Cranko seemed to be impeded by its vocal accompaniment, though the court dances of the period were effective and in character. The scenery and costumes of John Piper were resplendent and suitable, drawing short bursts of appreciative applause at the rising of the curtain. The production by Basil Coleman, who has an infallible eye for situation, kept a pageant play in motion by its ingenuity.

In the *Daily Telegraph* (9 June 1953), Richard Capell wrote:

Mr Britten is a composer who cannot write otherwise than stylishly. The whole score is evidence of his brilliant technique, and there are, in the hors d'œuvre, many characteristically attractive things – Essex's lute song 'Happy were he', for instance, in the first act, the choruses at the Norwich masque and the pavan and coranto at the Whitehall ball.

But it is probable that his heart was not in the enterprise. Nor can his poet's have been: for his characters are lifeless – puppets and not men and women. It is typical that we should be alienated from Essex in the very first scene, where he is represented as a mere quarrelsome featherpate.

In his Saturday column (13 June 1953), Capell offered further thoughts on the opera:

Gloriana [...] proved to be a problematical work. It raised no less a question than the limits of music.

Something has already been said about the pageantry of the new piece and the splendour of the stage show. But what of the essential action? The authors of *Gloriana* have drastically simplified the complicated characters of their principals, the ageing Elizabeth I and that spoilt darling of fortune, Devereux, Earl of Essex. This was perhaps inevitable.

As the evening wore on and nothing but a surface was shown of the pair, each the other's victim, the wild Essex the victim of the Queen's possessiveness and the Queen the victim of his rebellious temper, the reflection came that in all the great lyric dramas of the past the characters have been simple, their motives plain to every man [...]

That the authors of *Gloriana* soon despaired of their self-imposed task is shown by the large allowance they have made in their opera to trimmings or diversions.

An exposition of the relations between the Queen and her favourite, a searching exposition giving both their due, would have taken up three whole acts with no room for galliards and lavoltas, jolly though these are in their way – the lavolta at the Whitehall ball was one of the hits of the evening.

Whether any mortal men could have succeeded in such an enterprise may be doubted. Plomer and Britten have failed. Their simplification shows both Essex and the Queen in a more or less odious light.

The cruel humiliation inflicted by the Queen on Lady Essex in the scene of the ball – where the Queen somehow purloins the poor lady's all-too-gaudy dress and herself appears in it before the Court – may be justified by something in Lytton Strachey's book, but the episode takes up too much time in the opera, where, such a subject having been chosen, not a moment should have been wasted.

Mr Britten's score, ineffective though it is as a whole, should not lead to disparagement of his wonderful gifts; but it exposes the limitations of his art. All the breadth of style, the heartiness, the passionate flow, wanted to represent a sanguine age, are lacking. This queen and this swashbuckling courtier were once great people. They are dwindled, in spite of fine clothes, by such uneasily nervous, ungenerous music.

Scott Goddard, *News Chronicle* (9 June 1953), like several other reviewers, was wholly admiring of John Piper's designs, but held reservations about the music:

> As a spectacle *Gloriana* is indeed exciting. And then the music. Evidently we shall need more than one or two performances to get it into focus.
>
> At present it is the least memorable part of the show. One or two striking passages one recalls, things not swamped by the pageantry on the stage. The rest remains for the moment an intriguing background.

Outspoken Tory MP Beverley Baxter, *Evening Standard* (9 June 1953), expressed characteristically exaggerated views:

> The truth is that it was a perfect setting for an all-star production of *Merrie England*, and what a night the old piece would have made of it! Instead, we had Mr Britten, which was tough all round.
>
> Let us face the blunt truth. When the Arts Council decided to commission a Coronation opera and finance its production they should have asked Mr Britten his intentions. The idea was that he should centre his theme about the personality of Elizabeth I and bring the glory of the two Elizabeths across the span of the centuries.
>
> Instead of that Mr Britten and his librettist, William Plomer, decided to take the lamentable love story of the ageing Queen and the youthful Essex. For reasons which they no doubt felt were justified in the name of art they gave us a Queen with a red wig who was finally discovered by Essex (back from Ireland) without her wig. So the opera ends with the miserable old woman sentencing Essex to death for treason, plus the incident of the wig, and then telling us that she only wanted to live in order to serve her people.
>
> Not a mention of Drake or Shakespeare or any of that brilliant galaxy of daring, gifted men who won the sixteenth century for England. The Arts Council could not be bothered about that.
>
> However, let us admit that in an opera the music is all important [...]
>
> There are some delicate and exciting passages in the score of *Gloriana*. There are sustained passages of immense strength and never does the vitality of the composer flag. John Pritchard, who conducted splendidly, was obviously fascinated by the score.
>
> Yet for minutes at a time – minutes piled upon minutes – it was as clamorous and ugly as hammers striking steel rails. No melody emerged, no tune, no beauty in the sustained passages which, in the last act, took complete command. At least in *Peter Grimes* we had those deep haunting chords of the cruel sea, and in *Billy Budd* there was the soft singing of the sailors at dusk, but in the finale of *Gloriana*, Britten seems to be shouting: 'Ugliness is truth, and truth is ugliness!'
>
> My head throbbed with the clangour until I longed for the opera to come to an end [...]
>
> The audience was cold, and rightly so. In fact, at the close of the different scenes there was hardly enough applause to give the conductor a breather. Even at the end

there was only sufficient applause to keep the curtain up long enough to hand over the flowers to the women soloists.

Baxter expanded this *Evening Standard* notice as 'The One Sour Note of the Coronation', for the Toronto-based magazine *Maclean's* (1 September 1953).

Members of the foreign press corps also contributed accounts of the first night, with notices appearing in, for example, *Le Monde*, *Le Figaro* and *Die Welt* (all 10 June 1953), as well as the *New York Times* (9 June 1953), where Stephen Williams wrote:

Perhaps the libretto is partly responsible but the work certainly lacks dramatic tension and the clash of temperaments is not urgently brought out. It is pageantry rather than drama. On the other hand, those who dislike Britten's *Peter Grimes* and *Billy Budd* will like *Gloriana*. They will enjoy the continuous charm of this music that even deviates into melody here and there; in the powerful ensemble begun by the Queen in Act I; in the music of the enchanting masque, and in Essex's beautiful song to the lute.

Williams returned to *Gloriana* in the following Sunday's edition of the *New York Times* (14 June 1953), when he noted:

The intervals resounded with violent altercations between pro-Brittens and anti-Brittens. 'Not essential Britten at all,' said the pros. 'And a very good thing, too!' retorted the antis.

Writing in the *Manchester Guardian Weekly* (11 June 1953), Philip Hope-Wallace considered:

Suitable subject or not, in the circumstances, it had an undeniable piquancy, touched in as it is with the candour inspired by Lytton Strachey's famous essay. For those interested in the operatic problem as such it was, of course, an absorbingly interesting evening; what were the thoughts of those merely attending in the line of duty a modern three-act opera as long as *Aida* history does not record. What do they know of *Merrie England* who only Britten knew? In the event, a lot.

In such a gala, criticism if actually even admitted is at best rather lame. There will be other chances to evaluate a work, which, as those listening to the broadcast must have known quickly, is packed with clever and audaciously original strokes of operatic craft.

But here and now two things may be said: one, that the masques and Elizabethan jigs and ambles which are entirely suitable to a gala do tend rather to impede the movement of so fine-drawn a psychological study; and that, with a production as unobtrusive and muted as some of the singing, one is still, somehow, waiting at the end of the second act, two-thirds of the way through, and wondering if the opera will ever 'get off the ground'.

Pressure for seats at the gala opening meant that critics from the serious weekly journals were denied tickets. Martin Cooper, *Spectator* (12 June 1953), contributed his notice having listened to the broadcast of the premiere and acquired a vocal score:

It is a festival piece, such as eighteenth-century composers wrote for royal weddings – part pageant, part ballet, part cantata – an occasional work which should not be judged by the standards applicable to opera in general, where the music and the drama are their own masters. My impression is that Britten has understood this and fulfilled his commission with brilliant success. The subject was not in itself promising, for neither Elizabeth nor Essex makes a very attractive figure and the relationship between the ageing Virgin Queen and her youthful, ambitious captain and courtier – half maternal and half erotic – is in itself hardly a subject for glorification. It is in the scenes of court festivities, the masque offered to Elizabeth on her visit to Norwich and the crowd scenes, that Britten's music seems most successful – simple and forthright yet extraordinarily poetic, full of a sense of the occasion yet never derogating from a high musical standard. Excelling as he does in the expression of tortured or thwarted emotions and in scenes of nervous tension or outbreak, he has presented isolated moments in the lives of both Elizabeth and Essex with great power, though he has not attempted to present their characters as a whole or 'in the round'. In a warmer, more evenly flowing emotional scene – that between the lovers Mountjoy and Lady Rich – there seemed to be an element lacking, that sense of ordinary human life continuing all the time against the background of intrigue and personal enmities. If William Plomer, the librettist, designed this scene as a moment of contrast, Britten's music hardly follows that intention. The second scene of the last act, on the other hand, gives the atmosphere of the crowd in the streets with extraordinary vividness and the Blind Ballad-Singer's music, like Essex's lute songs, belongs to the most effective in the piece.

It will be easier to speak of the performance after seeing it in the opera house. Joan Cross's Elizabeth seemed dignified and dramatically moving. She spoke the lines in the last scene, where Elizabeth is haunted by spectres, with great dignity and feeling; but a fuller-bodied and larger voice would have been more effective. Peter Pears, frankly miscast as Essex, did his best to give a robust, heroic ring to a voice whose natural character is anything but that.

Desmond Shawe-Taylor, *New Statesman and Nation* (13 June 1953), had also attended the dress rehearsal:

Gloriana is a neat and serviceable text, poetic and imaginative on occasion, and free from the pretentious obscurity of the typical modern opera book; but it is more pageant than drama. Though Strachey's highly dramatized *Elizabeth and Essex* has provided a framework, it has not provided a play: that complex and tortuous relationship was not easy to recast in dramatically self-sufficient terms at the slow pace dictated by music. Bold manipulation and invention of fact might have produced a taut drama of amorous and political intrigue; but this was not the aim of author and composer. Before their Virgin Queen they have spread a sober cloak of historical truth, upon which she can pace forward safely, picturesquely, grandly – but without the clash and the tension which we expect from opera. Only now and again – most notably in the last act – are we emotionally affected by the human predicament set before us; in general, drama has been subordinated to spectacle and splendour. There was good reason behind this decision, though it will limit the future popularity of the work. Masques, dancing, ceremony – all these were required, not only in homage to the present Queen, but in order to present a vivid picture of the Elizabethan Age. The familiar attributes of the principal figures are recognizably outlined; but the work remains essentially decorative, a lavish picture book [...]

The most emotional passage in the score occurs in the first scene of the last act, in which we witness Essex's wild intrusion into the Queen's dressing-room. After his departure, and the Queen's sad comprehension of the hopelessness of his character, her ladies complete her toilet to a lyrical passage of great beauty which bears some resemblance to the folding away of the linen in *Lucretia*. The abortive rebellion of Essex in the City is 'covered' by a blind ballad-singer in a somewhat American-sounding ditty, *à la* Burl Ives, to a thrummed accompaniment. This odd treatment is justified, perhaps, by the historical ineffectiveness of the rising; but, in the theatre, the apparent triviality of the episode makes a curious prelude to the solemnity of the final scene. After the pleading of the Essex party before the Queen and her signature of the Earl's death warrant, there follows a foreshortened vision of her last years which is the most imaginative feature of the libretto. The Queen stands in a gradually contracting pool of bright light. Out of the surrounding gloom come visitors, to whom she speaks some of those famous sentences which have come down to us, while the orchestra, playing with a grave and sonorous amplitude the second of the Lute Songs, shows that her mind is elsewhere. At the very end, still erect on her feet, the fantastic monarch is enveloped in complete darkness, while a solo violin modulates from the elegiac C minor of the Lute Song to the fresh D major of the 'loyal' chorus, which is now distantly heard – 'Green leaves are we, Red rose our golden Queen...' It is a moving and poetic conclusion, which owes something, perhaps, to Lytton Strachey's account of another royal ending: '... and the trees and the grass at Kensington.'

Ernest Newman, in *The Sunday Times* (14 June 1953), relegated discussion of *Gloriana* to a third of his weekly column, preferring instead to concentrate on Glyndebourne's new production of Gluck's *Alceste*. As ever with Britten's operas, he was critical of the libretto:

Mr Britten has once more shown us how uncritical of his librettists he can be at times. Such dramatic life as there is in *Gloriana* goes to the credit of the historians; neither Mr Plomer nor Mr Britten has done much to reanimate the figures and the action in terms of his own medium.

The substance of the dramatic plan being too thin to spread itself with any strength over three acts, there is a great deal of padding, generally in the form of dance or pageant episodes. In general the music seems to me to fall far below the level we have come to expect from a composer of Mr Britten's gifts. It goes without saying that there are moments in the work when he looks like coming into his own as a musician, notably the quartette ('Good Frances, do not weep') in the second act and for a fairly long stretch in the last scene of all. Even here, however, the final fulfilment does not equal the initial promise; Mr Britten has put more genius into much the same sort of thing elsewhere.

The bulk of the music is hardly more than pastiche, sometimes very clever pastiche, sometimes not so clever. On the whole, Mr Britten will have to do something decidedly better than *Gloriana*, if he is to retain – or regain – the position he has won for himself in the operatic world with some of his earlier works. The performance, conducted by John Pritchard, was scrupulously painstaking, if hardly of National-Opera-House standard. Joan Cross was Queen Elizabeth and Peter Pears Essex.

Eric Blom, in the *Observer* (14 June 1953), wrote:

The choral writing in particular, including dances to unaccompanied singing, is infallibly telling, and it must be said that the splendid Covent Garden chorus is at its best here. The orchestration is dazzling, often with that peculiarly Brittenish brassy edge, and the bells of Norwich are made to sound with a realism matched only by Mussorgsky's in *Boris*, but produced by quite different and essentially very simple means. That Britten is one of the front-rank masters of scoring has long been evident, and here the fact is brilliantly confirmed by his knack, as remarkable in him as in Berlioz, of doing all sorts of things that had never been tried before – and, one wonders why, for they seem obvious once they have been done.

It is all very splendid and very interesting. It is also often rather superficial and unfeeling, so that it is far from certain how well *Gloriana* would fare in the ordinary repertory, without the backing of a festivity and with anything less than the breathtakingly lavish and beautiful Covent Garden production [...]

[What the audience] may properly be asked to answer is the question whether it has found *Gloriana* good enough. In other words, the opera must here be faced as a work of art and nothing else. For my own part I found it more than good enough, and if not superlative all through, I challenge anyone to name more than a dozen of the world's operas that are unquestionably so. A certain emotional aridity, found to some extent in all Britten's work, is not to be denied here, though partly to be excused by the deliberate showiness of much of the action. There is also a scrappiness to be noticed, which makes one often wish that a movement, once started, would go on longer and develop. But what scraps! Over and over again one comes across one of those short phrases, so many of which are now familiar in Britten's earlier operas, phrases never forgotten once they have been heard. They may seem quite ordinary – the kind of thing which composers ought long ago to have thought of, but just happened unaccountably to overlook. Whatever else Britten may lack, he is one of music's great epigrammatists, as he is one of its great orchestrators. And of course there is more, much more, in *Gloriana*. No doubt it is a weakness, a failing of great emotional inspiration, that Elizabeth's final, most significant and moving words should be spoken, not sung; on the other hand her dismissal of Essex in the dressing-room, where he has discovered her, ageing and divested of her trappings, is a moment of true pathos, musically as well as dramatically conveyed. It must also be said that though the arresting phrases most take the ear, many of the set musical numbers are beautifully constructed and give strength and shape to the work as a whole.

The vocal parts are less satisfying than the instrumental, except for the choruses: rather dry on the whole and remarkable for excellent declamation of the words rather than for sympathy with the voice. It must be added that the two principal parts, Elizabeth I (Joan Cross) and Essex (Peter Pears), are not sung with great richness or roundness of tone [...] But Miss Cross's impersonation of the Queen, make-up, bearing, understanding and all, will probably never be surpassed. Basil Coleman's production and John Pritchard's conducting leave nothing to be desired.

American Joseph Newman, in the *New York Herald Tribune* (14 June 1953), detached from the Coronation and nationalist fervour of his UK counterparts, summarized for his readership the London press notices of *Gloriana*:

Everyone expected *Gloriana* to be a tribute to the new sovereign – a glorification of Elizabeth I which would serve as a glorification of Elizabeth II and would ring the curtain up on a new Elizabethan Age.

It turned out to be nothing of the kind. Instead of pursuing and elaborating the sweet fairy-tale mood which had been woven around the Coronation in the streets of London and in the nation's press, Britten shattered it – at least for several hours – by bringing to life the full-blooded, down-to-earth tragedy of Elizabeth I, torn between her illicit love for a man who had betrayed the State and her duty as queen to execute him.

The thirty-nine-year-old composer and his librettist, William Plomer, either through innocence or defiance, had served a dish which London's critics felt was not fit for a queen, and the critics set up a howl in the newspapers.

He concluded:

Elizabeth II, unlike most of the others in the audience, obviously was not disturbed by the thought that Britten was violating the mood of the fairy-tale myth which was being woven around her and her Coronation. Having approved the score and script beforehand, she evidently preferred a dramatic production of a tragedy built around some of the stark realities of her ancestor to fanciful nonsense about a New Elizabethan Age. In this, Queen Elizabeth, while deserted by many of her subjects, was supported by some of the foreigners who witnessed the production.

For more on the social, cultural, artistic and personal background to the savage response to the work in the national press, see PBBG, pp. 1–16 and 49–65; HCBB, pp. 325–6, Donald Mitchell, 'Fit for a Queen?: The Reception of *Gloriana*', liner notes for *Gloriana* (Argo 440 213-2, 1993), and Heather Wiebe, '"Now and England": Britten, *Gloriana* and the "New Elizabethans"', *Cambridge Opera Journal* 17/2 (2005), pp. 141–72, a fascinating analysis of the opera's ambivalent position within the climate of national renewal prevalent at the time of the Coronation.

The negative critical response to *Gloriana* provoked a correspondence in the pages of *The Times*, beginning on 16 June with Anthony Lewis, then Professor of Music at the University of Birmingham:

The artistic merit of current productions is rarely a profitable topic for correspondence. My excuse for this letter on the subject of Mr Benjamin Britten's *Gloriana* must therefore be that in this case more than a personal reputation is involved. Her Majesty's command that a new opera should be written to celebrate the Coronation was not only a signal honour for the composer concerned but a source of deep satisfaction to the musical profession as a whole. The degree of success of the resulting work is thus a matter of more than usually wide concern. Perhaps because Mr Britten's outstanding gifts are taken for granted, comment on *Gloriana* in some quarters has been so guarded as to cause some anxiety among those who have not seen the opera.

May an independent musician, therefore, express his belief that on this historic occasion English music has been splendidly represented by Mr Britten's *Gloriana*? Page after page of music of superb richness and invention testifies to the continued excellence of the composer's creative powers, responding magnificently to the demands of the occasion. In the welter of indecision and frustration in which so much European music now finds itself, it is truly exhilarating to hear a score that unfolds with such masterly confidence, and yet with such originality. *Gloriana* is indeed a worthy execution of the royal command.

Vaughan Williams, never the staunchest supporter of Britten's work, nevertheless joined in the debate, writing to *The Times* (18 June 1953):

I do not propose, after a single hearing, to appraise either the words or the music of *Gloriana*. The important thing to my mind, at the moment, is that, so far as I know, for the first time in history the Sovereign has commanded an opera by a composer from these islands for a great occasion. Those who cavil at the public expense involved should realize what such a gesture means to the prestige of our own music.

Three further letters appeared on 19 June, two (from Harold W. Rhodes and Elizabeth Sellers) supporting Lewis; a third, from the writer and wit Caryl Brahms, however, concluded that the 'average taxpayer – as distinct from the musical taxpayer' might 'still feel that English history has been slighted by the librettist's choice of the petulant episode of Elizabeth and Essex from what was an age of vigour and adventure'. Labour MP Woodrow Wyatt defended the expense of *Gloriana* in a letter printed on 20 June 1953:

All those distinguished persons concerned wth the composition and production of *Gloriana* were rightly left free by the Government to do what they themselves thought best. One advantage of the hostile criticism that *Gloriana* has received is that one goes to Covent Garden, as I did last night, prepared to be bored or worse. Pleasure at finding that the Government have commissioned not a monstrosity but a work of art is consequently enhanced. Musically, dramatically, and scenically *Gloriana* is original and impressive. Nor is the objection to the subject-matter understandable.

It is true that we do not see a stylized and school-book picture of the first Elizabeth and her age: instead we see an effective representation of a remarkable queen in her varying aspects of dignity, greatness, generosity, tragedy, and human frailty against a background that is thoroughly English in concentration and atmosphere. The first-night audience is reported to have been frigid. If that is correct the reflection is on them and not on *Gloriana*. I shall have no hesitation in telling my constituents that their money has been well spent.

Counterbalancing Wyatt's letter was criticism from birth-control pioneer Marie C. Stopes, which appeared in the same edition:

Public resentment, intense and widespread, is not at the cost but that the opera was unworthy of the great occasion, uninspired, missing the main glories of the times, its music inharmonious and wearisome, and with at least two scenes profoundly affronting the glorious memory of Queen Elizabeth I, hence unsuitable for public performance before Queen Elizabeth II.

The correspondence came to a close on 22 June with support for Britten's and Plomer's treatment from R. M. Roberts, and the contrary view being expressed by an Aldeburgh resident, J. Thorburn Irvine, who considered that it was

on the score of this belittling of an heroic reign and age that the public may well be justified in cavilling at the expense, though the expense is a small matter as compared with the missed opportunity of creating something to inspire other than purely musical people.

Writing in the *Spectator* (19 June 1953), Martin Cooper concluded that the critical outburst had been prompted by jealousy of what was viewed as the composer's increasingly privileged position in Establishment circles and to 'an almost sadistic relish or glee that has little to do with the musical merit or demerit'. In many respects, it marked the spectacular culmination of a critical malaise that had already reared its ugly head at the time of the first performance of *Billy Budd* two years before: see BBMCPR, pp. 135–40, and Letter 718 n. 2.

A culturally fascinating – as well as amusing – example of the permeation of New Elizabethanism in the early 1950s can be found in Geoffrey Willan's and Ronald Searle's *Whizz for Atomms*, one of their 'Molesworth' books, first published in 1956, in which can be found 'How to be a Young Elizabethan', a chapter that originally appeared 'in that super smashing mag *Young Elizabethan*'. (Britten was interviewed by Scott Goddard for an issue of *Collins Young Elizabethan* in June 1953 and appears to have received copies of the magazine which he regularly forwarded to Roger Duncan.) No doubt the following exchange between Elizabeth I and the King of Spain would have registered with the composer's schoolboyish sense of humour:

Aktually Drake was pretty tuough and did more or less as he liked espueshully if there were spaniards about. Good Queen Bess was very keen on him in spite of the remonstrations of the king of spane who had a lisp like all spaniards.

THE KING OF SPANE: i tha, beth, that thcoundrel drake hath thinged my berd agane.
ELIZABETH: (*wiping her fhoes on his cloke*) La coz you furprise me you fimply fake me rigid.
THE KING OF SPANE: Tith twinthe thith week. Ith abtholutely off-thide.
ELIZABETH: Off-fide? Where are you fettaclef? He was on-fide by fix yardf.
THE KING OF SPANE: Yar-boo. Thend him off.
ELIZABETH: Upon my foul tif clear you do not kno the rules of foccer.
(*Raleigh, the Earl of Essex, John and Sebastian Cabot join in the brawl with vulgar cries. Which match are you looking at? Pla the game, ruff it up ha-ha, etc.*)

See Geoffrey Willans and Ronald Searle, *Molesworth*, with an introduction by Philip Hensher, p. 216. The headmaster of Molesworth's fictitious public school, St Custard's, is called Grimes, 'a monster of callous cruelty who fly into a bate at every opportunity' (p. 213).

Sixth Concert

ON WEDNESDAY 3 JUNE AT 8 P.M.
IN THE ROYAL FESTIVAL HALL

PROGRAMME

Spring Symphony . . . . *Britten*

INTERVAL

Symphony No. 1 in A flat . . . . *Elgar*
Allegro : Allegro-molto — Adagio : Lento-Allegro

ELSIE MORISON
(SOPRANO)

ANNE WOOD
(CONTRALTO)

PETER PEARS
(TENOR)

BBC CHORAL SOCIETY
(Chorus Master: Leslie Woodgate)

A Section of
WATFORD GRAMMAR SCHOOL BOYS' CHOIR
(Conductor: Frank Budden)

THE BBC SYMPHONY ORCHESTRA
(Leader: Paul Beard)

CONDUCTED BY
SIR MALCOLM SARGENT

Programme for the sixth of a series of eight concerts marking the Queen's Coronation

772 To Lennox Berkeley

4 CRABBE STREET, ALDEBURGH, SUFFOLK
[after 28 June 1953]

My dear Lennox,

I forgot to thank you for your nice letter about 'Gloriana' – it was nice of you to write, & about the CH too.[1] It makes (the latter!) me feel fairly old, but not (thank God) too respectable!

I was sorry that the Stabat Mater didn't receive a performance worthy of it, here. But all the same it made a very deep impression.[2]

See you some time?

Love from
BEN

Thank you also for writing such a nice variation.[3] I hope the recordings are good.

1 Britten had been made a Companion of Honour in the Coronation Honours List published on 1 June. He had written to Eric Walter White on 7 June to say he regarded his CH 'as a compliment to serious English music & what is more – opera. It is a big, & surprising, gesture.' The composer duly attended the investiture held at Buckingham Palace at 12.30 p.m. on 1 July.

2 Berkeley's *Stabat Mater* had been performed at the Aldeburgh Festival on 22 June by Arda Mandikian and Gladys Whitred (sopranos), Anne Wood (contralto), Raymond Nilsson (tenor), Thomas Hemsley (baritone), Norman Lumsden (bass), and the EOG Chamber Orchestra conducted by Norman Del Mar. This, the Sixth Festival, ran from 20 to 28 June, its highlights including a production of *Albert Herring* on 20 June. The Second Lute Song from *Gloriana* was performed by Pears with Britten at the piano at an 'Opera Concert' on 28 June; for details of other concert performances of the song during this period, which included airings at the Taw and Torridge Festival and at King's Lynn, see PBBG, p. 124 n. 44.

3 Berkeley had contributed the third variation, *Andante*, to the composite set of *Variations on an Elizabethan Theme*.

773 To Eric Walter White
[*Typed*]

4 Crabbe Street, Aldeburgh, Suffolk
30th June, 1953

My dear Eric,

We were very sorry that you missed the Festival this year which most people seem to agree was one of our best, and the filthy June weather was less foul than it has been on other festive occasions.[1]

Thank you for your nice remarks about "Gloriana". I am delighted that it seems to be going so well now. Certainly the audience's reactions when I have been there have been most exciting.

Auden[2] has come and gone, giving a most provocative [*handwritten*: (& fine!)] lecture,[3] but your request I quite stupidly forgot to pass on to him. I have no excuses to offer except that the Festival, as you know, is a very strenuous affair. Perhaps he is still in England, and you can get in touch with him at Faber's.

I hope the revision of the book is going well – if you want any help with it do not hesitate to ask.[4]

[Handwritten:] With love –
BEN

1 Britten refers here to the wet weather in London on Coronation Day, 2 June.

2 Wystan Hugh Auden (1907–1973), British poet (later naturalized American), Britten's friend and collaborator since the 1930s. See Letter x n. 3 (vol. 3, p. 78).

3 Auden gave a lecture in the Baptist Chapel on 26 June, entitled 'The Hero in Modern Poetry'. It was a lecture he gave elsewhere in the 1950s, for example in 1952 at the Arts Club of Chicago. To Elizabeth Mayer, Britten described Auden's visit as 'provoking and brilliant' (see Letter 777), but it was after this meeting – and Auden's criticisms of aspects of *Gloriana* – that Britten had minimal contact with the poet: see Addenda to vol. 2, p. 1340.

After seeing *Gloriana* at Covent Garden, Auden told Elizabeth Mayer (16 July 1953; quoted in Humphrey Carpenter, *W. H. Auden: A Biography*, p. 375): 'It has some of the best operatic music in it, I think, Ben has done yet, and the Piper sets were superb. Didn't care for the libretto and neither Joan Cross nor Peter should sing anymore on the stage.' Of his visit to the Festival, he told Mrs Mayer, 'Everyone was charming, but I was never allowed to see Ben alone – I feared as much, still, I was a bit sad.' In an earlier letter to Mrs Mayer (undated, but probably June 1953), prior to his Aldeburgh engagement, Auden had remarked, 'I hope, though faintly, that I shall be able to have a real talk with Sir Benjamin' (quoted in Carpenter, p. 375).

Responding to Letter 777, Mrs Mayer wrote:

I *was* so happy that Wystan was in Aldeb. He wrote me a long long and happy letter from England, happy, too, that he had heard *Gloriana* and liked the music immensely.

A later passage in this letter suggests she had already learned of the incipient rift between composer and poet:

But don't forget (I know you don't) that he is a truly *great* person and has, of course, *great* faults but also *great* qualities (not only as a poet but as a human being).

4 See Letter 780 n. 2.

774 To William Plomer

PORTLEDGE HOTEL, FAIRY CROSS, BIDEFORD, N. DEVON
[Postmarked 20 July 1953]

My dearest William,

It is ages since I heard of you, longer even since I saw you – & this is only a brief note to say that [it] is all much too long, & I miss seeing you very much indeed. I wonder how everything is going with you, whether you are moving to Brighton or have moved. I don't like the idea of you moving, I must confess, because it is that much further away from London, & the chances of seeing you will be even smaller, I suppose. But if you are happy there, that is the main thing, for you & Charles. Please drop me a line to Aldeburgh with the address.[1]

As you see from the odd heading, Peter & I are in Devon for a pleasant, successful & extremely damp Festival in Barnstaple & Bideford.[2] It is hard work & we long for some rest – but although we return East on Monday, the rest will be postponed for a couple of weeks, because there are still concerts to be done. But August means rest & Aldeburgh. I wish there were a chance of seeing you both there, but having moved (as I suspect) so recently you won't want to move – & I (I'm afraid) am rather under doctor's orders not to move myself.[3]

Gloriana came to a triumphant, & temporary, conclusion I gather last Saturday.[4] It has been an enormous success, from the box office, having on average beaten all other operas there this season. I expect that you, like me, have felt a bit kicked around over it – perhaps more than me, because I'm a bit more used to the jungle! But the savageness of the wild beasts always is a shock.[5] The fact remains that I've loved working with you, my dear, & that you've produced a most wonderful libretto, that it is impossible for me adequately to express my gratitude for – Please let us sometime work together again[6] – no hurry – just don't forget me –

with all my love, & to Charles –
BEN

Peter sends a lot of love too – I wish you could see his really charming MacHeath. It is a jolly good piece – that Beggar's Opera.

1 In June 1953 Plomer bought a house on the Sussex coast, at Rustington, moving in (with his companion Charles Erdmann) on 16 July; see Peter F. Alexander, *William Plomer*, p. 280.

2 Ronald Duncan, whose brainchild this first Taw and Torridge Festival was, recalls (RDWB, p. 120) that the venture had Britten's full support: the composer viewed the initiative as providing an additional venue for the English Opera Group and as a vital 'oasis' in an area of England that constituted 'a

cultural desert'. Britten and Pears had travelled on 10 July to Bideford, where the next day Pears was soloist in Britten's *Saint Nicolas* with the EOG Orchestra conducted by Norman Del Mar; among the Festival's several Britten-related events were performances of *The Beggar's Opera* (14, 16 and 18 July in Barnstaple (John Gay's birthplace), EOG conducted by Del Mar, with Pears as Macheath), and *Let's Make an Opera!* (16, 17 and 18 July, in Barnstaple, EOG again conducted by Del Mar), and Pears and Britten gave a special 'Soirée Musicale' on 19 July at Sir Hugh Stucley's Moreton House. Britten also accompanied at an operatic concert in Barnstaple on 12 July, introduced by Lord Harewood, with soloists Joan Cross, Nancy Evans, Rowland Jones and Michael Langdon, which included extracts from *Gloriana*; and Britten and Pears participated in a concert with the Wind Ensemble of the London Symphony Orchestra on the 15th in a programme that included Mozart's Quintet in E flat, K. 452; Schubert's *Der Hirt auf dem Felsen*, and Beethoven's *An die ferne Geliebte*. See also RDWB, pp. 121–2, though Duncan's memory of the occasion is often at variance with the Festival's programme. As he often did, Britten kept meticulous notes in his pocket diary of all expenditure on petrol incurred during the trip to Devon.

3 Britten was suffering from the effects of over a year's concentrated work on the composition and production of *Gloriana*, topped by the Aldeburgh Festival the previous month. In addition, he was experiencing severe pain in his right arm, subsequently diagnosed as bursitis, which was to plague him for the remainder of the year, severely curtailing his professional activities. Although the symptoms became more acute during the summer of 1953, it would appear that the original source of the trouble lay in Britten's conducting of *Billy Budd* in 1951–52. (In Letter 777 Britten tells Elizabeth Mayer that his arm 'has been troubling me for 2 years'.) Rest, treatment, and eventually an operation in March 1954 were to relieve the discomfort.

4 The final performance of the initial run took place on 11 July.

5 In his reply, dated 23 July, Plomer wrote:

> V. pleased to hear your news about *Gloriana*. Well, well, one could write a book about it all, and *them* all. On the whole I think we have seen a healthy reaction to a new work of art. All the ferocities, the knowingnesses, the superficialities, the stampeding sheep-in-wolves'-clothing, the second thoughts, the timidities, the jealousies, and so on, amount, it seems to me, to a real tribute to your powers.

6 The next project on which Britten and Plomer were to collaborate was the first Church Parable, *Curlew River*. Plomer was not an admirer of Henry James's *The Turn of the Screw* (see Letter 778 n. 3), and appears to have been happy for Myfanwy Piper to assume the responsibility for providing Britten with his next major libretto after *Gloriana*.

Following the initial run of performances of the Coronation opera, Britten made several minor revisions to the work and corrections to the performing materials during the autumn of 1953 in readiness for the revival

1 (*above*) Benjamin Britten in his vintage Rolls-Royce in the early 1950s

2 (*left*) Britten and Peter Pears in Canada, August 1957

3 (*above*) In the garden of Crag House, Aldeburgh: Imogen Holst, Pears, Sally and Sebastian Welford, Paul Rogerson, Maria Curcio, Britten and Roguey Welford

4 (*right*) Britten with his miniature dachshunds, Clytie and Jove

5 Nellie Hudson, Britten's housekeeper, with her cat Bang

6 Jeremy Cullum, Britten's secretary and driver

7 (*left*) London, 1953: Lord Harewood, Erwin Stein and William Plomer (librettist of *Gloriana*)

8 (*below*) Ski-ing holiday at Gargellen, March 1952: Pears, the Harewoods and Britten

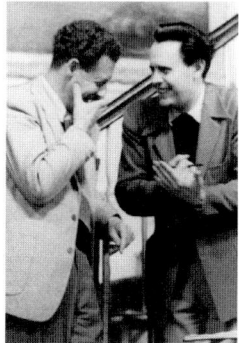

9 *Gloriana*, Royal Opera House, Covent Garden, May 1953: Britten and conductor John Pritchard share a joke during a rehearsal break

10 Piano rehearsal in the Crush Bar, with Pears (Earl of Essex), director Basil Coleman and Joan Cross (Elizabeth I). The repetiteur is unidentified.

11 (*top left*) *Gloriana*, Royal Opera House, Covent Garden, June 1953: Elizabeth I (Joan Cross)
12 (*top right*) *Gloriana*, Act III scene 1: Essex (Peter Pears) and Elizabeth I (Joan Cross)
13 (*bottom*) *Gloriana*, Act II scene 1: Queen Elizabeth's progress to Norwich – the masque presented in the sovereign's honour

14 (*top*) *Gloriana*, Act I scene 1, 'Happy were he': Essex (Peter Pears) sings his Second Lute Song to the Queen (Joan Cross)

15 (*left*) *Gloriana*, Act II scene 3: Elizabeth I (Joan Cross) humiliates Lady Essex (Monica Sinclair)

16 (*above*) *Gloriana*, Act III scene 3: Lady Essex (Monica Sinclair) pleads with the Queen (Joan Cross) for Essex's life

17 (*top left*) *The Turn of the Screw*, La Fenice, Venice, September 1954: Act I scene 5: the Governess (Jennifer Vyvyan) and Peter Quint (Peter Pears)
18 (*top right*) *The Turn of the Screw*, Act II scene 1, 'The ceremony of innocence is drowned': Quint (Peter Pears) and Miss Jessel (Arda Mandikian)
19 (*bottom*) *The Turn of the Screw*, Act II scene 2: Flora (Olive Dyer), Miles (David Hemmings), Mrs Grose (Joan Cross) and the Governess (Jennifer Vyvyan)

20 (*top*) *The Turn of the Screw*, Act II scene 5: Quint (Peter Pears) and Miles (David Hemmings)
21 (*above left*) *The Turn of the Screw*, Act II scene 3: Miss Jessel (Arda Mandikian) and the Governness (Jennifer Vyvyan)
22 (*above right*) *The Turn of the Screw*, Act II scene 8: Miles (David Hemmings) and the Governess (Jennifer Vyvyan)

25 Venetian gondola ride: Erwin Stein, Britten, Sophie Stein, Basil Coleman and Pears

23 (*top*) La Fenice, Venice, 14 September 1954, curtain call after the premiere of *The Turn of the Screw*: David Hemmings (Miles), Jennifer Vyvyan (Governess), Britten, Myfanwy Piper (librettist) and Basil Coleman (director)
24 (*above*) Street picnic in Venice during rehearsals for *The Turn of the Screw*; *left to right*: John Piper (designer), Britten, Pears, Myfanwy Piper, and Edward and Clarissa Piper

LETTER 774: JULY 1953

Cover of the *Gloriana* vocal score,
designed by John Piper

GLORIANA
AN OPERA IN THREE ACTS BY
WILLIAM PLOMER
Music by
BENJAMIN BRITTEN
(Op. 53)

Messrs. Boosey and Hawkes announce the publication of an edition limited to one hundred copies of the vocal score of this opera, numbered 1 to 100 and signed by the composer and the author. The edition is printed on finest hand made paper and is bound in parchment. The price is ten guineas net. Libretto 2/6

BOOSEY AND HAWKES LTD
295 REGENT STREET LONDON W.1

Advertisement for the first edition of the vocal score of *Gloriana*.
The edition was hastily prepared and as a consequence contained
several errors.

of the production in January 1954 (see PBBG, pp. 104–5 and 117), when it was conducted by Reginald Goodall at Covent Garden and during a provincial tour.

In her diary for 2 November 1953 (IHD, pp. 265–6), Imogen Holst details many of these revisions:

> He'd asked me to go round and work at *Gloriana* mistakes in the score: – he began by talking about general criticisms. Tony Gishford had felt the character of Essex was incomplete in the libretto. We discussed it, & he said again, what he'd said months ago, that Joan & Peter's love scenes were all right for a small theatre but wouldn't do in Covent Garden, and I said they were right because they'd got the right English restraint which was in keeping with the music and that that's how English opera ought to be, and when I quoted the hesitating low-level of Aeneas's first entry [in Purcell's *Dido and Aeneas*] he was *frightfully* pleased [...]
>
> He talked of altering several details – the bar before 'Love's better than fear' [Act I scene 2, No. 2] – which always hangs fire. He said was it wrong in the music? It always sounded wrong at each performance, yet when he played it on the piano it was all right. He decided to add horns. He also altered the strings' dynamics at Essex's first entry (Act I scene 2, No. 4), from *sfp* to *f* ($>$), and added a perc roll & cresc to take out the abruptness of the trumpets' quavers. And he marked down the muted trumpets at the 'Jackal' [Act I scene 2, No. 7] to *pp* from *mf* – I was enormously relieved, because it's always been too loud. At the beginning of the Masque scene [Act II scene 1] he took *all* the strings' dims out, saying that it had been an error of judgement, as the wind & brass had the dims.

The most significant change for the 1954 revival was the omission of the Norwich masque scene (Act II scene 1; see Letter 790 n. 1), though the scene was never deleted from the published score of the opera, and its omission was sanctioned only for the revival. The opera thereafter received no full performance in the UK for almost a decade, until Bryan Fairfax conducted a concert performance at the Royal Festival Hall on 22 November 1963 to mark Britten's fiftieth birthday. A new stage production at Sadler's Wells, for which further revisions were made (see PBBG, p. 150), opened on 21 October 1966. The opera finally established itself in the British repertoire following highly successful productions at English National Opera (1984; released on video in 1988) and Opera North (1993–94), and a recording by Welsh National Opera under Sir Charles Mackerras (1993).

II ABSOLUTE SINGLENESS, CLEARNESS AND ROUNDNESS: *THE TURN OF THE SCREW*

AUGUST 1953–SEPTEMBER 1954

PILL HOUSE HOTEL,
BARNSTAPLE,
DEVON.

TELEPHONE:
BARNSTAPLE 2535.

My dear Myfanwy,

So sorry about the pencil but I've left mine behind — Peter's using his.

The second version of the Prologue has just arrived — &, my dear, I am afraid I prefer the first, as the present idea stands I can't do the 2nd version

Britten to Myfanwy Piper, 1 August 1954: Letter 812

CHRONOLOGY 1953–1954

YEAR	EVENTS AND COMPOSITIONS
1953	
August	Experiences an increase in pain in his right arm and is ordered to rest; cancels many of his autumn concerts
5 September	Begins work on arranging the *Symphonic Suite: 'Gloriana'*
15 September	COMPOSITION *Winter Words*
17–23 September	Visits Denmark to record *Sinfonia da Requiem* (Danish State Radio Orchestra) and *A Ceremony of Carols* (Copenhagen Boys' Choir) for Decca
8 October	Harewood House, Leeds Festival: first performance of *Winter Words*; death of Kathleen Ferrier
22 October	Records *Winter Words* for BBC Third Programme (broadcast 28 November 1953)
October	Starts work on *The Turn of the Screw* with librettist Myfanwy Piper
14 November	Royal Opera House, Covent Garden, London: revival of *Peter Grimes*, with Pears as Grimes, directed by John Cranko and conducted by Reginald Goodall
5 December	Death of Noel Mewton-Wood
12 December	Auditions children (including David Hemmings) for the roles of Miles and Flora in *The Turn of the Screw*
14 December	COMPOSITION *Symphonic Suite: 'Gloriana'*
Christmas	Stays with the Prince and Princess of Hesse and the Rhine at Wolfsgarten, until early January 1954; during this visit Britten works on the libretto of *The Turn of the Screw*
1954	
January	Formal announcement by the Sadler's Wells Ballet that Britten and Cranko are collaborating on *The Prince of the Pagodas*

27 January	Re-auditions David Hemmings, who is cast as Miles in *The Turn of the Screw*
29 January	Royal Opera House, Covent Garden, London: revival of *Gloriana* in revised version, conducted by Reginald Goodall
31 January	COMPOSITION *Am stram gram*
4 March	Toynbee Hall Theatre, London: first performance of André Roussin's *Am stram gram* with Britten's incidental music
7 March	First performance (broadcast in BBC Midland Home Service) of *Choral Dances from 'Gloriana'*
16–17 March	Records *Winter Words* with Pears for Decca
23 March	Undergoes a procedure to treat bursitis at University College Hospital, London
30 March	Begins work on the composition draft of *The Turn of the Screw*
May	Publication of a new edition of Eric Walter White's *Benjamin Britten: A Sketch of His Life and Works*
12–20 June	Seventh Aldeburgh Festival: highlights include a celebration of George Crabbe's bicentenary and Janáček's centenary, the premiere of Lennox Berkeley's *A Dinner Engagement*, and Bach's *St John Passion*
17–18 July	Records *Seven Sonnets of Michelangelo* with Pears for Decca
23 July	Completes composition draft of *The Turn of the Screw* and immediately starts scoring the opera
1–6 August	Performs at the Taw and Torridge Festival, Devon
August–September	Rehearsals for *The Turn of the Screw* in Aldeburgh
September	COMPOSITION *The Turn of the Screw*
14 September	Teatro La Fenice, Venice: first performance of *The Turn of the Screw* (also broadcast live by Radio Italia and BBC Third Programme), directed by Basil Coleman and conducted by Britten
23 September	Town Hall, Birmingham: first performance of *Symphonic Suite: 'Gloriana'*

775 To William Plomer

4 CRABBE STREET, ALDEBURGH, SUFFOLK
August 14th 1953

My dear William,

I was very happy to get your nice letter with description of the delightfully scanning new home.[1] I long to see you & it, & hope for a chance to pop down when my enforced rest ends here. The rest is taking no enforcing, I need hardly say since the weather makes tennis, bathing, & of course 'motoring' so attractive! I expect you are having a similar rustication – & only hope you can pop into the sea at times. This weather must make even Charles reconciled to English sea temperatures.

I've been doing a little preparing of Gloriana for the more accessible Vocal score & have one or two queries which I fear I must bore you with ... see next page ...

[new page begins:] (Queries)

i) Stupidly I've set – Act 2. Sc. 2. Lady Essex 'Danger to all about us' (rather than 'is all about us'). Does that matter, or do you want me to reconsider it?[2]

ii) Act 3. Sc. 1. Queen E. . . . . 'The Earl Marshal of England is Himself a rebel' (instead of 'himself is a rebel'). Do you mind that very much – it is much stronger musically.

iii) Act 3. Sc. 2. The City Crier had to sing in performance (to get his words clearer) 'is this day proclaimed TRAITOR' instead of 'a TRAITOR'. Shall that go in the score, do you think?

iv) Shall Harington say at the end my Lord Deputy or my Lord Essex. The second, you may remember, we changed to at the last moment.

v) Last bore – in the cast list, several people have queried Penelope, Lady Rich – suggesting she's already (prematurely) a dowager. I don't know about social matters & of course leave this to you – but could we have Lady Penelope Rich – as I gather on occasions is possible.[3]

Just send a note, my dear, if not too bothersome, saying i) yes, ii) yes ... etc. (or even i) no, ii) no ... !)

We met Lady Cholmondely[4] in King's Lynn, & she very kindly showed us over Houghton the next morning.[5] What a lovely house, & how she loves it. She could scarcely have been more kind to us.

Just off to rub a brass or two[6] – so forgive scribble & haste this comes as always with my love.

and from Peter and to Charles
Yours ever
BEN

P.S. We see the Van der P's from time to time.⁷ Laurens always asks tenderly after you; he is very sweet, but rather sadder & older I feel.

1 In a letter to Britten dated 23 July, Plomer explained that his new address – Rossida, Stonefields, Rustington, Sussex – 'scans like this: - ᴗ ᴗ | - - | - ᴗ ᴗ | - -', and described the house as an 'extremely bijou bungalette'. He continued, 'It is rather like having not *a* but *the* change of life, after many fusty and fussy years in London.'

2 In his reply, dated 18 August, Plomer gently disagreed: 'I'm afraid "Danger *to* all about us" doesn't *quite* make sense there, so if we *could* have "is" instead of "to" . . .'

3 Plomer's reply indicated his agreement to points (ii) – (iv) inclusive, but he had this to say about the matter of Penelope Rich's status:

Cast list. I've never had an expert ruling on the question of Penelope's designation. I like it as it is, with Lady Rich in brackets. I don't agree that it suggests a dowager. After all, we've got 'Frances, Countess of Essex' just above. No dowager she. Short of a consultation with the Earl Marshal of England, who lives only 5 miles away but whom I don't know, I propose a *stet*.

I hope I don't seem *madly* obstinate?

4 Sybil Cholmondeley (1894–1989), a first cousin of Siegfried Sassoon, married the Fifth Marquess of Cholmondeley in 1913, and was largely responsible for the restoration of the Houghton estate, near King's Lynn, Norfolk. She was painted by John Singer Sargent, photographed by Cecil Beaton and among her illustrious guests was Henry James.

Plomer had first met Sybil Cholmondeley during the Second World War, though they did not become friends until after its conclusion; from 1949 until his death in 1973 he spent a week every summer at Houghton, as well as visiting the Cholmondeleys' London home. See also Peter F. Alexander, *William Plomer*, pp. 255–6.

5 Britten's diary shows that he was in King's Lynn on 26 July, where he and Pears had given a recital at the King's Lynn Festival, travelling back to Aldeburgh in time for a meeting on the subject of *The Turn of the Screw* with Myfanwy Piper on 28 July. On 18 August, Plomer wrote, 'Sybil Cholmondeley was delighted with you both.'

6 In his reply, Plomer recounts at some length for Britten's amusement a brass-rubbing anecdote concerning the character of Mrs Shamefoot in Ronald Firbank's *Vainglory* (1915), as she is escorted around the fictional St Dorothy's Cathedral by the Bishop with a view to 'planning her own monument'. She rejects the Bishop's suggestion that her remains be interred in the cathedral precincts on the grounds that, with the inevitable visitations by future generations of brass-rubbers, her husband was not likely to approve of 'persons on all fours, perpetually bending over me'.

7 Laurens Van der Post (1906–1996), Anglo-South African writer and conservationist, a friend of Plomer from his time in South Africa and Japan in the 1920s who made his name as a soldier, explorer and writer. In 1931, Van der Post had been a considerable moral support to Plomer at a time when the latter's sexual problems had compelled him to consider suicide (Alexander, p. 177). In the 1970s Van der Post became a close friend and adviser to the Prince of Wales (to whom he was introduced via mutual Suffolk friends), and was also close to Prime Minister Margaret Thatcher during whose premiership (1979–90) he received a knighthood.

Van der Post and his second wife, Ingaret, owned a cottage in Aldeburgh which they used as a retreat and summer home for over thirty years. They were part of Britten's and Pears's circle of Aldeburgh friends (Van der Post lectured at the 1957 Festival: see Letter 897 n. 6), and often played tennis with them and the Potters. In mixed doubles, Van der Post usually partnered Mary Potter, while Britten partnered Ingaret. Beth Britten recalled (MKBMM, p. 198) that when Britten was distraught on receiving news of Plomer's death in September 1973, Laurens and Ingaret Van der Post were a considerable comfort to him. See also J. D. F. Jones, *Storyteller: The Many Lives of Laurens Van der Post*, pp. 243–5.

776 To Ronald Duncan[1]

4 CRABBE STREET, ALDEBURGH, SUFFOLK

August 25th 1953

My dear Ronnie,

Most unfortunately Peter & I have got to be in London Sept. 3–4 – Doctors,[2] Income Tax, Dentist & happy things like that – perhaps we could meet & then talk a bit about T & T [The Taw and Torridge Festival] and the exciting idea of your Theatre Group.[3] I'm so sorry that it doesn't work for you to come down here, but I'm so full of holiday here that I can't really think or talk sense!

It's being a glorious month of tennis, bathing, brass-rubbing, & carnival that not even a sprained ankle could spoil (I must confess that a little work has gone on under the desk too, but – shush . . . !)[4] I hope eventually to be able to bully you all to coming here. Perhaps next holidays.

Love to you all – will you ring us (Welbeck 4652) if in London Sept. 3rd or 4th?

BEN

1 Rhodesian-born poet, playwright and publisher (1914–1982). His friendship with Britten, partly rooted in their shared pacifist convictions, dated from the mid-1930s. The most significant of the Britten–Duncan collaborations were *This Way to the Tomb* and *The Rape of Lucretia*. See also Letter 116 n. 1 and 1C1/2/3.

2 Britten's pocket diary lists consultations with Dr McCready at 3 p.m. on 3 September, then a Dr Barber on the same evening and again on the following day at 140 Park Lane, and on six further occasions that month.

3 Duncan's letter to Britten, to which Letter 776 is Britten's reply, has not survived. The 'Theatre Group' idea may have been Duncan's plan for a theatrical equivalent to the English Opera Group, realized with the formation of the English Stage Company, on whose Council both he and Lord Harewood sat.

4 Among the leisure activities in Britten's diary for this period are a cricket match against Framlingham (8 August), a 'rodeo party' (15 August), sailing (17 August) and the Aldeburgh Carnival and Regatta (24 August). Michael Tippett was a house guest for four days from the 18th. For further on Britten's recreation at this time, see Letter 777.

777 To Elizabeth Mayer

4 CRABBE STREET, ALDEBURGH, SUFFOLK
August 30th 1953

My dearest Elizabeth,

After all this long time, where does one start! It's difficult to remember even when one last wrote. But there are lots of things that you've heard of us; friends have given you bits of news, I'm sure, & you've maybe read this and that in the papers. Lots of things, good & bad, memorable & completely forgotten, have happened – but, although we've not written, you are still, my dear, so much part of our lives. We so often talk of you, wonder what you would say to so-and-so, wish you were with us. Letters are so feeble, unless one is a writer, that it seems senseless to bother to put pen to paper. I know I have a young secretary[1] now, but I refuse to dictate letters to you, that seems really impertinent! So these long gaps occur. I only hope that they mean as little in our friendship to you as they do to me.

I hope all goes well with all of you; that you & William are happy, and that you see a lot of your dear ones. How is Beata & the children? We so often talk of them, & hope you see them often.

We have had a difficult winter & spring, & now in the high summer, we have been having a lovely rest here in Aldeburgh – No work for a complete month, & although the weather hasn't always been beautiful, we have had a glorious time. The house is always full of friends, it seems, both old & young. Beth has a summer house in Aldeburgh, & we see a lot of her & her family. Bathing, tennis, sailing, motoring – a lot of 'brass rubbing' (making tracings of the incredibly beautiful old memorial brass figures that fill so many Suffolk gothic churches). It is glorious to feel free & well after the hectic months of hard work. As you probably know I gave up all my commitments this last winter to write an opera in commemoration of the Coronation. I enjoyed working on Gloriana enormously. William Plomer is a great man & writer, and a sweet man as well – so easy to work with, & always stimulating. The subject was profound & fascinating. We had wonderful people to work for – John Piper, whose visual sense & gifts were wonderfully suitable for the period. Joan Cross, born for the part of Elizabeth I, both vocally & histrionically. Dearest Peter, with style, temperament, & singing as ever so beautifully, at the moment. And as much collaboration from Covent Garden as they were, in a busy season, able to give.[2] It is difficult to write about the occasion calmly and objectively. Anyhow, can or should one be calm & objective about one's children? The work seems to me the best I have yet done. The performance in the respects I have above mentioned was perfect. The Queen was delighted & flattered by the occasion. The fact that the press failed to be in any way happy or receptive confused us all, but the public as usual, dear things, kept its head & at the end of the run was coming in large numbers & taking the work to its heart. But – there is no point in glossing this fact over – we all feel so kicked around, so bewildered by the venom, that it is difficult to maintain one's balance. I suppose it was ever thus, and it is wonderful that we have so many lovely friends of sense & courage to sustain us. I so wish that you & William could have been with us. I do think you would have been happy with us in 'Gloriana'. Otherwise, apart from the curtailed concerts because of working commitments, things have been the same. The Aldeburgh Festival was lovely – 'Albert Herring' in its real home, lots of lovely concerts (some are now recorded for Decca in a new Aldeburgh Festival series of records); Wystan [Auden] came, & was provoking and brilliant. We had lovely large audiences, but of course lost money – shall do, in fact, until we can build a theatre bigger than the Jubilee Hall.[3] But there are even plans for doing that now . . . building it high above flood level too. The town has recovered quite from the catastrophe of the winter, at least, this part has. The south part, Slaughden quay (if you remember it) is a shambles, & will, I fear remain so. This house is in spots very damp still; a fine day brings out great damp patches, even upstairs, & will continue to do so, I gather for months to come.

    Well, now, the holiday seems over. I go this week to Denmark for some recordings – the Sinfonia, & the Carols with an enchanting boys' choir which made such a success of them in the Festival in 1951.[4] Peter goes to London, to start work & also to complete the furnishing & preparation of our new little house in Chester Gate – just off Regents Park. We left Melbury Road with great regrets; it was simply not big enough, & getting too much for Sophie. But we see them a great deal, & are as ever the best of friends. Erwin[5] hasn't been well (he had a fall & complications) this last winter, & is rather older – but still the same sweet wise dear. Marion is very near her second baby – due in October.[6] She and David[7] (with George coming for odd days & nights) have been spending some time here. He is the most attractive, gay & intelligent boy, & adores the sea & Aldeburgh – & above all adores my car – 'Bim's Car' as he calls it. He seldom misses praying for it before bed. We had the annual cricket match – versus a neighbouring village[8] – & came near to winning. Peter & George excelled themselves – I not so good, but I have an excuse of a bad arm which has been troubling me for 2 years – affecting my conducting as well as my cricket! In fact I may not be able to conduct Peter Grimes at the Garden this November – which will be a disappointment.[9] Happily Peter will sing it, & Joan may – although she now says she is a one-part 'girl' (Gloriana, of course). We have many concerts to do this winter – Peter & I – here, and abroad – our first visit to Germany for recitals (Peter has been for solo dates, & I for operas, but never together).[10] I will let you know when we go, & how it seems – we don't yet know the itinerary. Then I have a new opera to write (the 'Turn of the Screw' for Venice Festival). I have just completed a set of Thomas Hardy songs which we do at Harewood House, as part of the Leeds Festival, next month. Wonderful, touching poems.[11]

Well, my dear, I could go on & on, but unless I stop tonight you won't get it for ages, & you've waited long enough!

My dear – I can't thank you adequately for your letters, & messages, & sweet presents that arrive (thin mints, included!) – but even without them, our dearest Elizabeth is dear in our thoughts, as dear as always – our deepest love – to you & to dear William,

love – Your devoted
BEN

Our love to all of the dear family of course.

1 Jeremy Cullum (1931–1999), Britten's secretary and driver for seventeen and a half years from late 1951. Cullum had attended St Paul's Cathedral Choir School (1941–45) on a scholarship, though because of the war his time was mostly spent evacuated to Truro Cathedral, Cornwall. When Cullum's father became Manager of Barclays Bank at Aldeburgh, and subsequently first Treasurer of the Aldeburgh Festival, Cullum came to Suffolk. Cullum senior sought Britten's advice about his son's career prospects in music and the composer suggested he continue studying piano, organ and music theory as well as acquiring the conventional secretarial skills of shorthand and typing, with a view to pursuing a career in music publishing or administration. From 1951 Cullum functioned as Britten's full-time secretary and driver, as well as acting as his page-turner at his recitals with Pears. He not

only dealt with Britten's business correspondence but was also responsible for the typing of the librettos (and their preliminary drafts) of many of Britten's operas, beginning with *The Turn of the Screw*. Although he was in Britten's employment during the composition of *Gloriana*, Cullum recalled that Elizabeth Sweeting had typed Plomer's libretto for that opera (see Donald Mitchell's interview with Cullum, Horham, 20 August 1998, at BPL). In the late 1960s, as it became clear that the composer would begin to moderate his hitherto frenetic pace of activity, Cullum began to look for a change of career. He and his wife Sylvia purchased (with Britten's assistance) the local music shop in Aldeburgh, which they ran together for twenty years.

In his interview with Mitchell, Cullum provided numerous – and often highly amusing – reminiscences of his long period in the composer's employment. Mitchell drew on three of these memories in the (unpublished) tribute he paid to Cullum at the latter's funeral in February 1999 (copy at BPL):

One memory of Jeremy's was altogether typical of him and the household where he worked. Britten's room [at Crag House], he recalled, faced the sea, 'which was fatal actually because we used to get in the middle of a letter and something would be happening at sea and everything would stop for a quarter of an hour while we watched it. But it was a lovely view. You'd see storms going past, extraordinary. Very sort of *Peter Grimes*-ish.'

But when Jeremy returned to the business in hand he could be marvellously – and drily down to earth. He was telling me once of a recording of one of Britten's choral works [*A Ceremony of Carols*] made without the composer in attendance and of the composer's shock at discovering at least twenty-four errors in the harp part. The recording company enquired nervously what was to be done about the recording and Jeremy was left to reply, which was brief and to the point: 'Re-record it,' he wrote.

One should remember of course that Jeremy had his own musical gifts and expertise. Another reminiscence of his brought to the surface his skills and imperturbability, qualities that were thoroughly exercised when, as he often did, he sat on the platform turning the pages for Britten. On one particular occasion, after a performance of a particularly complex twentieth-century piano trio [Bridge's Piano Trio No. 2 (1929), performed by Britten, Yehudi Menuhin and Maurice Gendron at the 1963 Aldeburgh Festival], Britten turned to him at the end and said: 'Jeremy, there were moments when I thought you were the *only* one who knew where we were.'

Also among Cullum's reminiscences to Mitchell were of his driving the composer to London by a route that would delay for as long as possible their arrival in the metropolis, visits to which the composer so dreaded. As Cullum put it, this involved driving 'sideways through Suffolk'.

In his wide-ranging interview Cullum recalled Britten as 'pretty good, mostly' as an employer, though

he could be a hard taskmaster ... not selfishly but because of the music. I remember having flu once, and you know how awful you feel after you've had flu – so I didn't go back to work for two or three days, until I felt strong enough to work. Ben said, 'When did your temperature go down?' So I said, 'Oh it went down about three days ago.' 'You should have come back to work then.' And that's what he used to do. He used to have the thermometer beside him in his bedroom if he was ill; as soon as his temperature was down to normal he was off.

In reply to questions about Britten's homosexuality, Cullum was matter of fact: 'Ben was too much of a gentleman to show this in normal life.' He further recalled:

He was rather keen on having these young boys to stay and then getting me to drive them in an open car while he sat in the back and had a bit of a cuddle, but whether it ever went further than that, I don't know. I think Peter [Pears] was much more likely to find extra little friends than Ben was. I think Ben was very loyal to Peter, and so how much these little friendships, how far they went, I don't know.

Cullum's interview concluded with memories of Britten's siblings:

Barbara was a sweetie, very nice. *Ever* so nervy – always terrified at the Festival of doing or saying the wrong thing. Beth became an unfortunate lady, I think, when her husband walked out on her. Ben was so worried about her. Ben never really got on well with Robert. I was very fond of Robert but Ben just couldn't see eye to eye with him. I think Robert very easily said just the wrong thing. And Robert married somebody that Ben didn't really get on with, and then of course Robert divorced her, which was even worse, because Ben couldn't stand people who were not loyal. I'm sure that was at the bottom of a lot of things: lack of loyalty. I think Ben liked the status quo . . . musically, it was difficult for him to have somebody upsetting his world.

See also plate 6, Cullum's contribution to PPT, p. 134, and Virginia Caldwell, 'Profile: Jeremy Cullum', *Aldeburgh Soundings* 10 (February 1998).

2 The diplomatic tone of this sentence makes an interesting contrast with Britten's anger at the Royal Opera House's inefficiency that boiled over in Letter 770.

3 The scheme for a purpose-built Festival Theatre was to be announced in 1954. In his 'Foreword' to the 1954 Aldeburgh Festival Programme Book, Lord Harewood wrote about the project:

By the time this Festival Book is in print, we hope that an announcement will have been made about the Festival Theatre which it is planned to build at Aldeburgh. This project has been maturing for two or three years, and the need for something of the sort has been apparent for quite a bit longer. At the moment, the number of people who can attend and thus help to pay for the Festival is entirely governed by the seating capacity of the Jubilee Hall. A bigger Theatre should enable more people to get into the performances, and so reduce the cost of the Festival as a whole.

The new Theatre is to hold between five and six hundred people, which seems to be about the top limit for a Festival of this kind, and, no less important, there is to be an adequately equipped stage, with improved dressing-room accommodation for the artists. The intention is to have the means to 'fly' scenery – the absence of any such arrangement has, in the past, proved a notable disadvantage when adapting scenery made for other theatres. No one need be afraid that what will be built will be too grand to fit in with the character of Aldeburgh and its Festival as we have always known them. It won't – the new Theatre will avoid the elaborate, if for no other reason than that this would cost far too much; but the intention is to design it in such a way that it can be added to as and how experience, and the money available, suggest. A site has already been chosen, well above sea level and with a good view, and has been approved as suitable for its purpose by experts from London and from Aldeburgh itself – in fact, the designs should be far enough advanced by the time of the Festival for a model to be on view for everyone to see.

The design and character of the Festival, as I have tried to emphasize, will not be altered by the building of the new hall. It will, in any case, and however closely it may be associated with the Festival, be administered and run by a separate body, but it is hoped that its existence will make it possible to remove some of the disadvantages which had acted as restrictions in the past, and that programmes will, as a result, be richer than ever before. For example, we shall perhaps no longer have to do without the performances of Bach cantatas in the Church, which were such a valuable (but expensive) feature of early Festivals, and on the improved stage and with the larger orchestra pit, we may, as we should like, be able to perform operas by Mozart.

But these things are not innovations; what we hope is that everyone who has known the Festival since its beginnings in 1948 will see this new venture as a necessary development of what has so far been achieved.

A leaflet outlining the theatre project and including a photograph of the architectural model on display at the Festival Club was produced for the 1954 Festival, and is reproduced in facsimile on p. 253.

A Foreword to the 1955 Festival Programme Book (written by Fidelity Cranbrook, Britten and Pears) lamented that the project had been postponed since 'expansion has had to yield to economy': among the cuts necessitated by the severe 'financial bottleneck' was the loss of the professional General Manager, Elizabeth Sweeting.

See also Letter 780, and Donald Mitchell, 'Introduction: Happy Families?', vol. 3, pp. 36–8.

4 Britten left for Denmark with his sister Beth on 17 September, rehearsed and recorded *Sinfonia da Requiem* with the Danish State Radio Symphony Orchestra on the 18th and 19th, and then tackled *A Ceremony of Carols* with the Copenhagen Boys' Choir and Enid Simon (harp) between the 20th and 22nd.

While in Denmark, Britten wrote Pears an undated letter from the Hotel d'Angleterre, Copenhagen:

Schnappy luncheon with Frank Lee [of Decca], who is quite a dear & got as tiddley as I did! Walked a bit in the afternoon, & had a rehearsal with the boys in the evening, which I must say was heaven – meaning, of course the way they sing. Wöldike has trained them beautifully, & I gulped all the time, naturally. Benny & Leif are still in it – Leif singing the top solos like an angel. After that we had a rather awful meal with the Tuxons (the conductor of the orchestra) & Ormandies [the conductor Eugene Ormandy and his wife] – all rather exaggerated (I eat lobster & died of it, nearly) terrific compliments, & rather boring – Beth stood up to it manfully. She is a dear & really enjoying herself, I think.

Today we have lunch with the Schiøtzs [the Danish tenor Aksel Schiøtz and his wife; Schiøtz had shared the role of Male Chorus in *The Rape of Lucretia* with Pears at Glyndebourne in 1946] and record again in the afternoon. One has to fight to get any free time, they are so madly hospitable.

5 Erwin Stein (1885–1958), Austrian-born conductor, editor, publisher and writer, one of Britten's closest colleagues and musical advisers, with whose family Britten and Pears had shared accommodation in London for a number of years; see also Letter XVIII n. 1 (vol. 3, p. 97).

6 James Lascelles, the Harewoods' second son, was born on 5 October 1953.

7 David Lascelles, the Harewoods' first-born, was three years of age in 1953.

8 The match, against Framlingham, took place on 8 August.

9 In the event, *Peter Grimes* was to be conducted by Reginald Goodall, who had conducted the opera's premiere in 1945: see Letter 779 n. 3. A letter written by Britten to Plomer on 9 November reveals that the composer attended the performance on 14 November.

10 This tour was cancelled because of Britten's bursitis.

11 The Hardy cycle *Winter Words*, which was given its first performance by Pears and Britten at Harewood House on 8 October 1953, as part of the Leeds Festival. The cycle was broadcast on 22 November 1953 on the BBC Third Programme (pre-recorded on 22 October). The songs were dedicated to the Pipers.

At least one of the settings – 'Wagtail and Baby' – was composed in March, shortly after the completion of *Gloriana*, and the drafts of three of the others were dated by the composer: 'At the Railway Station, Upway' (7 September 1953); 'The Little Old Table' (13 September); and 'Proud Songsters' (15 September). Thomas Hardy and the cycle's composition are mentioned in Imogen Holst's diary during this period (IHD, pp. 252–7):

2 SEPTEMBER
Ben was trying fragments over at the piano – perhaps bits of *The Turn of the Screw*? (No: Hardy songs).

5 SEPTEMBER
Ben said there was lots of work to do:– orchestral suite of dances in *Gloriana*, and Hardy songs. [...] He talked about Hardy:– said that *Jude* [Hardy's final novel, *Jude the Obscure*] wasn't unbearable – that he minded the first bit more than the last.

7 SEPTEMBER
When I went in at breakfast he thanked me for the 3 Hardy songs [she had made fair copies], said he'd written another the evening before:– couldn't find the right one to begin with – they were all so depressing. He wanted another philosophical one like

> **LEEDS MUSICAL FESTIVAL**
>
> Morning Concert
> HAREWOOD HOUSE
> (By courtesy of H.R.H. The Princess Royal and The Earl of Harewood)
> Thursday,   October 8th, 1953
>
> **WIND ENSEMBLE**
> of the
> **LONDON SYMPHONY ORCHESTRA**
>
> | | |
> |---|---|
> | EDWARD WALKER | Flute |
> | ROGER LORD | Oboe |
> | SIDNEY FELL | Clarinet |
> | RONALD WALKER | Bassoon |
> | JOHN BURDEN | Horn |
>
> PETER PEARS   BENJAMIN BRITTEN
>
> Kleine Kammermusik, No. 2.   *Hindemith*
>   1. Lustig mässig schnelle viertel
>   2. Walzer: durchweg sehr leise
>   3. Ruhig und einsach achtel
>   4. Schnelle viertel
>   5. Sehr lebhaft
>
> Divertimenti for Flute, Oboe, Clarinet and Bassoon   *Frank Bridge*
>   Prelude, Nocturne, Scherzetto, Bagatelle
>
> Three Short Pieces for Wind Quintet   *Jacques Ibert*
>   Allegro, Andante, Assez Lent, Allegro Scherzando
>
> INTERVAL
>
> Hardy Songs   *Britten*
>   (First Performance)
>
> Quintet in E flat (K452)   *Mozart*

Programme for the first performance of *Winter Words*, entitled 'Hardy Songs' on this occasion

'Before Life and After' [the final song of the cycle]. Peter had suggested calling them 'Winter Words', which is *good* [...] When I'd checked the *Gloriana* pages and mended the splits in the paper I went to the studio to copy out the next 2 Hardy songs.

8 SEPTEMBER
Asked if I could copy the new Hardy, 'At the Railway Station, Upway', and Ben said, 'Yes'. He also said, 'It's rather good.' He asked for the piano part on one stave, as in his sketch, 'as it's really violin music'. I took it back that afternoon:– meant to leave it for him but he came out of the sitting-room just as I arrived. I asked if he'd got another for me, and he said no, he'd been working all the morning trying to do one less depressing, but it wouldn't work, and they'd *just* got to be gloomy. I said it would be all right because of the last one [i.e. 'Before Life and After'], and he agreed.

11 SEPTEMBER

Peter told me that they'd been working at the Hardy songs that morning. I asked him if Ben had found the right poem for the first one yet, and he said no, that he'd been trying to persuade him to set the one about Proud Songsters, and when he'd told him that Finzi had set it, 'that seemed to spur him on a bit'. Going home in the car Ben said, 'The songs sound all right when Peter sings them.'

15 SEPTEMBER

Copied out 'The Little Old Table', and took it round. He'd already written another. 'Proud Songsters'; said Peter had probably wanted 'Down in a forest something stirred'!

16 SEPTEMBER

Copied out 'Proud Songsters', and took it round. They were discussing the order the songs should be in, and said they'd do them in the evening. Went round [. . .] and they sang the whole eight. At first Peter wanted to leave out the 'Wagtail', but Ben included it in the end. They are magnificent, especially both the railway ones ['Midnight on the Great Western' and 'At the Railway Station, Upway'], and the last.

28 SEPTEMBER

He was pleased with the present of G's [Gustav Holst's copy of Hardy's] *Return of the Native*.

Britten's list of possible poems for *Winter Words*, drawn up by the composer in the back of his copy of Hardy's *Collected Poems*. 'Proud Songsters' does not feature in this list.

LETTER 777: AUGUST 1953

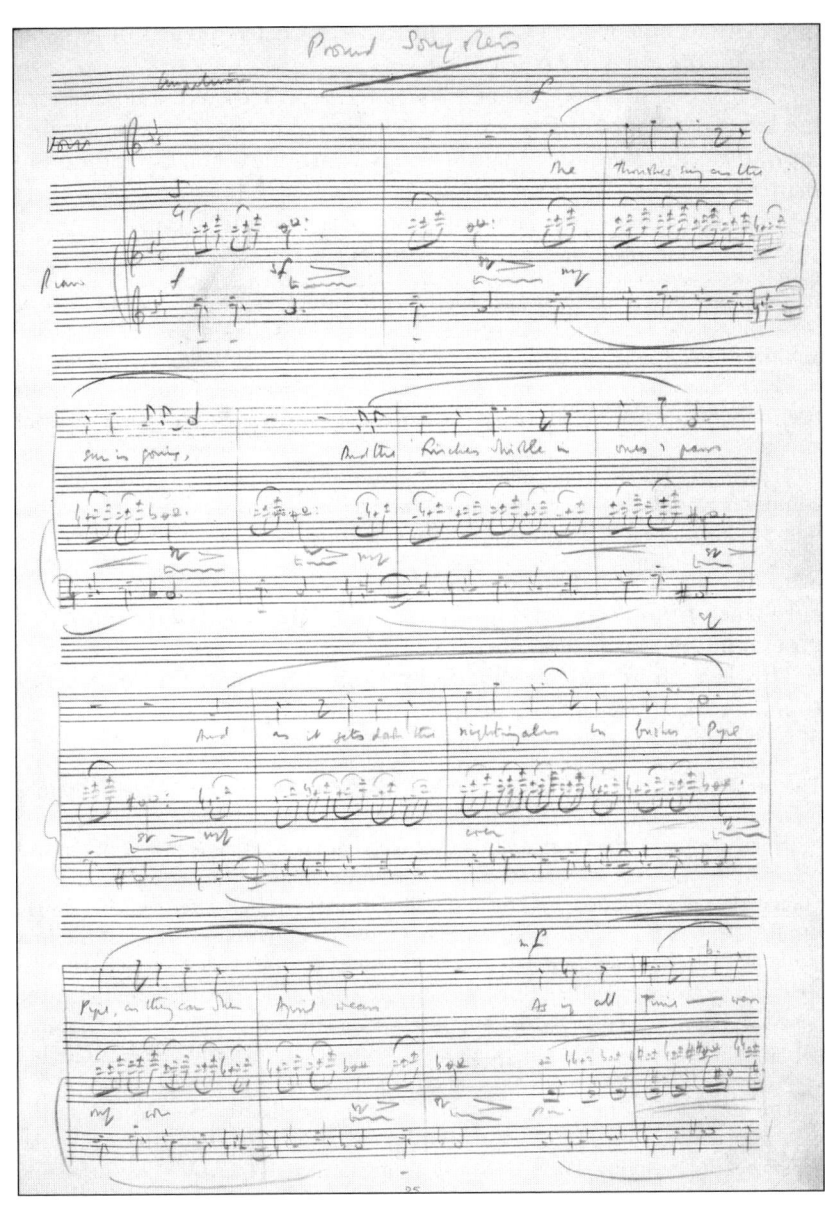

Britten's composition draft of 'Proud Songsters', the sixth song from *Winter Words*, composed 15 September 1953

Two Hardy settings were not included in *Winter Words*: 'If it's ever spring again' and 'The Children and Sir Nameless'. These were posthumously revived in 1983, and in 1994 were included as an appendix to the published score.

The copy of Hardy's *Collected Poems* from which the composer selected the texts for the cycle had been a present from Christopher Isherwood in

1949. The volume includes one of Britten's characteristic lists of possible poems for the songs: see p. 184.

The first performance, part of a shared recital with the Wind Ensemble of the London Symphony Orchestra, was reviewed in *The Times* (9 October 1953); the critic concluded that the songs 'constitute a notable addition to Britten's previous sets of songs and being less recondite than some others make an immediate appeal but still promise lasting satisfaction'.

Ernest Bradbury in the *Yorkshire Post* (9 October 1953) wrote:

In these eight new songs we find an even deeper musical expression than in some of the earlier works [...] The mastery over sounds is here again – see, for example, the accompaniment to the second song, 'Midnight on the Great Western', with its train noises, or the wonderful ending to No. 5 – 'The Choirmaster's Burial' – with its overtones of celestial singing, and the toneless line 'we buried the master without any tune'.

Britten and Hardy – one had not thought of the combination before. But the composer would seem to have realized the sombre, ironic quality, that essential non-pitying sadness in his music, even though not all of it is immediately obvious.

Bradbury mentioned that the 'songs do not form a cycle', a remark he must have taken from Pears, who introduced the songs, and whose annotated programme at BPL includes this same comment.

This last point was also made by Colin Mason in the *Manchester Guardian Weekly* (15 October 1953): 'Britten carefully describes them as a set of songs, not a song-cycle.' Mason continues:

They are in fact very mixed both in subject and style. What is curious about them is the ambiguous relation of these styles to Britten's recent music. It seemed at first hearing as though Britten had looked out and perhaps revised some early songs or had collected together some composed at various times. One at least was characteristic of an earlier phase of his style – the last, called 'Before Life and After', which strongly recalls Ellen's aria in *Peter Grimes*, 'Let her among you without fault cast the first stone'. Another, 'At day close in November' (No. 1) is, in its very English harmonic style, unlike almost anything Britten has written before. The character of his music has always been strongly English, but not its actual idiom. The prelude to *Gloriana* gave a hint, but this song is English in a different way, though still Brittenish in that only he could have devised within that style harmonies so ravishing.

The other songs are all slightly puzzling. They are like the later Britten in the greater austerity of their language, their rejection of the vivid pictorial stroke or the breath-taking harmony. There is word painting in them – the arpeggios suggesting the flick of the bow across the open strings in 'At the Railway Station, Upway, or The Convict and the Boy with the Violin' (No. 7); or the rattle of the train in 'Midnight on the Great Western' (No. 2) – but it is more subdued, more self-denying, less photographic than we are used to.

All this suggests the maturer composer now seeking to do more subtly what he knows he has the facility to do obviously. Yet the harmony seemed not to have the distinctive dissonance of Britten's recent work, which we missed as much as the striking consonance of the earlier ones. Perhaps the set marks a new stage in the evolution of his style.

778 To E. M. Forster
[*Typed by BB*]

4 CRABBE STREET, ALDEBURGH
sunday oct.?,,I(£/
[25 October 1953]

dearest morgan,

THANk you more than i can say for sending the DEVI Book.[1] i haven't quite finished raeding it yet, but what i have raed so far is entrancing, wise, & absorbing. THere's no doubt about it, it comes off magnificently. FRANKLY i was a little worried about it, much as I loved those letters which YOu read out to me here, that a series of letters wouldn't really make a book. But i need not have worried. The little inter_linking bits match the letters perfectly (without being too chatty)? & the result is a beuatifull wohle, most vivid & TOUCHing. Thank you my dear both for doing it & for sending it.

I am sorry to have to inflict this xentric typing on you, but the alternatives are dictateing it or left-handed writing which is as exhausting to do as to read. That is also why you have heard so little of me these last weeks. You see, i have had a horrid complaint boyling up for some time called BURSITIS.[2] All through the summer i have been fighting it, & trying this autunm to go on doing concerts as usual, but the doctors have at last put thier feet down - - - so here i am - - - at least 3 months without my mov - - ing the right-arm, & as far as poss. without strains of any kind (very easy). Incidently the last specialist i saw, and by far the best was called Higgs who loked after your ankel (i hope you liked him as much as he liked you).

I have to go to london eyery week (in the middle of the week) for treatment otherwise i am here trying to work a bit in order not to get depressed! Is there any chance of you spending a weekend with me? All except the 14th of Nov. when i hope to be able to go to Grimes at Cov. garden, would do. Billy [Burrell] has now married Barbara & is very happy, i think, living just across the road. Otherwise aldebrouhg is the same. Would you let me know if you'd like to come?

No news of William [Plomer] recently but i expect you've heard something of him.[3] How's Bob & May?[4] Are thay enstalled in Coventry yet? There is a vague chance that i may be driven over to Cambridge one of these days to see the Cranbrook boys & girls,[5] in which case i'll call on you, but i hope very much that you'll come& see me here before that.

Lots of love & more thanks than i can xpress for sending the lovely Devi.

from
BEN

[*Handwritten*:] Love from Peter

1 Forster's *The Hill of Devi*, his account of two visits he made to the Indian State of Dewas Senior in 1912–13 and 1921, first published by Edward Arnold in 1953. During the second visit, Forster acted as private secretary to the Maharajah of Dewas Senior. The volume consists largely of letters written home to his mother, and other relatives and friends, together with narrative passages commenting on his experiences in India. These visits provided Forster with much material for his final novel, *A Passage to India*.

2 By 27 October, Britten was clearly writing entries in his pocket diary with his left hand. He had continued to see a succession of specialists since September, principally Dr Barber but also a Dr Caldwell (12 October) and a Dr Ratcliffe in Leeds (2, 5, 6 and 9 October). Following Britten's return from Denmark on 23 September, Pears and Britten had given a recital in Nottingham on 1 October prior to their trip to Leeds for the Festival. A projected visit to the Netherlands scheduled for 19 October (Rotterdam, 20 October) had to be cancelled, but Britten and Pears were able to record *Winter Words* for the BBC Third Programme on 22 October.

Britten wrote to William Plomer on 29 October:

I am afraid i am the world's worst typer, but at the moment it is either that or dictating or writing with my left hand (which is a shambles) because my right arm is for the next 3 or 4 months out of action. I have been having pain in it for the last 2 years and now those doctors have jumped on me & said that unless . . . if i dont . . . etc. etc. So here i am, with everything cancelled, hobblxxing up to london Once a week for treatment, otherwise sitting gloomily here in Aldeburgh trying to learn to write music with my clumbsy old left-hand! As you'll see from my signature it looks as if i'm aged 6, but it's getting better, and Imo can DECIPHER it enough to transcribe it for the world to read. It does at least prevent one becoming absolutely suicidal - - having something to do - - but the situation, you can imagine, is pretty blackish: Peter & i should be, for instance, in Holland now, I should be doing Peter Grimes at Covent Garden next month and so on. ALL this induldgent gloom is naturally leading up to something, & that of course is - - can you possibly come and see me sometime? I can guess that you hate leaving the new house, that you are more than ever reticent to waste your time "week-ending"? but it would be a really charitable act. Besides we have a little work to discuss! Gloriana is coming back to the repertoire early next year (good news this) and there are one or two wee things I'd like to chat about with you. There isn't any hurry about it, but i am beginning to forget what you look like!

3 Plomer spent the weekend of 28–29 November with Britten at Aldeburgh, in the company of the Harewoods. It is evident from Plomer's letter of thanks, written on 1 December, that discussions had centred on *The Turn of the Screw*:

I like to think that also there was some usefulness in our discussions – let's say rather constructiveness.

I feel immense curiosity – immensely more than I did a week ago – about the way *The Turn of the Screw* is shaping (I prefer to think of it as *The Tower and the Lake*). I have written a word or two to Myfanwy [Piper] because she said she wanted to know what I thought and partly in the hope of drawing her attention to the task that ought to be, it seems, more in hand than it is.

Plomer had shown himself to be only grudgingly interested in James's novella. Lord Harewood recalls (*The Tongs and the Bones*, p. 139) a later meeting between Britten and Plomer at Aldeburgh after Myfanwy Piper had finished her libretto:

> Ben let me see it, and asked William Plomer to read it too. The next day was beautiful and we went for a walk. When William did not mention the new project, Ben could not contain himself and asked his opinion. Unexpectedly, William said that, having been born and brought up in South Africa where the supernatural was part of everyday life, he could not take Henry James's gingerly northern hauntings truly seriously. His imagination was not engaged, for all his admiration of the technique with which it was put across. Ben was disconcerted, even indignant, and needed much reassurance.

4 Robert (Bob) Buckingham (1904–1974), Forster's close friend, and his wife May (1908–?). See also Letter 658 n. 6. Buckingham retired from the police force in 1951 and embarked on a fresh career as a probation officer, moving to Coventry.

5 Lady Cranbrook's children and their cousins, some of whom by now were studying at Cambridge University. The young Gathorne-Hardys had provided the models for the children in *The Little Sweep*.

779 To Elizabeth Mayer
[*Typed by BB*][1]

4 CRABBE STREET, ALDEBURGH, SUFFOLK
Nov. 21st. 1953
[completed 24 November 1953]

My dearest Elizabeth,

You can't imagine how delighted we were with your sweet letter. Peter and I read it and reread it, and discussed every point. It was so good of you to write so fully, when especially you are working so hard, but it was appreciated to the full![2]

It is kind of you to inquire so tenderly about my silly arm. It is indeed being no end of a bore, not only for myself but also for all the people I must let down. Covent Garden, for instance, where at this very moment I should be conducting Peter Grimes.[3] Happily Goodall,[4] who did the first performance, can again do it, and a wonderful show it is too – perhaps the best all-round cast we have yet had, and a really fine new production by John Cranko (the young choreographer from Sadler's Wells, who also did the dances in Gloriana).[5] Peter, all agree, has grown greatly in stature, and gives a staggering performance. It is interesting to hear the old piece again, quite touching in the memories it brings back. But how one has grown, or at any rate changed!

My medical orders are – not to use the right arm for at least three months. They don't want to do any injections, and for the moment I'm only having short-wave treatments and a tiny bit of manipulation. How odd that Michael [Mayer] also had it, but it is very odd that, since mine was diagnosed as bursitis, almost everyone has had it or knows someone who's had it! Luckily they all seem to have recovered, because at the moment it seems as if I shall never get well, it is taking so long – however I'm getting on well with my left-handed writing, and I get fun in writing to my friends on this machine, with all the silly mistakes!

I'm sending you under another cover one of our new Aldeburgh Festival calendars, in the hopes that it'll give you pleasure, and that if it does you may be able to persuade some of your rich friends to send some to <u>their</u> friends! We are making a big effort to raise money for the Festival, and in order eventually to build our own little opera house, and Mary Potter, a jolly good painter who lives here (the wife of a nice writer Stephen P.) has got together with Piper and Clough,[6] done these nice local lithographs, a printer has made them very cheaply, and we are bombarding all our friends with them! They only cost 5/- (less than a $) and we'll send them post free. Enough of begging – but even if nothing comes of it, I hope it will give you pleasure, perhaps remind you of Aldeburgh, and entice you back again. William did mention the possibility of your coming next year in his note; is that likely? We've got rather nice programmes – Lucretia, a new opera by Lennox Berkeley,[7] St. John Passion, a visit of a swell French choir[8] and Poulenc, the Amadeus quartet[9] (good friends of ours) Crabbe bicentenary celebrations[10] with Morgan Forster, and endless P.P. & B.B. – doesn't that tempt you?

Please give all the family lots of love from both of us. I don't suppose that Muki [Wachstein] remembers those two odd English chaps at all, but they don't forget her! How very sweet she is growing. It is nice that you are getting to know Jennifer,[11] very nice for her, and I hope for you too. Esther, her mother, is rather lonely with her away, but realises that it is the best thing for her.

Since this letter was started your sweet birthday letter has arrived.[12] Thank you so very much for remembering! I had a lovely day, lots of friends around; Barbara and Beth, with Sally and Roguey (grown very nice and bright companions now),[13] and Basil Douglas was there – I'm finishing this in London – and we all talked of you and sent love.

Our London address is now: 5 Chester Gate, NW1, just off Regents Park, a sweet little house that Peter is slowly doing up with exquisite taste. He is upstairs now resting, because he's singing Grimes tonight. Otherwise he

Mary Potter's lithograph for 'June', from the 1954 Aldeburgh Festival calendar

would send lots of particular messages. We both went this morning to dear Kath Ferrier's Memorial service – a crowded Cathedral. A horridly sad occasion.[14]

A great deal of love to dear William. I will really answer his many and welcome notes very soon.

Sorry to bother you, my dear, with this calendar but I think you'll understand!

[*Handwritten:*] Love from

BEN

1 Letter 778 gives an accurate account of the standard of Britten's typing. This and subsequent letters typed by him while suffering from bursitis have been edited for ease of reading.

2 Elizabeth Mayer had written to Britten on 9 November, relating how she had read about his bursitis in the *New York Times*; she had also read about his recent trip to Denmark 'in some paper, where I always pick up news here and there, so that I can follow you with my thoughts'. She continued:

I am delighted about the plot of your new opera – my beloved H.J. [Henry James] and this grand story – and you'll find just the right eerie, beyond-this-world sounds – I still remember the evening in Amityville – we were all sitting together and Wystan [Auden] asked me – did I know *The T. of the S.* – I didn't at that time. Then he turned his almost uncannily penetrating glance on me and recited by heart the last lines from: I caught him, yes. I held him . . . He opened a door for me to H. J.

3 The revival of *Peter Grimes* at Covent Garden opened on 14 November 1953, with Pears in the title role, Sylvia Fisher (Ellen Orford) and Geraint Evans (Balstrode) under Reginald Goodall. There were further performances on 16, 20 and 24 November, and 4 and 9 December.

During the run of *Peter Grimes*, Pears also took part in an English Opera Group-promoted concert at the Royal Festival Hall on 17 November, conducted by Paul Sacher, the programme of which consisted of Stravinsky's Cantata (1952), with Joan Cross and Arda Mandikian, and Walton's *Façade* (with Cross).

4 Reginald Goodall (1905–1990), British conductor. As well as conducting the first performance of *Peter Grimes* in 1945, he shared the first production of *The Rape of Lucretia* in 1946. See also Letters 392 n. 3 and 517 n. 12.

5 Cranko said he had been responsible for 'patching up' Tyrone Guthrie's production. He later commented, rather oddly (quoted in John Percival, *Theatre in My Blood*, p. 97.),

Opera direction, essentially, is the art of making singers look not quite so bad as they really are. There are exceptions, of course, singers who can move and act, but basically the act of singing is so ugly [. . .] In a funny way, *Peter Grimes* is an effective opera to produce, because the movement is supposed to be clumsy and ugly.

6 Prunella Clough (1919–1999), British artist, who, with Mary Potter and John Piper, had contributed four lithographs each to a fund-raising 1954 Aldeburgh Festival calendar. See also Julian Potter, *Mary Potter: A Life of Painting*, p. 58.

7 *A Dinner Engagement*: see Letter 809 n. 1.

8 Britten had hoped to engage the Couraud Choir from Paris, as part of a French weekend at the 1954 Aldeburgh Festival. In the event, they did not come. See also Letter 786.

9 The Amadeus String Quartet – Norbert Brainin (1923–2005), Sigmund Nissel (b. 1922), Peter Schidlof (1922–1987) and Martin Lovett (b. 1927) – was formed at Dartington in 1947 and made its London debut at the Wigmore Hall the following year. The Quartet enjoyed a considerable international reputation for four decades. The Quartet regularly appeared at Aldeburgh, and gave the first performance of Britten's Third String Quartet. See also Christopher Driver's and Anne Inglis's obituary of Norbert Brainin, *Guardian* (11 April 2005), and the supplementary obituary by Philip Reed concerning Brainin's and the Quartet's relationship with Britten, *Guardian* (19 May 2005).

10 The 1954 Aldeburgh Festival celebrated the bicentenary of Crabbe's birth on 16 June. A lunch at the East Suffolk Hotel, at which Forster and Plomer were the speakers, was followed by an excursion to sights and houses associated with Crabbe, ending at Great Glemham House where Plomer read from a selection of Crabbe's writings. The Festival also mounted an exhibition of first editions, manuscripts and letters in Aldeburgh's Moot Hall.

11 Esther Neville-Smith's daughter, who married Max Wachstein, Beata Mayer's ex-husband.

12 Britten celebrated his fortieth birthday on 22 November.

13 Sally and Roguey, Beth's daughters, were currently aged ten and eight respectively.

14 Kathleen Ferrier died on 8 October 1953. Ronald Duncan recalls (RDWB, p. 130):

> Not long after Kathleen Ferrier's triumphant performance in Gluck's *Orfeo* [at Covent Garden] and her rendering of *Das Lied von der Erde*, with Bruno Walter, she was taken ill with cancer. All her friends including Ben and me were miserable and shocked. It was only Kathleen who was brave. She appeared to recover from the first operation. But shortly after, a secondary cancer was diagnosed of a more serious nature. At that time, I was writing a song-cycle for her with Adrian Beecham. In spite of her condition she insisted he played the songs to her. Ben, too, went to her flat frequently to play to her.
>
> Ben and I had not seen much of each other. After Kathleen Ferrier's tragic, wasteful death in October 1953, Neville Cardus brought us together. He approached both

of us with the idea that he should interview us for BBC radio about our memories of Kathleen. Naturally, we both agreed. The only time suitable to the three of us was when we'd all be at the Edinburgh Festival.

In a posthumous tribute to Ferrier ('Three Premieres', pp. 60–61; and PKBM, pp. 123–4), Britten recalled:

One of our most determined plans was to make a long-playing record of this programme [their 1952 recital programme featuring *Canticle II: 'Abraham and Isaac'*]. Several dates were fixed at the studio, but each one had to be cancelled because of new developments of her illness. Finally, the engineers inspected her bedroom – acoustically possible, they said. So we planned to go along one evening to record the Morley canzonets, the wonderful dialogue *Corydon and Mopsa* of Purcell, which we had all loved doing, the folk songs, and *Abraham and Isaac*. This time it seemed that there could be no hitch; although bedridden, her voice had lost nothing; the record was even announced. But another operation, the last, intervened, and in a few months Kathleen was dead.

There seemed to be one more chance, even so, of perpetuating what was for me one of her most delightful performances. We had made a broadcast of this concert, and this had been recorded and repeated several times. Could this not be issued commercially? It seemed it could, with one or two permissions to be obtained (and eagerly granted), and the receipts would go to the Kathleen Ferrier Cancer Fund. But there was another 'but'. At the very last minute it was discovered that the recording had been destroyed 'in the course of events'. Not overmuch imagination here; for quite a time it had been common knowledge how ill Kathleen was, and everything she did had a more than usual significance. Of course, there are many beautiful performances of hers recorded for our delight, but it is my own special selfish grief that none of my own music is among them – music that she sang with her own inimitable warmth, simplicity, and devoted care, as indeed she sang everything – as if it were the most important in the world.

780 To Eric Walter White
[*Typed*]

4 CRABBE STREET, ALDEBURGH
21st November, 1953

My dear Eric,

Your letters both personal and business have been received with pleasure, as well as the delightful Bealings Bells and Aldeburgh Ghost.[1] I think the latter could now be honoured with a poem too don't you think, although I admit that the subject is not quite so romantic as the Bealings one. I was sorry to see, by the way, that the Aldeburgh chap was such a sceptic.

Thank you for your kind and sympathetic remarks about the bursitis. I am sure that this rest will clear it up, and all one needs is a great deal of patience – easier said than done, actually. By the way I think I feel quite strong enough to read the proofs of your new book, in fact I am sure it would divert me not a little. So please get Boosey's to send them to me.[2]

LETTER 780: NOVEMBER 1953 195

In answer to your business letter (incidentally I suppose this part of the letter should be sent to St. James's Square, so please do not bother to read it in Cholmley Gardens but carry it with you next time you go to work) we are going ahead with the <u>plans</u> of the art centre which include either buying or first refusal of the site. I gathered that your advice was to get these two points cleared before we start to raise any money. Apropos your comments on the latter point, we shall certainly include a sum for maintenance, but I am not so frightened about this as you seem to be. For one thing I rather gathered from our talk at lunch the other day that whereas the Arts Council probably cannot help us to find the money to build the centre, that the Council could probably help us run it when it exists. Besides we would plan to use the centre on many other occasions than the Festival. We would try in the holiday seasons, when there is a large unemployed public, to run performances of opera, ballet and straight theatre, such as a week or so at Christmas, Easter and Whitsun, and a month or more in the summer. Then we hope to let it for periods to the Opera School[3] and other educational groups. All these functions will contribute to the management expenses of the theatre. We all think that this sounds sense.

I am in London for most of next week for treatments, etc., and will ring you and perhaps we can arrange a meeting to discuss our plans more thoroughly.

With best wishes,
Yours ever,
BEN B

1 White wrote to Britten on 8 November 1953:

I've bought *Bealing Bells* [*An Account of the Mysterious Ringing of Bells at Great Bealings, Suffolk in 1834*, by Major Edward Moor], and it turns out to be an account of some mysterious bell-ringings (Victorian household bells, not church bells) that took place at Great Bealings [a village near Ipswich] in 1834. The book was published at Woodbridge in 1841 and sold 'for the Benefit of the New Church'. It contains 'relations of farther unaccountable occurrences in various places' including Aldborough. I will type out the Aldborough letter for you on a separate sheet [which has not survived at BPL], for I know you are always interested in Aldeburgh *curiosa*! I wish I could write a poem on Bealings Bells à la Betjeman!

White's poem 'Bealing Bells' was included in his 1962 collection, *A Tarot Deal and other poems*, p. 28, Britten's and Pears's copy of which is in BPL.

2 Britten thanked White for his efforts, having received the proofs of the new edition of White's *Benjamin Britten: A Sketch of His Life and Works* from Anthony Gishford, in a letter dated 2 December. This letter contains much of interest, and shows the care and appreciation with which Britten checked White's material:

I must say I take my hat off to you for your incredibly industrious research. It is really rather frightening that nothing I do seems to be a secret from you! I am very glad you have made the book into this present shape. The chapters on the operas contain valuable things, and I was especially grateful for your sympathetic writing on Gloriana. In the excellent first part of the book your research is so detailed and accurate that I cannot forbear to make one or two comments here which you can use or not as you choose. But I suspect you will want to use them because your love of accuracy is so terrifyingly great.

Page 2. My mother was never a professional singer, only a keen amateur, one with a sweet voice. I did not learn the viola until I was ten or eleven, and actually my piano lessons did not start until I was about seven. I believe I started strumming like any other kid as soon as I could walk, and the composing business is supposed to have started as you say when I was about five.

Page 3. I did not join the G.P.O. Film Unit till 1935. I have never heard of the film "Cable ship" and presume that it is a slip of Basil Wright's or that the film, if it contained my music, was later than 1933.

Page 5. Music for "On the Frontier" [the play by Auden and Isherwood] seems to be lost, but as far as I can remember the scoring also contained parts for two trumpets.

Page 7. I seem to remember writing incidental music for broadcasts when I was in America, for Columbia broadcasts I think. One was certainly a remarkable monologue by Auden for Dame May Whitty [*The Dark Valley*]; the other I believe was for "The Rocking Horse Winner", but I am not certain and it does not seem of major importance. Peter's and my gruelling journey back from America was not in a crowded troopship but in a small Swedish cargo boat. Apropos this, an exciting sidelight on my mental struggle as to whether to stay in America or return to England was that this struggle was echoed by a physical illness, and as you can imagine Auden with his Freudian leanings was very interested! I was in effect ill with a streptococcus infection for the whole of 1940 and I went out in 1941 to recuperate. As I got well the decision to come back to Europe seemed crystal clear.

Page 9. One tiny point you have overlooked. You say here "the Ceremony of Carols written early in 1942" which is actually a repeat of information on the previous page. Incidentally it would be nice if you could mention Walter Hussey in connection with St. Matthews, Northampton, since if ever there were a case of one person being responsible for an idea [*Rejoice in the Lamb*] this is it.

These are my only comments on the first half of the book, and I have nothing to say about the second half as that is a case of your own opinions [...]

I am sending these proofs back to you. Perhaps that is not right but it is in case you have not got a copy by you to refer my comments to. Thank you very much again for taking so much trouble over the book; I can well imagine the time and energy it must have taken [...]

P.S. Tony Gishford queries two comments or two remarks on Gloriana you have made, and with which I must say I agree. On page 44 I do not feel that the comment 'platitudinous bathos' is quite just for Cecil's song of Government. Perhaps when it is more convincingly sung it may seem that the qualities are control and wisdom with a sly sense of humour – or rather I hope so. Page 45. Could you not find something a bit more dramatic for "helps the Queen to make up her mind". Technically you are accurate, but perhaps something stronger could describe the climax of the opera.

3 The Opera Studio (later National Opera School) founded in 1948 by Joan Cross and Anne Wood, which, for a time, operated under the aegis of the English Opera Group (see Letter 683 n. 4). Britten's outline proposal for the Festival Theatre at Aldeburgh foreshadows the pattern of performing and educational activities (for example, the Britten–Pears School for Advanced Musical Studies) at Snape Maltings during the early 1970s.

781 To Mary Behrend[1]
[*Typed*]

4 CRABBE STREET, ALDEBURGH, SUFFOLK
1st December, 1953

My dear Mary,

Thank you so much for your nice letter and for sending the Busch book.[2] He was certainly a remarkable musician and it is nice that he has jotted down so many interesting things for us to read. His political behaviour in Germany seems to have been courageous and clear sighted. I am sorry he did not live to bring the memoirs up to date because, selfishly, that is the period that I came into his life a little. You know, perhaps, that he conducted quite a few performances of my works, notably the "Sinfonia da Requiem", which he liked very much, and one of the first performances in America of the "Spring Symphony".

I was glad that your reactions to "Peter Grimes" were as strong as ever. I feel that the excellence of the production and performance at Covent Garden has something to do with it now. I hope when you rehear "Gloriana" after Christmas that some of your objections to the character of Essex will be removed. But make him into the traditional hero, or his relations with the Queen more simple and direct, we cannot. This part of the story must always remain elusive, but to me always fascinating.

Please give my love to Bow. I hope that he is well, and you too.

With much love and thanks,
Yours ever,
BEN

1 Mary Behrend (1883–1977) and her husband John Louis (Bow) Behrend (1881–1972) had been friends of Britten and Pears since the mid-1930s. They were well known as patrons of the arts, in particular of the work of Stanley Spencer, and generous supporters of the Aldeburgh Festival and the English Opera Group. Britten dedicated his Second String Quartet to Mary

Behrend in 1945. See also Diary for 14 March 1937, n. 1, IC1/2/3, and their son George's autobiography, *An Unexpected Life.*

2 The German conductor Fritz Busch's memoir, *Pages From a Musician's Life*, published in an English translation by Marjorie Strachey by the Hogarth Press in 1953; the book was originally published in 1949 as *Aus dem Leben eines Musikers.*

Busch (1890–1951) came from a family of musicians; his brother, Adolf (1891–1952), was a celebrated violinist and chamber musician. While serving as Music Director at the Dresden Staatsoper, where he gave notable premieres of operas by Strauss, Busoni and Weill in the 1920s, Busch first collaborated with the director Carl Ebert, with whom he worked closely at Glyndebourne both before and after the Second World War. With his son-in-law Martial Singher as soloist, Busch conducted the premiere of the orchestrations of Britten's French Folksong Arrangements in Chicago in December 1948 (see Letter 520 n. 1).

782   To Ralph Downes[1]
[*Typed*]

4 CRABBE STREET, ALDEBURGH, SUFFOLK
2nd December, 1953

My dear Ralph,

The enclosed explains itself, and I only want to add to you personally how deeply sorry I am that I cannot do the piece for you, but I hope it will only be [a] postponement, and that one day we may work on the concerto together.[2]

With every good wish,
Yours ever,
BEN B

1 British organist (1904–1993), who appeared in every Aldeburgh Festival during Britten's lifetime. He had been responsible for the innovative design of the new organ for the Royal Festival Hall. See also Letter 606 n. 1 and Charlotte Mullins, *A Festival on the River: The Story of the Southbank Centre*, p. 75.

2 Britten had agreed to compose an organ concerto to mark the installation of the new organ at the Festival Hall, and enclosed with this letter a copy of the official apology he had sent to Mr T. C. Bean at the Hall on 2 December when it became apparent that he would no longer be able to fulfil the commission:

My left-handed writing has been improving and I was sincerely hoping that I should be able to manage the organ concerto, but it now seems that a general rest is necessary as well as resting the arm, and I must now give up the idea of writing the concerto in time for March 24th. I know what this means to you especially as you were so kind [as] to change the date of the opening of the organ in order that I could write this piece, and I can only apologise very deeply for the great inconvenience that I know this decision will cause. I still intend some day to write a concerto specially for this organ if you will allow me, but I am afraid that at the moment I dare not even suggest a date since all my writing plans are thrown into confusion by my present illness.

I am sending a copy of this letter to Ralph Downes who will, I hope, understand what a disappointment it is for me not to be able [to] christen what will be I am sure a wonderful instrument.

No manuscript sketches of the projected organ concerto survive at BPL.

Britten wrote to his sister Barbara on 3 December to apologize for his decision not to spend Christmas in the UK:

I'm afraid I've decided after all to go off to Germany for a few weeks, because the horrid old arm won't get any better, and I feel that only a complete rest will do the trick. [. . .] I've decided to go to the Hesses, because there it is so comfortable, no trouble, and I can go on having my treatments so easily locally.

At the Hesses's home, Schloss Wolfsgarten, Britten began planning *The Turn of the Screw* in earnest, reporting to Myfanwy Piper on 3 January 1954 that he had been 'thinking & thinking about Act I & having lots of ideas' (see Letter 784).

783 To Erwin Stein
[*Typed*]

WOLFSGARTEN, EGELSBACH/HESSEN

Jan. 1st, 1954

My dear Erwin,

First of all, a very happy New Year to both you and Sophie. I hope it'll be a fruitful and quiet one – uneventful in the best sense of the word! I hope there'll be more wise and calm books, like the last,[1] forthcoming from you to give us pleasure. I wonder if you were both up in Harewood for the celebrations, as we were last year? or did you have to come back after the christening?[2] We of course talked a great deal about you all, your ears must have burnt. There is so much to tell you about that I don't see how I can start. It has all been so interesting, and full of new experiences and atmospheres – a world in every sense alien to us but bound to us by the warmth and bigness of Peg and Lu.[3] We have met so many people, familiar to you personally or by reputation. It is a curious, circumscribed, little world, this international Royal clan – there were, for instance, seven princes to the family Xmas dinner! Some are fascinating, Barbara of Prussia,[4] and Francis of Bavaria,[5] some dull or just effete(?). The stimmung of Xmas is so different too. I accompanied Peg to many feiers(?) and got more and more nauseated by "stiller nacht" & "o du fröhlicher"![6] but the seriousness and lack of commercialism was moving, tho' it is possible to confuse seriousness with slop. So much more to tell you, but it must wait till we meet. I think I'll be coming back to England next week, and to London the week after. I've been having treatment here, much the same as in London, but there is not much to report in progress, except for feeling better for the change.

    Thank you for sending Gloriana,[7] which looks lovely, and I've not found too many mis-prints!, and for your nice letter. I still feel it is risky to engrave the suite or the dances,[8] before we have heard them. After all they may not sound good, people may hate them even if we don't, they may be too long etc. etc. I know that for Roth[9] it is only a matter of salvaging something from the wreck, but why spend so much on a rear-guard action?[10] We can of course talk it over when I'm back, but my strong feeling now is to use Imo's score[11] until we see how they go. Nicht wahr? In the meantime I've been looking through the opera itself with interest. There are one or two bits which show signs of haste, notably Act 2 Sc. 1, and my old enemy Act 3 Sc. 2, but what I'm pleased with, and what has got people down, is the simplicity and directness, the fewness of the notes. This has been confused with thinness of invention.[12] Time will show if they are right about this, but from a point of view of attitude or technique I'm sure I'm right, for this work, at any rate. There is also room in the world for Lulu.[13]

    I long to hear about the way James took the Christening. Were you proxy for any of the absentees? I hope someone made sense of the dotty wire [i.e. telegram] that Lu and Peter sent, with all our help.

    Lots of love from Wolfsgarten to you both, tell Sophie that I've got lots of Darmstadt gossip for her. No news yet from Erwin, but he know where I'm staying if he wants anything.

Yours ever,
BEN

1 *Orpheus in New Guises*, published by Rockliff in 1953, which includes a chapter on Britten's music. Stein had given Britten a copy on his birthday, inscribing it: 'For Ben/with all my love/Erwin/22nd November 1953/Dear S. Cecilia,/I hope this book is no/heresy.'

2 Of James Lascelles, the second child of the Earl and Countess of Harewood.

3 Prince Ludwig of Hesse and the Rhine (1908–1968), German artist, art historian, poet and translator, head of the House of Hesse, and his British wife, Princess Margaret (1913–1997), who had been introduced to Britten and Pears by Lord Harewood in 1952.

Prince Ludwig and the Hon. Margaret Campell Geddes met while on holiday in Bavaria, he subsequently arranging a position as Third Secretary in the German Embassy in London in order to see more of her. Their wedding in 1937 was marred by tragedy: first, the marriage was postponed owing to the death of Prince Ludwig's father; second, four days before the re-arranged wedding in London, a plane crash near Ostend killed Prince Ludwig's mother, his brother George and his pregnant wife and their two young sons, the best man and two others, as they travelled to London. The wedding went ahead quietly (in mourning dress), and the Hesses returned immediately to Wolfsgarten for the ceremonial funeral. During the Second World War Prince Ludwig never became a member of the Nazi Party, though he was a reserve officer in the Wehrmacht despite being considered politically unreliable. In 1943, like all German princes, he was expelled from the army, and for the remainder of the war he and Princess Margaret were held under house arrest at Wolfsgarten, where she was able to undertake Red Cross work and house refugees.

Post-war, the Hesses did much to re-establish links between the British Royal Family and their German relatives (the Duke of Edinburgh was one of Prince Ludwig's relations). They made Wolfsgarten an important cultural and artistic centre, and the Hesses befriended many writers, artists and composers, as well as politicians. Hans Werner Henze was a notable recipient of their patronage, and it was they who introduced the young German composer to Britten and Pears in the mid-1950s.

'Lu' and 'Peg' became intimate friends of Britten and Pears from this period, and were staunch supporters of the Aldeburgh Festival from 1952 until the end of their lives. In 1959 Princess Margaret founded the Hesse Students Scheme, through which young people received free tickets to Aldeburgh Festival concerts in exchange for practical help; she endowed an annual lecture in memory of her husband in 1984, and became President of the Aldeburgh Foundation two years later.

Britten and Pears often stayed with the Hesses at their home at the Hesse family 'hunting lodge', Wolfsgarten, near Darmstadt (for example, in January 1971 Britten began to compose *Death in Venice* there), and the Hesses accompanied Britten and Pears as congenial travelling companions on several occasions, beginning with the Far East trip in 1956, during which Prince Ludwig kept a diary, privately published as *Ausflug Ost 1956* (see Part IV), and Italy in 1957 (see Letter 894).

Under the pseudonym Ludwig Landgraf, Prince Ludwig provided German singing translations for several Britten works, including *The Turn of the Screw* (see also Letter 906), *Noye's Fludde, Nocturne, War Requiem* (with Dietrich Fischer-Dieskau), *Curlew River* and *The Burning Fiery Furnace*. Britten dedicated his *Songs from the Chinese* to the Hesses, and his *Sechs Hölderlin Fragmente* to Prince Ludwig on the occasion of his fiftieth birthday. According to Christopher Headington, it was Princess Margaret of Hesse and the Rhine who mentioned to the Queen Mother Britten's depressed state in 1975, suggesting that a royal commission might well stimulate him; at this prompting the Queen invited Britten to compose *A Birthday Hansel* to celebrate her mother's seventy-fifth birthday in 1975 (see CHPP, p. 265).

See also Princess Margaret's *Dear Friends 1956–1986*, compiled by Edward Mace, and Virginia Caldwell, 'Profile: The Princess of Hesse and the Rhine', *Aldeburgh Soundings* (autumn 1986); obituaries of Prince Ludwig in *The Times* (1 June 1968), and of Princess Margaret by Philip Mansel, *Independent* (30 January 1997), *The Times* (31 January 1997), *Daily Telegraph* (1 February 1997) and by Edward Mace, *Guardian* (7 February 1997), and tributes by Marion Thorpe and Hans Werner Henze in the 1997 Aldeburgh Festival Programme Book.

4 Princess Barbara Irene Adelheid Viktoria Elisabeth Bathildis of Prussia (1930–1994).

5 Franz Bonaventura Adalbert Maria Herzog von Bayern, Duke of Bavaria (b. 1933), the senior co-heir-general of Charles I of England. During the Second World War the Wittelsbach family had been opposed to the Nazi regime and had emigrated to Hungary. After the occupation of Hungary, members of the family, including the eleven-year-old Franz, were arrested and sent to concentration camps, among them Oranienburg and Dachau.

6 As with the 'Aldeburgh-Deutsch' that Britten and the Russian cellist Mstislav Rostropovich employed in the 1960s as a means of communication, the German words and phrases in this letter to the Austrian-born Stein are not always correctly used. *Die Stimmung*: 'mood'; *die Feier*): 'celebration' or 'party' (the plural form is *die Feiern*; *Stille Nacht*: 'Silent Night', the first words of Franz Gruber's well-known Christmas carol; *O du fröhlicher!*: 'O how joyfully!' the opening words of the popular, early nineteenth-century German Christmas carol. In the next paragraph, Britten uses German again – *Nicht wahr?*: in this context, 'shan't we?'

7 Britten refers here to the second of the two editions of the vocal score of the opera, first published in 1953, in which the errors and misprints that had marred the first special edition of 100 copies printed on handmade paper and bound in real parchment, signed by both composer and librettist, were rectified; see PBBG, p. 116.

8 The two most significant concert pieces devised from the opera were the *Symphonic Suite: 'Gloriana'* and the *Choral Dances form 'Gloriana'*. The *Symphonic Suite*, comprising four movements (1 *The Tournament*; 2 *The Lute Song*; 3 *The Courtly Dances*; 4 *Gloriana moritura*), was first performed on 23 September 1954, in Birmingham, with Pears (the original Essex) as soloist and the City of Birmingham Symphony Orchestra conducted by Rudolf Schwarz. (Schwarz and his orchestra had rehearsed the suite in the composer's presence on 14 April 1954.) The titles of the movements were

suggested by Plomer. His title for the last movement, *Gloriana moritura*, was surely a felicitous one, though Britten, fearful as ever of pomp and circumstance, felt he needed a 'little time' to consider it before accepting it. The *Choral Dances from 'Gloriana'*, derived from Act II scene 1, were first performed on 7 March 1954, broadcast by the BBC Midland Home Service, with the BBC Midland Chorus conducted by John Lowe (see also Letter 524 n. 7).

Other concert pieces adapted from the opera include the *Second Lute Song of the Earl of Essex* for voice and piano (arranged by Imogen Holst), *Five Courtly Dances from 'Gloriana'* for school orchestra (arranged by David Stone) and Julian Bream's unpublished arrangement of the *Courtly Dances* for the Julian Bream Consort.

9 Dr Ernst Roth (1896–1971), British music publisher of Czech birth, who joined Boosey & Hawkes in 1938 as assistant to Ralph Hawkes. In 1949 he was appointed Managing Director, joined the Board the following year and later became Chairman. See also his autobiography, *The Business of Music: Reflections of a Music Publisher*, and Helen Wallace, *Boosey & Hawkes: The Publishing Story*, pp. 20–155 *passim*. Wallace (p. 20) describes Roth as 'the most consummate publishing professional the company ever employed'. See Letters 450 n. 1 and 527 n. 4, and 1C3.

10 Roth and Britten had already clashed over *Gloriana* in August 1953 when the proposed performances at La Scala, Milan, fell through. Roth wrote to the composer (10 August 1953) in exceptionally strong terms:

It is difficult for me in the present circumstances to speak of disappointment and regret. You have been told, I know, that I am not interested in *Gloriana* and this has not been contradicted by those of your friends who know better. The truth is that I am much concerned about *Gloriana*, apparently much more than those of your friends whose advice is more important and more welcome to you than mine. If you were willing to compare the facts with what you are told, I would not have to write to you what I hate even to think and you and I might be happier just now. In fact, I was hoping, particularly after our meeting in Aldeburgh last October, that a better understanding between us would develop. However, I do not seem to have an adequate weapon against persistent vilifications and your readiness to listen to them. Needless to say how profoundly disappointed I am.

Obviously I must leave future developments entirely to you; but, please, remember that I am always at your disposal (though not at the disposal of go-betweens) if you wish to make use of my advice and of my experience. I still feel it would be useful if we would meet after my return, sometime in September, and talk things over 'sine ira et studio' [without anger or prejudice]. Perhaps you let me know if you feel the same.

See also Letter 824 n. 1.

11 Britten refers here to a copyist's score made by Imogen Holst, which would have been kept up to date with the composer's latest revisions.

12   These last comments of Britten continued to resonate, and indeed resurfaced most conspicuously in a further letter to Stein dated 16 February 1954:

> I am so glad that Keller was so enthusiastic about them [the Hardy songs, *Winter Words*]. We did them in Dorchester, but I cannot pretend that the audience made much of them [but see Letter 793 n. 1]. I think it was Mitchell who made the observation that the easier my music gets the more difficult it is to understand it! I feel both 'Gloriana' and 'Winter Words' bear this out. But I am not going to be silly about the publication [of *Winter Words*] and will certainly let you have the work very soon.

Donald Mitchell cannot now remember making any such 'observation', either in written or spoken form. However, he does recall a comment made to him by Britten during one of the rehearsals for the *Gloriana* (either in 1953 or 1954). He was sitting close to the pit and at some moment when clearly something had gone awry, Britten walked past him, pausing only to say, 'The easier [or simpler] I try to make my music, the more difficult, it seems, it becomes to perform [or play].' (The parentheses take care of any possible variants.)

How curious it is to find Britten not only rewriting the message but misidentifying the messenger. The result, however, was his committing to paper (in two letters to Stein) some of the creative preoccupations and anxieties generated by the composition of *Gloriana*. Britten was rarely given to making statements about his own music, or his own aesthetic, for which reason his erroneous attribution to Mitchell of an observation that had in fact begun its life as something he himself had said proved to be the enabler that allowed him to say something important and revealing about his creative agenda, along with an assessment of the compositional ambitions and ideas involved: 'simplicity and directness, the fewness of the notes'. These were goals that, for all the complexity and diversity of the works Britten composed in the decades preceding his death, were never abandoned. As he was to write in 'Britten Looking Back', *Sunday Telegraph* (17 November 1963; PKBM, p. 250–54), an article published on the occasion of his fiftieth birthday, 'I haven't yet achieved the simplicity I should like in my music, and I am enormously aware that I haven't yet come up to the technical standards [Frank] Bridge set me.'

13   Britten refers here to Berg's opera, *Lulu*, which Berg left unfinished at his death in 1935. (Stein had been responsible for the piano vocal score during his time at Universal Edition in Vienna.) What Britten certainly had in mind was the complexity of Berg's score and complication of his compositional processes as compared with his own current preoccupations.

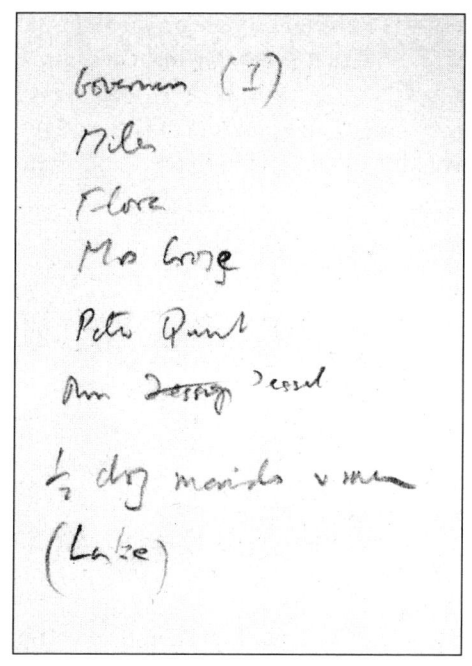

Britten's handwritten list of characters for *The Turn of the Screw*,
which he inscribed in his copy of Henry James's novella

784 To Myfanwy Piper
[*Handwritten, left-handed*]

WOLFSGARTEN, EGELSBACH/HESSEN
Jan. 3rd [1954]

My dear Myfanwy,
 A Happy New Year to you all! Personally I am rather glad to see the back of 1953, although it did have some good things about it, I suppose.
 I'm having a lovely time here; a wonderfully lazy time, but interesting things to do, if one is inclined. The German Xmas was very romantic; very holy & serious, but inclined to be a bit sloppy & "heilige Nacht".[1] But I won't strain your eyes or your patience by describing it now – it must wait till we meet, which I hope will be soon. I come back to England this week (6th or 7th) & will ring you up at once, & hope you aren't already gone to your Welsh fastness.[2] I long to see what you've been doing – hope it's a lot!![3] I've been thinking & thinking about Act I & having lots of ideas. I've got one idea about the school-room scene, which you may not like, but which we must discuss soon, as it affects the structure of the music.[4]
 I wonder if you have had a shot at the Ghosts' dialogue,[5] or have left it?

I know it's a corker, but I'm certain we are on the right track so far.

I hope John is well, & ideas & paint flowing. Give him lots of love & the kiddies too, of course.

I saw the ugliest opera ever in Frankfurt the other night, with a revolving stage, which wouldn't or couldn't keep still! Don't let's have any of that – – !!

Love from
BEN

1 Another instance of Britten's German; *heilige Nacht*: 'Holy Night', another phrase from the carol 'Silent Night'.

2 The Pipers' cottage in Wales.

3 Piper was drafting the libretto of *The Turn of the Screw*.

4 Britten's idea about the schoolroom scene (Act I scene 6) cannot be identified with absolute certainty, but it probably concerned Miles's 'Malo' song and/or the rhymed verse of twenty-nine nouns, beginning 'Amnis, axis caulis, collis' at the start of the scene.

It is evident from one of Myfanwy Piper's notebooks (at BPL) containing an early draft 'Synopsis of Scenes' that hers and Britten's dramaturgy for this scene incorporated the possibility of a specific song for Miles (though not yet the 'Malo' song) and its possible reprise in the opera's final scene:

Act I scene 6. Governess, Miles, Flora.
Interior, school-room, with blackboard or table.
A music lesson, singing – I should like if possible to get Miles' fool song in here. He could have written it and she could make them sing it in parts or canon. She could make clear that she thinks it an odd little verse but that she has so much respect for his inventions and brightness that she encourages it.

Later in the same notebook, in the entry for Act II scene 8 (the final scene of the opera), she writes:

I'd like if possible some sort of repetition of the fool song. I think it is the only good thing I have written so far and cling to it a bit but because it expresses for me the particular odd mixture [of] old-fashioned imaginativeness, bible-knowledge and poetry that such a small boy might have had. But there easily might be something far better. The things one clings to are usually terrible stumbling blocks.

The text of Miles's 'fool song' appears in Piper's draft libretto (BPL):

O say I am a fool
And a fool is a knave
O say I am a fool
And a fool is not brave
But I am a Daniel and a Lion too
And so I say beware to you
Beware of the brave knave
Of the only brave knave.

Interestingly, Piper's handwritten complete draft libretto of *The Turn of the Screw* contains no text for Act I scene 6 'The Lesson', which suggests that there was some uncertainty about this scene.

In the final version of the libretto, Miles's lesson is not a music lesson as originally planned but a Latin lesson. As Myfanwy Piper later wrote (DHOBB, p. 10):

[Britten] asked that Miles should have a short, very simple song, the tune and echoes of which could steer him through the work. Long before the many attempts to find the right words had been written and discarded, and Britten himself had decided to use the Malo rhyme from an old-fashioned Latin grammar that an aunt of mine produced, I conceived the idea that the song, hitherto only sung in Miles's childish voice, should be sung in the mature and tragic accents of the Governess, when she discovers that he is dead.

Andrew Plant has observed that no Latin grammar containing the rhyme has yet come to light, though he suggests it was most probably H. T. Riley's 1856 *Dictionary of Latin Quotations, Proverbs, Maxims, and Mottos* (see Jane Mackay, *The Turn of the Screw: Visual Responses to Britten's Opera*, with commentary by Andrew Plant, p. 17), further noting the apposite alteration in the third line from '*Malo*, than a wicked man' to '*Malo*, than a naughty boy' in Britten's opera. See also Christopher Stray, 'A Preference for Naughty Boys in Apple Trees', in *Ad Familiares* 20 (spring 2001), pp. 6–7.

The list of Latin nouns at the start of the scene – 'Many nouns in *is* we find/To the masculine are assigned' – is not present in Myfanwy Piper's libretto drafts, though on the verso of one folio there is the following: 'Come now – Latin – Miles/*Mensa*/*Mensam*/*Mensae*/*Mensa*/*Mensa*', which suggests she was trying to find something appropriate for a Latin lesson. Britten discovered exactly what he needed in Benjamin Hall Kennedy's *The Shorter Latin Primer*, first published in 1866. The copy at BPL, a new and revised edition published in 1948 (see p. 208), belonged to Richard Kihl, an Aldeburgh schoolboy befriended by the composer. After speaking to Kihl in 2000, former Director of the Britten–Pears Library Jenny Doctor wrote to Valentine Cunningham (see below) on 27 October 2000:

Until 1951, [Kihl] went to school at Sizewell Hall and took Latin, using this grammar book as text. In autumn 1951, he started to go to Framlingham College and no longer studied Latin, but still had the book on his shelf.

He remembers going for a long walk with Britten around the marshes, and Britten asked him lots of questions about Latin. Before I said anything about *The Turn of the Screw*, Richard mentioned that he remembered that this took place when Britten was working on *Screw*. Richard finally offered to go home to get his Latin grammar, which he did. Britten never returned the book to him. Richard says that he remembers the walk, the conversation and the loaning of the book quite clearly.

Much has been made of this list of nouns by the literary scholar Valentine Cunningham, who decoded them as phallic slang, as well as a line in the children's distorted Benedicite in Act II (see 'Filthy Britten', *Guardian* (5

APPENDIX I

(d) Aequor, marmor, cor decline   *sea, marble, heart*
    Neuter; arbor Feminine.   *tree*

(e) Of the Substantives in ŏs,
    Feminine are cōs and dōs: *whetstone, dowry*
    while, of Latin Nouns, alone
    Neuter are os (ossis), *bone*,
    and ōs (ōris), *mouth*: a few
    Greek in *os* are Neuter too.*

(f) Many Neuters end in *er*,
    siler, acer, verber, vēr,   *withy, maple, stripe, spring*
    tūber, ūber, and cadāver,   *hump, udder, carcase*
    piper, iter, and papāver.   *pepper, journey, poppy*

(g) Feminine are compēs, teges,   *fetter, mat*
    mercēs, merges, quiēs, seges,   *fee, sheaf, rest,* **corn**
    though their Cases have increase:
    with the Neuters reckon aes.   *copper*

Rule 2.—Third-Nouns Feminine we class
    ending *is, x, aus*, and *ās*,
    s to consonant appended,
    ēs in flexion unextended.

Exc. (a) Many Nouns in *is* we find
    to the Masculine assigned:
    amnis, axis, caulis, collis,   *river, axle, stalk, hill*
    clūnis, crīnis, fascis, follis,   *hind-leg, hair, bundle, bellows*
    fūstis, ignis, orbis, ēnsis,   *bludgeon, fire, orb, sword*
    pānis, piscis, postis, mēnsis,   *bread, fish, post, month*
    torris, unguis, and canālis,   *stake, nail, canal*
    vectis, vermis, and nātālis,   *lever, worm, birthday*
    sanguis, pulvis, cucumis,   *blood, dust, cucumber*
    lapis, cassēs, Mānēs, glīs.   *stone, nets, ghosts, dormouse*

(b) Chiefly Masculine we find,
    sometimes Feminine declined,
    callis, sentis, fūnis, fīnis,   *path, thorn, rope, end*
    and in poets torquis, cinis.   *necklace, cinder*

(c) Masculine are most in *ex*:
    Feminine are forfex, lēx,   *shears, law*
    nex, supellex: Common, pūmex,   *death, furniture, pumice*
    imbrex, ōbex, silex, rumex.   *tile, bolt, flint, sorrel*

* As melos, *melody*; epos, *epic poem*.

The schoolboy Richard Kihl's copy of Kennedy's *Shorter Latin Primer*, lent by him to Britten in 1954. The list of nouns marked by the composer in this copy are those sung by Miles in Act I scene 6 of *The Turn of the Screw*.

January 2002)). Cunningham argues that Britten's covert use of such slang – familiar to any public schoolboy (i.e. Britten and his circle) was a direct response to the rampant homophobia of the society in which he lived. But as Andrew Plant observes, Christopher Stray, 'who has closely examined all Kennedy's papers and consulted the author's surviving family over many years, has uncovered no evidence whatsoever for these claims; perhaps more especially since both Kennedy's *Revised* and *Shorter Primers* were largely written by his daughters'. Moreover, no evidence has come to light to suggest that anyone involved in the creation of the opera – the homosexual Britten, Pears, Coleman, Graham or Douglas, or for that matter the heterosexual Pipers – were aware of these hidden meanings of the Latin. It seems unlikely that during the period of the anti-homosexual campaign waged by David Maxwell-Fyffe, Home Secretary in Winston Churchill's post-war Conservative Administration (see also Letter 769 n. 3) Britten, ever the most circumspect of homosexuals, would have risked his reputation and the successful future of his latest opera by knowingly including phallic slang of this type. Britten himself refers in his correspondence to the delicate nature of aspects of the opera and his anxiety to avoid any hint of scandal (see Letter 800). See also Christopher Stray, 'Sexy Ghosts and Gay Grammarians: Kennedy's Latin Primer in Britten's *Turn of the Screw*', in *Paradigm* 2/6 (August 2003), pp. 9–13.

We are grateful to Dr Plant for sharing with us his fortuitous discovery of a hitherto unknown connection concerning the list of Latin nouns at the beginning of Act I scene 6. These same Latin nouns, 'amnis, axis, collis' etc., appear in Musorgsky's 1866 song, 'The Seminarist', composed in the same year that Kennedy's *Primer* was first published. As Dr Plant points out, Musorgsky's song not only sets the Latin nouns in a similar rapid pattern to that of Britten but also in F minor/F major – the same tonal centre as Britten's scene. See Mackay, p. 16.

5 The colloquy between Quint and Miss Jessel that opens Act II, for which Piper was obliged to invent dialogue between the ghosts, there being no direct model in James's novella. It is in this scene that a quotation of a line from W. B. Yeats's 'The Second Coming' – 'The ceremony of innocence is drowned' – is made.

785 To Carl Dolmetsch[1]
[*Typed*]

4 CRABBE STREET, ALDEBURGH, SUFFOLK
20th January, 1954

Dear Mr Dolmetsch,

I have to thank you for the very welcome present of two superb recorders which arrived yesterday. I am afraid my technique is, as yet, very inadequate, and I do not feel in the very few hours I have had playing on them since their arrival that I have fully exploited their possibilities, but I have realised in a very short time a little of their exceptional quality, and thank you more than I can say for the kind thought and generosity of your gift.

I have always been fascinated by the sound of recorders and cannot understand why I have not tried to play any of them before. It was, in fact, our very active music club here,[2] with its energetic consort, that spurred me on, and I am much enjoying my beginner's efforts. I am also discovering for myself some of the possibilities of the instrument which will be invaluable when I start to write for them, as I hope to soon.[3]

Peter Pears has tackled the bass recorder which, of course, is a more difficult affair,[4] but he has several months' start over me, and before long I hope we shall be playing duets.

With many thanks,
Yours sincerely,
BENJAMIN BRITTEN

1 British recorder-player and instrument-maker (1911–1997), son of Arnold Dolmetsch, the early music pioneer. Carl Dolmetsch, whose long career included a sixty-year duo partnership with the keyboard player Joseph Saxby, had many works specially written for him by composers including Lennox Berkeley, Arnold Cooke and Nicholas Maw. See obituaries by Shelagh Godwin, *Independent* (14 July 1997), and in the *Daily Telegraph* (15 July 1997).

   Dolmetsch was to write to Britten on 29 September 1954, requesting a work for recorder and harpsichord. The composer evidently gave Dolmetsch no firm commitment, suggesting only that he would like to write for the recorder at some point in the future. Dolmetsch made a further attempt in 1962; but Britten never did write a work for him. See also n. 3 below.

   Following his visit to Japan in 1956, Britten was to make a gift of a Dolmetsch recorder to Kei-ichi Kurosawa.

2 Founded by Britten, Pears and local amateur musicians, the Aldeburgh Music Club held its first meeting on 6 April 1952 at Crag House. During this early period of its activity there were three groups of musicians: recorder-players, string-players and singers. Both Britten and Pears took an active part but not in their professional capacity: Pears played the recorder, piano or organ, but did not sing; Britten usually played the viola or the recorder. Imogen Holst immediately took a leading role in the Club after her arrival in Aldeburgh, conducting a performance of Purcell's *Timon of Athens* on 26 October 1952 (IHD, pp. 157–8):

   Music Club *Timon* in the evening – went right through – not too bad on the whole, though bits were scared. It was lovely following the score in the Overture & listening to Ben's viola playing. Peter did the piano part beautifully. Then when it was over Ben suggested doing it all over again and wanted me to conduct because it was difficult to follow from the piano. I didn't want to do the overture because I'd never worked at it and didn't know the first thing about speeds or even cuts, but he made such a fuss, like a small boy, scraping his bow on his open strings, so I had to, and most, but not all of it went better the second time. Everyone radiantly happy. It is *wonderful* for the amateurs in Aldeburgh to have those two to play & sing with. Hadn't had anything like it since G [Gustav Holst] in Thaxted thirty years ago.

See also Patrick Walker and Valerie Potter, *Aldeburgh Music Club 1952–2002*.

3 Britten's initial pieces for recorder consort were the *Scherzo* (November 1954), written for the Aldeburgh Music Club, and the *Alpine Suite* (1955). Perhaps Britten's most striking and elaborate use of recorders is made in *Noye's Fludde*; for example, the solo representing the dove and the contribution the recorders make to the sound of the storm. In the second act of *A Midsummer Night's Dream*, Bottom is entertained by the 'tongs and the bones', an ensemble in which two sopranino recorders participate.

The gift of the Dolmetsch recorders was undoubtedly linked to a new publishing initiative from Boosey & Hawkes in 1953: *Music for Recorders: Recorder Pieces from the 12th to the 20th Century*, edited by Imogen Holst and Britten. Among the works proposed for the series were a 'Trio' by Britten (this turned out to be the *Scherzo* for recorder quartet), 'works by Lennox Berkeley (if Chesters agree)', a 'work by Arthur Oldham', and 'works by contemporary composers', including James Bernard, Robin Orr, James Butt, and Richard Rodney Bennett (see undated memorandum in Boosey & Hawkes file at BPL). See also IHD, pp. 271–2 and 285.

Imogen Holst records in her diary several occasions when Britten played the recorder: 'we played recorder duets & laughed till we cried' (7 December 1953; IHD, p. 275); '[Ben] produced his recorder and began practising and we did Tower Hill [by Giles Farnaby] as a duet – he enjoying having to remember the right fingering and got terribly angry with himself when he went wrong' (6 February 1954; IHD, p. 285); 'we went round to the Potters and practised recorders – Stephen back from Spain & two visitors who were very patient in putting up with the frightful sounds we made. Ben still gets the giggles badly, but Mary and Julian [Potter] were very good, & Peter is getting superb tone on his low notes. Drinks helped' (20 March 1954; IHD, pp. 289–90); '[Britten] played very well in the recorder 4tet and didn't laugh once' (21 March 1954; IHD, p. 290).

4 In his youth Pears had played the bassoon.

786 To Francis Poulenc
[*Typed*]

4 CRABBE STREET, ALDEBURGH, SUFFOLK
21st January, 1954

My dear Francis,

You may have heard already that we are planning a French weekend at the next Aldeburgh Festival.[1] In fact I am sure that Tony Mayer[2] must have mentioned this to you. Fournier[3] was going to come, but alas his commitments in South America forbid it, but the Couraud Choir from Paris, and a flute player called Rampal[4] will visit us, we hope. What this obviously needs is a crown, and who could that be but you! I have heard so much about the wonderful lecture of "Les Six"[5] that you give with exquisite illustrations on the piano. Would you be very sweet and come and do this for us? The Festival, as you may know, is quite a small and intimate affair, but we do good things and have a warm and discriminating audience. The Festival lasts from June 12th–20th, and the time which we were keeping open for you is Sunday afternoon June 13th, quite the peak time of the Festival! If the Couraud Choir comes we hope that either on the Saturday afternoon or Sunday evening they will give a performance of a big work or works by you, in which case perhaps you would accompany them on the piano if there is something you would like to do.

We all so hope that this idea attracts you and that the date is suitable. In which case would you write a note to me, and I will pass it on to the Festival Manager who will get in touch with you or your agent about the financial arrangements. Please forgive a type-written letter, but for the last few months I have been unable to use my right arm having been attacked by a horrid and so far resisting complaint.

I hope you are well. I was so sorry to miss you when you were at the Wigmore Hall before Christmas.[6]

[*Handwritten:*] With cordial greetings,
BENJAMIN B.

1 The planned events appeared as follows in the 1954 Programme Book:

13 June, at 3 p.m., Jubilee Hall, Aldeburgh: Lecture
'Francis Poulenc will speak in French, with music illustrations: Propos à batons rompus sur la musique'. The French Ambassador to introduce the lecture.

13 June, 8.15 p.m., Jubilee Hall: Chamber Music Concert
Programme includes Poulenc playing his *6 Improvisations* (1936–42)

14 June, 11 a.m., Cinema: Musique concrète
Programme introduced by Tony Mayer

But as Letter 811 makes clear, Poulenc was obliged to cancel his visit and other programmes were substituted.

In addition to these planned events, French music was further celebrated at the 1954 Festival by the inclusion of four songs by Poulenc in Pears's and Britten's recital on 12 June, and arias from operas by Berlioz, Debussy and Ravel in the 'Opera Concert' on the 20th.

2 French diplomat (1902–1997), who escaped to England following the fall of France in 1940 and the ensuing German occupation. During the next twenty-eight years as Cultural Attaché at the French Embassy, Mayer promoted a remarkable series of concerts of French music in London and elsewhere in the UK, in which French and British artists (including Britten and Pears) participated: see, for example, Letter 392 n. 1. It was Mayer who helped make arrangements for Britten's and Pears's trip to Paris in March 1945 (see Letter 496 n. 2). In London, Mayer also successfully promoted the cause of French drama and literature (see Letter 788). He contributed 'L'affaire *Gloriana*' to a symposium about Britten's Coronation opera in *Opera* 4/8 (August 1953), pp. 456–60; published a book about the English, *La vie anglaise*, in 1960; made a contribution about his friendship with Britten and Pears to PPT, pp. 62–3, and wrote 'Subtle Values of the Spirit: Les Concerts de musique française de Londres' for the programme book for the Aldeburgh October Britten Festival 1994, 'Britten and the French Connection', pp. 49–52. See also John Calder's obituary, *Independent* (6 November 1997).

3 Pierre Fournier (1906–1986), French cellist, for whom Poulenc wrote his Cello Sonata. Fournier was a close friend of Tony Mayer; in February 1952, Mayer had approached Britten on Fournier's behalf, with a request for a suite for cello and orchestra.

4 Jean-Pierre Rampal (1922–2000), French flautist, who was to give the first performance of Poulenc's Flute Sonata in 1957.

5 The group of six French composers – Auric, Durey, Honegger, Milhaud, Poulenc and Tailleferre – which had formed in 1917 when all six composers appeared together on the same programme. Though Satie was a watchful godfather to the group, its most enthusiastic advocate was Jean Cocteau.

6 On 25 November 1953 Poulenc had taken part in one of Mayer's 'Concerts de musique française', entitled 'A Programme of French Operatic Arias'. It was introduced by Lord Harewood, with singers Denise Duval, Raymond Amadé and Bernard Lefort, and Poulenc and Germaine Tailleferre at the piano. The programme included arias and ensembles by Grétry, Dalayrac, Gounod, Massenet and Bizet, as well as extracts from Tailleferre's *Le petit navire*, Messager's *Isoline*, *Fortunio* and *Véronique*, and extracts from Poulenc's *Les Mamelles de Tirésias*. The Tailleferre and Poulenc items were receiving their first public performances in the UK.

787 **To Anthony Gishford**
[*Typed*]

4 CRABBE STREET, ALDEBURGH, SUFFOLK
31st January, 1954

My dear Tony,

Thank you very much for returning the Spanish letter so beautifully translated. I shall reply in equally flowery terms.

Thank you also for the lovely party after "Gloriana";[1] we all enjoyed ourselves enormously. I hope you liked the performance. I thought it was a great improvement, and hope that the reception at the end may prove that the tide is slightly turning.

I am here working all this week in case anything arises about important matters – you know what I mean. May be with luck I shall be penning the first notes of the Henry James opera now provisionally called "The Tower and the Lake".[2]

I have just received the winter edition of "Tempo" and was delighted to see the Grimes photos.[3] Who took these? You could not bully whoever the excellent photographer was to send me a complete set for my collection, could you?

I hope you are warmer in London than we are here. We could scarcely be colder. With all the different types of heating known to man we are keeping a few rooms habitable although the plumbing has gone haywire.

With best wishes to you and many thanks for [*handwritten*: all] your support.

Yours ever,
BEN

P.S. Could you ask whoever controls these things to send me half a dozen catalogues of my works?

1 29 January 1954: the first night of the revival of *Gloriana* at Covent Garden, conducted by Reginald Goodall. Britten was to remark to David Webster in a letter of 2 February 1954,

> I hope you were as pleased as I was with "Gloriana" on Friday. In spite of first night tensions felt by some of the performers, I felt it was in every way an improvement on the summer performance.

2 In fact Britten was not to begin work on the composition draft of *The Turn of the Screw* until 30 March (see Letter 794 n. 2), though his composition draft is dated 'April 1st – July 23rd 1954'.

3 At this period Gishford was editor of the contemporary music journal *Tempo*, published by Boosey & Hawkes. The uncredited photographs, which appeared in *Tempo* 30 (winter 1953–54), pp. 18–19, were of the recent revival of *Grimes* at Covent Garden in November 1953.

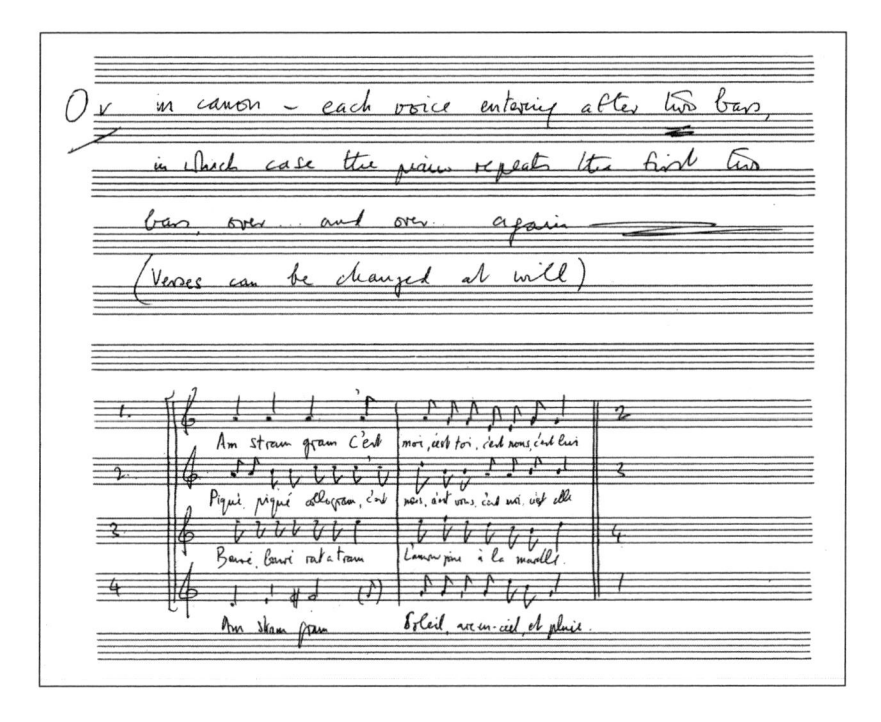

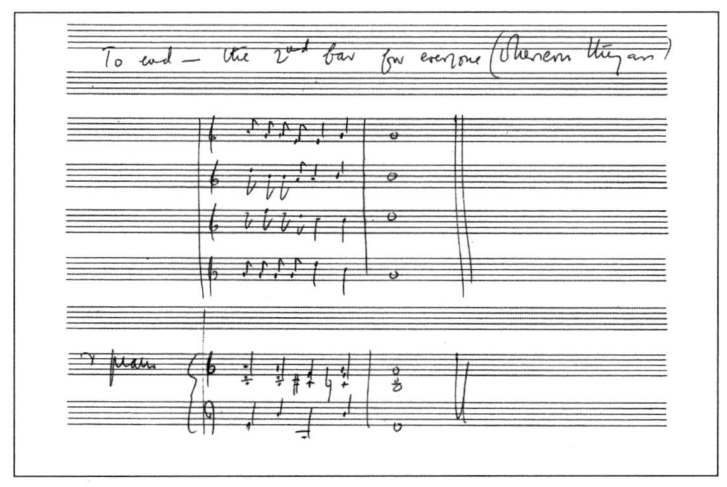

The second, canonic version of *Am Stram Gram* sent by Britten
to Tony Mayer, 31 January 1954; see Letter 788

788 To Tony Mayer
[*Typed*]

4 CRABBE STREET, ALDEBURGH, SUFFOLK
31st January, 1954

My dear Tony,

We were held up by snow and breakdowns over the weekend and so I have only [*handwritten*: just] had time to write this little masterpiece[1] for you, and send it in haste. I hope it is clear, the two different [*handwritten*: versions] (1) sung altogether, (2) sung as a quartet. I shall be here all the week so please ring me if any elucidation is necessary.

I did enjoy my lunch with you and Therese so much.

[*Handwritten*:] Looking forward to seeing you next Tuesday,
[*Typed*:] Love to you both,
BEN

1 *Am Stram Gram*, a single number that could be performed either as a unison song with piano accompaniment or as a four-part canon. It was Britten's contribution to the London French-language production of André Roussin's 1941 'comédie-farce en trois actes' of the same name first performed at Toynbee Hall on 4 March 1954, in a staging by Victor Azaria. See also Eric Walter White, 'Britten in the Theatre: a Provisional Catalogue', *Tempo* 107 (December 1973), p. 9, where the number was reproduced in facsimile. See also PRIM, pp. 561–2.

A review of the production in *The Times* (5 March 1954) noted, 'Mr Benjamin Britten composed a pleasant musical setting for a little song that Mr Tony Mayer wrote around the title, and which brought the curtain up pleasantly.'

789 To Myfanwy Piper
[*Typed*]

4 CRABBE STREET, ALDEBURGH, SUFFOLK
31st January, 1954

My dear Myfanwy,

Thank you so much for ringing up this morning. I was sorry to hear about the Fort,[1] but hope the new arrangement will be even more attractive than that sounded.

Here are the two new scenes typed by Jeremy [Cullum]. We will delay typing the whole until we get your first act corrections and any more you are able to send.

The end of the first act could be something like this:

At the climax Mrs. Grose appears at the window and the Governess at the porch. Quint and Miss Jessel disappear as Mrs. Grose drags Flora away and Miles runs down to Governess.

<u>Gov.</u>   Miles! What are you doing?
<u>Miles</u> You see, I <u>am</u> bad, aren't I?

<u>Curtain</u>

I like Miles' last remark because it is clear, bright, and in short phrases, which I think is right for the boy's character and his manner of singing.[2]

Much love,
BEN

1 See Letter 784 n. 2.

2 A typical suggestion from Britten, duly adopted by Myfanwy Piper. Some of the most memorable and significant lines in the librettos of Britten's operas were the work of the composer himself.

790 To William Plomer

4 CRABBE STREET, ALDEBURGH, SUFFOLK
Jan 31st 1954

My dear William,

If you were at C. Garden on Friday, I am sorry to have missed you; but I feel you would have shown yourself ... in pleasure or in anger. It went well, I thought, & the improvements Basil [Coleman] was able to achieve were advantageous – altho' <u>nothing like</u> as many as he, or we, wanted. The attitude there was "a revival, & not a re-production", & couldn't be budged. Everyone missed 'Norwich',[1] but many agreed the work gained in dramatic intensity, if it lost in open-airness or splendour. Musically it was way beyond anything yet heard – Cecil (Kraus)[2] will be good, but is yet a bit nervous, ditto the new P. [Penelope] Rich (who has a splendid voice).[3] Joan [Cross] was tremendous, & the end (without the ghosts)[4] worked well. Peter, rather under the (awful) weather, wasn't as euphoric as he'd have liked, but was gayer & sang well. I hope you'll manage to see it (if you weren't there on Friday, that is) on Tuesday. Just ring them for tickets. I can't alas be there as I'm now down here to work; but I hope to see you very soon all the same.

Please forgive short scrawl, but – this is my first letter written with my <u>right</u> hand, – painful, but definitely improving.

Much love to you, & to Charles [Erdmann]. I hope what kept you from our rehearsals (many thanks for telegram) was work and not misfortune of any kind.

BEN

Love from

PETER

1 For the revival the scene of Queen Elizabeth's progress to Norwich, Act II scene 1, was omitted. *The Times* (30 January 1954) observed:

> The excision, in spite of the musical loss, is fully justified, for it concentrates instead of dissipating attention on the developing character of the Queen. Furthermore, one scene of pageantry is enough for one act, and both the garden scene and the ball at Whitehall gain in dramatic point.

However, the excision of the Norwich scene ruptured Britten's and Plomer's alternating pattern of public and private scenes across the three-act span.

This revival was conducted by Reginald Goodall. There were two further performances at Covent Garden (2 and 16 February), followed by performances during the company's provincial tour on 11 March (Cardiff), 30 March (Manchester) and 13 April (Birmingham).

Britten wrote to Princess Margaret of Hesse and the Rhine (4 February 1954):

> It really went very well, was an improvement both from the production and from the musical angle, and seemed a big success; but it has still quite a lot of ground to make up, and the houses and critics aren't very cheering yet. But really I'm pleased with it, and it is a wonderful performance (I doubt if the Queen will ever be done much better, and Peter is most charming and touching as Essex). So that's that.

In this same letter Britten confided: 'I'm getting a teeny bit alarmed about this opera I've got to write for the autumn, for Venice; time's getting a bit short and writing is still very difficult. Still I expect the Lord will provide –.'

2 Otakar Kraus (1909–1980), British baritone of Czech birth, who had created the role of Tarquinius in *The Rape of Lucretia*. See also Letter 534 n. 4.

3 The 'new P. Rich' was the twenty-seven-year-old Australian soprano Joan Sutherland (b. 1926), who had made her Covent Garden debut as the First Lady in *Die Zauberflöte* in October 1952. During these early years of her career at Covent Garden, Sutherland created the role of Jenifer in Tippett's *The Midsummer Marriage* (1955), excerpts of which she performed at an 'Opera Concert' at the 1955 Aldeburgh Festival, and sang Madame Lidoine in the UK premiere of Poulenc's *Dialogues des Carmélites* (1958). Her assumption of the title role of Donizetti's *Lucia di Lammermoor* in 1959 coloured the course of the rest of her career, and thereafter she became a legendary exponent of the *bel canto* repertory. Britten's parodying of the early nineteenth-century *bel canto* school in the Pyramus and Thisbe play

in the final act of *A Midsummer Night's Dream* (1960) may have been connected with Sutherland's recent success as Lucia. She was made a DBE in 1979 and appointed a member of the Order of Merit in 1991, a year after her final performances.

With Pears, Sutherland recorded Handel's *Acis and Galatea*, conducted by Adrian Boult, for Decca in 1959; and in 1972, again for Decca, *Turandot* conducted by Zubin Mehta, with Sutherland in the title role and Pears as the Emperor Altoum.

4 Significant revisions to the opera's conclusion were made by the composer in two stages, the first (with which this letter is concerned) at the time of the revival, was to omit the procession of ghosts during the Epilogue. As Antonia Malloy has suggested, the identity of these ghosts (Sir John Harington, Elizabeth I's godson, the King of Scotland, the French Ambassador) remained unclear to the audience; see PBBG, p. 64.

In 1966, for a new production mounted by Sadler's Wells, further revisions were introduced which comprised abbreviations of the Queen's Soliloquy and Prayer and Cecil's Entry, and further amendments to the Epilogue; see PBBG, p. 150.

791 To Myfanwy Piper
[*Typed*]

4 CRABBE STREET, ALDEBURGH
4th February 1954

My dear Myfanwy,

Here in haste are Jeremy [Cullum]'s typings of Scenes 6 and 7 [of Act II]. You will see that I have changed the order of scene 6 a little. I worked on it this morning and found that musically speaking this seemed the best way round, especially if, as I suggest, you could write Flora a little jingle to sing about the cat's cradle. Miles can appear to accompany this on the piano if you like, which would give them a closer relationship.[1]

Thank you for the alterations which I have confirmed in my copy. Jeremy will now type the whole thing and I will bring a copy for you and send one to George Malcolm[2] whom it will help in the selection of children.[3]

Much love to you all. I hope Litton Cheney[4] is a success.

BEN

1 The duet for Mrs Grose and Flora, 'Cradles for cats/Are string and air' (Act II scene 6), which Miles does indeed accompany at the piano.

2 British harpsichordist, pianist and conductor (1917–1997), who was, from 1947 to 1959, Master of Music at Westminster Cathedral, where he trained

the choristers to produce a bright, Continental-style singing tone, much admired by Britten. Britten wrote his *Missa Brevis in D* for Malcolm and the boys of Westminster Cathedral Choir in 1959. Malcolm was to become a very close colleague of both Britten and Pears (for example, he trained the boy singers in *A Midsummer Night's Dream* and conducted the second and third performances of the opera at Aldeburgh in 1960), made frequent appearances at the Aldeburgh Festival (beginning in 1951 with the English Opera Group, conducting Purcell's *Dido and Aeneas* and Monteverdi's *Il combattimento di Tancredi e Clorinda*), and participated in many important recordings. Malcolm was Conductor of the Philomusica of London (1962–66), Associate Conductor of the BBC Scottish Symphony Orchestra (1965–67), and an influential collaborator with the Academy of St Martin in the Fields and the English Chamber Orchestra. See also obituaries in *The Times* (15 October 1997) and the *Daily Telegraph* (14 October 1997), and a tribute celebrating Malcolm's links with Britten, Pears and the Aldeburgh Festival by Rosamund Strode, which appeared in the 1998 Aldeburgh Festival Programme Book, p. 35.

Malcolm contributed two chapters to DMHK – 'The Purcell Realizations' (pp. 74–82) and '*Dido and Aeneas*' (pp. 186–97) – and 'Boys' Voices' to TBB, pp. 100–103.

3 Malcolm was evidently assisting Britten in his search for young singers to take on the roles of Miles and Flora.

4 The Pipers had gone to stay with Reynolds Stone (see Letter 792 n. 8) and his wife Janet in this Dorset village.

792 To Myfanwy Piper

4 CRABBE STREET, ALDEBURGH, SUFFOLK
Feb. 16th 1954

My dear Myfanwy,

That was a very enjoyable and also a very useful day we spent with you all. Thank you so much for putting up with us, & looking after us so well. My! – how you do work! I don't understand really how you manage to fit it all in.

I was very pleased with the work on 'the Tower & the Lake'. I think it is in very promising shape now, & I am longing to get down to finding the right notes. At the moment I am hunting for the right kind of singing game for the two children;[1] have you had any inspirations about this?

We enjoyed our Lancing weekend very much.[2] Edward[3] was in splendid shape, & very good company indeed. Clytie II[4] met us then & was made much of by the boys of course. We met the new head; an intellectual (Wykehamist) type; not altogether my cup of tea, but I think useful for the school at this juncture.[5]

St. Nicolas went well, & was fun, & appreciated by many, it seemed. By-the-way, I heard the boy (Robert Woodward) sing & he's a very bright & charming child – <u>excellent</u> type for 'Miles': I'm getting him up to sing to George Malcolm, but I fear that his voice may not last too long, he's already 15! But it is a good strong voice now, & he's a good performer.[6]

No more now – the hand & arm are rather playing me up (hence the awful scribble – but I wanted to thank you for a lovely day & night. It was fun. I often think of Portland Bill.[7] Love to all of you, from Peter (snowed deep under income tax at the moment).

BEN

Love to the Stones[8] – it was nice seeing them again.

1 *The Turn of the Screw*, Act I scene 2: 'Lavender's blue, diddle, diddle', and scene 5: 'Tom, Tom, the piper's son'.

2 Britten and Pears had been at Lancing College during the weekend of 13–14 February for a performance of *Saint Nicolas* and a recital.

3 Edward Piper (1938–1990), artist and photographer son of John and Myfanwy Piper. He exhibited at the Aldeburgh Festival in 1983 and collaborated with his father for over twenty years on the Shell County Guides. See obituaries by Sylvia Clayton, *Guardian* (14 May 1990), and Reg Singh and Fay Weldon, *Independent* (14 May 1990), and Sylvia Clayton, *Edward Piper*.

4 Britten's and Pears's miniature dachshund, which Pears had acquired from a litter bred by John Cranko. In a letter of 8 February 1954, Britten told William Plomer: 'Peter has a new passion, the smallest Dachshund ever, called Clytie, & our lives are completely changed now.'

5 The new headmaster was John Dancy, who had briefly taught at Winchester (where he had also been a student). He remained head until 1961. Basil Handford writes, in *Lancing College: History and Memoirs*, p. 260, that Dancy 'wanted to change things quickly and his relations with his staff were soured during his first year by the dismissal or resignation of no less than nine members of the staff [. . .] Somebody coined the phrase, "Dancy's Inferno".'

6 The role of Miles was eventually to be created by the twelve-year-old David Hemmings (1941–2003), who subsequently sang the role in London and on tour, until 1956 when his voice broke. In 1955 he not only recorded the role of Miles for Decca, but also the boy Nicolas in *Saint Nicolas* and Sam in *The Little Sweep*, all first recordings under the composer's baton.

Hemmings had been one of more than fifty boys and girls auditioned for the children's roles in *The Turn of the Screw* on 12 December 1953, at the Royal Court Theatre, London. Hemmings, who recited a poem by Robert Browning and sang Handel's 'Where'er you walk', was called at 12.30 p.m.

"THE TURN OF THE SCREW" AUDITIONS: 12.12.53.   Contd.

11.30 a.m.

   17. QUINTON WILKINSON. ☓

   18. MICHAEL INGRAM. ✓ voice good speaking

   19. WENDY ATKINSON. weak small

   20. PATRICIA WRAIGHT. Clavin Isleorm

11.45 a.m.

   21. PETER ~~SIMPSON~~. ?too personality but most voice in performance

   22. ANITA GERMAINE.   (Beatrice Hume) ☓

   23. LEE STRAUSS.   (-do-   ) No Form.

   24. CAROL FRYER. ☓

12 a.m.

   25. DAVID GODFREY.   Corona School. No Form. ☓

   ~~26. ROBERT STRUGGIN.~~   -do-   -do- ☓
   Margaret Downs
   ~~27. KIT PENNINGTON.~~   -do-   -do-
   Gillian Shrimp
   ~~28. EILEEN CUSHING.~~   -do-   -do-
   acquelnil walsh

12.15 p.m.

   ~~29. VALERIE WYNER.~~   -do-   -do-

   30. MAVIS SAGE.   -do-   -do-

   31. CAROL OLVER.   -do-   -do-

   32.   ?Boy -do-   -do-

12.30 p.m.

   33. DAVID HEMMINGS. ✓ voice strong. personality

   34. PEARSON DODD.

   35. PAT LAURENCE.   (Aida Forster)

   36. VALERIE POLE. good memory.

Myfanwy Piper's copy of the audition list of children for *The Turn of the Screw*, 12 December 1953. At 12.30 p.m. David Hemmings was auditioned, Mrs Piper commenting with a tick: 'voice strong. personality'.

Myfanwy Piper annotated her audition sheet with the comment 'voice strong. personality' (see facing page). (Among the other children heard that day was Michael Ingram (later Michael Crawford), who also worked with the English Opera Group in the 1950s, notably creating the role of Jaffet in *Noye's Fludde*.) Although this first round of auditions had proved somewhat unsatisfactory – for example, Britten realized he would have to jettison his idea of writing the role of Flora for a young girl – Hemmings was recalled for a further audition at Britten's London home on 27 January 1954. Britten's diary for that date has the entry: 'D. Hemmings & G. M. [George Malcolm] at Chester Gate'. Basil Coleman recalled (DHOBB, p. 41):

One of the few boys brought back for a second hearing was a very shy but quite personable little twelve-year-old, with a true but very small treble voice. Despite this it was decided to risk casting him, in the hope that the voice would develop and grow during rehearsals – the boy was David Hemmings.

According to John Bridcut (JBBC, p. 195), within months of the audition, Hemmings was living for two or three months at Crag House: 'It was one of the most wonderful times of my entire life,' recalled Hemmings, and he goes on to mention working with other members of the cast, 'gathered round the piano'. In his autobiography, Hemmings himself writes of his 'months with Ben at Aldeburgh', though it is possible that, in recalling childhood events of fifty years earlier, Hemmings exaggerated the period of time he spent in Aldeburgh. It should however be borne in mind that the composer often liked to have tangible visual stimuli such as stage designs by him during the period of composition (see PBMPG, pp. 82–3); the opportunity to have the boy who was to play Miles close at hand during the writing of *The Turn of the Screw* might have been desirable. In any case, Hemmings would have had to learn the role and Britten would have needed to be quite certain, particularly with such a tight composition schedule, that the boy would be able to sing it.

In this context, it is of interest to note that the 'Malo' song (or a version of it) was composed in advance of the opera's composition draft (see p. 225): this song was copied out by Imogen Holst on 19 March 1954 (see IHD, p. 289), and presumably given to Hemmings to learn. Britten's reasoning might well have been: if Hemmings could manage to sing this music, one of Miles's – and the opera's – key moments, then all was likely to be well for the remainder of the role. (In an interview with Roderic Dunnert, Myfanwy Piper recalled that Britten 'wanted to have a song for the boy to steer him through the piece, so that if he should get lost, he could listen to his own intervals, and sounds in the song. And I realized that this piece, which we'd neither of us yet found, was going to be extremely important to Ben': see Dunnert, 'A Close and Intense Collaboration', programme book for Welsh National Opera production of *The Turn of the Screw* (2000).)

Hemmings's autobiography, *Blow-Up and Other Exaggerations*, however, includes an account of a 'full day in his flat near Regent's Park', working at the 'Malo' song (p. 54):

[Britten] crouched over the piano and played the outline of what was to be Miles's aria 'Malo'. [...] I sang tentatively, reading the pencilled notes from the score in front of him (rather badly, for I was never a good sight-reader), and began gradually to learn its tricky phrasing. Britten would change the odd note, rubbing out a previous thought, and we would sing on, interrupted only by tea and crumpets in the mid-afternoon. Peter Pears was there too – looking on, I suppose, in consternation, though he was polite, generous and funny [...] After the session, my part in the opera was confirmed without it ever needing to be said.

Of his time in Aldeburgh when he stayed with Britten – and his autobiography mentions rehearsing with the other singers which rather tends to confirm the period as August–September 1954 – Hemmings recalled (p. 57):

If I was frightened when the winds were howling off the North Sea and it was easy to imagine Norse demons prowling across the churning grey waters, I would patter along to Ben's room and creep into his bed for security. I slept with him often, to be sure, when the dark got the better sense of my reason. It never occurred to me that there was anything untoward about this. Britten had quickly become an important and considerate father figure, making up, perhaps, for the lack of warmth in my own father; certainly he was more interested in my singing and, for that matter, my general well-being.

There was no question of anything that these days would be called 'inappropriate' but I have to say that it's a measure of the cynical, prurient world in which we live now that everyone would assume the worst of him. And I say this after I learned later in life that Ben, who was without question a homosexual, was for a while infatuated with me. Since then there have been many suggestions that our relationship was untoward, that Peter Pears was furiously jealous (he was, but I didn't know that until almost forty years later) and that Ben had cast me more for passion and personal favour than for talent. That may have been true, but if so, he was never to show it in any physical way, although there are those who have tried to imply otherwise over the years.

Both Humphrey Carpenter and John Bridcut have written about the strength of the relationship between the composer and Hemmings, in particular Britten's infatuation with the boy (see HCBB, pp. 356–8, and JBBC, pp. 194–210). It was an obsession that, as Hemmings retrospectively observed, evidently caused some friction between Britten and Pears, which was witnessed by EOG colleagues. Colin Graham, stage manager with the EOG on this production, considered that 'whatever people may say, Peter behaved angelically and with enormous understanding. He knew Ben too well and was too sure of him to be jealous – it was neither necessary nor realistic' (HCBB, p. 357). But after the composer's death, Pears discussed with the conductor Raymond Leppard Britten's feelings towards boys, describing the Britten–Hemmings relationship as 'nearly catastrophic' (HCBB, p. 357).

To Bridcut, Hemmings gave what turned out to be his final interview before his death, during which he spoke movingly – and frankly – about his friendship with the composer. This interview forms a memorable contribution to Bridcut's film, *Britten's Children*.

Britten's earliest version of Miles's 'Malo' song. It was composed in March 1954, ahead of the rest of the opera, for David Hemmings to try out. BL Add. MS. 60602

Hemmings gave an evocative account of the first night of *The Turn of the Screw* in an interview with Tom Sutcliffe in 2000, quoted by Sutcliffe in his Welsh National Opera programme article, 'Haunting Parallels Between Art and Life' :

'We had performed [the reprise of the "Malo" song] hundreds of times in rehearsal,' he says. 'But that night in front of an audience, when Jennifer Vyvyan really went right up there I was shattered – in tears in her arms, because the whole meaning of the opera in some way came together for me. I can't describe how appallingly wonderful that moment was, with Jennifer Vyvyan really ripping that aria back at the audience, right up there – with the pain and agony that she was going through at that point. And then there was old James Blades with those final soft taps on the timps. And gradually the curtain came down. And then for a moment we didn't know what had happened. It was one of those occasions when the audience can do nothing. There must have been fifteen seconds before they realized it was over, even though the curtain was down in front of them, so great was the emotional response. Then it started slowly, and soon there was this rush of enormous enthusiasm from the audience – which absolutely took you by the bowels and broke your heart. We didn't quite know what had happened. There was something like forty-three curtain calls. It was one of those special nights.'

The finale to the event for Hemmings was much later after the show had ended walking through empty St Mark's Square at four in the morning with Pears and Britten and the other singers following the Mayor of Venice's ball, and hearing Arda Mandikian (Miss Jessel) starting to rattle the rafters with Greek folk songs. Peter Pears at one corner and Jennifer Vyvyan at another joined in. (Arda Mandikian had taught everybody Greek songs.) Suddenly Jennifer Vyvyan snapped into the end of the opera – and St Mark's Square resounded with the "Malo" theme. Windows opened. People came out or looked down, or emerged from behind archways and colonnades. 'Ben', says Hemmings, 'was in the corner just smiling and standing there – just as if he was saying, "Look. This is my cast." Such a wonderful evening might influence one's life as a young boy – just a bit.'

(An appendix to Sutcliffe's article includes the first publication of four letters from Hemmings to Britten from 1954–55, which convey something of the flavour of the Britten–Hemmings relationship. None of Britten's correspondence with Hemmings has come to light.)

Although, in his interview with Bridcut, Hemmings claimed that Britten was no longer interested in him once his voice broke (see JBBC, p. 210) – Hemmings told Bridcut that it happened during a performance of *The Turn of the Screw* in Paris in May 1956 (but see Maureen Garnham, *As I Saw It*, p. 86, and Basil Douglas makes no mention of it in his report to the EOG Board (29 June 1956) about the Paris performances) – the surviving documentation at BPL suggests this is not quite the case. While it is true that the friendship cooled once Hemmings could no longer perform with the EOG, the composer certainly kept in touch with the boy. He had already secured for him a place at Gresham's, his own public school, and offered to foot the bill, and had also wanted him to train as a professional singer. But when these schemes failed after Hemmings launched almost immediately post-EOG into an acting career, Britten – judging by the few letters at BPL from

Hemmings to the composer – tried at least to keep in touch occasionally. Indeed, their last known contact by letter would appear to have been in May 1970 when, following an approach initiated on behalf of Britten, Hemmings was arranging to visit the composer with a view to assisting in raising money for developments at Snape Maltings. (In the event, the proposed visit was cancelled due to the illness of Hemmings's then wife.)

Hemmings's adult career as one of that new breed of charismatic British actors of working-class origins who emerged in the 1960s – others include Terence Stamp and Michael Caine – is well documented. In particular, he will be forever associated with London in the 'Swinging Sixties' because of his role as the young photographer in Michelangelo Antonioni's iconic film, *Blow-Up* (1966). Later film projects included the musical *Camelot* (1967) and *The Charge of the Light Brigade* (1968). Though he never completely abandoned his acting career, from the 1970s onwards Hemmings focused more on directing and producing, working mainly in American television series.

See also David Hemmings, *Blow-Up and Other Exaggerations*, pp. 51–8; Maureen Garnham, *As I Saw It*, pp. 12–86 *passim*; Davina Hughes, 'A Boy Finds Opera is Grand', *Illustrated* (9 October 1954), pp. 23–4; and obituaries in *The Times* and *Daily Telegraph* (both 5 December 2003), by Tom Vallance, *Independent*, and by Tim Pulleine, *Guardian* (both 5 December 2003), by Philip French, *Observer Review* (7 December 2003) and Philip Reed, *Guardian* (11 December 2003).

7 Britten and Pears had met with the Pipers and the Stones (see n. 8 below) while in Dorset. 'Portland Bill' is inscribed in Pears's diary for 11 February.

The South Coast at Portland was a landscape Piper frequently painted between 1948 and 1955, including the large-scale oil painting *Clymping* (Clymping Beach, near Littlehampton, Dorset) of 1953, which Pears purchased from the artist in 1954, and *Portland Foreshore* (1955), which Pears purchased from a dealer in 1955.

8 Reynolds Stone (1909–1979), British artist and illustrator, whose woodcuts were included in the volume of Britten's early Walter de la Mare settings, *Tit for Tat*, published in 1969. Stone was to design and carve Britten's gravestone, see PFL, plate 438.

793 To Mary Behrend
[*Typed*]

4 CRABBE STREET, ALDEBURGH
18th February, 1954

My dear Mary,

I owe you a reply to two very kind letters, and here is only a brief typewritten acknowledgement – very remiss of me I know, but it is written in between concerts in a brief visit to Aldeburgh.

I was so happy that you enjoyed "Gloriana" in the revival. We felt that it was a great improvement on the first performances especially musically. Reginald Goodall has much more intensity than Pritchard.

I was even more delighted that you enjoyed the Hardy songs because being the youngest child they are most precious at the moment. Peter and I are doing them around the country now, but I am afraid many people find them difficult or elusive.[1] Personally the poems move me very deeply and it is difficult to tell whether it is Hardy or my own notes that pleases me!

My arm is painful but much better, and I hope the little rather painful treatment I must face in March will complete the recovery. I hope you and Bow [Behrend] are well and not too worried about George[2] and the farm.[3] He seems much more confident about it, and I am sure that is a good sign.

This comes with belated thanks and much love.

[*Handwritten:*] Yours ever,
BEN

1 One listener who clearly did not find *Winter Words* 'difficult' or 'elusive' was the writer Sylvia Townsend Warner, who was later to befriend Pears. On 10 February 1954 she had attended a recital Pears and Britten gave in Dorchester, about which she wrote in her diary (Claire Harman (ed.), *The Diaries of Sylvia Townsend Warner*, pp. 206–7):

The Britten–Pears concert, with Britten's new cycle of Hardy poems. All have power, and his particular forthrightness, and poetic reading of the words: those I was most impressed by were The Travelling Boy ['Midnight on the Great Western (or The Journeying Boy)'], with its reiterated figure in the accompaniment, a bouncing futile phrase with the frustration of To Lincolnshire to Lancashire to buy a pocket-handerkercher; and the last, 'Before Life and After', which is noble like a slow dance, a sarabande-like solemn climbing. Pears was singing very well, his 'Nacht & Träume' superlative, and a Schubert I didn't know, 'Sprach der Liebe', most beautifully phrased. He began with a pounce like a weasel, and a total attentiveness and identification with the music. He has a goblin look, like the child in the Carpaccio *Annunciation* who peeps down when she ought to have been at her lessons.

2 The Behrends' son (b. 1922), who had known Britten and Pears since the mid-1930s. From 1946 until 1958 he often acted as Britten's and Pears's driver when on tour and was in particular a regular general assistant and driver at Aldeburgh Festivals. See also PPT, pp. 8–9; his autobiography, *An Unexpected Life*, pp. 376–606, in which Behrend gives a detailed account of his friendship with Britten and Pears, and Letter 866.

3 The Behrends owned a smallholding at Burghclere which they rented to a tenant farmer. By 1954 George Behrend was himself installed at the farm, delivering eggs and cream once a week to London's Garrick Club, and to many private customers for whom the English Opera Group offices were

DORSET MUSIC SOCIETY

With the support of the Arts Council

presents

Peter Pears

&

Benjamin Britten

at the

CORN EXCHANGE, DORCHESTER

Wednesday, 10th February, 1954

at 7-30 p.m.

Price 6d.

Dorchester, 10 February 1954: programme for a Pears–Britten recital that included *Winter Words*. Dorchester is close to Thomas Hardy's birthplace and where he lived for the latter part of his life, dying there in 1928; it appears in his Wessex novels as Casterbridge.

the collection point. Maureen Garnham, *As I Saw It*, pp. 16–17, recalls meeting George Behrend during her first week at the EOG in 1955:

I gathered that he had suffered a nervous breakdown, and when recovering his parents had set him up at the farm as a form of therapy; I doubt whether it was ever a commercial success.

794 To Myfanwy Piper
[*Typed*]

4 CRABBE STREET, ALDEBURGH
30th March, 1954

My dear Myfanwy,

I ought to have written days ago to thank you for your nice letter to U.C.H.,[1] only I have not felt very much like writing letters. I hope you will forgive my dictating this, but I want to save what little manual energy I have left for writing the opera! They were not too beastly to me at the hospital, but the whole affair was not very pleasant and the after effects are very painful. They will not know for two or three weeks whether it has done the trick, and at the moment I am left to my own resources; doing exercises very painfully to prevent the adhesions happening again.

However, in spite of all this I started the opera this morning and have quite good progress to report.[2] I have got well into the first scene, and am quite pleased with it. So far there are not many alterations in the words to suggest – nothing anyhow that cannot be done by writing. The best plan seems to me to be for me to go on working, and writing the suggestions of changes daily (or telephoning if they are more urgent), and when it seems to need your actual presence I will write to you suggesting it, and hope you may be able to fit it in. The alteration I would like to suggest in Scene I is the following:

Instead of the second paragraph, in order to keep the train of thought more continuous, and also for musical reasons, to lengthen the paragraph to read:

"Who will greet me? The children ... The children ... Will they be clever? Will they like me?"[3]

Be an angel and put your reactions to this on a postcard.

Thank you for your suggestions of titles. I do not quite feel that we have arrived yet, although something to do with "Bly"[4] is hopeful I think. I am not worrying about it at the moment until I am forced to, but I must confess I have a sneaking, horrid feeling that the original H.J. title describes the musical plan of the work exactly!![5]

[*Handwritten*:] Lots of love to you all. Hope it was nice getting home again. I'm very partial to getting home these days!

BEN

1 Britten was admitted to University College Hospital, London, on 22 March for a procedure on his arm to deal with the effects of the bursitis; he was discharged two days later. When he left hospital he resumed work on *The Turn of the Screw*, writing at first with his left hand.

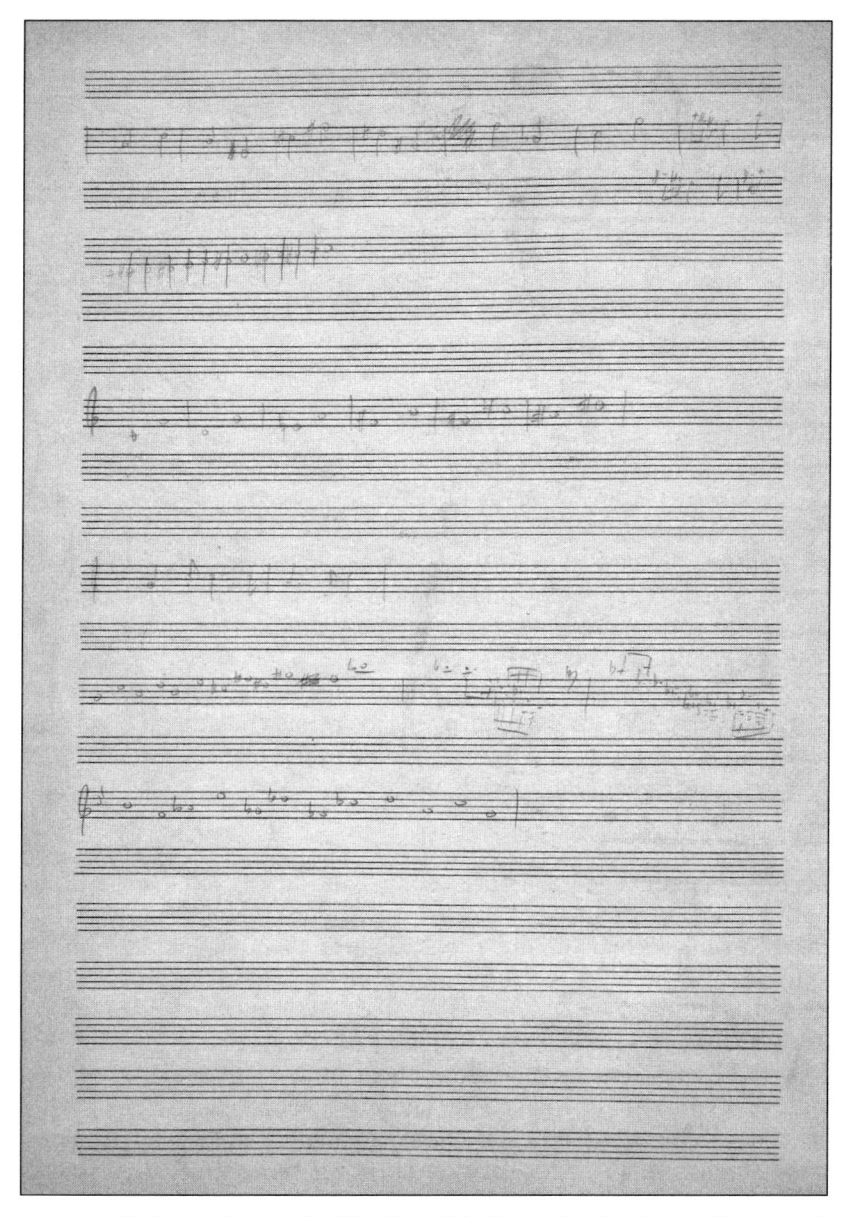

A page of Britten's sketches for *The Turn of the Screw* showing his working out of the twelve-note theme on which the sequence of variation-interludes is based.
BL Add. MS. 60602

Britten explained to Princess Margaret of Hesse and the Rhine (4 February 1954):

> I've played two concerts this last week, without any terrible results – only a bit stiff after. Actually the doctors say that the "bursitis" is mostly cleared now, and what is causing the pain and stiffness is that the shoulder is adhesed(?), in other words it is "frozen". So in a few weeks, I'll have to have it broken-down with a general anaesthetic, after which I hope I'll be as good as new – or rather nearly [...]

2   The pain had delayed Britten starting work on the composition draft of *The Turn of the Screw*. However, it would seem that he had attempted to make a start on the draft at the beginning of February (see Letter 787) but had come immediately on a difficulty: on 4 February 1954, Imogen Holst notes in her diary (IHD, p. 283) that Britten 'said he was stuck because he couldn't find the right tune [i.e. the twelve-note 'Screw' theme] for the variations in the opera'; and on 12 March (IHD, p. 288) she reports that Britten 'was slightly alarmed at the slowness with which he was getting down to the new opera'. Interestingly, Holst's entry for 19 March (IHD, p. 289) – 'Went in after breakfast and he gave me the boy's song in the new opera to copy' – indicates that Miles's 'Malo' song (from Act I scene 6) had been composed in advance of the main work on the composition draft (see also Letter 792 n. 6 and n. 4 below).

On 31 March 1954 Britten sent Mrs Piper a few textual queries from Act I scene 1, adding: 'I have finished this scene today, and am rather pleased with it. I look forward to having your reactions to these queries since I want Imogen to get on with the copying of it.'

3   Act I scene 1; Britten's words again.

4   Bly is the fictitious country-house setting of the novella and the opera.

Britten and Myfanwy Piper were reluctant at first to use James's own title for the opera, probably in order to distinguish their adaptation from the original. They might have been influenced by the existence of William Archibald's 1950 stage play after James, which was entitled *The Innocents*. The play formed the basis of the 1961 film of the same title, directed by Jack Clayton, scripted by Truman Capote among others and featuring Deborah Kerr as the Governess. In her contribution to TBB, p. 79, Myfanwy Piper mentions seeing Archibald's play 'after I had begun working on the libretto'.

In an undated letter that has survived at BPL among the libretto drafts for the opera, Mrs Piper suggested five titles for the new opera:

> The Servile Pair
> The Sacred Terror
> The Tale of Bly (not James)
> A Vision of Evil
> The Approaching Spirits (not James)
>
> O dear. They are not much help are they?
> I have thought a lot about Malo – even to my inadequate musical memory it haunts.

On 4 April 1954 Anthony Gishford suggested further possible titles for the opera: 'Shadowplay', 'Darkness Outside', 'The Governess's Story', 'A Mortal Struggle', 'The Little Children', 'The Interlopers' and 'Pity the Young'. In January 1954, the opera's working title was 'The Tower and the Lake' (see Letter 787).

5 Henry James's own title came to be adopted. The theme itself comprises all twelve pitches of the chromatic scale arranged in a series of alternating rising fourths and descending fifths. Beginning with A (the tonality associated with both the Governess and innocence), each successive scene of Act I rises by one diatonic step until A flat (Quint's tonality) is reached at the end of the act; in Act II the tonal centres fall from A flat down to A by the final scene. This tonal scheme, which produces an ever-increasing tension, encapsulates the image of the turning of a screw.

795 To Myfanwy Piper
From Jeremy Cullum
[*Typed*]

4 CRABBE STREET, ALDEBURGH
3rd April, 1954

Dear Mrs. Piper,

Ben has asked me to send you this suggested change in the libretto, since he has had to go to Norwich. He says it is what he should have talked to you about on the telephone.

After the Round[1] for the children and Mrs. Grose's tidying them up, and the bowing and curtseying, enter Gov. timidly.

Gov.	You must be Mrs. Grose. I am so happy to see you, so happy to be here.
Mrs. Grose	(curtseying) How do you do, Miss. Welcome to Bly.
Gov.	This must be Flora? and Miles?

The children curtsey and bow.

Gov.	(with Mrs. Grose) How charming they are, how beautiful too. The house and park so splendid, far grander than I am used to – I shall feel like a princess here. Bly I begin to love you.
Mrs. G.	(with Gov.) We are happy that you have come, Miss. Miss Flora and Master Miles are happy that you are here too. They are good children, yes they are, they are good, Miss. But they are lively, too lively for an ignorant old woman. They wear me out indeed they do. My poor head is not bright enough – the things that they think up! I am far too old a body for games, Miss, far too old, and now

	they will do better with a young thing as lively as they are themselves. Master Miles is wonderful at lessons, and Miss Flora's sharp too. Yes, they are clever, they are clever. They need their own kind, they are far too clever-clever for me! They'll do better now with a young thing (pardon the liberty Miss), they'll do better now you're here.
The Children	(interrupting) Come along, come along do. We want to show you the house. We want to show you the park. Don't stay talking here any more.

And the rest of the scene the same.

Yours sincerely,
JEREMY CULLUM

1 For Miles and Flora, Act I scene 2: 'Mrs Grose! Mrs Grose! Will she be nice?'

796 To Joy Bowesman[1]
[*Typed*]

4 CRABBE STREET, ALDEBURGH
12th April, 1954

My dear Joy,

We have just posted Dermot[2] off back to you, and enjoyed the weekend with him a great deal; although he was naturally rather overawed to start off with, he got much gayer, and soon was chatting quite freely, especially after his ping-pong successes!!

I had a bit of a talk to him about his future which he will probably tell you about in detail, but just in case the flavour of my remarks doesn't get accurately conveyed to you there are one or two things I would like to say.

I think it would be a great mistake at this point to say definitely what he is going to do when he grows up. He is very young for his age and has not yet developed the knack of handling people that he indubitably will sooner or later. Until we see how this knack develops I think it would be a mistake if he meets a director of Boosey and Hawkes. They might so easily not understand each other, and Dermot's diffidence might be misunderstood as lack of keenness. Besides these next years, perhaps months, will make such a difference to him that it is conceivable that he might even change his mind about what he wants to do. About his specialisation at school I made the point which I hope you will not think unwise, that he should now work at the things he most likes, which incidentally are those things which will come in most handy if he does eventually decide to take up music publishing. These include modern languages as thoroughly as possible, a basic amount of <u>maths</u> and <u>Latin</u>, and do not include <u>science</u>. I have suggested <u>to him</u> moreover to spend as much time on <u>music</u> as possible, perhaps learning a wind instrument (and I would urge the clarinet because that is the instrument Boosey and Hawkes makes principally) and concentrating getting his <u>reading</u> of music as fluent as possible. He probably knows the best ways of <u>doing</u> this, and here might come in that extra tuition which you said in your letter might be possible.

    Can we not see how this goes for one term, and then if he is consistent in his plans he might come here for a few days next summer and I will casually invite down one of the publishing directors who could talk to him and give us his unofficial advice.

    You must realise, of course, this is only after a very casual meeting with the boy, and I may be quite wrong, so please disregard it if you are in any way unconvinced by my reasoning. Please give my love to your mother and say I will try to call in on my way to London sometime next month, only it is impossible to say at the moment when that will be.

    Much love to you too, and of course to Dermot.

Yours ever,
BEN

1 The elder sister of Francis Barton, a childhood friend of Britten; see Letter 12 n. 3.

2 Joy Bowesman's teenage 'music-maniac' son – as his mother described him to Britten – was contemplating a career in music publishing and had written to the composer in 1954 having sung in a performance of *A Ceremony of Carols*. Dermot was to die of cancer in 1962. For Bowesman's account of her family's friendship with the composer, see Letter 12 n. 3.

797 To Myfanwy Piper
[*Typed*]

4 CRABBE STREET, ALDEBURGH
12th April, 1954

My dear Myfanwy,

    A very brief note reporting progress to date. I have now finished [Act I] Scene 3 and am very pleased with it. No alterations to speak of, only the following minor ones which I hope you will approve of.

1) <u>Gov</u>. Tell me, have you known Miles to be bad? (i.e. cut "ever")
2) I have made the Governess and Mrs. G. sing all the remarks over the children's nursery rhyme together, so the last five sentences on page one of this scene, and the first of page two are for both.

3) The tune I have used is "Lavender's Blue" which fits very nicely.
4) Do you mind: It is all a wicked lie (instead of mistake)?
5) Mrs. Grose. and what shall you say to him? (instead of "or say to him?")
6) Last sentence cut the first "Miss". (Bravo, and I'll stand by you). This is for musical reasons, and I think the intensity of the moment will prevent its sounding cheeky!

It has been lovely having Basil [Coleman] here, and we have done lots of work together on the piece. We have had one major discussion which he will talk to you about.[1] It arose out of a sudden fear that the work is going to be much too short. The first three scenes, incidentally, play only ten minutes. Please do not be shocked at his suggestion, and give it a fair chance. When you have thought it over we must meet at once because it may affect some of the scenes a lot.

[*Handwritten:*] Lots of love to all,

BEN

[*Handwritten:*] P.S. I don't want it to sound as if the proposed alteration comes only because the piece might be too short, because it has been in my head for some little time – – a prologue? ... the interview or the ghost-story party?[2] possibly spoken?

But I won't whet your imagination any more.

P.P.S. Please tell Edward [Piper] we've had Sebastian [Welford] here for the week-end & that he's quite right ... S. is quite charming, & very intelligent too.

Love,

1 The addition of a prologue: see Letter 812 n. 2.
2 Both of Britten's suggestions for the proposed Prologue are derived from Henry James: the interview between the Governess and the children's remote guardian and the 'short-story party' held 'on Christmas Eve in an old house' can be found in James's prefatory chapter to the novella.

798 To Myfanwy Piper

4 CRABBE STREET, ALDEBURGH
April 23rd 1954

Dear Myfanwy

– In great haste, here are the possible changes at the beginning of Act I Sc V for your consideration:

Both children: (coming in on hobby horses)

	"Tom, Tom the Piper's son
	Stole a pig and away he run.
	Pig was eat & Tom was beat,
	Tom ran howling down the street."
<u>Miles</u>:	Now I'll steal the pig!
<u>Flora</u>:	Go on then, go on!
<u>Both</u>:	"Tom, Tom . . . away he run."
<u>Miles</u>:	Now, chase me!
<u>Flora</u>:	I'll catch you!
<u>Both</u>	"Pig was eat . . . down the street." (<u>Squeals from children</u>.)
<u>Flora</u>	Let's do it again.
<u>Governess</u>	(<u>off</u>) Children! Are you ready! Run along then! (<u>coming in</u>)
<u>Children</u>	"Tom, Tom the Piper's son" (<u>running off</u>)
<u>Gov.</u>	I'll follow.
<u>Children</u>	"Stole a pig and away he run."

Would you like another remark from the Gov. / about looking for gloves, or something?[1] There's room if you would.

Lots of love –
BEN

P.S. Stupidly I forgot to post this yesterday – but it saves postage since I've got a fresh query after this morning's work –

Can I have a <u>longer</u> description of Quint please? For the moment I've written it thus (taken from H.J.)

<u>Gov.</u> "His hair was red, close-curling – a long pale face – small eyes – His look was sharp, fixed & strange – He was tall & active, yes, even handsome – But a horror!"[2]

Will that do? No other changes to speak of so far –

Would you let me have the possible Overture[3] soon, please.

1 The published stage direction reads: 'The Governess looks about for a moment, picks up a pair of gloves and is about to go out when she looks up and sees Quint appear suddenly at the window.' No additional remark materialized.

2 The passage in James (*The Turn of the Screw and Other Stories*, chapter v, pp. 146–7) in which the Governess describes the man she has seen to Mrs Grose reads as follows:

'He has red hair, very red, close-curling, and a pale face, long in shape, with straight good features and little rather queer whiskers that are as red as his hair. His eyebrows are somehow darker; they look particularly arched and as if they might move a good deal. His eyes are sharp, strange – awfully; but I only know clearly that they're rather small and very fixed. His mouth's wide, and his lips are thin, and except for his little whiskers he's quite clean-shaven. He gives me a sort of sense of looking like an actor.'

'An actor!' It was impossible to resemble one less, at least, than Mrs Grose at that moment.

'I've never seen one, but I suppose them. He's tall, active, erect,' I continued, 'but never – no, never! – a gentleman.'

My companion's face had blanched as I went on; her round eyes started and her mild mouth gaped. 'A gentleman?' she gasped, confounded, stupefied: 'A gentleman, he?'

'You know him then?'

She visibly tried to hold herself. 'But he is handsome?'

I saw the way to help her. 'Remarkably!'

3 The Prologue.

799 To William Plomer

4 CRABBE STREET, ALDEBURGH
April 24th 1954

My dear William,

May I bother you with two requests?

1) You know these Crabbe celebrations in the Alde. Festival, when you are so kindly coming to read some of his poetry in Glemham, start with a luncheon, in which speeches in honour of the old boy will be made?[1] Morgan is doing one, & the old Sir John Murray[2] was scheduled to do one too. He now writes that he feels he hasn't the strength, & would we excuse him. Could you face, dear William, making a (quite short) tribute after the meal, to which anyhow we were going to invite you? Do say yes, if it isn't too much worry for you. Jock Cranbrook[3] will be presiding, & will of course introduce you. We'd be all so pleased if you would.

2) In this "Symphonic Suite" I'm doing from Gloriana (which, incidentally I heard rehearsed in Birmingham & which sounds splendid), there is the little matter of titles. Could you give me your advice? There are four movements. I is the Prelude, including an orchestral version of 'Green leaves'. "Tournament and Homage to the Queen" – or just "Tournament". II is the 2nd Lute Song – so, "Lute Song" do you think? III is more of a problem. It is all the dances of Act II Sc. 3 all strung together, which makes a pleasant kind of Scherzo. Dances? The Ball? The Court ball? Any ideas? IV is the end of the whole work, without of course the speaking. As you'll remember it is a full version of "Happy were he". Could one say "Apotheosis", or is it too pompous? Or the Death – of Essex – or the Queen? Be a dear & put some ideas on a p.c., because I'm a bit at sea about it all.

I had, alas, to miss the readings on the 3rd Programme last week – the

Screw takes all my time & energy – & having heard you read the Ballads here, I regret it all the more. But couldn't you read them next year at the Festival, perhaps?[4]

Gloriana was a terrific success in Birmingham, again. It was most heartening. I hope you are well, my dear, and that the return of the native Charles, to Germany, won't be too worrying for you.

Much love from both Peter – and

BEN

Please forgive awful writing – arm's a bit stiff still.

1 Britten had suggested to Plomer (8 February 1954), that the writer 'might come & read some extracts from [Crabbe] as the culmination of the round-Crabbe-trip at the Cranbrooks (luncheon here, & unveiling of a plaque, Parham, Glemham, Rendham (another plaque), & then tea & reading (½ hour or less) in the drawing-room at Great Glemham [...] Date, June 16th (in the afternoon)'.

The Crabbe bicentenary was celebrated at the Aldeburgh Festival on 16 June along the lines Britten suggests in his letters to Plomer. Plomer and Forster paid their tributes after the lunch at the East Suffolk Hotel in Aldeburgh. The bicentenary was further marked at Aldeburgh by an exhibition of first editions of the poet's work held in the Moot Hall, and by a performance of extracts from *Peter Grimes* (the libretto of which had been based on Crabbe's *The Borough*) sung by Peter Pears and Joan Cross, with Britten (piano), at the 'Opera Concert', held at the Jubilee Hall on 20 June.

2 Sir John (Jock) Murray (1884–1967), British publisher, whose long-established family firm had published Crabbe. Murray was the last editor of *Quarterly Review*. For almost thirty-five years, he directed the affairs of Murrays with his nephew John Murray (1909–1993), whose friends (and authors) included John Betjeman, John Piper, Reynolds Stone and Kenneth Clark.

3 John (Jock) David Gathorne-Hardy, 4th Earl of Cranbrook (1915–1978), whose wife Fidelity was the first Chairman of the Aldeburgh Festival; see Letter 602 n. 5. The Cranbrook family lived at Glemham House. See also TBB, pp. 145–50.

4 On 19 June 1955, at the Moot Hall, Aldeburgh, Plomer, assisted by Nancy Masefield, indeed gave a 'Ballad Reading' as part of the Aldeburgh Festival. According to Peter F. Alexander (*William Plomer: A Biography*, p. 290), 'From the start [Plomer's ballads] had been written to be performed, or at least read aloud. Delivered in this way they are highly effective pieces of work, and perhaps his most characteristic productions.' Plomer published a collection of his ballads under the title *A Shot in the Park* in 1955, presenting an inscribed copy to Britten and Pears: 'For Ben & Peter/with love from William/March 1955.'

800 To Myfanwy Piper
[*Typed*]

> 4 CRABBE STREET, ALDEBURGH
> 26th April, 1954

My dear Myfanwy,

   I am getting on well with [Act I] Scene 5, but I have one major query which I must ask you to think about. Do you remember Mrs. Grose's big outburst after "O! he was a horror" (or in my new version "but a horror") – "Dear God, I can't abide such and their dreadful ways"? I have set this to a big dramatic phrase, and Peter on hearing it felt that it did not quite work, and I am inclined to agree with him. Where it was originally placed (on the next page) it was fine, but I feel that it does not quite fit Mrs. Grose's feelings at this place. It is neither universal enough, nor realistic enough. It is certainly a most complicated moment. Mrs. Grose has recognised Quint from the Governess's description, yet knows that the man is dead. Is this an outburst of terror at something she can't understand, and against which she is soon going to shut her mind; is it rather a cry of terror at the memory of Quint (in which case "Dear God, I can't forget him and his dreadful ways"[1] would perhaps be better)? The trouble is as usual that I have set the phrase as it stands, and the whole of the narration following is founded on it. If we want to change it therefore, I am afraid it must be to those notes. Here they are:

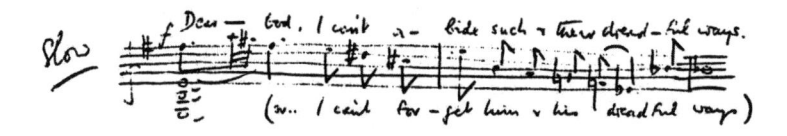

   Peter also made a rather good point about Mrs. Grose's last speech on the first page of Scene 5 ("when Quint made free with everyone"). He feels that "made free" is too particular and suggestive, and that we should save this particular phrase until the beginning of the next page. James merely says "Quint was too free with the boy". I think the sexy suggestion should only refer to his relationship with Miss Jessel, don't you? Incidentally it may help to avert a scandal in Venice!![2]

   [*Handwritten:*] Sorry to bother you so often, but we must 'keep together in these anxious days' of course.

> Love to all
> BEN

1 Finally, these words were chosen: 'Dear God, is there no end to his dreadful ways?' See also Letter 801.

2   In chapter VI (*The Turn of the Screw and Other Stories*, p. 150) James writes:

> [Mrs Grose] paused a moment; then she added: 'Quint was much too free.'
> This gave me, straight from my vision of his face – such a face! – a sudden sickness of disgust. 'Too free with my boy?'
> 'Too free with everyone!'

In the libretto, the final version of this passage reads as follows:

MRS GROSE   [...] But I saw things elsewhere I did not like. When Quint was free with everyone – with little master Miles –

GOVERNESS   Miles!

MRS GROSE   Hours they spent together.

GOVERNESS   Miles!

MRS GROSE   Yes, Miss, he made free with her too – with lovely Miss Jessel, governess to those pets, those angels, those innocent babes – and she a lady, so far above him.
Dear God! Is there no end!
But he had his ways to twist them round his little finger.
He liked them pretty, I can tell you, Miss – and he had his will, morning and night.

801 To Myfanwy Piper
[*Typed*]

4 CRABBE STREET, ALDEBURGH
28th April, 1954

My dear Myfanwy,

Thank you for your letter and the telephone conversation last night – most helpful both of them.

Jeremy [Cullum] has now typed [Act I] scenes four and five as I have set them. You will find a lot of little changes in Scene five which perhaps you could examine and let me know if there is something you don't approve of.

In the big phrase for Mrs. Grose, the word "finished" is awkward since one has to sing it short–long, and it is long–long in the musical phrase. Do you think "ended" would do instead, or is this too stilted? Also I had, before your card arrived, set "guardian" in the Governess's last paragraph. The whole of this demands to be set rather high, and "Uncle", also, as you will see, "peace", are awkward to manage in that part of the voice. Do you mind if we keep "guardian", and do you approve "quiet" in the latter case?[1]

In haste,
Much love to you,
BEN

1 The final choice of words for the Governess at the end of Act I scene 4 was: 'I must guard their quiet, and their guardian's too.'

802 To Myfanwy Piper
[*Typed*]

4 CRABBE STREET, ALDEBURGH
7th May 1954

My dear Myfanwy,

I am getting on slowly, but your new bit in Scene 7 is excellent.[1] I want to make one or two small additions to the geography rhyme, and have fitted a dotty pronunciation of Mediterranean to balance the end of it. I would also like some reactions from the Governess to Flora's virtuosity (to balance Flora's reactions to Miles in the previous scene). I suggest something like the enclosed.[2]

Here also is Jeremy's typed copy of Scene 6 which you forgot to take. Plans have gone slightly wrong for next week as Beth cannot get away on Thursday, but I will get in touch with you as soon as things are sorted out.

Much love to you all,
BEN

1 Myfanwy Piper had written (undated letter, 'Friday'):

> Here is scene 7. I think Dolly is all right now. Do cut anything you think – especially the last soliloquy which may have too much [i.e. the Governess's 'Miss Jessel! It was Miss Jessel.']. The Quint poem [presumably 'I am all things strange and bold', Act I scene 8] shall be redone tomorrow. I can't wait to get on with the Ghost Duologue [Act II scene 1] and I think it brilliant of you to suggest doing it next.

2 Britten refers to the Governess's interjections to Flora's catalogue of seas – 'Adriatic and Aegean', etc. – in Act I scene 7, and to the parallel passage in scene 6 when Flora mimics Miles's Latin lesson – 'Many nouns in –*is* we find', etc. The same 5/4 metre is employed in both places, thereby reinforcing the verbal parallel with a musical one. The enclosure Britten mentions sending with this letter has not survived.

803 To Myfanwy Piper

4 CRABBE STREET, ALDEBURGH
May 16th 1954

My dear Myfanwy,

Thank you so much for putting Beth [Welford] & me up so nicely on Thursday. We both loved it. Beth was thrilled to listen to some of the discussions & hopes she wasn't in the way. Once we'd got the thunder over,

I think we did some excellent work. It was maddening that the atmosphere had to go mad just as I was going to play the piece[1] – it always needs my full concentration & inclination, & because it had neither, I'm afraid it was a bad performance. But I hope it gave the visual boys an idea. I do think John's [Piper's] brainwaves are thrilling. He is a wonder. Whatever he touches has magic. Please tell him that when I come next to Fawley Bottom[2] to work he must put some of his pictures away – it is difficult to concentrate with so much wealth all around!

Our visit to Malvern was very useful, but it was a very long way (about 220 miles back to Aldeburgh yesterday) & rather tiring & frustrating coping with relations[3] – (We stopped to see, & report to, my brother[4] on the way back, as well!). But the glass in the Priory[5] was staggering. Do you know it?

I'm now well into the last scene, & pleased with it. What about a title for it? – – The night . . . ? – the Hauntings – the Tower & the Lake – – ?[6] Could you put something on a p.c. Also can the boy have more reaction to Quint – like Flora's to Miss Jessel perhaps. Or – I'm here, Quint. Any ideas?[7] I'm very pleased with the new end to that scene. You are a clever girl.

Much love to all – & many thanks again –
Yours ever,
BEN

1 On their journey by car to Great Malvern, Worcestershire, Britten and his sister had stopped off for a night at the Pipers (see n. 2 below), when Britten had played through as much of Act I of *The Turn of the Screw* as had been completed, i.e. to the end of scene 7. As the letter makes clear, the play-through provided an opportunity for John Piper, who was responsible for the set and costume designs, to hear some of the music for the first time.

On 3 May Britten had told Princess Margaret of Hesse and the Rhine that progress on *The Turn of the Screw* 'is very behindhand – going well, but slowly. I think it's going to be good, but it's jolly difficult to tell at such close quarters. What a story it is.'

2 Fawley Bottom Farmhouse, near Henley-on-Thames, Oxfordshire, the Pipers' home from the 1930s for the rest of their lives and to which they habitually referred as 'Fawley Bum'.

3 Britten and his sister had visited their aunt, Florence Britten (see Diary for 27 May 1931, n. 1), who was resident in a nursing home in Great Malvern.

4 Britten's elder brother, Robert (1907–1987), then teaching at Wellingborough. Neither Britten nor his sister Beth enjoyed an easy relationship with their brother.

5 Great Malvern Priory, noted for its fifteenth-century stained-glass windows.

6 Act I scene 8 was to be called 'At Night'.

7 In the final version of the libretto, Miles responds to Quint's calling him with short phrases echoing Quint's, such as 'I'm here, O I'm here', 'Gold, O yes, gold!' and 'Secrets, O secrets!'

804 To Eric Walter White
[*Typed*]

4 CRABBE STREET, ALDEBURGH
21st May, 1954

Dear Eric,

Many thanks for the new book[1] which arrived yesterday morning. I have not studied it fully yet because the new piece takes most of my time, but I hope before long to learn many things about me that I had never dreamed of! I do congratulate you on it, and thank you for the really incredible amount of industry. I am no judge of things written about myself (as you know), and so I won't pronounce it a masterpiece, but I know it will come in very handy, and settle many arguments for a long time to come.

The new piece progresses in a <u>circular</u> direction,[2] and I am pretty pleased with it. I am sorry it puts the book out of date a little, but not so much as you would think since it becomes the E.O.G.'s property, and therefore would not need such an enormous appendix as the other operas.[3]

With much love, and great gratitude to you,
Yours ever,
BEN

1 The new (second) edition, revised and enlarged, of Eric Walter White's *Benjamin Britten: A Sketch of His Life and Works*, first published in 1948 by Atlantis Verlag, Zurich, and Boosey & Hawkes, London; see also Letter 741 n. 3.

2 A reference to the 'turning' image of the theme's rotating intervals.

3 In the 1954 edition of his book, White had included (as Appendix B) a list of all the productions of Britten's operas to date. The forthcoming premiere of *The Turn of the Screw* would therefore render White's appendix immediately out of date. Britten's remark about the *Screw* not requiring as extensive a list as the other operas was because the English Opera Group was to enjoy a period of exclusivity over the opera, an exclusivity that was coupled to a generous financial arrangement in respect of the performing rights, in an attempt to place the EOG on a more secure financial basis.

805 To Peter Pears

4 CRABBE STREET, ALDEBURGH
May 28th (?) 1954

My darling P,

This is just a brief note to send my love to you now in Switzerland – although as I write it, you are still in Brussels.[1] I hope it isn't all too hectic, & that you've met some nice people, & that you get on well with the Fullers.[2] I shall try to listen to P.G. tomorrow night, but rather doubt if we shall hear anything. I suppose Lucretia isn't to be broadcast?

All goes well here – the work slow, but (I think) sure. Wish it weren't so slow, but I expect it'll be done in time. Imo likes Act II beginning alright.

The Goble recorders have come, & are lovely – Much nicer than the "monarchs of the plastic"[3] – nice sound, & very (almost too much) in tune. The tenor needs a finger piece (like your bass) I think, because neither Imo nor I can stretch far enough to cover the bottom hole. It is a lovely noise it makes, not too cow-like.

I've just seen Stephen Reiss[4] & he says our little Bonington is genuinely a B.[5] It is catalogued apparently in the original catalogue – a detailed description – "man with red cloak, before a tomb in a crypt with light coming through the door". Isn't that exciting? A jolly good buy of yours!

No other news. The fine weather broke yesterday with big thunderstorms (& a hurricane at Hasketon!),[6] & today is sunny, but windy & clouds too. I expect to play tennis this afternoon, but otherwise work – work – work.

I miss you dreadfully. It's almost worse you coming for just a day & then off again – but it isn't so very long. I'll try & find a way of collecting you on Whit Sunday.

Much love to you; enjoy yourself a bit,

B

Greetings to the Fullers – & to Arda[7] if she's with you.
I still love the Gwen John.[8] It is a beauty.

1 Pears sang Grimes in Brussels on 28 and 30 May, before travelling on the 31st to Geneva, where he was due to sing the role of the Male Chorus in *The Rape of Lucretia* on 1, 3 and 4 June at the Théâtre de la Cour Saint-Pierre. Arda Mandikian (see n. 7 below) sang the Female Chorus and Frederick Fuller (see n. 2 below) played Junius. Pears told Britten in a letter of 1 June that:

Brussels was up & down – A somewhat bumpy flight, in some ways desperate rehearsals – a rather dear M. Daniel Sternefeldt – wild fellow soloists in certain ways – Viccy very graty & breathy – Chorus in agony over the Mad Scene [in *Grimes*] –

wonderful old Astoria [Hotel] with an influx of French footballers on the last day – Finally not a wholly bad performance (did you hear it?) which made a great impression.

Later in the same letter Pears reports that 'Mme Ansermet was there last night [at *Lucretia*] & they both come tonight I think.'

2 The British baritone, writer and singing teacher Frederick Fuller (1909–1995) and his wife, Patricia; both were described by Pears as 'extremely nice & kind' (letter to Britten, 1 June 1954). Fuller made his debut in 1940 at one of the National Gallery concerts in London. In 1947 he joined the United Nations in Geneva as a translator and during the 1950s he gave concerts throughout Europe with Julian Bream. Patricia Fuller's correspondence with Britten and Pears suggests she ran a theatre or production company in Geneva. The Geneva *Lucretia* is described in the programme as 'presented by Phoenix Productions'.

3 The Dolmetsch recorders received in January 1954. The superior Goble recorders were made of wood.

4 British arts administrator, art historian and art dealer (1918–1999), who was General Manager of the Aldeburgh Festival, 1955–71, and served as General Manager of the English Opera Group, 1958–61. Following Reiss's resignation from the Festival administration (see vol. 3, Donald Mitchell's Introduction, pp. 30–48, and HCBB, pp. 520–29), Reiss held appointments as Director of 'Fanfare for Europe', 1972, and as Administrator of the London Symphony Orchestra, 1974–75. In 1975 his monograph on Aelbert Cuyp was published by Zwemmer. He subsequently returned to the world of fine art, first with Curwen Prints, 1975–80, before founding Business Art Galleries in 1978. From 1985 he owned a small gallery in Norwich, during which time he came to know the work of the painter Peggy Somerville, about whom he was to write two books and curate an exhibition for the Aldeburgh Festival in 1994.

Reiss was a pupil at Gresham's School, Holt, where he briefly overlapped with Britten, five years his senior; he remembered Britten playing in school concerts. Although Reiss went up to Balliol College, Oxford, he switched to studies at the Chelsea School of Art where he cultivated his interests in painting and art history. (Reiss came from a cultured background: his father, Richard Reiss (1883–1959), was a leading figure in the new towns movement, and his sister Delia was married to the artist Patrick Heron.) He served as an intelligence officer in the Second World War, and in 1945 was responsible for overseeing the revival of the cultural life of Lübeck and Schleswig-Holstein. With his wife Beth, Reiss moved to Aldeburgh in 1949 to make his living as a professional artist, a venture that failed. In 1953 he curated, at short notice, an Aldeburgh Festival exhibition of the work of the caricaturist William Haselden, and joined the Festival Council.

Two years later, following Elizabeth Sweeting's departure, he became

General Manager. Reiss recalled (in an interview with Donald Mitchell, 18 July 1998; at BPL) that Britten and Pears were

> very unhappy with the way things were developing because they felt the Festival had reached a sort of road block [...] They wanted a theatre and the Council was not happy about it, the financial aspect [...] They decided that [...] a change of management [was needed].

Reiss's tenure at Aldeburgh was extremely successful: he forged and maintained better relations with the Aldeburgh Town Council and church authorities than had previously been achieved; he supervised the expansion of the Jubilee Hall in 1960, for which Britten wrote *A Midsummer Night's Dream* (dedicated to Reiss); he took the Festival beyond Aldeburgh to churches elsewhere in East Suffolk (Blythburgh, Orford and Framlingham); and he founded and managed the Festival Club.

Reiss was closely involved in the conversion of the disused Maltings situated on the banks of the River Alde at Snape, which was to become the Festival's principal venue following its opening by the Queen in 1967. (It was, it seems, Reiss's idea to engage Arup Associates: 'I don't know why. I didn't know anything about Arups [...] I just happened to know that they were engineers as well as architects, so I felt that this was the kind of proposition which would be relevant.') His remarkable skills as an administrator were keenly tested by the destruction of the Maltings by fire on the opening night of the 1969 Festival, following which the entire Festival had to be rescheduled at other venues (principally Blythburgh Church), and were no less stretched by Britten's and Pears's insistence that the hall should be rebuilt in time for the 1970 Festival.

See also obituaries in *The Times* (13 October 1999); by Ian Collins, *Guardian* (14 October 1999); by Elizabeth Forbes and Ian Collins, *Independent* (19 October 1999), and by Alan Blyth, *Opera* (February 2000), pp. 181–2.

5 A painting by Richard Parkes Bonington (1802–1828), British Romantic artist, known for his landscapes and historical scenes, whose style attracted many imitators. The work Britten refers to in this letter is a small oil entitled *Crypt of a Church*, which was purchased by Pears in 1950. An exhibition of Bonington's paintings, including presumably Britten's and Pears's, was held at the 1954 Aldeburgh Festival. Stephen Reiss contributed an article about the artist to the Aldeburgh Festival Programme Book, pp. 11–12.

6 A village near Woodbridge, Suffolk, where Britten's sister Beth Welford and her family lived.

7 Arda Mandikian (b. 1924), Armenian soprano, who was to create the role of Miss Jessel in *The Turn of the Screw*. Other EOG roles included the title role in Holst's *Sāvitri*, the Sorceress in Purcell's *Dido and Aeneas* and the Female Chorus in *The Rape of Lucretia*, and she made several appearances at the Aldeburgh Festival during the 1950s. Maureen Garnham (*As I Saw It*, p. 16), writes:

She had a voice quite different in timbre from Jennifer's or Joan's [Jennifer Vyvyan and Joan Cross], but equally individual, and she was a good actress. She was a lively character, a personal friend of Basil's [Douglas] and also of Olive Zorian's, and I have always regretted not having been the proverbial fly on the wall when those three were together over a good meal and a bottle of wine; the conversation must have been well worth overhearing. Eventually, Arda returned to Greece, and though Basil kept in touch with her for a long time, and they met whenever she visited London, she moved house in Athens, and we failed to find her when we visited Greece in 1989.

Mandikian was born in Smyrna (modern Izmir) and studied at the Athens Conservatory with Elvira de Hildalgo and Alexandra Trianti. In 1951 she made her UK debut in the title role of Egon Wellesz's *Incognita* in a production by the Oxford University Opera Club. She first appeared at the Royal Opera House in Britten's *Peter Grimes* in 1953. Her very few solo recordings include Delphic hymns and folk songs from her native land, repertory that she sang at an open-air late-night concert during the 1954 Aldeburgh Festival. In 1971 she was a co-signatory to a pro-democracy petition in Greece (a subject dear to Britten's heart: see Letter 765 n. 11), and from 1976 was Vice-President of the Greek National Opera in Athens.

8 British painter (1876–1939), the sister of Augustus John. Britten probably refers to Gwen John's charcoal study for *The Messenger*, purchased by Pears on 24 May.

806 To Basil Coleman

4 CRABBE STREET, ALDEBURGH
May 29th 1954

My dear Basil,

Thank you for your very nice letter. I am so glad – much encouraged – that you like the way the Screw is Turning. I have never felt so insecure about a work – now up, now down – & it helps a great deal to know that you, who know so instinctively what I'm aiming at, like it so much.[1] The next Act goes on the same way. I wonder if you talked to Myfanwy about the churchyard scene? I feel so strongly, for the form & drama of the work as well as for the music's sake, that we <u>must</u> have something light and gay here, something for the children to be young & charming in (for the last time, almost, in the work) – & I think the idea of the hymn (a kind of 'choir procession') to be the best yet thought of.[2] Goodness – how <u>difficult</u> it is to write an opera with the librettist so far away! She is so good, but is so occupied with being a wife & mother.

I feel I'm being bad about your Canadian trip.[3] Myfanwy seems to have swung right round about it, & was quite cross with me when I disagreed. It is a great compliment to you, my dear, that your friends feel so strongly about your future! But for goodness sake don't take any notice of what they (we) say. Do what your instinct tells you. I certainly was swayed by M's arguments that you are so keen on this film & television business. Personally I don't feel it matters to be 'out of the swim' of things for a few months – especially when you have the EOG & School[4] to come back to. But it does matter to do something for convenience or safety's sake when there is something more important to be done elsewhere. – – There I go – advising again! Sorry. Ignore it!

I am sorry you can't be here next week, but perhaps it's just as well; I shall do more work, without the temptation to sit & talk to you!

Much love,
BEN

1 Coleman was to make his own contribution to the libretto of *The Turn of the Screw*. In an interview with Donald Mitchell (Aldeburgh, 29 October 2000; at BPL), he recalled:

There was a time when Ben and Myfanwy were stuck in the last scene for something they wanted, and I'm pleased to say there is one line that I contributed to the opera – the line 'What have we done between us?' in fact was my suggestion.

2 Act II scene 2, 'The Bells', in which Miles and Flora, 'walking in like choir boys', sing a sinister 'Benedicite' – 'O sing unto them [i.e. Quint and Miss Jessel] a new song.' According to Myfanwy Piper (DHOBB, p. 11), she 'could think of no way to parody a hymn until at last it was solved by a clergyman friend who said, "It must obviously be a Benedicite."' (Britten had already made ironic use of a Benedicite setting in Act II scene 1 of *Peter Grimes*, when it is sung offstage by the congregation during Sunday worship.)

In an undated letter probably written in early June 1954, Myfanwy Piper wrote to Britten:

Basil was here at the weekend and he and John did quite a lot of work. He is in very good form and has a lot of ideas about the piece [...]

I'm frightfully pleased with Act II scene 2 now. I think your idea of a chant was brilliant and I'm rather pleased with my canticle. I'm sorry I was so mulish and absurd about the hymn – all those excuses about it not going down were awfully thin. It was simply that I was unhappy and *couldn't* see why or what to do about it – not because I couldn't find another alternative that didn't have too much emphasis on his [Miles's] first syllables [...]

3 Coleman was to emigrate to Canada in the mid-1950s, where he spent several years directing drama in both television and the theatre.

4 A reference to the National Opera School (later the London Opera Centre).

(Ab) Var. VIII

Colloquy & Soliloquy ⟨CT⟩/II.

Scene I. ~~Hosts, Quint and Miss Jessel — nowhere.~~
The scene is undefined. The lights fade — & Quint, Miss Jessel —

Miss Jessel.	Ah, did you call me from my schoolroom dreams?
Quint.	I call? not I, you heard the terrible sound of the wild swan's wings.
Miss Jessel.	Cruel, why did you beckon me to your side?
Quint.	I beckon? no, not I, your beating heart to your own passions lied.
Miss Jessel.	Betrayer, where were you when in the abyss I fell?
Quint.	Betrayer? No! I, I waited for the sound of my own last bell.
Miss Jessel.	And now what do you seek?
Quint.	I seek a friend.
Miss Jessel.	She is here.
Quint.	No, self-deceiver.
Miss Jessel.	Ah, Quint. Do you forget? Quint!
Quint.	I seek a friend —
	Obedient to follow where I lead,
	Slick as a juggler's mate to catch my thought,
	Proud, curious, agile he shall feed
	My mounting power.
	Then to his bright subservience I'll expound
	The desperate passions of a haunted heart,
	And in that hour
	"The ceremony of innocence is drowned".
Miss Jessel.	I too must have a soul to share my woe.
	Despised, betrayed, unwanted she shall go
	Forever, to my joyless spirit bound.
	"The ceremony of innocence is drowned".
Quint – Jessel.	Day by day the bars we must break
	~~(Each day our hauntings closer take)~~ lest them do round,
	Break the love that ~~~~~~~~~~
	Cheat the careful, watching eyes.

"The ceremony of innocence is drowned." the Governess,
the lights fade a Quint, Miss J. + in a — P.T.O

Britten's working copy of the draft libretto for *The Turn of the Screw*,
Act II scene 1, 'Colloquy and Soliloquy'

807 To Myfanwy Piper

4 CRABBE STREET, ALDEBURGH
May 29th 1954

My dear Myfanwy,

   So sorry I was so short & sharp on the telephone this afternoon; only it's been a vile day, just on the edge of thunder, & work doesn't seem to come very easily, & figures on the top of everything is a bit much! Anyhow, I feel if I bother too much about them that there won't be any need for any figures at all – besides I've done my bit by suggesting the economies in Venice & Aldeburgh (& finding the house, cook & house-keeper here).[1] Lord knows what else we can save, except by not doing the Beggar's Opera out of the same funds, which seems to be the real trouble, I feel.

   I've done Scene I [of Act II], & there are one or two queries.

line 8:	Quint:	Betrayer? Not I, I waited …
		(to match the other phrases)
line 13:	Miss Jessel:	Ah, Quint, Quint – do you forget?
line 17	Quint:	Proud, curious, agile he shall feed.

   I'm awfully sorry, I've tried & tried to get the final quatrain to start with 'Each Day' – but it just can't work, & I'm not awfully happy about "Day by day the guards we break". Wouldn't 'bars' be better, or better still some kind of reversal of lines 1 & 2 such as:

Day by day the love we break
Break the bars that round them … ??[2]

Could you think about this please & send a p.c. along, because it ought to go to the singers fairly soon?

   There aren't any changes (except: 'Lost in my labyrinth I see no truth') in the next bit – only, where do we say the Governess is – not 'nowhere' like the ghosts I presume – or just 'rapt in thought' (wherever that may be!)[3]

   I look forward to playing you the scene. I think it's odd but nice! – & quite long, nearly 10 minutes!!

   I'm sorry about the Churchyard Scene worry. I feel sure that we must, for dramatic & musical reasons, have a set piece for the kids at the beginning of it, & what else can it be? I don't see how a gentle make-believe of a choir procession (unless done grotesquely) could offend anyone; and I don't see why the words should offend more than the music – most people would anyhow recognise the tune first, especially if they start it off-stage as I'd like. Anyhow I must go ahead & write something here;

& we can discuss the details of the production when we meet. Sorry to be so cantakerous – I think I'd better go & have a bathe! –

Lots of love,
BEN

I do hope you were able to discuss a little scenery this weekend, & weren't only stuck with those dreary figures.

1 Paul Kildea writes (PKSB, pp. 113–14):

Lulled into a false sense of security by the [Venice] Biennale Festival's fee, the Group allowed a period of several weeks for coaching, a full month of rehearsals, and a great enough financial incentive for the singers to forgo all other engagements during the rehearsal period [for *The Turn of the Screw*]. Almost £10,000 was spent fulfilling these commitments and covering running costs in Venice – considerably more than the production and running costs of Britten's previous operas.

Basil Douglas had written to Britten about these spiralling costs on 27 May 1954 (EOG Correspondence, 1954, at BPL). Despite his being preoccupied by the composition of the opera – 'I'm getting on quite well, but rather slowly. I hope to goodness there will be an opera ready in time for the Group to perform in Venice' (Britten to Myfanwy Piper, 28 May 1954) – the composer responded immediately to the financial crisis by suggesting the practical economies he mentions in his letter to Piper.

2 The final version of these lines reads: 'Day by day the bars we break, / Break the love that laps them round': see p. 250.

3 In the published libretto, the stage directions at this point read: 'The lights fade out on Quint and Miss Jessel and fade in on the Governess.'

808 To Joan Cross

ROYAL STATION HOTEL, YORK[1]
July 1st, 1954

My dear Joan,

I am so worried about the way that the "Mrs Grose" situation is developing that I feel I must write to you personally. There are so many indications that you are really not inclined to do the part; things that you have said, or not said; your unavailability in the first few days of the rehearsal period; your tiredness & apparent disinclination to look at the music, nor comment on it at Aldeburgh. Let me say immediately, my dear, that I am sure you can, if you will, do it superbly. As you know every note is written with you in mind, & I passionately want you to do it. But if you really don't like the part, or the story, or the idea of giving up your summer to work on it, I don't want you to strain your devoted loyalty to us over so

> # A New Theatre in Aldeburgh.
>
> EVERY JUNE hundreds of disappointed people are turned away from operas and concerts in Aldeburgh because the Jubilee Hall is not large enough to house its Festival audiences. And every year the organisers of the Festival are faced with a struggle to make ends meet, in spite of generous help from the Arts Council, donors, guarantors, subscribers and the strenuous efforts of the Friends of the Festival.
>
> If room could be found for all those who clamour for tickets, the budget could be balanced, and at the same time some cheaper tickets could be made available to bring the Festival within the means of many more people. The high standard of the Festival could be maintained without an ever increasing strain on the artists and on all who are concerned with it.
>
> It has not been found possible to enlarge the Jubilee Hall or to add to its seating capacity. Meanwhile the twelve members of the English Opera Group Orchestra have barely room to breathe or move in their pit, and nothing can be done to make their playing-space sufficient for a production of, for instance, a Mozart chamber opera. Miracles are performed on the small stage, but it is inadequate for the necessary lighting effects in Britten's new opera, "The Turn of the Screw," which is therefore having its first performance in Venice instead of in Aldeburgh this summer.
>
> Interest in the Aldeburgh Festival increases every year, but this welcome increase brings with it additional disappointments and anxieties, which are already threatening to endanger the future life of the Festival.
>
> ### It has therefore been suggested that a new theatre should be built in Aldeburgh.
>
> The photograph shows the model of the proposed theatre which would be of the utmost simplicity in structure and decoration, and entirely in keeping with the character of the Festival. The building would increase the seating from 290 to 600, or possibly 700. While avoiding any suggestion of luxury in its fittings, it would provide possibilities in accoustics and lighting which could make it one of the foremost small experimental opera houses in the country.
>
> An option has been taken on an excellent site behind Aldeburgh Lodge, on high ground, with an uninterrupted view over the marshes, and near enough to the sea for interval-promenading.
>
> The Arts Council of Great Britain and the English Opera Group have given their enthusiastic approval to the proposal, and the Aldeburgh Borough Council has agreed in principle subject to normal planning consents.
>
> If Festival audiences and the general public show sufficient interest in the scheme, the organisers of the Festival will send an appeal to the Board of Trade asking for permission to form an independent limited company for the purpose of building and maintaining a theatre in Aldeburgh.
>
> Everyone who is interested will be able to take part in the scheme. If you would like further information, please sign one of the books which are placed in the Festival Office and the Festival Club for this purpose.
>
> **The Model is on view in the Festival Club, White Lion Hotel.**

Leaflet publicizing the proposed Aldeburgh Festival Theatre, 1954

many years, & we must reluctantly release you from it. I hate to write this, & hope against hope that you will come in to it with us all, but I am too fond of you, & too much an admirer to want you to do something against your will. We have other possibilities for the part, but we cannot delay approaching them any longer, if your reply is negative – so please be a dear & reply as soon as possible.[2] I am here till Saturday & then London on Sunday & Aldeburgh on Monday.

Much of my anxiety is caused by nervousness about my youngest, & most precious offspring, nervousness about conducting & rehearsing such a complicated & intense piece, & for such a very special occasion. Dearest Joan, make it easier for us all, & help us with your inimitable art.

Much love,
BEN

1 Britten was in York where the English Opera Group was on tour, giving performances of *Love in a Village*, *A Dinner Engagement* and *The Rape of Lucretia*. On 3 July Pears and Britten gave the first half of a concert (songs by Dowland, Blow, Purcell and Rosseter, and a group of Schubert *Lieder*), the second half of which was a performance of Walton's *Façade*, with Pears and Edith Sitwell as speakers, and instrumentalists from the EOG Orchestra conducted by Vilem Tausky.

2 As Joan Cross explained in an undated letter in response to Britten's entreaty, her reluctance to commit herself had been because of the difficulty of leaving her elderly and frail mother throughout the extended rehearsal period (most of August and the first half of September) which the new opera would require. But this problem had been solved and Cross was now free to take part, telling the composer, 'I've started work on *The Screw* and am ravished by the music – surely the loveliest ever?'

809 To Lennox Berkeley

4 CRABBE STREET, ALDEBURGH
July 6th 1954

My dear Lennox,

Thank you so much for your nice letter. We are all <u>delighted</u> that Dinner Engagement[1] is such a success. We did it 3 times in York[2] & everyone loved it there too. I hope you were pleased with the performance – it seems to me an excellent cast & Billy Chappell[3] did a most amusing production, I think. There are most lovely things in the piece, my dear, which give one enormous pleasure, & we are proud, both Festival & Group, that you wrote it for us. There are one or two moments which either seem obscure or too long, & I'm not sure whether that is the 'tempo' or the writing. I want to hear it again, with a score, in Taw & Torridge;[4] dare I make some suggestions before Sadler's Wells,[5] if it seems necessary? Good luck to Nelson,[6] & wish me luck for the 'Screw'! – rehearsals start in a month & I have 5 scenes still to write ... O Law!

Love to all
BEN

> YORK FESTIVAL 1954
>
> ---
>
> THE ENGLISH OPERA GROUP
> General Manager: BASIL DOUGLAS
>
> # AN ENTERTAINMENT
>
> EDITH SITWELL -   -   *Speaker*
>
> PETER PEARS   -   -   *Tenor*
>
> BENJAMIN BRITTEN   -   *Piano*
>
> THE ENGLISH OPERA GROUP ENSEMBLE
>
> Conductor:
> VILEM TAUSKY
>
> ---
>
> THEATRE ROYAL, YORK
>
> Saturday, 3rd July, 1954, at 8-0 p.m.
>
> *Programme One Shilling*

Programme for an English Opera Group concert at York, 3 July 1954, in which Edith Sitwell and Pears were the reciters in Walton's *Façade*

1 Berkeley's one-act opera, Op. 45, libretto by Paul Dehn, was commissioned by the English Opera Group, which had given the first performance at the Jubilee Hall, Aldeburgh, on 17 June 1954, in a production directed by William Chappell and conducted by Vilem Tausky. The opera was dedicated to Basil Douglas, General Manager of the EOG. *A Dinner Engagement* shared the evening with Oldham's *Love in a Village*. See also Peter Dickinson, *The Music of Lennox Berkeley*, pp. 169–77, and *Staging History*, catalogue for the exhibition held at BPL, June 2001, p. 22.

2 Performances were given at the Theatre Royal, York, on 29 June, and 1 and 3 July.

3 William Chappell (1907–1994), British dancer, designer, writer, librettist and director. He studied at the Chelsea School of Art and, as a dancer, with Marie Rambert. He performed with the Ballet Club, with Ida Rubinstein's company in Paris (alongside Frederick Ashton), for the Vic-Wells Ballet and in revues for C. B. Cochran. For the Ballet Rambert he created a number of roles choreographed by Ashton. He had a significant career as a producer of revues, musicals and plays, at one point having an association with eleven concurrent West End productions. In 1938 he had danced in Berkeley's *The Judgement of Paris* at Sadler's Wells.

4 The Taw and Torridge Festival based in Barnstaple, Devon. The EOG appeared there, as did Britten and Pears in recital, in 1953 and 1954. Performances of *A Dinner Engagement* in a double-bill with *Love in a Village* were to be given at the Queen's Hall, Barnstaple, on 4 and 7 August.

5 Performances of *A Dinner Engagement* and *Love in a Village* were to be given in London at the Sadler's Wells Theatre on 7, 9 and 15 October.

6 Berkeley's three-act opera, libretto by Alan Pryce-Jones, first performed at Sadler's Wells on 22 September 1954 (director: George Devine; conductor: Vilem Tausky) and broadcast live by the BBC Third Programme.

810 To Myfanwy Piper

4 CRABBE STREET, ALDEBURGH
July 8th 1954

My dear Myfanwy,

Back here – thank God – & hard at work again. York was pretty exhausting – more so after you went, what with concerts, rehearsals & meetings; but quite useful I think. At the request of the orchestra, I played the Screw through again! They were most interested. Thank you so much for trekking all the way up there.

Thank you for your sweet & encouraging letter. You really are the best audience ever; but you must remember that if the piece moves you, it's partly your fault & (I suppose) old H. James! I'm feeling rather low about it at the moment; it's hard to pick up the reins again. I've done Miles' Bedroom[1] – pretty gloomy, but I hope it works, & now – the Temptation.[2]

Here are two corrected scenes, for your reference. Hope there's nothing in the new scene you don't approve of. 'Why, the candle is out' – comes from H.J.

I expect Don Giovanni[3] was terrific, at least to look at – I long to hear about it.

Hope Christie[4] wasn't too awful.

Love,
BEN

1 Act II scene 4, 'The bedroom'.

2 Variation XII, when Quint sings 'So! She has written./What has she written?', etc. This is the only variation in the opera to make use of the voice.

3 A revival of Carl Ebert's 1951 Glyndebourne production of Mozart's opera, conducted by Georg Solti, which John Piper had designed. See Michael Northen, 'Designs for the Theatre', in *John Piper*, the catalogue of a retrospective exhibition of his work at the Tate Gallery, London, p. 32; the design for a backcloth is reproduced in the same volume as plate 83.

4 John Christie (1882–1962), British opera enthusiast who founded the Glyndebourne Festival Opera, near Lewes, Sussex, in 1934. The early history of the English Opera Group was bound up with Christie's opera house, both *The Rape of Lucretia* and *Albert Herring* receiving their premieres at Glyndebourne, in 1946 and 1947 respectively. See also Letter 517 n. 11.

811 To Francis Poulenc

4 CRABBE STREET, ALDEBURGH
July 14th 1954

Mon cher Francis,

Je suis très desolé de lire que vous êtes si malade. Nous, Peter, moi & tout le monde, esperons qu'il va mieux avec vous, & que vous pouvez travailler & voyager comme vous voulez. C'était tragicque qu'il n'était pas possible pour vous venir ici. Tout était prêt de vous donner une bienvenu vraiment royale. D'avoir seulement 'Musique Concrête' n'etait pas du tout assez – – – !!

Ce qui porte cette lettre est un grand ami de moi, un jeune homme (il s'appele John Cranko), très très donné, vif et gai, que je suis sûr que vous aimerez assez que moi. Il fait les chorégraphie pour les ballets de Sadler's Wells, & a fait les choses vraiment remarquable. Je vais moi-même écrire un ballet (dans trois actes!) avec lui, dans le printemps prochain. Je ne sais pas si vous êtes à Paris, en ce moment, mais si vous êtes, s'il vous plaît, mon cher, soyez gentil et parlez un peu avec il.

Excusez cette lettre horrible et courte, mais écrire en français est formidable pour moi (!), & aussi il me faut ecrire trois scènes d'un opera qui sera répété dans trois semaines! . . . quelle horreur!

With much love & hoping to hear very soon that you are quite well, my dear Francis,

Yours ever,
BEN

Translation:

My dear Francis,

I am very sorry to read that you are so ill.[1] All of us, including Peter, hope you are feeling better and are working and travelling as you'd like. It's tragic that it wasn't possible for you to come here.[2] A truly royal welcome was awaiting you. 'Musique Concrète' just wasn't enough on its own!

This letter is being brought to you by a great friend of mine, a young man (his name is John Cranko) who is very, very gifted, bright and gay, and I'm sure you'll like him just as much as I do. He is a choreographer at Sadler's Wells and has done some really remarkable things. I'm going to write a ballet myself (in three acts!)[3] with him next spring. I don't know whether you're in Paris at present, but if you are, please, my dear, be so kind as to speak a little with him.

Please excuse this horrible, short letter, but writing in French is quite a business for me (!), and also I've got three scenes of an opera to write. Rehearsals start in three weeks! . . . quelle horreur!

1 Poulenc was suffering from severe depression due to the breakdown of his relationship with Lucien Roubert, a condition heightened by the copyright problems surrounding his opera *Dialogues des Carmélites*. See Claude Gendre, '*Dialogues des Carmélites*: the historical background, literary destiny and genesis of the opera', in Sidney Buckland and Myriam Chimènes (eds.), *Francis Poulenc: Music, Art and Literature*, pp. 274–319, and Sidney Buckland (ed.), *Francis Poulenc: Echo and Source: Selected Correspondence 1915–1963*, letters 250–59.

2 Poulenc had been compelled to cancel his visit to Aldeburgh and therefore his engagements at the Festival.

3 *The Prince of the Pagodas*: the project had originated as early as January 1954 when the Britten–Cranko collaboration was first announced by the Sadler's Wells Ballet.

Some confusion surrounds the circumstances of the ballet's genesis. According to the second of two articles published by Cranko at the time of the premiere of *Pagodas* ('Making a Ballet – 2', *The Sunday Times*, 20 January 1957; the full text is reproduced in Letter 882 n. 4), work had begun on a draft scenario and John Piper had been consulted on the question of scenery well before Britten agreed to compose the music:

> The decor was under way, but what about the music? No composer available to me seemed to have the kind of imagination the ballet demanded. One evening I asked Britten if he had ideas about composers, little dreaming that he would become excited enough with *Pagodas* to undertake it himself [. . .] the whole ballet was rediscussed, and Britten suggested various themes on which he would make variations short enough to provide the episodic dances, but which would give the work as a whole a sense of continuity.

> General Shape The Green Serpent. Act I.
>
> | 2 Clowns & Court Entry. | 3 mins |
> |---|---|
> | Court dance with king & Dwarf. | 3 mins |
> | Entry of Suitors & 4 Solos. | 7 mins |
> | Entry & Solo Malina | 2½ mins |
> | Entry & Solo Gracieuse | 3 mins |
> | Business with the crown intro to Adage with 4 suitors: ~~Coda quarrel suitors~~ Quarrel & suitors rejection of Gracieuse. | 4 mins
> 1 min |
> | Entry of Frogs & casket scene. | 4 mins |
>
> Total time 27½ min
>
> Act 2. Scene I.
>
> | Entrée of Clouds Gracieuse gets dress. Waltz of Clouds & Stars. | 4½ mins |
> |---|---|
> | Entrée of Water Gracieuse gets Necklace. Entrée, dance, dance, Coda Fishes | 4½ mins |
> | Entrée of Fire G. gets the Crown. Entrée. solo. solo. coda. | 4½ mins |
> | Gracieuse is deposited | ½ min |
>
> Total 14 min

A page from John Cranko's draft scenario for *The Prince of the Pagodas*, entitled 'General Shape The Green Serpent'

If this account is trustworthy (and it seems highly unlikely for such a major venture to have been planned without the composer in mind from the outset), the ballet must have been conceived well before the end of 1953. The formal January announcement (the existence of which disproves Cranko's hazy memory that the project was mooted in February – see John Percival, *Theatre in my Blood: A Biography of John Cranko*, p. 102) reveals that the ballet was intended to receive its first production as part of the 1954–55 season at Sadler's Wells.

Cranko had devised his own scenario for *Pagodas* which fused elements drawn from *King Lear, Beauty and the Beast* (which he had choreographed for Sadler's Wells in 1948) and the oriental fairy-tale *Serpentin Vert* (published at Milan in 1782 by Madame D'Aulnoy); a detailed draft scenario in Cranko's hand is preserved at BPL: see p. 259. The stage directions in the scenario differ from those in the published scores of the ballet in several respects, but Britten's composition sketch conforms to the handwritten scenario which must have been at his side as he worked. The document gives estimated timings for individual dances, mostly in units of three to four minutes, and these must have provided a convenient stimulus to a composer who had served his apprenticeship in the film industry. Cranko himself drew this parallel in 'Making a Ballet – 2', remarking that they worked out

> a sort of 'shooting script' for the whole ballet, almost as if we were planning a silent film [. . .] Then Britten started to compose. As the music grew, the ballet sprang to life and, carefully as Britten had followed my script, his imagery was so strong that the entire choreography had to be revisualized.

It is uncertain when Britten began work on the ballet score, but he had made some headway by spring 1955 when he received a letter from Cranko (dated 18 April) which makes specific reference to the Variation of the King of the West in Act I:

> I loved what you had done, and feel one could practically choreograph it now it all falls so perfectly in place. But a new doubt fills me about the intellectual variation [in which Britten parodies the serialism of Schoenberg] – I feel that perhaps it is not obvious to dance to [. . .] either rhythmically or melodically. It is quite possible to choreograph but I feel that it's an intellectual piece of music and not an intellectual *dance*. Also its fugal shape is not obvious enough to amuse and gets in the way of the theatrical shape [. . .]
>
> Sorry to be a bore, but I hasten to say this before you start the adage and get it all involved in the waltz.

By the time of his departure for the world tour in November 1955, Britten had just started Act II (see Letter 837). The sorry history of postponements which afflicted subsequent work on the ballet is charted in a number of letters between in Part V. See also MCBFE, pp. 90–98.

812 To Myfanwy Piper

PILL HOUSE HOTEL, BARNSTAPLE, DEVON[1]

[1 August 1954]

My dear Myfanwy,

So sorry about the pencil but I've left mine behind & Peter's using his.

The second version of the Prologue has just arrived – &, my dear, I am afraid I prefer the first, as the present idea stands I can't do the 2nd Version Recitative – it needs fuller accompaniment to match its nice lyric quality. I feel the ideal is a (slightly) shorter version of the 1st. I can then start with a few loud chords, set it naturalistically as recitative (Basil & I have talked a lot about how to get Peter to do it – with the MS in his hand, as if starting to read the story) then, at the end – perhaps overlapping – the orchestra, which is the story, starts.[2]

Please excuse the hasty scribble, but what with concerts, writing, & trying to get the score done for first orchestral rehearsal of the T of the S tomorrow, life is hectic. But nice, all the same – think of us tomorrow, with the first signs of life of our new child – – exciting!!

I've done a new end – better, but not still just right yet I fear.[3]

Lots of love from P [Peter] & B [Basil],

BEN

---

1 In addition to the English Opera Group's visit to the Taw and Torridge Festival, Pears and Britten were involved in four concerts: on 1 August, at the Queen's Hall, Barnstaple, they gave an 'Opera Concert' (Mozart, Verdi, Tchaikovsky, Britten), with Joan Cross and Frederick Sharp, introduced by Lord Harewood; on the 3rd, Pears sang in a Bach Concert in Barnstaple; on the 5th, Pears and Britten gave a recital at Holy Trinity Church, Ilfracombe; and on the 6th they performed *Winter Words* as part of a chamber music concert.

2 The question of introducing a prologue into the opera had been first raised by the composer in April, following discussions with Basil Coleman (see Letter 797). As Myfanwy Piper recalled (DHOBB, p. 11), this was a difficult problem to solve:

I had tried to get all necessary information into the Governess's journey [scene 1] and I was afraid a prologue would be repetitive, unless I rewrote Act I Scene 1, but it had already been set and time was short. I tried various things.

Mrs Piper described her second version of the Prologue – rejected by Britten in this letter – as

a rather gay scene from Henry James's introductory ghost story party [. . .] For literary as well as musical reasons it wouldn't have done, it had quite a different atmosphere from the rest, all right in James's story but wrong for the tightness of the re-created work.

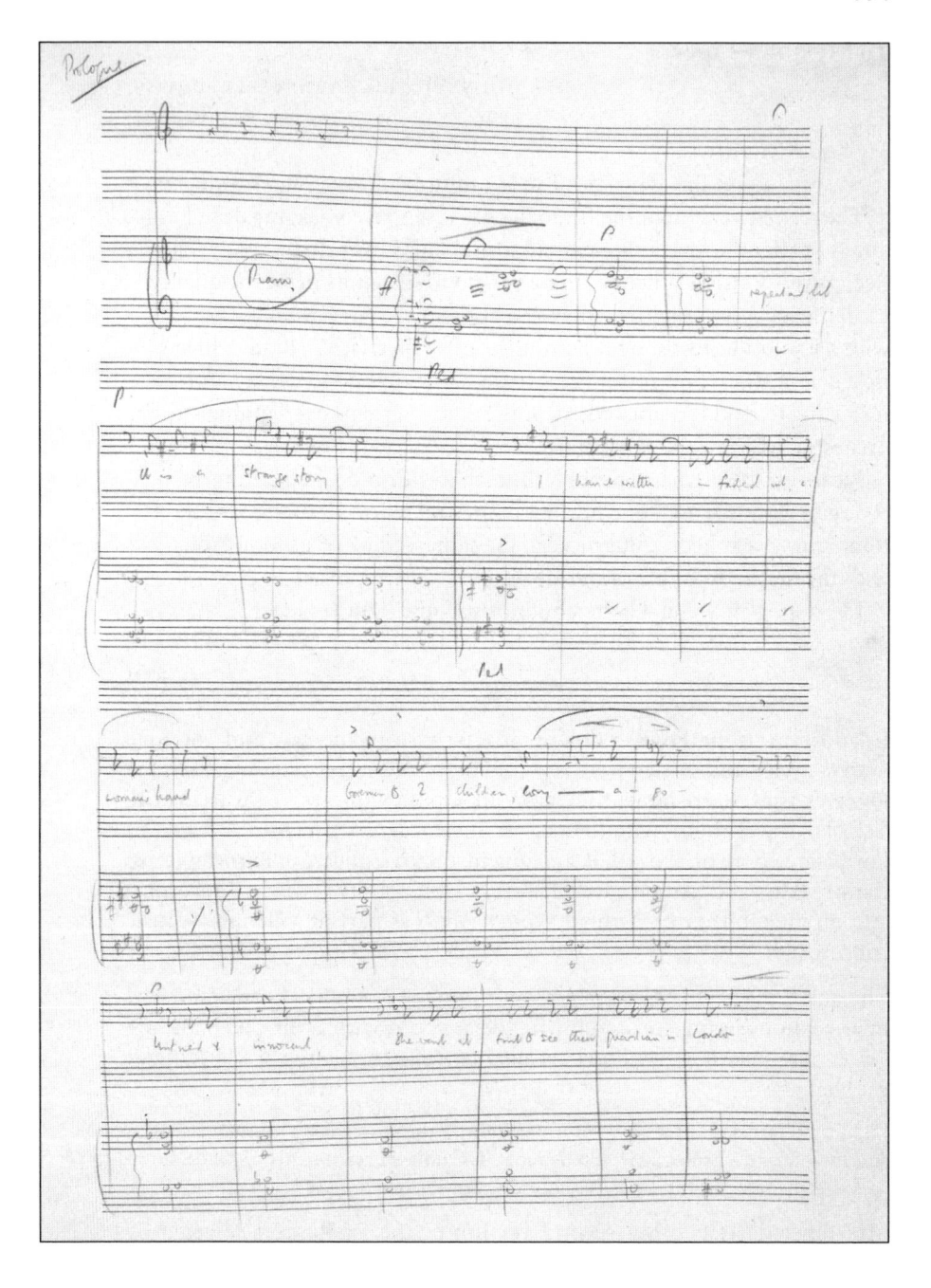

The opening of the discarded version of the Prologue from the composition draft of *The Turn of the Screw*, BL Add. MS. 60602. Note the three introductory knocks in the first bar.

LETTER 812: AUGUST 1954

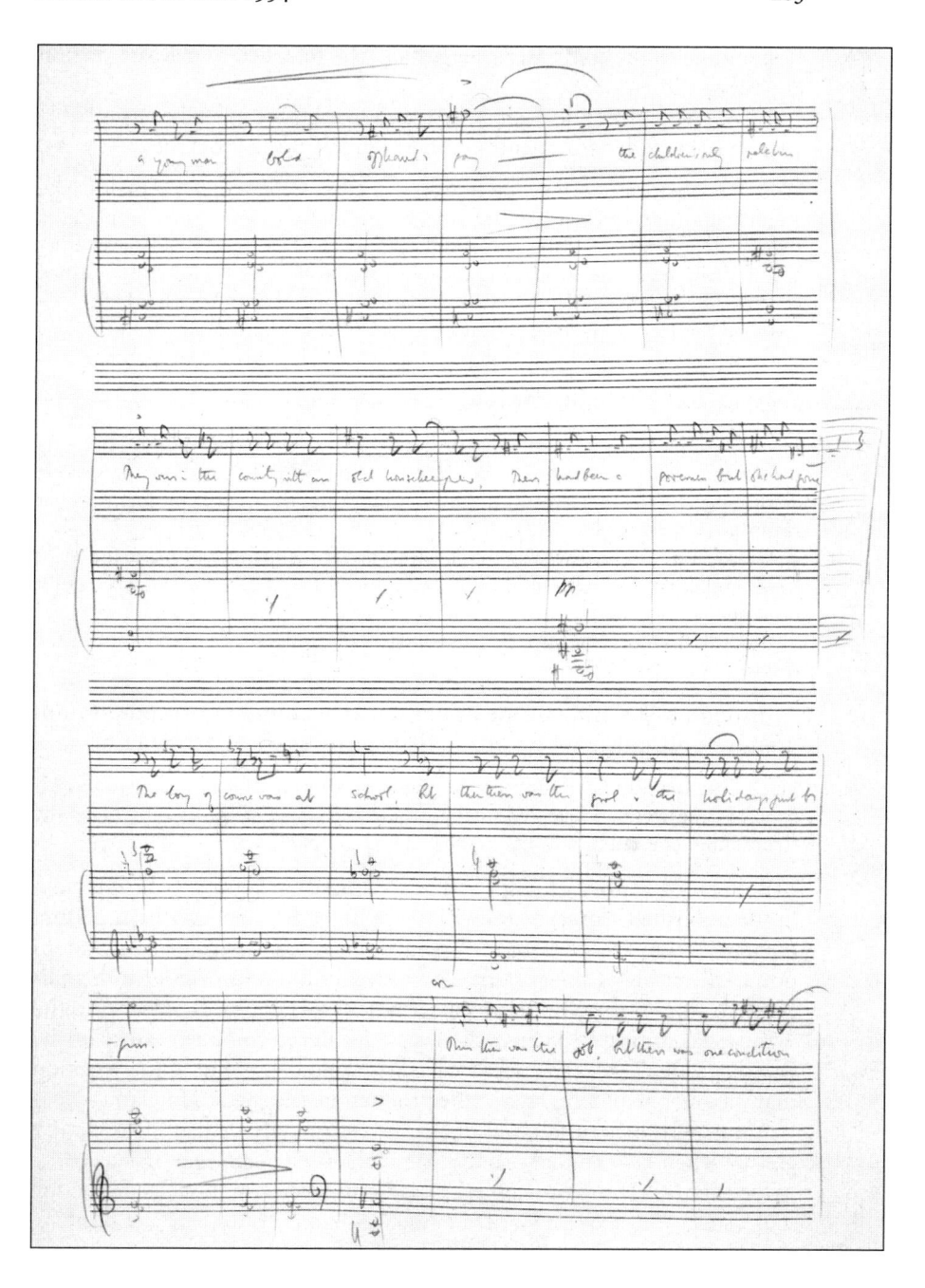

Responding to the composer's suggestion, she returned to her first version and revised it.

Two of Mrs Piper's letters to the composer, both undated but probably written in late July 1954, mention the two drafts of the Prologue:

Here is the prologue – at least it is the one we looked at; but I'm not entirely happy about it and I'm trying it another way – same substance but *much* simpler and slightly more lyrical. I feel that this and the first scene is too prosey and explanatory and potted James. The 1st scene is all right without it. It isn't quite distinguished enough. I had hoped to finish the 2nd try before post time but I'm afraid I shan't – so I send this to show willing. It needs a lot of rather intelligent attention [. . .]

I'm going on now with the prologue and will send it – possibly even today.

A second letter ('Monday') brought the redrafted version:

I feel this is much nearer – I'm not sure if it's right yet, but somehow, incorporating the fact that she was overcome by his charm, the only thing that we *really* have to get across (and the fact that she was not to communicate) with a little prologue proper seems more natural.

Please let me know what you think. If you prefer the manner of the first one I'll have another shot at that. I find I've typed it in a sort of free verse with caps but it need not be of course.

I found, thinking about it, that faded ink a bit unnecessary – and a lot of the rest too.

Britten's first setting of the Prologue (to be found in his composition draft) was discarded: see pp. 262–3. John Evans (PHTS, p. 66) describes it as

much drier than the lyric-recitative setting as we know it. The harmonic support is generally more static; repeated pitches in the voice part are often punctuated by strumming repeated harmonies in the piano accompaniment.

Both this discarded attempt and the second draft version (which is close to the published score), begin with three 'Introductory Knocks', a gesture borrowed from French baroque opera and classical theatre drawing attention to the rising of the curtain. The convention has its origins in the religious drama of the Middle Ages, with 'les trois coups' representing the Trinity. According to Evans, 'this was considered to be necessary at the Fenice, particularly as the opera starts with solo piano', but 'it was a notion that was later abandoned when the production returned to England'.

Amusingly, Britten fell foul of a more thoroughly British introductory gesture when he included a loud drum-roll at the beginning of *The Prince of the Pagodas*. The drum-roll is crossed out in the composer's conducting score, suggesting Covent Garden audiences had risen to their feet thinking they were about to hear the National Anthem.

3 The lines along which Britten was thinking are revealed in a scribbled pencil entry at the back of his 1954 diary, on a page dedicated to 'Sports Fixtures and Results':

Miles I have failed.
I have lost you.
Farewell.

The closing scene of the opera gave Britten particular trouble, as can be seen from the various discarded passages in his composition draft (for a discussion of this material, see PHTS, pp. 70–71). But changes to this scene were made even later than the composition draft stage, as Donald Mitchell fortuitously discovered when, in 1963, he came across a dyeline copy of Imogen Holst's manuscript vocal score in which the music from fig. 130 (Governess: 'Is who there, Miles? Say it! Say it!') to the end of the opera was significantly different from the published score. As Evans observes,

Britten had revised the end of the opera when scoring the final scene. The most remarkable aspect of that revision was the insertion of the duet for Quint and the Governess at fig. 131, which delays the climax of the scene and most brilliantly combines Quint's alluring song from the end of Act I ('On the paths, in the woods') with the Governess's persistent interrogation of Miles ('Who made you take the letter?').

The combination of these ideas superimposes the two crucial key centres of the opera – A flat and A. See Donald Mitchell, 'Britten's Revisionary Practice: Practical and Creative', *Tempo* 66–7 (autumn/winter 1963), pp. 15–22, ex. 4 of which reprints Britten's first version of this passage, the first time that Britten had consented to the publication of an example of his revisionary process in operation. (The article is reprinted in DMCN, pp. 393–406.)

After Britten had completed the score and Myfanwy Piper heard a complete play-through of their opera, she wrote a letter to the composer (undated, 'Wednesday', probably late August 1954) which begins by alluding to part of her libretto (Act II scene 3, '"Sir – dear sir – my dear sir –"', when the Governess writes to the children's guardian):

Sir, my dear, dear sir,
 So wonderfully beautiful it is: I wish I knew how to say so better. It would have been so easy to make it strange and to have left it at that – but you have given it such passion and such intensity. Richness and no splurge. Such a shape. I can't hear it enough – because the more I hear it, the more even my feeble capacities understand about the bones of it. I'm very much aware of how you have made use of every scrap of feeling and suggestion that has been given you in the script – and also of how much these feelings and suggestions have been the product of your generous, patient and imaginative sympathy with me in the early fumbling stages. I only hope that my part is good enough to carry what you have given it – and if it *is* a good deal of it is your fault – that is what I'm trying to say in rather a shapeless and splurgy way.
 There is something very special about those early play-throughs of yours. I know what Peter means, they have an emotion and tension all their own that one never gets in quite the same way again. I remember it particularly about *Billy Budd* [...]
 Bless you my dear for looking after me so well. I'm much happier about the overture [i.e. Prologue] now and think we have tightened up the whole conception into something that will work and really make a positive contribution.

813 To Princess Margaret of Hesse and the Rhine

4 CRABBE STREET, ALDEBURGH
August 15th 1954

My Dear Peg,

– awful that I haven't written before, but you can guess what things are like here . . . all the same I wish I'd written before to thank you for being so sweet to the young students at Ansbach.[1] We had delighted postcards from them; it was clearly a <u>great</u> experience. I'm so glad from your card that things were obviously going so well with the Festival. Next year . . . perhaps . . . who knows . . . we may be there! Peter was pleased that <u>they</u> were pleased with the idea that he might come to sing for them next time.[2]

Here, rehearsals are in <u>full</u> swing. A jolly good cast, in every way, we have for the 'Screw' and all working well together. It is lovely rehearsing here by the sea; & now that the weather is at last better, working, bathing, working, tennis & again rehearsing is becoming the order of the day. The opera itself isn't <u>quite</u> finished yet, alas, but it isn't altogether my fault. The beginning is again changed, & is going to be a prologue sung by Peter, & isn't yet written. Generally, though, I'm pleased. The dates in Venice are Sept. 14th & 16th, & in Sadler's Wells on Oct. 6th & 8th . . . any chances?

This letter, I suppose will follow you all around – are you in Tarasp[3] now? Sigrid[4] sent me a nice photo of Barbara P's wedding.[5] I must try & write to her, but what in the blazes do I call her?

Much love to you & Lu – & many apologies for the lateness & brevity of this; but it is only to remind you of our existence, & and to send lots of our love.

BEN

Basil Coleman, sitting out in the garden here, sends his greetings.

P.S. – an agitated P.S. too – We are <u>not</u> after all doing our German concerts in October, but in March, & we'll <u>do</u> our levelest best to fit in the Hauskonzert then. I'm so sorry it won't be possible to do it in October; the schedules have been switched round, & we're going to Scandinavia & Belgium in October.

1 In a letter of 3 May 1954 from Britten to Princess Margaret, Britten and Pears had suggested '3 young professionals to come to Ansbach' for the annual Bach Festival held in the German town each July. It would appear that Princess Margaret had generously provided financial support for these young musicians.

2 Pears first appeared at Ansbach in 1955 (see Letter 836) with further appearances in 1957 (see Letter 895 n. 2), when Britten visited as a member of the audience, 1959, 1963 and 1964: see PRPP, pp. 73–84.

3 Schloss Tarasp, the Hesses' summer home in Switzerland.

4 Countess Sigrid von Schlieffen, widow of Cavalry Captain Ernst-Albrecht von Schlieffen. At this period she and her two sons were staying at Wolfsgarten as refugees from East Germany. During his visit to the Hesses the previous Christmas, Britten had extended an invitation to the Schlieffens to stay with him in Aldeburgh during the summer of 1954, even offering (in May) to assist financially with the trip. However, the pressure of writing *The Turn of the Screw* meant the visit was cancelled.

5 Presumably the marriage of Princess Barbara of Prussia, whom Britten had met at Wolfsgarten the previous Christmas.

814 To John Ireland[1]

4 CRABBE STREET, ALDEBURGH
August 15th 1954

My dear John,

It is dreadful that this letter comes two days late for your birthday,[2] but I hope I can still send you my congratulations, & very many happy returns. Both Peter & I were very disappointed we couldn't be in your triumphant Prom. last week.[3] It would have been good to cheer you & greet you personally. But alas we are deep in the rehearsal here, of a new opera, and it takes all our time & energies. You were in our thoughts, though.

It is sad that we meet so seldom, but in our several ways we are all so rarely in the same place. Do you often come to London? I suppose you will not be able to come there in October? Peter has a nice house in Chester Gate (Regents Park) & it would be a great pleasure to welcome you there. Perhaps you would let us have a note if there were a chance of this?[4]

Please, John, forgive this brief note, but I wanted to send my congratulations, my best wishes & most sincere thanks for the warm attitude you have always had towards me, which has touched me very deeply.

Yours affectionately,
BEN

1 British composer (1879–1962) who had taught Britten at the Royal College of Music. The relationship had not always been smooth, but in later life Britten was to appreciate Ireland's guidance rather more than he had as a student. See also Letter 26 n. 14.

2 Ireland had celebrated his seventy-fifth birthday on 13 August.

3 Ireland's birthday had been celebrated at the BBC Proms by performances of his *London Overture*, *The Forgotten Rite*, the Piano Concerto and *These Things Shall Be*, conducted by Sir Malcolm Sargent.

4   In a letter of 26 August, Ireland explained that he visited London very little but would try to come up in October as Britten suggested. In his letter, Ireland goes on to pay warm tribute to his former pupil:

> You know well, my dear, dear Ben, the deep regard and admiration I have felt to you and your work ever since I first met you when you were still in your teens – you know also, I hope, that Europe holds no more loyal and constant supporter of you in the maze of jealousy your well-deserved success has aroused in the world of pygmies, who – well – I need say no more!

Ireland was among those who listened to the broadcast of the premiere of *The Turn of the Screw*, as well as a subsequent broadcast from London. Later in 1954 (quoted by Muriel V. Searle in *John Ireland: The Man and his Music*), he told Charles Markes,

> I have listened twice to Britten's new opera *The Turn of the Screw* [...] I am no judge of opera as such, but this contains the most remarkable and original music I have ever heard from the pen of a British composer – and it is on a firmly *diatonic* and *tonal* basis. Also, what he has accomplished in sound by the use of only 13 instruments was, to me, inexplicable; almost miraculous. This is not to say I *liked* the music, but it is gripping, vital, and often terrifying. I now am (perhaps *reluctantly*) compelled to regard Britten as possessing ten times the musical talent, intuition and ability of all other living British composers put together.

A letter of 4 June 1955 to Britten further reveals the deep impression made on Ireland by *The Turn of the Screw*:

> It is a wonderful piece of imaginative musical expression. What you have achieved with that small number of instruments and the normal tonality is nothing short of miraculous. Much more could be said (and no doubt has been) but at any rate your music held me spellbound from the first note to the last.

815   To Roger Duncan[1]

4 CRABBE STREET, ALDEBURGH
Sept. 1st 1954

[...]

How <u>very</u> nice of you to send us the chocolates. We both loved them, & shared them with some of the singers rehearsing the new opera here when they arrived. Thank you very much. As usual there is not time to write a nice long letter as rehearsals start in 10 minutes time!

We had a lovely Carnival here on Monday, in beautiful fine (!!) weather. A jolly good procession of decorated cars & people too. Peter & I went round in the Rolls[2] judging decorated houses – very good too. We also drove the Queen of the Carnival to visit the Fair, & she went on the Roundabout with us, & the Mayor too!! (Actually, & I put it in brackets, I <u>fell</u> off the Roundabout on Saturday & hurt my hand – wasn't I silly?)

Hope the weather is better with you now & that you've had some good surfing & bathing. Bathing is lovely here.

[...] thanks to you from Peter & me – & love to your father & mother & Briony too. We'll send a postcard from Venice.

BEN

1 This letter is one of the earliest of a large collection of correspondence with Roger Duncan (b. 1943), the son of Ronald Duncan, who occupied a notably strong place in the composer's affections at this period (see HCBB, pp. 366–8, and JBBC, pp. 218–25). With Britten's Welford nephew and nieces, Roger Duncan is one of the dedicatees of *Noye's Fludde*. To John Bridcut, Roger Duncan gave a interview about the years of his closest friendship with Britten, a period from around 1954 until Duncan's marriage in 1963 and subsequent emigration to Canada. As Ronald Duncan recollected in RDWB, pp. 131–3, Britten recognized the effect on both Roger and his elder sister Briony of the disruptive family life of their parents – the marriage of Ronald Duncan and his wife Rose-Marie was somewhat turbulent in the mid-1950s, though they never divorced – and the composer offered to have the children to stay in the holidays, especially Roger. For example, Roger spent part of August 1955 in Aldeburgh, as Britten reveals in a letter to Basil Coleman (25 September 1955):

> I had little Roger here for a fortnight – which was enchanting. He is a dear child, & a most sweet & gay companion. He stayed a few days with us in Chester Gate last week, seeing the operas before he went back to school. His is not an easy home life, as you know, & I think it's a relief to him to have an avuncular refuge! It was a pretty tearful parting, with the prospect of not seeing each other till Easter.

Britten formed an exceptionally close bond with Roger, one that led him to ask Roger's father (whom he had known since the mid-1930s) if he might be a surrogate father to the boy, not replacing the child's own father but sharing him. Ronald Duncan recalls (RDWB, pp. 131–2) that when Britten was visiting the Duncans in Devon (probably during the Taw and Torridge Festival),

> He asked me if I would walk out to the cliffs alone with him because he wanted to ask me a favour. Naturally I agreed and picked up a biro to take with me. But after we'd walked a couple of hundred yards, I discovered that he wasn't wanting a libretto [...] he stopped and turning to me said quite simply and openly, 'Ronnie, I've got a problem. I love children and as you know, I can't marry.'
> 'Yes, I know. Why don't you adopt one?'
> 'That's what I want to do.'
> 'Then there's no problem.'
> 'You don't understand. It's Roger I like. I want to be as a father to him. But I don't want to put your nose out of joint. Will you allow me to give him presents, visit him at school, and let him spend part of his school holidays with me – in other words share him?'

'Of course. He's fond of you too. And as you see, we've always got Briony.'

'You mean you won't be offended if I give him that bicycle he wants, and ask him to Aldeburgh for some part of his holidays?'

'Of course not.'

'Thank you. That fills a gap in me. But I wouldn't want you to think I was trying to replace you. I want to be as his father.'

We returned to the farm. It was as if I had given Ben three opera houses.

Ben took me at my word. Roger got his bike. For the next ten years Ben was a second father to my son, giving him affection and advice as he grew up. He wrote to him once or even twice a week [...] I have just had the privilege of reading this vast correspondence. I felt some shame at my own inadequacy, at my own lack that I had failed to give my son the support he had received from Ben. The only thing I can say in my own defence is that I knew Ben was writing these letters, visiting him at school, giving him a room in his house where he invariably spent part of his holidays. Even so, I must admit that if Ben had not assumed my role, I doubt if I would have been as conscientious as he proved to be. There is hardly a point in Roger's growth and development which Ben does not touch upon: he advised him on his football and tennis and his exams. When he had broken off from a girl friend, Ben writes and tells him how to let her down lightly; and when the continuity of my marriage was threatened he wrote to my son to alleviate his worries and give him the security of his own affection.

These letters show Ben at his best. They reveal his sympathy for and his understanding of children. Their language is childlike and often schoolboyish: they are not from a man writing down to a child, but letters from somebody who is relaxing into the nature of a child within himself.

Colin Graham commented on the composer's relationship with Roger Duncan (quoted in JBBC, p. 218):

I think he really felt a great need to help that boy in a most major possible way. And Roger Duncan was the closest . . . I mean right up to the very end of his life, he always regarded him as a lost son.

As Bridcut surmises (JBBC, p. 224), there was more to this friendship than Britten acting merely *in loco parentis* to Roger: 'love' would not be too strong a description of the feelings between the composer, then in his early forties, and the teenage boy. Though guarded in interview with Bridcut, Roger Duncan admitted that he realized Britten's interest in him was homosexual and that the composer was attracted to him: 'That was quite plain. But he respected the fact that I was not.' Remembering his own feelings at this period, Duncan told Bridcut: 'I admired him and enjoyed being with him. I enjoyed and liked his affection, his care, and the attention he gave me. But I wasn't attracted to him physically.' But Duncan recognized the importance of the relationship (JBBC, p. 226): 'I was very honoured and privileged to spend so much time across eight years with such an interesting person.'

Roger Duncan studied law at Cambridge and, following his marriage at the age of twenty and the completion of his degree, emigrated to

Vancouver. Though they kept in touch right until the end of the composer's life, the correspondence became less prolific. In the summer of 1975, Duncan visited Britten in Suffolk, the last occasion they met. Following Britten's death Duncan wrote Pears a moving letter of condolence (quoted in JBBC, p. 227):

You must know how much influence he had on my early years, for which I will always be most grateful and the memories of which I will always treasure. He was such a kind, wise, loving, knowledgeable person. He was indeed a second father to me. He always made me feel an equal, which I could never be of course, by not talking down to me, or treating me as a child. He gave me my enduring love for architecture, parish churches, and old buildings, which is still the thing I miss most of England. I loved him dearly as an adopted father/friend, and I consider myself so very honoured to have known him well for ten of the most impressionable years of my life.

2 Britten's 1929 Rolls-Royce Shooting Brake, which he had purchased in 1946. See PFL, plate 239, and Letter 536 n. 3.

816 To David Webster
[*Typed*]

4 CRABBE STREET, ALDEBURGH, SUFFOLK
3rd September, 1954

Dear David,

Thank you for your telegram about the new ballet. It was very nice of you to send it, and I look forward to getting your letter with details.[1]

I must confess I am rather alarmed at the prospect of my first ballet being given at Covent Garden, because I feel rather tentative. Also I am not quite sure whether the idea of this ballet is suitable for the large stage at the Garden. But I am seeing Cranko in Venice, and will discuss it with him and John Piper, and hope to see you when I return.

Excuse hurried note, but rehearsals press.

[*Handwritten:*] Yours ever,
BEN

1 Webster's letter (which has not survived at BPL) had been inadvertently sent to Britten's London address; Webster's telegram (which does survive at BPL) apologized for this mistake.

817 To Princess Margaret of Hesse and the Rhine
From Benjamin Britten and Peter Pears
[*Postcard: The Grand Canal, Venice*]

[Venice]
[after 14 September 1954]

Thank you for your wire – v. nice of you. It went <u>very</u> well[1] after some alarms brought on by Italian character & heat,[2] but we're now feeling exhausted & contented. We've been thinking of you both a lot these days, & hope skies will clear very soon. See you in London – do come![3]

Love from B to you both.

OXOXOXO

PETER

1 The first performance of *The Turn of the Screw* had been given at the Teatro La Fenice, Venice, by members of the English Opera Group conducted by Britten, on 14 September, with a second performance on the 16th. The performances were given as part of the International Festival of Contemporary Music, which was presented under the auspices of the Venice Biennale. The cast comprised: Peter Pears (The Prologue/ Quint); Jennifer Vyvyan (Governess); David Hemmings (Miles); Olive Dyer (Flora); Joan Cross (Mrs Grose), and Arda Mandikian (Miss Jessel). The premiere was broadcast by Radio Italia and also relayed in the UK by the BBC Third Programme.

Reprinted below is a selection of first-night reviews; the detailed musical commentary suggests that the critics had access to pre-publication vocal scores of the opera. Those critics reviewing the London premiere (6 October 1954) may also have attended the 'Introduction' to *The Turn of the Screw* presented by Lord Harewood at the Wigmore Hall, London, on 30 September, at which members of the original cast, with Britten at the piano, performed excerpts from the opera.

The traditionally anonymous critic (probably Frank Howes) of *The Times* (16 September 1954), wrote:

We all know by now that Mr Britten's sheer musical ability is equal to any demands made on it, that his invention flows most readily from the inspiration of words, and that as a result of the combination of the two factors he accepts in song and opera the challenge of the most recalcitrant material. His operas in fact have generally provoked criticism to ask not whether he has succeeded in his aim but why did he choose this subject, that story or a particular libretto. It is an improper question for criticism to ask, but it recurs so invariably that it must have some relevance to his art.

In the case of the new opera, *The Turn of the Screw*, which was performed for the first time last night at La Fenice opera house, he accepts two questionable handicaps – the need for a boy singer and the ambivalence of Henry James's ghost story. He saddles himself with a third – his choice of five soprano voices with no more than a solitary tenor for ballast, which is bad registration for the enunciation of important

THE ENGLISH OPERA GROUP

Direttori artistici:
Benjamin Britten - John Piper
Basil Coleman - Anne Wood

Impresario Generale
Basil Douglas

presenta in prima esecuzione mondiale

THE TURN OF THE SCREW
(IL GIRO DI VITE)

di
BENJAMIN BRITTEN

Libretto dal racconto di *Henry James*, di *Myfanwy Piper*
Scene e costumi su disegni di *John Piper*

Regia di
Basil Coleman

interpreti

Il Prologo	*Peter Pears*
L'Istitutrice	*Jennifer Vyvyan*
Miles } bambini affidati alle sue cure {	*David Hemmings*
Flora }	*Olive Dyer*
La Signora Grose, governante della casa	*Joan Cross*
Miss Jessel (ex istitutrice)	*Arda Mandikian*
Quint (ex domestico)	*Peter Pears*

Direttore *Benjamin Britten*

THE ENGLISH OPERA GROUP ORCHESTRA

Olive Zorian, primo violino - *Suzanne Rozsa*, secondo violino - *Cecil Aronowitz*, viola - *Terence Weil*, violoncello - *Francis Baines*, contrabbasso - *Enid Simon*, arpa - *John Francis*, flauto - *Joy Boughton*, oboe - *Stephen Waters*, clarinetto - *Vernon Elliott*, fagotto - *Charles Gregory*, corno - *James Blades*, percussione - *Martin Isepp*, celesta e pianoforte.

Direttore Tecnico e delle Luci: *Michael Northen*

Scenari della *Stage Decor Ltd.*, dipinti da *Harker Bros.*, sotto la supervisione di *Charles Bravery* - Costumi femminili di *Maria Garde* - Costumi maschili di *W. G. Rosdale* - Cuffie e bambole di *Christine Harold* - Parrucche di *Nathanwigs*, London - Attrezzatura delle luci della *Strand Electric & Engineering Co. Ltd.*

Direttore di scena *Geoffrey Manton* - Macchinisti: *Douglas Cornelissen, Colin Graham* - Capo elettricista: *Anthony Church* - Guardarobiera: *Christine Harold*.

La Fenice, Venice, 14 September 1954: from the programme book for the first performance of *The Turn of the Screw*

words. There are two schools of thought about Henry James: one regards *The Turn of the Screw* as a wonderful little work of art in which the aim is fully realized of achieving a sense of horror; the other, more sceptical, admiring its construction though boggling at the literary style, fails to attain the suspension of disbelief which is necessary for the enjoyment of a ghost story. Post-Freudian criticism of the story can be neglected. For the first school the opera will be successful if it seems faithful to James; its difficulty, if any, will be with Mrs Piper's materialization of the ghosts and with the words she puts into their mouths. On this count her quotation from Yeats, 'The ceremony of innocence is drowned', will seem wildly alien to James, and the first scene of the second act of the opera will appear not only redundant but offensive.

I myself, though belonging to the other school, which prefers William James to his brother Henry when the discussion is of human nature, find that scene, in which Quint and Miss Jessel behave like two too solid stage villains, an unnecessary inclusion. This school, which thinks that James strains credulity too far with his quite unreal children, is greatly helped to accept it in the theatre by the music, which is in Britten's most evocative vein. The whole of the first act by a series of 'turns of the screw' suspends disbelief, but the second, though it contains two dazzlingly brilliant episodes, that of the Sunday morning church bells [Act II scene 2] and that in which Miles plays the piano [Act II scene 6], strains it till we disbelieve once more – Miles is incredible.

Master David Hemmings played him extraordinarily well, but one cannot ask of a boy's singing the volume, the expressiveness or the dramatic power to achieve an impossible characterization. For Flora the English Opera Group were lucky enough to find an experienced singer in Miss Olive Dyer, who, by virtue of her diminutive person and pretty voice, has in the past made a specially appealing Gretel and Snowmaiden, and now adds another to her special roles.

It seems, therefore, as though one's valuation of the opera will depend on one's valuation of Henry James. But of one thing there is no doubt, the construction of the opera is as masterly as is that of James's story. The screw is turned sixteen times in as many episodes, which are connected by interludes, all of them variations on a leading motif that stands for the dramatic conflict of good and evil. The ingenuity of it and the fertility of the invention which makes a cumulative effect are rewarded by the complete theatrical success of the device. The production of Mr Basil Coleman similarly aided and abetted in all significant details the progressive sharpening of the emotional tension.

Miss Joan Cross gave one of her admirable character studies as the housekeeper who represents stability in a dissolving world. Miss Arda Mandikian sang well but was perhaps too positive for the shadowy Miss Jessel, and Mr Peter Pears showed his usual skill in significant gesture and articulation, but Quint should have been a *basso sepolcro* if he was to make our flesh creep. Miss Vyvyan's firm singing of the principal part was [...] a major triumph.

Colin Mason, *Manchester Guardian* (15 September 1954):

Not unexpectedly, Benjamin Britten's new opera, *The Turn of the Screw*, given its first performance [...] by the English Opera Group under the composer's direction in the Teatro La Fenice, proved the great occasion of this year's Venice Festival. What should an Italian audience make of a sung version in the original language of a story which English readers have been reading for years without ever really finding out what it means? Unlike the French at *Billy Budd*, however, they were not unresponsive [see Letter 736 n. 2]. Clearly their practice in Pirandello [the innovative Italian playwright, writer of *Six Characters in Search of an Author*] stood them in good stead, and they fell outside into dozens of little groups gamely, ingeniously, or obscurely explaining and counter-explaining, and all ready to die rather than look blank.

The libretto is by Myfanwy Piper, wife of John Piper, who has designed the scenery and costumes. She has been very faithful to the original, and has occasionally been insensitive to some of Henry James's silences and reticences, without the one conceivable justification of using a definite interpretation of them. The unhappiest example is the last scene of Act I, in which the episode with Miles on the lawn at night is expanded into a quartet in which the relationship between the children and the ghosts is made crudely explicit, and yet no more intelligible.

On the other hand, her idea of balancing this scene with another at the beginning of Act II, a duet for the ghosts alone, comes off very convincingly as an imaginative filling out and not a violation of James's silence. The rest is nearly all taken directly from the story, and if Mrs Grose is not an entirely satisfactory character that is James's fault. For once he uses his technical tricks of the passive confidant, characteristic of all his novels, rather maladroitly, so that she occasionally emerges obtrusively from that role. The same inconsistency is found in her in the opera. Otherwise the libretto is skilful and the book is made to yield very varied musical opportunities – obvious ones such as the journey [Act I scene 1] and the piano and church episode, those that lie naturally in the book such as the Governess's arias and duets and ensembles with Mrs Grose and the children, and ingeniously created ones such as a Latin lesson [Act I scene 6], children's rhymes and games [Act I scene 5], the ghosts' duet, and a duet between Miss Jessel and the Governess [Act II scene 3]. And Britten as always instantly seizes them and sets them so vividly to music that it seems absurd ever to have thought as many of us did that the story had not the makings of an opera in it. The piano scene [Act II scene 2], it is true, seems a shade naive and literal-minded, and some of Quint's appearances, such as the tempting of Miles to steal the letter [Variation XII and Act II scene 5] and his last phrases after the boy has died, give the impression of having been manufactured for the sake of the music and of giving Peter Pears something to sing. But the rest, with the exception of the finale of Act I is wholly convincing.

As generally happens at an opera premiere, it took some time to tune in to the music and in the early scenes its beauty and atmosphere could only be fleetingly caught – in the Governess's 'journey' passage, her aria immediately before her first sight of Quint, and the lesson scene. But from the following scene, the first appearance of Miss Jessel, it became almost continuously absorbing and gripping, which suggests that at a second hearing the early scenes will also be found so.

With the possible exception of *Billy Budd* it is in musical style the most difficult and tightly unified of Britten's operas. Technically, it carries this unification still further, in the even more pronounced symmetry of structure, and in that for the first time Britten consistently uses twelve-note technique. The opera is divided neatly into two continuous acts of eight scenes each, the scenes being all linked by orchestral variations on the twelve-note theme announced at the beginning of Act I. It would not be safe to assume from this that Britten had 'turned twelve notes', for the use of such a theme may, as has been suggested, have a special significance for this work – that it represents, by the revolution that (like all twelve-note rows) it undergoes before returning to the original note, the 'turn of the screw'.

Reduced to its most compact form of alternating rising fourths and falling minor thirds, it has in fact a screw-like movement, which might theoretically be continued indefinitely in the same direction as the alternation of two rising whole-tone scales a fourth apart. On the other hand, the actual title phrase never occurs in the opera, not even in the superfluous prologue (it would have been the one good reason for having it) and the theme may be interpreted as representing Quint, since in the last scene where the Governess presses Miles to utter Quint's name, the theme appears in the bass in the orchestra, first eight notes, then ten, then eleven, and finally as he cries, 'Peter Quint. You devil', the twelfth.

Britten no doubt meant this to be as ambiguous as James. What is perhaps more important about the twelve-note row is that its sequences of rising fourths allow Britten to establish and preserve classical tonality in the work, the more so by his layout of the theme, which, naturally, is not in its most compact form. His use of the note row is also very free, although it would not be an exaggeration to say that the entire opera is based on it. But what distinguishes the music above all is the variety of texture and invention and the unmistakable personality of Britten throughout it all.

The variations are not so called for nothing, and it is often they that set the character of the scenes that follow. These, while even more closely integrated in style than in *Billy Budd*, are at the same time more varied and show, as in Britten's earlier operas and as again in *Gloriana*, his Verdian gift for devising vivid, memorable, and inexhaustibly varied accompaniments and figurations to adorn his simple melodic lines. There are a few pages in the work that have the kind of sound generally associated with twelve-note music, and many more that have not, but they are all alike in sounding like Britten. He has tackled yet another problem, brought off yet another *tour de force*, and, it seems likely, created yet another masterpiece.

Martin Cooper, *Daily Telegraph* (15 September 1954):

Benjamin Britten's operas have always shown a plain enjoyment of the challenge presented by an awkward subject. Yet even *The Rape of Lucretia* hardly involved such problems as *The Turn of the Screw*, which was given by the English Opera Group at the Fenice Theatre here tonight, with the composer conducting.

Impalpable evil is wonderfully suggested by the ambiguities and prolonged sinuosities, the very omissions and sudden *sforzato* revelations of Henry James's narrative.

For the theatre Myfanwy Piper, the librettist, had no choice but to fill in, even to elaborate, what James surely deliberately left unexpressed in the nature of the ghosts and their influence.

They appear too often in this foreshortened version and say too much to maintain the effect of what should be nameless horror. Against them the children are not only powerless but colourless. They lack both the improbable charm and the faint scent of corruption with which James invested them [...]

The character of Britten's score is largely determined by that of the English Opera Group's orchestra. The sixteen scenes of the two acts constitute so many variations on a theme, in which the screw is ingeniously 'turned' through a circle of fourths and fifths.

The music abounds in effects of percussion and plucking – celesta, gong, drums, harps and pizzicato strings.

Familiar nursery rhymes (and even gender rhymes) appear, and dramatic prominence is given to one schoolroom doggerel in which two false quantities cast a serious reflection on Miles's schooling.

The whole effect is of great, almost excessive, refinement and intelligence, of a very personal taste and a tense nervous sensibility hard indeed to match.

John Piper's sets, excellently in tone with the music, are a brilliantly conceived series of gauze curtains, which reveal or suggest the different scenes in house or park.

Basil Coleman, the producer, has made the children as plausible as may be, and done his best to prevent the audience getting on terms of too easy familiarity with the two apparitions.

Felix Aprahamian, *The Sunday Times* (19 September 1954):

An elegant international audience, of the kind usually attracted by the Biennale, received Britten and the English Opera Group warmly, although some Italians seemed a little worried by his preoccupation with 'Morbidezza'.

For his libretto Britten has gone to Henry James's tale, told by a governess, of the demonic possession of her two small charges, Miles and Flora, by two sordid spirits, Peter Quint and Miss Jessel. Such an unprepossessing subject would seem little suited for operatic treatment; yet it has certainly fired Britten's creative imagination. Its peculiar brand of supernaturalism turns out to be no less apt for musical illustration than the squalors of *Wozzeck*.

Myfanwy Piper's adaptation of the text into a Prologue, followed by sixteen short scenes, divided equally into two acts, is admirably direct and clear, owing nothing to William Archibald's stage version of the story. Only at the beginning of the second act, where the two spectres evoke the past in unsentimental colloquy, does Mrs Piper permit herself a certain leaning towards a Celtic twilight, complete with 'the terrible sound of the wild swan's wings' and the quotation of a whole line of Yeats.

To bind the eight scenes of each act into a continuous whole Britten has used a form in which he has previously scored some notable successes: the variation. The orchestral interludes preceding each of the sixteen scenes, and fixing their tonal centres, are a series of variations of the theme which marks the orchestra's entry and links the narrator's piano-accompanied Prologue to the first scene. The sequence of keys rises in the first act and descends in the second. Thus, although each key has its own mood and colour, a unifying thread runs through the ritornelli as well as individual characterization. The composer solves his self-set problems as ingeniously as ever: unusual combination of voices (one treble, four sopranos, one tenor) yields acceptable ensembles up to a sextet, and the thirteen-piece orchestra is made to produce sounds ranging from the exquisite to the hair-raising. But *The Turn of the Screw* is much more than the sum of all this. It is not only Britten's most griping score: it is among his finest.

He has been fortunate in his interpreters: Master David Hemmings (making a remarkable debut at the age of twelve) and Olive Dyer as the children, Joan Cross as Mrs Grose, the housekeeper, Jennifer Vyvyan as the governess, Arda Mandikian as Miss Jessel, and Peter Pears doubling narrator and the evil Peter Quint, memorable in his recurring, muezzin-like invocation. John Piper has captured the phantasmagorical atmosphere of Bly, with its turreted towers, dream-like decors which, partially dissolving into each other, contribute to that sense of ambiguity and flux which characterizes the story [. . .] The real triumph is, of course, Britten's. It is a measure of his prestige abroad that the English Opera Group was invited to present this latest opera within the framework of the Biennale.

The foreign press corps was strongly represented at the Venice premiere of *The Turn of the Screw*. Among them was the composer Riccardo

Malipiero, nephew of the composer Gian Francesco Malipiero, who contributed a notice to *Il popolo* (15 September 1954, quoted in PHTS, pp. 134–5). His response to the opera is remarkably obtuse:

The subject [. . .] is a morbid and yet a fascinating one which conjures up vast frescoes of sound, dramatic and dazzling structures full of zest and colour, and sound-images rich in meaning.

We had imagined a use of colour as an expressive force similar to certain effects which were successfully created in *Peter Grimes* [. . .] we hoped that Britten would have been equipped to contrast the overwhelming feelings of the protagonists with their child-like natures, and that he could have cast light on the tragedy which develops in these innocent souls, involuntarily corrupted.

There is, indeed, an expressive crescendo in this opera of only two acts for the second part is more intense than the first. Nevertheless, this crescendo, instead of rising to the peak of the harsh mountain of psychopathic revelation, stops short halfway and remains literal and narrative rather than musical and poetic. Admittedly many things are said on the stage and there is a denouement followed by the flight of the girl, and there is the death of the boy and the torment of the governess who wants to arrive at an explanation but who succeeds only in precipitating the tragedy; but all this has no musical equivalent except in a well-moulded vocal line. But can human speech, set to music, expound and illuminate the abysses of a soul which does not know delight or love but only fear and depravity? This must be the role of music, music designed as a connecting fabric, as illumination, as leaven to the drama. This, however, can only partly be observed in the second act, or rather in the first half of the second act. The whole of the first act, although its function is preparatory and therefore only potentially figurative, is nothing; the drama is lost in a notable vacuity of expression, in fluent but undistinguished invention, as is also the end of the opera which reverts to these mistakes after having touched some sensitive chords in the first scenes.

The conflict between infancy and degeneration could have been brought out better, taking advantage of the dramatic structure of brief, episodic scenes. There are indeed contrasts here and there but they are not related to the drama: they do not strengthen it – they only decorate it. The music is made a humble serving maid.

This is a mistake: Benjamin Britten has wasted a good opportunity and has wasted it perhaps partly through presumption. Is it not perhaps presumptuous to entrust the musical texture to an instrumental group of a dozen or so performers? Such things can be done only when each of the instruments achieves an expressive power such as few, very few musicians have attained up to the present day! Otherwise one risks the customary poverty of chamber orchestras!

While listening to this opera we were reminded of neglected examples of musical illusion– Bartók, Ravel in *L'Enfant et les sortilèges*, Berg in the lake scene in *Wozzeck* – examples, alas, which have evidently not served as models to be copied.

The composer Virgil Thomson wrote the following review for the *New York Herald Tribune* (26 September 1954):

Not since *Peter Grimes* has this composer, whose gift for the stage has always been a powerful one, composed a theater piece so gripping and so intense.

At least, that was the reaction of this listener to his second hearing of it. At the dress rehearsal it had seemed to him slender, improvisatory, disappointingly casual.

On the opening night he was held throughout by its musical brilliance and dramatic intensity. Every time a ghost appeared he had a chill. And he was lost in admiration of Britten's ability to produce with thirteen orchestral players constant variety both coloristic and expressive. He did not find the Victorian Gothic sets of John Piper either apt or convincing, though his costumes were pretty in color. And the stage direction of Basil Coleman was stiff. But those are minor elements, no part of the script. *The Turn of the Screw*, words and music, is an opera that seems to me to have beauty and power in it. I predict it will travel.

Both the libretto by Myfanwy Piper and the composer's musical treatment of it seem to have opted for that theory of the tale in which the ghosts are all an invention of the Governess. We see them appear to the little boy when he is alone on the stage, but they remain invisible to the housekeeper. And the music seems to be telling us the whole story through the Governess, just as Henry James did. At any rate, such was my view of the authors' intent; and it was a legitimate reading of the tale. As a matter of fact, the ghosts, as well as the Governess, appeared frequently and all over the stage; they also sang a great deal. They were constantly around.

The singing of Peter Pears as the ghost of Peter Quint (also as a Prologue in sideburns), was the vocal delight of the evening. David Hemmings as the boy Miles was adorable all round, as child actors can be. Olive Dyer, the diminutive adult who sang little Flora, though not taller than her partner, was neither convincing in movement nor vocally pleasing. Neither was anybody else, for that matter, save Peter Pears, who was perfect in both ways, and Joan Cross who, as the housekeeper, stood and walked well. It is partly the composer's fault that the women singers did not sound well, because the tessitura of all their roles lies too high for comfort. The orchestra, which had come from England with the whole production, was excellent; and the composer conducted admirably.

Thomson registered the Eastern influences in the score:

Britten's music, as usual, has little stylistic tension; but it has fluency, aptness and a rich instrumental imagination. And the opera contains several moments, 'numbers' one might almost call them, of brilliant effectiveness. One is the florid tenor solo with which Quint's ghost first calls to Miles [Act I scene 8]. Another is the scene of Miles playing his piano lesson [Act II scene 6]. Equally striking perhaps is a passage for chimes that accompanies a graveyard scene [Act II scene 2], though the music heard in this scene from inside the church, if that is what it was supposed to be, seemed to me more oriental than Anglican. The modal melodic forms employed throughout the opera give, indeed, a somewhat Near East tone to the music, very much as a similar method of composition gives a similar tone to Menotti's operas. And in more ways than this Britten has hinted in *The Turn of the Screw* that he aspires to the success that Menotti has had with spooky subjects and with child singers, though he is no novice at handling either. His musical fancy is, I think, greater than Menotti's, his dramatic taste less sure.

In this work the numerous faults of dramatic taste that have weakened the punch of his recent operas seem to me almost wholly absent. On the contrary, two changes in the Henry James story were boldly made and are, I think, advantageous, though either could have changed the whole tone and meaning of it had they not been done with a sure hand. These are the turning of James's furtive and silent ghosts into overtly singing ones and the revelation of the sensitive bourgeois little Miles as a pianistic genius, a child virtuoso. The first risked making of the establishment a banal 'haunted house', of which there are thousands in the world. The other, by giving the boy that psychological protective armor which talent and skill provide, might have rendered him impervious to moral injury. That they did not vitiate the terror of the tale is proof of somebody's sound literary sense, possibly the librettist's.

That the opera has musical quality is all due to Britten of course. It sounds on first hearing improvised and facile, casual and only superficially brilliant. But is not. It is, in fact, elaborately constructed out of well-chosen themes and formal variations on them. Its prologue and eight scenes [sic] are separated, save for one intermission, by instrumental interludes that are highly fanciful and intensely atmospheric. These are integrated thematically, and ever so skilfully, with the vocal scenes. The music is ever professional, serious and full of that special energy that people used to call inspiration. It has sincerity, tenderness and brio. I did not perceive these qualities the first time I heard the opera, nor did some of the people who heard it only once. It is not difficult music to understand. But it does flower under acquaintance.

See also PHTS, pp. 130–38.

2 See HCBB, pp. 358–9, which includes reminiscences from EOG General Manager Basil Douglas and the company's stage manager Colin Graham. Douglas recalls that 'rehearsals were very fraught', while Graham, who had wisely taught himself some Italian specially for the occasion, found himself mediating with stage hands who were threatening strike action because of having to dismantle and re-assemble the *Screw* set to make way for concerts between rehearsals. Carpenter writes:

Lord Harewood, who had come out to Venice for the premiere, says it was to be 'a lower-keyed event' than the *Gloriana* gala first night. Nevertheless on the evening of 14 September 1954, Fenice Theatre was *en fête*, the air heavy with the scent of roses which had been set out in each box in the auditorium. The performance was to be broadcast live on the BBC Third Programme and several European stations, and Basil Douglas 'got more and more anxious, because we couldn't start on time because another broadcast was over-running. And there was slow hand-clapping going on.' At last the opera began. All went smoothly, though the numerous scene changes were noisier than had been hoped. During the interval the Italians in the audience could be seen in little groups, explaining the significance of James's tale volubly to each other. Harewood says that when the curtain came down it was obvious from the reception that the opera was a 'genuine success'.

3 Following the UK premiere on 6 October 1954 at Sadler's Wells, which launched a London run by the original cast that ended on 16 October, some of those UK critics who did not assess the opera the previous month had an opportunity to do so. Ernest Newman, 'Some Don'ts for Librettists', *The Sunday Times* (10 October 1954), offered the following views:

Everybody told us in advance, and we told everybody, that *The Turn of the Screw* simply couldn't be made into an opera; and everybody was right, for what Myfanwy Piper has done with it takes it quite out of the true Jamesian sphere. Of the sixteen short scenes one or two are rather superfluous, and one at least undesignedly comic – the one in which young Miles, quite the little virtuoso, gives us of his best at the piano; long before the recital was over I found myself wondering whether the scene of the dramatic action was really Bly Hall or the Wigmore Hall. The children tend, like most stage children, to be unduly stagey and a trifle tiresome at times; while the two evil 'influences', Quint and Miss Jessel, lose rather than gain by being materialized.

But when we come to consider the music there is a different story to tell. Mr Britten has given us an extraordinarily fascinating score; in much of it he has surpassed his own previous best. We must now eagerly await the publication of the score, and, after intensive study of that, see another stage performance; by which time we shall have managed to shake our various impressions of the whole into something like logical coherency. Last Wednesday's performance at Sadler's Wells under the composer left the audience in a state of high enthusiasm.

Eric Blom, *Observer* (10 October 1954), wrote:

The brilliance of Britten's technique can be taken for granted by this time, and his invention in *The Turn of the Screw* is as arresting as ever. What is chiefly remarkable, though, is that the two work inevitably and inseparably together. I know nothing about his way of working, but from a mere hearing it is evident that he does not, as biographers so often say of others, first 'compose' a work and then orchestrate it, but that for him the act of creation is one single process.

There are things in this opera which, for purely musical reasons, justify its *being* an opera, as one may doubt that the choice of Henry James's story itself did. In the fifth scene of Act I, for instance, the children sing a gay and quite uncomplicated little song while the goings-on in the orchestra are disturbingly sinister. This is rather like the *Peter Grimes* incident with the offstage church service in reverse [Act II scene 1]. A Henry James or an Ibsen may find means of devising undercurrents of the kind in a novel or a play, but not with the directness, the immediate intelligibility that a composer can contrive it in music-drama. Britten can also let music take charge of a whole situation, music that is not just interesting for its dramatic values, but strikingly compelling in a purely symphonic kind of way. Two scenes in particular come to mind in this connection: the former integrates church bells, the latter a performance on the piano, into the very core of the musical substance while these external sounds go on side by side with the dramatic action with a reciprocal heightening of effect.

One would have thought that after the realistic and yet artistic peals of Norwich Cathedral in *Gloriana* (inexcusably cut in the later performances) Britten could have found nothing more to do in that line; but the more humble parish church bells in the new work are quite different. In *Gloriana*, as in Mussorgsky's *Boris*, bells are suggested without any actual use of them; here tubular bells are part of the one-man percussion department of the chamber orchestra, yet they are only a sort of kick-off for a long-drawn and entrancing game in which everything becomes, so to speak, bell-conscious. The piano performance (very well mimicked by young David Hemmings, who has evidently memorized the whole long piece) makes use of a kind of furbished-up period music, rather like Dussek recollected by Poulenc, to construct another extended movement saturated in old-fashioned pianistry that could be heard with pleasure separately and at the same time fits the situation perfectly.

Part of Britten's individuality, of course, expresses itself by means of what an adverse critic might call tricks, which, however, are simply the hallmarks no creative artist can ever escape. We get once again those little trickles from the harp and the characteristic melodic use of that essentially harmonic instrument, the starved string quality, that makes even Britten's fully scored orchestral music rather lean and dry, those stealthy, panther-like pacings up and down of bass figures in fourths, those tiny pecking accompanying woodwind figures which a correspondent of mine (too unkindly, though I see his point) calls 'chicken-feed'. One may or may not like such things, or wish Britten would go on to something else; but they are part of his personality and that is [...] nothing short of genius.

Desmond Shawe-Taylor, *New Statesman and Nation* (16 October 1954), pp. 469–70, submitted the following assessment, which is reproduced here complete:

Who could have guessed that Henry James's ambiguous story of two children haunted and corrupted by the spirits of two wicked servants could be made to yield an opera – and opera unlike all other operas, yet within its strange terms of reference nothing less than masterly? This miracle Benjamin Britten and his fine-fingered librettist, Myfanwy Piper, have together performed. *The Turn of the Screw*, first produced by the English Opera Group last month in Venice and now being repeated with very great success by the same company at Sadler's Wells, can never take its place in any standard repertory: so much follows inevitably from the nature of the subject and the attendant difficulties of casting. But practical disadvantages, however regrettable, must not obscure the aesthetic issue – the unquestionable truth, as it seems to me, that down to the last quaver, the last barely audible whisper from bass flute, the little opera is a consummate work of art: a work of art quite in the high sense of James himself, who wrote about his story: 'The thing was to aim at absolute singleness, clearness and roundness ... the "roundness" in which beauty and lucidity largely reside.' Those words (which I have conflated from two separate sentences in James's preface) might well have been written to describe what composer and librettist – contrary to all expectation – have here achieved.

It is true that everything we know of Britten's talent – his skill in the creation of atmosphere, his intense sympathy with childhood, all his fine lightness and grace and rapidity of touch – marked him out as the only conceivable composer for such a task; but without a good libretto he would still have been helpless. The great virtue of Mrs Piper's contribution is that she has managed to do almost equal justice to the genius of Henry James and to that of the composer: her sixteen short scenes (eight to each act) combine without apparent effort a scrupulously exact unfolding of the Jamesian narrative and atmosphere with a pattern that has proved intensely stimulating to the composer's purely musical instinct. In consequence, the score, ingeniously illustrative though it is at every turn, stands on its own feet every bit as firmly as a symphony or a set of variations. The brief orchestral interludes by which we are led from scene to scene and prepared for the impact (idyllic or gay or sinister) of each successive episode are, in fact, a series of variations on a single theme; this theme consists of a series of alternate rising fourths and falling minor thirds, extended and modulating in such a way as to pass through all twelve notes of the chromatic scale. Like some of Berg's themes, Britten's material has thus, so to speak, a foot in both camps; but where Berg allows traditional tonality to hover like a mirage over his basically twelve-note idiom, Britten merely causes the suggestion of a twelve-note series to 'compromise' his normally lucid tonality; and it can easily be imagined how well this treatment suits the subject, so charming and ordinary on the surface, so tortuous and equivocal underneath. I apologize to the reader who may be puzzled by this technical description, and assure him that the music makes its effect in the theatre with the utmost clarity and immediacy by virtue of its melodic freshness, its endlessly fascinating variety of rhythm and texture, and a remarkable homogeneity of style which will become more apparent with every hearing. I doubt if any other opera of Britten's, even *Peter Grimes*, unfolds a musical argument so close, compelling and symmetrical as this. None, to my ear, is so drenched in the deep, pure flood of musical invention.

If this is true, the reason lies partly in a subject which has possessed the composer's imagination as nothing has since *Grimes*, and partly in the finely sensitive libretto. I come back to Mrs Piper's share in the work because a great deal – far too much, I think – is being made of her single failure. An obvious flaw does arise in her treatment of the two *revenants*, Peter Quint and Miss Jessel. In James they are silent, ineffably horrible: 'Make the reader *think* the evil, and you are released from weak specifications.' In opera it was inevitable that they should speak (that is, sing); but with every word they utter, with every step they take towards the footlights, their power is diminished – and of this the authors do not seem to have been sufficiently aware. These objections would largely vanish if the producer were more careful to keep the ghosts far back on the stage and dimly lit (except for the one chilling moment when the living Governess finds Miss Jessel seated at her desk [Act II scene 3]) – and if Peter Pears, the Quint, could be provided with a more plausible red wig. But two stumbling blocks would still remain: the last scene of Act I and the first of Act II. In the former, the voice of Quint is first heard, with admirably uncanny effect, in long quasi-oriental vocalises on the word 'Miles!'; but thereafter neither librettist nor composer has solved the problem that James was so careful to avoid. Quint's stanzas ('I am the riderless horse . . . the hero-highwayman', etc.) faintly reminiscent of Midir's 'Luring Song' in [Rutland Boughton's opera] *The Immortal Hour*, are quite too harmless for a devil whose utterances (if he *must* utter) ought almost to scare the Lord Chamberlain [responsible for the licensing of stage performances and empowered to insist on some censorship]. And the music at this point cannot supply (what music could?) the evil element missing in the words. The opening scene of Act II, a dialogue inspired by the 'Colloque sentimental' of Verlaine, in which the ghosts talk of their past relationship and present intentions, is in itself more effective, but dramatically redundant: we know it all, or can guess it, from what Mrs Grose, the housekeeper, has already told us.

From this single flaw, which could quite easily be removed, it is a pleasure to turn to the extraordinary virtues of a text which has inspired the composer to scene after scene of radiantly beautiful music. Some of his happiest inventions arise from the seemingly innocent games of the children, their schoolroom rhymes and affectionate teasing of their elders. Wonderful art is shown in such things as the setting of 'Tom, Tom, the piper's son' [Act I scene 5], with its galumphing hobby-horse accompaniment, the tune rising, along with the high spirits of the children, first from A to B, then – with a huge jump – to E. Right into the middle of one of these schoolroom scenes – and this is the finest of all the librettist's strokes, a *trouvaille* of genius – Miles suddenly drops the mnemonic quatrain which plays on several different senses of the Latin *malo* : 'Malo, I would rather be; malo, in an apple tree; malo, than a naughty boy; malo, in adversity.' The slow, drooping, infinitely sad little tune to which Britten has set these lines forms the still centre of the whole musical design; constantly alluded to by the orchestra, it becomes at last the boy's epitaph.

By such means, and by the dramatically and musically brilliant episode of Miles's piano-playing, the children are kept well in the forefront of the action without having too much to sing. The main vocal burden of the opera falls on the Governess's shoulders. To her is given the most immediately taking 'number' in the score, the vesperal aria in Act I, with its ravishing orchestral prelude, in which she meditates on the beauty of Bly ['How beautiful it is', Act I scene 4], and the dramatic letter scene of Act II [scene 3], in which she first writes her letter to a fiercely agitated orchestral accompaniment, then reads it over to a calmer version of the same musical idea. It is hardly too much to say that, in this setting of a prose text, there is no recitative: only free melody and arioso. There are many telling ensembles, although it is true that the presence in the cast of four sopranos and one treble makes it at times difficult to distinguish the several vocal strands. The scoring contrives to wring fresh miracles of sound from the now familiar chamber orchestra: it is notably free from all 'spikiness' except where such a quality is positively wanted.

The performance, from singers and players alike, was just about perfect. The composer conducted a cast which included Peter Pears and Arda Mandikian as the ghosts, Jennifer Vyvyan as the Governess, Joan Cross as Mrs Grose, Olive Dyer and Master David Hemmings as the children (alas, how difficult it will be to replace either of them!). John Piper's decor was beautifully in key; so, in general, was Basil Coleman's production.

Britten wrote to Princess Margaret of Hesse and the Rhine on 10 October 1954:

What pleasure your sweet letter gave us – coming right in the middle of premières (& worries, colds & temperaments, which are the necessary adjuncts of premières of course). We are all bitterly disappointed that you & Lu aren't coming over [to London] for the Screw, because this performance is so remarkable & it may never be the same again ... It has had a really exciting effect on the public, & all performances were immediately sold out; but it has had the usual effect on the old newspapers, & fur is flying ... o dear, o dear, how I sometimes wish I were respectable & dead, & that people wouldn't get so cross. Venice was really nice tho'.

III ON THE THRESHOLD OF A NEW MUSICAL WORLD:
TOWARDS *THE PRINCE OF THE PAGODAS*

OCTOBER 1954–OCTOBER 1955

4 CRABBE STREET
ALDEBURGH
February 3rd 1955

My dear Basil,
 Irony that the only letter I've written to you should be just as you are leaving to come home! — I'm so sorry I have been so bad about writing, but it hasn't been altogether a happy winter. The strains (& lack of holiday) in the Summer told heavily on us both, & although víz

neither of us has been seriously ill, we've been pretty low. Peter had a bad cold (& flu really) on the first night of Walton's opera, & was only put through by drugs & champagne — 'put through' is a slight understatement since he literally stole the show with a really long comedy performance. (But he told you so recover from it) We are now off abroad — a week's concerts in Belgium & Switzerland — & then, a then, a fortnight's ski-ing in the mountains, which

Britten to Basil Coleman, 3 February 1955: Letter 829

CHRONOLOGY 1954–1955

YEAR	EVENTS AND COMPOSITIONS
1954	
6 October	Sadler's Wells Theatre, London: conducts the first UK performance of *The Turn of the Screw*
17 October – 1 November	Recitals with Pears in Switzerland, Belgium, the Netherlands and Sweden
October – November	Planning a children's opera with William Plomer on a classical Greek story; the project is shelved in January 1955
27 November	COMPOSITION *Canticle III: 'Still falls the Rain – The Raids, 1940, Night and Dawn'* (words by Edith Sitwell)
3 December	Royal Opera House, Covent Garden, London: first performance of Walton's *Troilus and Cressida*, conducted by Malcolm Sargent, in which Pears creates the role of Pandarus
1955	
2 January	Performs Tippett's *Boyhood's End* with Pears at Tippett's fiftieth birthday concert
3–7 January	Records *The Turn of the Screw* for Decca
16 January	Performs Poulenc's Concerto for Two Pianos, with Poulenc as fellow soloist, at the Royal Festival Hall, London
27 January	Attends first performance of Tippett's *The Midsummer Marriage*, at the Royal Opera House, Covent Garden
28 January	Wigmore Hall, London: first performance of *Canticle III* given by Pears, Dennis Brain and Britten, as part of a concert in memory of Noel Mewton-Wood
6–13 February	Concert tour with Pears to Belgium and Switzerland, followed by a ski-ing holiday in Zermatt, with Pears, Mary Potter and the Duncans. First discusses projected *St Peter* oratorio with Ronald Duncan

February	COMPOSITION *Alpine Suite*
April	Composing Act I of *The Prince of the Pagodas*
13–14 April	Records *Saint Nicolas* for Decca in Aldeburgh Parish Church, with David Hemmings, Pears, and the Aldeburgh Festival Chorus and Orchestra
26 May – 6 June	Conducts *The Turn of the Screw* at Schwetzingen, Munich and Florence
18–26 June	Eighth Aldeburgh Festival: highlights include *The Turn of the Screw*, *Saint Nicolas* and Schubert's *Die schöne Müllerin*
7–20 July	Performing at Holland Festival, including *The Turn of the Screw*
Summer	COMPOSITION *Hymn to St Peter*
August	Begins composing Act II of *The Prince of the Pagodas*
September	Planning *St Peter* with Ronald Duncan
28 September	Duke of York's Theatre, London: 'Old friends are best' (a setting of a text by Plomer) included in *The Punch Revue*
September & October	Records English song recital with Pears for Decca, including songs by Lennox Berkeley, Bridge, Holst and Oldham
October	Revises *A Boy was Born*; records *The Little Sweep* for Decca

818 To Edith Sitwell[1]

4 CRABBE STREET, ALDEBURGH
September 27th 1954

My dear Edith,

Will you and Osbert[2] be in Renishaw[3] at the beginning of March next year? Peter and I are performing in Manchester on March 8th, & we would love to come to you on 7th & sing those songs for you that we talked about.[4] It may be, of course, too soon for you to have any idea of what you may be doing then, but that is for us the most convenient date.

The other thing I wanted to bother you about is this – a young friend of mine, a pianist, whom you may have known, died under terrible circumstances last year – Noel Mewton-Wood.[5] We are doing a memorial concert to him next December, & I want to write a piece specially for the occasion. Would you allow me to attempt to set your very great poem from the war years – 'Still falls the rain'?[6] I feel very drawn towards it, & in its courage & light seen through horror & darkness find something very right for the poor boy. Also playing in the programme is that most wonderful of all horn players, Dennis Brain,[7] & I was contemplating setting it for Voice, Horn, & Piano. Would you be so kind as to let me know what you feel about this? If you agree, my publishers will naturally approach Macmillans for the formal arrangements but I first want to know what your reactions may be.

I suppose there is no chance of your being in London at all, the first half of October? It would be lovely to see you, & I should so like you to see 'The Turn of the Screw'.[8]

With every good wish,
Yours sincerely,
BEN (BRITTEN)

1 British poet and critic (1887–1964), with whom Britten and Pears enjoyed a warm friendship during the 1950s. She performed at Aldeburgh Festivals, Britten set her poem 'Still Falls the Rain' as his *Canticle III* (see n. 6 below), and Pears joined her as speaker for several performances and a recording of Walton's *Façade*. See also Letter 639 n. 1 and 1C3.

2 Sir Osbert Sitwell (1892–1969), British poet, essayist and novelist, brother of Edith, probably best known for his five volumes of autobiography (published 1944–50). In 1938 there had been a possibility that he would collaborate with Britten on a ballet for Colonel Wassily de Basil: see Addenda 2 n. 8, vol. 2, p. 1335. See also *The Sitwells and the Arts of the 1920s and 1930s*, catalogue for an exhibition at the National Portrait Gallery, in particular the chapter 'Osbert', with an essay by John Pearson.

3 Renishaw Hall, Derbyshire, the Sitwells' country seat. Osbert Sitwell commissioned John Piper to undertake a series of paintings of Renishaw Hall in the early 1940s. For an amusing account of the atmosphere in this supposedly haunted house, and Edith Sitwell's attempt to exorcise it, see Susana Walton, *William Walton: Behind the Façade*, p. 56.

4 Were these songs perhaps *Winter Words*? Sitwell responded on 6 October, telling Britten that unfortunately both she and her brother would be abroad in March 1955.

5 On 5 December 1953, following the death of his partner, Bill Federick, the distraught Mewton-Wood took his life. There had already been one failed suicide attempt. On 4 December he had written to Britten – one of many such letters the pianist wrote to his friends – in which he betrayed nothing of what he was planning. News of Mewton-Wood's suicide reached Britten in Aldeburgh on 6 December in the middle of a drinks party. Imogen Holst records in her diary (IHD, p. 274): 'Ben came back looking distraught saying that Noel had killed himself. He didn't let everyone know, and carried on being host.' On 7 December, she writes (IHD, pp. 274–5):

He was looking grey & worried, & talked of the terrifyingly small gap between madness and non-madness, and said why was it that the people one really liked found life so difficult. Peter had rung up and was 'in a state'. He also talked of the difficulty of finding anyone else to take his [i.e. Mewton-Wood's] place. He'd had an awful time being rung up by newspapers.

And on 11 December, in London (IHD, p. 275): 'Afterwards, sitting by the fire, he talked of Noel's death and of how all his friends had done all they could to help him.'

Mewton-Wood had received high acclamation for his interpretations of Arthur Bliss's Piano Concerto and Piano Sonata (the latter dedicated to him in 1952), and Bliss declared in a broadcast obituary transmitted on 24 January 1954:

Mewton-Wood was much more than an outstanding pianist. His was one of the most inquiring and far-reaching minds I have met in a young man. A study of his bookshelves would show the serious and varied range of his reading. He had a great love of poetry. He admired modern painting, and knew how to add to the collection left him by his uncle, the poet Walter Turner [...]

Noel Mewton-Wood's repertoire was a very wide one. He was a staunch exponent of modern music. It is rare to get a great virtuoso who will play modern music with understanding and enthusiasm, and with his death we composers of today have lost one of our greatest champions. I remember wonderfully authentic performances of Bartók's Sonata for two pianos and percussion, of Stravinsky's Concerto and *Capriccio*, of Michael Tippett's Sonata [No. 1], of Hindemith's *Ludus Tonalis* [...]

Earlier on I said that Noel Mewton-Wood felt music from a composer's standpoint. It may be news to many that he was himself a composer of many works. I confess I did not know this myself. He was so modest both on the platform and off that I never knew what really lay behind that keen mind. Thanks to his mother, who has shown me his scores, I now know that he had written two symphonies (the second was composed during a South African tour), three piano concertos, two string quartets, piano and violin sonatas, and many songs. Remember his age – thirty-one.

Bliss then played the recording of Tippett's song-cycle *The Heart's Assurance* made by Mewton-Wood with Pears in 1953. See Gregory Roscow (ed.), *Bliss on Music: Selected Writings of Arthur Bliss, 1920–75*, pp. 215–17.

6 Sitwell told Britten in a letter of 6 October 1954: 'To have my "Still Falls the Rain" set by you would fill me with pride and joy; I think I need not say that.' The resulting work was *Canticle III: 'Still Falls the Rain – The Raids, 1940, Night and Dawn'* for tenor, horn and piano. It was completed on 27 November, just one week before the memorial concert for Mewton-Wood, which had been scheduled to take place at the Wigmore Hall on 4 December (almost exactly the first anniversary of the pianist's untimely death). However, the premiere of *Canticle III* had to be postponed due to an indisposition on the part of Pears, as Britten explained in a letter to Elizabeth Mayer written on 6 December:

It is being a difficult autumn–winter for us. We are both feeling the effects of no holiday this summer (and complete lack of sun too), & little illnesses are, through tiredness, inclined to develop. Poor old Peter has had a horrid 'flu cum trachyitis (??) – & had to get out of bed (literally) to sing a big part in the new Walton opera at Cov. Garden. It was a noble effort, & he has been much acclaimed for it – but honestly the work itself isn't very interesting; he makes a charming thing of his own part, though, & the Waltons are great dears, & so we are delighted with its great success, although slightly bewildered (as usual!) with the critical standards.

Pears had created the role of Pandarus in Walton's opera *Troilus and Cressida* at the Royal Opera House on 3 December, and wrote to Mary Behrend on 13 December:

I was so sorry to hear that you had come all the way up for Noel's memorial concert – Oh dear! I think it was announced as cancelled in the Telegraph, but perhaps not in The Times.
   I wonder how you enjoyed 'Troilus' on Monday – I don't really think much of it – Badly shaped – too long – lacking in ideas – and looks pretty terrible, don't you think? but I can't complain – I have the best part!

For further information on Pears's participation in *Troilus and Cressida* and on the uneasy relationship between Britten and the Waltons, see CHPP, pp. 168–70 (where the author notes that Pears did not sing in the four remaining *Troilus* performances in December). See also Susana Walton, *William Walton: Behind the Façade*, pp. 122–6, Michael Kennedy, *Portrait of Walton*, pp. 129–33 and 179–81 and Malcolm Hayes (ed.), *The Selected Letters of William Walton*, p. 248.
   Canticle III was given its rescheduled first performance (by Pears, Brain

Britten's fair-copy manuscript of *Canticle III*: variation v and verse vi

LETTER 818: SEPTEMBER 1954

and Britten) at the Wigmore Hall on 28 January 1955. The performance was reviewed in *The Times* (29 January 1955):

From Britten came a third canticle, a setting for tenor, horn, and piano of Edith Sitwell's passionate comment on the *Blitzkrieg* of 1940, 'Still falls the rain'. The words of the title recur as a refrain, and Britten has set them for a ghostly melismatic semitone step against a bare fourth accompanimental chord; but here the poem and this musical refrain can be enhanced by the interludes in which the horn and piano, between verses, recount the horror that may be taken as a cosmic symbol of warfare in the personal human intellect. The musical effects which the composer has devised for these interludes are themselves staggeringly brilliant *trouvailles*; but they are less than the terrible impact of the whole, or the effect in the closing lines when horn and voice, in note for note counterpoint, produce a composite sound as, in a technically similar yet emotionally different way, did the two singing voices who, in Britten's second canticle, also enact the voice of God.

Desmond Shawe-Taylor reviewed the memorial concert in the *New Statesman and Nation* (12 February 1955), p. 210:

The concert given at the Wigmore Hall in memory of the pianist Noel Mewton-Wood by a group of his friends and colleagues proved to be in itself a memorable event. It had a worthy object in the establishment of a scholarship for Australian pianists; but it was in the first place a gesture of affection and regret for a young, rare, vigorous talent untimely swept away. Mewton-Wood was widely admired for his musical powers, much loved for himself. His intellectual vivacity and apparently limitless fund of friendliness and high spirits were the counterpart of his playing, so bold and vivid and downright, so acutely intellectual, yet capable too on occasion of a sudden intimacy and charm [...]

Benjamin Britten, whose bare and tender *Lachrymae* for piano and viola (Herbert Downes) had made a perfect introduction to the evening, also contributed the most important novelty in his Third Canticle, a setting of Edith Sitwell's 'Still falls the rain' for tenor, horn and piano. The form of this piece is original. The refrain is invariably delivered in a sorrow-laden, hieratic recitative, turning in and back on itself after small excursions of a semitone or a tone above or below the starting point. Between each appearance of the refrain, horn and piano execute a series of increasingly bold variations, in one of which the horn indulges in fiery chromatic runs; at the end, horn and voice move together in equal note-values but in contrary motion suggesting, by a device similar to that of the two voices in *Abraham and Isaac*, the voice of God. The nature of the poem (a meditation on the raids of 1940) is such as to preclude the childlike and profound lyricism to be found in Britten's two earlier canticles; but the new piece is no less masterly in its translation of a poetic idea into musical shapes that are strange and new, yet seemingly inevitable.

For Sitwell's reaction to the work, see Letter 831 n. 1.

A recording of a 1956 performance given by the original artists was issued on the BBC 'Britten the Performer' CD label in 1996. *Canticle III* was later incorporated into a programme of further Sitwell settings and poetry entitled *The Heart of the Matter*: see p. 460.

Canticle III occupies the same world of concentrated musical economy that characterized *The Turn of the Screw*, the work that immediately precedes it. As with the opera, the Canticle employs a twelve-note theme as the basis for a sequence of instrumental variations, which are presented as interludes between the setting of the stanzas of Sitwell's poem. Britten himself recognized that this pair of works marked a change in his compositional style: see Letter 831.

7 British horn-player (1921–1957). Britten had known Brain since 1942 and both *Canticle III* and the *Serenade* were composed with his beauty of sound and technical virtuosity in mind. See also Letter 392 n. 2; Walter Legge's obituary tribute to Brain, first published in the *Gramophone* (November 1957) and reprinted in Alan Sanders (ed.), *Walter Legge: Words and Music*, pp. 121–5; Britten's obituary, 'Dennis Brain 1921–1957', *Tempo* 46 (winter 1957), pp. 55–6 (reprinted in PKBM, pp. 158–60); and Stephen Pettit, *Dennis Brain: A Biography*.

8 As is indicated by Letter 831, Sitwell had still not seen the opera in April 1955.

WIGMORE HALL
Wigmore Street, W.1

The English Opera Group
General Manager : Basil Douglas

presents

THE EARL OF HAREWOOD

in a talk, illustrated by the original cast, on
Benjamin Britten's new opera

THE TURN OF THE SCREW

Thursday, 30th September, 1954 at 8 p.m.

THE ENGLISH OPERA GROUP
25, WIGMORE PLACE
LONDON   :   W.1

PROGRAMME
ONE SHILLING

819 To Edward Sackville-West[1]

5 CHESTER GATE, REGENT'S PARK, LONDON, NW1
October 16th, 1954

My dear Eddy,

Peter & I leave for a tour at crack of dawn tomorrow,[2] & today is full with meetings & rehearsals & the last 'Turn' tonight, so there is only a moment in which to thank you for your letter. It gave me great pleasure, my dear, to learn that you like the new piece, & appreciate it so fully. I am happy with it, but very surprised that the <u>general</u> public has reacted to it so strongly. It seemed, as I was writing it, to be so intimate, so personal, & so odd, that only a few friends would take it. Imagine the surprise when the Fenice rose to it . . .! It only shows that one can never gauge these things. I'm very pleased with the performance, & want Decca to record it as soon as possible[3] – before, at any rate, David's [Hemmings's] voice breaks! Isn't he a stunning little performer?

As I said, we are off tomorrow, to Holland, Belgium & Sweden for 2 weeks or so – when I come back, can we meet? What about a weekend in Aldeburgh? Would that attract you at all? I'll write & suggest one.

In the meantime, my dear, lots of thanks for writing so nicely.

With love,
Yours ever,
BEN

1 British writer (1901–1965), a cousin of the writer Vita Sackville-West; see Letter 416 n. 4. For an account of Sackville-West's sympathetic critical writings on Britten in the 1940s, see Letter 414 n. 1. The relationship between critic and composer is discussed in Letter 416 n. 4, and the correspondence between them from 1942 to 1945 is examined in Donald Mitchell's essay, '"I love being with you and picking your brains"', vol. 3, pp. 111–34.

2 Britten and Pears travelled to Zurich on 17 October, in time for Pears to fulfil an engagement that evening in Donaueschingen; they both rehearsed in Brussels the next day and then gave a recital in Rotterdam on 19 October, returning to Brussels on the 20th for their concert. Further engagements followed in the Netherlands: a broadcast recital from Hilversum on the 21st and a recital in Amsterdam on the 24th (Purcell, Handel, Schubert, *Winter Words* and folksong arrangements). They then travelled to Stockholm for a recital on 30 October and an orchestral concert on the 31st before their return to the UK the following day.

3 The Decca recording of *The Turn of the Screw* took place between 3 and 7 January 1955 at the Decca Recording Studios, West Hampstead, London, with the original cast under Britten's baton: this was the first of Britten's operatic works to be recorded in full, as the composer himself notes in

Advertisement for the English Opera Group's 1954 London season

Letter 826. The monophonic discs were originally released in 1955 and the recording has (at the time of writing) never been out of the catalogue in over fifty years.

820 To William Plomer

AMERICAN HOTEL, AMSTERDAM, HOLLAND
Oct. 25th 1954

My dear William,

I've been meaning to scribble you a note before this week, but our rushings round Holland & Belgium have taken one's tiny energies & time I'm afraid. We are flying off to Stockholm in a few minutes, this morning, so it really still isn't the ideal moment for telling you some of my ideas of what the new little opera might or might not be.[1] Actually letters are probably not the way to decide such a thing. The main thing, I feel, is that we should meet. I plan to be in Aldeburgh all of November. Would a day or a weekend, or longer if you will, be possible – (as far as I can remember – any day is possible except the 12th) – for you & Charles to visit me?

I don't remember whether I made the 'data' clear about the new piece? It ought to fit with the 'Little Sweep' into an evening – to be between 30–45 minutes about – have a cast of not more than 6 children (4 boys, 2 girls) & 5 adults (3 women, 2 men). We <u>could</u> use the audience as chorus if we want, also.

The idea, just to give you a little something to think about, that is in my mind, is a Greek story, translated into present day children's world. I wonder whether Phaeton wouldn't be possible.[2] A little boy teased into borrowing his father's racing car & driving it into disaster ... But I know you have other ideas, & long to hear them.

We get back from Scandinavia Nov. 1 or 2. You wouldn't have a moment on Nov. 3rd, which, I believe is a Cape day?[3] Perhaps a p.c. to 5 Chester Gate, NW1? Lots of love to you both – from a rather weary couple – weary from over-work, over-eating & drinking & over-travelling – but still game,

BEN

1 Plomer and Britten had been toying with the idea of a children's opera since at least August 1951, when they discussed a preliminary scenario for a stage work to be based on Beatrix Potter's *The Tale of Mr Tod* before abandoning the project because of copyright difficulties (see Letters 711 and 714, and Peter F. Alexander, *William Plomer*, pp. 269–70). Next came a project on the theme of space travel under the working title *Tyco the Vegan* in the spring of 1952, which was to have included audience participation of a similar nature to that in *The Little Sweep*. The energies of the two men were then chan-

nelled into *Gloriana*, but the plans for a children's opera, which were never to be realized, were resumed with the present letter. It was not until *Curlew River* (with its lengthy gestation from 1957 until 1964) that another Britten–Plomer project reached fruition. See also Letters 823 and 828.

2   Phaethon (in the customary spelling) was the son of Helios, who asked his father's permission to drive the horses that pulled the sun. He was unable to control them, and Zeus intervened by striking Phaethon dead with a thunderbolt lest he should set fire to the world. The tears of his mourning sisters (the Phaethoniades, who were transformed into poplar trees) became amber. Phaethon's fate is related in the second book of Ovid's *Metamorphoses*, a literary source to which Britten was no stranger in the 1950s: he had already treated the same tale in the second of his *Six Metamorphoses after Ovid* for solo oboe. The stories of Arion and Icarus were also under consideration as alternative topics: see Letter 823.

3   A 'Cape day' was one of the days on which Plomer worked at the offices of the publishers Jonathan Cape in London. Britten returned to England on 1 November, but his diary for the 3rd is blank. Letter 823 reveals that a meeting between the two men was planned for 17 November, but this date is also blank in the diary and the only tentative reference to Plomer appears on 26 November ('William?'). Britten wrote to Plomer on 18 November:

> How disappointing that you are ill, how wretched for you. I am so sorry, & hope that the germ is by now almost, if not quite, gone. But I hope that your visit here is only postponed, & that we can fix a date soon. Next week isn't wonderfully good for me – the middle of it, that is to say – but I suppose Friday 26th isn't possible? Otherwise, I am afraid it must wait till the beginning of December (I have to be away 30th–Dec. 6th), unless we had a little get-together in London. Anyhow, my dear William, the main thing is, get well quick; don't hurry up too soon – portentous colds can be treacherous, you know – and when you're well we'll fix a meeting. I can't say how I look forward to it, nor how disappointed I am that you're not here now as we'd hoped.

Clearly, Britten and Plomer could not have met on 17 November, in spite of Alexander's assertion to the contrary (p. 299).

821   To Eric Walter White

4 CRABBE STREET, ALDEBURGH
5th November, 1954

My dear Eric,

Just a brief thank you for your touching letter. I am delighted in your reaction to my latest baby – one is always so delighted that one's sympathetic friends find the last work the best.[1] It was certainly a difficult work to bring off both technically and spiritually. The thing that pleases me so much about its reception is that it is not taken solely as a story of horror, but as something deeper as well. I am sure Henry James intended that.

By the way, do you know another short story of James' called 'Owen Wingrave' with much the same quality as the Screw?[2]

With many thanks again.

Yours ever,
BEN

1 White had seen a performance of *The Turn of the Screw*.
2 This constitutes a remarkably early testimony to Britten's interest in the James tale which was to serve as the basis for the BBC television opera *Owen Wingrave* in 1970.

822 To Desmond Shawe-Taylor[1]

4 CRABBE STREET, ALDEBURGH
November 6th, 1954

My dear Desmond,

Your very nice letter arrived just as I was leaving with Peter for a strenuous tour abroad, on which there wasn't a second for writing letters ... hence the delay in answering you. I am so glad you liked the 'Screw' so much. It <u>does</u> work as an opera I feel, & I think in many ways you are right about the subject being, as it were, nearest to me of any I have yet chosen (although what that indicates of my own character I shouldn't like to say!) I don't, frankly, see your point about the ghosts, but we must thrash that out one day. I'm sure I'm right to make them sing, hence the necessity of words, & consequent removal of one layer of <u>mystery</u> from the ghosts.[2] But I feel Myfanwy has done this well, & there is jolly little explicit in what the ghosts say. The trouble is, if you admire the H. James story (which I do), one is inclined to condemn any divergence from it. But it <u>must</u> be an opera in its own right, & must stand or fall by that.

We hope to record it very soon, by the way; I am very proud of the performance.

I am here working for a bit now – but I shall be in London for quite a time in December, & we <u>must</u> meet.

Thank you again for writing – I was much touched by the warmth of your letter, my dear.

Yours ever,
BEN

1 Anglo-Irish music critic (1907–1995), at this period music critic of the *New Statesman and Nation*; see Letter 602 n. 2. For his detailed assessment of *The Turn of the Screw*, see Letter 817 n. 3.

2 Britten's round rebuttal of Shawe-Taylor's criticism of the decision to make the ghosts in *The Turn of the Screw* sing shows the composer to have been very much aware of the dangers inherent in an operatic adaptation of James's elusive story. Much critical verbiage has been expended on the theory that Britten's singing ghosts can no longer be interpreted as the product of the Governess's feverish imaginings, as some argue they should be in the James story (for a rather one-sided view, see PHTS, pp. 1–22). Subscribers to this viewpoint singularly fail to demonstrate why the ghosts' singing (itself the natural means of communication in an operatic context) could not equally well be imagined by the Governess: even a scene in which the Governess takes no part (e.g. the first section of Act II scene 1) could be deemed to exist solely in her subconscious, as Patricia Howard concedes (PHTS, pp. 48–9). Among early reviewers only Virgil Thomson noted that Britten's approach could be deemed to be in accordance with such an interpretation (see Letter 817 n. 1). Shawe-Taylor's opinion became something of a hobby-horse, but his much later remarks in *The Sunday Times* (31 October 1976) to the effect that he could not agree with the interpretation of the tale whereby the ghosts were seen as 'figments of the Governess's overheated imagination', when he goes so far as to say that the James story does not 'lend any colour to such a theory', seem curiously at variance with his critical stance in 1954.

In a letter to a young friend, Neil Saunders (28 June 1955), Britten was to give an unequivocal indication of his interpretative position, especially in respect of the opera's final scene:

This particular story arouses the wildest disagreements of interpretation, and you must know that your own interpretation of the last page is very much the minority one; but when you get to know the opera better I hope you will find that Myfanwy Piper and I have left the same ambiguities as Henry James did, and in the particular case you mention the boy's final cry ['Peter Quint, you devil!'] is addressed to no one on the stage at all. I am afraid both you and your friend must have been too carried away with your own idea to notice that David Hemmings says the word directly to the <u>audience</u> – otherwise, facing upstage he would not have been heard clearly enough.

823 To William Plomer

4 CRABBE STREET, ALDEBURGH
Nov. 8th 1954

My dear William,

I am delighted that you can manage the 17th, & look forward immensely to your coming.[1] I'm glad you think you can stay till the Saturday – but if you change your mind & want to stay over the weekend, it's OK by me – to coin a phrase – & I'm sure by the Hesses too.

I've read Arion with great pleasure.[2] It is a sweet story and sweetly told. But for the life of me I can't think of a way to fit it naturally to a contemporary setting, nor of making him a boy. A boy doesn't (well, normally) make a fortune out of his gifts, although he could fall overboard on to the back of the equivalent of a dolphin, I suppose. Have you thought any more about Phaeton, to which I am still loyal? Or what about Icarus,[3] which is such a good, & up-to-date story. Don't bother to reply, of course; we can wrangle over all this when you come, which will be lovely.

love to you & C.
from P. & me

Thinking of other stories with a boy in – I suppose Medea & Absyrtus[4] is too awful. What a girl she was.

1 A visit that did not take place.
2 Arion, a poet living in the seventh century BC, was (according to Herodotus) thrown overboard by the crew of a ship carrying him to Corinth, only to be rescued by a dolphin which bore him safely home. Arion is otherwise famous for his development of the dithyramb.
3 In one of the most famous stories of Greek mythology, Icarus (son of Daedalus) used wings fashioned from feathers and wax in order to escape from the island of Crete. He flew too close to the sun, against his father's advice, and when the wax melted he plummeted to a watery death. As with Phaethon, Britten presumably knew the tale in its version by Ovid (*Metamorphoses* 8); he might also have been familiar with Auden's 1938 poem 'Musée des Beaux Arts', a response to Pieter Brueghel's painting *The Fall of Icarus*.
4 Absyrtus was Medea's brother, whom she is reputed to have killed during their flight from their native Colchis. Medea went on to kill her own children in the temple of Hera as an act of revenge against their father Jason, whose new bride she also managed to poison before herself committing suicide.

824   To Anthony Gishford

4 CRABBE STREET, ALDEBURGH
December 28th, 1954

My dear Tony,

What a lovely pot of Stilton to thank you for. It was extremely kind of you, & added greatly to our Festive gastronomic gaiety. I wonder if you went away, or whether you sported in Highgate. We had a quiet, but extremely pleasant Christmas with a few intimates here. My toothache, a constant companion for three weeks, elected to disappear on Christmas eve, the threatened floods subsided at the eleventh hour, & the weather was fine & beautiful, so all was rosy. Now work starts again, & it is rather a gloomy thought. Luckily I'm getting interested in the ballet, so it isn't as gloomy as it might be.

A very happy New Year, successful in every way to you, Tony. I confess I feel more confident about the New Year than I have for ages, & one of the reasons is certainly the new & improved relations at B. & H. That is certainly due to your splendid, & tactful efforts in 1954.[1] I do understand a little of your problems there, enough to admire & be very grateful for your solving of them. To me personally your understanding & sympathetic presence there is comforting, & encouraging – to say the least.

Many thanks again & every good wish from both
PETER &
BEN

1 Earlier in 1954 Leslie Boosey had responded to Britten's concerns about his relationship with Boosey & Hawkes and in particular the composer's wish to see the firm more actively involved in publishing the work of younger composers. He proposed a series of lunch meetings, to be attended by himself, Britten, Stein, Gishford and Roth, through which the composer would have a regular opportunity to make his views known. Boosey recognized the need for a better working relationship between Roth and Britten to be forged and very much hoped these meetings would make that possible. As Stein's involvement in the company decreased, Gishford had taken on responsibility for the composer's affairs at Boosey & Hawkes. See also Helen Wallace, *Boosey & Hawkes: The Publishing Story*, p. 94.

825 To Michael Tippett
[*Typed file copy*]

[Aldeburgh]
12th January, 1955

Dear Michael,

Your charming note to Peter and me gave us great pleasure, although we felt our contribution to your birthday celebrations rather inadequate.[1] It is not a work to do in cold blood, especially when the blood is rather tired and 'fluey as it was that night. Anyhow we were both glad it gave you pleasure.

It was not exactly the moment to raise the matter of your previous letter[2] which, of course, was received with affection and sympathy; but you did not in replying make any comment on our idea of putting a note in the score of your Divertimento to the effect that the second movement was originally variation two of the Aldeburgh piece.[3] I still feel strongly that this is the only way to clarify the confusing situation. I am, by the way, at Sacher's[4] request going to perform the Aldeburgh Variations for him in Switzerland,[5] but also at his request I have furnished him with a similar note saying how the one piece comes to be included in two different works. I know you are up to your eyes in "Midsummer Marriage",[6] but please do find a moment to talk to Schott's about slipping the score[7] to this effect.

I hope all is going well at the Garden, and you are not too exhausted with the incredible preparations that all opera seems to need.

[BEN]

1 Britten and Pears had performed Tippett's 'cantata for tenor voice and piano', *Boyhood's End*, on 2 January 1955 at the Tippett 50th Birthday Concert held at Morley College. The work had been composed for the two artists in 1943: see Letter 430 n. 4. Tippett thanked Britten in a letter of 3 January 1955 (Thomas Schuttenhelm (ed.), *Selected Letters of Michael Tippett*, p. 205):

You should not have been out and about for my sake and so ill. I was deeply touched, but also deeply worried.

Of course, yours and Peter's contribution stood so out, that that was all there is to it. Music only really speaks when performed thus. That got borne in on me every moment.

2 In an undated letter (probably from the end of 1954; Schuttenhelm, p. 204), Tippett had written to Britten about his *Divertimento on 'Sellinger's Round'*, a performance of which was planned for the 1955 Aldeburgh Festival:

One of my intentions had been to incorporate a bit of your music, not Sullivan, into the last movement of the piece [where Tippett quotes from Sullivan's *The Yeoman of the Guard*]. But I abandoned it, because of my self-imposed secrecy. But if a second one ever came, say for a Mozart orchestra, I really shall ask you if I may. As you are the only English composer of nowadays I care at all about, it would be a way of saying so.

3 Tippett's *Divertimento on 'Sellinger's Round'* had begun life as a single movement contributed to the composite work *Variations on an Elizabethan Theme* for string orchestra. Tippett's movement (*Andante espressivo*) incorporated references not only to the Sellinger theme but also to the aria 'Ah, Belinda' from Purcell's *Dido and Aeneas*, on an edition of which Tippett was working at the time of composition. The movement then found its way into Tippett's *Divertimento*, commissioned by Paul Sacher for a performance with the Collegium Musicum in Zurich on 5 November 1954.

As Britten's letter of 12 January 1955 suggests, the re-use of the Aldeburgh movement had been a source of tension between the two composers. In a

LETTER 825: JANUARY 1955 305

letter to Anna Kallin (10 December 1954; Schuttenhelm, p. 367), Tippett explained about his *Divertimento*:

The second movement was written first, in the series of variations (by different composers) on the tune 'Sellinger's Round' for Aldeburgh Fest. last year. Mine was the best! So I took it out and back to make the Divertimento for Sacher. Have now (10 days past) sent B.B. a score of the Divertimento and a nice letter. But at *Troilus [and Cressida]* he cut me twice dead. So I've had it. *Er ist äusserst empfindlich!* [He's extremely touchy!]

See also n. 5 below.

It was the common movement from his *Divertimento* and the *Variations on an Elizabethan Theme* that Tippett copied out in 1960 as his contribution to the auction held at Christie's, London, on 23 March 1961, in aid of the Aldeburgh Festival. See Schuttenhelm, pp. 211–12.

4 Paul Sacher (1906–1999), Swiss conductor and an influential patron of the arts, who commissioned many works from contemporary composers. See also Letter 617 n. 9, and obituaries in *The Times*; the *Independent*; by Sibylle Ehrismann, *Guardian* (all 27 May 1999), and in the *Musical Times* 140 (autumn 1999), pp. 9–10, and Lesley Stephenson (with Don Weed), *Symphony of Dreams: The Conductor and Patron Paul Sacher*.

5 Britten and Pears embarked on a concert tour of Belgium and Switzerland on 6 February 1955, giving recitals in Brussels (7 February) and Antwerp (8 February), both of which included *Winter Words*. They arrived in Zurich on 9 February and spent two days in rehearsal for a concert at the Tonhalle on the 11th: this was the venue where Tippett's *Divertimento* had been given its first performance three months before. Britten's anxiety that Sacher might have been perplexed by the appearance of Tippett's Sellinger variation in two entirely different works was justifiable. The tour concluded with a private recital at the Sachers' home on 12 February (Britten's diary has the entry: 'PP BB Schonenberg Hauskonzert') and a concert in Geneva on the 13th, shared with the Motet de Genève, before the duo embarked on a skiing holiday at Zermatt (see Letter 838 n. 2).

6 Tippett's first opera, *The Midsummer Marriage*, was in rehearsal at the Royal Opera House, Covent Garden, where it was to receive its first performance on 27 January 1955. The conductor was John Pritchard and director Christopher West, with costumes and scenery designed by Barbara Hepworth and choreography by John Cranko.

Britten attended the premiere of *The Midsummer Marriage*. Tippett wrote to him on 29 January 1955 (Schuttenhelm, p. 205; the editor's slight mis-transcription of the text has been corrected here):

Dearest Ben,

It meant a lot to have you there on Thursday; however the music takes you or not. Most deeply it meant an outward sign of affection. And then it is that, for better or worse, we two are the most interesting English music has at the moment.

I shall soon again try something new for the theatre – and that will put *The Midsummer Marriage* into better perspective. The reasonable view that it's good music wasted on nonsense is a valid one. But for those to whom it speaks as a whole, it has a haunting and exhilarating power. They *seem* to be chiefly young ones.

For myself, I can't regret – for that's no use. It came as it came. The symbolic world is exhausted for the time being and I'm sure forever. I shall go down some fresh road.

Forgive my little confessional note. I needed to communicate with someone who can know where we kind have to stand. Don't answer.

Blessings,
MICHAEL

The Midsummer Marriage had been received in the press largely with bafflement: see the exhibition catalogue, *A Man of Our Time*, pp. 70–77.

7 Inserting a note on a separate small sheet into the score after it had been printed.

826 To Erwin Stein

4 CRABBE STREET, ALDEBURGH
January 12th, 1955

My dear Erwin,

Thank you for dealing with Manoug & the Violin Concerto for me.[1] I haven't yet had time to go into his comments or suggestions thoroughly, except to come to the conclusion that the doublestops must remain (even if only in small notes).[2] After all they have been played adequately, & it'll sound all wrong to leave them out. Anyhow we can talk about that when we meet, which cannot alas be Saturday, since Peter & I have to go to Birmingham on that day.[3]

I don't quite, apropos the recording business[4] see how I was inconsiderate or 'awful'. After all I rather presumed that it was your job now to look after such things from B & H point of view (at least) – you are responsible for my things, aren't you? Also, I don't see how one can, as you ask me from time to time, make strong representations to Leslie Boosey to allow you to come abroad to important performances, if the first complete operatic recording of mine happening on your own doorstep isn't important enough for you to attend. I know it would have been hard to return from Harewood [House] in time, but I don't honestly think it made a wonderful impression on Tony [Gishford] that you couldn't arrange to attend a panel meeting the previous week, which would have been easier for all of us (even without illness, for me to attend one, between two recording sessions, wouldn't have been the happiest arrangement). I don't say this, my dear, because of pique that you dismiss the matter as "all this is not important",

LETTER 826: JANUARY 1955   307

but really because it seems to be imperative from everyone's point of view that when your present interim arrangement with B & H finishes you prove yourself to have been indispensable to them, & so they continue your connection with the firm – always supposing you want it, that is.

Much love to you & Sophie. I hope you've recovered from that horrid ballet evening.⁵

I always forget to thank you both for the lovely wine bottle carriers – we feel very grand now using them, almost like Blades.⁶

Lots of love,
BEN

1 Manoug Parikian (1920–1987), British violinist of Armenian origins, who led the EOG Orchestra between 1949 and 1951 and participated in Aldeburgh Festival concerts, chamber, orchestral and operatic. See Letter 617 n. 12. Parikian had suggested emendations to the solo violin part of Britten's Violin Concerto. Stein had written to Britten on 9 January, enclosing his comments on the markings Parikian had added to a copy of the solo part. Britten wrote to Stein again on 16 February to say, 'Please keep the violin part of the Violin Concerto until I come to London when I shall arrange a meeting with Parikian to discuss the whole matter.' The revised version, incorporating both the 1954 changes as well as some made in 1950, was published in a piano reduction and solo part in 1958.

2 Stein had written that Parikian suggested simplifying the double-stopping in sixths, octaves, tenths and harmonics in the second movement: 'His contention is that the clear and clean tone is preferable to difficulties which hardly anybody can solve satisfactorily.'

3 This was a hectic week for Britten and Pears: not only did they give a recital in Birmingham on 15 January, but Pears was also singing in Walton's *Troilus and Cressida* at Covent Garden (14 January) and Britten preparing for a performance of Poulenc's Concerto for Two Pianos which took place at the Royal Festival Hall on 16 January. (He and Poulenc had previously performed the Two-Piano Concerto together in January 1945; see Letter 491 n. 8.) The timing of the 1955 performance was significant: the work derives some of its musical material from the Balinese gamelan, and it may have reopened Britten's ears to these distinctive sonorities while he was at work on *The Prince of the Pagodas* (see MCBFE, pp. 15–17 and 104). Britten was to visit Bali himself exactly one year later (see Letters 850–52).

Donald Mitchell contributed a review of Poulenc's and Britten's performance of the Concerto for Two Pianos to the *Musical Times* 96 (March 1955), p. 153, reporting, 'The concerto was well done, M. Poulenc most expertly demonstrating his prowess as a pianist, Mr Britten lavishing as much care upon his notes as if he had written them all himself.'

4 The Decca recording of *The Turn of the Screw* one week earlier, which Stein had failed to attend. Stein had apologized in these terms:

> I am frightfully sorry to have disappointed you. Had I known that you really wanted me at the recording, I should have coped with my own affairs differently (workmen in the flat, proofs, articles). You composer friends are awful people. You are of course an angel compared with Schoenberg, and also more considerate than Alban [Berg] was. But you know I am there if you want me and should say so. It is sometimes a bit awkward to sit during rehearsals, just to satisfy my curiosity, while I think I could be of some help. But all this is not important.

5 On 6 January 1955 Britten, Pears and the Steins had attended the opening night of two new ballets choreographed by Frederick Ashton, performed by the Sadler's Wells Ballet at the Royal Opera House: *Rinaldo and Armida* (music by Malcolm Arnold), in which Svetlana Beriosova danced the role of Armida; and *Variations on a Theme of Purcell*, which used Britten's *Young Person's Guide to the Orchestra*. Of the latter, the critic of *The Times* (7 January 1955) considered Ashton's choreographic invention to be 'copious and calls for virtuosity in its execution'. According to David Vaughan, *Frederick Ashton and His Ballets*, p. 276, Peter Snow's design 'featured a pedestal on which stood a bust of Purcell which was turned round at a certain point to show a bust of Britten on the reverse.' Although present at the dress rehearsal, this device failed to survive to the first night.

Anthony Gishford wrote to Britten from Boosey & Hawkes on 7 January to say:

> I shall be interested to know what you thought of the ballet last night. I myself should have enjoyed it more had the orchestra and performers both been better rehearsed. Alexander Grant's dance seemed to me an excellent piece of work and perfectly suited to the music, but on the whole I do not think that making a ballet from an existing orchestral score is really a very good idea.

Alexander Grant's role was a combination of court jester and master of ceremonies, with a camp parody of Anton Dolin's *Bolero* during the percussion variation. As Britten's remark to Stein suggests, neither of these Ashton ballets was particularly well received.

6 This reference remains obscure. Was Blades a smart restaurant, hotel or club they both knew, or is Britten referring to the fictional private club from Ian Fleming's James Bond novels (Bond's boss 'M' was a member), located somewhere in central London and celebrated for its gourmet catering and gambling card games?

827 To Norman Del Mar

4 CRABBE STREET, ALDEBURGH
January 25th 1955

My dear Norman,

We have again had to change our plans about the big (for us!) orchestral concert in the Festival this year, about which Peter spoke when in the North with you. Markevitch[1] cannot come after all, & we were wondering whether you could possibly conduct it for us? The programme isn't of course fixed, but if you will still be in England (Peter had an idea you were going abroad) & would like to do the concert on June 21st (& the BBC preview the week before), we could discuss the details.[2] What we were considering was something like the 2nd Haydn Horn Concerto (with Dennis [Brain]), the Holst 2 Violin Concerto (with Olive[3] & Suzi[4]), the Frank Martin 7 wind-instrument Concerto,[5] & perhaps if he can manage to write it, a Concert piece for Horn & Strings by Arthur Bliss[6] (first performance). (If he can't do it we were considering asking H. Searle).[7] Because the BBC will broadcast the concert from the studio the week before we are assured of plenty of rehearsal – the date of that will of course be arranged with you.

I do hope you will want to do this concert – we should all be most happy if you will agree.

Peter & Dennis much enjoyed their concerts with you, I hear.[8] I wish I could have heard them. Did *Gloriana* go well?[9]

Yours ever,
BEN

1 Igor Markevitch (1912–1983), Russian-born composer and conductor. See Diary for 31 March 1931, n. 6.

2 The concert duly took place at the Aldeburgh Festival on 21 June 1955 with the soloists mentioned by Britten; the event was conducted not by Del Mar but by Walter Goehr. The programme consisted of Tippett's *Divertimento on 'Sellinger's Round'*, Holst's Double Concerto, Searle's *Aubade* (see n. 7 below), Haydn's Horn Concerto No. 2 in D, the *Six Sketches* for string orchestra by Skalkottas and Schubert's Symphony No. 5 in B flat. The reasons for Del Mar's inability to accept the engagement are obscure, but at around the time of the event his relationship with Britten was under some strain. Writing to the composer on 30 June 1955, Del Mar apologized for his apparent inability to present Britten's point of view at an EOG meeting, commenting,

> Your last paragraphs disturbed me very much. Please believe me that I am neither so narrow and conceited to have written in this way out of any sense of pique. Nor am I so selfish as only to want the personal plums as you suggest, at the expense of the group team-work.

Britten had evidently written a stern reproof to the conductor, in much the same manner as Letter 826 had taken Erwin Stein to task. See Richard Alston, *Norman Del Mar*, p. 21.

3 Olive Zorian (1916–1965), British violinist who in 1942 formed the all-female Zorian String Quartet, which not only gave many notable premieres and early performances of works by young British composers, including Britten (Second String Quartet) and Tippett (Third String Quartet), but also introduced quartets by Bloch and Bartók to UK audiences. The quartet disbanded in 1949. Zorian was leader of the EOG Orchestra, 1952–57, and a member of the Julian Bream Consort. Between 1948 and 1955 she was married to the broadcaster and writer John Amis, who writes in his autobiography, *Amiscellany*, p. 17:

Olive's own playing was not virtuosic, though she could most capably negotiate things like Mozart concertos, the first fiddle-parts of Britten, Bartók and Tippett, as well as Stravinsky's *Duo Concertant*. Her strongest point was her instinctive musicianship and, above all, her ability to float and spin a line. You can hear the best of her in the old 78 rpm recordings of Britten and Tippett Second String Quartets and, on LP, the original recordings of Britten's *Saint Nicolas* and *The Turn of the Screw*.

Of the end of Zorian's leadership of the EOG Orchestra, Amis notes (pp. 181–2):

It was decided by Ben and Peter that poor Olive was no longer the right player to lead the orchestra, but in typical Aldeburgh fashion neither Ben nor Peter had the nerve to tell her. [Letter 909 bears this out.] A situation arose when she was the only person in the organization who did not know that she was for the chop. So many artists and people connected with Ben and Peter were dropped. Yet, some years later, when Ben needed Olive for something, he was charming and she went back.

See also the obituary in *The Times* (18 May 1965) and Maureen Garnham, *As I Saw It*, p. 15.

4 Suzanne (Susi) Rozsa (1923–2005), Hungarian-born British violinist, who studied in Vienna and, following the *Anschluss* in 1938, emigrated to Britain where she completed her studies at the Royal College of Music and the Guildhall School of Music and Drama. At the College she met her husband, the cellist Martin Lovett; through her Lovett met the violinist Norbert Brainin and, together with Sigmund Nissel (violin) and Peter Schidlof (viola), formed the Amadeus Quartet. Rozsa was a founder member of the English Chamber Orchestra and a distinguished chamber musician, performing with the London Polish Quartet, the Dumka Trio, and in partnership with Paul Hamburger. She was principal second violin of the EOG Orchestra during the 1950s.

Maureen Garnham (*As I Saw It*, p. 15), recalls Rozsa as 'a strong personality [...] a Hungarian refugee, whose words tumbled over each other [...] She was a good and loyal colleague as well as a fine player.' See also the obituaries by Anne Inglis, *Guardian* (17 November 2005), and in the *Daily*

LETTER 827: JANUARY 1955   311

Telegraph (18 November 2005) and *The Times* (19 November 2005), Daniel Snowman, *The Amadeus Quartet: The Men and the Music*, and Muriel Nissel, *Married to the Amadeus: Life with a String Quartet*. Rozsa herself compiled a privately published volume *The Amadeus: Forty Years in Pictures and Words* (1988), in aid of the Amadeus Scholarship Fund.

5   The projected Martin performance did not materialize. Britten's contacts with the Swiss composer Frank Martin (1890–1974) extended back at least as far as October 1946 when he heard a rehearsal of Martin's *Le Vin herbé* in Amsterdam. Martin wrote to Ernest Ansermet in November 1946 (quoted in Jean-Claude Piguet and Jacques Burdet (eds.), *Ernest Ansermet–Frank Martin, Correspondance 1934–68*, p. 28):

Britten [...] told me that he found my harmonies captivating, because with essentially chromatic means I achieved the feeling of solid tonal construction [...] Moreover, he is going to try to mount *Le Vin herbé* in London with Pears as Tristan. That would be magnificent. To begin with, they will do together my *Jedermann Monologues*. Britten is a marvellous accompanist.

Although no performance of *Le Vin herbé* appears to have been mounted by Britten, in 1948, he and Pears broadcast the *Sechs Monologe aus Jedermann* for the BBC. This performance, broadcast on 9 January 1948, was the UK premiere of the *Monologues*, nos. 1–3 and 6 of which were released on CD in 2005 by Pearl from an off-air recording owned by Lord Harewood.

Martin wrote to Ansermet on 20 April that year (ibid., p. 44):

We recently returned to London where the BBC gave two broadcasts devoted to my music: one of chamber music and the other in which Peter Pears sang my *Jedermann Monologues*, slightly transposed for his voice, in a manner which moved me. If by a great chance you would think of engaging him for a concert (it would certainly be worthwhile), I could orchestrate these six pieces.

Martin did indeed orchestrate the work in the following year, but specifying baritone or alto voice and entrusting the first performance to Elsa Cavelti and Rafael Kubelík. Pears and Britten repeated their performance of the *Monologues* at the 1952 Aldeburgh Festival.

In later years Martin was to be greatly moved by Britten's *Cantata Misericordium*, first performed in a programme that included the premiere of Martin's *Inter Arma Caritas*, describing the Britten work to Ansermet as 'inspired in its simplicity' (ibid., p. 123). Ironically, it had been Ansermet's prior commitment to conduct the early performances of Martin's opera *Der Sturm* in 1956 that prevented his accepting the invitation from Covent Garden to conduct the first performance of *The Prince of the Pagodas*: see Letter 862 n. 2 and MCBFE, p. 94.

6   British composer of American descent (1891–1975), who was Director of Music at the BBC, 1942–44, and was appointed Master of the Queen's Music in 1953. See also Arthur Bliss, *As I Remember*, and Letter 625 n. 8.

7 Humphrey Searle (1915–1982), British composer who had studied with Webern in Vienna from 1937 to 1938 and who was compositionally much influenced by Schoenberg and his twelve-note method. In 1947 Pears commissioned *Put Away the Flute* from Searle. See also Letter 561 n. 9.

The Bliss piece did not materialize, with the result that Searle contributed his *Aubade* for horn and strings. Britten was to write to Searle on 27 March 1956 acknowledging receipt of a score of *Aubade*:

> I was delighted to get it, & especially delighted to read the dedication! I think it is a very beautiful piece & I look forward to hearing it again soon.

8 No programmes for these concerts survive at BPL, but Pears's diary suggests that he gave performances of the *Serenade* and the *Suite of Songs from Orpheus Britannicus* with Dennis Brain in Keighley (11 January 1955) and Hull (13 January 1955).

9 No details survive at BPL to clarify this reference, though it seems likely that Britten refers not to his opera but to a performance of the *Symphonic Suite: 'Gloriana'*.

828 To William Plomer

4 CRABBE STREET, ALDEBURGH
Jan. 26th 1955

My dearest William,

So very sorry not to have answered your nice letter before, but I've been, & am still, up to my eyes, & over, with horrid pressure of work, & a certain dreary amount of worry & illness too. But that's <u>not</u> a tactful thing to say to you who are certainly drowned in an excess of all those horrid scourges, & I've no reason to complain.[1]

Please <u>don't</u> worry about the Children's Opera, at any rate. See how the land lies in the Spring, & let's consider it again.[2] You see, Peter & I are off abroad at the beginning of February, & apart from a few days in early March we'll be away for two months. I must confess I'd love to do the Lear piece,[3] but just let your ideas simmer, my dear, & let's meet if we can around Easter & talk. I hope in the meantime that the time isn't too horrid for you or for your father. I do sympathise with you. Take care of yourself; occasionally be a little selfish & let things go hang. Anyhow you know you have the warm thoughts of both of us, wherever you are & whatever happens.

Love to Charles,
Please forgive hasty scribble,
BEN

1 The health of Plomer's father had been seriously deteriorating; Plomer informed Britten of his death in a letter of 29 January. Plomer's family situation was a factor contributing to the lack of progress on the children's opera (see Peter F. Alexander, *William Plomer*, p. 299).

2 There was to be no further consideration of the project: by the time Britten returned from Japan in 1956 he had become caught up in Japanese Nō theatre, an interest – fostered by Plomer – that was to lead to their collaboration on *Curlew River* (see Letter 897 n. 5).

3 Plomer had written to Britten on 29 December 1954:

> All of this [i.e. attending to his father's needs and affairs] doesn't prevent me from waking up in the night and devising a chorus with 'Propter's Nicodemus Pills' as a refrain, or from inventing an encounter between Uncle Arly and Mr and Mrs Discobbolos.

It would appear that in addition to the proposed children's opera, Britten and Plomer were planning a work based on characters created by Edward Lear. (Like the children's opera, the project was to remain unrealized.) Britten and Pears were both enthusiasts for the work of Edward Lear (1812–1888), the British artist, illustrator and author of nonsense verse and limericks. They owned a copy of *The Complete Nonsense of Edward Lear*, edited and introduced by Holbrooke Jackson, published in 1947, and one of the most treasured paintings in Pears's art collection was a large landscape by Lear entitled *Ravenna* (1867). Other paintings by Lear in the collection include a small watercolour entitled *Parnassus*, an oil sketch *Girgenti*, and a watercolour of Grant's Castle, Gozo, Malta.

829 To Basil Coleman

4 CRABBE STREET, ALDEBURGH
February 3rd 1955

My dear Basil,

Irony that the only letter I've written to you should be just as you are leaving to come home! – I'm so sorry to have been so bad about writing, but it hasn't been altogether a happy winter. The strains (& lack of holiday) in the Summer told heavily on us both, & although we've neither of us been seriously ill, we've been pretty low. Peter had a bad cold (& flu really) on the first night of Walton's opera, & was only got through by drugs & champagne – 'got through' is a slight understatement since he literally stole the show with a really lovely comedy performance. (But he took ages to recover from it.) We are now off abroad – a week's concerts in Belgium & Switzerland – & then, o then, a fortnight's ski-ing in the mountains, which we both feel will put us back on our feet, ready for your return!

I am so glad to hear from friends, & also from your letter, how successful your trip has been – I hope happy too. I am sure you must have been dreadfully tired at the start – & what a tempestuous start too! – but you must be heartened that you had strength of body & will enough to pull everything off in spite of it. I long to hear all your news first hand. We'll be in this country for the first half of March & hope to see you then.

Things have been difficult for the Group – lots of possibilities which have evaporated for lack of money or time. Basil D. [Douglas] has been ill & tired &, like us, hopes that his coming holiday will restore his vitality. I hope we'll have quite a few Turns of the Screw anyhow, although, I'm afraid you'll have to face quite a bit of simplification of the production & lighting plans when you get back. In order to perform it at all we've had to cut down the number of days necessary in the theatres. Just to put an idea into your head for you to consider on your journey back – I think we'll have to reconcile ourselves to complete blackouts between the scenes. I'm not sure anyhow that formally that isn't best. The recording went well – everyone (except Joan [Cross] who had a beastly cold) on tremendous form. David H. [Hemmings] was a good boy – I've seen quite a lot of him & am fond of but puzzled by his two completely opposite sides. He's no Roger [Duncan], I'm afraid!

No more now, my dear – I'm just off to Norwich to conduct the Serenade for Peter.[1] He sends lots of love to you – & to all the friends of ours you may see – my godchild (& parents), Peggy Rooke[2] – etc. etc. We long to hear your news. Hope Twelfth Night went well.[3]

Love from
BEN

1 Britten had stepped in for the indisposed Heathcote Statham to conduct a performance of the *Serenade*, with the Norwich Philharmonic Society, at St Andrew's Hall, Norwich, on 4 February 1955, in which Pears and Brain were the soloists.

2 The identity of Britten's Canadian godchild remains unknown. Peggy Rooke, who was based first in Ottawa and later Toronto, corresponded with the composer between 1953 and 1962; she helped promote the work of the English Opera Group and advised Britten about the proposed Aldeburgh Festival Theatre.

3 Coleman had directed a production of Shakespeare's comedy in Canada, probably at the Crest Theatre, Toronto.

830　To Trevor Harvey[1]
　　　　[*Typed*]

4 CRABBE STREET, ALDEBURGH
27th April, 1955

Dear Trevor,

　　Fancy those old pieces turning up.[2] I am afraid technically the scores of The Company of Heaven and The World of the Spirit belong to the B.B.C., so perhaps you would be kind and get in touch with the appropriate power there. If they don't want them I will of course take them, but I don't know where they will go as my shelves are so full of rejected masterpieces already.

　　Thank you very much for your good wishes. I am well and busy, and perhaps flourishing too. I hear good things about <u>you</u>.

Yours ever,
BEN

1　British conductor (1911–1989), a friend and colleague of Britten in the late 1930s and early 1940s. See also Letter 172 n. 2.

2　The manuscript full scores of *The Company of Heaven* and *The World of the Spirit*, two 'radio cantatas' composed by Britten for the BBC National Programme in 1937 and 1938 respectively. Harvey had conducted the original broadcasts, but had then mislaid both manuscripts at his parents' country home. In response to a letter from Harvey further seeking his permission to broadcast excerpts from *The Company of Heaven*, Britten wrote on 25 October 1955:

> By all means go ahead and try and arrange a broadcast of some of the music you have discovered, only I can trust you only to put the good bits of music in and leave out the bad, can't I?

Harvey was to organize a broadcast of a concert version of *The Company of Heaven* (comprising nos. 2, 6, 7, 8 and 11) on 20 July 1956 performed by April Cantelo (soprano), John Carolan (tenor) and Charles Spink (organ), with the BBC Chorus and St Cecilia Orchestra. The genesis of the work is described in full in Letter 106 n. 1; for a full critical discussion, see Philip Reed, 'A Cantata for Broadcasting: Britten's *The Company of Heaven*', *Musical Times* 130 (June 1989), pp. 324–31.

　　The Company of Heaven was published in a concert version, prepared by Donald Mitchell, by Faber Music in 1990 (rev. edn, 1992), following the first concert performance of the score at Snape Maltings on 10 June 1989. *The World of the Spirit* was published by Oxford University Press in 2001, following a concert performance of a shortened version at Snape Maltings on 27 June 1998. The first recording of *The World of the Spirit* was made by the BBC Philharmonic conducted by Richard Hickox in 1996, the liner notes for which include a detailed commentary by Donald Mitchell and Philip Reed.

831 To Edith Sitwell

4 CRABBE STREET, ALDEBURGH
April 28th, 1955

My dear Edith,

In the hopes of catching you before you leave for Italy I am scribbling this short note to thank you most heartily for your lovely letter, & for the telegram which preceded it. It has thrilled me beyond measure that you approve so warmly of the new Canticle.[1] I must confess I was nervous about writing it; it is such a great poem, & I was well aware of the responsibility. Where I think I <u>have</u> succeeded is to have the wit to put nothing in the way of the wonderful words, & that of course is largely why the effect on the listeners is so intense. I can only be grateful to you, my dear Edith, for having written them. But in another way too I am grateful to you; writing this work has helped me so much in my development as a composer. I feel with this work & the Turn of the Screw (which I am impatient for you to hear) that I am on the threshold of a new musical world (for me, I am not pretentious about it!).[2] I am worried by the problems which arise, & that is one reason that I am taking off next winter to do some deep thinking.[3] But your great poem has dragged something from me that was latent there, & shown me what lies before me.

Peter & I were most happy with you & Osbert [Sitwell] after the concert. You gave us a most wonderful meal, & were both so kind to us at what is always a difficult time – immediately after a long & difficult concert. It was a great joy to be with two such great & good people.

We are in Florence June 4th & 6th,[4] & will reserve tickets for you & Osbert on 4th, & may we suggest coming to Montegufoni[5] on 5th? The "Still falls the rain" will be given in the Aldeburgh Festival on June 22nd[6] & the "Turn of the Screw" on 23rd[7] – if you would care to come to those nothing would please us more than for you to stay here for those days or longer if you want.

My love to both of you, & may the miracle happen & Osbert be restored to health.

And with warmest thanks for your lovely letter from

BEN

1 Britten wrote in response to a letter from Sitwell dated 26 April (Richard Greene (ed.), *Selected Letters of Edith Sitwell*, pp. 362–3), in which the poet expresses her admiration for his setting of 'Still Falls the Rain':

I am so haunted and so alone with that wonderful music and its wonderful performance that I was incapable of writing before now. I had no sleep at all on the night of the performance [28 January 1955]. And I can think of nothing else. It was certainly one of the greatest experiences in all my life as an artist [...] I can never begin to thank you for the glory you have given my poem [...]

WIGMORE HALL

A Concert

in memory of

NOEL MEWTON-WOOD

∞

Postponed from

**Saturday, 4th December
1954**

to

Friday, 28th January, 1955

Programme

BENJAMIN BRITTEN (born 1913)
"Lachrymae": Reflections on a song of Dowland
for Viola and Piano (1950)

ALAN BUSH (born 1900)
Two Pieces for Horn and Piano
(a) "Autumn Poem", Op. 45
(Written as a tribute to the memory of Noel Mewton-Wood)
(b) "Trent's Broad Reaches", Op. 36
(First performance of both pieces)

ARTHUR BLISS (born 1891)
"Elegiac Sonnet" (to Noel Mewton-Wood)
Words by C. Day Lewis
for Tenor, String Quartet and Piano
(First performance)

INTERVAL — FIFTEEN MINUTES

BENJAMIN BRITTEN
Canticle No. 3: "Still falls the rain" (Edith Sitwell)
(In Memoriam Noel Mewton-Wood)
for Tenor, Horn and Piano
(First performance)

BENJAMIN FRANKEL (born 1906)
Sonata, Op. 13 for Violin Solo

NOEL MEWTON-WOOD (1922–1953)
"As ye came from the Holy Land" (words by Walter Raleigh)
(Written when the composer was 15)
for Tenor and Piano

MICHAEL TIPPETT (born 1905)
"Remember your lovers" (words by Sidney Keyes)
(The last song of "The Heart's Assurance")
for Tenor and Piano

Further praise for the new work came from Anthony Gishford, to whom Britten had written on 4 February 1955:

> Thank you very much for your kind letter about the Canticle no. 3 & other things besides. I am so gratified that you appreciated it, & more important that you feel that there is something stirring – !! I was deeply moved by the poem, & felt at last that one could get away from the immediate impacts of the war & write about it.

Britten's strong reaction to the poem may be accounted for, not only by its latent pacifism, but also because the composer found in 'its courage & light seen through horror & darkness [. . .] something very right for the poor boy [Noel Mewton-Wood]'.

2 The 'new musical world' mentioned by Britten must to some degree be connected with the intense, emotionally concentrated economy of material that characterizes both *The Turn of the Screw* and *Canticle III*. It was this tendency which, after 1956, Britten developed with the aid of techniques borrowed from Far Eastern music and an increased interest in the serial techniques he had first systematically explored in both the opera and the canticle.

3 Britten made this portentous remark six months before the concert tour that took him halfway across the globe for five months in the winter and spring of 1955–56 and provided him with the opportunity for 'some deep thinking'. The significance of those travels in exposing the composer to vivid first-hand experiences of various Asian musical traditions, and the surface impact these had on his own style, have long been recognized. But Britten's identification with Far Eastern music went far deeper than the obvious borrowings from the Balinese gamelan to be heard in *The Prince of the Pagodas* or the emulations of the Japanese Nō theatre and Gagaku court music in *Curlew River* would suggest. Britten's style was at a turning point in the mid-1950s, as his remarks to Sitwell attest: the intense motivic economy and dodecaphonic techniques in *Canticle III* and *The Turn of the Screw* had clearly left him wondering in which direction his style would now develop. The Asian adventure, with perfect timing, opened his ears to other traditions of musical economy and structural clarity while his compositional thinking was clearly running along similar lines.

4 The EOG undertook a short European tour of *The Turn of the Screw* to Schwetzingen (26 and 28 May 1955), Munich (31 May and 1 June 1955) and Florence (4 and 6 June 1955). In addition, Pears and Britten gave a recital at Schwetzingen (30 May). The Sitwells attended the performance of *The Turn of the Screw* on the 4th.

Britten described the tour in a letter to Roger Duncan (9 June 1955):

> Well, we had a tremendous tour with the opera – "The Turn of the Screw". All the company went, with scenery, orchestra & all – Peter of course, & little David Hemmings as Miles (you remember the story?), & I conducted. We played in three different theatres, two in Germany & one in Italy (Florence), & what with all the

travelling & lots of rehearsals in each place, there wasn't much time for fun! Florence was terribly hot, hotter than I can ever remember being anywhere; so it's been rather difficult coming back to Suffolk with its N-E. Gales! I am glad to say we were a great success, with packed theatres & great clappings – it's always a toss-up how different countries will react to things. We had a bad, a horrid journey, flight home – in a chartered plane, a private one, just for the opera company; & the weather was so bad before we left that the pilot wouldn't take some of the instruments (the drums, for instance) in case they got loose inside the plane & rushed about hurting people & smashing up the place! ... You can imagine we felt cheerful! And we weren't allowed to land in France because the visibility was so bad. However, we bumped our way across Europe, & apart from one or two people feeling sick (& being it) no one was hurt & we arrived safely.

5 Near Florence, the Castello di Montegufoni was Edith and Osbert Sitwell's Italian home. Britten, Pears and Basil Douglas were duly invited to lunch there on 5 June. It was a lavish building, with over a hundred rooms and included a chapel and a seventeenth-century frescoed bathroom; it had been purchased by the Sitwells' father in 1909. Montegufoni remained Sir George Sitwell's home until the Second World War forced him to abandon it and relocate to Switzerland. (During the war it was used to store many famous paintings from the Uffizi Gallery in Florence.) Both Osbert and Edith Sitwell used the house frequently in the 1950s, usually in the spring or autumn, and from 1965 Osbert made it his permanent home. John Piper made a series of paintings of Montegufoni at Osbert's invitation in 1947. See *The Sitwells and the Art of the 1920s and 1930s* (exhibition catalogue), pp. 184–5.

6 *Canticle III* was performed by Pears, Brain and Britten in Aldeburgh Parish Church, as part of a concert given by the Dennis Brain Wind Quintet.

7 The performance on 23 June was the last of three performances of Britten's latest opera given at the 1955 Aldeburgh Festival. The cast at the performance on the 23rd was the same as at the Venice premiere in September 1954, except for Lotte Medak replacing Joan Cross as Mrs Grose. Other highlights of the 1955 Festival included Britten playing Schubert's 'Trout' Quintet with members of the Amadeus Quartet and Francis Baines (double-bass), Pears and Britten performing Schubert's *Die schöne Müllerin*, and a choral and orchestral concert of music by Purcell, Handel and Britten (*Saint Nicolas*) conducted by Britten and Imogen Holst.

Neither Osbert nor Edith Sitwell was able to take up Britten's invitation to come to Aldeburgh.

832 To Ronald Duncan

4 CRABBE STREET, ALDEBURGH
May 9th, 1955

My dear Ronnie,

So sorry about yesterday, but the day got hopelessly involved – & Peter & I are just off to this friend's funeral.[1] I'm up next Monday for quite a few days then, & we must meet. I'm enclosing the Punch revue number, because I don't see how I can help you there.[2] I've thought about it a great deal, & feel that to do the piece justice & get the revue off to a good start a lot of work must be done on it. It's by no means an obvious thing. I wish I could think of the right composer for you – I hear excellent things about Donald Swann (Airs on a Shoe String)[3] – Julian Slade (Salad Days),[4] but if you don't want this kind of person what about Arthur Benjamin who writes very good light music (Jamaican Rumba).[5] If you've got a straight-forward lyric I will certainly set it for you; but otherwise there's only the Auden songs.[6] Imo [Imogen Holst] will get Calypso & Funeral Blues to you, the other from Erwin [Stein] –

Lots of love to you both from
BEN

1 At Coombs Parish Church (North Lancing) on the afternoon of 9 May, Britten and Pears attended the funeral of Esther Neville-Smith, who had died in a car accident near Oxford. She had been the wife of one of Pears's schoolmasters at Lancing College, and was a literary scholar in her own right. Pears contributed an obituary of her to *The Times* (10 May 1955) and sang Pérotin's *Beata viscera* at a memorial service held subsequently in London. See CHPP, p. 175.

2 Although he returned the text of Duncan's revue number with this letter, Britten did, in fact, contribute to the project: he later provided a waltz setting of Plomer's verse 'Old friends are best' as well as giving permission for two of his Auden *Cabaret Songs* to be performed. See Letter 838.

3 British composer and writer of Russian extraction (1923–1994). A conscientious objector in the war, he had served with the Friends' Ambulance Unit. Best remembered for his collaboration in revues with singer Michael Flanders, independently he was a prolific composer of musicals, music for young people, choral and sacred settings, and songs, writing for artists such as Joyce Grenfell, Rose Hill and Carl Dolmetsch. *Airs on a Shoestring*, a successor to *Penny Plain* (see also Letter 557 n. 2), was devised by Laurier Lister and staged at the Royal Court Theatre, London, opening on 22 April 1953; it subsequently toured until 5 March 1955. It included the Flanders-and-Swann spoof, 'A Guide to Britten'. Flanders and Swann introduced the song on their album *And Then We Wrote . . .*:

Our big success in *Airs on a Shoestring* was undoubtedly 'A Guide to Britten', which is a comprehensive musical tour of all Benjamin Britten's operas, and all other works up to that date. Laurier Lister liked it very much – he thought it was a bit highbrow, he warned us that while the show was on the pre-London tour, we could expect no reaction at all from the audiences. This actually didn't happen, and the very first time when it was played, which wasn't a sort of cultural centre, by any means, everybody loved it. I think revues at that time did rather under-rate the growing general knowledge and intelligence of audiences everywhere, and this was part of their downfall. This is how we first did 'Guide to Britten' at the read-through.

> Who?
> Who is
> Benjamin Britten,
> Benjamin Britten,
> Benjamin Britten?
> Benjamin Britten,
> Benjamin Britten,
> Benjamin Britten?
> Please don't send him up again,
> Please don't send him up again.

MF: *Edward Benjamin Britten, born Lowestoft 1913 . . .*
DS: *That is approximately.*
MF: *. . . entered the Royal College of Music, studied under Frank Bridge . . .*
DS: *. . . according to Percy Scholes.*

> His work was soon in rehearsal,
> Because he always usèd . . . Purcell!

> A rising young composer,
> He published every spring,
> An olde English folk song
> For Peter Pears to sing.

> The judges at each festival
> Admired his *Sinfonietta*,
> They voted it the best of all,
> They'd never heard a better.

> 'Twas applauded by the masses,
> The middle classes too,
> And even by the Harewoods and the county set,
> Yes, even by the Doggy Doggy Few.

MF: *Art songs,*
DS: *Quartets,*
MF: *Cantatas,*
DS: *A Spring Symphony for Sackbut, Psaltery and Siffleur.*
  But this was not all . . . No!
MF: *Whenever he had a spare half-hour,*
  It was always:

DS: *Let's make an opera!*
MF: *Ummmmmmmm! (Foghorn.)*
DS: *Peter Grimes*
MF: *Cribbed from Crabbe.*
    Ummmmmmmm! (Foghorn again.)
DS: *Peter Grimes*
MF: *Sung all over the civilized world. And in America.*
    Pierre Grimes!
    Pedro Grimo!
    Pyotr Grimsky!
    Peter J. Grimes!

   Of the first *Beggar's Opera*,
   They used to say
   That it made Gay rich,
   And it made Rich gay,

   Revived by our hero
   After all these years,
   It made bundles for Britten,
   And piles for Pears.

   The Rape of Lucretia
   Was splendid fun,
   And night after night,
   Was discreetly done,

   But best of them all,
   We should like to state,
   Was the night when the curtain
   Came down too late.

   His mother kept *Albert Herring* in curls,
   He was never allowed to go out with girls.
   His terrible fate he long endured,
   Until *Albert Herring* got pickled, and cured.

MF: *Nor did Uncle Benjy forget the dear little children, composing for them:*
DS: *The Young Person's Guide to the Orchestra!*
MF: *In which are explained the capabilities of each instrument, such as, the pianoforte.*
    You can play on the white notes,
    You can play on the black notes.
    You can screw up the stool,
    You can screw it down.
    The turn of the screw.
    You can raise the lid,
    And you can shut it again.
DS: *Aarg!*
    So much for the pianoforte.
DS: *Back to opera, and Billy Budd*
    (Lyrics by Alan Melville)

> With floggings and hangings,
> And pitch and toss,
> And nothing but men,
> Oh, it made Joan Cross.
>
> As for *Gloriana*
> DS: *Gloriana!*
> That *Gloriana*,
> Was a social success,
> It turned out a regular orgy,
> And Bess.
>
> So rule Britannia, while Britten rules the staves,
> All the music-loving public are his slaves.

Of course, we'd both admired Benjamin Britten's music very much, we'd hoped that he might have come along and even enjoyed that affectionate parody, but he never did. However, the Royal family came to *Airs on a Shoestring*, they didn't understand a word of it, or course. Bang goes me peerage.

The published lyrics included a few more lines about *Gloriana*:

> As for *Gloriana* ... !
> As Covent Garden discovered all too soon!
> You can pay John Piper
> But you can't call the tune!

A notice of the revue in *The Times* (23 April 1955) observed: 'If any particular item is to be singled out it must be a witty lyric by Mr Michael Flanders smothering Mr Benjamin Britten with genial chaff.' Britten's views on the Flanders and Swann spoof, which quotes from several of Britten's works, are undocumented.

The good-humoured, affectionate nature of the Flanders and Swann 'Guide to Britten' was to be replaced in 1961 by an altogether more acerbic satire both of Britten's compositional language and Pears's voice, in the shape of Dudley Moore's 'Little Miss Britten', an item from the celebrated satirical revue *Beyond the Fringe* which was devised and performed by Moore, Peter Cook, Alan Bennett and Jonathan Miller. Moore was an accomplished classical and jazz musician (he had been an Oxford organ scholar) whose acutely analytic ears honed in on the essential characteristics of Britten's folksong arrangements – 'Little Miss Britten' is a spoof setting of the nursery rhyme 'Little Miss Muffet' – which he then exaggerates to punishing effect. No less effective in performance was Moore's cruel mimicking of Pears's vocal mannerisms.

Neither Britten's nor Pears's reaction to 'Little Miss Britten' is known. While Pears could be tolerant of, even amused by, similar take-offs (see HCBB, pp. 302–3, where John Amis's impersonation of Pears is recalled), Britten was less thick-skinned: undoubtedly, he would have been made furious by Moore's song. The *raison d'être* of *Beyond the Fringe* was to ridicule the Establishment, of which, by the early 1960s, Britten was popularly regarded as very much a member. He and Pears were, therefore, as justifiable targets for Moore and his colleagues as Macmillan's Tory Administration or the Royal Family. And Britten would have realized that he could do nothing about 'Little Miss Britten'. The title of Moore's spoof also hints at Britten's and Pears's homosexuality, which had been an open secret among the music profession for years, but was still very much in the closet as far as the wider world was concerned.

Moore later selected 'Little Miss Britten' as one of his choices when appearing on BBC Radio 4's *Desert Island Discs*. He told the presenter Roy Plomley, 'I do this out of absolute love and admiration for Britten and with no malice aforethought at all' (see Peter Cook and Dudley Moore, *Goodbye Again*, edited by William Cook).

4 British lyricist and composer (1930–2006). The modestly ambitious musical *Salad Days*, written in only six weeks, was a contrast to the currently popular large-scale American shows in the West End, and ran at the Vaudeville Theatre, London, for a record-breaking 2,288 performances from August 1954.

5 Australian–British composer and pianist (1893–1960). He had been Britten's piano teacher at the Royal College of Music from 1930 to 1933. See also Letters 25 n. 6; 58, and 517 n. 2. His popular *Jamaican Rumba* clearly influenced Britten's cabaret song 'Calypso'.

6 See Letter 126 n. 2, for a full discussion of Britten's *Cabaret Songs* (1937–39).

833 To Ronald Duncan
[*Typed*]

4 CRABBE STREET, ALDEBURGH
11th May, 1955

My dear Ronnie,

Here are Calypso and Funeral Blues with a new end specially written for the occasion to the former. Erwin [Stein] can supply you with "Love, the truth about, tell me"[1] if you want it.

I was so sorry to have to write that letter to you last Monday, and still suffer qualms of guilt about having let you down. You would not like me to approach any of the composers I mentioned for you? But I cannot pretend that that is necessary even if it would salve my conscience a little.

I was very happy indeed to get a copy of "The Death of Satan" – I have read most of it, and find it as exciting to read as it was to see. I do hope you will find a chance of getting it put on in London very soon.[2]

[*Handwritten:*] Lots of love to you both
from
BEN

Britten's new ending for 'Calypso', revised in May 1955 for the *Punch Revue*

1 'Tell me the truth about love' (1938), another of the cabaret songs.
2 Duncan's one-act verse play *The Death of Satan* was first performed by a local group at the 1954 Taw and Torridge Festival. It was later to be staged in a double-bill with Duncan's *Don Juan* by the English Stage Company in its opening season at the Royal Court Theatre in May 1956 – the same month that saw the first production of John Osborne's *Look Back in Anger*, part of

the surge of new theatre writing that swept away the heightened dramatic language that interested Duncan. *The Death of Satan* was published by Faber and Faber in 1955. Britten's copy, inscribed by Duncan 'for Ben/with much love/Ronnie/1955', is at BPL.

834 To Roger Duncan

4 CRABBE STREET, ALDEBURGH
May 19th 1955

[...]

This can't, I'm afraid, be the long chatty letter I'd like to write to you, because I'm just ever so, terribly, busy – almost as bad as Tests! But I'm going abroad in a few days time & I wasn't sure when I'd get a chance to write & thank you for your nice last letter which I loved getting. I'm glad you are all right, & getting lots of tennis: I hope the back-hand is improving – don't forget to stand sideways to the net when you hit; it is much easier to hit that way, & the same with fore-hand & serving . . . I must really give you some coaching in the summer![1] I was sorry to hear about the second test (the 12/20 one) – did that mean rather painful results?? . . . hope not! or had I better send you some cushions to sit on?

I enjoyed my trip over to Holland (did you get my post-card?).[2] The opera was very well done, & I had a ter-mendous reception, & was given a large laurel wreath standing on the stage! It was rather difficult to manage, trying to bow with a thing as big as a life-belt in my arms, & weighing a ton. My sister Beth & I went, by boat both ways, & had a fearfully rough crossing back (it takes 6½ hours from Hook of Holland to Harwich). I wasn't sick, but for the first time in my life I felt horribly wobbley – most annoying!

When I see Peter I'll ask him for his autograph. If you like I'll get all the cast of the Turn of the Screw for you – they are quite famous – including Master David Hemmings, aged 13, but jolly good. When I get back from abroad I'll go through my letters & see if I can find any good ones, but the trouble is when you know a famous person well they always end up – "with love, Tommy" which isn't much use to you, is it?

The weather is horrid here – storms, & snow, & wind & thunder & lightning (did I tell you my Mill at Snape[3] was struck the other day?) – so the only thing to do is work, which is in fact what I've got to do. [. . .] hope everything goes well – – – –

BEN

[...]

LETTER 835: JULY 1955

1 Britten had given Duncan a tennis racquet as a present, and was obviously delighted that the boy so enjoyed the game at which he himself excelled.

2 Britten sent a postcard to Roger Duncan (postmarked Amsterdam, 13 May 1955): 'Just here in Holland for 18 hours – saw my opera Peter Grimes at the theatre last night, & just off to catch the boat again!' The Netherlands Opera production of *Peter Grimes*, with Frans Vroons in the title role, Greet Koeman (Ellen Orford) and Caspar Broecheler (Balstrode), was directed by Friedrich Shramm and conducted by Alexander Krannhals. The production, which had been first staged in March 1955, used the sets and costumes designed by Kenneth Greene for the original 1945 Sadler's Wells production.

3 The Old Mill at Snape, the converted windmill where Britten lived from 1937 until 1947.

835 To Edith Sitwell

4 CRABBE STREET, ALDEBURGH
July 28th, 1955

My dear Edith,

Thank you very much for the book.[1] I have taken it around with me on a wild series of visits and concerts these last few days, & it is so wonderful that it never fails to stimulate or comfort. Wonderful things in it, by you & the others.

It was sweet of you to send it. I treasure it. Peter is still abroad.[2] He rushed back[3] for Façade in King's Lynn on Sunday, & then off to Germany. He will be writing I know when he 'stays put' for a moment! We were both disgusted by that asinine attack on you (& us).[4] You do suffer most terribly from beastliness & stupidity – I'm afraid, a true sign of greatness to be so subject to pettiness of this sort. It is difficult to take no notice. I have, by hard practice, managed to get my minding down to about 24 hours!

We may be driving up to Harewood at the end of August. Will you still be in Renishaw? We would love to call & see you & Osbert.[5]

In haste, but with a great deal of love & thanks,

BEN

1 Edith Sitwell had sent Britten a book which it has not proved possible to identify – it was possibly an anthology which she had compiled. She wrote to Britten on 22 July 1955: 'The book has been out some time, but I am sure neither of you have it, and I want you to, for my own pleasure. First copies have just reached me from America.'

On 15 June 1955, Pears, Brain and Britten had given a performance of *Canticle III* as part of an English Opera Group concert at the Royal Festival Hall, which also included Sitwell reading two groups of her poems and, in the second half, a performance of Walton's *Façade* (with texts by Sitwell), in which Sitwell was joined by Pears as the second reciter, and members of the EOG Orchestra conducted by Anthony Collins. The same forces had recorded *Façade* for Decca in 1954. Maureen Garnham recalls (*As I Saw It*, p. 48) the performance was given behind a screen painted by John Piper, in the manner of the original performances in the 1920s. Garnham described Sitwell's appearance at a rehearsal for the concert (ibid., pp. 47–8):

> A tall figure with a long white face, black flowing robes, and an assortment of jewellery, and resembling a medieval representation of Death, swept through the doorway, stopped in its tracks in front of me and held out a long, beringed hand, palm downwards. For an instant I was not sure whether I was meant to shake it or kiss it, but settled for the former, which fortunately appeared to be acceptable.

2 Pears was singing at the Ansbach Bachwoche in West Germany: see Letter 836.

3 Britten and Pears had attended the Holland Festival between 7 and 20 July, Pears needing to return to the UK for two performances: in Norwich (Britten's *Saint Nicolas* on 21 July, with the Norwich Philharmonic Society conducted by Heathcote Statham); and in King's Lynn on the 24th (Walton's *Façade*, with Irene Worth as the other speaker, and the EOG Ensemble conducted by Vilem Tausky). Highlights in Holland had included EOG performances of *The Turn of the Screw* in Rotterdam (8th), The Hague (11th), Amsterdam (13th) and Arnhem (15th), and a difficult staging in the Casino at Knokke in Belgium under trying circumstances (see Garnham, p. 50). The opera had previously been given three performances at the 1955 Aldeburgh Festival, opening on 18 June, and a single performance at the International Eisteddford at Llangollen, Wales, on 5 July.

4 The precise form and content of the 'asinine attack' remains unidentified; perhaps it was no more than a waspish notice of one of their concerts together. However, during this period Sitwell had been continually subjected to hostile and personal criticism. She wrote to William Plomer (18 June 1954), 'I am glad to have been made a Dame, because it has slapped down all the miserable little pipsqueaks in the *New Statesman and Nation* and *Spectator*, who have been persecuting me for months.' Her conversion to Roman Catholicism in 1955 again attracted comment in the press. The novelist Evelyn Waugh, himself a prominent Roman Catholic, warned the priest who was to receive her into the Church, 'What I fear is that the popular papers may take her up as a kind of Garbo–Queen Christina [...] There are so many malicious people about to make a booby of a Sitwell. It would be tragic if this great occasion in her life were in any way sullied.' (See Victoria Glendinning, *Edith Sitwell: A Unicorn Among Lions*, pp. 311 and 318.)

5 The visit to Harewood House took place between 26 and 29 August, but neither Britten's nor Pears's diaries records a meeting with the Sitwells during this period. However, Edith Sitwell wrote to Britten on 9 August

1955: 'Osbert is delighted at the thought of you & Peter coming to Renishaw. He says do stay the night, alas – alas, I shall not be there.'

Britten told Roger Duncan (1 September 1955):

> Peter & I went up to Harewood for the weekend – lovely drives, & the open Rolls went like a bird several times doing over 80 [mph]. The weekend was fun; lovely to see George & Marion & the children; but somewhat of a strain because Princess Mary was there & one has to behave so well – – – ! She is nice, of course, but being Royal likes things just so. We saw a nice film of their visit to Jugoslavia with your father. It looks a nice place; & we look forward to our visit in November.

836 To Benjamin Britten
From Peter Pears

~~5 Chester Gate, Regent's Park, London N.W.2~~
Hotel Stern, Ansbach [West Germany]
Saturday 7 A.M. [30 July 1955]

My darling Honey bee

Thank you so very much for your telegram – I do hope you are well and happy & that your Dorset dash[1] was all right & the car didn't wobble too much.

Here everything has been really very moving.[2] My concert went off yesterday morning very well, it seems. It was in a curious rather lovely little old Gothic chapel, very German, with curious old ugly tombstones all round – very resonant acoustic, too much, but allright-ish when full. Everyone was, on the surface anyway, bowled over by your favourite tenor, and I think I sang quite well, although I had to wait from 10.30 until 12.0 before I sang! owing to a sort of Council meeting going on & on. Peg & Lu [Hesse] are of course very much here, in very good form, a lot of late nights! – very sweetly they have asked us (all 3 chaps & me)[3] to spend a night at Wolfsgarten – We have of course discussed the world tour a lot (Peg's brother David[4] + wife have been here till today) & everyone advises us not to cross the Pacific, v. expensive & tiring – Much better they say to come back same way or over the top. In any case I suggest we agree to cut the Pacific & Mexico etc, & either come back the way we came more or less, or stay longer everywhere & then dash back over the old North Pole. But more of that when I'm back.

This Festival is very instructive – Gosh! what lots of money there is for art here! The tickets are very expensive & the audience smart, snob to a certain extent, but Bach is safe that way! Performances frightfully efficient, jolly accurate in every way & with about as much charm as a type-writer. The great rage is a young man called Karl Richter,[5] played a complete organ recital by memory on a hideous organ – The line seems to be straight & narrow Bach with no room to expand – an occasional, very, ornament played pokerfaced, to show we know about them – Plenty of lively down-beats but precious little living rhythm. My players were as usual better wind than strings – oboe good, flute young & a bit silly, violin a shy adequate Brucknerian from Munich, rather sweet girl harpsichordist. But all the musicians are young and passionately keen, and play for their lives. It is in many ways curiously touching. It makes me sure that we ought to have our musicians at Aldeburgh for the whole of the week before the Festival – !

Ros[6] and Noreen and Philip[7] are of course wild with excitement – They live in a hostel with 13 East German music students – & the stories are pretty dreary and make them think quite a bit.

Everyone here sends lots of love to you, my B. We think of you & talk of you often – It will be lovely to see you again –

Please give lots of love to Roger [Duncan] & Imo and Clytie –

& to yourself, my own dear B,
from a very loving
P.

I think NO to Tureck[8] – Too awkward during August Sept Oct.

1 Britten's diary entry for 28 July reads 'Fetch Roger'. Roger Duncan, who was at All Hallows prep school (in Somerset, not Dorset), was to keep Britten company at Aldeburgh during Pears's absence.

2 Pears was participating in the Ansbach Bachwoche, the annual Bach Festival established in 1948. He had left the UK via Ostend on 25 July and arrived in Ansbach two days later. His one engagement took place on 29 July. According to a handwritten note by Rosamund Strode in the programme book (at BPL) for the 1955 Ansbach Festival, Pears's concert (Bach solo cantatas) is unmentioned in the programme book as it was 'a private, by-invitation-only, affair'. His long drive back to Aldeburgh began on the day he wrote this letter to Britten.

Pears was to return to Ansbach in 1956 (where he first sang with the baritone Dietrich Fischer-Dieskau); 1957 (when Britten visited as a member of the audience), 1959, 1963 and 1964. He was one of very few non-German singers, and the only British singer, invited to work with Karl Richter (see n. 5 below) at this time, a reliable indication of Pears's high reputation in Germany. See also Pears's 1959 Ansbach Bach Festival diary, in PRPP, pp. 73–84 and 207–13.

3 Pears had arranged for three young professional singers – Rosamund Strode (see n. 6 below), Noreen Willett and Philip Todd (see n. 7 below), all of whom were members of the Purcell Singers – to attend the Ansbach Bachwoche as students.

4 David Geddes (1917–1995), younger son of the 1st Lord Geddes, and a director of Jardine Matheson Hong Kong, 1953–57, and his wife Pytt (see Letter 854 n. 4). The world tour party (Britten, Pears and the Hesses) were to stay with David Geddes and his wife, who lived on Victoria Peak in Hong Kong, in the first week of February 1956 as part of their Far Eastern itinerary: see Letter 855. The tour itself is chronicled in Part IV: the route adopted did indeed avoid crossing the Pacific Ocean, the party returning home westwards from Japan.

5 German organist, harpsichordist and conductor (1926–1981), who was appointed Organist of the Thomaskirche, Leipzig (Bach's church), in 1947. In the early 1950s he founded the Munich Bach Orchestra and Choir, with whom he performed and recorded all Bach's major choral works, including a representative cycle of the church cantatas. In 1958, Pears was one of the soloists in a recording of three Bach cantatas conducted by Richter.

6 Rosamund Strode (b. 1927), British musician and soprano, who studied at the Royal College of Music and with Imogen Holst at Dartington. She was a founder member of the Purcell Singers, through which she came into closer contact with Britten and Pears, having first met them at Dartington in 1948. She acted as a freelance assistant to Imogen Holst during the 1950s and early 1960s, and then worked part-time at Aldeburgh from 1963 before succeeding Holst as Britten's music assistant the following year, a position she retained until the composer's death in 1976; she was subsequently Secretary and Archivist to the Britten Estate/Britten–Pears Foundation until 1992. She is the dedicatee of Britten's *A Wealden Trio: The Song of the Women* (1930, revised 1967). She was awarded an Honorary MA from the University of East Anglia in 1990.

A key member of Britten's Aldeburgh staff, Strode has written several articles about her association with the composer and Pears, including 'Working for Britten (II)' in CPBC, pp. 51–61; 'Reverberations' in PPT, pp. 89–90; an obituary of Pears, *RCM Magazine* 82/2 (1986), pp. 39–42; and 'A Death in Venice Chronicle', in Donald Mitchell (ed.), *Benjamin Britten: 'Death in Venice'*, pp. 26–44. She made a substantial contribution to Christopher Grogan (ed.), *Imogen Holst: A Life in Music*. See also Alan Blyth (ed.), *Remembering Britten*, pp. 108–10, and Philip Reed (compiler), 'Rosamund Strode: A Tribute', 1992 Aldeburgh Festival Programme Book, pp. 70–73.

In an undated letter, probably written in the late 1960s, Britten told Strode, '[. . .] your simply incredible skills, loyalty, & understanding is something beyond my range & I never cease to be grateful for & touched by it.'

7 Philip Todd, British tenor, whom Pears taught during the early 1950s when Todd was singing in Canterbury Cathedral choir; he was a member of the Purcell Singers. Todd was the tenor soloist in Britten's recording of *Rejoice in the Lamb*. See CHPP, pp. 171–2 for Todd's memories of lessons with Pears

at this period. In 1970 Todd was teaching singing at the University of Auckland, New Zealand, and hosted Pears and Britten when they visited Auckland during their trip to Australia and New Zealand: see CHPP, p. 236.

8 Rosalyn Tureck (1914–2003), American pianist and teacher, particularly known for her all-Bach cycles.

837 To John Cranko
[*Typed file copy*]

[Aldeburgh]
15th August, 1955

My dear Johnny,

I am sorry to have to write this letter to you, but I hope you will understand. I got back here from the Continent at the end of July absolutely exhausted – not surprisingly because I have been at it for months, even years, without a break. With considerable effort, with only a short break, I made myself start on Act II of the ballet last week, but for the above reason and for a variety of others, work went very slowly. The other reasons were – the feeling that I had to have the bulk of the ballet finished by early September when you go off to America to rehearse it;[1] the ghastly dateline for the full score to be ready by the time I go off for the world tour at the end of October; the tension with John P. over the decor-battle (Flute versus Ballet);[2] the (as far as I know) non-existence of a conductor,[3] in fact the non-existence of a date for the first night (about which I hear nothing but rumours, never a direct communication from Covent Garden, not even a twitter to say they are serious about the whole matter).

I have therefore come reluctantly to this conclusion: I cannot make myself ill with worry and over-work about anything so vague. I will continue to sketch the work in what time I have in these next two months. I hope, but cannot guarantee, to have the piano score completed before I leave.[4] I will be back mid-March, and will if necessary complete the sketches and write the full score then.

The obvious solution seems to be the postponement for at least six months which will allow the work to be completed, the conductor engaged, and solve the problem of Piper having to do two major productions on top of each other.[5]

The one thing that has never varied in spite of these vicissitudes has been my interest in the ballet itself, and I hope eventually to write the work worthy of you and the Company. That I fear may be your only crumb of consolation in the rather dreary matter.

Yours ever,
Benjamin Britten

1 Presumably Cranko had intended to begin work on *The Prince of the Pagodas* with the ballet company while on tour in the United States.

2 Piper had been engaged by Covent Garden to design a new production of Mozart's *Die Zauberflöte*, directed by Christopher West and conducted by Rafael Kubelík, which premiered at the Royal Opera House on 19 January 1956 and was mounted to mark the bicentenary of Mozart's birth (27 January 1956). According to Michael Northen, 'Designs for the Theatre', in the exhibition catalogue for Piper's eightieth-birthday retrospective at the Tate Gallery, p. 34: 'The production was designed almost entirely with painted gauzes, a medium which had been used with great effect in *The Turn of the Screw* and which Piper found more and more interesting to use.' The production was revived on several occasions that year, including in November with Pears as Tamino and Joan Sutherland as Pamina.

The tension to which Britten refers presumably concerned the closeness of this project and the original schedule for *Pagodas*; as Britten suggests, the postponement of *Pagodas* alleviated this difficulty.

3 The lack of a conductor for *Pagodas* was to continue to be an anxiety for many months more: see Letters 862, 869 and 870.

4 As Letter 862 reveals, this was something of a rash statement on Britten's part: he had not completed the piano score in April 1956, some eight months later, when he reported he was still only 'in the middle of the second act'.

5 Britten sent a copy of this letter to David Webster at Covent Garden, with a covering note which read: 'Here is a copy of a letter I've had to write to Johnny Cranko; it's a pity, but it had to be done. Shall I be hearing from you?' A new February deadline for completion of the score was scrapped, and the ballet was duly postponed until July 1956. Britten wrote again to Webster with increasing irritation on 1 October 1955, one month before his departure on the world tour, to say:

> But if the main reason [for meeting] is to discuss the dates of the ballet surely that has been done already – Ninette [de Valois] came down to Aldeburgh to do this, and we thrashed it all out thoroughly. As she will have told you in America the earliest I could possibly manage would be the last half of July, and that is only possible if you can somehow extend the season. She was going to let me know your reactions to this, but I have heard nothing. With my complete absence from England and work this winter you will realise that this is going to be a tight squeeze, and I do not see how I can <u>guarantee</u> completion by that date, try as I will. Why can we not postpone the work till the autumn without further ado?

Webster replied on 18 October, agreeing to abandon the July deadline.

It was, in the event, highly propitious that Britten should have had Act II of the ballet in his mind when he arrived in Bali, since it was into this act that he was to incorporate material from the gamelan music that he encountered there (see Letters 850–52). When he returned from the world tour the following March, Britten was uncharacteristically forced to cancel concerts in order to make available the time necessary for the completion of *Pagodas* (see Letter 859).

838 To Ronald Duncan

4 CRABBE STREET, ALDEBURGH
Sept 2nd 1955

My dear Ronnie,

Thank you for your letter. I am glad the Punch Revue seems to be going well, & that you liked the little piece I did for William's verses.[1] I wasn't altogether happy about it – I don't feel any longer I can knock off a thing like that; but if it doesn't let the side down too badly, that's fine.

Most unfortunately I can't come to the 1st night because I have a performance that night, but I am sure I can catch it later.

I have to be in London on 18th & 19th (according slightly to rehearsals) & could work on St. Peter on the evening of 18th if you like.[2] Or we could wait till you come up for Punch (or the Scala Season which I hope you can attend some of).[3] But it would be nice to have a talk on 18th if possible – –

Lots of love to you all –

BEN

1 Britten's (unpublished) polka-cum-waltz setting of Plomer's 'Old friends are best', a contribution – along with two of the *Cabaret Songs* – to the *Punch Revue*, which had been devised and directed by Vida Hope, and opened on 28 September at the Duke of York's Theatre. The production was reviewed on 29 September in the *Daily Express* and *The Times*. Although the review in *The Times* does not mention the Britten–Plomer contribution, it does note one of the Britten–Auden *Cabaret Songs*:

What the writers lack in theatrical guile is compensated for to a great extent by Miss Binnie Hale, who is full to her finger tips of theatrical guile. How superbly she puts across Mr W. H. Auden's earnestly scientific lyric 'O tell me the truth about love', for which Mr Benjamin Britten has composed the music.

The anonymous reviewer concluded,

The dancing is gay; the decor as various as might be expected; and, though there are moments when we seem to be assisting at a faint stage parody of a number of *Punch*, the general effect is striking.

Vida Hope had written to Britten on 20 June, enclosing a copy of the Plomer text and explaining how tableaux were to be derived from famous *Punch* cartoons:

I leave it entirely to you as to how you wish to set it, naturally. I think it seems to fall automatically into waltz time, but I should like to explain that when the girl has finished the number, it leads into a very brief ballet-mime in which we see such figures as 'the Stout Party collapsing', the 'Curate opening his egg' etc. If you are very pressed for time, therefore, and do not wish to write special ballet music for this purpose, we can elaborate your melody for the lyric into dance form.

I do not know if Ronnie has told you that on the six weeks tour of this show we shall use two pianos and a drum, but when we come into town we hope to have a small orchestra of about six pieces. I am not quite sure whether you will wish to score this song yourself, or whether, in view of your busy life, you prefer to leave it to be done by someone else. I imagine if you have time, you would prefer to do it yourself.

I am also longing to hear the settings which Ronnie has told me you have done of two lyrics of Auden's [*Cabaret Songs*] and I gather from him we have your permission to include these items in our Revue.

Plomer had been working on the text earlier in the year, telling Britten in a letter dated 14 April 1955 that

I am a bit out of my depth with the technicalities of writing a scenelet or sketchkin for the *Punch Revue*, but the maternal hand and expertness of the produceress are guiding me. I have an idea the whole thing may be rather a lark. The final text of 'Old friends are best' runs as follows:

Too clever by half! Too clever for me! I'm dumb, I'm frustrated!
These jokes aren't explained! They may be all right in their way –
They're too smart for me, to items like this my response is belated –
I feel such a clot when I can't see the point till next day.

I'm not asking much! They used to put once, before we were thought of,
'Collapse of stout party', and things of that kind, down below –
If only they'd do it again! You know, *explain* it all, sort of,
I shouldn't feel dumb and frustrated! I'd see the whole point! I should *know*!

So give me back-numbers
   With drawings by Keene,
And Du Maurier girls in
   A drawing-room scene;

Sir Gorgius Midas
   Is my glass of port,
And 'Dropping the Pilot'
   And things of that sort!

I'm a raging escapist,
   I'm now on the run!
I want some back-numbers
   And old-fashioned fun!

Plomer wrote to Britten on 21 June 1955 to say, 'I am amazed and delighted to hear that you are going to set a trifle I wrote for the *Punch Revue*', indicating that when he wrote to the composer in April the possibility of Britten's collaboration had not been discussed. The revue was in rehearsal during August, when Duncan told the composer,

The number you wrote with William is excellent and everybody is delighted and grateful. I am especially pleased because it makes my point: that revue music need not be tied to the ghastly tin-pan-alley-on-a-shoestring rhythms.

It was in response to this letter, which is simply dated 'Aug 55', that the present letter was written. Although Britten was unable to see the show, Plomer caught a provincial preview in Brighton and reported to the composer on 20 September and declared: 'What a pretty and haunting tune you have hung upon that little peg I provided for the *Punch Revue!*'

Britten wrote to Roger Duncan on 17 August 1955, after having received Ronald Duncan's letter dated 'Aug 55':

You remember the piece I wrote in the garden (for the Punch Revue), with Clytie on my knee (just as she is now) & you playing your 'Owzat' cricket to interrupt me – well they are very pleased with it, & think I'm clever! I told them that it was only because I had something very handy to clean my india rubber on ... it makes such a difference!

2 Duncan had written in his 'Aug 55' letter: 'Let me know when you think you could put in some more time with me on "Peter" [*St Peter*] and I will come up to London for it. Would somewhere about the 17th September be any good?' Britten wrote 'Ronnie evening?' in his diary for 18 September, but then crossed the entry through.

The *St Peter* project is described by Duncan (RDWB, pp. 128–30) as having originated during the Zermatt ski-ing holiday they took together during February 1955. Britten was now, according to Duncan, anxious to compose an oratorio for York Minster, the patron saint of which was St Peter. Duncan proposed a work in two parts, the first ending with Peter's betrayal and Christ's crucifixion, the second with the crucifixion of Peter. Duncan relates (RDWB, pp. 128–9):

On returning to London, he and I worked out a musical synopsis for *Saint Peter*. This synopsis was most precise. Ben knew how many stanzas he wanted for this aria, where the chorus should enter, and which part should be a trio and so forth.

In order to concentrate wholly on this *Saint Peter* libretto, I left London and went alone to Gerald and Gamel Brenan's house at Churriana, outside Malaga. My only luggage was the *Apocrypha* [...] The libretto went very well. Just as in the *Lucretia* libretto I had deliberately written lines like:

It runs after him with steady beat
Like a lost child with tireless feet

describing Lucretia's yearnings for Collatinus with an image about childhood which I knew would release Ben musically, I again had recourse to this device of playing upon his sympathies or susceptibilities, using precisely those images where he was vulnerable and raw.

For example, I made as much use of the boats and the sea as I could knowing what *Grimes* had revealed, but not exhausted. Similarly, I deliberately introduced the boy, the urchin dogging Peter's feet like an unwanted mongrel, and then on the last page showing that this gamin was Christ by Peter's side. The libretto was found still in Ben's desk after his death. A pity – no, that's not the word – but there is no other word. Ben was not unaware of these tricks I had played on him, nor ungrateful.

I was pleased with my work, and after a fortnight I returned to London and took it to Ben in his house at Chester Gate. I have seldom seen him so grateful or excited.

'This is precisely what I wanted,' he cried. 'I'll start setting it immediately.'

I returned to Devon [and] I heard nothing more of this composition. After a year or so, I wrote and asked Ben how it was going. He replied that he still intended to set it. But I knew his impulse for this oratorio had been carefully diverted into the *War Requiem*.

A letter from Duncan to Britten written in Malaga on 22 November 1955 is full of excitement concerning the project:

I've been here a month now sitting in a rather lovely garden which is full of orange trees and pomegranates. I have just finished the first draft of *St Peter*. We must have planned better than we knew, for it's gone very well. I really am excited about it and can hardly wait to work with you on it. Of course, you must buy 2 pairs of scissors in Tokyo – for it needs cutting, etc. But that'll be easy. What does please me is that it's worked out so dramatic. The Trial scene and the scene with the Boy particularly. As I say, I can hardly wait till you give this thing its wings.

Two copies of a typed first draft for the *St Peter* libretto are preserved at BPL, along with a full, typed synopsis. The latter appears to be based on a rough outline for the work written by Britten on his 4 Crabbe Street headed notepaper. The typed synopsis bears several annotations by the composer, the most interesting of which is the insertion of congregational hymns along the lines of *Saint Nicolas*. The draft libretto typescripts are dated 'Churriana, Nov. 1955', and one copy was annotated by Britten.

Britten was to write to Duncan on 12 June 1956 implying a continuing interest in the *St Peter* project (see Letter 871). In Letter 861 Britten discusses the possible York Minster commission which might have brought the project to completion, but by February 1957 he had decided against pursuing the idea (see Letter 887). See also Letter 116 n. 1, for details of Britten's other unrealized projects with Duncan, including, for example, *Mea Culpa* (see Letter 518 n. 2).

Britten's initial thoughts for an oratorio were not immediately linked to St Peter and are mentioned by Imogen Holst in her diary on several occasions during the summer of 1953. On 22 July, shortly after Britten's return from the Taw and Torridge Festival, and the very day the composer learned of Paul Rogerson's intention to become a Jesuit, she writes (IHD, p. 234):

While Ben & I were standing on the wall opposite the garden gate he began telling me what he meant to write next, and how the Devon festival had proved that *Saint Nicolas* is the answer to a great need, and he'd been discussing with Ronald Duncan the possibilities of other Saints, and then afterwards he'd decided that he'd do a life of Christ. I was so excited that I nearly knocked him off the wall. He said that he and Peter would do the libretto themselves, using the Apocryphal acts. And that it would be for the 1955 festival; – that he'd have to do it fairly soon because there'd be a lot for the chorus to learn, and that I must promise to stay for it.

On 6 August (IHD, pp. 239–40) Imogen Holst reports:

I told Ben about the apocryphal St John's reasons for having a holiday and his eye lit up when it got to the bit about the bow not always being stretched. He talked about the infancy legends and said he must read them again.

And that evening, 'we talked about the apocryphal legends when we were finishing our wine in the sitting-room'.

The second occasion was on 11 August (IHD, p. 243):

He talked again of the apocrypha and asked me which five or six incidents I'd have if it were me: – he said he thought *not* the resurrection, as it was to be the human [bits]. I suggested the temptation, and he said, 'yes – a time of agony' and he went on to speak of Gesthamene.

Britten asked Holst about Conrad Noel's *Life of Jesus* on 16 August, 'and I said I'd been trying to get a copy for them & Peter said they'd got one somewhere' (IHD, p. 247).

3 The English Opera Group's 1955 season at London's Scala Theatre included performances of Britten's *The Turn of the Screw* and *Let's Make an Opera*, and a double-bill comprising Lennox Berkeley's *A Dinner Engagement* and Walton's *Façade*. For a description of the poor facilities at the Scala Theatre, see Maureen Garnham, *As I Saw It*, p. 54. The season closed on 1 October; two days later there was a live BBC broadcast of *The Turn of the Screw*, in which Gerald English replaced an indisposed Pears as Quint (though Britten insisted that Pears perform the Prologue: see Garnham, pp. 54–5).

IV AS COMPLICATED AS SCHOENBERG: EASTERN ENCOUNTERS

OCTOBER 1955–MARCH 1956

Britten to Imogen Holst, 17 January 1956: Letter 850

CHRONOLOGY 1955–1956

YEAR	EVENTS AND COMPOSITIONS
1955	
31 October	Britten and Pears leave for their world trip, travelling first to Amsterdam for engagements, then to Dusseldorf, Stuttgart, Geneva and Zurich
13–17 November	Concerts in Vienna and Salzburg
20 November	St Peter Mancroft, Norwich: first performance of *Hymn to St Peter*, choir of St Peter Mancroft, conducted by C. J. R. Coleman
22 November	Grosvenor Chapel, South Audley Street, London: first performance of the revised version of *A Boy was Born*, Purcell Singers, conducted by Imogen Holst
20–30 November	In former Yugoslavia, with concerts in Ljubljana, Maribor, Zagreb and Belgrade
30 November – 11 December	In Turkey, with concerts in Istanbul and Ankara
8/9 December	COMPOSITION *Timpani Piece for Jimmy* (unpublished)
11 December	Britten and Pears fly overnight from Istanbul to Karachi (via Beirut), arriving in Pakistan on the 12th; they fly on to Bombay on the 13th
13 December – 2 January 1956	In India, visiting Bombay (13th–19th), Delhi (19th–24th), Agra (24th–26th), Delhi (26th) and Calcutta (27 December–2 January 1956)
1956	
2–7 January	In Singapore, where Prince Ludwig and Princess Margaret of Hesse and the Rhine join Britten and Pears for the remainder of the trip
7–8 January	In Sumatra, with a concert in Palembang

8–12 January	In Java, visiting Bandung and Semarang. In Bandung on 8 January, Britten has his first live contact with Indonesian music, and on the 11th visits the gong factory in Semarang
12–25 January	In Bali, where the Bali Hotel, Denpasar, serves as their base, although they spend time outside the capital, notably at the beach resort of Sanur and at Ubud, the island's artistic centre. The party hears many Balinese gamelan
25–31 January	Return trip to Java
31 January – 2 February	In Singapore, before flying to Hong Kong (via Bangkok) on 2 February
2–8 February	In Hong Kong, with a visit on 4 February to the Portuguese colony of Macau for a recital
8–19 February	In Japan, where Britten and Pears give two concerts for the Japanese broadcasting authority NHK; during the visit the party attends two performances of the Nō play *Sumidagawa* and visits the Imperial Palace to hear the Gagaku orchestra. Britten and Pears join the members of the Tokyo Madrigal Singers in an informal concert at the British Council in Tokyo
19 February	The party returns to Hong Kong for twenty-four hours before flying to Bangkok
21–22 February	In Bangkok, returning to Singapore on the 22nd
24 February – 8 March	In Sri Lanka, where Britten and Pears give a recital and take part in an amateur performance of Bach's *St Matthew Passion*
8–15 March	Return to India, staying in Madras (where the final recital of the trip takes place on the 11th) and Bombay
15–16 March	The party flies back to Europe; after spending a night at Wolfsgarten, Britten and Pears return by train then ferry to the UK (Harwich) on the 17th

839 To Leslie Periton

PARK HOTEL, STUTTGART
Nov. 7th, 1955

My dear Leslie,

I was sorry not to have had a chance to ring you before we left – but those last days were hectic! Anyhow, I expect you will have gathered that the wills were finished, & that we signed them, & I hope by now are in Isador's[1] hands (Jeremy [Cullum] was bringing them to London) – & also the power of Attorney was signed – for us both. I hope that won't be a bore for you. I told Jeremy to ask you for larger cheques than he could sign – wages for instance – and he may appeal to you for occasional help or advice – which I'm sure you won't mind giving. I expect by now you will have our addresses (such as they are, so far), & so you can write, if you are in any way worried!

Thank you very much for your help, in so many ways; it is a real relief to know you are around and in charge! Here things go according to plan . . . very busy, but wonderful audiences, & exciting receptions. We go to Switzerland the day after tomorrow.[2]

I hope you & Muriel are well.

With kindest regards from both Peter & me –
Yours ever,
BEN

1   Isador Caplan (1912–1995), Britten's and Pears's solicitor and legal adviser from the mid-1940s, who was later to become an Executor of both Britten's and Pears's Estates and a senior Trustee of the Britten–Pears Foundation. Caplan served on the board of the English Opera Group from 1951. See also Letter 590 n. 11.

    In an undated letter to Caplan, probably dating from the late 1960s, Pears was to write: 'I just wanted to put down on paper our (Ben's and my own) intense and very real gratitude to you for all that you do for us.'

2   Britten's and Pears's movements in the early days of their five-month world tour can be reconstructed from the entries in their pocket diaries, Pears's travel diary (PRPP) and and the detailed account Britten himself gives in Letter 840. By Tuesday 1 November, they had arrived in Amsterdam. On 4 November they caught a train to Dusseldorf, moving on to Stuttgart on the day this letter was written. They performed in Geneva on 10 November and Zurich on the next day, leaving Switzerland for Austria on 12 November.

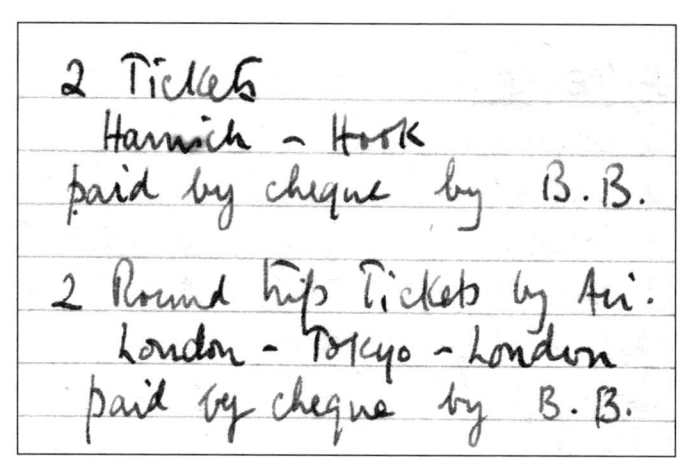

> 2 Tickets
> Harwich – Hook
> paid by cheque by B.B.
>
> 2 Round trip Tickets by Air.
> London – Tokyo – London
> paid by cheque by B.B.

The opening entry in Pears's expenses notebook
for the world trip

840   To Roger Duncan

HOTEL NEUES SCHLOSS, ZURICH
Nov. 12th [–18th] 1955

[...]

I am sorry not to have started on the great series of letters before this, because, even though we have visited three countries & are just leaving for the fourth, they are all old European ones, & I don't feel the Tour has properly started.[1] Anyhow this is just to report, if briefly, on progress up-to-date, & to thank you for your long & newsy letter, which incidentally was the first letter I received on the journey – well done, old thing! I am not, in these letters, going to talk a lot about your news, not because I'm not interested (you know I am, in everything you do), but because there's going to be so much to say about what we do, that there wouldn't be time to get it all in. Anyhow, briefly, glad about the fireworks & the conjuror, awfully sorry about Kit's[2] concussion (give him my love & tell him to get well quick), and I'll try and write Christopher Hewetson a note about the English Opera Group, although I haven't a clue as to what he wants.[3]

Well, we started off nearly two weeks ago,[4] by car to Harwich, Jeremy drove & Imo came too. It was horrid to say good-bye to Aldeburgh, & Clytie, and I must confess I still feel a teeny bit homesick for it all, & look forward to Easter, & to seeing you too.

We crossed on the day boat to the Hook, where Peter Diamand[5] (our agent chap) met us, & took us in his car to Amsterdam. Driving, you know, in Holland is ghastly, & one always feels thankful when one gets back to one's hotel ... they drive too fast, & badly; in Amsterdam the streets are narrow, with trams too. They have a flag flying in the centre of the town & when someone gets killed on the streets they pull it down to half-mast – it's never, as far as I can see, at the top! However, we got to Amsterdam safely, & checked in at the American Hotel, where we always stay, & where we know the porters, & people. I don't know whether it was the injections, or exhaustion after the packing & arrangements to leave England for 5 months, or whether just because we have given so many concerts in Amsterdam, but we were both <u>fearfully</u> nervous at the concert we gave the next day. We didn't think we did at all well, but luckily the audience was kind & seemed to like what we did: anyhow Peter sang well.[6]

The next days we stayed there still, rehearsing ourselves for forthcoming concerts, meeting old friends – we went over to the Hague for dinner with the British Ambassador (Sir Paul Mason)[7] & his wife, most musical, kind, & amusing people. They gave us names of ambassadors & people we may meet in the Near & Far East.

On Friday (4th) we took the train to Germany, Düsseldorf – a large industrial town on the Rhine. There we enjoyed our concert enormously;[8] we've been before, & they really like what we do a lot. The very nice Consul-General, Bill Marchant, gave us a party after, to which many people, some nice, some rather dotty, came. Mr. Marchant, by-the-way, used to teach modern languages at Harrow; he must think it a good school because he's sending his own small son there in a year or two – you must get to know him, & be kind to him because he'll be junior to you![9] We stayed in Düsseldorf three days in a very posh hotel, but just opposite a clock-tower which chimed (<u>fortissimo</u>) every quarter, & I just couldn't sleep, & I hate not sleeping, don't you? The nice Consul General & his wife drove us over to a town called Wuppertal for another concert – a hideous textile town, but with a lovely audience, mostly young people, who loved the rather difficult programme we did – so much so, that even in the interval they came round asking us to come & give another concert in December, no <u>two</u> concerts; but we had to explain we'd be in Turkey! We had a bit of an adventure arriving there – it was dark, & we had trouble in finding the Town Hall, where we were told the concert was. At last we found it, & when we presented ourselves – they'd never heard of us! So we went out again into the street, looked everywhere for a poster with our names on, found the name of the <u>right</u> hall, & after difficulty found that one! But we were so late, that there wasn't much time to try the piano before the audience came in ...[10]

The next day we took the train for Stuttgart, a journey of about 5 hours. We stayed in a nice hotel, with <u>another</u> beastly clock chiming all night!

But, in spite of feeling rather weary the concert was all right[11] – & we went on the next day to Geneva (a lovely, though rather long journey in the train). We stayed with some friends there, which was nice after so many hotels . . . but I was rather ill, must have eaten something in the train, & the concert there was rather agonising.[12] However I felt better for the next concert (Friday 11th) in Zürich[13] – the journey wasn't long, although it is the other end of Switzerland . . . Switzerland is only a small country. The next day

HOTEL GOLDENER HIRSCH, SALZBURG, GETREIDEGASSE 37

we flew to Vienna – about 2 hours in the plane. We had rather a funny arrival. You see, in Austria, musicians are rather important people, & our arrival was quite a big event. They had cameras out, & everything we did was filmed – including losing our luggage (we must have looked very worried), getting into the bus (they had to turn people out of their seats to take the shots), & we had to smile & wave . . . just like film stars. All Vienna was in fête, because the Opera was being re-opened having been rebuilt after its destruction in the war. There were tremendous parties, & lots of concerts, all on the occasion of the re-opening, of which we gave two – one in which I had to conduct an orchestra.[14] It was all very exciting, as music always is in Vienna, & although I don't always like their taste, it is nice to be liked so much, as they like us . . .!! We had a grand lunch at the British Embassy, & a party at the British Council.[15] We went one night to see a performance (not a very good one) at the Opera[16] – we didn't have to pay for our seats luckily, as they would have cost 2000 shillings (nearly £30!) – but the Opera House itself is wonderfully beautiful all gold & glittering, with immense foyers and passages – makes poor old Covent Garden look rather drab. Then yesterday (you see this is a week later than when I started the letter!) – Nov. 17th – we caught an early train to Salzburg (about 4–5 hours) & did a concert last night here[17] – & today and tomorrow we have nothing to do except walk around this lovely little town in the mountains, & maybe, tomorrow, take a car & go up high into the snow . . . although it has been snowing hard here most of the day. You may have heard of Salzburg because it is where Mozart was born, & where streets, houses, & restaurants are called after him. Peter & I have been this evening to see some of his manuscripts & letters kept in a Mozarteum (music college) near this hotel – letters, some written when he was touring when a boy of 14 in Italy – very funny ones, full of jokes – & one rather terrible one about him being kicked downstairs for not obeying some arch-bishop – nearly as fierce as some headmasters!

LETTER 840: NOVEMBER 1955 347

So that brings us up to date. Don't you think you've got to read all this – but I hope the next letter will be more interesting, because on Sunday we leave for Jugoslavia[18] – & then for Turkey – & then we're well away to India!!

[...]
BEN
[...]

1 Britten had promised to chronicle his world tour in writing to Roger Duncan, who was twelve at the time. The tone of the series of letters that resulted from this promise is noteworthy for the apparent ease with which Britten could adopt preparatory-school jargon for the benefit of his young correspondent.

On his return from the world trip, Britten was to ask Roger Duncan to return his sequence of letters in order that he could have typed copies made. Britten wrote to him on 18 May 1956:

I'm asking Jeremy [Cullum] to send "the" letters back to your mother, & I'm making some (tiny) alterations in them – do you think I should publish them; are they interesting enough?

The letters to Roger Duncan recording the events of the world trip remained unpublished in Britten's lifetime; the minimally edited typed copies – the alterations Britten mentions amount to no more than a tidying up of the text – were retained by the composer in his archive. The versions of these letters presented here revert to the composer's handwritten originals, which, together with the remainder of Britten's extensive correspondence with Roger Duncan, have been acquired by BPL.

2 Kit Barrington, a school friend of Roger's at All Hallows school.

3 Roger Duncan had enclosed a letter from Christopher Hewetson with his own letter to Britten, of which Letter 840 is Britten's response. The nature of Hewetson's request remains unclear.

4 In a letter to Basil Coleman (25 September 1955), Britten states that he and Pears were due to depart on 31 October. There is no entry in his pocket diary for this date, however, which has 'Amsterdam' written in for 1 November. This entry records the date of their concert after arriving in the city; the following day (2 November) carries the entry 'Recording Amsterdam' (probably a reference to a radio recording). Pears's engagement diary carries the entry 'to Am–d' on 31 October.

5 Dutch-naturalized administrator of Austrian birth (1913–1998), who, as their European agent at this period, encouraged Britten and Pears to make regular tours of the Netherlands. Among the posts he held during his career

were Artistic Director of the Holland Festival and the Edinburgh Festival, and General Manager of the Royal Philharmonic Orchestra. See also Letter 538 n. 2.

6 The recital (Haydn, Schubert, Bridge, Rainier's *Cycle for Declamation*, Britten's French folksong arrangements) took place on 1 November in the Kleine Zaal of the Concertgebouw, Pears writing home to his distant relation Janet Stone (Reynolds Stone's wife) in a letter 'begun in Istanbul about December 1st!':

> Why is it that though we have given oh twenty recitals in Amsterdam in the last 8 or 9 years we are always shaking with nerves there? The audience is always very warm and we have lots of friends but somehow each time one feels more responsibility, & less confidence in shouldering same. Well, the concert was adequate, I suppose, & then there were two blessed days without work, in which we could see our friends. Ben practised the Mozart 2 Piano Concerto and the Schumann Andante & Variations for 2 Pianos for the Aldeburgh Festival next year (one can't escape from Suffolk so quickly) & we visited Simon Goldberg & his wife, and had a very happy 'Yes' as answer to our invitation to him to come to the Festival.

The full text of this letter is reproduced in PRPP, pp. 118–20; the works by Mozart and Schumann were duly performed at the 1956 Aldeburgh Festival by Britten and Maria Curcio (the wife of Peter Diamand), with whom the composer rehearsed during his free time in Amsterdam. The American violinist Szymon Goldberg also participated in the 1956 Festival.

7 British diplomat (1905–1978), Ambassador to the Netherlands, 1954–60, and UK Permanent Representative on the North Atlantic Council, 1960–62. He served as High Sheriff of Nottingham in 1970 and was Treasurer of the University of Nottingham from 1972.

8 Pears's letter to Janet Stone continues:

> On the journey to Düsseldorf, a passport man shook us by telling us that we needed visas to perform in Germany. We had none. However he was kind and let us in. The whole of the Ruhr is immensely prosperous; the big Mercedes-Benz is known as the Volkswagen of the Ruhr. But whatever you find to say against the Germans, they love music, & our audience at the Robert Schumann-saal was wonderful. Nice German couple took us home in their car; talked about contemporary German painting: next morning they had sent us a woodcut by Gerhard Marcks [German sculptor (1889–1981)], and a medallion by Ewald Matare [German sculptor (1887–1965)]; both very distinguished contemporary German artists. Most kind and generous. Our life in Düsseldorf was very much helped by the extremely pleasant & helpful British Consul General, and his wife, who gave us a lift to our next concert in Wuppertal, which was again extremely pleasant, in a small hall [see n. 10 below].

The recital programme in Dusseldorf consisted of six Haydn canzonets, *Lieder* by Schubert and Schumann, together with Britten's *Winter Words* and *Seven Sonnets of Michelangelo*: see PRPP, p. 19.

LETTER 840: NOVEMBER 1955 349

9 Roger Duncan was shortly to sit the scholarship examination for Harrow School. His father was to write to Britten on 22 November 1955:

> Roger is going to Harrow in May, a term before the other new boys. I've agreed to this because the housemaster wanted it. Was I wrong? I dunno. It'll mean he's the *only* new boy. But it does give him a summer term extra & surely the *whole* of the school won't turn and bully him?

10 The recital in Wuppertal (early English songs, *Winter Words*, *Michelangelo Sonnets*, Rainier's *Cycle for Declamation*, Britten's French folksong arrangements) took place at the Stadthalle on 6 November. Pears noted in his letter to Janet Stone: 'Asked back in April: Ben can't do it, so offered Julian Bream and me instead: accepted.'

11 The Stuttgart recital took place on 8 November, in what Pears described to Janet Stone as 'a rather too large newish hall; the audience was kind if not enormous; "but next year – "; mad young man who spent the whole concert photographing us off stage – !!'

12 The Geneva concert was held on 10 November in the Théâtre de la Cour St-Pierre, with a programme similar to that given in Dusseldorf. Pears revealed to Janet Stone that the 'friends' referred to by Britten in this letter were Patricia Fuller, wife of the singer and translator Frederick Fuller, and Sidney Shaw. Britten was taken unwell and had to recourse to some rather different 'old friends' (PRPP, p. 20):

> Ben started one of his tummies, apparently very bad, visions of operations, cancelling concerts etc. However he got through with the help of old friends Brandy & Glucose. Concert in rather dreary little theatre, run by hard-faced impresari-ette, who gave us out of stinginess an appalling piano, an 1890 Steinway continually used for Boogy-woogy; Ben almost overcome but managed somehow.

13 Pears's letter to Janet Stone records that the Zurich concert was followed by dinner with Martin and Bettina Hürlimann, who had been responsible for commissioning Eric Walter White's pioneering book on Britten in 1948: see Letters 574 n. 2 and 605.

14 One of the two Vienna concerts was a recital featuring *Winter Words* on 13 November, and the other an orchestral concert on the 16th with a programme including Britten's *Serenade* and *Sinfonietta*, and his arrangements of Purcell's Chacony in G minor and six songs from *Orpheus Britannicus*.

15 The lunch at the Embassy took place on 14 November, and the British Council reception in Britten's and Pears's honour on the following day.

16 Britten and Pears attended a performance of Wagner's *Die Meistersinger von Nürnberg* conducted by Fritz Reiner. See Letter 841.

17 Britten and Pears had travelled on to Salzburg by train on 17 November, giving a recital the same evening in the Grosser Saal of the Mozarteum and

staying until the 19th, attending a performance of Johann Strauss II's *Der Zigeunerbaron*: see PRPP, pp. 21–2.

18 Letter 841 confirms that the trip to Yugoslavia took place on 20 November, although Britten wrote the departure and arrival times one day earlier in his diary.

841 To Anthony Gishford

HOTEL GOLDENER HIRSCH, SALZBURG, GETREIDEGASSE 37

19.11.55

My dear Tony,

Forgive this rather brief note from the wilds of Austria (& pretty wild it looks now in the snow), but time presses, as it always will I fear during this little Tour! So far everything goes well. We were nearly dead after Vienna – a wicked schedule of concerts & travelling – but things will loosen up a bit now (Jugo-Slavia tomorrow). The Concerts have been really very successful – Winter Words much liked everywhere, especially Vienna![1]

We went to the Opera – wonderful house, but dreary performance (Meistersinger) – saw a lot of Seefehlner,[2] who has now gone to the opera as second director to Böhm[3] (whom we also saw). S. is a remarkable chap, with remarkable ideas for a Viennese, but struggling rather helplessly against usual Viennese intrigue & incompetence. We've known him for ages as head of the Konzerthaus (which he still is). I think he deserves encouragement.[4] He wants very much to do the Screw next year (at the Redoutensaal), & possibly Lucretia too . . . I was non-committal about the former; & definitely the Ballet (!) too. He said he would write to Ernst R. [Roth] about this, & I said I'd put a word in to you about it. I think he & Böhm <u>really</u> mean to do it, but whether they will succeed is about as doubtful as – well, the Scala, for instance!

We had a curious worry over the score of the Purcell Chacony (G minor)[5] which was lost until the middle of the first rehearsal in Vienna. Do you think you could check this with the Hire department? I was cross because I was accused of having kept it – I presume from Aldeburgh, where I last saw it. The parts, by-the-way, of Orpheus Britannicus[6] need looking into – they are awfully small & inaccurate. The concert, actually, went very well, with a really good performance of the Serenade – & the old Sinfonietta too!

I hope things go well with you & yours. Think of us occasionally, alternately freezing & boiling, these next months. We have moments of absurd home-sickness, but when we get to more exotic parts of the world, I daresay we'll cheer up!

With love from us both,
Yours ever,
BEN

P.S. I got a slight rocket from Fritz Reiner[7] for not allowing him to do the first performance of Gloriana Suite in U.S.A. – furious at New Orleans doing it!!?? Can David Adams[8] enlighten us? – but he is a peppery person & may easily have mucked it himself. He's just had a good performance of Variations [*on a Theme of Frank Bridge*] in Chicago, he said.

1 While in Vienna, Britten also attended a reception given by the British Council on 15 November, where he met the Austrian composer Joseph Marx (1882–1964).

2 Egon Seefehlner (1912–1998), Austrian arts administrator, who was Secretary General of the Vienna Konzerthausgesellschaft, 1946–51, Deputy Director of the Vienna Staatsoper, 1954–61, under Karl Böhm and, later, Herbert von Karajan, and was appointed Deputy General Manager of the Deutsche Oper in West Berlin when it was established in 1961, becoming Director General in 1972. In 1976 he returned to Vienna as General Administrator at the Vienna Staatsoper, where he remained for a decade.

3 Karl Böhm (1894–1981), Austrian conductor, Director of the Vienna Staatsoper, 1943–45 and 1954–56. The performance of Wagner's *Die Meistersinger* was conducted by Fritz Reiner (see n. 7 below). In the audience was the conductor and Mahler disciple Bruno Walter, with whom Britten and Pears renewed their acquaintance: see Letters 554 n. 10 and Letter 556.

4 In a letter from Istanbul, Britten was to write to Lord Harewood on 9 December 1955:

We saw Meistersinger, at least Acts I & II of it – but, honestly, pretty dreary. An enormous (physically & vocally) [Walter von] Stolzing [one of the tenor roles in Wagner's opera], but he apparently gave out in the last Act, & I don't wonder – since he made so much noise in the other Acts. [Irmgard] Seefried [as Eva] was incredibly competent & coy – not to my taste, honestly – but the whole conception of the work ([Herbert] Graf) was conventional, & not for me. However, that's the way things are there now, I gather. Böhm, very pleasant, is pretty narrow, & the whole atmosphere is traditional. The man I really respect there, who is 2nd to Böhm now, is Seefehlner (he is head of Konzerthaus as well), who is enterprising, with fine ideas, & fighting hard against the reactionary & stuffy elements in that curious old city. I think he should be supported if you get the chance.

5 Britten's arrangement of Purcell's Chacony in G minor, z.730, which he had conducted in Vienna on 16 November. His edition of the work had already

been performed at the Aldeburgh Festivals in 1948 and 1955; it was published by Boosey & Hawkes in 1965 and recorded by Britten with the English Chamber Orchestra in 1969.

6   The suite of six songs by Purcell, edited and arranged with accompaniment for small orchestra by Britten and Pears, and published by Boosey & Hawkes in February 1956.

7   Hungarian conductor and teacher (1888–1963) who had become a naturalized US citizen in 1928. He studied with Bartók in Budapest and worked closely with Richard Strauss at Dresden. In later years, at the Curtis Institute, Philadelphia, his pupils would include Leonard Bernstein and Lukas Foss.

8   British music publisher (1909–2000), President of Boosey & Hawkes Inc. following the death of Ralph Hawkes, and later Director Music Publishing in London, in succession to Roth; he retired in 1974. When Hawkes died in 1950, Adams was managing the Canadian office. Helen Wallace (*Boosey & Hawkes: The Publishing Story*, p. 78), quotes from a colleague of Adams:

> David was charming, and became seriously popular in New York: Copland and Stravinsky regarded him as a friend. But he was timid and indecisive. He lacked judgement when it came to composers and he was shaky as a manager.

See also *The Times* obituary (14 November 2000).

842   To Imogen Holst
From Benjamin Britten and Peter Pears

ISTANBUL HILTON, ISTANBUL
December 1st, 1955

My dearest Imo,

You cannot imagine how pleased we have been with your letters; three lovely long ones which we have almost literally <u>eaten</u> with pleasure! It is so good of you, & we do feel a tiny bit guilty that we've written so little ... but, quite honestly it's been so hectic this far (Jugoslavia was, alas, much worse than we'd expected) & the only day off we had before coming here we spent fast asleep in bed ... !! ... admittedly we'd travelled the night before, & had a concert that evening. Anyhow, thank you so much for all the news. It's glorious that Miss Hudson & Clytie are getting along so well together; both from yours, & Mary [Potter]'s (to say nothing of a superb letter signed by <u>both</u> of them) descriptions we can picture them vividly. No news, since Switzerland, or communications from Jeremy, alas; but letters are madly unreliable – I got, for instance, <u>all</u> my birthday communications a week late[1] – & I expect there's a package on the way. So sorry that things were worrying for the 1st Boy was Born,[2] but relieved that you enjoyed Lancing. I'm sure it sounded glorious there. I long to hear it from you – do let's arrange a performance when we get back – somehow. Beth was looking forward to your trip down to the South coast – I'm so glad you could go with her.

About the Aldeburgh Opera situation; I'm disappointed that Basil [Douglas] doesn't like the Herring idea – I still think we could have done it, & that it might have been useful for the EOG later, but there were so many queries of mine he didn't answer that it is difficult to comment. I think definitely not Screw again. The best idea seems to be Venus & Adonis, and Savitri – if we can afford it – the E.O.G. I mean.[3] In which case, I think it would be a mistake to start on the Friday (one needs a real 'first performance' draw for that) – couldn't we do the Monday, & the second Saturday (& drop the French mime). I say 'I' all through this – it means 'us' really. So very glad about Chichester coming – that's thrilling.[4] Any news about Edith Sitwell?[5] I didn't see Sacher in Switzerland, but I'm writing him about programme.[6]

Now for a little of our news. Jugoslavia was, in every way, an experience. They are, especially in the North, a charming people; very poor, but struggling manfully, & from what we could see, in a healthy way. They are madly unbusinesslike – in fact our week was really wrecked by being faced with an extra concert (the 4th in 6 days) in another city, which plus all the entertaining, & etceteras – at least 2 receptions, & 2 interviews, a day – nearly broke us.[7] But, in spite of ghastly hotels, difficult travel, & hopeless tiredness our memory of the country is a happy one, of fresh young people, & lovely exciting audiences, adoring what we did. We saw Peter Grimes in Zagreb – not alas very good, but, thank God, enough good that one needn't be only critical afterwards. We went to a reception given by Tito, curiously attractive personality, & met quite a few members of his government, all cultured & sympathetic.[8] And then we've come on here yesterday, & have 4 blissful days off – which really one needs anyhow to get used to a completely new world. It's really the East now – our room in this incredibly new & expensive hotel faces Asia across the Bosphorus, looking much nearer than Thorp Ness![9] It's a bit overwhelming at first, & even the incredible beauty of many of the Mosques & above all St. Sophia, hasn't acclimatised me yet. The cleavages [i.e. divisions] of the people are terrifying – & the dotty, hopeless, money situation: the exchange is mad – a shoe-clean, or a piece of bread costs nearly 3/- at the present rate! How the people exist one doesn't know. We're here till 5th then Ankara for a few days, back here, then – India! . . . I'll write again there with news of that! I'm sure there are lots of things to say – but I'm sleepy & I'll just send lots of love & stop. Peter's writing a long letter to Mary (I'm so relieved she's better) but will add a few lines to this. He really seems a little less tired now, but it's taken all his strength & stamina to get through – 14 concerts in 28 days, plus all that travel & effort! I hope your mother is fine & fit –

love to her - & <u>lots</u> to you,
BEN

Today we saw Santa Sophia[10] which is <u>superb</u>! On Sunday we start at 10 AM to hear Byzantine Greek chanting (I have no great hopes as the finest church along with God knows how much else was destroyed 3 months ago in the <u>appalling</u> anti-Greek riots here) & then go on to a concert of <u>modern</u> Turkish music. What <u>will</u> that be like? At 11 A.M.? Here one's first name is the important one. "Any mail for Mr. Britten?" "No." "For Mr. Benjamin?" "Oh Yeeess, Mr. Benjamin!" It's something to do with the Harem system, I'm told.

Much much love to you. Wish we were in Aldeburgh!
PETER

1 Britten had celebrated his forty-second birthday on 22 November (see n. 7 below).

2 Britten had revised *A Boy was Born* in October, shortly before his departure from the UK. Imogen Holst directed the first performance of the revised version on 22 November in London's Grosvenor Chapel, South Audley Street; the performance was repeated at Lancing College, and on both occasions the work was programmed alongside choral music by Weelkes and Purcell.

   Britten went on to record the revised version under his own direction in January 1957, in a Decca recording featuring the Purcell Singers and the treble Michael Hartnett, who in the same year replaced David Hemmings as Miles in the English Opera Group's production of *The Turn of the Screw*. Britten was to write to Frank Lee of Decca (11 January 1957):

   I think we have made a good record of "A Boy Was Born"; we were all delighted with the singing of the Purcell Singers.

   In response to a letter from Rosamund Strode, who had taken part in the recording as a member of the Purcell Singers, Britten wrote on 14 January 1957:

   It was very kind of you to write so nicely about that wretched piece; not "wretched" for me who enjoyed the recordings enormously, but I am afraid "wretched" for Imo and you all who have had so much difficulty and worry over it. Anyhow I hope that the recordings will be so good that all the troubles will be forgotten – in fact I am sure we shall all be delighted with the results!

3 Both John Blow's masque *Venus and Adonis* (c. 1685) and Gustav Holst's chamber opera *Sāvitri* (1916) were performed at the 1956 Aldeburgh Festival, the former in a realization by Imogen Holst. John Cranko had been engaged

LETTER 842: DECEMBER 1955

Pears's expenses notebook – including the entry for a bank deposit in Belgrade

as director for both works, but withdrew at a late stage because he had double-booked himself (an early indication of the more serious problems that were later to arise between Britten and Cranko during the preparations for *A Midsummer Night's Dream* in 1960). In one of the 'three lovely long' letters (dated 16 January 1956) written by Imogen Holst to Britten at this time, she reveals her intention to finance the staging of *Sāvitri* with £100 drawn from the income for performance of her father's suite *The Planets* (Christopher Grogan (ed.), *Imogen Holst: A Life in Music*, p. 300):

My mother's performing fees have been going up quite a bit during the last 18 months, and if they stay as high as this I shall ask the Trustees to let me spend some of what's to spare on getting some of his music performed the right way.

The EOG was labouring under severe economic difficulties in this period, and its 1956 tenth-anniversary season was to prove financially disastrous: see Garnham, *As I Saw It*, pp. 71–2 and 87.

4 The Bishop of Chichester since 1929, George Bell (1883–1958), who had been invited to attend the 1956 Aldeburgh Festival. As a close friend of Dietrich Bonhoeffer, Bishop Bell was well informed of the German resistance to the

rise of Nazism and was instrumental in organizing the emigration to England in the late 1930s of nearly a hundred members of pastors' families at risk because of their Jewish origins. During the war Bishop Bell had spoken out repeatedly against the indiscriminate bombing of German towns, a stance that some commentators believed cost him the See of Canterbury.

A friend of Gustav Holst, Bell had hosted Holst's Whitsun weekends at Canterbury (when he was Dean) and then at Chichester. After her father's death in 1934, Imogen Holst maintained the friendship with Bell. She had originally put his name forward as a possible Aldeburgh Festival preacher in July 1953 (see IHD, p. 52).

5 Sitwell was to take part in *The Heart of the Matter*, a sequence of poetry and music, at the 1956 Aldeburgh Festival: see Letter 867.

6 Britten did not write to Sacher about the conductor's appearance at the 1956 Aldeburgh Festival until after his return to Aldeburgh in March 1956: see Letter 860.

7 Pears described their experiences in Yugoslavia in a letter to Mary Potter also written from Istanbul on 1 December:

The first part of Jugoslavia was absolutely heaven – ravishing weather – beautiful country – sweet welcoming people – lovely audiences – no advertisements so that you could really see the landscape – nice looking peasants, dear oxen, an occasional lorry with a puncture, stately geese, silly turkeys, bony horses, all fair game for our driver who enjoyed near misses, except for one chicken who had it. Nice old place called Ljubljana with an open market by a fine river, & a nice piano; darling old place called Maribor (we were suddenly told when we arrived that we had an extra concert – oh dear!) with a terribly nice crowd of provincial professors etc. who welcomed us, & a chandeliered room in the opera house, holding at a pinch 300 seats into which were squeezed two hundred standing students as well (my! the heat & the smell) & a piano which Ben played throughout with the soft pedal down & it still jangled like an old barrel organ; then Zagreb, which was heavenly – terribly nice pair at the Brit. Council, & a wonderful producer called Vlado Habunek whom we both fell for & "Peter Grimes" in Serbo-Croat! Very slow indeed, & an Ellen with a cold, a dull production, but a good-singing rather dim Grimes & an enormous loud good chorus: then Belgrade, a ghastly grey hotel, with endless official luncheons etc., questions to Ben (what is the future of modern music?), one or two terribly sweet occasions, a students' choir singing English songs (wonderful sound) & terribly keen & grateful! Oh! it's all been most moving & exhausting, & now for a day or two off before we tackle the Turks!

Britten gave his own account of Yugoslavia to Lord Harewood in a letter dated 9 December 1955:

Jugoslavia nearly killed us, but with kindness, enthusiasm & genuine interest. We really feel for it in a big way. Vlado Habunek is a real dear, & most intelligent & brave. You may have heard our great plans to return there (Dubrovnik) for the first two weeks of August [1956], to do some concerts, & with luck (if the dates work) to take part in Lucretia. Can't you both come too, or do you think you've done

Jugoslavia? (As an inducement, we've left lots of money there!!) Peter Grimes in Zagreb was rather disappointing – the singers not bad (you'll curse me for only remembering one name – Fransel who sang Grimes – the Ellen was Female Chorus [i.e. in a production of *The Rape of Lucretia*], & Swallow [Drago Bernadic] is singing Sarastro at Glyndebourne – splendid voice, but very silly) & chorus excellent – but, oh, the Tempi (conductor is nice but incompetent – Baksic(??) & the production. There is obviously a crisis there, because Vlado should have done it, & intrigue & politics interfered. It was an awkward situation for us, as you can imagine, being bad liars anyhow.

The concert in the Slovenian capital Ljubljana took place on 21 November, the performers receiving 40,000 dinars and staying in the town for two nights at the Hotel Slon (see CHPP, p. 181). The recital at Maribor followed on 22 November, Britten's birthday, and they moved on to Zagreb the next day. They had originally intended to see the performance of *Peter Grimes* on the evening of the composer's birthday, Britten having written to the Steins from Salzburg on 20 November (in a German message presumably drafted by Pears): 'Ich habe ein nettes Geburtstagegeschenk in Zagreb – – – Peter Grimes!!' ('I'll have a lovely birthday present in Zagreb – *Peter Grimes*.') In the event, they did not reach Zagreb until 23 November. In a letter to Oliver Holt written from Zagreb on the day after the performance, Pears commented (CHPP, p. 181) that it 'wasn't half bad, though I don't believe Croat is a very easy language to translate into!' On 24 November the two men had lunch at the British Council, staying a second night in the Hotel Palace and moving on to the Serbian capital Belgrade the following night after a farewell party with the director of *Grimes*. Pears wrote in his travel diary (PRPP, p. 24):

6AM arrival posse of greeting. Sleep all day in Hotel Moscow & concert that evening [26 November] apparent success but agony of tiredness: composers supper after: no English.

These events were further described by Britten in a letter to Roger Duncan written from Istanbul on 3 December:

We went by train from Salzburg to Ljubljana which was the first place we visited in Jugoslavia. Train was packed with people – many going home, & bringing with them lots of things you can't buy in Jugoslavia. One woman seemed to be carrying everything including the kitchen stove, & the customs man made her unpack everything – (customs and passport examination usually happen on these big International trains). One poor man, an American, had clean forgotten to get himself a visa, & was turned off the train. God knows where he spent the night; it was already late, & a pretty terrible place.

We arrived in Ljubljana, & the most surprising thing was no cars (or practically none) – certainly no taxis. We got a porter to wheel our luggage to the Hotel on a barrow . . . Jugoslavia you see is very poor. They have had terrible wars, civil & foreign, but, as far as one can judge, are being very brave and honest about building it up – necessities (new houses) first, & luxuries (cars, & paint, & new hotels) later. The only luxuries they allow, if you call them so, are the arts. They adore music, &

```
                KONCERTNA POSLOVALNICA
                MARIBOR


                    PETER PEARS
                    TENOR

                    BENJAMIN BRITTEN
                    KLAVIR

                    DUO IZ LONDONA
```

1. J. Haydn:
   PET ANGLEŠKIH PESMI
   Mornarjeva pesem
   Naklonjenost
   Nikoli ni govorila o svoji
       ljubezni
   Prodorni pogled

2. F. Schubert:
   PET PESMI
   Na mostu
   Spomladi
   Spev nad vodo
   Noč in sanje
   Sin muz

   ✶

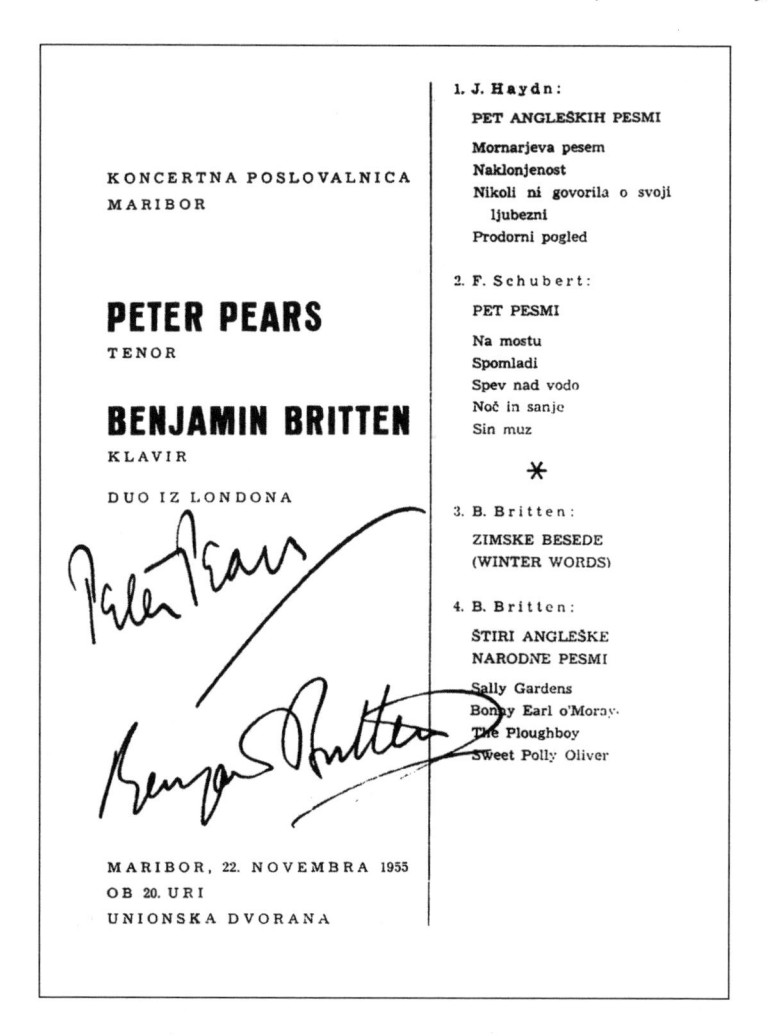

3. B. Britten:
   ZIMSKE BESEDE
   (WINTER WORDS)

4. B. Britten:
   ŠTIRI ANGLEŠKE
   NARODNE PESMI
   Sally Gardens
   Bonny Earl o'Moray
   The Ploughboy
   Sweet Polly Oliver

```
                MARIBOR, 22. NOVEMBRA 1955
                OB 20. URI
                UNIONSKA DVORANA
```

flock to their operas & concerts – & the wonderful thing about concerts there is that most of the audience is very young. At one concert people stood all round the sides, up in galleries, & even on the platform (just behind me was a little boy, not more than 10, who stood dead-still for the whole programme!). We were supposed to do three concerts there (in Jugoslavia), but when we arrived they said: "O yes, concerts in Lujbljana, Zagreb, & Belgrade, & of course Maribor tomorrow." We said: "What, where" – we'd never heard of Maribor – but they said: "O yes, all arranged, & sold out; you must go" – we said, "We can't, that's too many concerts" – they said, "Please, please" – so of course we had to go; but luckily the British Council chap sent us in a car which took two hours, instead of a dirty train taking five – so it wasn't so bad, but more than we'd bargained for! Everywhere we went we met nice, friendly people, but all terribly poor. I expect your father or George & Marion [Harewood] after they came back from Dubrovnik said the same thing. But I'd

26 (*top*) Benjamin Britten, Ronald Duncan and Peter Pears on their way to Aldeburgh's public tennis courts

27 (*left*) Britten marking out the grass tennis court at the Red House, Aldeburgh

28 (*above*) The Red House, 1950s. Britten, partnered by Mary Potter, playing tennis when the house still belonged to Mary Potter and her husband, Stephen

29 (*top left*) Journey East, 1955–56: Pears and Britten

30 (*above left*) 20 January 1956, Ubud, Bali: Pears, the Hesses and Britten pose in traditional Balinese costume. Princess Margaret wrote the next day that 'Ben [. . .] looked like a governess at a fancy dress. Peter looked like a Rhine maiden and Lu like a *Fasching* Rajah! We laughed so much we could hardly be photographed!'

31 (*top right*) Britten in Tenganan, a village in the hills to the east of Bali

32 (*right*) Bali, 1956: a young girl is given a dancing lesson to the accompaniment of a gamelan

33 (*above left*) Britten playing the *shō*, with encouragement from Kei-ichi Kurosawa, Tokyo, February 1956

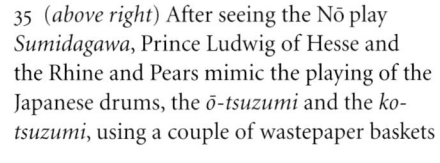

34 (*top right*) 8 February 1956, Tokyo: Pears and Britten arrive in Japan

35 (*above right*) After seeing the Nō play *Sumidagawa*, Prince Ludwig of Hesse and the Rhine and Pears mimic the playing of the Japanese drums, the *ō-tsuzumi* and the *ko-tsuzumi*, using a couple of wastepaper baskets

36 (*mid-left*) Pears and Britten (back row, respectively seventh and fourth from the right) join the Tokyo Madrigal Singers, conducted by Kei-ichi Kurosawa

37 *and* 38 (*bottom left*) 9 February 1956, Tokyo: Britten and Pears give their first televised recital, for NHK

39 (*top*) The Artistic Directors of the 1956 Aldeburgh Festival – Imogen Holst, Britten and Pears – meet in the garden of Crag House
40 (*mid-left*) A meeting of the Aldeburgh Music Club at Crag House; the recorder quartet comprises Julian Potter, Imogen Holst and Mary Potter (descants), with Britten (treble)
41 (*above*) Britten rehearsing for an Aldeburgh Festival concert; Imogen Holst is page-turner
42 (*mid-right*) Imogen Holst and Basil Douglas
43 *and* 44 (*bottom right*) Noel Mewton-Wood, who accompanied Pears during 1952 and 1953, and Dennis Brain, the horn-player for whom Britten composed *Serenade* and *Canticle III*

45 (*top left*) Birmingham, 22 January 1952: Pears, Kathleen Ferrier and Britten on a tour in aid of the English Opera Group, during which *Canticle II: 'Abraham and Isaac'* was given its first performances
46 (*top right*) Britten in rehearsal
47 (*mid-left*) Julian Bream and Pears in the mid-1950s
48 (*below*) Britten and Francis Poulenc, possibly photographed during rehearsals for a performance of Poulenc's Concerto for Two Pianos, in which they were soloists, at the Royal Festival Hall, London, January 1955

49 (*above*) Royal Opera House, Covent Garden, January 1957, *The Prince of the Pagodas*, Act II scene 2: the appearance of the Prince (David Blair) as a salamander

50 (*left*) The choreographer John Cranko, who devised the dances in *Gloriana* and collaborated with Britten on *The Prince of the Pagodas*

51 (*above*) *The Prince of the Pagodas*, Act II scene 2: the Prince (David Blair) and Belle Rose (Svetlana Beriosova)

52 (*right*) David Webster, General Administrator of Sadler's Wells (subsequently Royal) Ballet and of Covent Garden (subsequently Royal) Opera companies, 1945–70

53 (*above*) Roger Duncan, a snapshot probably taken by Britten

54 (*right*) Roger Duncan and Britten, *c.* 1955

55 (*left*) Paul Rogerson on Aldeburgh beach

56 (*below right*) David Hemmings and Clytie, Aldeburgh, August 1954

57 (*bottom right*) Britten and Hemmings playing marbles, Aldeburgh, August 1954

LETTER 843: DECEMBER 1955 359

honestly rather have a country like that, where everyone is working together, and not where there are terribly rich & terribly poor side-by-side. I know they are communist, but it is really as far as I can see a kind of socialism – a genuine attempt to work things out. I expect you've heard of Tito – who is the present Dictator – we went to a big reception at the palace, saw him, & met his wife, & they made a nice impression. Of course, all of this is only a foreigner's superficial idea, but certainly we liked it so much that we are planning to come back. I'd like to show it to you – perhaps, who knows . . . one day!!

8 Britten's meeting with Josip Broz Tito (1892–1980; President of Yugoslavia from 1953 until his death) took place on the evening of 29 November after a performance by the university choir mentioned by Pears in his letter to Mary Potter. In the morning of the same day, Britten and Pears had made a radio broadcast. The day before had been National Day, Pears noting in his travel diary: 'National day at opera house Tito present.'

9 Thorpeness, as seen from Aldeburgh along the Suffolk coast.

10 The masterpiece of Byzantine architecture, built in the first century AD as the Cathedral of Constantinople; the building was later a mosque, and is now a museum.

843 To Anthony Gishford

ISTANBUL HILTON
Dec. 2nd 1955

My dear Tony,

Thank you so much for the birthday wire & your nice letter which we got in Belgrade. I feel guilty that I haven't written adequately on this tour, & probably shan't be able to in the future either, but it is terribly difficult to find any time . . . When one hasn't concerts, there are receptions, & interviews galore, to say nothing of sight-seeing, & sleeping (welcome activity!). Anyhow, if you can brace yourself for it, when we get back, I'll give you a full description of the tour, with film accompaniment!

Glad things go well with you. I'd like to hear your new gramophone – sounds superb. Thank you for your conciliatory – Boston – efforts – I'm sorry, I thought they were resigned about it.[1] Please give Leslie my sympathies about the court case – really bloody mindedness, that seems.[2]

Since I last wrote we have had a most touching time in Jugoslavia. I was everywhere most thrilled that people knew so much of my stuff, & the audiences were absolutely extraordinary – packed, with tremendous % of young people, mad with excitement. That sounds exaggerated, but it is typical of that country, young, fresh & struggling. I can't tell you how many musicians we met, all eager for contact with us – they don't seem to be able to get music there, & I've said I'd try & send things to them.

I attach a list of requests; do you think you can send them out for me (I'm quite prepared to pay myself, if you can manage the sending???). Peter & I have agreed to spend first two weeks of August in Dubrovnik & Split – & if possible conduct & sing in Lucretia there.[3] Couldn't you arrange to come too? – I can't tell you how much you'd like the people & the atmosphere. I saw Grimes in Zagreb – some excellent singers, poor conductor & dull production: but they were all cross about it, & say Lucretia was much better. All the same P.G. is very successful.

We've come on here – & we really are in the East now . . . We see Asia close across the Bosphorus opposite the Hotel![4] And everything is difficult & strange – wonderful town & Mosques (you should see Santa Sophia!) – but so far our impressions are rather confused & rather troubled. The blessing is that we've a few days off from concerts (not from interviews or parties though!) – rather necessary, because the first 4 weeks nearly killed Peter; however he survived & sang wonderfully. Thank you again for writing, & sorry to burden you with these requests; I wouldn't if I didn't think it important. Is Screw out yet?[5]

Love from us both –
yours ever,
BEN

1 No information has come to light at BPL to explain this reference. It is likely to have been concerned with the Boston Symphony Orchestra.

2 Nothing is known at BPL about the court case.

3 This projected return visit to Yugoslavia did not materialize. Worn out by intensive work on *The Prince of the Pagodas* after his return from the world tour, Britten spent most of August 1956 recuperating at Schloss Tarasp, the Hesses' home in Switzerland (see Letter 877). Britten had, however, at some point written journey times from Zurich to Zagreb in his pocket diary under 5 August and 'Dubrovnik' under both 6 and 13 August: all three entries were subsequently deleted. Britten and Pears were to return to Yugoslavia in the winter of 1959 (accompanied by the Prince and Princess of Hesse and the Rhine) and in August 1961 when Britten conducted *Lucretia* there.

4 Pears had written to Mary Potter on 1 December:

Well, we have reached this glossy glamorous pub. & from our windows we can see Asia! It looks pretty good, as we see it from the 7th floor on top of a hill, and the Bosphorus which flows between is very beautiful with twinkly ships at night, & extraordinary layers of dusty pink and grey at twilight. We arrived yesterday from Belgrade (which I will tell you about later) by plane two hours early in the rain with no one to meet us, and a little Turk was very helpful (he was clearly either a pimp or a secret police agent or both) in finding us a taxi & we ploughed through the mud of half made roads to this great slab of House & Garden. It was opened in June & is surrounded by swimming pools – bedroom furniture by Hille of London, close fitting carpets in lemonpeel, Siamese pink or gunmetal, coffee & rolls in bed costs £1 and a hair-cut-and-wash 30/-, but it's worth it (we hope!) for a few days anyway, after our very gloomy hotel (the Moscow!) in Belgrade.

5 Britten was awaiting the publication of the vocal score of *The Turn of the Screw*.

844 To Imogen Holst

ISTANBUL HILTON, ISTANBUL
[10 December 1955]

My dearest Imo,

Here is a silly little piece for Jimmy Blades[1] – written in the maddest hurry, in the only free morning for ages – – – ! I don't know whether it is what he wants, but he can chop it about as he wants; hope you can read it – could you possibly do a copy for him & send it to him?[2] Sorry to bother you with it. (I hope you'll like the echo of Planets in the middle bit – quite accidental!)[3]

No time for a letter. We'll write properly about Turkey from India. It is a disturbing country in many ways, but also lovely. We've heard Turkish music, galore – & also a lovely Greek sung Mass – but more of that later.

Hope Mary [Potter] is better. Lots of love to her, & Miss Hudson & Clytie,

& of course loads to you,
Sorry to bother,
BEN

1 James Blades (1901–1999), British timpanist and percussionist, who began his career in orchestras accompanying silent films and playing in dance bands. He was also involved in many film-music recordings in the early days of the sound film, including some of those by Britten for the GPO Film Unit (notably *Night Mail*). Among the most universally familiar of his recordings were the Chinese tam-tam strokes that accompanied the production title credits of Rank films and the V-for-Victory signal for BBC wartime radio. He became principal percussionist of the London Symphony Orchestra in 1940 and until his retirement was a regular freelance player with most of the major British orchestras, notably the Melos Ensemble and the English Opera Group. His close working relationship with Britten dates from 1953 when he was invited to join the EOG Orchestra, and Britten frequently sought Blades's advice on how to create

Britten's fair copy of *Timpani Piece for Jimmy*, composed 8/9 December 1955, Istanbul

LETTER 844: DECEMBER 1955

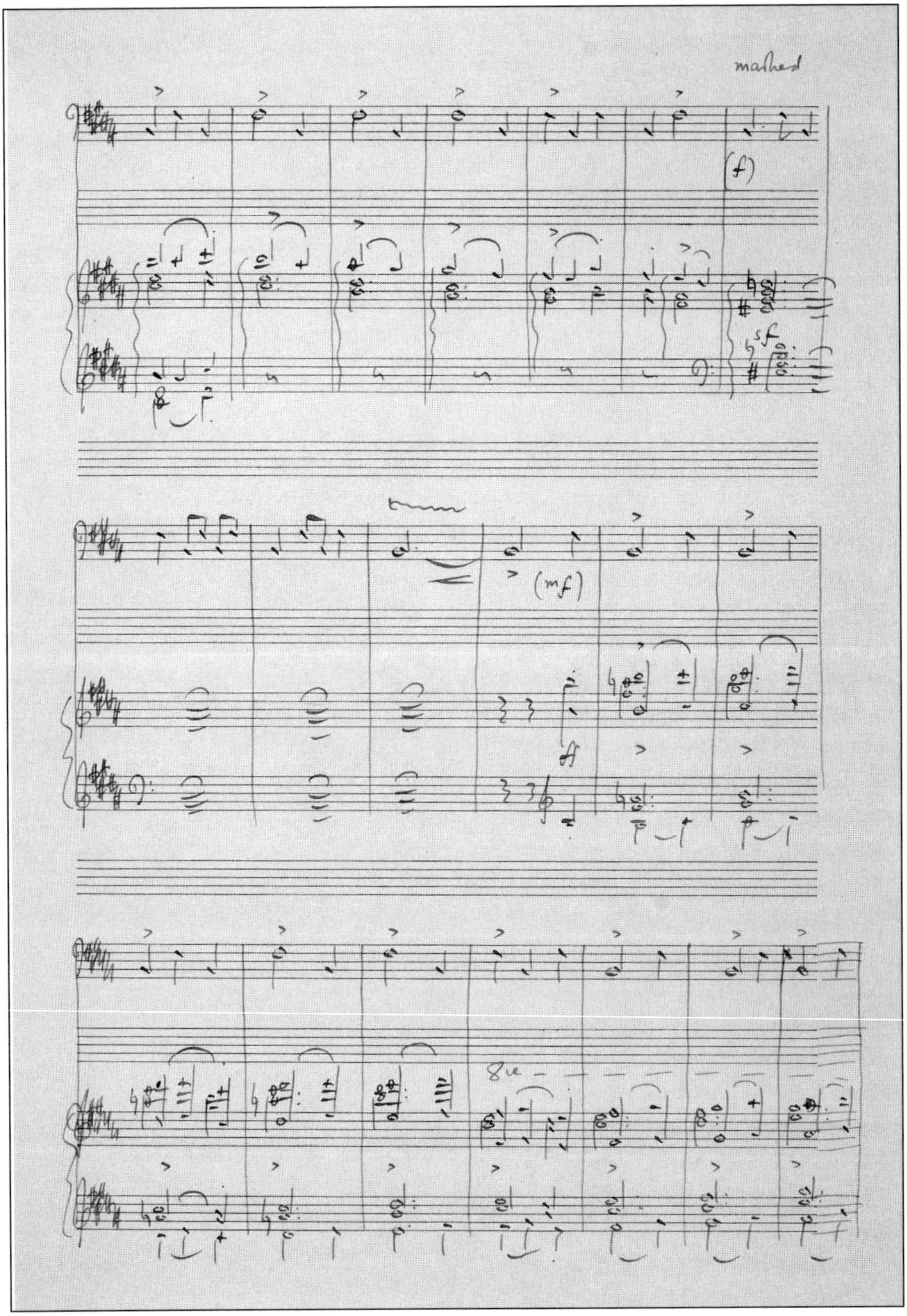
marked
(f)
sf
(mf)
ff
8va

(f) marked
DA
sf molto dim
dim
rall
always dim
(Piano)
pp Ped
(slow)
Then Coda

particular sound effects he had in mind (see Letter 853 n. 1). Blades, who had trained as an engineer in his youth, was often able to devise special instruments with a sound that satisfied Britten. Blades's skill in this respect found notable applications in Britten's Church Parables of the 1960s. Blades was a gifted communicator with children and adults alike (see n. 2 below), and gave lecture recitals on the history of percussion instruments almost to the very end of his life.

Among his writings are *Orchestral Percussion Technique*, *Percussion Instruments and their History*, with a foreword by Britten, and two volumes of memoirs: *Drum Roll: A Professional Adventure from the Circus to the Concert Hall* and *These I Have Met . . .: Reminiscences*. See also Maureen Garnham, *As I Saw It*, pp. 16–18, and obituaries by Graham Melville-Mason, *Independent* (24 May 1999), and in *The Times* (25 May 1999).

In his Foreword to *Percussion Instruments and their History*, Britten wrote (in 1970):

Everyone knows that James Blades is one of our great percussionists. He plays all the various instruments with accuracy and an infectious sense of rhythm, and his timpani playing is noted for its impeccable intonation and beautiful tone. I have been a lucky composer because, under my direction, he has played in ten of my operas, and also in those two difficult percussive nuts to crack – the *Nocturne* and Cello Symphony.

For Blades's thoughts on Britten's inventive use of percussion, see *Percussion Instruments and their History*, pp. 420–24.

2 Britten composed his *Timpani Piece for Jimmy* (previously unpublished) for timpani and piano during his stay in Turkey, i.e. between his first full day in Istanbul on 30 November and departure on 11 December. Since the Greek sung Mass mentioned in this letter took place on 4 December, and the period 5–7 December was full of various engagements, it is likely that the work was written on either 8 or 9 December when Britten's pocket diary records no commitments. In *Drum Roll*, p. 229, Blades recalls Britten discussing the 'sketch' of *Timpani Piece for Jimmy* with him 'on a train journey between Munich and Venice'. Blades often performed *Timpani Piece for Jimmy* as part of his lecture recitals with his second wife, Joan Goossens. Together they recorded it as a track on *Blades on Percussion* in 1972, as part of the series *All About Music*.

3 The work's middle section ('fast waltz') contains a theme resembling the lumbering melody of *Uranus* from Gustav Holst's *The Planets*; see p. 364.

845 To Roger Duncan

TAJ MAHAL HOTEL, BOMBAY
Dec. 19th 1955

[...]

You will be cursing me for not having written before, & probably now writing so late that I can't even send you Christmas greetings in time ... But since we left Turkey a week ago, & arrived here via Karachi (Pakistan), we haven't had a second to ourselves. I am afraid that this kind of thing will happen all round the World – that people are going to haul us around, killing us by kindness, so that altho' we do manage to see lots of things & meet lots of people, we nearly die in the attempt, & never have time to write to you about it all!

Turkey was no exception. Although we flew there from Belgrade not much more than two weeks ago (Nov. 30th), it seems a year or more, so much did we do & see – and I don't know how I am going to tell you all about it. Anyhow ... briefly ... we spent most of the time there in Istanbul, apart from four days in Ankara. Altho' Istanbul is by far the bigger & more exciting town, Ankara is the capital. I don't know how much you know of Turkish history – I knew precious little! – because it is difficult to understand what's going on there without some idea of the past. We borrowed books & mugged up a bit of history, which did enable us to understand a bit.

Istanbul (Constantinople) was until 1500 & something the Christian capital of the East (with Rome the capital of the West); it was then taken by the Turks who had come from central Asia somewhere. They were a warlike tribe – & have never really <u>absorbed</u> the places they conquer, & at one time practically all Europe up to Vienna was conquered by them. The result is that they still sit on Turkey like a lid on a boiling kettle, & in the kettle are Greeks, Armenians, Jews, Christians & all kinds. They still have riots (on Sept. 6th this year, they tried to destroy everything foreign in Istanbul, & jolly nearly succeeded – they burnt 28 Greek churches). You nearly always find that the interesting people have <u>other</u> nationalities besides Turk, even if they have Turkish names. The place is very uncomfortable. There were soldiers round the Hotel where we stayed – in case of more riots; the nice Greeks go around in fear of their skins. But it is a <u>wonderful</u> city, besides. Full of incredible things. We stayed in a large hotel, looking right across the Bosphorus to Asia (to Scutari, where Florence Nightingale[1] worked during the Crimean [war]), & even across to the Sea of Marmora. The buildings are fantastic – Santa Sophia, which was a Christian church, turned into a Mosque by the Turks (Moslems) & then after the Great War turned into a museum by Attatürk[2] (another bit of history I can't go into), is one of the most wonderful buildings I have ever seen. There are other little churches which had been turned into Mosques – the Turks were all Moslems & don't allow any decorations so they either destroyed all the mosaics (the Byzantine form of picture wall decoration) or covered them up with plaster. That plaster is now being taken off, & the result is the mosaics look as if they were made yesterday, instead of 1000 years ago . . . incredible!

But the people live in poverty & dirt, & everything is disorganised. After Jugoslavia it was a great shock.

As I said, we went to Ankara for a few days.[3] That is Attatürk's capital – when he took over Turkey after the Great War, he wanted to have a place less cluttered up by history & moved it to the middle of the desert, around a fantastically old village on the top of a hill. There you meet, like in most capitals, diplomats & Government officials, & it's a bit dull & formal (we had an incredible reception in which we met over 200 people (talking French or German) – & where we stood for nearly 3 hours!). But we saw a wonderful museum of Hittite remains – wonderful carvings of Bulls, & people, made about the time that David was playing to Saul on his Harp!

What was also exciting about Turkey, was the keenness of the young people about music – <u>our</u> Western music, that is. They have themselves their own Turkish music, Oriental stuff, which honestly I think pretty poor & boring (nothing like Indian music), & one of the things Attatürk did was to encourage, along with all things Western, European music. So you have a great split – the older people liking their own monodic stuff, & the younger craving for our stuff, & sometimes doing it well. I met one very good composer, Cemal Reşid,[4] whom I'm trying to get published in England, & one boy (of twelve!) who was frightfully promising & a jolly nice kid as well. Our concerts were a wild success, & were just like giving a thirsty person a long drink of champagne![5]

So then we flew to India[6] – but that must come later – and I must send this off now to you, since we leave in ten minutes for Delhi.

I hope you have a lovely Christmas & holidays. Write & tell me what you do in them. I'm hoping there'll be a letter from you in Delhi.

I'm going to send this scribble off & without even reading it through – so forgive all the mistakes . . .

Lots of love [. . .] to you & your mother & father & Briony (will you thank your father for his nice letter which I'll answer . . . when . . . ???) & from Peter too,

BEN

[. . .]

LETTER 845: DECEMBER 1955   369

1 British reformer of hospital nursing (1820–1910), who took nurses out to the Crimean War in 1854 and revolutionized conditions at the barrack hospital. She was christened by the wounded 'the Lady with the Lamp'.

2 Kemal Atatürk (1881–1938), Turkish political leader who, following the First World War, was the leader of the Turkish nationalist movement and became President, 1923–38, of the new Turkish republic. He was a West-orientated reformer who modernized his country's educational, legal and economic systems, but who largely ignored his own political institutions and ruled as a benevolent dictator.

3 Britten and Pears flew to Ankara at 10 a.m. on 5 December, Pears remarking in his travel notes that they found it in snow. Both men's pocket diaries record a 'cocktail party' on the evening of their arrival – presumably the diplomatic occasion mentioned by Britten in this letter – which was described by Pears as a 'huge endless party of 200 people' (PRPP, p. 25). They gave a concert in the city on 6 December, and visited the Hittite museum on the next day. An intriguing entry in Britten's pocket diary suggests they saw a rehearsal or performance of *Let's Make an Opera* in Ankara immediately after the visit to the museum; a full day concluded with Verdi's *Un ballo in maschera* at the local opera house in Ankara, Pears singling out a 'good Turkish soprano' for comment in his travel notes. They finally returned to Istanbul on 8 December.

In a letter to Lord Harewood dated 9 December, Britten wrote:

We heard Ballo at the opera there [Ankara], a sad experience again – some good voices, & chorus – but oh, the conductor & the production. Everywhere seems the same. Good material, & bad use of it. Most depressing. There's one soprano there they all think the world of, & whom you probably know about – Leyla Gencer. She's a nice woman (we had lunch with her), intelligent, immensely ambitious – sings a lot in Italy & Trieste – but she wasn't really on form enough to judge, that night. But you might keep an eye on her – big personality, good big voice (in a small theatre), ham acting & performance really (but I suspect could be shaken out of that), & I think good technique. Ulrica [a role in the opera] was good, but the men simply unbelievably awful – even Peter hadn't a good word to say about the tenor!

Turkish soprano Leyla Gencer (b. 1928) went on to sing regularly at many of the leading European and American opera houses, including La Scala, Milan (in 1957 she sang Madame Lidoine in the premiere of Poulenc's *Dialogues des Carmélites*), the Royal Opera House, Covent Garden, and the San Francisco Opera. A celebrated figure in Turkey, in 2007 Gencer was appointed by Riccardo Muti to oversee the direction of La Scala's training programme for young singers. In the 1979–80 season she sang the only Britten role of her long career: Lady Billows in a production of *Albert Herring* at Piccola Scala, Milan.

4 The Turkish pianist and composer Cemal Reşit Rey (1904–1985) was born in Jerusalem and studied in Paris and Geneva before settling in Istanbul in

1923 and promoting Turkish nationalism in classical music. He was Professor of Piano at the Istanbul Conservatory, Director of Music at Ankara Radio and responsible for the foundation of the Istanbul Philharmonic Orchestra. He wrote primarily piano and chamber music, and worked under the stage name Djemac Rechid. Britten had presumably met Rey at a morning concert of modern Turkish music held in an Istanbul cinema on 4 December. Britten wrote to Anthony Gishford on 29 December 1955:

> I expect you've heard about the Turkish composer from Erwin [Stein] (Djemal Rechid) – I hope his music will have arrived by now, & that you think it worth considering.

5 Two public recitals were given by Britten and Pears in Turkey: one on 6 December at the opera house in Ankara, and the other (a morning concert) on 11 December in Istanbul a few hours before their departure from the country. Their other activities had included a trip up the Bosphorus on 10 December, and a private recital for members of the Istanbul Philharmonic Orchestra the same evening.

6 The flight to Karachi via Beirut departed at 10.15 p.m. on 11 December. They arrived in Pakistan at lunchtime the following day and spent one night in Karachi's Palace Hotel before travelling on to Bombay on the morning of 13 December.

846 To Basil Douglas

MAIDEN'S HOTEL, DELHI
Dec. 22nd 1955

My dear Basil,

It is awful that I haven't answered your long letter before this,[1] but the amount of time one has for letters is just nil – so filled is every moment of our time, with travelling, concerts, entertainment, & the most devastatingly organised sight-seeing. We've got this far, as you see from the address, and the interest in everything increases rather than diminishes. I can't begin to tell you all about it, it must wait till the Spring – but Yugoslavia is adorable – wonderful people, young, enthusiastic, brave and musical (nice mixture!): Turkey fascinating, beautiful, sordid, alarmingly tense; India, all one imagined.[2] We lost our hearts to Bombay, & so far Delhi doesn't really compete, although last night's concert was one of the nicest to date, & yesterday we had a small informal lunch with Nehru[3] who is a wonderful saintly man, yet gay as well. We are going up to Agra for Xmas – Taj Mahal in the moonlight and all that . . . ! Then Calcutta, & so on . . . We rather wish we were pointing west, homesickness occasionally hits us, but Spring isn't so far away, really.

Now, my dear, to your letter & your problems. I am sorry that the tour[4] has been a disappointment altho' I hear excellent <u>outside</u> reports of it. I do hope the Court goes well, & that financially we recoup a bit.[5] Give my love to the cast & every good wish. I hope by now that something has developed about Paris, & Scandinavia. I feel strongly that <u>you should go</u> to these places as soon as you can manage it – on the spot you always manage so well. You don't mention Cheltenham, or has that faded away? I hope you got the messages about Aldeburgh from Imo. I think Venus & Savitri the best alternative but I strongly advise rearranging the week so that we <u>don't</u> start the first Friday, but have the performances on the Monday & 2nd Saturday – expensive in fares I know, but dangerous to have a <u>non</u>-1st perf. outside the usual span of the Festival. I think Arda [Mandikian] should be in Savitri, incidentally.

Now, about the larger problem of you & the Group. I feel you've given nearly five years of your time & energy to it, & that if you feel you want a change that is only natural. <u>You</u> must decide that, & we can only grin(?) & bear it! But if you <u>do</u> go, then I feel the whole Group situation must be thoroughly discussed & my feeling is that a new form should be evolved – either a drastic curtailment, for instance merging it with Aldeburgh (creating an ad hoc company, & occasionally touring from there) or a drastic enlargement.[6] I only hope that no decision need be taken till we come back, that you are able to push through at least one more year (achieving your particular babies, the Scandinavian & U.S.A. tours),[7] exploiting Lennox's new opera,[8] & further exploiting the Screw. But of course you mustn't miss any opportunities that may arise.

I can't help feeling that a lot of your depression may have arisen (I hope it's gone now!) from, apart from the Let's Make tour, outside causes, your really worrying time with your mother & the house, & possibly your health – because you have really done superbly this year, & you may be sure that we all feel that no one could ever adequately replace you. It is of course difficult for you that Peter & I are away, that won't happen for so long ever again. But you are quite right that as the Group now stands, it shouldn't rely so much on our active participation (it'll always have our interest & responsibility). But I must re-emphasise that if an ideal job for you comes along (if the BBC Television materialises) you must take it, & between us we'll find a way of coping with the immediate problems.

About Blickling.[9] I am afraid Peter & I cannot do August Bank Holiday. We have agreed to spend two weeks in Dubrovnik & Split (taking part in Lucretia, 2 concerts & a holiday), after Peter finishes with Ansbach. But why won't Whitsun do? If Paris materialises the dates I've got are 26th–28th (the following weekend) & we can easily do the Screw (if the cast's the same) in 2 days. Even if the Amadeus [String Quartet] can't do that, Thelma de Chair[10] agrees to 2 concerts only, & if necessary we can think up new programmes. Peter is writing direct to her, & making other suggestions of dates, but we feel Whitsun is still best.

I hope you've got the future addresses from Jeremy [Cullum] – the last month may be slightly reshuffled, but we'll let him know every change. I do hope he's been some use in the office, but there's been an ominous silence about all that!

This will be too late for Christmas, but we do wish you, Martyn [Webster] & your mother a very happy New Year – let's hope it'll see happy solutions to at any rate <u>most</u> of our problems!

With lots of love from us both,
Yours ever,
BEN

1 Douglas had written to Britten on 3 December 1955 during the English Opera Group's visit to Norwich to lament the loss of over £800 in box-office takings due to poor ticket sales. He ventured to suggest in his letter that perhaps the time had now come for Britten 'to find someone stronger than myself who can manage the Group's fortunes more independently', and that he had been contemplating taking a job with the BBC as the organization's first Head of Television Music. As Maureen Garnham has noted, when the relationship between Douglas and Britten finally broke down irreparably two years after the present letter was written, the composer was quick to remind Douglas of this earlier correspondence: see Letter 908.

2 For a full account of Britten's activities in India, see Letters 847 and 848.

3 Jawaharlal Nehru (1889–1964), Indian political leader and statesman, who was the the first person to hold the office of Prime Minister in India after its independence from the UK (from 1947 until his death).

4 The EOG took *Let's Make an Opera* on tour between October and December, giving a week of performances at each of the following cities: Cambridge (Arts Theatre), Oxford (Playhouse), Bath (Theatre Royal), Norwich (Theatre Royal) and Birmingham (Alexandra Theatre). At the conclusion of the tour, the production received a month-long run at London's Royal Court Theatre.

5 The four-week run of performances of *Let's Make an Opera* at the Royal Court Theatre, Sloane Square, did not secure the EOG as much revenue as the composer had hoped. Audiences in the week before Christmas were 'dismal', and by the end of the season on 19 January 1956 only £105 in profits had been made (see Garnham, *As I Saw It*, p. 66). Further complications were caused by the sudden attempt of David Hemmings's father to have his son's fee increased by a third (ibid.).

6 The future of the EOG was to be decided in 1957, when Douglas's post was not renewed by Britten and the composer (characteristically) avoided explaining the situation to him personally: see Letter 908 For further information on the Group's financial problems at this time, see Garnham, *As I Saw It*, pp. 90–91 and 96.

7 Basil Douglas had spent a holiday in Scandinavia in the summer of 1955, during which he had begun negotiating with several local agents and theatre directors in Stockholm and Copenhagen; these negotiations soon came to naught owing to the expensive nature of touring even chamber operas abroad (see Garnham, *As I Saw It*, p. 75). The EOG was to tour Canada in 1957 (see Letters 901–5), and the possibility of a tour to the USA was still under discussion in 1958, although this idea foundered (ibid., p. 93).

8 Lennox Berkeley's *A Dinner Engagement*.

9 Blickling Hall, Norfolk (by tradition the birthplace of Anne Boleyn, Henry VIII's second wife and mother of Elizabeth I), where Douglas was trying to fix a performance for the EOG or Pears and Britten (it remains unclear) at the request of Thelma de Chair (see n. 10 below).

10 Thelma de Chair, née Arbuthnot (1911–1974), divorced from Somerset Struben de Chair, Conservative MP for South-West Norfolk. She remarried in 1960, another Tory MP, Major Sir Jocelyn Morton Lucas.

847 To Mary Potter

MAIDEN'S HOTEL, DELHI
Dec. 23rd 1955

My very dear Mary,

Your lovely Christmas card has just arrived, & you've no idea how homesick it has made us feel – for you, Aldeburgh, Zermatt,[1] & Europe! It's a lovely little Potter, & will go around with us everywhere we go, you may be sure! . . . We shan't throw that away. I hope you'll have got a collective telegram for Christmas from us – sorry it was so 'collective', but honestly cables are rather expensive, & rupees a bit on the short side; we hope you didn't mind a few telephone calls, but didn't expect you to ring up all the Friends of the Festival, nor all the Music Club!

We'll be spending our Christmas at Agra, looking at the Taj Mahal. We have a few days off between our concerts here & in Calcutta, & are having a lovely time lazing in the sun & sight-seeing.[2] India, I'm afraid, has rather bowled us over. To start with, the heat – we left Istanbul in the cold (we'd had 10° of Frost in Ankara, & snow) & arrived in the sweltering heat of Bombay. But it wasn't really only the physical warmth, it was the warmth of the people & the landscape. They're so relaxed & calm, & much is incredibly beautiful – if poor & dirty too; somehow squalor is less squalid there, though tragic, since (especially further South) they have this tremendous dignity. We haven't seen much art yet – some caves, with remarkable, complicated sculptures (much less ponderous than it looked in photos).[3]

Yesterday we had our first real taste of Indian music, & it was tremendously fascinating.[4] We had the luck to hear one of the best living performers (composer too), & he played in a small room to us alone – which is as it should be, not in concerts.[5] Like everything they do it seemed much more relaxed & spontaneous than what we do, & the reactions of the other musicians sitting around was really orgiastic. Wonderful sounds, intellectually complicated & controlled. By jove, the clever Indian is a brilliant creature – one feels like a bit of Yorkshire Pudd. in comparison.

We had lunch with Nehru & his daughter[6] – what a man, & so gay too! ... considering what responsibilities & problems, & that he'd just made an hour's speech in Parliament. Imagine Churchill[7] relaxing, petting his Panthers, talking gay nonsense, followed by discussing what he's said – & insisting we should eat some Melon brought by Bulganin![8] – to absolute strangers!

We're sitting now in the hot sun (although Delhi isn't half so hot as Bombay), with the oddest little birds, & occasionally a vast Indian Vulture, & monkeys playing around us. We've seen only a very few snakes (thank goodness) but where we had dinner last night, the jackals were making a terrific noise in the jungle across the road. O, there's so much to tell, but so little skill & time to write it in. Spring's not so far away though, & how we'll bore you then! We may after all not go to Japan; things have fallen through a bit & we may spend longer in Ceylon & come back to the real South of India which we've not yet seen.

This comes with both of our warmest wishes for a wonderful, fruitful 1956, & no more wobblyness & lots of big oils & tiny watercolours –

Love to the boys, & lots to you, my dear,

BEN & PETER

We sent two scarves to you from Bombay – hope they arrive alright. One for you & one for Imo (pink & white respectively).

1 A nostalgic reference to the ski-ing trip Britten and Pears had taken in February with Mary Potter, the Duncans and Beth Welford. During this holiday Britten composed his *Alpine Suite* for recorder trio. Mary Potter injured herself on the first day and this brief suite was written to give her something to practise while she recovered. The suite is dedicated to her, and

was first performed by members of the Aldeburgh Music Club on 26 June 1955 at the Meare, Thorpeness, as part of the Aldeburgh Festival.

2 Britten and Pears were free from official engagements from 22 to 26 December inclusive, moving on to Calcutta on 27 December (see Letter 852 n. 3).

3 The excursion to the caves at Poona, which took place on 18 December, is described in greater detail by Britten in Letter 848.

4 Britten first became aware of Indian music in the 1930s. On 6 May 1933 the composer attended a programme of Indian dance, writing in his diary:

I go to Amb. Th. [Ambassadors Theatre] at 8.45 – ticket paid for by Miss [Marjorie] Fass – to see Uday Shan-kar & his Hindu dancers (inc. Simkie & Robindra – quite young) & musicians (inc. Vishnu Dan – marvellous drummer & Timir Bawan). I haven't seen anything for ages which has thrilled me more. Marvellously intellectual & perfectly wrought dancing. Finest I have yet seen. Music, full of variety, rhythmically & tonally. One perfect creation of Shan-kar – an ecstatic dance. Tandawa Nrittya was a longer ballet with a very exciting fight.

Britten singled out Indian drumming for special comment during the final stages of the world tour (see Letter 857), and Indian musicians were invited to appear at the Aldeburgh Festival in 1958 and 1965: see MCBFE, pp. 214–15.

Britten heard live Indian music again during his return visit to the country in the spring of 1965 (see PRPP, pp. 85–97). On this occasion he visited a settlement of Todas (aboriginal nature-worshippers) near Ootacamund, and appears to have remembered the excursion when working on *The Burning Fiery Furnace* since the musical sketches for the second Church Parable contain a fragment labelled 'Toda welcome song'. This curious melody (transcribed in MCBFE, p. 214) did not ultimately find its way into Britten's music, however. Britten's latent interest in Indian music had to wait until 1968 to surface in his compositions when, in *The Prodigal Son*, he made an explicit borrowing from a gramophone record of Indian music in his possession (a performance by the flute player Pannalal Ghosh of two ragas, *Yaman* and *Shri*). The composer was so captivated by Ghosh's rendering of *Raag Yaman* that he incorporated sizeable portions of the melody into the third Church Parable, adapting the material for alto flute. A full transcription and discussion of Britten's use of this Indian raw material is found in MCBFE, pp. 215–19, and Ghosh's *Raag Yaman* is included on the CD accompanying the book.

5 The occasion was a performance of Indian music by the sitarist Ravi Shankar, which took place in a studio of All-India Radio on 22 December 1955. Pears wrote in his travel diary (PRPP, p. 30):

Ravi Shankar, a wonderful virtuoso, played his own Indian music to us at the Radio Station & we attended a Broadcast. Brilliant, fascinating, stimulating, wonderfully played – first on a full orchestra of about 20 musicians, then solo on a sort of zither [sitar]. Starting solo (with a plucked drone background of 2 instruments always) & then joined halfway through by a man playing two drums; unbelievable skill and invention.

6 Indira Gandhi (1917–1984), Prime Minister of India, 1966–67 and 1980–84. Britten was to meet her again, in 1965.

7 Sir Winston Churchill (1874–1965), British Prime Minister, 1940–45 and 1951–55.

8 Nikolai Aleksandrovich Bulganin (1895–1975), Soviet political leader, who served as Soviet premier, 1955–58, during which period he often accompanied Communist Party Secretary Nikita Khrushchev on foreign visits.

848 To Roger Duncan

MAIDEN'S HOTEL, DELHI
Dec. 23rd [– 26th], 1955

[. . .]

Your nice, newest letter has just arrived, full of nice newsy news, & Christmas wishes. This will be too late for Christmas, but with luck I'll finish it in time for the New Year. We're going up to Agra (where the Taj Mahal is) for Christmas i.e. tomorrow we take a plane up there. We've been in India for about ten days. We had a long, rather nerve-racking flight from Istanbul – with a stop of three hours (1 a.m. to 4 a.m. – what gloomy hours!) in the airport in Beirut (Lebanon), & then bumped our way, mostly through cloud, arriving early afternoon in Karachi, where we got out of the plane and immediately started boiling – whew! the heat. We went on next day by plane down the coast into Bombay – India (Karachi is Pakistan) where we bought the thinnest clothes we could find & proceeded to get used to the heat! . . . which after 10 degrees of Frost in Ankara is pretty bewildering . . . it's rather like being socked over the head with a pillow.[1] But we immediately loved the Indians, most of all the simple ones one sees wandering around the place, sleeping on the streets, occasionally standing on their heads in a completely unselfconscious way! There is something lovably warm, graceful, athletic about them, & the women dress in Saris (about 6–8 yards of wonderful material, beautifully draped around them) which is the most becoming form of dress I've ever seen.

LAURIE'S HOTEL, AGRA
Dec. 26th

The worst happened, & I couldn't finish this letter as I had hoped, because of being hauled off to see something, or meet something – if I've complained about being organised elsewhere, it's nothing to India! In Bombay we were literally run by Parsees (an old sect of Indians, originally Persian, who live mostly in the West, & are the business back-bone of the country) & once a Parsee lady gets her teeth into you, there's no hope. They are charming, intelligent, brisk, & businesslike. They hauled us off at every moment of every day, to see the beauty spots, meet the interesting or wealthy (not so interesting) people, to receptions, where we were introduced to about 200 people – Bombay is "dry" – no alcohol – & although I'm not any more alcoholic than most other people, a little gin does help to get through such functions; I begin to wilt rather, without. We were in Bombay about 6 days, if I remember right; we didn't enjoy our concert there much – an enormous cinema, & we both felt that people had come for snobbish reasons than for musical.[2] After all they are Indian, & they have a wonderful Indian music of their own, which we heard in Delhi, & especially after their independence from England, their whole inclination is away from Europe (although they are extremely generous to visitors from England). But one must face the fact that most Parsees are snobs: we had a dotty evening with an old tough business woman called Lady Bomangee, at Bomangee Hall – who talked about English Royalty, & living at Scarborough & Windsor, incredibly rich & absolutely tasteless – her house (with private theatre, and marble everywhere) hideous.

We had one glorious day, driving out into the country from 7 a.m. to 11 p.m. – all the way to Poona, stopping at some caves with some fine but rather obscure sculptures in them (Khala Caves), having breakfast at the side of the road watching a family (all ages from an old man to a very young boy) threshing rice, having lunch in a Dak Bungalow (a sort of road-house for government officials), motoring on to Poona, which used to be the great British military centre. We did other excursions from Bombay, including a wonderful one by boat across the bay to the Elephanta caves (with beautiful Bhuddist carving). Then we came on to Delhi by plane, seen off, of course, by lots of Parsees.[3]

Delhi is a gigantic place – really two cities: Old & New – New was largely built in the 20's as a government capital of India. It is very spacious, a bit too spacious really, & the distances are enormous, especially for us who were living the other side of Old Delhi, & all our engagements were in New Delhi – rather like living in Hampstead & working in Chelsea. We saw lots of nice people, & lovely things – a tremendous Red Fort, & a wonderful Mosque. We went to lunch with Nehru the Prime Minister, a wonderful saintly man, who was amusing & gay as well as being wise. His daughter came to our concert, which was rather a nice one, & a great success.[4] We came up here on Christmas eve to a nice little hotel.[5] It's been a funny Christmas, the first I've ever spent without family or friends. Peter & I didn't even say 'Happy Christmas' to anyone (except a curious couple who'd brought their caravan from England – quite a drive across deserts, if you look at your map); but we weren't unhappy, & had a lovely time sightseeing – the Taj Mahal, you've probably heard of it, is a superb building, wonderfully beautiful – made of white marble with inlays – & with a superb dome floating (or apparently – in the moonlight) above it. We also drove about 25 miles to a curious place called Fatehpur Sikri, which was a capital built by Akbar the Great in the 16th Century, a gigantic affair, & then deserted after about 16 years – no one knows quite why. The place, houses, mosques, meeting places, parliament buildings are just falling down now, completely unlived-in.

I am writing this in the hot sun (December!) sitting in the garden. We have just had a snake charmer doing his stuff for us – not much fun really, rather gruesome; about 3 or 4 cobras hissing away swaying to a curious moan from a wind instrument he played. But we've just also seen the famous bird charmer too, which was fascinating – three little Indian canaries doing fascinating tricks, catching coins thrown up, hopping through rings, threading beads on cotton, selecting little numbered coins – quite amazing. We're flying back to Delhi this afternoon.

~~LAURIE'S HOTEL, AGRA~~
Grand Hotel, Calcutta

Yes we did fly back on 26th, & had a most interesting sightseeing trip, & then stayed the night with a friend of Peter's sister & brother-in-law, who were in Burmah-Shell.[6] All over India are the representatives of this Petrol & oil firm, & they have often entertained us. They live superbly out here, I mean, the average business people do – loads of servants, who are very cheap – you see, the average Indian gets paid still very little. We have a "bearer" in this hotel, & he asked to be paid 3 rupees (3/9) a day, for looking after me entirely (fetching meals, washing clothes, pressing, packing, doing the room etc. etc.) Things seem to be getting better for the poorer people, but it is a slow business – it is a colossal country; one never quite gets used to seeing so many people!

We found the nice telegram from all of you when we got back to Delhi on Monday – thank you ever so much for sending it; it reminded us that there <u>had</u> been a Christmas which we'd rather forgotten! I bet you had a lovely one.

I'm going to send this long rambling letter off now – sorry it's so dull, but the impressions we are having are too close to us to be able to see

LETTER 848: DECEMBER 1955 379

them properly. I'm just putting things down as they happen like a kind of diary, to tell you what sort of things we've been doing.

[...]

BEN

[...]

1 A good example of Britten's careful choice of imagery in order to appeal to his young correspondent. The allusion is to the dormitory pillowfights common among school boarders of Roger Duncan's age.

2 Britten and Pears had arrived in Bombay on 13 December, and stayed until their departure for Delhi on 19 December. The Bombay concert, held for the combined charities of the Time and Talents Club, took place on 15 December at the Regal Theatre. The programme comprised six canzonets by Haydn, five songs by Schubert, Britten's *Winter Words* and four of his folksong arrangments. In Bombay, they stayed at the Taj Mahal Hotel on Apollo Bunder, and were required to have an official permit to consume alcohol (hence Britten's complaint in this letter). Other activities while in the area included a boat trip to Elephanta Island to see Hindu sculptures on the day after their concert, and the visit to Lady Bomangee later on the same day.

3 From this point onwards, Pears began to write a detailed account of their travels on Taj Mahal Hotel notepaper. The travel diary may be read in parallel to Britten's epistolary account of their journey, which it often supplements and augments. Pears continued his diary on lined notepaper after they left India, but during their stay in Bali he abandoned prose descriptions in favour of hastily jotted aide-mémoires cataloguing their experiences in Japan and Sri Lanka.

Pears describes their first two days in Delhi as follows (PRPP, p. 29):

Delhi: rather dull flight from Bombay over brown landscape dotted with trees: airport a long way from town: drive in with Parsee lady secretary of Music Club & Sikh founder, late of Cambridge: have chosen to stay at Hotel in old Delhi, miles from New Delhi, which is modern centre: pity in certain ways, involves long drives in every direction: nice old Cheltenham type hotel, large rooms; much cooler here than Bombay, downright cold in evenings, no question of thin suits: nice British Council Robinsons, helpful: afraid we are bad sight seers, always arrive at a mosque five minutes before closing time; easily daunted by distances, e.g. Red Fort v. impressive (& red) from outside but vast. Can one face tramping all through its interior? Sikh gentleman kindly lends car, reception for us at Gymkhana Club [on 20 December], dry (no drink in Delhi on Tuesdays), various Ambassadors etc, nice, supper after with B. Council – very agreeable.

4 Pears described the incident-filled preparations for their broadcast recital in Delhi (recorded on 21 December) in his travel diary (PRPP, pp. 29–30):

Concert on Wednesday went well in pleasant small Y.W.C.A. hall [the Constantia Hall]. Nice Indian situation – wonderful new Bösendorfer concert grand bought a year ago, always tuned by one particular tuner, but piano was moved by a certain firm who insisted on their tuner doing the piano. So when we arrived to rehearse, No. 1. was in middle of tuning; we stopped him & worked & balanced for radio; enter No. 2 tuner: everyone busy hiding one from t'other: delicate situation, unsolved. Also memorable moment in evening – P & B arrive for concert, glance at piano & mike to make sure in same place, Indian radio-lady at first sure not moved but P. thinks it has been, Indian r-lady worried suggests re-balance; as audience in hall already, r-l draws curtain behind mike, P & B utter a few chords & squeaks ppp with thick curtain between music and mike; radio-lady eagerly listening with headphones 2½ yards off-stage, expresses complete satisfaction. Stifled laughter from P. & B. Next day two minutes of tape recording showed Indian radio-lady's balance-judgement not reliable. Invitation to tea next day by I.r-l. (name Mrs. Dutt): accepted: went & were treated to many sandwiches & rich cake, in company with Indian general and others, also 2 Americans. Hostess played on piano excerpts from Ballet written for Pavlova! also sang long song about the Ascent of the Soul: music mixture of Alec Rowley and Ketèlbey: composer said sadly, coyly. "I try to fuse Indian ragas with Harmony. I am a Rebel!" This tea-party mercifully was preceded by an hour or more of the real thing.

5   At Agra, where they stayed from Christmas Eve until Boxing Day when they returned to Delhi for one last night before moving on to Calcutta on 27 December. Pears provides a full account of the Agra excursion in his travel diary (PRPP, pp. 31–2):

Awoken at 6.45, we take a small aeroplane (a Heron) from one of the Delhi aerodromes. Confusion intense at getting off from hotel, paying bill etc. Tips are a burning problem in India; there is a row of entirely unknown faces, eager, perhaps worthy, people who have cleaned one's shoes, washed one's clothes, mended them, dusted one's room, brought breakfast, laid the fire, made the bed, lift boys, porters, waiters, all different, how many does one tip & how much? Embarrassment on all sides. B and P mutter furiously "Have you any small change?" "I've told you once, No!" Finally one tips two people far far too much & the others not at all. Impossibly difficult.

Journey to Agra all right over progressively more fertile plain: signs of floods but not excessive. Arrival at nice colonial-style hotel. Snake charmer immediately noticeable, with python & mongoose. Whenever B or P are visible on way to or from room, he blows a squirl at us from his absurd shawm. Irresistible. When will we succumb? Arrange to visit Taj [Mahal] with dear old guide, in taxi, also Red Fort. Both turn out v. impressive. Red Fort vast walled palace built by Akbar in 1569(?) in red sandstone: ravishing marble mosque-let & wonderful carved lattice screens. Taj quite perfect, noble elegy: gentle and not oversize: exquisite inlay work throughout: dome superb & yet not oppressive. Late lunch, lazed in garden all afternoon. Early to bed. Hotel has several (10?) English guests. We don't speak.

Dogs bark loudly most of night; uncomfortable beds, pillows filled with cotton-wool rocks. B. sleeps little: P. enough. Tea brought by ex-Sepoy at 7.30 A.M. After breakfast, off with guide in taxi to Fatehpur Sikri, Akbar's capital for 16 years, built in 20(?) years employing 20,000 workmen: vast city, depressing, only beautiful thing, tomb of Holy Saint who foretold Akbar's son, in marble again. Gosh! how good marble is compared to red sand-stone? Man dived from roof 70ft. into dirty water for us: curious what tourists pay for! Back for Christmas Day lunch; mince-pies etc. Forced into conversation with British pair, man & wife, doctors, caravanning from London to Singapore; Druids, prefer Stonehenge to Taj Mahal; hair-raising stories of punctures in Afghanistan, etc: very odd: on to Calcutta in their Land-Rover. Lazy in sun all afternoon, tea, drinks, then dinner (plum pudding, oh dear, my waistline.) Then to the Taj by moonlight. Too much mist, too many silly noisy people, too little moon, but grand, beautiful, haunting, touching all the same. Another deafening night with dogs howling near & far and a terrible cough just outside the window; Indian music on the wireless starts at 7 A.M. and goes on to 9 P.M. with few breaks. Ultra-lazy morning in the sun. Ben: "I want to do just this for three weeks". Great decision: asked snake-charmer to perform at a charge of Rs 5. (7s/6d). Appeared with a sleepy python, 3 cobras, a krite(?) (you're dead in 20 minutes!) a two-headed snake (rather a dear) and a depressed mongoose. Charmer rather like a one-eyed Malcolm Sargent, limited repertoire; dull tune, snakes didn't dance, merely sat up & spat. Malcolm Sargent offered to drape python round one's neck, no danger, refused; cowardly?

During the wait for the Air-Bus, succumbed to another Tourist lure. Man with three little so-called Indian canaries, attached by the leg to a cross-stick. He frees them & throws coins, rings etc into the air which they catch, they put betelnut into his mouth, cottonwool into his ear, one threads half-a-dozen beads with needle and cotton, another picks up the card with the number you chose on it; very talented, dear little creatures; owner learnt it from his father, produces fat book of references and appreciations, signatures & photographs. Charges 7s/6d for demonstration. Reasonable? Early at the Airfield, we lie for half an hour in the sun in a ruin – not of a 4th century temple – but of an open air film theatre. Oh India! Land of contrasts!

6 Pears resumes the narrative in his travel diary, describing the return to Delhi on 26 December (PRPP, pp. 32–3):

Good flight to Delhi, met by nice Eric da Costa, Economist, who motors us to see two more of the 9 (at least) cities which have been built on or near Delhi in 1000 years. Very curious tower called Q'tub [Qutab] Minar – part of vast mosque built in 12th century by Turkish invaders – very tall and – as it were – waisted with pleats at every storey – most curious and beautiful effect. Thence to Tuglakabad [Tughlaqabad] – immense fort built in 13th century (in 18 months) – with vast impressive panorama – left empty after 3 years. India full of such deserted horrific ruins, always reminding one of the length of this continent's history and its vast scale and senselessness.

Stayed the night with Philip Wade of Burmah-Shell in house which used to be inhabited by my brother-in-law John [Blackwell, married to Pears's sister Jessie]. Extremely comfortable, & kind host. Roaring open fire most acceptable. Nevertheless I started a cold which was not helped by 1¼ hrs. shivering wait from 7 A.M. to 8.45 at Delhi airport [on 27 December], nor by the ventilation of the Skymaster which bore us towards Calcutta & which swung wildly from icy breeziness which made one cower under a rug, to blasts of heat which set one gasping. Arrived shattered.

849 To Imogen Holst

CATHAY HOTEL, CATHAY BUILDINGS, SINGAPORE
Jan. 4th 1956

My dearest Imo,

It is awful how little we have written, but I'm sure you understand how taken up one's time is. Even when there is no concert, the days are crammed full of fascinating things, & the people are after one more eagerly than any of the wild animals one sees around!

India was lovely – we quite lost our hearts to it. Of course we didn't see much – only three weeks, & only in the North. But we plan to come back via the South, around Madras, where we gather the best dancing is.[1] We haven't really seen the best of that yet, although we have heard lovely & exciting music: I can't write about it, it'll have to wait till we get back, but I was pleasantly surprised that with only a little instruction, we were able to get so much from it.

We went around the countryside – to Poona, & Khala from Bombay – to Agra from Delhi (spent Christmas gazing at the Taj Mahal!) – to the foothills of the Himalayas from Calcutta. We had lunch with Nehru & his daughter, who wanted your address to write to you; he was greatness & charm personified.

We met some slightly ridiculous Indians – the richer & snobbier Parsees, the pathetic Westernophile musicians – but on the whole we were touched & moved greatly by their grace, beauty, warmth & oh – – – their calm! The way they squat on their heels & do nothing for hours; how I wish I could do it too! We met also a charming family (Mookerjee)[2] – friends of the Elmhirsts.[3]

And then Singapore – like living in a Turkish bath – except when you go into air-conditioned rooms, when one shivers! A wonderful position, but rather ugly modern commercial town. We have to give two concerts (including Dichterliebe & Schöne M.) in a vast bath-like hall – – horrid thought.[4]

We have just had another lovely long letter from you – you are angelic to write so much & so often, & we almost eat your letters! So sorry about your mother – what a dreadful nuisance for her.[5] Lots of love to her. We loved the Aldeburgh news, especially Rhoda & Biddy[6] on the recorders! ... What a good thing for the music club that will be. No news is good news we are presuming about the Festival-opera situation.

There are moments when one longs to be back, but enough when we enjoy ourselves hugely to keep one going.

    Love to all – Mary [Potter], Clytie, Miss Hudson & to yourself –
        loads of it – Happy New Year –

BEN

1 See Letter 857 n. 8.

2 The family of the Indian businessman and politician Sir Birendra Nath Mookerjee (1899–1982) and his wife Lady Ranu Mookerjee. When she was sixteen years old, Ranu Mookerjee had been a companion to Rabindranath Tagore, the Indian educationalist, poet and social reformer, following his wife's death: see Michael Young, *The Elmhirsts of Dartington: The Creation of an Utopian Community*, p. 88. In his travel diary, Pears describes the encounter with the Mookerjees (PRPP, p. 33):

> Pleasant dinner at Lady Mookerjee's (friend of Leonard Elmhirst). Family of son, daughter & d-in-law, all arguing furiously and presto about everything. Sir Brien [*sic*] M. holds forth lengthily about finance & socialism. House built 1880? full of wild Victorian pictures & furniture, surprising since Lady M. is a great patron of contemporary painting.

3 Leonard Elmhirst (1893–1974), British agricultural economist and philanthropist, and his American-born wife Dorothy (1887–1968), who was a notable patron of the arts and of education. For four years, beginning in 1921, Elmhirst worked in India with Tagore and he maintained close connections with the Subcontinent for the rest of his life. In 1925 he married Dorothy Straight, the daughter of the millionaire businessman and politician William Collins Whitney, and in the same year the Elmhirsts purchased the Dartington estate near Totnes, Devon, where they established a progressive school, undertook restoration of buildings, and financed new construction and land development. Although he relinquished personal ownership and control of Dartington in 1932, Elmhirst remained Chairman of the Dartington Hall Trust until 1972. Throughout their married life, the Elmhirsts, particularly Dorothy, were generous patrons of the arts, and painters such as Cecil Collins, Ben and Winifred Nicholson, the sculptor Henry Moore and the potter Bernard Leach were all involved with Dartington for a time and their work collected by the Elmhirsts.

Through their friendship with Imogen Holst, who was Director of Music in the Arts Department at Dartington (1943–51), Britten and Pears came to know the Elmhirsts, who gave significant financial support to the English Opera Group, particularly in its earliest days (see Letter 504 n. 3). Britten and Pears often visited Dartington to give recitals, and several Britten works received early performances there. Britten composed his *Five Flower Songs*, for unaccompanied chorus, to celebrate the Elmhirsts' silver wedding anniversary in 1950; all five songs received their first performance at Dartington Hall on 23 July 1950, when they were given by a student choir conducted by Imogen Holst, though Rosamund Strode (who was herself at Dartington at that time and took part in the performances) recollects that some of the songs had already been performed on the anniversary itself (3 April 1950). As Britten explains in Letter 707, the *Five Flower Songs* 'were written about flowers because they [the Elmhirsts] are both keen amateur botanists'.

After the death of his first wife, in 1972 Leonard Elmhirst married Susanna Isaacs, daughter of Hubert Foss (see Diary for 29 February 1932, n. 1), the founding editor of the Oxford University Press Music Department.

See also 1/C3 and Michael Young, *The Elmhirsts of Dartington: The Creation of an Utopian Community*, and Peter Cox, *The Arts at Dartington, 1940–1983*.

4 Pears and Britten gave two recitals during their six-day visit to Singapore: Schumann's *Dichterliebe* on 4 January, and Schubert's *Die schöne Müllerin* on the 6th. Pears wrote in his travel diary (PPPR, p. 36):

> I sang like a pig at both concerts [...] in one of those ghastly good-for-nothing great halls built in the middle of the nineteenth century to glorify municipalities, useless for meetings (speaking voice inaudible), vile for concerts (music goes up to the ceiling and stays there, churned around by fans). The artist's room icy with air-conditioning, the hall stifling with airlessness, sweat pours down one's shirt, and one shouts oneself hoarse to be heard by the poor people at the back of the great hot barn of a place. Ugh!

Princess Margaret of Hesse and the Rhine noted in a letter home dated 11 January that on 6 January (the day of the Hesses' arrival in Singapore): 'Ben and Peter gave an excellent concert – rather too hot for them.'

5 Isobel Holst (1877–1969), widow of Gustav Holst, lived in Dunmow, Essex. Her declining health from the mid-1950s was a cause for concern and involved Imogen Holst in securing live-in companions for her mother: see Christopher Grogan (ed.), *Imogen Holst: A Life in Music*, p. 319.

6 Rhoda Backhouse and Biddy Row, local amateur musicians who were members of the Aldeburgh Music Club. Both were violinists and members of the string quintet with whom Britten (on viola) had played through Schubert's C major String Quintet in 1954. See also Patrick Walker and Valerie Potter, *Aldeburgh Music Club 1952–2002*, pp. 7–10.

850 To Imogen Holst

Ubud, Bali[1]
Jan: 17th 1956

My dearest Imo,

We have just had another lovely letter from you – taken rather a long time to get to us – but everything is completely and deliciously casual in Indonesia – no trains, jolly few roads, & occasionally eccentric planes (as we discovered to our cost, trying to get round Java to do some concerts!) – hence the posts are a bit odd. Descriptions of our trip since India must really wait till we get back – I am really no E.M.F.[2] – and anyhow they would take pages & pages. India continued fascinating, but we haven't yet seen the south, where one gathers the best music & dancing are – anyhow, all that music is put out of one's head by this extraordinary island. We went up to the hills for 2 days from Calcutta to a tea plantation. We came on to Singapore,³ which had a hellish climate, & honestly, except for the kindest people & an interesting bit of Chinese opera, not madly interesting – except for a really hair-raising incident when we went by car up Malaya (on the mainland) to visit a rubber plantation – what heroism to live as they have done for 8 years armed to the teeth, surrounded by barbed wire, guns, & searchlights, against the bandits!⁴ We were pretty scared, especially when our car got stuck for an hour in a thunderstorm. But after a week of hectic concerts & dotty travelling in Java,⁵ we came on here – the island where musical sounds are as part of the atmosphere as the palm trees, the spicy smells, & the charming beautiful people. The music is fantastically rich – melodicly, rhythmicly, texture (such orchestration!!) & above all formally.⁶ It is a remarkable culture. We are lucky in being taken around everywhere by an intelligent Dutch musicologist,⁷ married to a Balinese, who knows all musicians – so we go to rehearsals, find out about & visit cremations,⁸ trance dances,⁹ shadow plays¹⁰ – a bewildering richness. At last I'm beginning to catch on to the technique, but it's about as complicated as Schönberg.

 The dancing would thrill you – usually done by minute & beautiful little girls,¹¹ & of a length & elaborateness which is alarming, but also by wonderful elderly men with breath-taking grace & beauty; & little boys with unbelievable stillness & poise. The stories of Bali being spoiled are quite untrue – in Denpasar (the only town of any size) there are about 8 Americans, & 7 Dutch (& a Viennese danceband trio!!) – but it is quite amazing that it's not spoiled; because the art is so easy, & the people so charming – just too far away I suppose.

 I am writing to Stephen R.¹² about Festival things (had a long letter from him), so he'll tell you anything important. So glad he's being so wonderful – what a relief. Dead silence from Basil [Douglas], Jeremy [Cullum], & EOG – but I suppose that means good news. Wish I'd heard Marsh Flowers.¹³ Love to your mother (hope Munich agreement endures a bit) –

& lots to you, my dear, from us both,
BEN

1 Britten, Pears and their tour companions, the Hesses (see n. 3 below), flew from Java to Bali on 12 January and stayed on the island for two weeks, leaving for Java once more on 25 January. The Bali Hotel, Denpasar, served as their base, but they were to spend long periods away from the capital, particularly at the bathing hut rented by Prince Ludwig at the south-eastern beach resort of Sanur, and at the inland village of Ubud.

Even today, Ubud is a haven from the hectic tourism of Sanur and Kuta beaches which was already well advanced when Britten visited the island. Since the 1930s, when the German painter Walter Spies lived in the village (Colin McPhee was simultaneously researching gamelan music on the island), Ubud has remained Bali's artistic centre: the distinctive brand of Balinese painting its artists have cultivated was profoundly influenced by the Western style of Spies (see Miguel Covarrubias, *Island of Bali*, pp. 160–204). Most of the Balinese music and dancing witnessed by Britten during his stay took place in the vicinity of Ubud.

The party's first night in Bali was spent at the Sanur bungalow, where Bernard IJzerdraat (see n. 7 below) introduced them to the music of Java, Bali and Borneo by playing a number of tape-recordings (LHAO, p. 38). The Sanur district housed many *seka* (traditional music clubs) and during the second evening here Britten witnessed an ensemble of jew's harps at the home of Mr Pandy (a Sanur art dealer) and saw a female processional dance called *rejang*. Both events were recorded by Britten on his manuscript sketches made on Bali, which list 'Gangong (Jew's Harp)' and 'Redjang (Purification)'. On the morning of 14 January, the group travelled by car to a village on the other side of Denpasar (i.e. to the west or north) where Britten saw for the first time a full gamelan taking part in a temple ceremony (LHAO, pp. 43–4):

A gamelan, that is to say an orchestra with at least one gong and one drum, is seated at the roofed assembly point in front of the entrance to the over-ornate temple with its many areas. There are about twenty instruments: metallophone, gongs, drums. They play beautiful, extremely complicated music, without looking at one another, with the sureness of sleepwalkers, while smoking cigarettes [. . .] The gamelan orchestra plays on the move, in a small procession around the region. An old priest mutters nasally from the top of a tall bamboo kiosk in front of the temple. He is presented with flower-garlanded gifts, or they are taken from him. He plays refined finger games, sprinkles the water from the flower-stems all around and waves a small handbell to and fro.

Britten may well have had this gamelan procession in mind ten years later when he instructed the instrumentalists to process around the church in *The Burning Fiery Furnace* and then resume their places beneath the image of the Babylonian god Merodak. The use of bells in Balinese religious ceremonies must also have appealed to a composer who had already revealed a liking for this type of instrument (cf. *The Turn of the Screw*, Act II scene 2) and was to employ bells tellingly in later works (e.g. the handbells in *Noye's Fludde* and the tolling of the chapel bell in *Curlew River*). In *Peter Grimes*, the tolling church bells of the 'Sunday Morning' interlude had been inspired by a specific Balinese source (see Letter 312 n. 12 and MCBFE, pp. 32–4).

The same evening was spent with Mr Pandy in relaxed entertainment at Sanur (LHAO, p. 45):

We sit down in chairs behind the gamelan which contains many bamboo xylophones. The music begins, luring from behind the curtain one girl after another, each of which performs her own dance to the same music. The *joged* 'bung-bung' is unrestrained, even smiles and ogling are permitted. IJzerdraat really distinguishes himself. He knows the delicate movements and is highly musical. One of the trio ventures to dance and naturally looks clumsy and comical, as he should. I am spared, Ben declines.

The *joged* is intriguing on account of its social rather than religious orientation, the idea that onlookers can join in being a unique feature. For information on this dance, and on the others seen by Britten in Bali, see Beryl de Zoete and Walter Spies, *Dance and Drama in Bali*. Although Britten made no musical sketches on this occasion, he included the words 'Djoged (luring dance)' on one manuscript page (using the old Dutch-influenced spelling) and it seems likely that the style of the music played by the *joged* xylophones (*rindik*) subsequently influenced the xylophone and marimba writing in *Death in Venice*. See MCBFE, pp. 232–5.

On 15 January the group made an excursion into the foothills of Gunung Agung, Bali's 3,140-ft volcano. Stops were made at Klungkung, the eighteenth-century capital famous for its highly decorated Kerta Gosa (Hall of Justice) and Bale Kambang (Floating Pavilion). Towards evening the party arrived at Ubud, where they were to stay for two nights.

Prince Ludwig's extensive travel diary *Ausflug Ost 1956* (LHAO) offers a complementary, detailed account of Britten's activities in the later stages of the world tour. Representative extracts in English appear in TBB, pp. 56–66 (translated by Prince Ludwig), and throughout MCBFE. The translation used in this present volume is by Richard Stokes (the first of the complete text) and is available at BPL; page references are to the German edition.

2 A reference to E. M. Forster's novel *A Passage to India*.

3 In Singapore, on 6 January, Britten and Pears joined forces with Prince Ludwig and Princess Margaret of Hesse and the Rhine, who had departed from Frankfurt on 27 December 1955 and spent eight days in India *en route* to the Far East (see Letter 852). On the evening of their arrival, Britten and Pears performed Schubert's cycle *Die schöne Müllerin*, after which the party repaired for a Chinese dinner at Britten's hotel.

4 This excursion is described more fully in Letter 852. Day trips to Malaysian rubber plantations have now become such staple fare for tourists that it is easy to forget how traumatic such an excursion must have been during the State of Emergency that had existed in the country since June 1948. The bandits referred to in this letter were Chinese Communist guerrillas who, after the disbanding of the Malayan People's Anti-Japanese Army in 1945, had, under the leadership of Chin Peng, infiltrated the trade unions and attacked European planters. The security forces under Lieutenant-General Sir Harold Briggs slowly began to restore law and order, but the State of Emergency was not lifted until July 1960.

In 1957 Britten was to be approached to compose a national anthem for the newly independent Malaysia: see Letter 897 n. 3.

5   The party flew from Singapore to Palembang (Sumatra) on 7 January where they spent two days, Britten and Pears giving a further concert. They arrived in Java on 9 January and stayed for three days, spending the first in Bandung and the remaining two in Semarang. It was at Bandung that Britten first experienced live contact with Indonesian music by attending a dancing lesson. The event is described by Prince Ludwig (LHAO, pp. 30–31):

> Siesta. Then Mr IJzerdraat, who is to be our guide throughout Indonesia, takes us to a schoolhouse behind our hotel. Sounds of clapping and drum-beats, as we approach. All the rooms inside are full of little girls learning to dance to the accompaniment of a small orchestra, consisting mainly of percussion. Swinging bodies, hands bent back, gliding, holding. The children in the youngest group are about five years old. Over European children's clothes, each girl wears a batik sarong with a body wrap, from which two sashes hang which they hold delicately from time to time. Zither and flute players enter the adjoining room. Very large zither [*siter* or *celempung*], in the form of a ship, strung above the surface with many metal strings. The nails of both index fingers are kept long for the purpose of plucking the strings. The bamboo flute [*suling*] has six holes, with the mouth-piece wedged into a small opening and held in place by creeper-like string.
>
> The zither begins, as though feeling its way, the flute joins in. I cannot follow the whole thing, can only hear the watery tone of the flute and the wail of the zither, as they intermingle, seemingly independent of each other. Then a song with a forward-moving melody develops, which they play in unison. The pieces end slowly, without any stressing of the final note. Ben and Peter can hear the melody, and the ornaments added by the artist. I lack the ear and the knowledge for such an understanding. The players are pleased when Ben sings them the scale on which the piece is based. They laugh.

Britten's perception of the Javanese scale is significant in the light of the musical sketches he was subsequently to make in Bali and his own specific use of the equivalent Balinese scales (see Letter 851 n. 1). It should be noted that Prince Ludwig's description of the flute may be inaccurate, since the Javanese *suling* traditionally has only four or five fingerholes. See Neil Sorrell, *A Guide to the Gamelan*, p. 42.

6   In an undated postcard showing a beach scene, Britten told the Steins:

> Wish I could get a photo of a Balinese Gamelan to send you – they are fantastic, most complicated & beautiful, & they are <u>everywhere</u>! [...] the air is always full of the sound of gongs, drums, & metallophones!

Britten had first encountered Balinese music through his friendship with Colin McPhee during his wartime sojourn in the USA. For a summary of the connection between the two men and the early impact of Balinese music on Britten's style, see Letter 312 n. 12, and MCBFE, pp. 23–49. Britten's visit to Bali provided him with his first opportunity to witness Balinese music at first hand, although it seems likely that McPhee would have played Britten his tape-recordings of gamelan music while they were working together on McPhee's *Balinese Ceremonial Music*. Britten owned four gramophone recordings of gamelan music (see MCBFE, pp. 101–2); it is not known when he obtained them, but they were all issued before his world tour and indeed before the composition of *The Turn of the Screw*, which betrays obvious gamelan influences in its percussion writing and layered textures: see, for example, Variation VII.

Britten's strong interest in Balinese music is evinced by the care with which he compiled a detailed set of musical sketches from the live performances he saw while on the island. These are preserved at BPL on all four sides of a single complete folio of fourteen-stave manuscript paper; they are reproduced in facsimile and their content discussed in detail in MCBFE, pp. 75–85.

7 Bernard IJzerdraat (?–1986), known affectionately as 'Penny', for a time played in the famous gamelan at Peliatan – a rare privilege for a Westerner. As a musician proficient in gamelan performance, IJzerdraat must have been in a position to explain many technicalities to Britten and this no doubt accounts for the accuracy of the annotations the composer made to his on-the-spot musical sketches.

IJzerdraat's connection with Peliatan, a village situated just to the south of Ubud on the main road to Mas and Denpasar, is significant. The Peliatan gamelan had toured the West under the guidance of John Coast in 1952: the story is told in Coast's book *Dancing Out of Bali*. The gamelan made two long-playing records from the live performances they gave during their tour, both of which were in Britten's possession during the composition of *The Prince of the Pagodas* (see n. 6 above). Britten undoubtedly visited Peliatan during his sporadic stays in Ubud (15–17 January and 21 January): the most likely date for the visit is 17 January, when the party strolled through the rice fields and neighbouring villages. One of Britten's sketches is labelled 'Penny's gamelan (near Ubud legong)'. Britten made use of material from the Peliatan gamelan's recordings of the overture *Kapi Radja* and *Tamililingan* in Act II of *Pagodas* (see MCBFE, pp. 101–9; an extract from *Kapi Radja* is included on the CD accompanying the book). The manuscript sketches he made from the Peliatan recordings probably date from after his return from the world tour, and are written on manuscript paper identical to that used for the composition sketch of the ballet. For an account of the fascinating connection between *Kapi Radja* and Britten's *Young Person's Guide to the Orchestra*, see Donald Mitchell, 'An Afterword on Britten's *Pagodas*: The Balinese Sources', *Tempo* 152 (March 1985), pp. 7–11.

8 Balinese cremations are impressive affairs: poorer families often bury their dead for several years until such time as they can afford to exhume the bodies and bid them farewell with the traditional cremation rites. Several of Britten's gamelan sketches are labelled 'cremation', and they include a distinctive theme which he subsequently incorporated into *The Prince of the Pagodas* at fig. 73 in Act II. This melody undoubtedly reminded him of the second of McPhee's *Balinese Ceremonial Music* transcriptions, where it

also appears. See Letter 312 n. 12, and MCBFE, pp. 32 and 102–3. McPhee's transcription is entitled 'Gambangan': the *gambang* are sacred bamboo xylophones employed in cremation ceremonies. See McPhee, *Music in Bali: A Study in Form and Instrumental Organization in Balinese Orchestral Music*, pp. 272–81.

9   Britten lists the 'Sang Hjang Dedari (Trance dance)' on his manuscript sketches, but provides no music for it. For a description of the *sanghyang dedari*, see De Zoete and Spies, *Dance and Drama in Bali*, pp. 67–80. The *sanghyang* is traditionally presented with the famous monkey dance called *kecak* (ibid., pp. 80–85).

10   The Balinese shadow play (*wayang kulit*) is performed with leather puppets viewed in silhouette behind a translucent screen. Prince Ludwig mentions only one visit to the *wayang*, on the group's last day in Bali (24 January), but the present letter implies that they had seen it at least once before then. Britten already knew a representative piece from the *wayang* repertory: McPhee's first *Balinese Ceremonial Music* transcription ('Pemoengkah') consists of the opening music to the shadow play. Britten made two musical sketches from the *wayang* in 1956, one labelled 'Pemungkah'. On his return to England he notated a scale from a gramophone recording of a *gender wayang selendero*), and 'Pemungkah' itself forms one of the tracks on the tape-recording made for him in Bali (see Letter 851 n. 1). The music for the *wayang kulit* employs the anhemitonic pentatonic tuning called *saih gender wayang*, familiar to Westerners as approximately equivalent to the intervallic patterns of the black notes of the piano keyboard. See McPhee, *Music in Bali*, pp. 204–33.

11   Britten refers to the celebrated *legong* dance, of which he had seen a rehearsal in Ubud on the evening of 15 January. See PFL, plate 297. The occasion was described in detail by Prince Ludwig (LHAO, pp. 49–50):

Already during dinner we could hear in the distance a gurgling and grumbling: the gamelan rehearsing. We then walk with torches through the pitch-black, slippery night into a little hall with bamboo walls, where the entire orchestra of about thirty or forty players is squatting on the ground and hammering away under paraffin lamps. The noise in the small space was sometimes simply deafening. Then the *legong* is rehearsed – at which point five little girls appear and perform for about forty-five minutes a strictly choreographed dance, in which they move delicately and decoratively exactly like insects. At the end they are bathed in sweat [...] Basic position: feet turned outwards, knees bent, shoulder-blades back, arms held horizontally outwards, hands bent back with fluttering fingers. The children, who seem to dance for ever, as well as the continually rising and fading storm of the rhythmical gamelan in the little hall, remain unforgettable.

Britten returned to see the *legong* rehearsal again on the following day, and on 21 January he watched another *legong* specially organized for him by Çokorde Gde Agung in Kuta. The 'Ubud-legong' figures more than once in

Britten's manuscript sketches. For a description of the dance, see De Zoete and Spies, *Dance and Drama in Bali*, pp. 218–32; the musical accompaniment is discussed by Colin McPhee in *Music in Bali*, pp. 150–90.

12 Stephen Reiss had succeeded Elizabeth Sweeting as Secretary of the Aldeburgh Festival. Sweeting had stepped down at the conclusion of the 1955 Festival.

13 The third of Britten's *Five Flower Songs*, of which Imogen Holst had presumably conducted a performance. The text of 'Marsh Flowers' is by George Crabbe.

851 To Ninette de Valois
[*Telegram*]

Denpasar, Bali
23 January 1956

CONFIDENT BALLET READY FOR MIDSEPTEMBER LOVE BRITTEN[1]

1 The timing of this telegram, which sounds a note of confidence concerning *The Prince of the Pagodas* for the first time in many months, is significant: it was on this very day that Britten arranged to have tape-recordings made of the Balinese music that would serve him as musical raw material for his continuation of Act II of the ballet after his return to England. Prince Ludwig's diary entry for 23 January (LHAO, p. 65) reads as follows:

In the morning to Denpasar, where Penny [IJzerdraat] is recording with the best gamelan in Ubud the pieces which particularly interested Ben. The temperature in the little studio is as hot as a Turkish bath. After almost two hours the instruments are satisfactorily distributed in the room. Two pieces, each 26 minutes long, are played. The head rings at every fortissimo. None the less we are hugely impressed by the fantastic discipline and the astonishing changes in tone and rhythm. We are all drenched with sweat, the artists, who have been rehearsing from nine to one o'clock, likewise. In the afternoon three more pieces are recorded (without me).

The identity of what Prince Ludwig describes as 'the best gamelan from Ubud' remains a mystery: in many ways the Peliatan group would fit this description, but no one connected with the gamelan recalls the event, and (if the speed at which the tape was recorded is reliable) the tuning does not match. In a diary letter to Wolfsgarten written on 29 January, Princess Margaret noted that it was the first time these pieces had been recorded.

The recording session contributed to the contents of a reel-to-reel tape (edited from various sources) which Bernard IJzerdraat sent to Britten on 7 June 1956 after the composer's return to England. Both the tape and IJzerdraat's covering letter are preserved at BPL. The letter reads as follows:

Dear Ben,

It was with the greatest pleasure that I received those four long-playing records you sent me. You have no idea at all how much I appreciate this precious gift.

Your telegram reached me after a long tour I had to make. In the meantime the tapes are sent through the diplomatic mailbag.

During the past months we did not have any good tape-recorders (except mine) in running condition. Not even Philips! [A reference to the recording company and audio-equipment manufacturer from IJzerdraat's native Netherlands.] This is the reason for the delay in copying the tapes, and I am truly sorry for this. Now I have finished them.

Enclosed you will find a list with all the titles. There are actually more than what we have arranged before, among which you will hear the 'katjapi' players, which we saw in Bandung before. [See Letter 850 n. 5.]

Well, Ben, I hope to hear from you again . . .

The tape contains ten different items from Bali, Java and Borneo, some of which may have been copied from the miscellaneous recordings IJzerdraat played to the tour group on 12 January. One track comprises music to the shadow play, a rendering of *Pemungkah* performed by an ensemble from Denpasar which was in all probability the group Britten witnessed on 24 January in the same Radio Indonesia studio where the recordings with the Ubud gamelan had taken place the day before (LHAO, p. 66). A full track listing is given in MCBFE, p. 73.

The most important track on the tape is undoubtedly a performance by the Ubud gamelan of *Tabuh Telu* (tracks 3 and 4), which must have been made at the session on 23 January. (Although the title is identical to that of the third of McPhee's *Balinese Ceremonial Music* transcriptions, the content is different.) On the sketches he brought back from Bali, Britten notated the *Tabuh Telu* melody with its accompaniment under the heading 'Tabu talu' with a ballpoint pen, not the pencil he habitually used in all the remaining sketches. This suggests that it may have been added to the sketches from the recording after the tape had been received at Aldeburgh and the composer was back at work on the ballet score. The melody was directly incorporated into the ballet as the theme associated with the Prince in his Salamander guise. The accompanimental figures were recaptured with the help of the Peliatan gamelan's recording of *Tamililingan*. For a discussion of Britten's use of this Balinese material, see MCBFE, p. 103; Britten's private recording of *Tabuh Telu* is included on the CD accompanying that volume.

852 To Roger Duncan

Oeboed [Ubud], Bali
Jan. 18th 1956

[...]
    I am writing this early in the morning. The sun is already up, & it is as warm as a lovely English mid-day. I am sitting outside Peter's & my room in the courtyard of a palace in this little Balinese village.[1] The palace is owned by a prince who takes guests, specially selected (but paying too!); but it isn't a palace in the Buckingham ditto sense, since it's really a collection of innumerable thatched tents, nestling around a complicated & exotic-looking Hindu temple. Even at this hour there is a sound of a musical gong; in fact the air is always filled by the sound of native music – flutes, xylophones, metallophones, & extraordinary booming gongs – just as it is filled by the oddest spicey smells, of flowers, of trees, & of cooking, as one's eye is filled by similar sights plus that of the really most beautiful people, of a lovely dark brown colour, sweet pathetic expressive faces, wearing strange clothes, sarongs of vivid colours, & sometimes wearing nothing at all. Sorry, old boy, to write in this "high-falutin'" way, but one is really knocked sideways by the newness of the experience of coming to this tiny island in the middle of Indonesia – about half-way between Singapore & Australia – where people live, & things grow, in a way one had never dreamed of. Peter & I have been in Indonesia for about two weeks. The first week was spent doing concerts in Java (the capital island of the country), which were not much fun – in a hot, sticky climate, to enormous & predominantly Dutch audiences (who were even more correct & stiff-necked than they are in Holland).[2] We flew everywhere, in nice fast little four-engined planes called Herons – had some very bumpy journeys because it is the rainy season here (with <u>tremendous</u> thunder-storms), & one gloomy day waiting all day at the <u>air-port</u> at Bandung, because the plane failed to turn up, & of course there was no telephone to ring up with. We came on to Indonesia from Singapore, & to there from Calcutta, & there from Delhi where I think I last wrote to you from – so I'd better tell you a bit about Calcutta.
    Calcutta[3] is an enormous sprawling city – millions & millions of people living on top of each other. It was hot, but not so hot as Bombay. We did the usual concert in a large (but quite nice) cinema,[4] sweating profusely, the usual broadcast, with old-fashioned microphones casually shoved around the place, on an old & badly tuned piano;[5] and of course the usual round of cocktail parties & receptions meeting English business people, some stuffy some nice, sympathetic Indians very nervous, & talking, talking oneself hoarse & drinking too much to give oneself courage. But the

nicest thing we did was to go up to the foot-hills of the Himalayas to a tea plantation. A fan of ours wrote to us out of the blue suggesting we should go, & we got up one morning at 2.15 caught a plane at 4.0 (a very rickety old jungly aeroplane) & landed on a large field near some wonderful hills, & were driven by our friend for about an hour through real jungle, seeing monkeys, jungle cocks, deer – & hearing the strangest noises & cries.[6] We spent a day going over the tea plantation, & went in the afternoon to a look-out in the jungle to see if any wild animals were about. We heard elephants, but apart from some incredible birds, large & highly coloured, didn't see anything new. We did see Katchenjunga, the second biggest mountain in the world, gleaming through the clouds; & met someone who'd seen the tracks of the Abominable Snowman, who actually <u>does</u> exist . . . a kind of large near-human ape.

We flew all through the night to Singapore and arrived in blazing, & dripping, humid heat.[7] It is an enormous modern city, built on swamps; a tremendous international port, with a mixed population, predominantly Chinese. We didn't like our concerts there much – in an enormous, old-fashioned hall, hot as anything – called Victoria Memorial Hall. We met nice people who took us around; stayed in a modern hotel with air-conditioning so cold, that indoors we froze & outdoors we boiled – & got colds as a result! – – Sore throats on the Equator! One day we drove up on to the mainland of Malaya for about 30 miles, right into the bandit country, to see a rubber plantation. There's been a war on for about 8 years with the bandit-communists – who were more-or-less started by the British in the war to fight the Japanese, & of course now fight the British! – & we had a taste of what it's like to live always armed, & in fear of one's life. The manager of the estate met us in an armed car, with soldiers, & guns, & we went on an interesting tour of the estate, but I must confess I was always looking over my shoulder, watching for shadowy figures! . . . (A week before we were there a coolie had had his head cut off, & the day before a car was machine-gunned.) We had no incidents and left in the afternoon, full of admiration for the heroism of the people, old & young, black & white, who go on quietly working under those conditions, – ran slick into the most tremendous tropical rain & thunder storm, which swamped the car, stopped it dead – & there we stuck for an hour! – waiting every moment for the rattle of machine-guns. Luckily the Bandits hate rain as much as we do, so they left us alone, & we managed to hail another car who got through the rain & took us back to Singapore . . .

We were joined there by our friends the Prince & Princess of Hesse, who are coming with us from now on. They are intelligent, gay & very sweet, & it's lovely being with them. So we flew together to Java, where after a week we came on to Bali (where this letter started). We spent 3 days in a very simple little hotel by the sea – bathing in the war<u>m, r</u>eally warm, sea, inside the coral reef so there were no sharks. We went to see dancing in the evenings, mostly done by small girls, about 7–10 years old, the most incredibly complicated & long dances. The music accompanying them is so unlike any we know in Europe that it is difficult to describe. It's mostly played on metal xylophones (sometimes wooden, bamboo), of all sizes,[8] with gongs of tremendous size, long thin drums,[9] and occasionally a curious one string fiddle,[10] & instruments rather like our treble recorders.[11] They have bands of 20–30, always men, sometimes including quite tiny boys. But although it is quite unlike our music, it is worked out technically & rhythmically, so that one can scarcely follow it. It isn't '<u>primitive</u>' at all, & neither are the people. They have been living quite cut off from the Western world, & have a highly organised life of their own, a most intelligent & sympathetic life too. I won't go on about all this now, partly because we've only just started to get to know it, & anyhow because I'm not good at writing about it. It'll have to wait till I see you.

We expect to get back about March 18th.[12] When do you break up? Write & tell me, & then we must make a plan about coming to see or fetch you. I hope you'll have a good last term at All Hallows. Do you have a pre-Harrow exam? Good luck to it, if you do.

[. . .] see you really pretty soon now –
only 2 months!!
[. . .]
BEN
[. . .]

P.S. One of the many things I forgot to tell you was Peter's & my first Chinese meal in Singapore. We went one evening to the Chinese restaurant in the Hotel Cathay (where we were staying); there was a kind of cabaret act going on. One man stood with another balancing on his head –

head to head, [figure] pretty clever! – especially as the man upside down

then played a long, funny Chinese solo on a trumpet! – & then drank a glass of coloured water, upside down too! and kept it down (or up!). We then ordered our meal; not understanding what things were, I ordered three dishes, exactly the same – rather tasteless bamboo shoots & rice, pretty boring![13] But to eat them with chopsticks was awful; I couldn't get the stuff to my mouth, and after an hour I gave up, still hungry, & quite exhausted. The only people who enjoyed it were the waiters, who laughed themselves silly.

Actually, since then we've had other Chinese food, much nicer – shark's fin soup, & bird's nest soup too ... one eats the oddest things in these parts of the world, but often they are very nice, if you can forget what it is you are actually eating.

1 The palace was described by Princess Margaret in a letter home dated 16 January:

> A temple gate and courtyard separates us from Ben and Peter's house. We are 'paying guests' with a Bali Prince who though no longer ruling but has many feudal rights. Each 'house' has its bathroom, a W.C. and bath. The W.C. is only a C. and made out of stone, as if done by Henry Moore! The 'bath' [an Indonesian *mandi*] is a sort of horse trough in the corner and one sloshes the water out of it, over oneself and everything else. No light (coconut oil light in one open courtyard only), no furniture except two small hard clean beds covered with mosquito nets with holes in it, hard pillows and a 'dutch wife' [bolster].

According to Prince Ludwig, the reference to the British sculptor Henry Moore was a pleasantry of Britten's: see LHAO, pp. 48–9.

2 Java and Bali were part of the Dutch Empire until 1949, the Netherlands having had trading interests in the region since around 1600. The story of the Dutch occupation of Indonesia is largely one of bloodshed and exploitation, culminating in a series of sporadic but violent campaigns against the Balinese which lasted from 1846 until 1914. The most important ethnomusicological research in Indonesia after McPhee's pioneering work in Bali was conducted by a Dutchman (Jaap Kunst).

3 Britten and Pears had arrived in Calcutta (on a Skymaster flight from Delhi) at lunchtime on 27 December, staying until the early hours of 2 January when they departed for Singapore. In his travel diary (PRPP, p. 35), Pears wrote:

> One of the features of Calcutta life which we were most sorry to leave was the very persistent pimp outside the Grand Hotel, who might whisper ardently to us at any time of day or night we appeared. At first his words were quite unintelligible, (possibly Hindi or German?) then after a day or two 'You like girl?' was audible, which grew into 'schoolgirls?' (*con espressione*) and then 'English schoolgirl?' (ah! that's got him); finally, in despair, to a quite unresponsive Ben, 'FRENCH SCHOOLGIRLS?!!' We got rather fond of him.

4 According to Pears's travel diary (PRPP, p. 33), the concert took place on the day after their arrival (28 December):

> Next day our concert, in surprisingly acceptable theatre-cinema. Went all right, though I was so hot during first part that I imagined that the great drops of sweat splashing off me were clearly audible and visible from gallery. Not so, I'm told.

On 29 December they visited an exhibition of the work of local painters and saw a performance by Martha Graham's ballet company which Pears

LETTER 852: JANUARY 1956   397

thought marred by 'basically pretentious and sentimental American folksiness'.

5   On New Year's Day 1956, Britten and Pears made a half-hour broadcast for the Calcutta studio of All-India Radio.

6   The excursion took place on 29 December, and was hosted by Martin Hawes; Britten and Pears flew back to Calcutta after breakfast the following day. In Calcutta, they attended a New Year's party at the house of Desmond Doig (a friend of Hawes), where they saw Tibetan and Nepalese dancing. Pears wrote in his diary (PRPP, p. 35):

> We left early, but not before Ben had been cornered by Martha Graham and asked for a Ballett about Heloise & Abelard, to be made as a Coloured Film!

In the 1940s Britten had considered the story of Abelard and Heloise as a possible subject for an opera and a cantata: see Letter 572 nn. 2 and 3.

7   Britten and Pears arrived in Singapore on 2 January and remained in the city for five days, departing (with the Hesses) for Java on 7 January. Pears recalls in his travel diary (PRPP, p. 39) that some embarrassment was caused by their having to cancel a dinner engagement with the Governor scheduled for the evening of their departure date.

8   The various types of gamelan orchestra are composed primarily of idiophones, a category of instruments that includes metallophones, gong-chimes, gongs and cymbals. Almost all the metallophones (generic term *gangsa*) have bronze keys which hang over resonating tubes made from bamboo. When Britten mentions instruments made from wood and bamboo, he probably refers to the *gambang* and *rindik* xylophones, the latter employed in the *joged* (see Letter 850 n. 1) and to cheaply made bamboo instruments (see McPhee, *Music in Bali*, pp. 23–6).

It is evident from the gamelan-inspired music in *Pagodas* and *Death in Venice* that Britten was well aware of the method of polyphonic stratification that characterizes the musical idiom of the largest Balinese ensembles: as the size of the metallophone decreases, so the melodic figurations become more rapid. For a representative example of Britten's emulation of this technique, see *The Prince of the Pagodas*, Act II, figs. 72–4.

9   The larger gamelans include two double-headed drums, called *kendang*, which lead the ensemble. Britten adopted some of their characteristic rhythmic patterns in both *Pagodas* and *Death in Venice*, where he employs Western tom-toms doubled by cello *pizzicato* notes to re-create the *kendang* sonority: this scoring device appears to have been borrowed from McPhee's *Tabuh-tabuhan* (1936), also based on Balinese material, the score of which McPhee may well have shown Britten during the course of their association in the USA. See MCBFE, p. 28–9, 108 and 109. In *Pagodas*, the prominent tom-tom cadenza at fig. 70 in Act II was borrowed directly from a *kendang* passage in the Peliatan gamelan's recording of *Kapi Radja* (see MCBFE, p. 107).

10 The *rebab*, which in fact boasts two strings.

11 The bamboo *suling*, which Britten imitates in *Pagodas* and *Death in Venice* by employing one or two Western piccolos, the latter sometimes doubled by artificial string harmonics.

12 See Letter 857 n. 10.

13 Pears noted in his travel diary (PRPP, p. 36) that Britten's tastes were much less adventurous than his:

> I had been bold and had ordered fascinating things like fried prawns, & some sort of odd meat in rice, but Ben thinking of his tummy had ordered safe-sounding things which turned out to be identical dishes i.e. Chicken Soup with beans, beans with noodles, & chicken chop suey or something, all quite uneatable with chopsticks. After an hour we went to bed, Ben exhausted with frustration and still hungry [...]

853 To James Blades
[Postcard: Gongs]

Indonesia
[postmarked 25 January 1956]

I've heard Gongs of all shapes, sizes, and metals here – producing fantastic notes – you'd be very interested.[1] I hope to bring back some tapes of the music here – fantastic stuff. Hope all is well with you –

greetings from
BEN B
& PETER P

1 James Blades was to act as Britten's specialist percussion adviser after the composer's return to England, suggesting Western equivalents for the Balinese instruments imitated in the gamelan reconstructions in Act II of *The Prince of the Pagodas* and providing the various exotic percussion instruments required in the Church Parables. See Blades, *Percussion Instruments and Their History*, p. 130. Blades recalls that Britten seemed well versed in gamelan techniques and required little help when working on the ballet score; his suggestions were restricted to the use of jazz tom-toms as substitutes for Balinese drums (*kendang*), and a vibraphone without motor to emulate the sound of the *trompong* (personal communication).

On 11 January Britten had visited a gong factory at Semarang, traditionally regarded as the centre of gong manufacture in South-East Asia (see Blades, p. 94). This provided the composer with his first introduction to gamelan instruments, and the occasion is described by Prince Ludwig (LHAO, pp. 34–5):

But first we visit the famous gong factory. In an alleyway off the main street. Black smithies in the building at the rear of the factory, like a thousand years ago. Infernally hot. Pitch black, except for two glowing charcoal fires, fanned by two men with bellows, pumping air from beneath. One of the blacksmiths sits alongside and rotates with a long pole the crude form of a large gong in the fire. Then, accompanied by groaning cries, the tempo is increased, the man holding the bellows becomes frenzied. More cries, a third man, holding tongs, pulls the gong from the fire and lays it on the soft clay of the ground, where three other men rhythmically pound the middle, with large hammers and great accuracy, in order to create the central boss, characteristic of Javanese gongs. Coal, dust and sparks fly up. A shout – and the gong flies back into the fire, to be heated once more. In the anteroom IJzerdraat shows us a metallophone. Rectangular bronze slab with cylindrical metal resonators below. Sweet, flute-like tone. Played with the hand [a reference to damping technique] and little hammers. Another rack carries small, pot-like, round gongs with the characteristic boss at the top and the opening at the bottom. Bright bell tone. Then a large, genuine xylophone of ironwood from Borneo, the best in all Java, which all instruments are tuned by. It has a sweet, reverberating, limpid flute tone.

For a discussion of Britten's frequent compositional use of gong strokes in the manner of the gamelan's scheme of slowly moving colotomic (i.e. 'dissecting') punctuation, see MCBFE.

854 To Imogen Holst

Hong Kong
Feb. 8th 1956

My dearest Imo,

Awfully sorry to have been silent for so long, but – work and play, – one is so absorbed & occupied that letter-writing is too difficult. I had Stephen's two communications about the theatre site;[1] & answered the first fairly fully. I expect you've seen or heard about it, & I do hope you don't think I'm being too wet-blanketty. Quite frankly I was a little alarmed by the reticence of Stephen's (& Gifford's[2]) approval of the whole Theatre project (much doubt being expressed by both as to whether it's a good idea), & without that can one really go ahead & raise money for the Site? That's a kind of responsibility that I can't alone face. Anyhow his second letter makes it clear that the sale won't be before late March, & so major decisions needn't be taken before we return. But I do think the Board or Committee situation should be argued out before. We're so very sorry that so many difficulties are arising over the Festival itself – it's a time of year when they do! I think the producer question, & casting, is safe in your & Basil [Douglas]'s hands. I still hanker after not starting on the Friday, & cutting the French mime – but suppose that's impossible.

Sorry this is all business, but there's so much to tell & no time . . . Bali was heaven, scenicly, musically, dancicly. It was a glorious holiday of 12 days too. Unfortunately the holiday was rudely dispelled by our return to Java,³ where <u>everything</u> went wrong, & I got ill & had to cancel a concert, & Hong Kong, where they've given us 4 concerts in 5 days – blast them! But Hong Kong is a sweet place, very interesting, & we've been beautifully looked after by Peg's charming brother David & sister-in-law (Norwegian dancer, whom you'd love).⁴ We had a trip up to Macao⁵ – a declining Portuguese town, of curious charm. Today, rather unwillingly, we go on to Japan, but it shouldn't be too bad, if I can get over my antipathy to the place & the people. We have revised our return schedule so as to include a holiday on Ceylon, & a visit to Southern India. Jeremy should by now have the dates so I won't bother you. We're not sure yet about the exact date of return, since we may stay a day or so with Peg & Lu in Wolfsgarten – but that we'll say later. It's exciting to think of returning, especially today, when as usual I have an awful bout of homesickness heading for a new country, & when the weather so resembles a glorious English Spring day. I do hope you've managed to keep warm – the cold spell sounded terrifying from the papers. Thank you so much for your sweet & newsy letters, they have been great comforts to us.

Lots of love from Peter – & Peg too
& heaps from me –
BEN

1   The scheme for a Festival Theatre at Aldeburgh, first under discussion in 1953 and postponed in 1955 (see Letter 777 n. 3), had been revived. See also Letter 875. This proposal would fail to materialize for a second time and was eventually to be abandoned in favour of a remodelling of the Jubilee Hall in 1960. The Aldeburgh Festival was not to have its new concert venue until 1967, when the former maltings at Snape was converted into a concert hall/theatre.

2   Charles Gifford (1909–1994), British economist and diplomat, who first came to Aldeburgh in 1954 and was to serve as Treasurer of the Aldeburgh Festival for twenty years from 1956. Gifford was a key figure in the management of the Festival's major fund-raising programmes that led to the conversion of Snape Maltings in 1967 and its reconstruction after fire destroyed the building in 1969.

3   The tour party had flown to Surabaya on 25 January, spending the following week in Java. Britten fell ill with a serious gallstones attack during the last three days of their stay, but not before he had managed to take in two further cultural events: on the day after his arrival he heard a Javanese gamelan and attended a popular folk play with musical accompaniment in Surakarta. Both experiences were chronicled by Prince Ludwig (LHAO, p. 69–71):

In a long, empty, stable-like hall we take our places on raffia mats on the stone floor. The orchestra of about fourteen players, with many instruments, sits in front of us on the ground. Every player has about three instruments in front of him and at his side [. . .] Metallophones, a vertical fiddle, a flute, gongs, etc., similar to Bali, but decked out more richly and splendidly [. . .] The music is beautiful and sweet-toned, heavy and slow in rhythm. I am not able to follow the course of its labyrinthine movement [. . .]

Set off at about eleven o'clock to the theatre, where a folk play is being performed. Large, cinema-like, open-air space for some 600–800 spectators. Stage with painted back-drop and pieces of scenery [. . .] Three clowns with white faces cause paroxysms of laughter. Regal girls and boys speak with stiff gestures and monotonous, tearful, high-pitched voices, occasionally breaking out into bleating song. Noisy Gamelan accompaniment.

The Princess of Hesse wrote home from Jakarta on 29 January:

We stayed with kindest Dutch consul in Surabaya – concert programme a great success and then we moved on at 6 a.m. by train [. . .] We ended up in a smallest hotel belonging to the Islamic political party – 5 beds in each room, tiny windows, no sheets, no towels and the sanitary arrangements were such you simply couldn't use them.

A nightmare visit – our money ran out, we travelled 11 hours (800 km) yesterday living on bananas and warm beer! The 'porters' are ganged boy thugs [. . .] We borrow money from the taxi man and arrived here (British Embassy) exhausted last night [. . .]

In Surajakarta [*sic*] we saw Javanese dances and heard Javanese music – quite different from Bali. Very beautiful and less wild.

See also Letter 855.

4 Gerda Meyer ('Pytt') Geddes (1917–2006), Norwegian-born wife of David Geddes, who had trained as a dancer before marrying her husband in 1948, soon after he had secured a position in Shanghai with the Far East traders Jardine Mathieson. It was during her time in the Far East, first in Shanghai then later in Hong Kong, that she first became interested in *t'ai chi ch'uan*, the Chinese system of callisthenics characterized by co-ordinated and rhythmic movements, and received instruction in this ancient practice. On the Geddes' return to the UK, Pytt Geddes was to become the first European to teach *t'ai chi ch'uan* in Britain, and gave courses at the Britten–Pears School for Advanced Musical Studies during the 1970s. See also her obituary in the *Daily Telegraph* (21 March 2006).

5 For Britten's comments on the trip to Hong Kong and Macau, see Letter 855.

855 To Roger Duncan

> Between Hong Kong & Tokyo
> High up in the air (17000 ft.)
> Feb. 8th 1956

[...]

    I was so very happy to get your letter here in Hong Kong – I must confess I was wondering what had happened to you all these weeks without a letter! But apart from not having addresses, I can imagine you had lots to do in the holidays, & not much time for writing. It's funny to be sitting here miles up in the sky, over the Pacific Ocean,[1] seeing nothing but clouds below us, writing to you, in Somerset hard at work at school. So you've got your schol. exam this term, have you?[2] Don't worry too much about it. If you work reasonably hard, & get the right kind of questions, it'll come out all right. But there's an awful lot of luck in it. I'll be thinking of you on March 6th, or whenever it is. By-the-way, haven't you got a birthday sometime then? Let me know, so that I can think about you then too. Do you want anything particular for it – but that must wait till we get home which will be about March 18th, we hope. I'll fix something with your parents about you coming to Aldeburgh in the holidays, don't you worry.

    It was in Bali that I last wrote to you. We had a wonderful time in that little Island, as I think I told you. We saw wonderful dancing – most of it by little girls aged about 10 or less – wonderful little creatures, doing dances of tremendous complication – lasting ½ hour or more![3] Some by men, with masks on, & one wonderful one where two men together have a kind of lion-tiger-horse animal over them, & they dance a very funny affair, with battles & tricks;[4] all these are part of religious ceremonies acted around & inside the temples which are everywhere all over the island.

    We went to one temple which would have amused you. It was in the side of a cliff by the sea, & had at least 5000 bats clinging to the roof, screaming, fluttering, & occasionally dropping to the ground where two enormous black pythons were waiting to gobble them up. The noise & smell made one feel sick. We stayed many days by the ocean, where we bathed (when it wasn't too hot!). It was protected by a coral-reef about ½ mile from the shore, & they said sharks didn't come inside it, but one evening when I was walking along the beach, I saw three within a yard of the shore – triangular fins swishing through the surf, & then great bodies shooting out of the waves. I was rather glad I wasn't swimming just then, altho' they say sharks are frightened of men – I think it must be mutual!

    I must tell you all about Balinese music when I see you, & perhaps play you some (I am bringing some recordings back with me) but what would have amused you was one Gamelan (the Balinese orchestra), made up of about 30 instruments, gongs, drums, xylophones, glockenspiels of all shapes & sizes – all played by little boys less than 14 years old.[5] Jolly good they were too, & enjoying it like fun!

Then on Jan. 25th (what ages ago it seems) we all, the Prince & Princess of Hesse, Peter, me and the very nice Dutchman who was our guide everywhere, flew back to Java – to the Eastern end of the island & gave a concert in Surabaya. Indonesia was owned by the Dutch until a few years ago – now it is independent, but the Indonesians don't really know how to run their country & get into terrible muddles. Letters, telegrams take ages to get to places, and all the simplest kind of transport goes wrong. We had two horrible days after leaving Surabaya, when we went into the centre of

the Island to a place called Solo, where there was supposed to be wonderful music & dancing. To start with, there we were turned out of our hotel because the President of Indonesia[6] was coming (because we were European, & he hates Europeans); all we could find was a very primitive kind of pub, with no lavatories (only holes, small ones, in the ground); we got lost in rickshaws, couldn't speak the language, couldn't get on to planes to fly to Djakarta, & then, because no letters had got through, ran out of money & had to live on bananas during a train journey lasting 12 hours, bumping through bandit country & past smoking volcanoes! This doesn't sound tremendous when one writes about it, but when one does it, & there are lots of little details one forgets, it's worrying enough to send one to bed with Tummy Trouble, as it did to me when I got back to Djakarta. We should have gone to Sumatra (another part of Indonesia) for a concert in Medan, but I was too ill, & so we flew straight to Singapore[7] & then on to Hong Kong (via Bangkok) on Feb 2. Hong Kong is much cooler than the other places (at least in the Winter it is), & a jolly good spot it is too. It is a series of islands off the coast of China, very beautiful, surrounded by blue sea. It is nice to be in a place administrated by English people, where you can telephone someone & get through, & where you get your letters &

telegrams & don't feel so cut off as you do in Java or Bali. We stayed with a brother of the Princess of Hesse (she is English, & he & his wife are awfully nice),[8] who lives on the main island, high up the mountain. They say that the level of your house on the 'Peak' corresponds to your income! He is one of the directors of a great East Asian trading company called Jardine Matheson. Although not as old as the East India Company, they've been going since about 1705, and they practically run the colony – banks and all. It was lovely to be cool again (although we read in the papers that you were having the coldest spell of the century!) & we enjoyed our 5 days in Hong Kong. We did one concert in a great Cinema (to about 1300 people), one concert on the radio,[9] & one in a private house of a curious man,[10] obviously a pirate or a smuggler; one of those odd creatures one meets in the East, half Chinese, or Siamese, & half Jew or Portuguese. We did lots of trips, on to the mainland, & looked at Communist China over the border, but particularly we went in a boat for about three hours, across the delta of the Pearl River to a Portuguese Colony called Macau.

Macau is a very old Colony, & why it isn't recaptured by the Chinese is difficult to say, because it is entirely surrounded by Islands (all communist) & attached to the mainland of China. I suppose it is useful to the Chinese – it is the only spot on the Continent where one can gamble, for instance! We all went to a gambling den after our concert,[11] & it did seem a silly sport. A chap had a lot of buttons; he made a special pile of some of them, & you had to bet on whether there would be 1, 2 or 3 left over or whether it would come to exactly 4 – and people lost <u>pounds</u> and <u>pounds</u> on it (I suppose some <u>made</u> something, but we never saw them). Pretty poor fun, we thought, & yet they go on 24 hours a day, & people flock to it. (We have just flown over Formosa [Taiwan], by the way, & I have got to stop this letter in order to fill up a horrible form so that we can land in Tokyo, customs, & visas and so on . . . !)

And so we go on to Japan.[12] I must say I don't want to, awfully. I don't like what I know about the country or the people – I certainly don't like the way they look (the Yellow races look very strange & suspicious – whereas the Brown, the Indians, or Indonesians, look touching & sympathetic, & can be very beautiful) – and judging by the difficulty Peter & I had in getting our visas, they don't like me any more than I like them.[13] We had to send cables to the agents, to the British Ambassador, & the [British] Council in Japan, & our agents – costing nearly £50 (really!) – before we could get permission to come here! But I mustn't be silly, & must try to like them. I'll write you another letter soon to tell you all about it.

I do hope these letters aren't too boring for you, old boy – it is extraordinary how things that are exciting to do are difficult to describe – I wish I were a writer like your father! but although boring, they give you an idea of the kind of life we are living, & are a kind of diary, to remind one in years to come of how we spent these five curious months of travel.

[...] I hope the term goes well – work, games, & play and all. How's Christopher Barrington, & the other Christopher [Hewetson] too? There'll be lots to talk about when we meet –

not so long now.
[...]
BEN

P.S. One thing I forgot to tell you about Bali (or did I?) is that the animals there are the nicest you ever see, splendid cows, water buffalos (usually with little naked boys riding them) & the cleanest, finest sows & pigs ever. The only exceptions are the dogs, which are dirty thin & mangy; they obviously despise them. They say they are the ghosts of dead uncles & aunts![14] Shades of poor Clytie! – I wonder who she is the ghost of; but someone nice I think, don't you?

1 Britten would have flown over the East China Sea, not the Pacific Ocean.

2 The entrance examination for Harrow School.

3 A reference to the *legong*: see Letter 850 n. 11.

4 Britten describes the *barong*, a mythical creature of good fortune not dissimilar to the Chinese New Year's Lion. It was on 20 January, shortly after being photographed in traditional Balinese costume (see plate 30), that the tour party encountered the *barong* dance at an unspecified village in the vicinity of Kuta (LHAO, pp. 60–61):

> The gamelan on the ground to our left. Music. The *barong* appears in the gateway; two men disguised as a wild, grimacing lion that has been terrifyingly adorned [...] The drama ends with a fierce fight between the *barong* and the evil demon. The *barong* disappears through the gate [...] A magnificent performance lasting some ninety minutes. The rise and fall of the gamelan music accompanies the action [...] Ben, who is probably the most sensitive of us, is greatly affected by the realistic mad raging of the handsome, murderous warriors.

Prince Ludwig notes (LHAO, p. 67) that on their final day in Bali (25 January 1956),

> Peter accepts from Penny [IJzerdraat] the gift of a whole miniature *barong*. We others foresee endless difficulties dragging along this substantial souvenir. Peter finally carries it beneath his arm like a Balinese Skye terrier.

The model of the *barong* survives at BPL.

5 As appears to have been the case with the Balinese temple procession that subsequently found its way into *The Burning Fiery Furnace*, the memory of

this adolescent gamelan may have stimulated Britten's creative processes many years later when he opted to accompany the children's beach games in *Death in Venice* with gamelan-inspired musical material. The children's gamelan described here was also singled out for enthusiastic comment by Prince Ludwig (LHAO, pp. 50–51):

> Another very large orchestra of boys up to the age of about fourteen. The instruments sound somewhat tinny; the players are magnificent.

Prince Ludwig's diary informs us that the encounter took place in Ubud on the evening of 16 January.

6 Achmed Sukarno (1902–1970), leader of the Indonesian National Party, who had become the first President in 1945. Initially a unifying influence, he gradually drew Indonesia closer to Communist China, suspending the constitution in 1957 and introducing what he termed 'guided democracy'. He declared himself 'President for Life' in the early 1960s, but was overthrown in a coup in 1967 and spent his final years under house arrest.

7 The party flew to Singapore from Jakarta on 31 January and found the island republic in the midst of bombings by Communist terrorists. The two days they spent there were taken up with sight-seeing, but Britten's pocket diary records that on 1 February he was to 'Ring Miss Hill (Straits times about prodigy)'. The 'prodigy' remains unidentified. The *Straits Times* is Singapore's daily national newspaper.

Britten and Pears called in once more at Singapore on their way home in order to give a concert to celebrate the centenary of the Anglican Cathedral on 23 February: see Letter 856.

8 Princess Margaret was in fact Scottish. She described the group's arrival in Hong Kong in a letter home dated 5 February:

> We were very V.I.Pish, Ben and Peter surrounded by press and an interview for the radio. Dave [Princess Margaret's brother] whipped us away into smart Jardine [Mathieson] motor boat across the bay into cars and up and up on winding steep roads to their house on the Peak. A charming house with a wonderful panoramic view [...] Dave and Pytt lent us their room, Ben and Peter the spare room [...]
>
> Next day [3 February] we were again given a super Chinese lunch – really wonderful dishes – very subtle and good tastes. We bought masses of old and rare silk and Thai silk in magnificent colours [...] Ben and Peter, who are really exhausted, gave us another concert, this time to 1,300 people including the governor. We all stood up when H.E. [His Excellency] arrived! Concert was greatest success, encores and praise and autograph hunters nearly finished Ben and Peter off! [...]

The recital took place in the Empire Theatre (Cinema), when the programme comprised songs by Dowland, Purcell and Schubert, Britten's *Michelangelo Sonnets* and folksong arrangements.

9 Britten's pocket-diary entry for 6 February reads 'Broadcast H. K.' In addition to their broadcast recital, Britten and Pears gave a joint interview for Hong Kong Radio's weekly *Music Magazine* programme.

10 On 7 February, for which Britten's diary notes 'Dichterliebe H.K.'

11 The recital in Macau was given on 4 February in the eighteenth-century Pedro V Theatre, under the auspices of the colony's Music Circle. The programme included songs by Dowland, Purcell and Schubert, Britten's *Michelangelo Sonnets* and folksong arrangements.

12 The six-hour flight from Hong Kong to Tokyo's Haneda airport took place in the afternoon of 8 February.

13 If this expression of anti-Japanese sentiment on Britten's part seems rather surprising, coming as it does some eleven years after the end of the Second World War and the natural antipathy towards the Japanese that the conflict had engendered in the West, it should be remembered that Britten's own contacts with Japan had also been less than happy. For an account of the fate of *Sinfonia da Requiem* in Japan in 1940, see Letters 211, 297, 298 and 299. See also Letter 856.

That Britten's visit to Japan entirely changed his outlook on the country is shown by the text of a warm address he broadcast on Japanese Radio (NHK) as a New Year's message on 1 January 1958:

> It gives me great pleasure to send this New Year's greeting to the music-lovers of Japan. Although my acquaintance with Japan is very limited, the short time I have spent there remains very vividly in my mind [. . .] We were treated with great courtesy and friendship [. . .]
>
> And I should like to take this opportunity to thank those Japanese who were so courteous and helpful to us, helping us to appreciate the beauties and subtleties of their great country [. . .]

The full text of Britten's address, which was recorded at Bush House on 3 December 1957, is given in PKBM, pp. 156–7.

14 The Balinese place small food offerings to ancestral spirits outside their homes. The fact that the scavenger dogs described by Britten almost immediately devour the morsels corroborates the superstition that the animals embody spirits of the departed.

856 To Roger Duncan

In the air between
Hong Kong and Bangkok
Feb. 21st 1956[1]

[. . .]

Since I wrote to you last, about two weeks ago, we have been to Japan and returned to Hong Kong, and now are on the way (in a rather bumpy aeroplane) back to Singapore (and via Bangkok) and it seems an age! There has been no news from you, which may have been because of the very irregular mail in these parts, but also it may be because you are tremendously working up to March 6th & the great <u>Exam</u>! This may be the last letter I can get to you before that day, so I wish you all luck, old thing, but don't worry too much about it, will you? We plan to get back to England on March 18th, the day before your birthday, which is nice – I'll ring you up at school, & see how you are, and how it has all gone. Judging by the papers we have seen, you have been <u>freezing</u>! I hope it isn't being too horrid, but so far, Somerset hasn't been mentioned as being the worst part affected. We have had quite a bit of snow, in Japan, & it was very cold, but that is one of the funniest parts of this trip ... the way one goes from Arctic to Tropic. Today, for instance, in the morning it was bitterly cold in Hong Kong. This afternoon, after only 5 hours flying, we shall be in Bangkok which is one of the hottest places we'll touch. It's funny to think of going from December to August in a few hours!! Difficult to know what to wear!

    We spent nearly 2 weeks in Japan. I really didn't want to go there. I didn't like what I had heard about the people & the country, and in a way I was right. It is far the <u>strangest</u> country we have yet been to; like, in a way, going to a country which is inhabited by a very intelligent kind of insect. Very industrious, very clever, but very different from us, very odd. They have very good manners, they bow & scrape all the time; they have most beautiful small things, all their houses, their flowers, the things they eat & drink out of, are wonderfully pretty, but their <u>big</u> things, their cities, their way of thinking, and behaving, have all somehow got wrong ... this may seem silly to you, feeling cold in Cranmore, & worried about Mr. Dix[2] and the exam, but they <u>do</u> affect us, and can cause a great deal of harm & trouble in the world, because they are so clever & industrious, and also so very brave, and don't worry about pain or death ...! like their behaviour in the last war, with prison camps and all.

    We arrived late one evening in Tokyo, after a long flight from Hong Kong (but with tremendous fuss about getting visas – having had to spend nearly £50 on cables to get them – just pure fuss) – and were met by hundreds of cameras and reporters. Japan is photography <u>mad</u> – Peter & I had every movement photographed on our first few days there, getting out of cars, going up lifts, meeting people, talking to people, getting up, sitting down.[3] We did a big concert on the second day we were there, for Radio & Television, and another big concert (in which I conducted an orchestra) on the day before we left.[4] In between we went out of Tokyo, south to a place called Kyoto, the old capital of Japan, on a very interesting visit.[5] It was about 8 hours in the train, a lovely journey, some time along the sea (rather like south Cornwall), & for 3 hours we went round Fuji-Jama, the great volcano, that appears in so many Japanese pictures – a tremendously tall, cone-shaped, beautiful mountain.

LETTER 856: FEBRUARY 1956   409

The Japanese Islands are volcanic, & Tokyo especially has earthquakes quite frequently (it was practically destroyed about 1923, & so houses are built quite small). We had two while we were there, a very funny feeling – like being in a lift.

While we were in Kyoto, we stayed in a Japanese Hotel, and that really takes some describing – I don't know if I can do it here![6] It is entirely made of wood (except that the walls are made of paper!); there aren't any chairs – you squat on the floor, & my goodness, how stiff you get!! There aren't any beds; they put down quilts on the floor. The baths are quite different from ours, small & deep, & filled with boiling water. You wash before you get in, because everyone uses the same water, & there aren't locks on the doors (which anyhow are just sliding screens), so people can easily come in & out – no one minds! But all these things, like the food, & the green tea (which they can sometimes take 2 hours to make, while you squat around on your heels, saying polite nothings, but getting slowly relaxed), you get used to gradually ... it somehow fits with these curious little people, & their curious landscape, with its temples, and hills, and odd twisted trees, and gardens made of stones. We saw some wonderful things, temples, and museums, old palaces, one gigantic Buddha (made in 700 A.D., so big that once a man hid for 3 days in its eye, and one can climb into its nostrils.

(This letter must stop now as we are just descending into Bangkok (with great big bumps!) and the Captain has just told us the temperature on the ground is 92 degrees – think of us, in your snow!!)

One thing that I unreservedly loved in Japan was the theatre.[7] They have two principal kinds – the Noh, & the Kabuki. The Noh[8] is very severe, classical – very traditional, without any scenery to speak of, or lighting and there are very few characters – one main one, who wears a mask,[9] & two or three supporting ones[10] & usually a very small boy too.[11] There is a chorus that sits at the side, chanting,[12] & a kind of orchestra of 2 drums (who also moan in the oddest way) & a flute, that squat in the centre of the stage, almost in the middle of the action.[13] At first it all seemed too silly, & we giggled a lot. But soon we began to catch on a bit, & at the end it was very exciting. It's funny that if you are a good enough actor, just one movement suggests lots of things, & in the Noh, there are very few movements (& those are all written down in the text books, & are never changed).[14] There was one called 'Sumida River' which we saw twice.[15] The other theatre, Kabuki,[16] is the great popular one – with dancing, music, tremendous stage effects (a revolving stage) & wonderful lighting ... It made Covent Garden or Drury Lane seem rather dull from that point of view. It was madly exciting.

There is so much to tell you about Japan that would take ages – it is a most interesting place, & we had wonderful experiences. And yet, when we left, I wasn't sure I wanted ever to go back (in spite of the Theatres, the Temples etc.), because I felt rather uncomfortable there, as if, in spite of their exquisite manners & lovely things, one didn't quite know what they were thinking, nor quite trust them. But I expect I'm wrong.

Anyhow, when we arrived in Hong Kong on Monday (20th) I was relieved to see the Chinese, who seem simpler & warmer people, & of course it is a very beautiful place as I think I told you before. We spent only one day there this time – but saw some more lovely things, drove around the Island, & saw again the Princess' charming brother & sister-in-law (the Geddes), who gave us a lovely evening.

We set off for Bangkok the next day (when I started this letter) and had the usual bumpy flight one always seems to get round these parts. Hong Kong airport is a very difficult affair (pilots are said to dread it), being too small, surrounded by water & high mountains. The plane is scarcely off the ground before it is over water, & then has to bank steeply so as to avoid hitting the mountain!

We enjoyed Bangkok, altho it was blisteringly hot. We only stayed there for one day, but managed to see quite a bit. The people are small, & neat, & after the Japanese & Chinese, to my eyes very beautiful. Their temples are very elaborate, like tremendously highly coloured cream cakes. Rather exciting. We went down the river in a launch, which I adored – seeing all the tremendous businesses of loading & unloading going on. They live, many of them, right on the river, bathing in it, falling into it, pouring all their refuse into it, drinking it – but seeming to survive! We had a nice, but rather stiff lunch with the Ambassador there[17] – as we usually do in such places, which is pleasant (one meets nice people), but difficult for me to behave well – rather a strain!! Then we flew on here[18] last night (22nd), very late, arriving at ¼ to one in the morning – staying here one day only, with the Archdeacon[19] who is an old school friend of mine (you met his sister Mrs. Stone when we stayed with her & her family near Dorchester last summer) & Peter & I are going to do a concert for his Cathedral fund tonight – and oh, what a horrid thought doing a concert is! That's one of the boring things about this tour, mixing seeing sights, & then suddenly having to switch over to doing a concert – like doing Latin Prose in the interval of a play.

[. . .] best of luck on 6th. I'll write again from India, & then home –

& I'll soon be seeing you.

BEN

[. . .]

LETTER 856: FEBRUARY 1956   411

1   As shown by the dates in the final two paragraphs of this letter, 24 February was the date of posting. The composer's pocket diary confirms that the flight from Tokyo to Hong Kong took place at 1 a.m. on 20 February: the connection to Bangkok left at 4 a.m. on the next day, and the flight to Singapore followed on 22 February. The group left Singapore for Columbo (Sri Lanka) on 24 February.

2   One of Roger Duncan's teachers at All Hallows.

3   The most intimate photographs of Britten and Pears in Japan were taken by the Kurosawa family, the party's hosts for the duration of their stay in the country. Kei-ichi Kurosawa (?–1978) and his son Hiroshi (known to his English friends as Peter) greeted them on their arrival at Tokyo's Haneda airport and escorted them to the Hotel Imperial where they were to be based. Pears noted in his travel diary that the hotel had been built by Frank Lloyd Wright in 1922, and Princess Margaret described it (letter to Wolfsgarten, 10 February 1956) as 'built to look more like a temple than Hotel [...] bathrooms like small individual swimming-pools – one notices the US occupator by the amount of chlorine in the water'.

   Kei-ichi Kurosawa had active connections with the two bodies that had organized Britten's visit to Japan: the British Council and the Japanese Broadcasting Authority (Nippon Hoso Kyokai). He had been educated at Trinity College, Cambridge, in 1925–28, and had inherited the highly successful typewriter company founded by his father Teijiro at the turn of the century. In 1929, he founded the Tokyo Madrigal Singers and the Tokyo Polyphonic Orchestra, and was awarded an honorary OBE in 1976 for his services to Anglo-Japanese relations, especially for his promotion of British music in Japan. Following Kei-ichi Kurosawa's death, his son Peter took over leadership of the family firm and the direction of the Tokyo Madrigal Singers. In 1956, he acted as chauffeur to Britten and Pears: his recollections of the period allow us to reconstruct their activities in considerable detail.

4   The first concert took place on 9 February, Britten already having had a hectic day with a press conference at 11 a.m., a lunch party with Bill MacAlpine (Deputy Director of the British Council), and rehearsals all afternoon. The recital by Britten and Pears was broadcast simultaneously on radio and television from the NHK annex auditorium at 7.30 p.m.: photographs of the occasion are reproduced as plates 37 and 38, and a video recording of the event is preserved at BPL. The recital was reviewed in the *Asahi Shimbun*; on 11 February (translation by Yukiko Kishinami):

   Pears's voice may not have been excellent but was polished and beautiful in tone. The sweet melody of 'The Salley Gardens', characteristic to the Irish folk songs, sounded even sweeter with his clear voice.
   Britten's *Seven Sonnets of Michelangelo*, accompanied by the composer himself, was most interesting. They are songs about love and employ complex harmonies peculiar to Britten, but their controlled Italianness made them familiar and accessible, and the singer and accompanist perfectly complemented each other.

The British folk songs ('The Miller of Dee', 'Oliver Cromwell', etc.) were all arranged by Britten. The long-lived and widely sung folk songs have become works of art – using the modern compositional method but not trying to make them eccentric or difficult. There is much to learn from them. Their music bore the sophisticated elegance of the English gentlemen, just like their appearances.

Princess Margaret noted in a letter written the next day:

Yesterday Ben and Peter were televised – we went along to watch them being made up and then in front of 3000 *invited* guests we enormously enjoyed their concert. Programmes hand printed on sort of velvet flock paper! All this sounds very dry, but we 4 laugh and fool so much and so many funny things happen we are a sort of travelling circus!

The second concert took place at 8 p.m. on 18 February, Britten conducting the NHK Orchestra with Pears as soloist in *Les Illuminations*. The programme also included the *Sinfonia da Requiem* and *The Young Person's Guide to the Orchestra*, and the concert was recorded for broadcast the following day on NHK Radio 2. The inclusion of the *Sinfonia* constituted a satisfying tying up of a compositional and diplomatic loose end (see Letter 855 n. 13). For a humorous anecdote from the rehearsals for this concert (which took place on the evenings of 16 and 17 February), see PRPP, p. 66.

Britten recalled both these concerts with pleasure in his 1958 New Year's broadcast to Japan:

I was there [in Japan] in the early spring of 1956 for two weeks, and had the great pleasure of conducting a concert of my works with the NHK orchestra, and of giving with Mr Peter Pears (also for NHK) what in fact was our first recital for television anywhere in the world [. . .] I was very impressed with the high standard of playing of the orchestra, and with the players' considerable understanding of my music. We greatly enjoyed these two concerts. In fact we were both (and I can include Mr Pears in this) astounded by the enthusiasm for and knowledge of Western music we met everywhere. One of the nicest examples of this was the

These cards accompanied bouquets of flowers for Britten and Pears following their concert with the NHK Orchestra on 18 February 1956

excellent little group of Tokyo Madrigal Singers, under their intelligent conductor Kei Kurosawa, which we heard at a party given for us. We even, after the serious part of the programme was over, took part light-heartedly in the singing ourselves.

The performance by the Tokyo Madrigal Singers referred to by Britten took place in the library of the British Council on 16 February. Peter Kurosawa recalls that Pears specifically requested a rendering of John Wilbye's madrigal 'Sweet Honey-sucking Bees', and Prince Ludwig reported (LHAO, p. 105): 'Enormous joy that Ben and Peter join in.' See plate 36.

5 The excursion from Tokyo took place between 12 and 14 February. On their first evening in Kyoto, Britten and Pears had dinner with the English poet D. J. Enright, who recorded the event in his book *Memoirs of a Mendicant Professor*, p. 45:

[We had] some visitors who gave as good as they took, like Benjamin Britten and Peter Pears, at a magnificent dinner which the Broadcasting Corporation of Japan gave for them at the Tsuraya, a notable Kyoto teahouse. The most highly regarded *shamisen*-players and singers were brought in to entertain the guests. As they performed, Britten scribbled down the musical notation while Pears (an even greater feat, I should think) swiftly made his own transliteration of the words. Then Britten borrowed a *shamisen* and plucked at it while Pears sang – the result being an uncanny playback. The effect on the *geisha*, a race who tend to be excessively conscious of their inimitability, their cultural uniqueness, and aggravatingly assured of the pitiable inability to understand their art inherent in all foreigners, was almost alarming. They paled beneath their whitewash. A more violent people would have seen to it that their guests' throats were cut the moment they left those sacred halls. This was one of the few indubitable triumphs for British art or artists which I noticed in Japan – and probably the most striking.

The *shamisen* referred to by Enright is a three-stringed banjo-like instrument played with a plectrum, the traditional accompaniment for *geisha* singing. Britten's jottings from this extraordinary evening have not survived. Britten and Pears had already heard a *geisha* performance on the evening of 11 February in Tokyo, and they were to do so again in Kyoto on 13 February.

On 13 February the party went sight-seeing in Kyoto, visiting the Imperial Palace and Nijo Palace in the snow, and then calling in at a textile museum (described by Pears as 'ghastly' in his travel diary) before seeing the Detached Villa at Katsua. The following morning they were driven to Nara, described by Princess Margaret in a letter to Wolfsgarten written on 23 February:

A most lovely old town, with huge Buddha statues, old bronze bells and shrines filled with images which have stood there since AD 600. We fed the famous holy deer and took part in the most impressive, complicated and full of deep meaning ceremony – the Tea ceremony – it takes (or took us) about two hours and at the end one has drunk three mouthfuls of very bitter and strong and excellent green tea.

This occasion in Nara is almost certainly that recorded in PFL, plate 293, where the caption gives Kyoto as the location: the photograph also appears as the frontispiece to MCBFE. A second tea ceremony took place on the next day, this time in Kyoto, but in the more intimate surroundings of a family home. We learn from Pears's travel diary and Princess Margaret's correspondence that the evening was enlivened by an impromptu performance by Pears of an aria from Puccini's *Tosca*, the singing of rounds, and a rendition of Brahms by Britten and Pears. As was the case many times during their fortnight in Japan, the party was disturbed by the constant presence of the Japanese press wielding tape-recorders and cameras.

Oddly, Britten does not mention in this letter the most significant event of his three-day excursion to Kyoto. This was his purchase of a *shō* at Tōzaburō Satake's Japanese Old Musical Instrument Company (see Letter 868). The *shō*, a bamboo mouth organ comprising seventeen pipes activated by a metal reed attached to a simple windchest, is used in the ancient Japanese court music called Gagaku which Britten witnessed at the Music Department of the Imperial Household Agency (Kunaicho-Gakubu) in Tokyo on 18 February. According to Peter Kurosawa, Britten saw Gagaku on two occasions: the first may perhaps have taken place before the trip to Kyoto, thus explaining Britten's interest in the instrument at a fairly early stage during his stay in Japan. Britten learned how to play the *shō* with the aid of a manual by Leo Traynor, an American resident in Japan working for the US government, who was a member of the Tokyo Madrigal Singers and a virtuoso on the *shakuhachi* (Japanese bamboo flute). His wittily entitled 'A Young Britten's Guide to the *Shō*' was accompanied by a set of miniature photographs illustrating the hand positions used to hold the instrument. These were sent to Britten after his return to England with a covering letter from Kei-ichi Kurosawa which read:

I wonder how you are getting on with this mysterious instrument. We shall be pleased to write further to you on the subject when you come across any particular difficulties.

Under the separate cover I am also sending you a back number of *Journal of the Society for Research in Asiatic Music* [in the BPL collection] in which you will find a diagram showing the positions of the various notes in Traynor's article on the '*Shō*'.

One of the Kurosawa family's photographs shows Britten investigating *shō* technique in Japan with the aid of Mr Kurosawa (see plate 33). For a discussion of Britten's subsequent adaptation of the *shō* idiom in the organ part of *Curlew River*, see Mervyn Cooke, 'Britten and the *Shō*', *Musical Times* 129 (1988), pp. 231–3, and MCBFE, pp. 181–5. Britten's interest in Gagaku is further discussed in Letter 868 n. 1.

6 Britten describes a typical *ryokan*, where one traditionally sleeps on a futon. The inn was described in detail by Princess Margaret in her letter home dated 23 February:

> ① Should be warmed slightly & obtain proper vibrations of the reeds. Too much heating will cause the wax to melt & the bamboo pipes will come out.
>
> ② Right hand finger to be inserted to stop the ⊙ inside.
>
> ③ The instrument will play either by exhaling or inhaling.
>
> ④ Outside holes when stopped, the pipes will respond.
>
> K.K.

Kei-ichi Kurosawa's instructions to Britten on
how to play the *shō*

At the entrance to the inn, which was hidden away in a plain little street lined with wooden walls of other houses, all the maids in kimonos greeted us with deep bows – kneeling on the ground and touching the floor with their heads. We all took off our shoes at the door and feeling over life size and rather 'British' we flapped along the polished floors to our rooms. All doors (and most of the walls are doors) slide and people pop in and out at any corner of the room and you never feel alone, you can't lock anything [. . .]

   At night our beds replaced the red lacquer table – quilts to lie on and quilts to cover you. We were all rather cold and a bit overcome till we were given *saki* (hot rice wine) in great quantities. Our gentle maids never left our sides and tried to read in our eyes our next wish. Ben (who is the most conservative of the lot) looked worried and like a wet depressed dog: he could find nowhere for his long legs and was cold and worried by the kimono he was made to wear! [. . .] Never can I describe how we four laughed at this inn. We nearly became hysterical and Ben, Lu and Peter were so funny and looked so odd my sides ached from laughing [. . .]

7 William Plomer, subsequently to be the librettist of *Curlew River*, had recommended Britten to make the most of this opportunity to witness the Japanese theatrical arts for himself. In a programme note written in 1968 for productions of the three Church Parables at the Edinburgh and City of London Festivals, Plomer commented:

In 1955 Britten was planning a journey to the Far East. Knowing that I had lived in Japan when young, he asked if there was anything he should particularly see or do while there. I strongly recommended the Japanese theatre in its various forms, Kabuki, Bunraku [puppet theatre] and Nō – particularly the Nō. I remember describing a Nō play and imitating some of the gestures used by the actors.

As becomes evident in the course of Britten's long correspondence with Plomer during the gestation of *Curlew River*, the writer's role in shaping Britten's interest in Japanese culture was analogous to Colin McPhee's in the sphere of Balinese music. See Letter 868.

In his 1958 broadcast message to Japan, Britten commented:

I shall never forget the impact made on me by the Japanese theatre – the tremendous Kabuki, but above all the profound Nō plays. I count the last among the greatest theatrical experiences of my life. Of course it was strange to start with, the language and the especially curious kind of chanting used; but we were fortunate in having excellent literal translations to follow from, and we soon became accustomed to the haunting sounds. The deep solemnity and <u>selflessness</u> of the acting, the perfect shaping of the drama (like a great Greek tragedy) coupled with the strength and universality of the stories are something which every Western artist can learn from.

8 A medieval theatrical development, Nō took shape during the Muromachi period (1336–1568). It was formalized from early folk entertainments by three successive generations of one acting family: Kan'ami Kiyotsugu (1333–1384), his son Zeami Motokiyo (1363–1443) and grandson Jūrō Motomasa (1395–1431), who became head of the school in 1422 and wrote the play *Sumidagawa* (see n. 15 below) on which Britten was to base the first Church Parable, *Curlew River*.

The Nō theatre evolved specifically to fit the tastes of the aristocratic warrior class (Samurai), who forbade the uninhibited expression of emotions: this consideration was clearly crucial to the formulation of an art characterized by extreme stylization. It was the central paradox of Nō, namely that by increasing the limitations on expressive techniques a greater emotional profundity is correspondingly achieved, that attracted Britten to the genre. As Kunio Komparu puts it in his definitive study of Nō, *The Noh Theater: Principles and Perspectives*, p. 17:

This is a highly sophisticated concept that envisions the performer as one who first denies the subjective with the objective and then goes beyond the objective to find another subjective truth.

In addition to Britten's emulation of the dramatic style of Nō in the trilogy of Church Parables he composed in the 1960s, the innovative musical idiom he created in *Curlew River* cultivated an optimum balance between extreme economy and maximum expressiveness wholly in keeping with the Nō aesthetic.

9 The central performer in Nō is the *shite*, each play treating a single event in the life of the character he portrays. The five types of *shite* determine the five types of Nō play (god, warrior, woman, lunatic and demon), and the roles are played by masked male actors even though the majority of parts are female. The mask (*nōmen*) identifies the spiritual state of the character and denies the actor the use of facial expression. In *Sumidagawa* (and hence *Curlew River*), the *shite* is the Madwoman: the play belongs to the fourth category of Nō (lunatic plays, of which madwoman pieces form an important sub-category), and occupies the very intense penultimate place in the five-play cycle in which Nō is usually performed. See MCBFE, pp. 134–7, and Komparu, *The Noh Theater*, chapter 6. In the first production of *Curlew River* the use of masks was extended to all the main characters, a departure from Nō conventions. The concept of a single central character remained clear in the second Church Parable (Nebuchadnezzar in *The Burning Fiery Furnace*), but became somewhat diluted in *The Prodigal Son*: see MCBFE, pp. 199 and 211–12.

10 The *waki*, a deuteragonist whose function is to evoke the thoughts of the *shite* in dialogue: he may be assisted by a second or third actor (*waki-tsure*). In *Sumidagawa*, both *waki* (Ferryman) and *waki-tsure* (Traveller) are present.

11 The presence of a child performer (*kokata*) is by no means as common in Nō as Britten suggests, but he would have seen one portraying the ghost of the dead child in *Sumidagawa*: they are also employed to play the parts of revered characters such as deceased emperors. It seems likely that the *kokata* in *Sumidagawa* was particularly potent for Britten since the child's role embodies the composer's lifelong preoccupation with youth and innocence.

12 The Nō chorus (*ji-utai*) consists of six to ten men who sit in two rows on a side stage, their function being to keep the plot in motion, to set the scene (in the absence of realistic stage representation) and often to voice the thoughts of the *shite* or *waki*. They sing in monophonic chant, a technique emulated by Britten in *Curlew River* where a chorus of similar size sings mostly in unison. See MCBFE, pp. 134 and 171–2.

13 The Nō instrumental ensemble comprises a simple bamboo flute (*nōkan*) and either two or three drums, *Sumidagawa* requiring only two as mentioned by Britten in his letter to Roger Duncan. The emphasis Britten

subsequently placed on solo flute and drums in *Curlew River* is an obvious debt to his Nō model: see MCBFE, pp. 166–8.

A photographs (see plate 35) from the tour shows Pears and Prince Ludwig humorously demonstrating Nō drumming technique with the assistance of wastepaper baskets, the scene no doubt reflecting their initial inability to take the genre seriously (to which Britten alludes in the next sentence). In his diary, Prince Ludwig described the overall effect of Nō as 'comically strange' (see n. 15 below).

14 For a detailed discussion of the widespread use by Colin Graham of specific Nō gestural conventions in the first production of *Curlew River*, see MCBFE, pp. 157–9.

15 The performances took place on 11 and 19 February. Peter Kurosawa recalls that the venue was the old Suidōbashi Nō Theatre (which no longer stands), and the performers the Umetani Group of the Kanze School with Takehisa Umewaka as the *shite*. The first occasion was to be described in detail by Prince Ludwig (LHAO, p. 89):

The audience sits before the front left side of the stage, which is connected by a footbridge, lined with a balustrade and little trees, to a door at the same height in the left rear corner of the auditorium. The actors emerge here through a draped door, after the curtain has been excitedly drawn back, and make their way over the bridge on to the stage. In the rear right corner of the auditorium there is a tiny door through which the stooping chorus, etc., make their entrances and exits. No scenery. The stage is enlarged to the front right by a balcony-like addition, where the chorus of about twelve black men squat on the ground. Placed a little higher, in the middle of the stage, sit two drummers who from time to time make clicking and banging sounds on their drums which are wrapped all round with many-coloured pieces of braid. While doing this, they sing cum recite in a remarkable strained and strangled voice [. . .] The chorus recites in a similar manner, and sometimes actually sings – in a powerful monotone [. . .]

Everything happens in slow motion. The actors move as slowly as possible, lifting up their stockinged feet before they enter. They wear what are clearly ancient costumes, mostly rich in form and colour. At first sight the whole thing seems to us comically strange. But through reading the texts we become utterly spellbound by this highly stylized, hierarchical but humanly moving art. Particularly by the play about the Sumida river. A ferryman waits by the river, a traveller arrives, tells him that a woman will appear. The madwoman is looking for her lost child, she comes to the ferryman on the bank of the river, who refuses initially to take her. He then ferries traveller and mother to the other side and tells long stories on the river about a child that was kidnapped by robbers and died of exhaustion on the other side of the river. The mother weeps and then finds her child's grave on the other bank. She grieves. The mother is played by a tall man in women's clothing with a small wooden woman's mask. Symbolic props are used to explain the story: a bamboo twig indicates madness, there is a staff for the ferryman, a small gong to express grief. When they are no longer needed, these props are taken away by servants. The mother's grief, the high swelling and subsiding *Sprechstimme*, the way she put her hand to her weeping eyes, the gentle banging of the little gong: the grieving by the grave, the

> Sumidagawa (NOH) abt. 12.30
>
> Tamura (singing only)
>
> 15 minutes interval

The programme for the performance of *Sumidagawa* Britten attended on 19 February 1956

remarkably tense, dejected voices, the sudden stamping of a white foot [. . .] The play made a great and moving impression. Ben was greatly affected.

Prince Ludwig was again present at a second performance on 19 February, when the party was augmented by the company of Reginald Close, Head of the British Council in Tokyo (LHAO, p. 110):

Ben wished to see another performance of the 'Sunigawa [*sic*] River' play with a different cast. Once more we are bewitched, although in my view 12–2 o'clock is not the ideal time for emotional drama.

Britten acquired a reel-to-reel tape-recording of a performance of *Sumidagawa* for his own use. The tape (which is preserved at BPL) is entitled

'Sumi-Kawa'; extracts are included on the CD accompanying MCBFE. The origin of the tape-recording was recounted by Reginald Close (quoted in PRPP, p. 64):

> As we were leaving the theatre [on 19 February], Peter put a wad of notes into my hand, begging me to get them a record of the *Sumidagawa* music. I got the Noh company to make a recording, and Lady Gascoigne, who was then on a brief visit to Tokyo, took it back to London and delivered it personally to Ben and Peter, who were then living in Chester Gate, Regent's Park.

Britten made no sketches from Nō music to correspond to those he made in Bali; however, Nō music is notoriously difficult to represent in Western notation.

Britten's and Plomer's transforming of the *Sumidagawa* text into the libretto of *Curlew River* is examined in detail in MCBFE, pp. 137–53. See also Peter F. Alexander, *William Plomer*, pp. 299–306, and his 'A Study of the Origins of Britten's *Curlew River*', *Music & Letters* 69 (1988), pp. 229–43.

16 Britten's single visit to the Kabuki theatre – a genre almost completely antithetical to Nō, as shown by Britten's accurate description of its spectacular nature – took place on 17 February. Princess Margaret noted in a letter home that they stayed at the theatre for four hours. It seems possible that the experience was remembered by Britten and Pears during work on *The Burning Fiery Furnace* in 1966, since Pears's spirited and witty interpretation of the role of Nebuchadnezzar would not seem out of place on the Kabuki stage. (Pears confessed himself to have been 'knocked sideways' by Kabuki ten years before, describing it in his diary as 'popularized, colourful, dramatic, brilliant, dazzling, amusing, skilful': see MCBFE, pp. 124 and 197–8.) The second parable's colourful and sometimes humorous style thus maintains a debt to Japan while achieving an effective contrast to *Curlew River*. At the same time, the second parable retains many of the features borrowed from Nō and Gagaku in its parent work: see MCBFE, pp. 190–205.

17 Sir Berkeley Gage (1904–1994), British Ambassador to Thailand from 1954 to 1957. In later years he was to give the eulogy at the London memorial service for Chiang Kai-Shek, and in 1989 published his memoirs under the title *It's Been a Marvellous Party*.

18 Singapore. Britten presumably wrote the second half of this letter there on 23 February, having interrupted it for the landing in Bangkok two days earlier.

19 The Reverend Robin Woods (1914–1997), British clergyman, who served as Archdeacon of Singapore from 1951 until 1958. Woods was appointed Dean of St George's Chapel, Windsor, and domestic chaplain to the Queen in 1962. He was Bishop of Worcester from 1971 until 1981.

Britten and Pears had met Woods during their first stay on Singapore: Britten had written 'Concert for Robin Woods' in his engagement diary for

1 February, but then deleted the entry. In addition to his being Britten's former schoolfriend, Woods was also a cousin of Pears. In his travel diary (PRPP, pp. 38–9), Pears described Woods and his cathedral as follows:

> He is a man of considerable charm and enormous energy who has built up a large and enthusiastic congregation (may one call a congregation enthusiastic?) in his vast parish. He has the major advantage of a large and really splendid Victorian Gothic cathedral (c. 1850) built by some civil engineer (from a book of plans by Pugin, I should think). Standing in a green grassy close and shining brightly all over with white paint, it makes a typically English but v. successful contribution to the Singapore sky-line.

St Andrew's Cathedral is still situated on Coleman Street, and has changed little since Pears described it in 1956.

See also Woods's *Robin Woods: An Autobiography* and obituaries by Michael De-la-Noy in the *Guardian* and by Alan Webster in the *Independent* (both 23 October 1997), and in *The Times* (24 October 1997).

In his autobiography (p. 24), Woods recalled his schooldays at Gresham's with Britten:

> Benjamin Britten arrived as a new boy in the upper school in the same term as I did. His quiet enthusiasm and obvious gifts [. . .] singled him out as someone quite exceptional, and whether I was playing a flute in the school orchestra or the piano or organ for school prayers, I was enormously stimulated by him. He and I not only arrived together but left together. At one of our last morning assemblies we accompanied 'Praise, my soul, the King of heaven' at the piano with four hands. Ben announced the plan: he would improvise between the verses and modulate in such a way that each verse started a semitone higher than the one before. C major for the first verse was easy, C sharp not so straightforward, D major was about the right level, and E flat a bit high for the voices – and quite a strain on me! However, the three hundred boys voices responded superbly. Although we did not often meet, my friendship with him continued, and duets were to be played again later with him in a very different setting.

857 To Roger Duncan

RAJ BHAVAN
Madras
March 11th 1956

[. . .]

This looks as if it will be the last letter of the Great Tour; in fact I shall probably be back in England, & have rung you up before you get it, because apart from a short break in our journey in Bombay, tomorrow we set our faces directly home, & expect to be in Aldeburgh early Sunday morning. I got your nice last letter in Ceylon last week. You have been a good boy to write so often, and your letters have all amused & interested me – even the news of rugger & Latin Prose; they kept me really in touch with England. Not of course that other people haven't written a great deal too – but you & Imogen have easily written the most often. By a funny coincidence Peter & I gave a concert last Monday in Colombo at the very moment you were setting out for the exam. at Harrow, & probably not feeling any more happy than I was. I thought about you as I was feeling (as always) nervous & sick – 'well Roger is feeling just the same at this moment', & it made me feel a bit better.

I think the last letter I wrote was from Singapore. We flew on (on Feb. 24th) after our concert (which went very well, & we made a lot of money for the Cathedral fund for which we were doing it), right across the Bay of Bengal to Ceylon – a long, but not too rough flight, in a fine Super Constellation air-liner – Qantas line. Actually the Australian airline (Qantas) has proved easily our favourite on this tour – best planes, big & roomy, & very comfortable, with excellent service & food. Pan-American has been easily the worst – crowded planes (no room for legs) & stupid badly cooked food. We arrived in Ceylon, the usual photograph arrival, & drove straight to a hotel on the edge of the sea – Mount Lavinia Hotel – not a wonderful hotel, but superb position with lovely bathing, with big waves, & hot sea! It was generally hot there, but not so bad as Singapore, less humid, & more air.

Ceylon (I am writing this now in the plane to Bombay on Monday 12th – hence the change to Biro – sorry!) is a most beautiful island – lovely tropical beaches, with palm trees galore, and lagoons, and funny fishing boats called Catamarans, made of a trunk of a tree hollowed out, & with a curious kind of outrigger contraption sticking out one side to balance it. Then in the middle of the island you get tremendous jungle out of which really big hills & mountains stick where they grow tea & rice, especially the former. We stayed by the sea for 4 or 5 days, nice lazy days with only a few official parties or receptions to spoil them! It was lovely to see the Indian (or Singalese – people from Ceylon) bodies and features again; lovely warm people, with kind expressions, & slim graceful figures. The only snag with them seems to be this terribly boring begging for money, which starts almost as soon as they are born, & continues all their life. Lu (the Prince of Hesse) & I went for a walk one day through a fishing village just north of Colombo, & we were followed the whole time by a crowd of little boys, some not more than 2 foot high!, shrieking 'munny, munny, sir, munny, munny' all the time. Some may have been hungry, but the government is trying to stamp it out, saying there are relief funds etc. Only when one father came out of his hut, & chased his son away with a bamboo rod, did we get any peace. But all the same I love the Indian race.

Then on the Wednesday we all hired a nice big car (& driver) & drove into the centre of Ceylon to the old capital called Kandy – staying with a young man who had a splendid bungalow.[1] We saw some interesting dancing, & heard some magnificent drumming in the evening, in a little hut outside the town. One boy, of 14, was a particularly fine dancer of great grace & energy too. The next day we motored to another even earlier capital of Ceylon called Polonnaruwa which was abandoned in the 8th Century, & completely overrun by the jungle (things grow so fast in the tropics that unless people take care the jungle covers buildings in almost no time). It was rediscovered about 50 years ago, & the jungle cleared away, & the ruins of temples & shrines, with most wonderful stone Buddhas (one enormous one lying on its side) are now visible in a glorious park. We stayed the afternoon there & then drove back through the jungle to Siginja. On this journey (of about 50 miles) we saw some exciting things: lots of monkeys of course, sitting on the road & leaping through the trees, some wild cats (with long striped tails), the car was charged by a large water buffalo (luckily it missed!), and, finally just after it got dark, a <u>LEOPARD</u> streaked across the road in front of the car! We couldn't believe our eyes, so we stopped the car & sat waiting, and it came back on to the grass verge and watched us, for nearly two minutes, & we could see it baring its teeth at us in the lights of the car! People consider us very lucky since they are now very rare – although, personally I was glad to be in the car, safely!

We spent the night in a rest house (very simple hotelly hut place) in this village Siginja, & then climbed to the top of the famous lion rock, which is shaped like a gigantic lion. 1000 years ago it was plastered & white-washed, but now all that remains of the detail is the lion's paws, about two thirds of the way up. In the cool of the early morning we climbed nearly 1000 steps to the top, with a wonderful view over a great deal of the island. That evening we went to a big ceremony in Kandy, when the Prime Minister[2] made a long speech in Singalese, but with a little bit at the end in English, sort of summing it up – a kind of rather dreary political speech. Ceylon like India has just got its independence from England,[3] & is going through the same kind of growing pains – but without the wise & patient leaders that India has – like Nehru, & many others. They are madly nationalistic, & trying to get rid of the Southern Indians (Tamils) who have lived there for ages & do all the organising & hard work. This is having awful effects on a lot of the business of the country – rather like Indonesia, I told you about. The next day we had a superb drive right up to a tea estate, very high, & very cold compared to the rest of the island. When we drove down to Colombo the next day it seemed unbearably stuffy – like an oven. Peter & I did two concerts, one on the Monday (sweltering in the heat, but otherwise a nice one, with a friendly audience) & one on the Wednesday, when we took part in a local performance of Bach's Matthew Passion (which Peter sings so wonderfully).[4] We did it really to encourage the Singalese musicians, who were putting it on, because they have so little Western Music (as opposed to their own). But they didn't show much skill or understanding; & it was a pretty dreadful evening, as well as being gruellingly hot. Generally those last three days weren't much fun – one always crowds too much into the end of a visit, & this was no exception. We had endless lunches (one nice one with the British High Commissioner,[5] a charming & gay man), receptions (at one there was a bewildering Indian trick – rather boring too, when a man memorised a whole pack of cards spread out in any old order) a tea party with Folk music, rehearsals of course, visits to Income Tax office, & customs (to send some luggage back) etc. etc. Whew! Then on 8th (Thursday) we flew on to Madras, a lovely big southern Indian city in a superb position along the sea. We were staying in the Governor's house (Raj Bhavan), because he[6] is a friend of the Mountbattens[7] (cousins of the Hesses) & although he isn't in Madras at the moment, lent us his wonderful house, where we live in splendid state, looked after by hundreds of servants, guarded by sentries who spring to attention whenever we go in or out! They have a lovely bathing beach where we went & bathed a lot; not much swimming (we weren't supposed to go too far out because of currents & sharks), but lovely fooling around in the surf. We enjoyed our few days in Madras a lot; saw some most wonderful dancing, heard some astounding music (again with very complicated & fine drumming), & met some nice people. It was pretty hot, but the house was very airy, & as cool as could be expected. We made one lovely all day expedition, about 40 miles south along the coast, to a ruined city (rather like Polonnaruwa in Ceylon) called Mahabalipuram; with some fine temples, one nearly in the sea. There was only one tiny private broadcast concert to break our holiday, so that wasn't so bad.[8]

Then we flew on to Bombay (& on the flight I changed over to Biro (see page 2!)), but couldn't write much because it was such a terribly bumpy journey, & one had to hang on to one's seat like mad). We are breaking our journey home in Bombay – where I wrote to you from, months ago – in order to see some particularly lovely temples about 250 miles from there. We flew out yesterday (13th), very early in the morning to Aurunjabad, & then at mid-day motored about 70 miles through hot dusty country to Ajunta. We spent the afternoon looking at the temple caves – carved magnificently out of the side of a hill, out of rock – but the heat was so tremendous that it was rather difficult to take in! But one couldn't miss the wonderful sculpture & extraordinary painting, & extraordinary skill of hollowing these extraordinary caves out of pure rock – good to remind one that India was doing these feats as early as 150 B.C., when there wasn't much going on in our part of Europe – rather puts one in one's place! Then very early this morning we motored about 20 miles to see Ellora, a rather similar kind of place, but with more sculpture – wonderful Buddha & Shiva figures, some dancing, superb Elephants, again all carved out of the side of the hill. It has been worthwhile, this trip to see perhaps the two great masterpieces of Buddhist art – altho' now, 3.30 p.m. on 14th, as we are waiting in vain for our aeroplane to take us back to Bombay to catch our plane to Europe tomorrow morning, & if it doesn't turn up (already two hours late & no sign of life), a prospect of a hot night sitting up in the slow train thro' the dusty desert, our spirits are rather on the gloomy side!

Well the plane did turn up, only seven hours' late, & tired with waiting & worrying we got into Bombay at about 10.30. That of course is the greatest snag about flying, the tremendous delays that occur.[9] One can't expect planes to run like trains or buses, as regularly I mean – too many factors come in, weather of all kinds, engine reliability – can't take any risks there! – fitting in with other planes etc. etc. We didn't suffer too badly really, only this wait & then one final flight from Karachi (where we went the next morning after arriving in Bombay) to Germany. We should have left at 10 p.m. on Thursday 15th; well, we were told that it wouldn't go till 2 a.m., and then till 10 a.m., & got pretty desperate. But they then fixed us up on a Pan-American which left at 5.0 a.m.; they woke us up at 4.0 & told us it was leaving, so we dragged ourselves out of bed, & almost literally fell into it. We flew in 17½ hours right across Iran (Persia) & Iraq, stopped for an hour in Beirut (Lebanon) flew on, over Cyprus over the Greek Islands (looking very exciting), thro' Greece, Jugoslavia, across Austria & landed, pretty whacked, at Frankfurt in the evening. Spent the night with the Hessens, & are now in the train speeding across Holland, to the Hook, & then . . . Aldeburgh![10]

(I forgot to add that in the plane with us were several members (including the captain) of the ill-fated MCC Cricket Team which had so badly blotted their copy-books.[11] They looked pretty dismal, as they flew back to face the music!!)

So that will end our tour. It's been quite an experience I must say, tiring, but well worth while. We've flown (not counting boats & trains) about 25,000 miles, visited 16 countries, packed & unpacked just on 100 times, given nearly 40 concerts, heard nine quite different kinds of musical traditions, seen countless different arts, talked to Turks, Indians of all sorts, Chinese, Indonesians, Malayans, Siamese, Japanese – not counting the many kinds of Europeans. And feel much richer for it. I hope these letters have given you some little idea of it all – but I'm not a good letter-writer I'm afraid, & I'm sure a lot of it has been rather boring. One thing I <u>am</u> keen on is that you should yourself go & see these places for yourself. Being told about it isn't enough, one must go & look, & when you are young enough too, to be influenced by these wonderful people, living full & rich lives, quite different from our own.

I'm looking forward to seeing you [...]; we'll arrange something for the holidays, don't worry. Can't say definitely at the moment till I get home & see what awful things have happened & just what I'll have to do!

So your voice is breaking! I wonder if you'll be talking a deep bass over the telephone when we talk these next days!

[...] see you very soon,

BEN

[...]

1 The trip to Kandy took place on 29 February, and the party stayed at the home of John Gibson. On the evening of their arrival Gibson introduced them to local musicians, as Princess Margaret noted in a letter home written on the same day:

In Kandy we all four stay with an artist and he has arranged dancings, singings and drumming for us. We have even borrowed a tape-recorder for Ben and Peter to record the new music.

Although Prince Ludwig provides a detailed description of the dancing in LHAO, he makes no mention of the recordings, but a tape marked 'Singalese drumming (Kandy)' is preserved at BPL.

2 John Kotelawala (1897–1980), the third Prime Minister of Ceylon, 1953–56. He supported the continued British military presence in Ceylon, while criticizing the racist attitudes of some British colonial officials.

3 Ceylon had been a dominion of the British Commonwealth since 1948, but did not become an autonomous republic until 1972, when its name changed to Sri Lanka.

4 No description survives of the recital on Monday, 5 March, in Columbo: the Hesses were not present for the event (having taken a trip to a Lipton's tea plantation owned by friends of theirs), Prince Ludwig commenting in his diary that they felt like traitors since this was the first Britten–Pears concert they had missed on the tour. Pears wrote in his diary (which by this stage of the trip had taken the form of abbreviated notes which he presumably intended to expand on a later occasion but never did; PRPP, p. 68):

down to Colombo, oh so hot. Galle: face fuss over rooms. Hot concert. Ben's tummy. Party after, oh! Rehearsal for St. Mat. perf, heat, amateur, – fans.

The amateur performance of the *St Matthew Passion* took place on Wednesday, 7 March, by which time the Hesses had returned from their excursion to learn that the first concert had been a great success in spite of Britten's stomach upset. The Bach performance was described by Prince Ludwig (LHAO, p. 142):

> In the evening the *St Matthew Passion*, without orchestra, with choir, piano (Ben) and organ in a medium-sized church. Peter sings the Evangelist with quite indescribable beauty, very well accompanied on the continuo by Ben. Otherwise a very mediocre performance of the work, which had been severely mutilated by cuts. The very pleasant choir mauled the splendid chorales unbearably to the point of sentimentality. The soloists were hardly adequate.

5 Malcolm MacDonald (1901–1981), the former Labour MP, Secretary of State of the Colonies and Dominion Affairs, and Minister of Health during the Second World War. He was the son of the former British Prime Minister Ramsay MacDonald.

6 Sri Prakasa (1889–1971), the President of Madras, whose residence was the former Governor's House. He had been a leading figure in the struggle for Indian Independence, following which he served as the first High Commissioner to Pakistan and as a cabinet minister in Nehru's administration from 1950 to 1952.

7 Lord Louis Mountbatten of Burma (1900–1979), great grandson of Queen Victoria. His family name of Battenburg was changed during the First World War in response to popular anti-German sentiment. A captain in the Royal Navy, he was appointed by Winston Churchill Head of Combined Operations Command in 1941. In 1947 Clement Attlee made him Viceroy of India to oversee the creation of the independent states of India and Pakistan. His wife, Edwina Ashley (1901–1960), accompanied him to India. He was murdered by the IRA in a bomb explosion on board his boat off Mullaghmore, County Sligo.

8 The party flew to Madras on the morning of 8 March, and stayed until 12 March. They attended an amateur performance of *The Mikado* by Gilbert and Sullivan on their first evening, and visited All-India Radio on the following day to hear local music at the invitation of the directors (see LHAO, pp. 145–6). The concert referred to by Britten took place on the evening of 11 March at the British Council, and was the last performance of their tour. The recital programme included songs by Haydn, Schubert and Schumann, five songs from *Winter Words* and folksong arrangements. After the concert Lionel Billows, the British Council representative whom Britten and Pears had first known in Switzerland in 1946 (see Letter 528 n. 5), hosted a reception.

9 In LHAO (p. 161), Prince Ludwig jokingly refers to their carriers as 'British Overdue Airways' (a play on British Overseas Airways Corporation (BOAC)).

10 Britten's pocket diary reveals that he and Pears had originally intended to fly directly to London from Frankfurt in the afternoon of 16 March. Instead, they stayed at Wolfsgarten overnight and travelled by train to the Dutch coast for the sea crossing to Harwich on the following day. The entry in Britten's pocket diary for 18 March reads, 'Arrive home.'

11 The Marylebone Cricket Club's touring team had performed badly in their matches with Pakistan, and laid the blame on a number of disputed rulings made by the local umpires. On 26 February, in an episode described by the *Evening Star* in Karachi as 'unparalleled in the history of cricket', one of the umpires involved – Idrees Begh – was kidnapped by seven Britons, drenched in water and forced to drink alcohol. The MCC subsequently cabled its 'deep concern at regrettable incident' to the President of the Pakistan Board of Control in Karachi. (See the *Guardian*, 26, 27 and 28 February 1956.)

THE BRITISH COUNCIL

MADRAS

The Regional Representative

invites

Dr. & Mrs Narayana Menon

to a Broadcast Recital

PETER PEARS (tenor)

accompanied by

BENJAMIN BRITTEN (piano)

at 150-B, Mount Road,
on Sunday, March 11th, at 7-30 p.m.

Invitation to the final recital of the world tour

858 To Princess Margaret of Hesse and the Rhine

4 CRABBE STREET, ALDEBURGH
March 20th 1956

My dearest Peg,

Not really a letter (you'll have had enough of them to read the last few days without my adding to them) but just to ask you the name of the Boys' Home in Madras,[1] & what do I do with the £25?? It seems quite easy to send money from here – hope it's the same with you. Could you get your sec. to write address on a p.c.?

The return has been all one expected, & more: Lovely in many ways, but, oh, oh, the problems . . .! Bali, Noh plays, Polonnaruwa, & Henry Moore Lavs, all seem years away now, as one settles into the domestic, Aldeburgh Festival, Sue[2] (blast her!), & Opera Group crises. I've not had a chance of even starting to put on paper those ideas I was so broody about.[3]

Thank you both more than I can begin to say for coming with us; it wouldn't have been quarter the experience, the fun, & the thrill without you. It's so lovely too to end a trip like this with one's love & respect for one's friends doubled.

All love to you both, dear Peg,
from
BEN

Peter would send love, but he's in London, coping with the wreck!

1   Prince Ludwig writes in his diary entry for 9 March 1956 (LHAO, p. 145):

At midday, Peg and many other ladies, having been shown a blood-bank and hospitals, were invited to visit the very pleasant Mrs Clubwala Jadhav, social welfare minister without portfolio. We arrive after lunch and visit an extremely good, state-subsidized local art shop. After which we go to a very nice and moving orphanage, which accommodates about 100 children, whose fees are mostly paid by foreign sponsors. The children, almost black, are delightful, the women who care for them, clever and confidence-inspiring. The whole place is imbued with a fine spirit, and a genuine effort is made to turn these children, who have been dogged by poverty and disaster, into good, educated, solid citizens. Peg and I intend to sponsor a child, partly as thanks to the entire East for this journey.

Britten decided to join the Hesses in sponsoring a child, whom he and the Hesses met during a return visit to India in 1965 (see PRPP, pp. 85–97). Britten told the treble John Newton in a letter dated 1 February 1965:

A remarkable Indian woman, called Clubwala, has started many homes for orphans, or unwanted children, and gets people to pay for their keep. Peg Hesse (Princess Margaret) and I "adopted" one when we were here last, and today we see them for the first time (they were only babies before). I have been writing to mine occasionally, and we have a very touching reunion. He is a sweet boy of about 13, very dark, good-looking, but shy [. . .] We go to the home where he lives, and they all perform for us, doing some dances and gymnastics – they are very lithe creatures, and perform brilliantly and neatly.

2 Susan (Sue) Pears (b. 1931), Pears's niece who kept house for her uncle in London during the early 1950s and who, from 1958, was Britten's and Pears's agent, first at Ibbs & Tillett and then independently from 1965, in which capacity she often accompanied them on their recital tours.

Her crisis (see also the postscript to Britten's letter) concerned the recent ending of her engagement to the composer Malcolm Williamson. See also Anthony Meredith and Paul Harris, *Malcolm Williamson: A Mischievous Muse*, pp. 66–67. She was later to marry the arts administrator Jack Phipps.

3 Britten presumably refers to the gamelan-inspired material which he was anxious to incorporate in Act II of *The Prince of the Pagodas*.

V BEYOND BALI: THE COMPLETION OF
THE PRINCE OF THE PAGODAS

MARCH 1956–JANUARY 1957

4 CRABBE STREET
ALDEBURGH

December 4th 1956.

My darling,

It was one of the most horrid moments I can remember – yesterday afternoon in Frankfurt station. It was unbearable seeing you steaming off into the cold darkness towards Munich, so many hundreds of miles away from Aldeburgh. But one mustn't be silly. it really isn't for so long, & when you get this half the time of separation will probably be over. I am living for Saturday week,

and & the meantime you are so very much in my thoughts. It is lovely to think of you enjoying Bach, & with people around who love & appreciate you. But no one can, or could, more than I do; you are a most adorable man & artist, intelligent, gifted, simple, loving & noble, and with the lightest touch too. I am really very, very lucky to be alive with you around — & 'how' around!

My journey was long & excessively boring — train was ½ hr late & I froze in the station, & then boiled in the carriage.

Britten to Peter Pears, 4 December 1956: Letter 880

CHRONOLOGY 1956–1957

YEAR	EVENTS AND COMPOSITIONS
1956	
30 March	COMPOSITION *Antiphon* (text by George Herbert), for choir and organ
early April	Visits the Pipers in Oxfordshire and then travels on to Devon to stay with the Duncans; while in Devon Britten works with Ronald Duncan on the libretto of the *St Peter* oratorio
by mid-April	Has resumed composition of *The Prince of the Pagodas*
6 May	Wigmore Hall, London: first performance of three Folksong Arrangements ('I will give my love an apple', 'The Soldier and the Sailor', 'The Shooting of his Dear') for high voice and guitar by Peter Pears and Julian Bream
8 May	Music Hall, Cincinnati: first US performance (concert performance) of *Gloriana*, conducted by Josef Krips, at the Cincinnati May Festival
10 May	Reaches the end of Act II of the composition draft of *The Prince of the Pagodas*
17 May	COMPOSITION *Three Songs from 'The Heart of the Matter'* (Prologue, Song, Epilogue; texts by Edith Sitwell)
22–23 May	Théâtre des Champs-Elysées, Paris: Britten conducts performances of *The Turn of the Screw* with the English Opera Group as part of the Festival of Paris
15–24 June	Ninth Aldeburgh Festival: Imogen Holst joins Britten and Pears as an Artistic Director. Festival highlights include Handel's *Samson*, chamber music by Mozart (Amadeus String Quartet and Britten), symphonies and concertos by Haydn and Mozart (conducted by Britten) and an orchestral concert (with Poulenc as soloist and Paul Sacher conducting)

21 June	Aldeburgh Parish Church: first performance of the Sitwell sequence, *The Heart of the Matter*; Edith Sitwell, Pears, Dennis Brain and Britten
30 July	Finishes the composition draft of *The Prince of the Pagodas*
4 August	Travels to Munich and then on to Schloss Tarasp, where Britten works on the scoring of *The Prince of the Pagodas*
9 August	Covent Garden issues a press release announcing that the scheduled premiere of *The Prince of the Pagodas* on 19 September is cancelled
13 August	Begins full score of Act II of *The Prince of the Pagodas*
26 August	Begins journey home by car, reaching Aldeburgh on 4 September
29 September	St Michael's College, Tenbury Wells: first performance of *Antiphon*, by the Choir of St Michael's College and Kenneth Beard (organ)
October	Britten conducts EOG production of *The Turn of the Screw* in London
7 November	COMPOSITION *The Prince of the Pagodas*
13–27 November	Recital tour of West Germany with Pears
December	Rehearsals in London for *The Prince of the Pagodas*

1957

1 January	Royal Opera House, Covent Garden, London: first performance of *The Prince of the Pagodas*; Sadler's Wells Ballet, Orchestra of the Royal Opera House, conducted by Britten

859 To Ronald Duncan

4 CRABBE STREET, ALDEBURGH
March 27th 1956

My dear Ronnie,

This is only a scribbled note to say how very, very sorry I am that I've had to say 'no' to May 8th in Barnstaple.[1] I expect George [Harewood] gave you the reason, how I've cancelled every concert for some time now in order to get on with the Ballet[2] – & have had considerable trouble in getting out of a concert with Peter on May 4th, only a few days before – & I think the agents would go up in smoke if they heard (& I don't see how they could avoid doing so) I was doing it. More important perhaps, I'm afraid the time I'd have to take off to rehearse & travel would be impossible, because I'm really fearfully worried about work – – –

I'm so sorry, because I love the T & T [Taw and Torridge] Festival & would do anything possible to help. I do hope you understand.

I look forward to coming down next week. I've got to call on John Piper & one or two others on the way so I'm not sure quite which day I can arrive – but certainly before the week-end; does it matter? I suggested to Roger [Duncan] that he might like to take a train to somewhere on the route & drive down with me (somewhere like Reading or Newbury on the Wednesday, for instance). If you think the boy'd like it, I'll ring up over Easter & fix details.[3]

You can't think how I'm looking forward to being with you all; it'll be a real oasis in this desert of fidget & fuss! – and St. Peter;[4] that's going to be really exciting.

Lots of love – & to Rose Marie. I hope she's less shingly[5] now.

BEN

1 It would appear that Britten had declined an invitation to take part in a concert in aid of the Taw and Torridge Festival.

2 Britten's diary records that he met John Cranko, presumably to discuss *The Prince of the Pagodas*, on 23 March (one week after his return from the world tour) and resumed discussions with Ninette de Valois at Covent Garden on 29 March.

3 Britten's diary reveals that he called in on the Pipers on the evening of 3 April and stayed overnight. (The composer wrote in a letter of thanks to Myfanwy Piper on 12 April: 'I only hope I didn't bore you with too many tales of the Far East!') He met Roger Duncan at Salisbury the next day and stayed in Devon until at least the weekend of 7–8 April, bringing with him a present of a watch for the boy. His apparent freedom of movement at this time was not unrelated to the fact that Pears was away on a concert tour of

Germany during this entire week. Britten wrote to Princess Margaret of Hesse and the Rhine on 13 April:

> I had a very pleasant week driving around the West of England seeing friends (Pipers, Duncans, etc.) that I hadn't seen since our Great Tour; country was looking divine – a ravishing spot this England – even compared with Haputale [Sri Lanka]! And now I'm back here, nose to grindstone, with the Ballet to be ready in 2 months – but feeling refreshed for all our adventures & experiences, I must say.
>
> Peter loved his hours with you at Wolfsgarten – lucky blighter, he gets all the fun – & was wildly excited by Lu's photos. He <u>is</u> a clever creature, & I'm madly jealous. The big ones Peter brought back make <u>one</u> very homesick. I hope the photos I'm sending on from Kei Kurosawa produce a twinge of the same sadness in <u>your</u> breast, my dear. My what a time it was – for me, never to be regretted or forgotten.

4 Britten's and Duncan's projected oratorio.

5 Duncan's wife was suffering from shingles.

860 To Paul Sacher
[*Typed*]

4 CRABBE STREET, ALDEBURGH, SUFFOLK
27th March, 1956

My dear Paul,

We are at last back from our tour which has been a wonderful experience in every way, and I long to tell you and Maja[1] all about it. I wonder how many of the countries we visited you know.

Since I got back I have been doing some research into possible pieces to complete your programme in the Aldeburgh Festival (and on the B.B.C.) to which we are all looking forward. I have the following suggestion to make which I hope you will like. Do you know the Notturni of Haydn, originally written for small orchestra including two <u>lire organizatte</u> (whatever they may be)?[2] Haydn later substituted flutes for these obscure instruments. I have the scores of two of them (Bärenreiter), and the second particularly looks charming. In the rearranged edition the scoring would be two flutes, two horns, two clarinets (Haydn later substituted violins for these too, but that seems to me to make it less interesting), two violas, cello and bass. Have you got the scores of number two for instance? If it is difficult for you to get it I could certainly send you mine. I think the music quite lovely, like a little formal 18th Century symphony, but with charming instrumental colour.

My suggestion for the programme is this:

1) Notturno No. 2 in C, Haydn.[3]
2) La Creation du Monde, Milhaud.[4]
   Interval.

3) Serenade in C Minor, Mozart.[5]
4) Aubade, Poulenc.

It would be a nice gesture to end the whole programme with Francis playing his Aubade, and incidentally it makes a better end than the Milhaud.[6] I should be most interested to know your reactions to these suggestions.

With love to you both,
Yours ever,
BEN

1 Sacher's wife.

2 Haydn composed seven *notturni* for two *lire organizzate*, and also wrote five concerti for the instrument. The *lira organizzata* is a form of hurdy-gurdy, which originated as a medieval stringed instrument: the body was shaped like a viol, but the strings were operated by a rotating wheel controlled by a handle. Haydn's specification of the instrument has been misinterpreted as a reference to the *lira da braccio*, but there is no doubt that he intended to use hurdy-gurdies (perhaps of the type to have small organ pipes attached to them, hence the term 'organizzata').

3 In the event, Sacher conducted the Fourth Notturno in F major (1790), scored for flute, oboe, two horns, two violins, two violas, cello and double-bass. Writing to Britten on 3 April in response to this letter, the Swiss conductor revealed that he possessed scores and parts of the work himself, and commented that the two violins hired for the concert should replace the clarinets, as otherwise they would be required only for the Milhaud. Sacher tentatively suggested a different (strictly chronological) programme order, but Britten wrote again on 13 April with characteristic practicality to say:

> Peter and I have again discussed the order of the programme, and we still feel that Haydn, Milhaud, Mozart, Poulenc is the best. It separates the two contemporary ballets and also the two piano obbligatos; it also gives a chance for the poor, wretched first oboe to relax before she tackles the Mozart Serenade.

The programme went ahead on 24 June 1956 as originally planned.

4 Milhaud's 1923 ballet score.

5 The Serenade in C minor (K. 388).

6 Poulenc did indeed appear as soloist in his *Aubade: concerto chorégraphique* for piano and eighteen instruments (1929). For the BBC broadcast of this same programme, recorded in London's Camden Theatre prior to the Aldeburgh performance, Poulenc also played the piano part in the Milhaud, though, as Maureen Garnham relates (*As I Saw It*, pp. 82–3), Poulenc and Sacher found it exceptionally difficult to co-ordinate perfect ensemble with the orchestra:

Conductor and pianist were yelling at each other, 'Un, deux, trois, quatre, un, deux, trois, quatre', but with Poulenc never yelling at precisely the same moment as Sacher, who was energetically trying to hold the piece together.

By the time of the Aldeburgh performance a few days later, Basil Douglas had shrewdly engaged an experienced orchestral pianist to take Poulenc's place in the Milhaud:

Basil of course then had to break the news to Poulenc. He found him, he later told me, in his room at the Wentworth [Hotel], sorting lovingly through the attaché case full of every kind of medicament which as a confirmed hypochondriac he always carried with him. Tentatively, Basil suggested that possibly Francis might like to be relieved of the Milhaud piece and just play in the *Aubade* [. . .] Poulenc almost fell upon Basil's neck. 'Oh, I am so glad, so glad!' he exclaimed; and was seen about the streets of Aldeburgh proclaiming joyfully to anyone who would listen, 'I am so happy! I have not to play in the Milhaud!'

861 To Anthony Gishford
[*Typed*]

4 CRABBE STREET, ALDEBURGH
13th April, 1956

My dear Tony,

Thank you for your letter. I am sorry that I have clearly forgotten giving permission for the organ piece to be recorded, but I obviously did so and as a result it is clear that we can do nothing about this present situation.[1]

Thank you for translating the letter from Caracas. I shall be writing to the Festival authorities to say that pressure of work forces me to refuse reluctantly their kind invitation.

I had a nice weekend with Ronnie Duncan in Devon, and I am pleased with the way the libretto for St. Peter is progressing, although it is a big work and surprisingly enough I am refusing to be hurried over it, which may disappoint the York Festival next year, but I am afraid it cannot be helped. While I was down there Peter Diamand paid a surprise visit to me with a formal request from Philips and the Holland Festival to be allowed to record the coming performance of "Peter Grimes" in Amsterdam. I am afraid I had to discourage him and them, since Decca seem to be determined to do it this coming year; in fact, at Frank Lee's[2] request I spoke to David Webster yesterday to propose a collaboration in the spring of next year, which excited David Webster not a little.[3] There is, however, many a slip ... and I have written to Peter Diamand telling him not to give up hope yet. Somehow, with all these offers, Grimes must be recorded soon, but I am determined it shall be well done. We discussed the ballet schedule thoroughly, David Webster, Dame Ninette and I, and I think with luck it will work.[4] The details are much as I mentioned on the telephone to you the other day.

There is only one other tiny point, and that a serio-comic one. I am being somewhat bothered by a woman who calls herself my "devoted wife".[5] So far the bothering has only taken the form of letters and a package, but yesterday I received a telegram asking me to meet her at Paddington station, and I am getting slightly alarmed. She always addresses me c/o Boosey and Hawkes, but should she appeal to anyone in the firm for my address could she please be denied at all costs; the one thing I dread is a love-lorn female appearing on Crag Path. It has happened before and fails to amuse me. Could you please warn the people concerned? Sorry to bother you.

Yours ever,
BEN

1 According to Charles H. Parsons (*A Benjamin Britten Discography*, p. 126), Britten's *Prelude and Fugue on a Theme of Vittoria* had been twice recorded before 1956. Both recordings dated from 1954 and featured performances by Andrew Wyton and Richard Elsasser.

2 The artists manager of Decca Records, with whom Britten and Pears had an exclusive recording contract from the 1950s.

3 On the same day this letter was written, Britten also wrote two letters to Peter Diamand, a formal letter for the benefit of the Holland Festival and a covering note which added a personal gloss. The formal letter reads as follows:

Thank you very much for taking the trouble to come so far to discuss the proposed recording of "Peter Grimes". I was very flattered that both Philips and the Holland Festival are so keen to record this work, and I should like you to give both institutions my warmest thanks, but I am writing to tell you at once that after further conversations since you left the proposed recording by Decca and Covent Garden looks more and more likely. They are both most keen to undertake it, and only the details remain to be fixed. The most likely date for this would be in the spring of next year.

I should, of course, be very delighted if Philips and the Holland Festival went ahead with the recording of this excellent performance in spite of this other proposal, but I shall quite understand if this is not thought practicable, especially as I fear I must insist that the English recording comes out first – since it will be recorded under my own supervision, and with a cast of my own choice, and I set much store by first recordings.

I shall be much obliged if you could communicate this to Philips and the Festival authorities with renewed thanks.

In his covering note Britten added:

As you see, the Covent Garden–Decca situation is not fixed yet; personally I have no doubt it will materialise, but from your point of view there is just a chance that the dates or something go wrong.

Five days later, the composer wrote to Frank Lee at Decca to say:

Following our conversation I have talked to David Webster on the lines you mention, and his immediate reaction was of great excitement. He is most keen to collaborate with Decca in the proposed recording of this opera, and there only remains to find dates to fit in with their operatic schedule. He promises to let me know this as soon as possible, but warned me that they could not be before February next year, but I do not expect that this delay will worry you too much.

On 1 May Britten wrote to Webster to inform him of Ansermet's provisional agreement to conduct *Pagodas* (see Letter 862 n. 2), and added a brief reminder at the end: 'Any news of Peter Grimes?' The correspondence then falls silent on the matter.

Peter Grimes was eventually recorded by Decca, under the composer's baton, in December 1958 at Walthamstow Town Hall. An Amsterdam connection already existed, however: in 1947 the Concertgebouw under Eduard van Beinum had recorded the *Four Sea Interludes* for Decca (see Letter 564 n. 4) and in 1954 the same orchestra and conductor had re-recorded the '*Grimes' Interludes* for Decca and *The Young Person's Guide to the Orchestra*. Philips released a full-length recording of *Peter Grimes* in 1978 (with Jon Vickers as Grimes).

4 The date for the premiere of *The Prince of the Pagodas* had been set at 19 September 1956, but one month after writing this letter Britten was seeking a postponement (see Letter 869 n. 4).

5 This unfortunate situation was recalled in some detail by Ronald Duncan (RDBB, pp. 134–5). According to Duncan, Britten claimed to have received a proposal of marriage from his admirer, who had been sending him a series of amorous postcards from Huddersfield. Britten's 'wife' then began to write to him from an address in Sussex Gardens, Bayswater, whereupon Duncan's wife and secretary called at the address in a piece of amateur detective work – only to find that it was false. Later, the offending woman allegedly burst in at the stage door after a performance of *The Turn of the Screw*, screaming, 'Ben . . . oh Ben!' The intruder was removed by four pairs of hands and borne away in a taxi, but returned on the following night. By this time her family had intervened and she was committed as mentally unstable. Duncan's account of the incident is interesting for the light it sheds on Britten's dismayed and anxious reaction to the predicament of his 'wife'; he thought poorly of Duncan's jocular dismissal of his fears, and sympathized with the woman's distress.

862 To Ernest Ansermet[1]
[*Typed*]

4 CRABBE STREET, ALDEBURGH
17th April, 1956

Mon très cher Maître,

I was delighted to have a telephone call from David Webster this morning saying that there was a good chance of your being able to conduct my new ballet at Covent Garden this autumn.[2] May I say how thrilled and honoured I shall be if you can really find time and inclination to do this. I have hopes that the music will interest you. As Webster most likely told you, it is a three act ballet, and I am doing my best to follow the conventional classical ballet forms – quite a task these days!

I am afraid the full score will not be ready for a little time; I am busy with the piano sketch (in the middle of the second act) so that the rehearsals can start soon. If it would interest you to see a piano version of the first act we can send one to you almost immediately.

I hope you and Madame Ansermet are well. As you may know, Peter Pears and I have just finished a fascinating tour of the Near and Far East up to and including Japan. The art we saw and heard baffles description. Have you ever, for instance, been to the Noh plays in Japan, some of the most wonderful drama I have ever seen?

This comes with every good wish to you both, and in the greatest excitement that I may have the chance of working soon again with my favourite conductor.

Yours ever,
BEN
(Britten)

---

1 Swiss conductor (1883–1969), who had close friendships with several composers, most notably Debussy, Ravel and Stravinsky. He had conducted the first performances of *The Rape of Lucretia* at Glyndebourne in 1946 and in 1963 he was to conduct the first performance of *Cantata Misericordium*. See also Diary for 27 January 1932, n. 2, and Letter 525 n. 20.

2 Ansermet replied from Geneva (in English) on 27 April 1956 (Claude Tappolet (ed.), *Ernest Ansermet: Correspondances avec des composituers Européens (1916–1966)*, vol. 1, p. 60), his letter indicating that September had been scheduled for the initial performances of *Pagodas*:

My very dear Ben,
I thank you immediately for your kind letter and am very proud from your confidence and your appeal. I would be very glad to accept. A difficulty is that I have a concert here on Sept 28, with rehearsal on 27 Sept. I am hoping to postpone both from, at least one day – more is impossible, and I am writing to Mr Webster in order

'The Pagodas revolve like merry-go-rounds': Britten's evocation of Balinese gamelan in Act II scene 2 of *The Prince of the Pagodas*, in the composition draft. Note that below the first system Britten has written, 'Gamelin'.

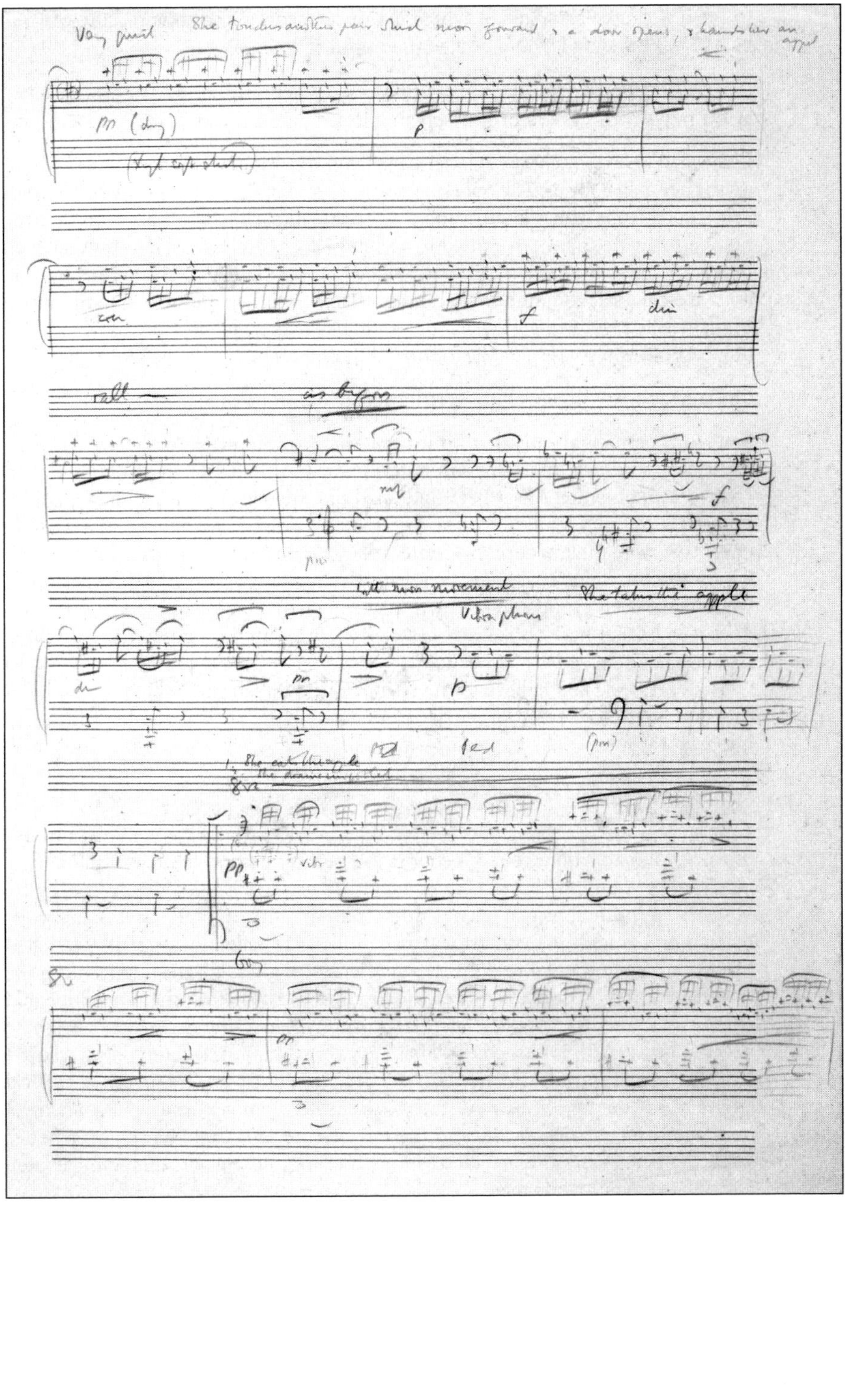

to see if it can be arranged. Anyhow if you can send me the piano score of your ballet for a few days I would be glad to know it [...]

The first night had been scheduled for 19 September. Britten passed the good news on to Webster himself in a letter dated 1 May 1956:

I have had an extremely sweet letter back from Ansermet who seems most keen to do the new ballet for us. The only snag seems to be dates in Geneva on 27th and 28th September, from which he is trying to extricate himself. Does that mean that the first performance has been shifted to a slightly later date? I must confess that even those few days would be a blessing, since although the work is progressing well, there is a colossal amount to write, and the date-line is beginning to keep me awake of nights. He says, by the way, that he would like to see a piano score of whatever is done. Could you please arrange for one of the copies of Act I to be sent to him?

On 11 May 1956, however, Ansermet wrote again to the composer:

You know perhaps already that I must renounce to conduct your ballet. I feel tired and I have so much to do this summer – namely with the opera of Frank Martin [*Der Sturm*, of which Ansermet conducted the premiere at the Vienna Opera on 17 June] – and till the middle of August, that, if I don't have some holiday and the necessary time for my cure at Montecatisir, I will not be able to undertake my winter season. I am terribly sad as I was extremely interested in your work and I would have been proud and happy to make the baptism. My only hope is to conduct it later, as I have spoken with David Webster about a possibility of taking (later) a new activity with the Ballet [...]

So, forgive me and believe to my deep regret. I am so sure that you are one of the two or three true composers of our time and that your ballet will be an important work.

Britten replied one week later:

Your letter was not entirely unexpected. When I knew what a tremendous amount of work you had before you as a conductor, not to mention the hours and energy needed for your new book [*Les Fondements de la musique dans la conscience humaine*, published in 1961], I was quite frankly rather apprehensive about your finding time to do the first performance of the new ballet. I was terribly touched that you felt you wanted to do it so much that you initially agreed to it, but quite understand that on thinking it over you feel it would be too much. I only hope that when you come to Covent Garden later you will do some performances [these never materialized]. I must confess that I am very disappointed, not only because I have such trust in your great gifts as a conductor, but I was hoping for practical advice from you during the rehearsal periods since I am very conscious of being a newcomer to the ballet world, and there is no-one who could have been a better guide than yourself. However, I look forward to your hearing or conducting it later, and will hear your views then!

See Letter 869 for Britten's comments to Webster on other potential conductors for the first production of *Pagodas* once the Ansermet plan had fallen through.

LETTER 863: APRIL 1956 445

863 To *The Times*
From Benjamin Britten and Peter Pears
[Typed draft]

[4 Crabbe Street, Aldeburgh]
30th April, 1956

Sir,

Having recently returned from a concert tour which took us through fourteen countries of the Far East and back, may we offer for your appraisal a few observations which are not entirely irrelevant to some recent correspondence in your columns?[1]

We went as British artists bringing mostly British music, and were soon made conscious of the tremendous interest in all branches of this country's art, and of the enormous goodwill towards us, at any rate on the cultural level. Our welcome was touchingly warm and enthusiastic, but our visit was as a drop of water in the desert. On a tour such as ours you will meet with musicians, dancers, actors from every country but our own; Russians in Delhi, Austrians in Tokyo, Poles in Madras, and Americans all over South East Asia. Every government but our own realises the importance of cultural propaganda – it must, we suppose, be called that. Four years ago the English Opera Group visiting the Wiesbaden Festival with a complete company of twenty-four was, absurdly enough, considered the most costly Festival Company, and that in competition with a full-scale performance of "Aida" sent at Italian expense from Rome. In Tokyo, the Stuttgart Chamber Orchestra was being flown out by the German Government. This year at Aldeburgh the Dutch Government is offering us, entirely free, a famous Dutch male voice choir.[2] Examples could be multiplied. In Djakarta they had had Martha Graham's[3] Ballet Company and the Symphony of the Air,[4] as well as a lot of similar stars, all at Uncle Sam's expense. Indeed, we ourselves were invited in the first place to give thirty concerts in Indonesia by that admirable Dutch-State spirited organisation, the Association of Art Circles of Indonesia.

Now at last the British Foreign Office has sent a group of British musicians to Moscow. Will this be the thin end of the wedge? Dare one hope that the British Council, which started twenty years ago as a good idea and is now a national necessity, will soon be able to vote a less inadequate sum of money to the export of our cultural achievements?

Goodwill and enthusiasm are waiting, and in our experience the representatives too, representatives who, we would like to say, throughout our independent tour were models of efficiency, tact and kindness, and, shamed almost into despair at the amount they can do with the money they are given, and with continual carping from home, work themselves into near-illness, buoyed up presumably by missionary zeal and the desire to save their country's face.

We should by now have realised that the arts can play a valuable part in the export drive. Other countries which do so export their achievements, and hospitably await ours. Their goodwill should not be allowed to wither.

We are,
Yours etc.,
[Benjamin Britten; Peter Pears]

1 A heated correspondence had been initiated by one R. O. Dunlop, who wrote to *The Times* to complain that British artists were insufficiently represented abroad. His letter was published on 12 April, and two days later the newspaper printed a rejoinder by the poet and critic Sir Herbert Read, who declared:

> The artists who have written to you to complain that their works, and the works of their friends, have not been exhibited abroad by the British Council should produce evidence of a demand for such exhibitions [...]
>
> The Fine Arts Committee of the British Council, of which I am a member, does not act arbitrarily; it does not impose its own tastes on foreign countries. It is guided by an accurate knowledge of the conditions abroad, of the prevailing climate of public opinion, and it tries to satisfy the legitimate curiosity of its patrons. To send abroad unwanted works of art would be next to impossible, for no reputable gallery would give them houseroom; and even if exhibition space were to be hired at the expense of the British taxpayer there are no means of persuading the unwilling foreigner to go out of his way to view, for example, some tepid exponent of the English watercolour school [...]
>
> As a nation we make ourselves internationally ludicrous by clinging to outworn fashions in art, as in everything else [...] but in the export of ideas (which is the sphere of the British Council) as in the export of goods it is only the new fashions that have the remotest chance of finding a market.

Read's extraordinary notion of artistic 'fashion' was openly challenged in three letters published on 17 April, two more over the following two days, and a sixth (wittily penned by novelist L. P. Hartley) on 21 April. The correspondence then lapsed, as readers began to air their views on the current political unrest in Cyprus, on premium bonds, and on other matters of less direct interest to Britten.

In writing his contribution nine days after the last offering on the subject Britten was aware that it was unlikely to be published. Sending a duplicate of this letter to Anthony Gishford, he commented:

> A copy has gone to Seymour Whinyates at the British Council for her approval [...] I believe there is a certain amount of haste because of the previous correspondence in the Times.

In any case, *The Times* had recently published another letter to which Britten had been signatory: a discussion of the implications of the Copyright Bill and the recording of music on long-playing discs, co-signed by Vivian Ellis, Howard Ferguson, Peter Racine Fricker and Billy Mayerl. The content of this missive, written in response to a letter on the subject signed by Ralph Vaughan Williams and Arthur Bliss which had appeared on 27 March, was disputed by R. S. Elkin (Chairman of the Mechanical-Copyright Protection Society) on 10 April. Britten and Pears again wrote to *The Times* in early June 1956: their letter, published on 6 June, returned to the theme of the present draft and asserted that, while it might be possible for individual performers to tour abroad on their own initiative, State support was essential for opera and ballet companies and orchestras.

A slightly modified version of the present letter (the expression 'in your columns' having been replaced by 'in the press') was sent to the *Manchester Guardian* on 7 May, and subsequently appeared in print three days later. The *Guardian* letters editor slightly shortened the text as submitted by cutting the last two sentences of the second paragraph.

2 The choir, which remains unidentified, did not appear at the 1956 Festival.

3 Pioneering and influential American dancer, choreographer and teacher (1894–1991), whose work predominantly explored the mythical heritage of Europe and America. Britten and Pears had also encountered Graham in India. See Letter 852 nn. 4 and 6.

4 After Toscanini's retirement as principal conductor of the NBC Symphony Orchestra in 1954, some of its players decided to form a new group, which was known as the Symphony of the Air. In 1955 Leopold Stokowski was appointed its Principal Conductor.

864 To Jonathan Harvey[1]

4 CRABBE STREET, ALDEBURGH
May 7th 1956

My dear Jonathan,

I have just heard from your father about the St. John's Scholarship, & send you my warmest congratulations. It is excellent news & I'm very happy about it. I wonder what your papers were like, & what musical subjects you had to take. Did you play the cello?

How has your composition been going – have you been writing a lot? I shall be away for most of the summer holidays, I'm afraid; but, with luck if you are in this part of England I could see you here in September before you go back to school, & have a look at what you've been doing.

Many congratulations again; I hope you have a good term,

Yours,
BENJAMIN BRITTEN

1 British composer (b. 1939), who began to compose at an early age with the encouragement of his father. Harvey had been brought to the composer's attention while still a pupil at Repton. Following recommendations from Britten he studied privately with Erwin Stein and, after Stein's death, with Hans Keller. Harvey won an Open Scholarship to St John's College, Cambridge, where he was an undergraduate from 1957 to 1960. Harvey was later far from complimentary about his time at Cambridge, recalling that 'I could quite easily have got away without studying any of the Viennese classics [...] I learned the usual things, which were not very useful, except for ear training and acoustics' (quoted in Paul Griffiths, *New Sounds, New Personalities*, p. 49). When he graduated, Harvey lost no time in moving on to Glasgow University where he completed his doctorate in 1964, submitting a thesis with the title 'The Composer's Idea of his Inspiration' ('Cambridge wasn't keen on the idea').

While his earliest music was influenced by Bartók and Britten, Harvey later absorbed the serialism of the Second Viennese School, the exoticism of Messiaen, and electro-acoustic techniques at IRCAM in Paris. In parallel with his career as a composer, he has been a university teacher. See also Harvey's interview in Griffiths, pp. 46–53, and Arnold Whittall, *Jonathan Harvey*.

865 To Roger Duncan

4 CRABBE STREET, ALDEBURGH
May 10th 1956

[...]

You can't imagine how happy I was to get your letter. I didn't expect to hear for some days, even weeks, as to how you were getting on, because I knew you would be ever so busy. Anyhow, thank you a lot for writing.

I'm glad it's all going well – sorry about 'boiling' every afternoon, but that's partly the weather which has been incredibly hot – even in Aldeburgh! When I drove up to London last Sunday in the Rolls, we had the hood down, & it was almost <u>too</u> hot! I drove up in the morning, heard Peter's <u>lovely</u> concert with Julian Bream[1] on the lute & guitar (they did my folk-songs marvellously), & then drove back in the evening – sad, only that you weren't with us, as you had been the previous week-end.

I thought about you on that Sunday, struggling with studs, collars & things. I hope you managed alright. But it was nice that all you three were in the same boat – all new boys with stiff collars! I know exactly what you mean about your French & Mathematics. It is one of the most infuriating things I know, to be ahead of your class – much more maddening than being behind, really! Did I ever tell you that I <u>never</u>, all the time I was at my public school, caught up with the Maths standard that I'd reached at

LETTER 865: MAY 1956 449

my Prep. school. Gosh, I was bored! But I hope other subjects are more interesting. Any cricket yet?

It's been a lovely week here – sea & country looking really wonderful – almost bathable in (the sea, I mean). I'm feeling triumphant to-night, because I've just finished the Second Act of the great new Ballet – well up to schedule! I think it's nice too – hope you'll like it. But I've worked & worked & worked! Now, for the 3rd & last Act.

Another reason I'm feeling mildly triumphant tonight is that – d'you know the Coronation Opera I wrote – called Gloriana, & which caused such a fearful fuss? – well, it was performed the day before yesterday in America, & all yesterday telegrams were coming in saying it was a "sensational success" – & I feel rather justified. It was a work I always thought alright myself; & it's nice that other people are now beginning to see it too!![2]

I've just been over to the Cranbrooks to look at a wonderful barn that's been built near there, & which could be the basis for our new theatre here. A tremendous one, built out of an old hangar. And now I'm just off to dinner at the Potters. Peter comes down tomorrow for a short week-end.

[...] hope things go well. Hope you can swim in 'Ducker'[3] soon – 1,000,000 gallons would be enough even for me to swallow (I always swallow waves when I swim). Is it fresh water? – but
I suppose it must be – or rather chlorinated. I'll keep the week-end July 13–16 free,[4] if you want – but don't you have a half term before that?

[...]
BEN

I've got very pleased with Mary's picture of you.[5]

1 British guitarist and lutenist (b. 1933), who studied with his father and at the Royal College of Music. During his fifty-year career, Bream exerted enormous influence in assuring the position of the classical guitar as a serious instrument with audiences throughout the world. In 1952 he made his debut at the Aldeburgh Festival and formed a recital partnership with Pears in which they explored the Elizabethan lute-song repertoire in recitals and recordings. In a 1988 BBC radio feature, *The Instrument of His Soul*, produced by John Evans (quoted in CHPP, p. 173), Bream recalled that Pears had

a great passion for lute songs, because he loved not only the songs themselves but the poetry; with the lute he felt he could add a very expressive nuance to the line. So from time to time, particularly when Ben Britten was composing or busy on some opera and Peter wanted to do a few recitals, I was asked to accompany him.

Their recital partnership also encouraged several contemporary composers to write for them, including Lennox Berkeley (*Songs of the Half-light*), Henze (*Kammermusik 1958*), Tippett (*Songs for Achilles*) and Walton (*Anon in Love*). Britten was also inspired by the possibilities of Bream's artistry, both as a soloist and in partnership with Pears: he wrote six folksong arrangements for voice and guitar between 1956 and 1958 (three of these – 'I Will Give My Love an Apple', 'The Soldier and the Sailor' and 'The Shooting of his Dear' – were first performed at the Wigmore Hall on 6 May 1956), and composed *Songs from the Chinese* for tenor and guitar in 1957 (see Letter 910 n. 4). In 1963, Britten dedicated his *Nocturnal after John Dowland* for solo guitar to Bream. See also HCBB, pp. 422–3 and 483; Tony Palmer, *Julian Bream: A Life on the Road*, pp. 167–9, and Emma Baker, 'Fingers on the Strings', *Gramophone* (January 2007), pp. 44–7.

2 Josef Krips had conducted the US premiere of *Gloriana* (a concert performance) in the Music Hall, Cincinnati, on 8 May 1956, as part of the Cincinnati May Festival, with a cast that included Inge Borkh (Elizabeth), John Alexander (Essex), Suzanne Danco (Penelope Rich), Kenneth Smith (Mountjoy) and Theodor Uppman (Cecil and Cuffe), an amateur chorus of over two hundred and fifty voices and the Cincinnati Symphony Orchestra. Between 1954 and 1960 Krips was Director of the Cincinatti May Festival.

Britten told Anthony Gishford on 9 May 1956:

> Telegram just received from Kripsy – "Gloriana sensational success Cincinnati work good performances I think excellent arriving London Airport May 15 9AM Pan-american Flight 100 going to Amsterdam 1 pm" – not sure about the grammar of the first bit, but perhaps it's the P.O.'s [Post Office's] fault (they aren't very bright since the "office of origin" was spelt "Sinsinati" – but perhaps they <u>are</u> bright!). I don't see <u>how</u> I can lead a deputation to meet him on 15th – the Ballet must come first – but <u>should</u> I send <u>another</u> telegram???

Gishford responded (14 May 1956) telling Britten that he planned to meet Krips the following day at London Airport on his way from Cincinnati to Vienna and would report back to the composer about the performance of *Gloriana*. In the event, Gishford forwarded a letter to Britten which Krips had written to Gishford in his slightly idiosyncratic English the day after the performance, but then not posted:

> Nobody could expect a success like this; an audience not at all familiar with Britten was excited from begin to the end and there was more applause than after any other concert. I made the interval after the Norwich scene, and there should be the end of the First Act also in stage performance. That shows Elizabeth on the heights of her power and popularity. The second act should start with Penelope Rich and Mountjoy [. . .]
>
> I had a wonderful cast [. . .] The whole thing was an occasion. Many American critics were there and I think *Gloriana* would be the great event in a New York performance.

3 The open-air swimming pool at Harrow School.

4 See Letter 871 n. 4.

5 Mary Potter's watercolour portrait of Roger Duncan remains part of the BPL collection.

Britten's composition draft of his arrangement of the folk song 'The Shooting of his Dear', for voice and guitar

866 To George Behrend

4 CRABBE STREET, ALDEBURGH, SUFFOLK
May 13th 1956

My dear George,

You are an angel to write so fully. It has helped me enormously, not only for Theberton Hall decisions but for the situation generally.[1] I shall take your document to London & discuss the whole business thoroughly with Leslie P. [Periton]. I think I see it all much more clearly now – the expenses & the responsibilities. Since your letter came, Peter has been down & we've been over & explored <u>round</u> the situation, not of course going in or giving the game away. He very much agrees with my maturing view, that while being a very lovely place it is too far from the sea, & is very much in embryo – i.e. everything from making a garden to building the house will have to be done. While neither of us know a lovelier spot than Eastbridge, the fact that this is in Eastbridge doesn't disguise the fact that the situation isn't ideal. That's not to mention the farm side, which looks good, although very costly – which actually one could have faced in spite of snags, had other things been equal.[2]

So, can we leave it like that? Go on generally & gently keeping an eye out, & if a <u>more</u> suitable spot occurs be ready to pounce. If this place doesn't get snapped up at once, well, perhaps the price might come down & one might reconsider in a year or so!

In haste, but with <u>much</u> gratitude for all your trouble,

& love,
BEN

P.S. Roger's getting on well at Harrow – seems to be enjoying himself – thought you might like to know.

1 Britten had commissioned George Behrend to find a new home for himself and Pears away from Aldeburgh. The place Behrend had found – Theberton Hall, situated a few miles north of Aldeburgh in the hamlet of Eastbridge – was described by Norman Scarfe in the 1960 edition of his *Suffolk: A Shell Guide*, p. 99, as 'reduced', a description borne out by Britten's letter. In November 1957, Britten and Pears were to move to the Red House, Aldeburgh: see Letter 911.

2 Behrend had managed a farm on his father's estate (see Letter 793 n. 3), and it would seem that Britten and Pears were considering inviting him to do so for them had they proceeded with the purchase of Theberton Hall.

867 To Edith Sitwell

4 CRABBE STREET, ALDEBURGH, SUFFOLK
May 13th 1956

My dear Edith,

Since we had that charming lunch with you, & since I knew Basil Douglas was going to be able to see you this weekend, I have got very excited about a new way of opening & closing your reading at the Aldeburgh Festival,[1] & I wonder how you will react. I have always been keen not to write just another song, but to make a true frame for your poems: a real prologue & epilogue. I have devised a kind of question & answer (each preceded and maybe 'postceded' too by a fanfare for the horn). I want to take a phrase or two from your big religious poems – for a question something like "Where are the seeds of the Universal Fire/To burn the roots of Death in the world's cold heart?" and "When in this world/Will the cold heart take fire?" – & perhaps a line or two more from The Two Loves. And for an answer, either the last lines from Metamorphosis ... "Out of the dark, see our great Spring begins" & so on; or some of the last lines of 'Invocation', starting "O Spirit moving upon the waters/ Your peace instil ..." I know these are not a true question & answer, but more like opening the door to your great religious thought, & then gently closing it.

I do so long to know what you think of this idea. If a telephone call is easier for you than a note, I'm in every morning & evening – Aldeburgh 323 (Toll call).

Much love to you,
Yours,
BEN

1 Sitwell's reading was due to take place on 21 June 1956, and the composite work that resulted from this proposal was entitled *The Heart of the Matter*. Sitwell clearly responded in the affirmative to Britten's letter, since the composer wrote to her again on 17 May to say,

I was so happy with your reactions to our Prologue & Epilogue idea – thank you very much for so promptly wiring & writing. I have set them, & I think they may be suitable for this occasion. As you suggested I have set the shorter version of the Questions, but in order to get adequate space, I have once or twice repeated phrases – for instance – "When in this world will the cold heart take fire – take fire – take fire?" I hope you don't mind. Similarly, in the Answer, I have repeated two phrases of Metamorphosis "The heart of Man! The heart of Man!", & "O, the new temper of Christ, in veins & branches! O! the new temper of Christ." I do hope this doesn't distress you.

In working on these pieces, getting more & more excited by your lovely poetry, I thought it might

Here the letter text breaks off, having been preserved incomplete.
The scheme finally adopted at the Aldeburgh concert was as follows:

Prologue: Fanfare
Song: 'Where are the seeds of the Universal fire'
Readings: 'An Old Woman'; Fanfare; 'Most Lovely Shade'; 'The Youth with the Red-Gold Hair'
Song: 'We are the darkness in the heat of the day'
Readings: 'Song' ('Now that fate is dead and gone'); 'Dirge for the New Sunrise'
Canticle III: 'Still falls the rain'
Readings: 'Invocation'; 'Holiday'; 'The Canticle of the Rose'
Epilogue: Fanfare; 'So out of the dark . . .'

(This order is derived from the BBC Transcription Service recording of the concert, which differs slightly from what appears in the specially printed programme for the event: see p. 460.)

The Heart of the Matter was never again performed in Britten's lifetime. After the composer's death, however, Pears made a shortened version of the sequence, the readings for which incorporated lines from a single poem by Sitwell, 'The Two Loves'. This new version was first performed by Pears (as reader), Neil Mackie (tenor), Richard Watkins (horn) and Iain Burnside (piano), at the Wigmore Hall in 1983. The following year Pears and Mackie recorded *The Heart of the Matter* for BBC Radio 3; the tapes of Pears's readings on this occasion were incorporated, after Pears's death in 1986, into Mackie's 1987 EMI recording of the musical settings from *The Heart of the Matter*, when he was joined by Barry Tuckwell (horn) and Roger Vignoles (piano). See also John Evans's liner note to the recording, and Philip Reed's introductory note to 'Three Songs from *The Heart of the Matter*'. A choral arrangement of 'We are the darkness in the heat of the day', prepared by Imogen Holst, appears not to have been performed during Britten's lifetime (see PBCPW, p. 111).

One of the poems read by Sitwell in 1956 – 'The Youth with the Red-Gold Hair' – was to be considered by Britten for his orchestral song-cycle *Nocturne* in 1958: a rejected, incomplete setting survives at BPL.

868 To William Plomer

4 CRABBE STREET, ALDEBURGH, SUFFOLK
May 13th 1956

My dearest William,

This little note will be a surprise to you after months of silence. It isn't that I've not thought often about you, & often longed to write – but since we got back from our great Tour, I have been plunged into a whirlpool of hectic work, & been made quite dizzy by it – the Ballet for Cranko

LETTER 868: MAY 1956

has got to be ready for the Autumn & is only ½ written – and so on.

But what compels me to write even this scribble is not my incredibly strong reactions to Japan – that really must wait until we meet – my pen fails me – but the fact that Gloriana in her entirety has just been first performed in America, & has apparently been a knock-out. It was only a concert performance, but it seems an excellent one at the Cincinnati May Festival – but wires pour in from not only performers but organisers, & all equally warm. It doesn't necessarily mean that the poor old girl is immediately waking up from her long winter sleep, but it may, & that soon people may realise that she's still alive! I'm very pleased, but more for your sake than for mine, because I've got more operatic balm for my wounds than you have, & anyhow I've always felt that your part was so magnificent in the work, & more undeserving of those brick-bats than mine ...

I long for news of you & Charles. I alas can seldom get to London – work ties me here – but when I can manage a Wednesday (is that still Cape day?) I'll let you know, & pray we can meet – & talk about those Noh plays, that Court music (I've brought a Shō back with me),[1] Nara,[2] that charm & bewilderment ... ad infinitum. Do you know the play Sumidagawa by the way?[3]

Lots of love to you both, & from Peter too (up in London singing),

Yours ever,
BEN

1 Britten refers to Gagaku, the oldest surviving form of traditional Japanese instrumental music, which developed from musical styles in T'ang dynasty China, Korea and Manchuria. Britten was captivated by Tōgaku, the so-called 'Left' School of Gagaku, especially the category known as Kangen which comprises purely instrumental music in contrast to the danced numbers of Bugaku. Britten had gone out of his way to obtain a *shō* for himself, and Peter Kurosawa's photographs taken on the day of the party's departure from Japan show the composer clutching the instrument with great care at Tokyo's Haneda airport (see MCBFE, plate 6, p. 128). Pears posed outside the Satake Instrument Company in Kyoto, wearing a mask used in a Bugaku dance. While in Japan, Britten acquired two Columbia long-playing discs of the Tōgaku ensemble he had witnessed on his two visits to the Music Department of the Imperial Household Agency.

Britten recalled his reaction to the Court Music in his New Year's message broadcast on NHK Radio, Tokyo, on 1 January 1958:

[...] we had the tremendous joy of hearing a performance of some of the Imperial Court Music in the Imperial Palace. I think it is true to say that we expected this music would be utterly foreign and incomprehensible to us. Actually we [were] impressed immediately by the great beauty of the sound, especially of that wonderful instrument the *shō*, by the stately melodies, and the subtlety of the rhythms. I immediately set out to discover gramophone recordings of some of this wonderful music, and brought them home to England. This great impression has been deepened by repeated playings of them. Incidentally, our friend mentioned before, Mr Kurosawa, who was so kind to us during our visit, obtained a beautiful *shō* instrument, which I brought home with me. Although in no way a competent player, I derive great pleasure from making what seem to me beautiful sounds on it, and reminding myself of that memorable morning in the Imperial Palace.

Britten later went on to capture certain distinctive technical characteristics of Tōgaku in the musical language of *Curlew River*: see MCBFE, pp. 174–89. He was not the first twentieth-century composer to do so: Messiaen had included a movement entitled 'Gagaku' in his *Sept haïkaï* for piano and small orchestra, a work conceived during the first Japanese performance of the *Turangalîla-symphonie* in 1962.

2 Britten, Pears and the Hesses had visited Nara on 14 February 1956 (see Letter 856 n. 5).

3 Plomer replied on 14 May:

It is a very great pleasure to me, and somehow not altogether a surprise, that your response to Japan was instant and strong. You see now how fortunate I was to be able to live there for a couple of years in my twenties. It struck me as a gong or bell is struck, and the vibration set up in me will last till I drop. I must hear more from you soon, viva voce.

Their correspondence then remains silent on the subject of Nō plays for over a year until Plomer rekindled Britten's interest in July 1957 (see Letter 897).

869 To David Webster
[*Typed*]

4 CRABBE STREET, ALDEBURGH
28th May, 1956

Dear David,

I had already had an extremely nice letter from Ansermet saying that he could not after all conduct the ballet, but saying that he had been in touch with you. As this was over a fortnight ago, I am afraid I hoped that you had already spoken to Kubelik,[1] who was you remember the next on our list. After him, as far as I can remember, came Markevitch, Sacher and Schwartz,[2] but I suppose at this late date it is going to be difficult to find anyone of this calibre who can fit in exactly with our dates.[3]

May I add in parenthesis that any postponement of the first night would be a god-send to me,[4] struggling to get the work finished in time – hence the brevity of this note!!

Yours ever,
BEN

1 Rafael Kubelík (1914–1994), Czech conductor who took Swiss nationality in 1973. Following studies in Prague, Kubelík served as conductor of the Czech Philharmonic Orchestra for two periods between 1938 and 1948, separated by an appointment as Musical Director of the Brno Opera, 1939–41. In 1948 he left Communist Czechoslovakia and settled first in London and later in Switzerland. An appointment as Musical Director of the Chicago Symphony Orchestra, 1950–53, was followed by his succeeding Karl Rankl as Musical Director of the Covent Garden Opera Company, 1955–58. During his three seasons at Covent Garden, Kubelík conducted important UK premiere productions of Janáček's *Jenůfa*, Berlioz's uncut *Les Troyens* and Poulenc's *Dialogues des Carmélites*, as well as two productions in which Pears was involved, *Die Zauberflöte* and *Die Meistersinger von Nürnberg*. Though he conducted many of the world's leading orchestras, it was as Principal Conductor of the Munich-based Bavarian Radio Symphony Orchestra from 1961 that he consolidated his reputation as a conductor of twentieth-century repertoire, notably Mahler's works. Britten was on friendly terms with Kubelík, whom he had known since at least 1946 (see Letter 538 n. 5). See also Lord Harewood, *The Tongs and the Bones*, pp. 159–63, Norman Lebrecht, *Covent Garden: The Untold Story*, pp. 183–90, and John Tooley, *In House: Covent Garden – 50 Years of Opera and Ballet*, pp. 22–6.

2 Rudolf Schwarz (1905–1994), Austrian-born conductor, who took British citizenship after the Second World War, during which he was incarcerated in Auschwitz and Belsen concentration camps. Was he perhaps present at the recital Menuhin and Britten gave at Belsen in August 1945 (see Letters 504 n. 4 and 505 n. 5)? He held positions with the City of Birmingham Symphony Orchestra, the BBC Symphony Orchestra and the Northern Sinfonia.

Britten was an admirer of Schwarz's conducting. During Schwarz's first week as Chief Conductor of the BBC Symphony Orchestra, a position he held from 1957 until 1962, Britten wrote to him (21 October 1957), congratulating him on a performance of the *Bridge Variations*:

It had great understanding, and great warmth. I realize that once or twice perhaps the orchestra did not do exactly what you wanted; but it was all such wonderful music making, and that is what I enjoy the most [...] I am sure it is a great thing for English music that you have undertaken this very important position.

Schwarz and the BBC Symphony Orchestra performed other Britten works during the conductor's first season with the orchestra, including the *Sinfonia da Requiem* on 23 November 1957; see also Letter 889 n. 3. In 1958 he was to conduct the first performance of Britten's *Nocturne* for tenor and orchestra.

During Schwarz's tenure, Britten was approached for a new piece for the BBC Symphony Orchestra for the 1957–58 season but declined owing to existing commitments; he did, however, accept a commission from the BBC for a piece to mark the centenary in 1960 of Mahler's birth, a work that remained unachieved. According to Nicholas Kenyon, 'it was also rumoured that he [Britten] was unsympathetic to performances by the Symphony

Orchestra' (*The BBC Symphony Orchestra: The First Fifty Years 1930–1980*, pp. 276–7), a point that is difficult to comprehend in the light of the composer's admiration for Schwarz.

3 In the event, Britten was to conduct the first performances of *The Prince of the Pagodas* himself in January 1957.

4 On 9 August Webster issued a press release from Covent Garden informing the public that the premiere projected for 19 September had been abandoned due to illness on the part of the composer. According to the *News Chronicle* of that date, 'Mr Britten was said yesterday to be worn out after his recent world tour.' *The Times* added, 'The piano score, however, is ready, and this is to be used for some rehearsals.' See also Letter 870.

870 To Anthony Gishford
[*Typed*]

4 CRABBE STREET, ALDEBURGH
5th June, 1956

My dear Tony,

Thank you for your letter about a possible commission for the Swiss male voice choir.[1] I think the best answer to all invitations of this kind is a gentle but firm no, but saying that if such a work is written in the near future the people concerned will be notified, and can give the first performance (for a slight consideration?). Only in that case we must keep a list of the various people so that we can let them know – or shall I?

The ballet is pushing on steadily in spite of innumerable interruptions for rehearsals, concerts, festivals etc.[2] The sketches are only a week or so off completion, and then there remains just the full score to be written (!) It is going to be a rush to get it done by the prescribed date, September 19th, but I think it will be possible.[3] In the meantime, Covent Garden have not got a conductor to do it. Ansermet eventually refused, needing a holiday; Webster delayed telling me for a fortnight, and consequently delayed approaching the next person on the list i.e. Kubelik. The date is now getting alarmingly close for a first-class conductor to be able to rehearse and do a reasonable number of performances. I tell you this only to prepare you for the stand I am going to make, refusing to let the work be performed inadequately. Oh dear! will nothing ever make them wake up?

Yours ever,
BEN

1 The conductor Kurt Rothenbühler had enquired of Boosey & Hawkes whether Britten might be interested in receiving a commission for a piece

for male-voice choir and instrumental ensemble. In his letter to Britten dated 1 June 1956, Gishford reports that Rothenbühler was soon to conduct the German premiere of Britten's *The Ballad of Little Musgrave and Lady Barnard*, for male voices and piano.

2   Two weeks before this letter was written Britten had travelled to Paris with the English Opera Group to conduct two performances of *The Turn of the Screw* at the Théâtre des Champs-Elysées on 22 and 23 May, which were given as part of the Festival of Paris: see Maureen Garnham, *As I Saw It*, pp. 75–6. Britten described the visit to Roger Duncan in a letter dated 29 May 1956:

We had an exciting time in Paris; the opera (the Screw) was a tremendous success, in spite of our worries about it; but it was a pretty strenuous week-end. Nice, also because George & Marion [Harewood] were there too, & we spent a nice long time with them, including a trip up the Seine in a boat. The journeys weren't much fun; we went by a kind of private air-line (Skyways) which left from Lympe (pronounced Lim) in Kent; & the journey there took 4 hours, & over two hours from where we landed in France (Beauvais) so it probably took longer than the boat & train journey, & was much more tiring (awful, ricketty busses). A man in the theatre, during the interval of the dress-rehearsal, jumped onto the violin case of the leader of the orchestra, & went right through the violin inside – & it was Whit Sunday, & we couldn't borrow another to go on with! – besides of course being a very valuable instrument too! Panics!

Peter & I had to do a dreadful television interview [. . .] there, a fearful shambles: the interviewer thought I was the leader of the orchestra, & Peter the composer – – – ! – all in French (but I made a joke, which they understood – ha! ha!). (It was along with film stars & cabaret singers!)

Now I'm back here & working hard at – you'll never guess – the ballet . . . !!

A week or so following this letter to Gishford, Britten was plunged into the Aldeburgh Festival (15–24 June 1956), in which he was involved in a particularly heavy schedule of concerts, which included playing harpsichord continuo in Handel's *Samson* and piano in a recital of chamber music by Mozart with members of the Amadeus String Quartet, conducting symphonies and concertos by Haydn and Mozart (including Mozart's two-piano Concerto in E flat, K. 365, in which he and Maria Curcio were soloists); a Schumann centenary concert; the Sitwell sequence *The Heart of the Matter*; accompanying at the piano an 'Opera Concert' (with a quartet of soloists including Joan Sutherland), and a recital of music by Telemann, Bach and his own *Donne Sonnets*.

3   Compare Letter 869, where Britten shows himself to be markedly less confident about meeting the September deadline. See also Letter 876.

The Parish Church, Thursday, 21st June, 1956

THE HEART OF THE MATTER

A programme of religious verse *by* Dame Edith Sitwell, with music *by* Benjamin Britten.

Spoken, sung and played *by* Dame Edith Sitwell, Peter Pears, Dennis Brain and Benjamin Britten

1. PROLOGUE
    Where are the seeds of the Universal Fire
    To burn the roots of Death in the world's cold heart?
    When in this world will the cold heart take fire?
    (The Two Loves)

2. POEMS
    (a) An old woman
    (b) Harvest
    (c) Most Lovely Shade
    (d) The Queen Bee sighed
    (e) The Youth with the Red-Gold Hair

3. SONG
    "We are the darkness"

4. POEMS
    (a) Now that Fate is dead and gone
    (b) Dirge for the New Sunrise

5. CANTICLE No. 3.
    "Still falls the rain"

6. POEMS
    (a) The Winter of the world *(from Invocation)*
    (b) Holiday
    (c) Heart and mind
    (d) The Bee-keeper
    (e) Canticle of the Rose

7. EPILOGUE
    So, out of the dark, see our great Spring begins—
    Our Christ, the new Song, breaking out in the fields and hedgerows,
    The heart of Man! O, the new temper of Christ, in veins and branches!
    (Metamorphosis)

871 To Ronald Duncan

4 CRABBE STREET, ALDEBURGH, SUFFOLK
June 12th 1956

My dear Ronnie,

Thank you (?) for sending Miss T.'s letter.[1] Mercifully I've been spared recently, but poor Isador [Caplan] is being bombarded for me. She's got her teeth firmly into me, so with luck you won't catch it yet ... but if you do, tell Isador & he'll handle it.

When do the Women's J.[2] want the MS. of the Ballet? Certainly I can send them a page of the scribbles (sic!), if you'll tell me where & when – will they mind pencil?

I enjoyed my visit to Harrow a lot[3] – Roger was a charming host, & showed me around. He seemed happy, & busy. He'll have told you of our plot about the Lord's Exeat week-end.[4] Couldn't you & Rose Marie come on down here, or would it be a bore?

Lots of love; the ballet's going swimmingly, & then when the decks are cleared ... St. Peter!

BEN

P.S. Our Festival's just breaking over us (illness galore!) – How's yours going?

1 See Letter 861 n. 5.

2 In an undated letter, Duncan asked Britten to send to a Miss Currant of the *Women's Journal* 'two or three bars' of *The Prince of the Pagodas*, adding 'I have already sent them a few bars of [Rudolf] Benesh's MSS of the choreography of Belle Rose's solo. He came round to the cottage to see me: interesting bloke.'

   In September 1955 Rudolf and Joan Benesh had given a public presentation at the Royal Opera House of their newly devised method of movement notation, and the following year published *An Introduction to Benesh Dance Notation*. Their method has become the most widely used means of recording and re-staging dance. Presumably Duncan had written an article (not traced) for the *Women's Journal* about the Beneshes' revolutionary dance notation, relating it to Britten's forthcoming ballet.

3 Britten had met Roger Duncan at his school on 9 June 1956.

4 Britten's diary for 13 July 1956 has the entry 'Roger – Lords Exeat'. After attending the cricket match at Lords Cricket Ground, the home of the Marylebone Cricket Club and Middlesex County Cricket Club, the composer brought Roger Duncan back to Aldeburgh for the remainder of the weekend. It remains unclear whether either of Roger Duncan's parents also came to Aldeburgh for the weekend.

872 To Peter Pears

4 CRABBE STREET, ALDEBURGH, SUFFOLK
July 20th 1956

My darling P.,

This is to send my love, & say how I'm thinking of you all the time, hoping the drive is going well, & not too much rain & traffic, & also not too much of a strain. I long to know you've arrived, & hope there'll be a message on Monday or so![1]

Poor old Jeremy [Cullum] is still stuck in London – the blinking old Rolls won't start still! . . . what a car; I think I'll buy a Morris 8 Station wagon!

Anne Holt[2] has been here, talked a lot with Miss Hudson about the arrangements for August, & seemed very happy with the house. I gave her lunch.

Johnny Cranko has just arrived, plus Clytie[3] – it is nice to have the three generations together.

Just dashing off to the Festival meeting – hope it goes well, & that there aren't too many fireworks – but I expect Fidelity [Cranbrook] will control them.

I'll write properly in a day or so.

Hope the Festwoche goes well – & that you begin to enjoy the pieces. Don't forget to talk to Fischer-Dieskau[4] about the Winter Reise,[5] & mention the possibility of Aldeburgh to Yehudi,[6] will you?

Lots of love, & bon voyage, my honey,

B

Love to Peg & Lu when they arrive.

1. Pears was participating in the Ansbach Bachwoche, in which he had appeared in the previous year.

2. The wife of Pears's friend Oliver Holt. Pears had first met Holt in Germany in the 1930s and was to remain in touch with him until the end of his life. See CHPP, pp. 36–8. It would appear that the Holt family was going to use Britten's house in Aldeburgh as their base for a holiday while the composer and Pears were abroad during August.

3. Presumably Cranko had brought with him his own miniature dachshund bitch Clytie, the mother of Britten's and Pears's bitch of the same name, who had recently had a litter of puppies, see Letter 874.

4. Dietrich Fischer-Dieskau (b. 1925), German baritone, one of the leading singers of his generation, who also recorded the majority of his extensive repertoire. Following studies in Berlin during and after the war (he was drafted into the German Army and taken prisoner in 1945), he made his

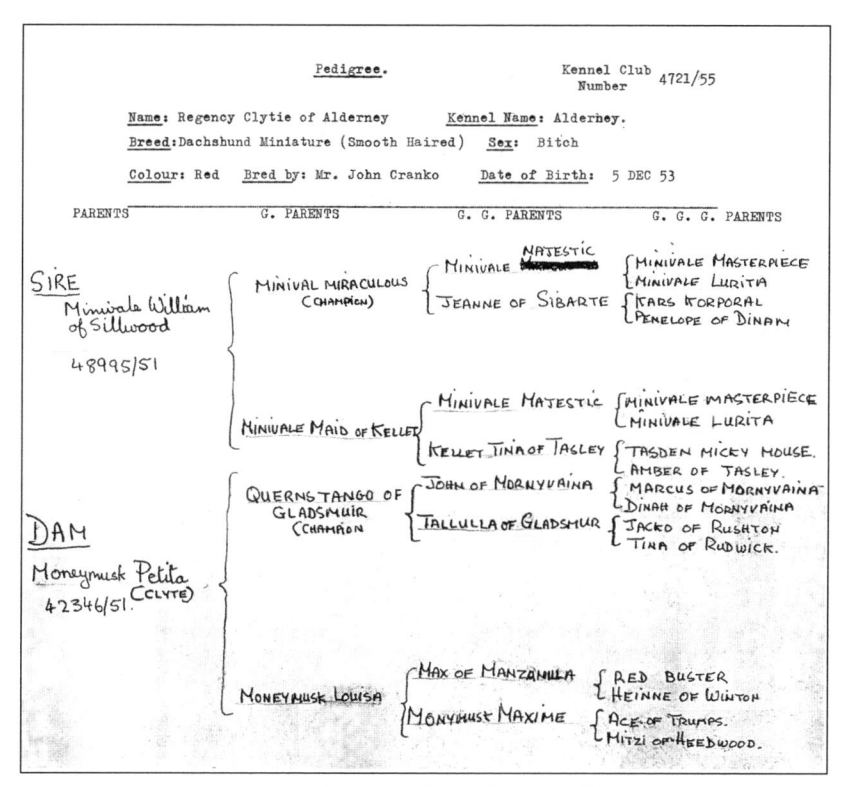

The pedigree certificate for Clytie II

concert debut in 1947 and his operatic debut a year later. Throughout his long career, which lasted until his retirement in 1992, he appeared at the leading opera houses and festivals, including the Vienna Staatsoper, the Bavarian Staatsoper and Bayreuth, singing most of the major baritone roles from Mozart to Berg. He made his London debut in 1951, and in 1955 made the first of several recordings of Schubert's *Die Winterreise*. Many contemporary composers wrote for him, including Britten, Henze (*Elegy for Young Lovers*) and Reimann (*Lear*).

It remains unclear when Britten first heard Fischer-Dieskau, but it must have been before Pears sang with him at Ansbach in 1956. Britten was to compose three works in the 1960s that involved Fischer-Dieskau: the baritone parts in *War Requiem* and *Cantata Misericordium*, and the cycle *Songs and Proverbs of William Blake*, all of which Fischer-Dieskau premiered and subsequently recorded with the composer. At least two projects from the early 1960s were devised for Fischer-Dieskau but remained unachieved: an operatic adaptation of Shakespeare's *King Lear* (with the baritone in the title role and Pears as the Fool); and a chamber vocal piece for what Britten called the 'Dieskau Consort' which was also to involve the baritone's first wife, the cellist Irmgard Poppen. Her death during childbirth in December 1963 put paid to this scheme, and it was replaced in 1965 by the Blake cycle; Britten's dedication of the latter work – 'To Dieter – the past and the future' – may well be a coded reference to this tragedy.

Britten invited Fischer-Dieskau to the Aldeburgh Festivals of 1965 and 1972. During the 1965 Festival, in addition to giving the premiere of the *Songs and Proverbs of William Blake*, he gave a recital of Brahms *Lieder* (with Sviatoslav Richter), sang Britten's realization of a secular cantata attributed to Purcell, 'When Night her purple veil had softly spread', Bach cantatas and Britten's *Cantata misericordium*, conducted by the composer. In 1972 Fischer-Dieskau gave a recital with Britten of Schubert and Britten (Blake songs), and took part in a performance of Schumann's *Szenen aus Goethes 'Faust'*, conducted by Britten (and subsequently recorded by Decca). With Prince Ludwig of Hesse and the Rhine, Fischer-Dieskau was responsible for the German translation of the Owen poems used in *War Requiem*.

In 1985 Fischer-Dieskau contributed to PPT (p. 36), a letter addressed to Pears:

> I count the experience of working with you among the most important ingredients in a life that has not been poor in significant encounters. But beyond that, such a fusion of humanity and artistic greatness as yours is rare indeed. When one grows older recollection acquires a new and more important function. I have only to think of you and Ben for it to warm my heart.

See also Dietrich Fischer-Dieskau, *Echoes of a Lifetime*, translated by Ruth Hein; H. A. Neunzig, *Dietrich Fischer-Dieskau: eine Biographie*, and Kenneth S. Whitton, *Dietrich Fischer-Dieskau Mastersinger: A Documentary Study*.

5 By 1956 Fischer-Dieskau enjoyed a considerable reputation as an interpreter of Schubert's song-cycle *Die Winterreise*. Presumably Britten's reminder to Pears was concerned with inviting Fischer-Dieskau to perform the cycle at Aldeburgh, though in fact he did not perform at the Festival until 1965 (see n. 4 above).

Pears and Britten were not to give the first of their own equally celebrated interpretations of *Winterreise* until the 1961 Aldeburgh Festival.

6 Yehudi Menuhin was to make his first appearance at the Aldeburgh Festival in 1957 (see Letter 895 n. 3), returning in 1958, 1959 and 1963.

873 To Peter Pears

4 CRABBE STREET, ALDEBURGH, SUFFOLK
July 26th 1956

My darling,
Your letter has just arrived & I was so relieved to get news of you. I am afraid it is all being a bit of a strain for you, but I hope you're beginning to

enjoy it now – just relax about your German . . . it really doesn't matter making mistakes, & anyhow, as we all know, mistakes are so charming![1]

Glad the car ran well. You can imagine how worried I was about you, going off in that weather & feeling so tired! But it was jolly good that you managed to get to Wolfsgarten.

Jeremy is doing the chores, photos to [Miss A.] Sellström,[2] & sending 2 programme-books in another envelope for you to show (or give) Yehudi.

There are quite a lot of things to tell you, but not much time to write fully, because I'm slaving, slaving at the old ballet: trying at the moment to get the music of Act III written. We got Act I score off last week. Tony's suggestion to Webster of postponing had the usual Webster reaction (nothing at all). But I'm trying to get it done for Johnnie's sake. He is still here; lazing around & enjoying the complete rest, before plunging back into work next week. The weather has suddenly become madly hot. Do hope it isn't too hot with you – because I could imagine that Bavaria could be baking.

Here, it has been almost too hot to sit in the garden. You can imagine that working's not easy, with all the little naked figures disporting on the beach to distract one!

We had a ghastly council meeting; but there's nothing really to worry about, & we are in excellent hands: Stephen [Reiss] & Fidelity are in tearing form.

Erwin & Sophie [Stein] come tomorrow for a long weekend – Erwin to work on the ballet, of course. George & Marion [Harewood] came down last weekend which was terribly nice. They are darlings.

Well, my darling – enjoy yourself, a bit – remember how good you are (the best ever), & see you very soon.

All my love,
Your
– B. OXXXXOO

Afraid we get in very late on 4th[3] – the only possible plane to Munich that day – arriving at 10.50 at the airport (Lufthansa) – we'll come straight to 4 Jahreszeiten Hotel.

1   Pears had written from Ansbach on 23 July 1956:

   I arrived here last night about 9.45 pm, having lost my way a few miles back & therefore being 45 mins. late. Not that it mattered. The Morris has gone without a hitch – no trouble – in fact the first day (Friday) I drove through to Köln & stayed at the Dom Hotel, then rang Peg in the morning & came to Wolfsgarten for the night. It was lovely to be there again, & to see them, & to talk to you. How I wish I were with you! I am very much the new boy here, and although everyone is really very kind I feel like hiding in my room all day. Why don't I speak German & when shall I learn it? Never. Fischer-D. doesn't come till next Sunday night, I think. Yehudi [Menuhin] comes on Thursday to play his solo Sonatas, & does 2 more concerts of Sonatas with cembalo & flute. Karl Richter who is very much in charge & is conducting me all 4 times is really rather nice, I think, & musical (in the German way). The players are very efficient but hard & overplay – Arias with Solo are boring because they play so loud! We did [Cantata] Nos 110 & 171 this morning – very difficult – B Minor 2 Flutes [i.e. the *Domine Deus* from the B minor Mass] tempo fearfully hard – no room for breath.

We have 3 rehearsals today – interrupted for meals and sleep – tomorrow 2 – 1 & a concert on Wed.

Tuesday morning

Rehearsals went all right – Am beginning to enjoy some of it – wonderful music – difficult some of it – but Richter is a terribly efficient & admirable German type – Wish we had more of them. My solo cantata is going quite well & Richter sees what I'm at & appreciates it, I think – My German is ghastly but I hope it will sich verbessern [improve]. – My fellow singers might be a whole lot worse as people and as singers – Two nice useful Sopranos, a big Alto, & a Papageno from Hamburg – I'll write again soon –

2 A representative of the Westdeutscher Konzert agency who was promoting a recital by Pears and Britten in West Berlin.

3 Britten, accompanied by Imogen Holst, travelled to Munich on Saturday, 4 August, and arrived at the Hesses' Swiss castle (Schloss Tarasp) on the following day. He remained abroad until 4 September and, as Letter 877 shows, had gone to Switzerland with the intention of devoting a period of uninterrupted work to the scoring of *The Prince of the Pagodas*. He had explained to Princess Margaret of Hesse and the Rhine in a letter dated 19 July 1956:

We've had meetings discussing the machinery of the business of score, photography, part-copying etc. etc. & it seems that if I'm going to get the Ballet ready for September the only way is to get away from here [Aldeburgh] as soon as possible, to as quiet as possible a place – & to come to Frankfurt/Tarasp on August 4th seems to be the answer to our prayers!

874 To Peter Pears

4 CRABBE STREET, ALDEBURGH, SUFFOLK
July 28th 1956

My darling,

Lovely to get your letter just now – I must say it sounds the tiniest bit dreary for you, & such hard work too – I hope you don't have to yell all the time! Don't feel you have to work hard with your dear Teutonic friends & colleagues, let them entertain you – try to be a grand & aloof great artist occasionally. It'll probably be nicer when Yehudi turns up & Diskauer [*sic*] too – at least they speak a decent language![1]

Here all goes to plan, I've just on finished the music of the ballet

(Thank God!!!),² & now I get down again to the score. There's a good old row developing between B. & H. [Boosey & Hawkes] & Covent Garden (Webster is the pink limit (a good term for him, don't you think?)), but no sign yet of postponement alas.³

Erwin (to get on with copying) & Sophie are here – Johnnie [Cranko] goes tonight – all nice, but I do wish I could have the house occasionally to myself (with one exception).

The puppies are thriving & adorable – even their puddles are adorable, & Miss Hudson worships them. Alison Pritt⁴ has gone mad at the idea of the bitch, & the black . . . well, we'll see! Clytie's run-downness is better, & her skin is improving. (We get her away from the pups as much as possible.)

I nearly knocked myself out playing tennis yesterday – hit myself on the temple running for a difficult one . . . don't actually <u>think</u> I've got concussion, but I wonder what complex that means!

I say 'hear, hear' to roll on 4th. So sorry the plane's so late, but it's the only one, & let's pray there's no delay.

Good luck to everything my honey – don't get too tired. Love to Peg & Lu, & see you <u>very</u> soon now.

Love you,
B. XXOOXX

1 Pears was to write to Britten on 31 July–1 August 1956:

I am now at the end of 10 days really rather attached to this whole set-up. Weymar (the hon-director) & his wife are both really <u>very</u> nice. [Karl] Richter is all right & amiable – & the chorus have taken to me it seems, and the orchestra are very appreciative. Tonight after the concert I go to abendessen [dinner] with the Choir at Windsbach where they live in a big house. They are really very sweet, madly keen. At first the men were all very critical of me (tiny voice! not as good as our [Ernst] Häfliger etc) but my Solo Cantata won them round – & the girls adore me!

As far as I can make out, I shall hardly see Fischer-Dieskau at all. He is being grand, living in Ansbach – only came to the 2nd rehearsal (last night) ½ way through & left after. This morning (our General Probe [full rehearsal]) he came at 11 – (we started at 9.30) and left after. I have shaken hands twice – that is all, & I suppose tonight will be the same. He seems very nice, & is very musical, but grand – A pity.

Richter wants me to do Matthäus [Bach's *St Matthew Passion*] with him in München though I can't manage dates this year – & they seem to want me to come back to this Bachwoche again – so I can't be quite such a phlop as I thought! [. . .]

Wednesday morning

Dietrich Fischer-Dieskau will be in Berlin when we are there.

Last night was really very moving. Fischer-Dieskau sang beautifully the Kreuzstab Cantata [Bach's Cantata No. 56] – & Richter did "Wachet auf" Cantata [No. 140] in mem. of Günther Ramin (ex-Leipzig Cantor) with great dignity & intensity. It was a good end to a remarkable week. After, I went up to the Choir –

very sweet – lots of speeches, toasts, & singing. The Germans are very devoted to music & damned efficient. More of all this later.

2 Britten's pocket diary notes that the music of Act III was required by 30 July; he was completing the sketch just in time.

3 The long-awaited postponement was to be made official on 9 August. See Letter 869 n. 4.

4 Alyson Pritt (b. 1941), daughter of Lyn Pritt, the owner of the Wentworth Hotel, Aldeburgh. Her puppy was also called Clytie.

875 To Edith Sitwell

4 CRABBE STREET, ALDEBURGH, SUFFOLK
July 29th 1956

My dearest Edith,

I am afraid it is going to take all your kindness & goodness, aided by (I hope!) your friendship for us and the Aldeburgh Festival to forgive this letter! I am going to ask you a great favour.

You know, I am sure, that for a long time we have been planning to build our own proper theatre here ... we suffer so much, artistically & financially (it holds less than 300 people) from the Jubilee Hall, that now, really to survive, we must go ahead with this plan. In fact next week we hope to buy the site for it, an excellent one on top of the hill, & therefore to launch the campaign to raise money for the actual building of the theatre. We are having a grand Bazaar, Garden Party, on September 8th. All the local people are working desperately hard for it, and we are looking for the most terrific, film-starry person to open it, to bring as many people in as possible, to make the greatest possible publicity for the scheme. Because you always say how nice & simple, & also interested in "cultural" things, she is, I wonder whether you could help us approach Marilyn Monroe.[1] I don't know her at all, & in fact am slightly disturbed by her friendship with the Oliviers (who don't I gather really approve of us much),[2] so a word from you would help enormously. Could you either write to her yourself, or write me a short note (a testimonial that the Festival is a really serious hard-working affair!) to enclose with an invitation to her? The date is September 8th, in the afternoon – but all details can be given by the authorities here, you needn't bother with that. Dear Edith, you give us so much in so many ways, that I hate to ask for more, but I feel this might find your sympathy – or if not, I know you won't hesitate to say no!

My love to you & Osbert,
BEN

P.S. I'm off to Switzerland on Saturday, so perhaps your (or her!) reply could come to me c/o Festival Office, Aldeburgh, who will be handling my letters.

1 American actress, pin-up and film star (1926–1962); on screen an extreme example of the iconic dumb and sexy blonde, Monroe showed signs of craving for artistic respect, studying method acting with Lee Strasberg at the Actors' Studio and in 1956 setting up her own production company to make films such as *The Prince and the Showgirl* and *Bus Stop*. On 29 June 1956 she had married the playwright Arthur Miller.

In 1954, *Life* magazine had brought together Edith Sitwell and Marilyn Monroe – in journalistic terms, an irresistible juxtaposition. The writer was to describe the actress in her 1965 autobiography, *Taken Care Of* (quoted in Victoria Glendinning, *Edith Sitwell: A Unicorn Among Lions* (p. 305)):

> She was very quiet, and had great natural dignity (I cannot imagine anyone who knew her trying to take a liberty with her) and was extremely intelligent. She was also exceedingly sensitive [...] In repose her face was at moments strangely, prophetically tragic, like the face of a beautiful ghost – a little Spring-ghost, an innocent fertility-daemon, the vegetation spirit that was Ophelia.

When Monroe came to London to film an adaptation of Terence Rattigan's *The Prince and the Showgirl* in the summer of 1956, the acquaintance was renewed and excited comment in the press.

Sitwell responded to Britten's request in a letter of 30 July 1956:

> I'd better let you know at once, so there will be no delay in getting someone else. Alas, there *isn't* a *hope* that we can get Miss Monroe. For both she and her husband told me, when they came to see me, that she is filming – or rather *will* be filming, for she hadn't, then, actually started – twelve hours a day.

2 Laurence Olivier (1907–1989), British actor, director and theatre administrator and his wife, the Indian-born British actress Vivien Leigh (1913–1967), who had achieved worldwide fame with her performance as Scarlett O'Hara in the 1939 film *Gone with the Wind*. The casting of Olivier and Monroe in *The Prince and the Showgirl*, which Olivier was also directing, reflected the culture clash of the two main characters and brought together two highly skilled performers drawn from irreconcilable schools of acting. Tensions on set were exacerbated by Olivier's frustration with Monroe's erratic behaviour and poor time-keeping.

The Oliviers' apparent 'disapproval' of Britten and Pears was no doubt coloured by the actors' close friendship with William Walton, who could be cutting about Britten and Pears in private. (Olivier had commissioned Walton to provide the scores for his three Shakespeare films, *Henry V* (1944), *Hamlet* (1948) and *Richard III* (1955).) Although Walton's biographer Michael Kennedy notes that Walton was untroubled by Britten's pacifism and homosexuality, there are several documented instances of

Walton making thinly veiled homophobic remarks about Britten; one such jibe was even made in front of Tippett, who was himself homosexual. The Oliviers would also have been conscious of Walton's jealousy of Britten's meteoric success in the post-war years, which came at a time when Walton's own fortunes as a composer were taking a downward turn. See Michael Kennedy, *Portrait of Walton*, pp. 130–33.

In her letter of 30 July 1956 to Britten, Sitwell wrote: 'Apropos of what you say about Sir Laurence Olivier, the man is a fool, anyhow. His outrage on *Hamlet* [the 1948 film] proves that!'

876 To Ronald Duncan

4 CRABBE STREET, ALDEBURGH, SUFFOLK
August 2nd 1956

Dearest Ronnie,

Just off & you're in the middle of your [Taw and Torridge] Festival, I believe; so won't write more than a note.But I wanted to tell you that the Prince of P's is postponed till at least Christmas[1] – I can't get the 600 pages of score written in time – I'm too old & tired to keep up the 14 hours a day schedule which it entails. It's all disappointing, but since the music's now all written, & I like it, I suppose it isn't the end of the world (but I expect D. Webster thinks it is!). Just off to Switzerland to try & recover.

Hope all goes well with you & nice audiences.

Lots of love,
BEN

1 The first performance of *The Prince of the Pagodas* finally took place at the Royal Opera House on 1 January 1957.

877 To Anthony Gishford

Schloss Tarasp, Unter Engadin
August 18th 1956

My dear Tony,

Just a greeting from our mountain fastness. This is a staggering place – a mediaeval castle, rebuilt, with incredible taste & luxury, at the beginning of this century, & now passed on to Ludwig of Hesse. Both of them (the Hesses) came from Munich (where Imo & I met Peter) & settled us in here, spent a week showing us the countryside & all, & have now gone away, she to England, he to the Mediterranean. It is a wonderful place to work in, still nicer to rest in – & because of the news you will have heard on your return,[1] one does have now a bit of respite from old crotchets &

quavers. All the same, Imo & I are now approaching the end of Act II,[2] working on the average I'd say about 4–5 hours a day. How we should [have] fared if we'd tried to finish the whole, I can't imagine; & I think you will understand when you see the fragment of Act II posted 3 days ago to Erwin!

I hope you had a good holiday, with passable weather. It hasn't been too bad here – quite a lot of sun. I suppose you are now back, & probably soon off to Edinburgh. I hope that's enjoyable.

While Lu Hesse was here he & we passed idle moments in translating the 'Screw' – I should think finishing about ¼ of it or more – in fact what we could remember of the text, having no music or libretto with us. It was great fun, & I think he's done a remarkable job. He is of course an accomplished poet, & we could all help in making it fit. I think it'll be very useful, especially if the 1st German performance takes place in Darmstadt as Ernst [Roth] seems to think it might.[3] Ernst, by the way, was splendid over the Ballet crisis; most understanding & helpful.[4]

We leave here on 26th – to motor slowly back across France, arr. in England on Sept. 4th. When will you be around?

Love from Imo & Peter – & from me,
Yours ever,
BEN

1 The postponement of the first performance of *The Prince of the Pagodas*.

2 Britten wrote 'Act 2 score' in his pocket diary on 13 August, presumably the date on which the orchestration of the act was begun. Britten was to write to Roger Duncan on 29 October 1956: 'I've been madly busy (still am – at that blinking Ballet – just 100 pages [of full score] to go!'; and in the postcript of a letter to Prince Ludwig of Hesse and the Rhine, dated 7 November 1956, Britten reported: 'That b. Ballet is FINISHED, & I feel as if I've been just let out of prison after 18 months hard labour.'

3 The Darmstadt production of *The Turn of the Screw* (staged at the Landestheater) was to take place in 1957: see Letter 906. Prince Ludwig's German translation of the libretto was also published in 1957.

4 This would appear to be a rare occasion in the usually stormy relationship between Britten and Roth when the composer was prepared to acknowledge his publisher's negotiating skills in what had been an extremely difficult situation in respect of the delay with *Pagodas*.

878 To Anthony Gishford
[*Typed*]

4 CRABBE STREET, ALDEBURGH
25th October, 1956

My dear Tony,

I am afraid it is the usual "no" to Walt Disney.[1] At the moment my policy about films is a negative one, unless it is a particularly interesting project in which music is an integral part, and in which I could be involved from the start. This is clearly not the case in the present instance.

I have just returned from a very touching performance of St. Nicolas at Southwell[2] given by the Southwell Minster Grammar School on the occasion of its millenary (one does not often have the opportunity of performing in a <u>millenary</u>, so Peter and I went and did it for love). I wish you could have been there because it really sounded nice in that wonderful building. Incidentally, their very enterprising musical staff is thinking of doing a stage performance in the Minster of "Abraham and Isaac". Quite a good idea, don't you think?[3]

I have just had a touching letter from Budapest (posted July 17th!) about some very successful performances of "Let's Make an Opera!" there; did you know about this?

Yours ever,
BEN

1 American film producer (1901–1966) who pioneered the production of animated cartoons starring such anthropomorphic animals as Mickey Mouse and Donald Duck; in 1937, Disney produced his first animated feature, *Snow White and the Seven Dwarfs*. In the 1930s Britten often enjoyed Disney's Mickey Mouse cartoons and 'Silly Symphonies'.

   Howard Connell, Production Manager of Walt Disney British Films, had written to Gishford on 22 October, with a proposal for Britten to compose the music for a thirty-minute travelogue entitled *Wales*. Between 1953 and 1960, the Disney company produced a series of seventeen such travelogues, designed mainly for children.

2 The performance took place on 23 October, with a rehearsal the previous day.

3 Although Britten here approves of the proposed staging of his *Canticle II: 'Abraham and Isaac'*, the practice does not seem to have caught on during his lifetime and it received no further encouragement from the composer.

879 To Anthony Gishford

HOTEL VIER JAHRESZEITEN – RESTAURANT WALTERSPIEL,
MUNCHEN, MAXIMILIANSTRASSE 4, SCHLIESSFACH 1

Nov. 27th 1956

My dear Tony,

I was awfully glad to get your wire – very good of you to remember.[1] I also stupidly (under the shadow of EOG finances) forgot to thank you for 'St Peter',[2] which I've read with great interest, & not a little disillusion – it's extraordinary how much scholars prove we don't know when they get going. Still I think the oratorio will grow, in spite of them!

Here all goes well – madly strenuous, & one feels uneasy from knowing & not-knowing the news. Everyone is very panicky here.[3] Still the concerts are full & seem successful.[4]

I've asked a lot about the ballet situation, but probably Ernst [Roth] knows it as well as I do. Munich seems the best (but only if Carter[5] is there, & his position seems uncertain). Düsseldorf is madly keen to do it, but they all say there is no company at all yet, & they'd more or less have to form one to do it properly. Frankfurt is a possibility, especially if they'd get someone like Kurt Jooss[6] to produce it. Wuppertal has the best reputation, but is clearly too small. My preference honestly would be Munich (with Carter) or Frankfurt (with Jooss), but I've no idea whether they are interested, & Düsseldorf certainly is.[7] P'raps Ernst can find out.

I get back next Tuesday – & will ring you to find out how everything is. I hope the Ballet material progresses without being too much of a head-ache.

Greetings to all, & thanks again,
Yours ever,
BEN

Peter sends his love too.

1 Probably a birthday greeting, Britten having celebrated his forty-third birthday on 22 November.

2 A volume relevant to Britten's and Duncan's projected oratorio on the subject. No such book can be traced at BPL.

3 The autumn of 1956 was an acutely tense period in international relations. On 23 October students and workers took to the streets of Budapest, demanding greater personal freedom and the dismantling of control by Soviet Russia. On 31 October the newly appointed Prime Minister, Imre Nagy, announced that Hungary would withdraw from the Warsaw Pact. On 4 November, Soviet tanks rolled into Budapest, crushing the short-lived attempt at liberalization. About thirty thousand people are believed to have died in the fighting; Nagy was executed and buried in an unmarked grave,

and over two hundred thousand people fled to the West to avoid reprisals. By 14 November Soviet authority had been re-established.

During the same weeks the Suez crisis was unfolding. President Gamal Abdel Nasser of Egypt nationalized the Suez Canal, taking it from the British and French companies that had previously owned it. Britain and France responded by planning a joint invasion and occupation of the Canal zone. Despite denials at the time, collusion between Britain, France and Israel was later exposed. Israeli troops invaded Egypt's Sinai Peninsula on 29 October. After Nasser refused Britain's and France's offer of temporary occupation, British and French forces attacked and invaded Egypt. The Soviet Union threatened to intervene on Egypt's behalf and America, under President Dwight D. Eisenhower, pressurized the Europeans to withdraw, which after a month they did, leaving Soviet influence in the region strengthened, and tensions heightened between Israel and her neighbours.

4 Britten and Pears had travelled to West Germany together for a concert tour that began in Frankfurt on 13 November and continued with recitals in Dusseldorf (15th and 23rd), Wupperthal (16th), Brucksaler (20th), Cologne (22nd), Ingoldstadt (26th) and Munich (27th). Having spent a few days at Wolfsgarten, Britten wrote to Princess Margaret of Hesse and the Rhine on 25 November 1956 from Ingoldstadt:

My birthday after we left Wolfsgarten fell to a pretty low ebb – Köln was big & seemed unfriendly & cold – although the concert went well, but in a gigantic kind of modernistic dance hall – fearful place (one's getting a pretty good idea on this tour of how not to build concert halls!); & after the concert we went with some pretty dreary chaps & dames to a keller & tried to be happy – but, oh, so different from Wolfsgarten! Düsseldorf was better, because of the sweet British Consul couple who looked after us so well, & a nicer hall, & our faithful Düsseldörfers.

And now we're here – bitterly cold, coming thro' some snow on the journey – but rather a sweet town. The nice musik-direktor took us to Eichstadt this morning, & what we could see of the Dom, & town through our tears (from the cold) was lovely. And in half an hour or so we are off to our concert in an enormous bier-keller! . . . What a life. But then München, Stuttgart, & Baden-baden, where we'll see you – something to look forward to.

5 Alan Carter (b. 1920), British dancer, choreographer and ballet director. In the mid-1950s Carter and his wife, the ballet mistress Joan Harris, were bringing to the Munich Ballet the traditions and discipline that can be traced back to Diaghilev's Ballets Russes and Dame Ninette de Valois's Sadler's Wells company and school.

6 German dancer and choreographer (1901–1979), who mixed classical ballet with theatre, developing what has come to be known as dance theatre. His best-known work remains the strongly pacifist *The Green Table* of 1932. The following year he fled Germany after refusing to dismiss the Jewish members of his company. He eventually settled in England, founding the Jooss–Leeder School of Dance with Sigurd Leeder, who had been teaching at Morley College, at Dartington Hall, where the Ballets Jooss was resident

from 1935. Jooss was a charismatic teacher and his influence can still be perceived in the work of a number of contemporary European choreographers. See also Diary for 3 October 1935, n. 5.

7 Of these projected German venues for *The Prince of the Pagodas*, only the Munich performance came to fruition (in March 1958). Cranko also staged the ballet at Stuttgart on 6 November 1960: see John Percival, *Theatre in my Blood: A Biography of John Cranko*, pp. 130–32. The ballet scored something of a success in Stuttgart (due in part to a major overhaul of the original choreography), Cranko immediately being invited to take up the position of Ballet Director of the Württemberg State Theatres during the following January. By this stage, Cranko's relationship with Britten had foundered, principally through the choreographer's inefficiency when producing *A Midsummer Night's Dream* at Aldeburgh in June 1960 (see HCBB, pp. 392–6), which Britten could not tolerate. So bad had relations between the two men become that, when Cranko wished to revive the Stuttgart production of *Pagodas* in 1968, he felt unable to approach Britten to request alterations to the score.

No doubt some strain had initially been placed on the relationship between Britten and Cranko as a result of the lukewarm critical response (see Letter 882 n. 4) to the first production of *Pagodas* at the Royal Opera House, which opened on 1 January 1957 (Britten conducting) and ran for a further twenty-two performances. The ballet was recorded for Decca in February, drastically shortened by over forty cuts sanctioned by the composer.

The Prince of the Pagodas returned to the Covent Garden stage in 1958 (five performances), 1959 (three performances) and 1960 (three performances) but was then dropped from the repertory in spite of a triumphant production at La Scala, Milan (May 1957; see Letter 894 n. 3) and a well-received staging in New York (October 1957). The ballet was staged by the Kirov Ballet in Leningrad as part of their 1971–72 season (on which occasion Britten agreed to make changes to the score), and the British public's interest in the work was revived by a performance of large sections at the 1988 Aldeburgh Festival by the London Sinfonietta under Oliver Knussen. These performers recorded the entire (uncut) score for Virgin in 1990, by which time the ballet had returned to the Royal Opera House in a new staging choreographed by Kenneth MacMillan (1989). Although MacMillan's revisions to the original Cranko plot made nonsense of many of Britten's dramatically effective motivic transformations, the staging was a welcome return for a major Britten score that had been neglected in its native country for almost thirty years.

In the late 1990s, the ballet score received a new lease of life in the form of an extended suite for concert performance, compiled by Donald Mitchell and Mervyn Cooke, which was first performed by Vladimir Ashkenazy and the Deutsches Symphonie-Orchester Berlin on 4 June 1997 at the Concertgebouw, Amsterdam.

880 To Peter Pears

4 CRABBE STREET, ALDEBURGH
December 4th 1956

My darling,

It was one of the most horrid moments I can remember – yesterday afternoon on Frankfurt station.[1] It was unbearable seeing you steaming off into the cold darkness towards Munich, so many hundreds of miles away from Aldeburgh. But one mustn't be silly, it really isn't for so long, & when you get this half the time of separation will probably be over. I am living for Saturday week, and in the meantime you are so very much in my thoughts. It is lovely to think of you singing Bach, & with people around who love & appreciate you. But no one can, or could, more than I do; you are a most adorable man & artist, intelligent, gifted, simple, loving & noble, and with the lightest touch too. I am really very, very lucky to be alive with you around – & 'how' around!

My journey was long & excessively boring – train was ½ hr late & I froze on the station, & then boiled in the carriage. With a bad meal after Eindhoven, into the bargain. But the boat wasn't too full, & passage fairly calm after a tossing beginning. Poor old Jeremy [Cullum] dragged himself from a 'flu bed to meet me, & I packed him off back to bed. Miss Hudson & the dogs are in spanking form; Jove's grown tremendously & is excessively naughty & attractive. Clytie gave me a sweet welcome, but looked over my shoulder to see whether he was there too, & was disappointed to find it wasn't the boss himself! I've seen Mary [Potter] for lunch, & she's very excited at the idea of us all being back for Christmas. I shall get on with Christmas arrangements this evening – & see if I can track down a 'conjuror'. This is scribbled off to send you a letter or two – they are mostly very boring!

The best of luck for all the concerts – & all, all my love for always, my honiest of honeys,

Your
B

1 Britten returned to England on 3 December to allow himself plenty of time to prepare for the imminent rehearsals of *The Prince of the Pagodas*, which began one week later. Pears remained in West Germany as he was due to perform Bach's *Christmas Oratorio* under Eugen Jochum in Munich on 6 and 7 December (Parts I–III) and 13 and 14 December (Parts IV–VI).

In her interview with Donald Mitchell (Aldeburgh, 22 June 1977), Imogen Holst shared her memories of the rehearsals for the first performance of *The Prince of the Pagodas*:

He was never meant to conduct *Prince of the Pagodas*. Covent Garden persuaded him against his will and said that they couldn't do it without him. And I was in the stalls at Covent Garden [during a rehearsal] when Ninette de Valois came and sat down by his side and argued, cajoling – I could've killed her – and I saw, then and there, Ben being defeated by this woman and having to give way. And it wasn't of course just by the woman, it was that he, I suppose, realized that if the thing had got to be done he'd got to do it himself. It wasn't only that his arm was bad but in those days he'd *no* experience of conducting a *huge* orchestra in a *very* long work in an orchestral pit for dance [. . .]

Ninette de Valois was impossible about [Svetlana] Beriosova, and wanted Beriosova's most beautiful solo to be altered [. . .] She came up, again, in the stalls, and said, 'But you see, Ben, she's a tall girl, she's got a very long back.' My *God* – that's nothing to do with Ben's *music* – that's John Cranko's [responsibility], and it was appalling, what he'd given that woman to do. It was nothing but physical tests of strength and endurance [. . .]

When it got very near the end, the last orchestral and stage rehearsal, Ben couldn't carry his own case with the music in it because his arm was so bad, so of course I did that for him. He wanted to ring up his doctor about having treatment for it, and so I did that, you know, from the office, and came back and said he would see him. Peter had come in to listen to some of the rehearsal and I must tell you that I got the impression very strongly throughout *The Prince of the Pagodas*, which lasted a long time and was a terrible burden to Ben, that Peter had no interest in it because it hadn't got singing things in it, and that therefore all that support that he gave Ben in all his compositions with a part for him in, which kept Ben going, was absolutely cut off at the main.

The climax of that lack of interest was very painful – I think it was the last full rehearsal before the performance, when Peter, having blown in for a little while, in the coffee break, halfway through, said to Ben, 'Well, I'm going now. I'm going to have a haircut.' And walked out of the theatre, leaving Ben bewildered and in pain – no one to get him a taxi, no one but me to carry the bag or anything, and it wasn't my job to encourage Ben, because I didn't do that side. I did it through the music, but nothing else. I thought it was *ghastly*. I thought if there was ever a moment in a composer's life when he needed his very, *very* nearest beloved just by his side [. . .] If Peter had been singing in Glasgow, well, of course he wouldn't have had him around, but he was going shopping and having a *haircut*. I found that terrible.

881 To Nancy Evans
[*Typed*]

4 CRABBE STREET, ALDEBURGH
3rd January, 1957

[*Handwritten:*] My dearest Nancy,

This year we are celebrating the Tenth Aldeburgh Festival. We have, we think, found the ideal event to celebrate such a momentous occasion, and I hope you will agree: this is to perform "Albert Herring" in the Jubilee Hall on the first night with, as far as possible, the cast that played it there in our first Festival in 1948. Joan [Cross] has very sweetly agreed to sing Lady Billows for us, and warmly joins me in hoping that you will come and sing Nancy.

The performance would be on Friday, June 14th, and in order to take as little of your precious time as possible we are planning to have a day's rehearsal in Aldeburgh on the 13th, and a dress rehearsal on the morning of the 14th. If you felt inclined we could have a musical brush up in London the previous week on a day to suit you.

All practical arrangements will be made by Stephen Reiss, the Festival Secretary, and Basil Douglas.

[*Handwritten*:] I am afraid that just one day's rehearsal may seem mad – but it will be a rather light-hearted occasion. Please join us, dear Nancy![1]

Much love,
BEN

1 Nancy Evans was unable to sing the role of Nancy in the gala performance of *Albert Herring*, given in the presence of the then Princess Royal (Lord Harewood's mother), at the Jubilee Hall as the opening event of the 1957 Aldeburgh Festival, as she was already engaged by Glyndebourne for *Die Zauberflöte*; the role was performed by Margaret Lensky. However, Britten was successful in persuading six members of the original cast – Joan Cross (Lady Billows), Gladys Parr (Florence Pike), Peter Pears (Albert), William Parsons (Mr Gedge), Norman Lumsden (Superintendent Budd) and Roy Ashton (Mr Upfold) – to join him for this performance, which he himself conducted. Britten was to write to Eric Crozier (26 June 1957): 'We did a lovely performance of "Albert Herring" at the beginning of the Festival. It was glorious to have Joan and many of the original cast back, but of course we missed Nancy.'

For this performance Britten rewrote several passages of Lady Billows's role, lowering some of the higher-lying tessitura in deference to Joan Cross, who came out of retirement to sing in the performance. The vocal score with Britten's emendations to Lady Billows's vocal line is part of the EOG Collection at BPL.

882 To David Webster

5 CHESTER GATE, REGENT'S PARK, LONDON, N.W.1
Jan. 4th 1957

My dear David,

This is just a note to thank you for your extremely encouraging wire on the first night of the 'Pagodas'. I am so glad you like the score, & I hope the public will like the Ballet & continue to come to it. I am sorry to have let you down about conducting the other performances – but who am I to argue with an extremely fierce doctor?¹ I'll let you know about other performances as soon as I begin to recover a bit! (In the meantime, please don't count on me).

I am so sorry about Ninette² – sorry for her sake, but also sorry as there were quite a few things I wanted to say to her about the Ballet Co. – especially the musical side – while they were fresh in my mind. But they must now wait, but not too long I hope.³

Are all things right now with Johnnie Cranko?⁴ I do hope you've had your talk with him, because the poor boy's <u>really</u> worried.

With thanks & love,
Yours ever,
BEN (B)

1 Britten conducted the first three performances of *The Prince of the Pagodas* (1, 2 and 3 January) but then had to withdraw from the remaining seven performances (between 5 and 22 January) on doctor's orders. Programmes surviving at BPL for 19 and 22 January suggest the subsequent performances were conducted by Robert Irving and Kenneth Alwyn; the performance on 19 January was shared between them, Alwyn conducting the first act and Irving the second and third.

Britten wrote to William Plomer (25 January 1957):

> I was really knocked out by that Ballet. I never wished to conduct, was already seedy when the rehearsals started, & the performances were really agonising. After three of them, my doctor put his foot down, & here I am [in Aldeburgh], for a month, doing absolutely nothing, on a dreary diet, & thoroughly low!

2 De Valois had been in hospital since 6 January and, according to her letter to Britten of 30 January, had seen only part of the second performance. She told the composer:

> You did a great thing for the English Ballet, stimulating the interest that was so very much needed. I thought John's work, as a whole, was a remarkable achievement – although there are spots where I feel that he has 'visually' moved away from the music. But it is a remarkable choreographic effort for one barely 30 – and it has had a great success.

3 Britten wrote to de Valois (4 February 1957):

> I plan to come back to London to start on the recording of the new Ballet next week; may we have our lunch one day then, because there is so much to talk about?

An entry in the composer's pocket engagement diary suggests they met on 22 February. At the top of Britten's agenda would have been not only his serious concerns about the musical standards of the ballet company, which undoubtedly made their own contribution to his difficulties in preparing *Pagodas* for performance, but also the standard of the dancing, particularly within the corps de ballet and the smaller roles (see Letter 886).

The Prince of the Pagodas

(*A Fairy Story*)
BALLET IN THREE ACTS
Music by Benjamin Britten
Choreography and scenario by John Cranko
Scenery by John Piper
Costumes by Desmond Heeley
Lighting by William Bundy

ACT I

THE COURT OF THE EMPEROR OF THE MIDDLE KINGDOM

The Fool, a good servant	PIRMIN TRECU
The Dwarf, a flattering servant	RAY POWELL
The Emperor of the Middle Kingdom, father of Belle Epine and Belle Rose	LESLIE EDWARDS
His four Councillors	CHRISTOPHER NEWTON, DAVID SHIELDS, JOHN SALE, RICHARD FARLEY
His Courtiers	MARY DRAGE, GERD LARSEN, BRENDA TAYLOR, VALERIE TAYLOR, MERIEL EVANS, STELLA FARRANCE, CATHERINE BOULTON, YVONNE CARTIER, FRANKLIN WHITE, RONALD PLAISTED, DEREK RENCHER, DOUGLAS STEUART, DAVID DREW, DAVID BOSWELL, ARNOTT MADER, KEITH ROSSON

The King of the North	⎫ All anxious to marry ⎧	DESMOND DOYLE
The King of the East	⎬ the ⎨	PHILIP CHATFIELD
The King of the West	⎬ heiress to the crown ⎨	PETER CLEGG
The King of the South	⎭ of the Middle Kingdom ⎩	GARY BURNE

Pages to the Kings	CHRISTINE BECKLEY, MAVIS OSBORN, DEBRA WAYNE, ANN HOWARD, ANTOINETTE SIBLEY, JOAN BENESH, DOROTHEA ZAYMES, ANGELA WALTON
The Princess Belle Epine, favourite daughter of the Emperor and heiress to the crown of the Middle Kingdom	JULIA FARRON
The Princess Belle Rose, the much neglected younger daughter of the Emperor who has only her beauty and simplicity for her dowry	SVETLANA BERIOSOVA
A Vision of the Prince of the Pagodas	DAVID BLAIR
Four Frogs, messengers from the Prince of the Pagodas	KEITH MILLAND, BASIL THOMPSON, WILLIAM WILSON, WILLIAM MORGAN

INTERVAL
Warning bells will be sounded five minutes and two minutes before the rise of the curtain

ACT II

Scene 1 BELLE ROSE'S STRANGE VOYAGE TO THE KINGDOM OF THE PAGODAS

The Princess Belle Rose	SVETLANA BERIOSOVA
Four Frogs	KEITH MILLAND, BASIL THOMPSON, WILLIAM WILSON, WILLIAM MORGAN
The Stars	MERLE PARK, SHIRLEY GRAHAME, MARGARET MERCIER, DEBRA WAYNE, GEORGINA PARKINSON, ANN HOWARD

Programme for the first performance of *The Prince of the Pagodas*, Royal Opera House, 1 January 1957

The Clouds	DAVID SHIELDS, RONALD PLAISTED, DAVID DREW, DEREK RENCHER, KEITH ROSSON, DOUGLAS STEUART, CHRISTOPHER NEWTON, JOHN SALE, ARNOTT MADER, DAVID BOSWELL
The Moon	ANYA LINDEN
The Fishes	DOREEN WELLS, JUDITH SINCLAIR, PIRMIN TRECU, PETER CLEGG
The Rulers of the Fire	BRIAN SHAW, MARYON LANE

Scene 11 THE ARRIVAL AND ADVENTURES OF BELLE ROSE IN THE KINGDOM OF THE PAGODAS

The Princess Belle Rose	SVETLANA BERIOSOVA
The Green Salamander afterwards Prince of the Pagodas ...	DAVID BLAIR
The Six Pagodas	JENNIFER GAY, DOREEN EASTLAKE, SALLY LEWIS, PATRICIA THOROGOOD, JACQUELINE WATCHAM, CHRISTINE BECKLEY

INTERVAL
Warning bells will be sounded five minutes and two minutes before the rise of the curtain

ACT III

Scene 1 THE COURT OF THE EMPRESS OF THE MIDDLE KINGDOM

The Empress Belle Epine	JULIA FARRON
The Dwarf	RAY POWELL
Her Courtiers, unhappy under her tyranny ...	MARY DRAGE, GERD LARSEN, BRENDA TAYLOR, VALERIE TAYLOR, MERIEL EVANS, STELLA FARRANCE, CATHERINE BOULTON, YVONNE CARTIER, FRANKLIN WHITE, RONALD PLAISTED, DEREK RENCHER, DOUGLAS STEUART, DAVID DREW, DAVID BOSWELL, ARNOTT MADER, KEITH ROSSON
The ex-Emperor, ill treated by his daughter the Empress ...	LESLIE EDWARDS
The Fool	PIRMIN TRECU
The Princess Belle Rose	SVETLANA BERIOSOVA
The Green Salamander	DAVID BLAIR

Scene 11 BELLE ROSE'S TRIUMPHANT RETURN AND MARRIAGE TO THE PRINCE OF THE PAGODAS

Pas de Six	ANYA LINDEN, BRYAN ASHBRIDGE, MERLE PARK, GARY BURNE, MARYON LANE, DESMOND DOYLE
The Fool	PIRMIN TRECU
The Prince and Princess of the Pagodas ...	SVETLANA BERIOSOVA, DAVID BLAIR
The Father of Belle Rose, once Emperor of the Middle Kingdom	LESLIE EDWARDS
Subjects of the Prince of the Pagodas	MARGARET MERCIER, DEBRA WAYNE, GEORGINA PARKINSON, ANTOINETTE SIBLEY, DOREEN EASTLAKE, MARGARET WING, HYLDA ZINKIN, CHRISTINE BECKLEY, DAVID SHIELDS, CHRISTOPHER NEWTON, JOHN SALE, DOUGLAS STEUART, RICHARD FARLEY, DAVID DREW, RONALD PLAISTED, DAVID BOSWELL
Pagoda Ladies	JENNIFER GAY, JACQUELINE WATCHAM, SALLY LEWIS, PATRICIA THOROGOOD, AUDREY HENDERSON, PATRICIA HANCOCK
Heralds	KEITH MILLAND, BASIL THOMPSON, WILLIAM WILSON, WILLIAM MORGAN

4 Britten refers to the criticism of *The Prince of the Pagodas* in the press. The critic of *The Times* (2 January 1957) wrote:

This new British ballet, which was enthusiastically received on its first performance at Covent Garden last night, is the joint work of four British artists: Cranko and [Desmond] Heeley [the costume designer] are both young, Britten and Piper more mature but still dedicated to adventure in artistic creation.

If there is a disappointment, it is in the premises of Cranko's scenario. Himself an inventive and thoughtful choreographer, he has decided to accept not only the fairy-tale subject of the classic Russian and French full-length ballets but also the conventional claims of *divertissement* which were natural once but which seem today to exercise an unsatisfactory restraint on the flow of the drama. So it is that, after a highly effective expository first act which has ended with the abduction of the Cinderalla-style heroine by a *cortège* of flying frogs, the first part of the second act is devoted, *à la Casse-Noisette*, to a depiction of her journey through air, water, and fire; and when at length Belle Rose wins her prince the third act is prolonged by a formal *divertissement* again – there has already been something of the kind in the first act, when North, South, East, and West send their kings as courtiers.

These *intermezzi* make the ballet appear too long but, like some of the balletic interludes in French grand opera, they have subsidiary qualities of some charm and individuality: the costumes and the music in the first scene of the second act are splendid; the *pas de six* and *grand pas de deux* of the closing scene show both Britten and Cranko in their most original and engaging form.

Once alive to the causes of these sags in tension we can wholeheartedly enjoy the inventive qualities and the style, the exhilaration and the florid spectacle of *The Prince of the Pagodas*. The oriental and fantastical elements in the story give it a novel twist, and they are matched by winning *trouvailles* of music, choreography, and *décor* alike. The logic of fairy story is quite often obscure, and so we may find our own solutions for the Prince's apparently heartless treatment of Belle Rose when he has brought her to his land of magical pagodas. But a ballet which brings together several demonstrations of airborne travel, transformations, metamorphoses, and working model structures as well cannot but beguile the child in every spectator – and this Everyman is well spoiled, too, by the gay colours and shapes of scenery and costumes, and by Britten's supply of lilting tunes and evocative sonorities.

It is a ballet for the young, and it was danced, for the most part, by young dancers, the stars of tomorrow. Mr Blair and Miss Beriosova in their heroic parts, Miss [Julia] Farron as a proud villainess, another Odile, Mr [Ray] Powell, a vile sycophant in the image of Sir Laurence Olivier's Crookback, have the lion's share. But this is a cake too full of plums for summary accounting; everyone must be his own Jack Horner.

Martin Cooper (*Daily Telegraph*, 2 January 1957) reported:

A three-act ballet with music by Benjamin Britten would be a feather in the cap of any opera management, and Covent Garden is to be congratulated on the commission.

The Prince of the Pagodas, which had its first performance there last night, is an infinitely superior pantomime based on 'Beauty and the Beast' and the story follows, often in considerable detail, many of the incidents of the *Sleeping Beauty* ballet.

The hints of political satire in Act I, where the court recalled King Dodon's in *The Golden Cockerel*, were not followed through and the major interest of the work lay in the magnificence of the spectacle and the beauty and ingenuity of isolated numbers.

Ingenuity and acrobatic display were certainly the chief characteristics of John Cranko's choreography, in which complicated patterns were developed at great length for their own sake and many of the lifts suggested the circus or the Folies Bergère. In fact this fairy story was carried on by wit and virtuosity rather than by the more conventional engaging of the emotions.

The same was for the most part true of Britten's score, which he conducted himself. He has made no attempt to disguise his indebtedness to other writers of ballet music.

Even so the music is unmistakably his own in sonority, texture and colour, even down to the pastiche of a Javanese [*sic*] gamelan. (Cranko's parody of Indian dancing was much less happy.) John Piper's sets were most successful when most exotically fantastic.

It was the prettiness of the toy pagodas in the second act which made up for the disappointing colour and architecture of the conventional 'Moorish' interior of Act I.

The rarity of lyrical feeling in the rest of the work enhanced the importance of Svetlana Beriosova's role, in which emotional expressiveness was combined with a wellnigh flawless technique and beautifully controlled art of of mime.

Julia Farron's evil princess was on rather too small a scale, though well conceived in detail, and David Blair skilfully combined the roles of prince and salamander, 'dancing' almost as expressively rampant as upright. In a huge cast Ray Powell's Dwarf, Leslie Edwards's Emperor and the members of the Pas de Six in Act III all deserve honourable mention.

The 'London Ballet Critic' of the *Manchester Guardian Weekly* (5 January 1957) contributed an extensive critique of Cranko's choreography:

> The most famous ballets have been made from fairy stories. *Swan Lake*, say, or *The Sleeping Beauty* turn happily into choreography, partly because the stories have the sort of butterfly fantasy which suits the artificialities of ballet's convention and not strain its very limited powers of dramatic narrative. Partly too because, in the world of fairy tales, it does not matter a bit if the story stops for a while to make room for dancing. But that does not mean that, even in ballet, a fairy story can do without some sort of plan; there must be a kind of coherence in its fantasy. And as with the scenario so too with the choreography: even in a choreographic fairy tale the dancing should not be all bits and pieces. It must show signs, as it were, of architecture, of planned development – as is so wonderfully shown, for instance, in the long familiar sequence of *Swan Lake* Act II or in almost the whole of *Giselle* or, for that matter, in the first act of Ashton's *Sylvia*.
>
> These points come to mind after a first view of John Cranko's *The Prince of the Pagodas*, an important addition (because it is this young choreographer's first attempt at a full three-act work) to the repertory of the Sadler's Wells Company. This ballet, which is rendered all the more important by the score which Benjamin Britten has composed for it, was first performed last week at Covent Garden, with the composer as conductor. It is made from a fairy story which Mr Cranko himself appears to have compounded out of 'Beauty and the Beast', 'Cinderella' and many tales besides; and just as the story, even within its fantastic idiom, is wild and

woolly, so too the choreography is bitty and inconsequent. That – the big fault in a work of great but intermittent interest – has the effect, among others, of making the ballet seem unduly long. It seems forever to be stopping and starting again.

Nevertheless the second of its three acts is, on the whole, a startling and lovely success. One long sequence of dance for 'clouds' and 'stars' and 'the moon' makes beautifully imaginative use of lifts, and of groups of dancers in a seemingly perpetual rise and fall of movement; and, in the same act, the 'fire dances' are, in their sharp, staccato style, almost as good. In the third act there are pleasant variations but here, as in the first one (which is much the weakest act) there is really not enough to compensate for the unrewarding air of 'bittiness'. Besides, in all but the very best passages of his choreography, Mr Cranko tends to lapse into a facile angularity – almost a 'smart' little skit on classicism – which is not quite suitable to the music.

There are, however, two great compensations throughout the ballet. One is the music, which is rich, tuneful, various, and strong (as ballet music should be) in rhythm; this is ballet music which will certainly stand up to the challenge of the concert hall. To the choreographer it must have been a challenge – with its many variations of rhythm and of mood – but a challenge with a big reward. The ballet's other consistent virtue, on Tuesday's showing, is in the standard of its performance. It cannot, perhaps, be said that Mr Cranko's choreography has always been kind to Beriosova (in the leading role), but her very special quality of cool, fluent grace is always apparent and always dominates her scenes. David Blair, Bryan Ashbridge, Gary Burne, Anya Linden, Julia Farron, Desmond Doyle – all these, and others besides, show a quite remarkable mastery. The standard of the company does, indeed, improve. The settings and costumes by John Piper and Desmond Heeley are pretty enough: and the ballet is brimful of the stage 'magic' which pleases us in pantomime.

This is Mr Cranko's most ambitious work to date; if it is far from being a complete success it is certainly abundant with promise, and it has moments which are superb.

The Sunday Times (6 January 1957) fielded two critics, one responsible for the dance, the other for the music. Cyril Beaumont considered

the result is not completely successful; for, despite Cranko's fertile invention, he sometimes usurps considerations of mood and style, and delighting to exploit his personal vein of humour, allows satire to become burlesque.

The ballet, supposedly self-explanatory, disdains a synopsis. A certain Emperor (resembling King Lear) has two daughters: his heiress, Belle Epine (another Goneril), and the charming Belle Rose. Add the suitors' episode from *Sleeping Beauty*, the meeting and wedding of Beauty and the Beast, called Green Salamander after D'Aulnoy's 'Green Serpent', and you have a theme with choreographic possibilities, but insufficient for three acts.

Felix Aprahamian was lukewarm in his response to Britten's music:

Unlike *The Turn of the Screw*, and despite a brilliant score, Britten's latest major work breaks no new ground. Although he may have matched John Cranko's scenario with music more significant than it deserves, this may not be enough to ensure the score's independent career.

The quasi-Balinese sounds in the second act of the ballet are contrived with Britten's usual skill, yet they remain pastiche, and there is little in the music more memorable than this colourful splash of oriental timbre.

An exception might be made of the arresting, fanfare-like music of the prelude, which recurs. Other ideas in the first act are no less admirable for recalling Stravinsky's best neo-classical manner, and elsewhere some of the purely descriptive music is enchanting. But the substance of the *divertissement* in Act Three is thin, and in the *grand pas de deux* for the Prince and Princess inspiration has flagged. Once again, Britten is seen responding best to definite dramatic or descriptive concepts; in their absence the music suffers.

Britten's music is no stranger to the ballet, but hitherto existing works such as the *Simple Symphony*, *Les Illuminations* and the Purcell and Frank Bridge *Variations* have been pressed into service.

Now, in the task of supplying Covent Garden with a full-length ballet score, the first by a native composer, Britten has succeeded; throughout the work, he has shown himself capable of writing effective dance music. He has still to prove – as did Delibes, Tchaikovsky, Ravel and Stravinsky – that this need be neither ephemeral nor insubstantial.

Aprahamian was not alone in singling out for criticism Britten's borrowings from gamelan. The static tonal effect caused by the relentless use of Balinese scales was seized on by Peter Heyworth, in the *Observer* (6 January 1957), who felt 'the difference between establishing atmosphere and giving a scene musical movement is all too apparent in the Balinese aura of the pagodas scene'. Donald Mitchell (while stressing the significance of the score as a 'brilliant amalgam of maximum dramatic effectiveness and maximum musical adventurousness'), singled out the pagodas scene for criticism in his lengthy review of the work in the *Musical Times* 98 (February 1957), p. 91:

The work's remaining 'new' aspect – the incorporation into the second act of an Indonesian (?) percussion band (a consequence of Mr Britten's recent travels) – though dramatically justified, was a major musical error: once the ensemble's tinkling has been savoured, its motivic stagnation becomes painfully tedious, all the more so since it is surrounded by music so richly inventive. In any case, this Oriental interlude is wildly out of stylistic place, though a transitional passage or two elsewhere proved that Mr Britten could, if he had insisted less on authenticity, have built his Oriental inflections into his score without disrupting its consistency. It is a pity that the second act should be marred by an indiscretion not only inappropriate but boring.

These comments are noteworthy in drawing attention to those ostensibly insignificant moments in Britten's score which attempt a fusion of Eastern and Western techniques in a manner looking directly ahead to the consummate synthesis of gamelan characteristics with Western motivic techniques that was to characterize Britten's final opera, *Death in Venice*. Donald Mitchell later explained his early response to the ballet (DMDV, p. 207, n. 16) on the grounds that the culture shock that the gamelan music in *Pagodas* presented was altogether too much for me, which may explain, though not excuse, my inept response to it – an indication, however, of how novel the experience was that Britten's gamelan offered and how sharp was its impact.

On the later critical reaction to *Pagodas*, see MCBFE, pp. 245–8.

It was perhaps in response to the negative criticism of his contribution that Cranko contributed two substantial articles – 'Making a Ballet – 1' and 'Making a Ballet – 2' – to *The Sunday Times* (13 and 20 January 1957). While his first article was concerned with the art of the choreographer, the second focuses on his collaboration with Britten and the designers John Piper and Desmond Heeley:

About three years ago I was asked by the Sadler's Wells organization to submit a scenario for a three-act ballet. How was one to provide a vehicle for creative choreography, rather than 'classical' pastiche, which would still have the immediate box-office appeal required? I decided that the mythological fairy tale would supply the framework needed.

In his ballet *Parade* Cocteau created such images as 'The Little American Girl', 'The Manager on Horseback', and 'The Chinese Conjurer', but found that, because he had given no narrative relationship to these characters, his ballet was not 'understood'. My idea was to make a series of images from traditional fairy stories, linked by a thread of plot which was as important or unimportant as the audience chose to make it. These images would provide the various *divertissements* I wished to make.

My choreography was to take Petipa as a starting point, but there were to be differences. Firstly, no 'deaf and dumb' mime passages. Relationships of dancers to each other or to objects, or the quality of their movement, were to convey all the meaning. The classical dance was to be quite freely interspersed with acrobatics or popular dance steps as long as these were used poetically, and not merely as stunts to steal a cheap gasp from the audience: the moon would be like a white trapezist swinging in a crescent through the air, the fishes would tumble and somersault through the waves. The result of these deliberations was a first rough scenario of *The Prince of the Pagodas*.

When I explained these ideas to John Piper he understood and was excited about them. We decided in favour of relating the 'Pagodas' to the strange edifices of [Saul] Steinberg and Paul Klee, and against making a pastiche of eighteenth-century chinoiserie by using sharply defined shapes in contrasting colours which advanced or receded, we would make our feeling of space, and the Palaces and Places would be in the imagination, rather than realistically represented.

The scenery was to move, too, and become a part of the dance. That is, its movements would have a beauty of their own and not be merely illustrative, such as realistic storms at sea, volcanoes erupting, and so on; in short, nothing was to be conveyed by scenic effect which could not be conveyed in the dance. Piper began his first drawings and with Desmond Heeley designing the costumes, soon our ideas became real.

The decor was under way, but what about the music? No composer available to me seemed to have the kind of imagination the ballet demanded. One evening I asked Britten if he had any ideas about composers, little dreaming that he would become excited enough with *Pagodas* to undertake it himself.

The whole ballet was rediscussed, and Britten suggested various themes on which he would make variations short enough to provide the episodic dances, but which would give the work as a whole a sense of continuity.

Together we worked out a sort of 'shooting script' of the whole ballet, almost as if we were planning a silent film. For example:

Belle Rose enters sadly and looks offstage to see if she is alone. (Short introductory bars.)

She dances her loneliness. (One minute.)

She sees a vision of a prince dressed in green. (Slow music, to allow for smoke to spread, then quickening when she sees prince, whole time not more than four minutes.)

The prince vanishes. (Some sort of crash, but very rapid.)

Then Britten started to compose. As the music grew the ballet sprang to life, and, carefully as Britten had followed my script, his imagery was so strong that the entire choreography had to be revisualized. This is often the case with specially composed ballets. There are stages of metamorphosis like a butterfly. Firstly the scenario; then the emotional and rhythmic framework provided by the music; and last of all the movements; thus a choreographer may find his original idea grown and developed differently from his first conception by the time he actually goes into rehearsal.

When the piano reduction of the first act was ready I began rehearsals with the ballet company. I was nervous of misunderstanding the music: by this I mean that a piano skeleton is very different from a full orchestration, and very often when one hears the final effect one is horrified at the difference in quality between what one had imagined, and the actual sound. In this case I was lucky, because Britten's descriptions of his musical intentions were so clear that there were very few surprises.

Very slowly the ballet began to 'jell'. Everything was done to facilitate rehearsals. Dame Ninette was forced to keep the company's repertoire as simple as she could for dancers' and stage staff's sake. [...] A whole programme had to be pulled out of a hat because, unfortunately, the production had to be postponed owing to Britten's illness.

This ballet was not by any means a 'safe play'. There were many enormous risks, not the least being a young choreographer, two young dancers not yet star names, and soloists taken mainly from the ranks of corps de ballet. This was done by the Directors of Covent Garden as a gesture of faith in the younger members of the company and the future of British ballet. If we have in any way justified that faith, we shall be proud of the achievement.

In an interview with Michael Oliver (London, 9 January 1992), John Tooley, who joined Covent Garden in 1955 as assistant to David Webster, recalled his impressions of the relationship between Britten and Cranko around the period of *The Prince of the Pagodas*:

The collaboration was not quite as Ben would have liked it to have been and consequently when he came to write the ballet and finish it he was largely doing it in a vacuum which, interestingly enough, is what persuaded him to look seriously at the notion of making some cuts and some alterations to the score at a later point, and more particularly when I took [the choreographer] Kenneth Macmillan to meet him some time in the early 1970s.

That was my first encounter with Ben both as a composer and as a conductor, because he conducted those early performances, and I have a vivid remembrance of the rehearsals and the way Ben rehearsed, and became aware of the enormous demands which Ben made upon the players, both in terms of what was actually in front of them, in terms of the written score, but also in terms of how he expected them to deliver what he'd written.

Ben, according to what he told me, had always been admiring of Tchaikovsky and the big classical ballets, and it was to Tchaikovsky that he turned in fact as he came to think more about writing *Pagodas*; and when he got to the point of writing it, he found that he had a narrative which was not complete, and he also found that Cranko was singularly unavailable, according to what Ben told me. There were moments when Ben wanted consultation with him about a passage and found that Cranko was unavailable at the end of a telephone, and so he went ahead and wrote in a bit of a vacuum. He actually wanted the collaboration. Ben was clear about this to me: he said, 'I really wanted precise direction of the number of bars that he [Cranko] actually wanted. I didn't want to be the person who dictated the length of the music. I wanted the choreographer to tell me.'

In response to a question about working with dancers, Tooley said that Britten

both enjoyed it and I think was quite awestruck by dancers and these phenomenal techniques that they had, their ability to do all sorts of wonderful things with their bodies. And he was – I think he was both surprised and amazed at what could be achieved and how expressive dance could be.

Tooley recalled that during orchestral rehearsals for *Pagodas*

there were odd moments when impatience set in, and Ben could become spiky and difficult and irritated by a musician's failure to respond in the way that he wanted him or her to respond. As I understood him and the way that he composed, he was totally clear about the sound picture that he wanted and how in the case of *Pagodas* each movement was going to be. He was somebody with this extraordinary vivid imagination and ability to hear, without the music being written down, how he wanted it to be.

He also witnessed at first hand

a great feeling of support for Britten [from the orchestra] because it arose from very considerable admiration for him as a musician, as a composer. While some players might well have thought, 'Well, he's being a bit too demanding. I don't quite know what he's doing'; they were on the whole a minority, and players in fact were only too happy to work with a great musician. They wanted to learn, they wanted to develop, they wanted to stretch themselves, and they found here, in the case of *Pagodas*, both the composer and the conductor making heavy demands on them.

According to Tooley, Britten did not at first understand the relationship between stage and pit in terms of ballet:

There is something very special in relating movement and music and having a true understanding as a conductor of how those two are related, and related in such a way that the end results can be achieved without miserable compromise. Ben discovered things pretty rapidly and a lot of what Ben had written and Cranko had devised was not putting Ben into the position which a conductor would be in conducting – what shall we say? – *Swan Lake*, where in fact there's infinite room for movement and change of tempi and demands made by dancers for it to be slower or faster. I think Ben was largely spared that. And I think the other side to that was that the dancers were much too afraid to go and ask anyway.

The piece failed to win lasting popularity with the public (but see Letter 886). The Royal Ballet, having revived it on a few occasions, took the decision to drop it from its repertory. Tooley argued that

there was some awareness that maybe it needed revision and uncertainty about how that might be achieved; and I regret very much that the easy way out was taken at that moment which was to drop it, and it took an awful long time to get it back into the repertory again, far too long.

See also John Tooley, *In House: Covent Garden – 50 Years of Opera and Ballet*, pp. 135–6.

VI IN THE NAIVE MEDIEVAL STYLE: *NOYE'S FLUDDE*

JANUARY–DECEMBER 1957

Did I ever thank you for those splendid socks, which I love so? I'm afraid not — how awful. Please forgive me.

4 Crabbe Street Jan. 13ᵗʰ 1957
Aldeburgh
Suffolk

My dearest Elizabeth,

We have both been thinking so much about you these last weeks, & how we resent those wretched 3000 miles of water between us, & those silly engagements which prevent me hopping into a plane & crossing them. One would give so much for the chance of seeing you and embracing you, at this moment when personal contacts are so very much needed. But for the moment we must put up with scrappy notes like this, & thank God, there seems a chance that in the Summer at least we will be crossing the ocean, & can be with you, even if only for a short time.

I'll let you know as soon as the Group's visit to Stratford, & possibly U.S.A. too, is definite, but it seems most likely at the moment.

The greatest comfort to us, away over here, is that your family, so devoted & united, are with you, & I know are helping you in these moments of intense loneliness & bewilderment. I hope that, for instance, Christopher could let me have a note saying how you are, & what your plans are. Will you stay on in Gramercy Park, that you loved so, or is it too full of memories, & too far away from the others? It is in these moments I know that the very young, the sweet grandchildren which I know you have, can be so helpful. Ask one of the children to write us a word.

Peter & I are so very happy that we could see William

Britten to Elizabeth Mayer, 13 January 1957: Letter 883

CHRONOLOGY 1957

YEAR	EVENTS AND COMPOSITIONS
1957	
1 January	Royal Opera House, Covent Garden, London: first performance of *The Prince of the Pagodas*; Sadler's Wells Ballet, Orchestra of the Royal Opera House, conducted by Britten
5–8 January	Conducts recording of *A Boy was Born* with the Purcell Singers for Decca
January	Planning a Mass (subsequently abandoned) for the 1958 Leeds Festival
February	Shelves the planned oratorio on St Peter (libretto by Ronald Duncan); agrees to a proposal from Rathbone Books to co-write (with Imogen Holst) *The Story of Music* (published in 1958)
from 12 February	Conducts recording of abridged *Prince of the Pagodas* with the Orchestra of the Royal Opera House for Decca
25 February	Records *Canticle II: 'Abraham and Isaac'* with Norma Procter and Pears for Decca
April	Approached by Associated Rediffusion about contributing a work to the television company's schools' programmes: this proposal leads to the commissioning of *Noye's Fludde*
15 April – 7 May	In Europe for recitals in Vienna (23rd) and Graz (24th) before holidaying in Italy with Pears and the Hesses
9 May	La Scala, Milan: attends rehearsals and first Italian performance of *The Prince of the Pagodas*; Britten and Pears return to Aldeburgh via France with the Pipers
14–23 June	Tenth Aldeburgh Festival: highlights include *Albert Herring* (with many of the original cast) and Blake song competition; Pears appointed CBE in the Queen's Birthday Honours List
9–10 July	COMPOSITION Malaysian National Anthem (revised 25 July)

17 July	Guest at a lunch at Buckingham Palace hosted by the Queen and the Duke of Edinburgh
29–31 July	Attends the Ansbach Bach Festival at which Pears is singing the B minor Mass and *St John Passion*
August – September	English Opera Group tour of *The Turn of the Screw* to Stratford, Ontario, Canada (20 August – 6 September); during the voyage Britten begins planning *Noye's Fludde*
1 September	Dennis Brain killed in a car accident
Autumn	COMPOSITION *Songs from the Chinese* (texts by Chinese poets, translated by Arthur Waley), for high voice and guitar; volume 4 of *Folk Song Arrangements* (*Moore's Irish Melodies*)
2–5 October	Conducts *The Turn of the Screw* at the Berlin Festival; later in the month changes in the structure and personnel of the English Opera Group lead to the termination of the employment of Basil Douglas (General Manager) and Olive Zorian (orchestra leader)
27 October	Begins composition draft of *Noye's Fludde*, which is finished on 18 December
21–23 November	Moves from Crag House to the Red House, Aldeburgh, Britten's home until his death in 1976
20 December	Landestheater, Darmstadt: attends the first performance of *The Turn of the Screw* in Prince Ludwig of Hesse and the Rhine's German translation

883 To Elizabeth Mayer

4 CRABBE STREET, ALDEBURGH, SUFFOLK
Jan. 13th 1957

My dearest Elizabeth,

We have both been thinking so much about you these last weeks, & how we resent those wretched 3000 miles of water between us, & those silly engagements which prevent one hopping into a plane & crossing them. One would give so much for the chance of seeing you and embracing you, at this moment when personal contacts are so very much needed. But for the moment we must put up with scrappy notes like this, & thank God, there seems a chance that in the Summer at least we'll be crossing the ocean, & can be with you, even if only for a short time. I'll let you know as soon as the Group's visit to Stratford, & possibly U.S.A. too, is definite, but it seems most likely at the moment.[1]

The greatest comfort to us, away over here, is that your family, so devoted & united, are with you, & I know are helping you in these moments of intense loneliness & bewilderment.[2] I hope that, for instance, Christopher [Mayer] could let me have a note saying how you are, & what your plans are. Will you stay on in Gramercy Park,[3] that you loved so, or is it too full of memories, & too far away from the others? It is in these moments I know that the very young, the sweet grandchildren which I know you have, can be so helpful. Ask one of the children to write us a word.

Peter & I are so very happy that we could see William in the Summer for even that short time.[4] He was so sweet, so gay, so typically William – excited about being there, being with Heckel, & in Europe again. It was a lovely & wild evening we all had together, & we felt so close to him, & to you, as if these years of separation didn't exist; and really for the amount Peter & I talk about Amityville, they don't exist.[5] You cannot imagine, dearest Elizabeth, what importance your & William's friendship, devoted, trusting loyalty & faith, had for us. In every way they were formative years; we were children before, men after. You both gave us strength, & courage to see ourselves & to face what we saw. You were both rocks who knew & loved the past, & yet were not daunted by the future. That is why, although out of my forty-three years, three isn't long, those years play such a large part, assume such proportions in my development, & I know Peter would say the same. After all Peter grew from that time – the Peter who through his voice & personality brings such comfort & deep enjoyment to audiences all over Europe, that need it so terribly at this moment. Our tour last November & December all over distressed Germany showed that clearly. Forgive this ramble, my dear, because you do not need to hear all this, but it gives me comfort to say it.

I wish you could see the new Ballet – it has wonderful things in it – hear it, you will soon because I am to make a complete recording of the music next month,[6] which I will certainly send you, at once. Incidentally if there is any record of ours you haven't got, & want, always write, won't you?

Have you, for instance Peter's new record[7] with Julian Bream, a wonderful young lutenist? At the moment I am compulsorily resting here, having overdone it a bit (I had, against my wishes, to take over the conducting of the Ballet); Peter is in London rehearsing Meistersinger (he is singing David!)[8] & singing Magic Flutes – how I wish you could hear the latter, the best Tamino ever, with wonderful [John] Piper sets, with splendid majesty & flow.[9] He is also singing the B minor Mass twice this week[10] – which I alas shan't hear – a secret, my dear, I am just starting a Mass myself, a rather sad 20th century, European, affair.[11]

My deepest love for you, dearest Elizabeth, & to all of yours too. I long for a scrap of news.

Your devoted
BEN

Did I ever thank you for those splendid socks, which I love so? I'm afraid not – how awful, please forgive me.

1 The English Opera Group was to tour *The Turn of the Screw* to the Stratford Shakespeare Festival, Ontario, Canada, in August 1957: see Letters 901–5. The USA leg of the tour failed to materialize.

2 William Mayer had died on 11 December 1956.

3 1 Gramercy Park, New York City, where William and Elizabeth Mayer lived.

4 Mrs Mayer told Britten (18 February 1957): 'I was so happy that William saw you both in Germany and how happy he was!' Photographs surviving at BPL indicate that while they were staying at Schloss Tarasp, Britten, Pears and Imogen Holst met William Mayer and his friend the German Expressionist painter Erich Heckel (1883–1970) on 26 August 1956. At that time Heckel lived in Hemmenhofen, near Lake Constance.

5 Britten refers to his and Pears's years in the United States (1939–42) when they formed a close friendship with the Mayer family, Elizabeth in particular, and with whom for most of that period they lived at Amityville on Long Island. See Letters 172–371 and 'The American Dream' from Donald Mitchell's 'Introduction' to vols 1 and 2, pp. 30–49.

6 *The Prince of the Pagodas* was recorded for Decca by the Orchestra of the Royal Opera House conducted by Britten, at the Walthamstow Assembly Hall in February 1957, beginning on the 12th. It was originally to have been recorded during the period 5–9 February, but these dates have been cancelled in Britten's pocket engagement diary.

The recording was not, as the composer suggests in this letter, the 'complete' *Pagodas* but in fact a cut version of the score (approximately twenty minutes of music were omitted, from single bars to entire numbers) to enable it to fit on to four LP sides. The first complete recording of *The Prince of the Pagodas* (Virgin Classics) was not released until 1990, by the London Sinfonietta conducted by Oliver Knussen. See also David Matthews's 'A Note on Cuts', in the preliminary matter to the published study score of *Pagodas*, and Mervyn Cooke's CD liner note, '*The Prince of the Pagodas*: An Introduction', for the Virgin Classics recording.

7 Of songs by Dowland, Ford, Morley and Rosseter.

8 Pears's appearance (at the age of forty-six) as David, Hans Sachs's apprentice, in a new production of Wagner's *Die Meistersinger von Nürnberg* at Covent Garden in January and February 1957, conducted by Rafael Kubelík and directed by Erich Witte, with Joan Sutherland (Eva), James Pease (Sachs) and Geraint Evans (Beckmesser), was the only Wagner role of his long career, though some (including Harold Rosenthal in PPT, p. 118) believed he could have been an impressive Loge in *Das Rheingold*, while Hans Keller claimed that he should have sung Tristan (presumably in a small theatre), arguing, 'we didn't hear him in everything he wholly understood' (PPT, p. 51). Rosenthal wrote in *Opera* 8/3 (March 1957), p. 186, that Pears 'sang David's music with style and taste; he was too refined an apprentice though, and looked too much the aristocrat to be convincing'.

The reason for Rosenthal's failure to be convinced by Pears's interpretation of David was a criticism frequently levelled at the tenor's impersonation of the fisherman Peter Grimes. Even when playing Captain Vere in *Billy Budd*, a role well suited to Pears's natural patrician bearing, the tenor was criticized for his lack of authority as a convincing man of action, notably in the muster scene at the end of the original Act I. See also BBMCPR, p. 140; CHPP, p. 161, and PPT, p. 114, plate 7.

Britten wrote to Roger Duncan (3 February 1957) to say he had

> heard Peter in Mastersingers – but, was it boring? – we got into the theatre at 6.0 & didn't leave till nearly 12.0! I was also a bit embarrassed because just as I was leaving Chester Gate, fully changed as far as my coat, I discovered that my dinner jacket had been left in Aldeburgh. In a panic I searched, found Peter's, & dashed to the taxi in that – about 3 sizes too big. I did look a fool. Kept my overcoat on at the theatre till I nearly boiled, & then my scarf – but I looked like a starved refugee with borrowed clothes. Saw your mother & father there. Peter did awfully well, looked & sang charmingly.

9 This was a revival on 12 January 1957 of a production first seen in 1955: see Letter 837 n. 2.

10 Pears sang in two broadcast performances of Bach's B minor Mass in an edition by Walter Goehr, the first on 16 January (BBC Home Service), the second on 17 January (BBC Third Programme). The other soloists were Heather Harper (soprano), Helen Watts (contralto), John Carol Case

(baritone) and David Ward (bass), with the BBC Chorus and the Goldsbrough Orchestra, conducted by Goehr. Pears wrote to Ursula Nettleship (undated letter, but probably 28 January):

> I am so glad you enjoyed the Benedictus; a lovely flute player [Richard Adeney] I thought; so much better on the Flute than the Violin [Bach did not specify the instrument for the obbligato line; Pears refers to the practice, derived from the nineteenth-century Bach Gesellschaft edition, of assigning the obbligato to the violin]. The performance was curious & full of Goehr's weaknesses, but with considerable virtues too I thought – very exaggerated & hysterical sometimes, but not without good fresh musical ideas – & (in the studio) very clear & resonant.

Goehr's edition, which used an increased orchestration including doubled winds, was the subject of some adverse criticism: see John Butt, *Bach: Mass in B minor*, p. 39.

11 Comments about this projected Mass in a letter to Lord Harewood (31 October 1957) suggest the work was conceived for large mixed chorus and orchestra, intended for Harewood's first Leeds Festival as Artistic Director in 1958, the festival's centenary year. Britten writes:

> About the Mass, I've been thinking it over. By the time I come to London for Grimes rehearsals (Jan. 15th [1958] onwards?) I shall have a good idea of how it's going, and if you like we can make that a dead-line for a decision. There's no hope whatever of getting chorus parts by the end of January. I spoke to Erwin [Stein] yesterday and he agreed that it should be a quick job, getting chorus parts out, and so I should have said that by the end of February, middle of March, if the work's going to be ready at all, there'll be something for the chorus to start on. Now, if the chorus master (Bardgett?) thinks this impossible, we'd better call it all off, but I can't see why he should, and as I'm most keen to get it done for you, let's put pressure on him to reconsider it. But anyhow I'll accept your decision either way.

Herbert Bardgett (see Letter 643 n. 10) was Chorus Master of the Huddersfield Choral Society and the Leeds Triennial Music Festival, and had conducted a successful early performance of *Spring Symphony* in place of the composer at Leeds in 1950 (see Letter 678).

Harewood responded to Britten on 14 November 1957:

> *Mass*: The timetable implied in your letter has now fitted beautifully into place as far as I am concerned. Originally, for some reason which I now cannot satisfactorily analyse, there was a notion that January was the deadline for choral parts of the Mass. I took the opportunity while I was in Leeds for my meetings last week, to see Bardgett and look at the whole situation with him. He agreed with me in every detail, and himself fervently hopes that we shall have the work to perform at the Festival. When he went through week by week to see how he should fit in the work with his chorus, he came to the conclusion that he could not possibly reach your Mass until April! May I then suggest as a 'deadline' for choral parts, April 1st, 1958? This would give Bardgett three weeks in which to digest it, and he would still have the practices which he needs in order to inculcate it into his chorus by the end of the summer.

I have always tried to avoid being too importunate about this work, but I must take this chance of saying what a vast difference it will make to the Festival if it can be ready in time. I know that you have never said any more than that you hoped you could finish it so that it could be performed in Leeds, but we all hope very much indeed that we shall be lucky. It would be the crown of the second half of the Festival.

If we could confer again as early in January as is convenient, I should still have time to make alternative arrangements if absolutely necessary.

Britten expressed his relief about the schedule in his next letter to Harewood (27 November 1957):

That gives us plenty of time if the work "jells", and also plenty of time to tell you so that you can replace it if it does not. Anyhow we shall be much in touch towards the end of January when a decision can be reached.

Harewood replied on 5 December 1957:

I am glad that the new time-table for the Mass will make it a bit easier – I do hope that ideas are pouring out, and that not all your thoughts have been on a purely mundane, not to say TV, level of recent weeks. As I watch the Festival programme, as I had hoped for and as I planned it, gradually evaporating, for reasons over which it seems to me I neither have, nor ever have had, any control whatsoever, I begin to see why most finished results are nothing but a rushed together, make-shift, last-minute hotch-potch. However, that is not news – and the only place where it does not apply is Aldeburgh.

At some point during December 1957 or January 1958, Britten evidently abandoned the proposed Mass setting, suggesting in its place what would become the *Nocturne*, for tenor and orchestra. Harewood wrote to the composer on 22 January 1958:

It is sad we have not got the Mass for Leeds, but we have at least 90% compensation in the promise of the new work for Peter and orchestra. When do you think I might contemplate an announcement of this? It is almost the only part of the programme not yet given to the public, and though there is no immediate hurry, I would like to be able to say it in the not too distant future. I have, of course, already talked to [Rudolf] Schwarz, who is delighted that he has at least something of yours to conduct.

Schwarz was to conduct the first performance of *Nocturne*, with Pears as soloist and the BBC Symphony Orchestra, at the Leeds Centenary Festival, in Leeds Town Hall on 16 October 1958. See also, Harewood, *The Tongs and the Bones*, p. 141.

While the shape of Britten's intended Mass for Leeds remains shadowy, it seems plausible that some aspects of the projected setting – not least because of the composer's telling description of it in his letter to Elizabeth Mayer as 'a rather sad 20th century, European affair' – were to resurface in his *War Requiem*, commissioned for the Coventry Cathedral Festival of 1962. In this context, it is significant that the initial approach by the authorities at Coventry was made in October 1958, the year the Leeds project was abandoned; unlike Leeds, the Coventry proposal afforded Britten a generous time-frame in which to plan and execute the work. The composer told Alec Robertson on 2 January 1959: 'The Mass idea has rather undergone some changes – & will come out somewhat differently – but for Coventry Cathedral, I think.'

884 To James Lawrie[1]

[*Typed file copy; with many amendments in Britten's hand*]

4 CRABBE STREET, ALDEBURGH, SUFFOLK
16th January, 1957

My dear Jimmie,

For obvious reasons I should very much like immediately to have a long talk with you about the E.O.G., but because I am stuck here for a month under doctor's orders I think it is best if I put my ideas down on paper, which you may like to pass on to the Directors, the Arts Council and Basil [Douglas].

Last year was the tenth of the Group's life; the year started with an enormous success in the Paris Festival, and ended with a disappointing season at the Scala Theatre, which nearly jeopardised financially the whole future of the Group. I feel a moral can be drawn from the year. It seems that the E.O.G. idea flourishes under special circumstances; briefly one could define these circumstances as:

1) Festivals – where the audiences are specialised, and therefore prepared to accept operatic works other than the traditional ones.

2) In countries where opera is a part of the daily bread, such as Germany. This can be demonstrated by the Group's repeated success there, and by the considerable number of independent productions of works like Lucretia, Herring, Beggar's Opera and "Let's Make an Opera!" However, in England the general public is operatically much more conservative, and our financial backing has not been adequate for us to do enough performances to win it round. I should like to say here that all of us have made strenuous efforts over the last ten years to increase this backing, by appealing to Trusts, business firms, and individuals – but without marked success.

What is the solution? The Opera Group could cease to exist altogether, but I think I am speaking for all the artistic directors when I say we wish to continue to produce similar works to those in the past, and festivals like the Aldeburgh Festival continue to want (although are not always able to afford) such productions. We should hate, therefore, to see the Group die;

but on the other hand our administration expenses, which are needed to exploit these works (needing a London office and staff) are too expensive to continue on the present Arts Council grant (under the circumstances a generous one); besides in these last ten years there have been increasing demands on the time and energy of the Artistic Directors from outside sources, which have made them less available for such exploitation. This suggests that the Group is more cut out to be a creator than an impresario.

I make the proposal, therefore, that the E.O.G. should narrow itself down, that it should move its office, staff and storage to Aldeburgh. In discussions with Stephen Reiss it seems the Festival Office could absorb a localised E.O.G. without much extra expense. The E.O.G. would therefore ask the Arts Council for less money rather than more. The immediate aim would be to mount operas for each Aldeburgh Festival, but when the new Aldeburgh Theatre is built ways could surely be found for using these works locally in the summer and holiday months, and of course touring, if financially guaranteed, could continue – to festivals in England and abroad. The E.O.G. activities would actually therefore be much the same as in the past, but without the annual season in London, undertaken at its own risk – but it would not, of course, rule out a London season if guaranteed.

Now where does the proposed season in conjunction with the Ballet Rambert at the Lyric, Hammersmith, come in?[2] I suggest that there is only one method of achieving this; it must be done by an independent young E.O.G. organisation. Our Directors have convincingly argued that it should anyhow be run by an independent company; I would go further and say now that it should have its own musical director and production director, and that the company should be chosen from younger singers and players (and we know that there is considerable talent around from our auditions for the Royal Court Theatre concerts).[3] It should also have largely its own individual repertoire, and suggestions for this have already been discussed; in other words it should profit by the experience and advice of the Artistic Direction of the old E.O.G., but should stand on its own legs. To press the point, not only is this desirable <u>artistically</u>, because in the past we have seldom been able to afford the risk of using unknown younger performers at important festivals, and it is something we have all wished to do; but also practically it would be impossible to use our older and more established performers regularly in such a season because salaries and commitments would forbid it. This highly desirable venture should be run, I suggest, from one office shared with the Ballet Rambert for economic and practical reasons.

I see therefore the Festival E.O.G. being centred on Aldeburgh, doing productions for the Festival each year, possibly with summer seasons when the Theatre is built, and fulfilling invitations to other festivals here and abroad, and a young E.O.G. sharing the Lyric, Hammersmith, with the Ballet Rambert, and with its own artistic leadership, but advised and helped by the Artistic Direction of the present E.O.G.[4]

Yours ever,
[BEN]

1 British businessman and financier (1907–1979), a member of the Board of the English Opera Group from its early years who served as Chairman from 1950 to 1960. See also Letter 651 n. 3.

2 According to Maureen Garnham, *As I Saw It*, p. 96:

There was an attempt, in the last two months of 1956, at salvaging the finances of the EOG by a long-term collaboration with the Ballet Rambert. The two companies would share the EOG orchestra, and would present a series of joint seasons at the Lyric Theatre, Hammersmith, starting with four months from October 1957. The EOG would be provided with storage facilities at the theatre in place of our damp railway arch, and would have a rehearsal platform there. Basil [Douglas] had several meetings with the management of the Ballet Rambert, but the high artistic standards which Dame Marie Rambert had once achieved with the company had slipped since her active involvement had ceased, and it did not appear at this period that her successors in the artistic direction of the company would be likely to revive its reputation. (This situation improved markedly in due course, but too late for us [i.e. the EOG].) It was thought that our own reputation might have been compromised by the association, so the scheme foundered primarily on artistic grounds.

3 The EOG promoted two series of concerts at the Royal Court Theatre, London, during the 1956–57 season: Sunday evening 'celebrity concerts', which included Britten playing the fortepiano with the Amadeus Quartet, and the Purcell Singers in Britten's *A Boy was Born*; and a Thursday lunchtime series given by young artists such as Malcolm Williamson, who played his own Piano Sonata, and horn-player Barry Tuckwell. See Maureen Garnham, *As I Saw It*, pp. 88–90.

4 Britten was to write to the Artistic Directors of the EOG (Basil Coleman, Michael Northen, John Piper and Anne Wood) on 31 January 1957, following the Directors' Meeting on 28 January:

As none of you were able to be at the Directors' Meeting of the E.O.G. last Monday, I thought I would write you a line in addition to the minutes which Basil Douglas will doubtless soon be sending you.

I think I can honestly describe the agreement to the proposal of moving the E.O.G. administration to Aldeburgh as wholehearted, even enthusiastic. Jimmie Lawrie put the case of "creation rather than exploitation" very clearly as being in tune with our financial situation, and with the situation of absorption with other work in which we all find ourselves; in fact in terms of agreeing with the long letter

I wrote him on 16th January. I believe that you all received copies of this letter, and of one in reply which Basil Douglas wrote to him. I had had no reactions to these letters from any of you (except John [Piper]) before the meeting, so I presumed that you did not feel strongly about this matter. I of course did not take your names in vain at the meeting (again with the exception of John's), but a decision had urgently to be reached, and I hope you will not feel ill-treated. The Arts Council is wholly behind the decision; it seems they would welcome the considerable reduction in administrative costs which would allow the Group to be more flexible. The plan at the moment is to absorb the administration of the E.O.G. into the Aldeburgh Festival office. For any outside Aldeburgh activities, such as visits abroad or to other festivals in England, the staff can be engaged ad hoc. Stephen Reiss has given considerable thought to the matter, and feels that the basic administration cost (including storage) would be not more than £800 a year (the administration costs for 1955 approached £4,000). The Arts Council has suggested it might be possible to give us £500 each year towards this figure (the £300 would not be difficult to raise elsewhere), and to consider sympathetically our requests for production costs as they arise each year. The feeling was that if we did no new production one year for Aldeburgh the request would be small, but so would the invitations to take it around; but with a new production the larger sum needed could be justified by probable visits to other festivals as well as abroad.

Although many attending the meeting felt it was advisable to keep the present board of directors, no agreement was reached as to whether it was possible or not under the new circumstances. Isador Caplan is examining the position. From many points of view it would be essential to keep the E.O.G. Association alive; and I don't think that would be difficult, especially with its close contact with the Aldeburgh Festival, & with concerts & functions given by people who would continue to have contact with the new form of E.O.G.

Underneath the surface all through this meeting was a feeling of deep regret that such a scheme would not include the services of Basil Douglas, who has worked so hard and loyally these last six years, but I have felt that the extreme worry of the recurring financial crises, especially in the last few years, have been really bad for him; besides, if the money can be found for the new venture in conjunction with the Ballet Rambert at the Lyric, Hammersmith, the suggestion is that he should be Operatic Manager for it. If this does not materialise another suggestion has been that he should act in some form or other as London booking agent for the Aldeburgh Festival and for the E.O.G. This, of course, all depends on his availability, which is not by any means certain, since he has shown in the last year or so interest in other jobs which were certainly full-time.

I should like, in concluding, to reiterate my hope that I have not transgressed your wishes in the matter, and also to say how strongly I feel that this is the right move. We are all so busy elsewhere that our interest is surely in the business of making things, and not in pushing them round the world (unless they go of their own accord); anyhow, with the proposed building of the Festival theatre in Aldeburgh we would at last have the working centre which we have felt for so long essential to this work.

885 To Dennis Brain
[*Carbon copy*]

[4 Crabbe Street, Aldeburgh, Suffolk]
21st January, 1957

My dear Dennis,

Thank you for your letter. I am looking forward very much to hearing the broadcast of your Haydn concerto tonight;[1] being a fan of yours and his I know I shall enjoy it, so anyhow let's do it in your concert here next June.[2]

We all strongly disagree with your wife that it would be unwise for Leonard[3] to play the solo in the Fricker[4] Concertante; in fact we should like to say that the work was written for him, and in a note to feature the Brain family musical tradition.[5]

About the new work, could we leave that to you, i.e. choice of composer and kind of work? There is no one particularly we have in mind, although our inclination would be to choose someone young (one is more likely to get the work written in time, and for it to be enterprising and interesting!). I would privately like to murmur the name Thomas Eastwood[6] to you – I think he is very interesting and talented, and certainly very practical.

By the way, you have forgotten the Mozart fragment.[7] We should dearly love to have this. If you agree I suppose the obvious place would be before the Malcolm Arnold[8] in the second half. The programme therefore would be:

Mozart Symphony No. 33 in B flat
Fricker Cor Anglais Concertante (soloist Leonard Brain)
Haydn Horn Concerto No. 1

New work
Mozart fragment of Horn Concerto
Malcolm Arnold Divertimento

I think that looks a nice programme.[9]

With best wishes,
Yours ever,
[BEN]

1 Brain was the soloist in a broadcast of Haydn's D major Horn Concerto (H. VIID:3), with the BBC Midland Orchestra conducted by Leo Wurmser. The performance was preserved by the BBC Sound Archive and was released on BBC Legends in 2001.

2 Brain was conductor and soloist in an 'Orchestral Concert' at the Jubilee Hall on 15 June as part of the 1957 Aldeburgh Festival, with the Dennis Brain Chamber Orchestra.

3 Leonard Brain (1915–1975), British oboist, brother of Dennis Brain. Like his brother, Leonard Brain had played in the RAF Central Band during the Second World War, as well as in various orchestras, and was a member of the Philharmonia Orchestra, 1945–46; the RPO, 1946–73, and the Dennis Brain Wind Quintet and Ensemble, from 1946.

4 Peter Racine Fricker (1920–1990), British composer, whose Concertante No. 1 for cor anglais and strings was composed in 1950.

5 Not only were the Brain brothers professional musicians, but their father Aubrey (1893–1955) and uncle Alfred (1885–1966) were both professional horn-players, as was their father before them.

6 British composer (1922–1999), who, after private lessons, studied with Boris Blacher in Berlin and Erwin Stein in London, and first came to public notice with his String Trio, which was the prizewinner in the 1949 Cheltenham Open Competitive Music Festival. He worked extensively in theatre, television and radio. His chamber opera, *Christopher Sly* (1960; libretto by Ronald Duncan), based on Shakespeare's *The Taming of the Shrew*, was considered by the English Opera Group but rejected. (There is a small exchange of correspondence at BPL between Britten and Eastwood concerning *Christopher Sly*: Britten looked through the score in January 1959, following which Eastwood made many revisions.) Eastwood's song 'At Baia', for soprano and harp, was written for, and first performed at, a 'Recital of Twentieth-Century Music' given at the Jubilee Hall on 18 June 1956 as part of the Aldeburgh Festival.

7 The 99-bar fragment of a Horn Concerto in E (K. 494a). In his obituary of the horn-player, 'Dennis Brain 1921–1957', *Tempo* 46 (winter 1957), pp. 55–6, reprinted in PKBM, pp. 158–60, Britten recollected Brain's performance of this fragment at Aldeburgh:

> He came many times to play for us at the Aldeburgh Festival, but last June he came primarily to conduct. Here again he showed many of the same fine characteristics – musicianship, intelligence, enterprise and hard work – and one felt that his conducting would soon possess the same ease and persuasion as his horn playing. However, what one remembers most clearly of that evening was not his conducting, but his playing in this same concert of the unfinished movement of Mozart's fragmentary Horn Concerto in E. The tutti started with its glorious richness. Delicate phrases followed with warm and intense counterpoint; brilliant passages for the violins, soothing oboe melodies. Then the solo entered – firm, heroic, and all seemed set for the best of all the wonderful Mozart horn concertos. And then suddenly in the middle of an intricate florid passage, superbly played, it stopped: silence. Dennis shrugged his shoulders and walked off the Jubilee Hall platform. That night, as always, he drove back home to London after the performance. Aldeburgh is not so far from London as Edinburgh [Brain was killed in a car accident on 1 September 1957 following a concert at the Edinburgh Festival], but far enough after a heavy day of rehearsals and performances, both conducting and playing. One protested, one always did, but off he went, laughing. That was the last time I

ever heard him play, the last time I saw him. That Mozart fragment sticks in my mind as a symbol of Dennis's own life. But it is not so easy for us to shrug our shoulders.

8 British composer (1921–2006), whose Sinfonietta No. 1, Op. 48, for two oboes, two horns and strings, was the final work in the Aldeburgh Festival concert. Though only eight years younger than Britten, Arnold was never close to him; he preferred instead to ally himself to the older Walton. Only a handful of works by Arnold was heard at Aldeburgh during Britten's lifetime, though these included two premieres: the Guitar Concerto, Op. 67, for Julian Bream, in 1959; and the Second String Quartet, Op. 118, in 1976.

9 The order of programme as given in the 1957 Aldeburgh Festival Programme Book was as follows: Telemann: Suite in F, for two horns and strings; Haydn: D major Horn Concerto; Mozart: Symphony No. 33 in B flat; Mozart: Fragment of Horn Concerto in E; Stravinsky: Concerto in E flat ('Dumbarton Oaks'); Fricker: Concertante No. 1; Arnold: Sinfonietta No. 1.

Another letter from Britten to Brain (22 February 1957) suggests there was further discussion of the shape of the programme, chiefly because Brain felt it was too late to commission a new work, as had been the original plan. Suggestions and counter-suggestions were made, Britten putting forward Copland's *Quiet City* – 'We should very much like to have a piece by Copland in the Festival' – and Janáček's Concertino (1925), 'which no one knows'.

886 To Basil Coleman

4 CRABBE STREET, ALDEBURGH, SUFFOLK
Jan. 31st 1957

My dear Basil,

I've been meaning to write to you for ages, but you know what it is like, with these long-distance letters! There is always some good reason to put it off, that the news will be better next week, or at any rate different, or that there is nothing <u>particular</u> to say, only heaps of rather boring news in arrear! There are plenty of particular things to say now, anyhow, rather too many – but I'd rather start off with questions. How are you? What are you doing now you've left the Crest,[1] or do you pay spasmodic visits back there? How did the Television idea work out?[2] Basil D. [Douglas] seems to be in touch with you, but I never hear anything but boring business details – never the personal things that one minds about! Anyhow there does seem a chance of seeing you this Summer, if the Stratford thing comes off, & if we manage (Peter & me) to fit it in – it comes in the middle of such a hectic period that I can't see us surviving! – or perhaps that's the rather understandable feeling at this low moment. We were all delighted with your telegram for the Ballet, & it was sweet of you to remember about the occasion to send the message. It was, of course, the usual Cov. Garden panic. They all behaved disgracefully to Johnny [Cranko], in fact he got no help & very little support over the gargantuan matter. I wasn't much help either, being involved with the huge job of conducting it, & the beginnings of not being well. John & Myfanwy [Piper] were rocks – but in, as you can see, rather a rough sea! Considering everything, it went well. Honestly, with a few exceptions, I think the dancing is disappointing. Beriosova,[3] & Blair[4] (a splendid chap) are lovely, & there are others – but the general level of small parts & corps de ballet is pretty poor, even to my novice's eyes. Johnny's part is full of wonderful invention, although there are some moments of inexperience, & not altogether absorbed classical idioms. But all of this we can alter & improve, certainly by the time it goes to Milan (if it does – shades of Gloriana!)[5] & certainly by later performances at the Garden . . . it is a terrific success, playing to packed houses, & they've just added 10 more performances – snooks to the critics! John's [Piper] part is up to his usual standard, i.e. miraculous. I hope you'll like the music – a lot of it I honestly think is good, altho' a 3 acter is a colossal task. Anyhow you can judge for yourself because we are to record it complete in a week or so! Of course, as you may have heard, I went & laid myself out again, & after 3 performances had to retire under Doctor's Orders, & have been here feeling like death for 2 or 3 weeks. The death-like feeling has been helped by the poor old E.O.G. situation, which the enclosed letter may tell you about a little.[6] The trouble is that I don't know how much you know, whether Basil D. has written about it or not, whether you've had minutes etc. In brief (& my own personal point-of-view strictly) the situation has been getting worse & worse – the Scala [Theatre, London] was disastrous, the financial aspect honestly hasn't been well-handled, poor old B.D. has been laid low by worry – his health makes him a fine-weather sailor I'm afraid – we've performed less & less & the administrative costs soar. In discussion with Jimmie Lawrie, Tony Gishford, Pipers & Stephen Reiss (who's handled the Aldeburgh Festival triumphantly) we decided to propose cutting our losses, move down to Aldeburgh, & to perform only when & what we like, & to hell with having to try & perform. (The Arts Council is tremendously keen on the plan, & have promised help.) Of course there's loads more to it than all this, & one's affection & admiration (in certain ways) for Basil remains constant. But as you know the poor dear gets out of his depth easily, & the burden falls more & more on all of us, with less time & energy than ever to receive it. Don't worry about it; with the above mentioned, the Group's in good hands, & I'll report developments.[7]

Peter's well, fearfully busy – just sung his first (& I hope last) Wagner part – David in Meistersingers – at the Garden. He was quite charming, & looked & sounded about 18! He's tremendously booked up now, with great success in Germany, wanted all the time, which is nice for him – & vicariously for me, because we are as we always were! I see more & more of little (now quite big!) Roger [Duncan], as his parents get more & more unhappy. He spends about ½ his holidays from Harrow here, & is an enchanting & deeply affectionate boy. Mary [Potter] is well – Imo in terrific form (the Ballet was really her child) & all send love with a great deal of mine, my dear Basil –

BEN

1 The Crest Theatre, Toronto, founded in 1953 by Donald and Murray Davis with the support of their sister, Barbara Chilcott, presented its first season in 1954 which signalled the beginning of an indigenous, commercial theatre in Toronto. Until then, audiences interested in professional theatre saw mainly touring productions from Britain or the USA. Coleman had originally gone to Canada in 1954 and 1955 to direct several productions for the Crest Theatre. See also the transcript of William Kerley's interview with Coleman (28 May 2004) at BPL.

2 Coleman had relocated to Toronto in the mid-1950s after he began working as a director in television with the CBC.

3 Svetlana Beriosova (1932–1998), Lithuanian-born ballerina, who created the role of Belle Rose in *The Prince of the Pagodas*. She accepted an invitation from Ninette de Valois to join the Sadler's Wells Theatre Ballet in the early 1950s, transferring to Covent Garden in 1952 where she danced all the great classical roles. In addition to Belle Rose, Cranko created the title role in his *Antigone* for her, and Frederick Ashton choreographed for her a series of leading parts, including Elgar's wife in his *Enigma Variations*. Following her retirement in 1975, she occasionally coached. See also A. H. Franks, *Svetlana Beriosova; A Biography*, and obituaries by Clement Crisp, *Financial Times*, and by Mary Clarke, *Guardian* (both 12 November 1998), and by Nadine Mesiner, *Independent*, and in *The Times* (both 13 November 1998).

4 David Blair (1932–1976), British ballet dancer, who created the role of the Prince in *The Prince of the Pagodas*. Blair joined the Sadler's Wells Theatre Ballet in 1947 and was soon dancing principal roles. He created the part of Captain Belaye in Cranko's *Pineapple Poll* (1951) prior to transferring to Covent Garden where he undertook many of the classical roles. Among the leading parts he danced at Covent Garden were roles in Cranko's *Lady and the Fool* and *Antigone*, Mercutio in Kenneth MacMillan's *Romeo and Juliet*, and Colas in Ashton's *La Fille mal gardée*. He partnered Margot Fonteyn for a brief period in the early 1960s until the arrival of Rudolf Nureyev. See also the *Times* obituary (2 April 1976).

5 *Il principe delle pagode* opened at La Scala, Milan, on 9 May 1957. The production was a tremendous success and well received by the Italian press. For this production Cranko revised his choreography, which had been much criticized by the UK press at the ballet's premiere. In a letter to the Pipers from Milan, April 1957, Cranko confessed he was 'keen to remedy the defects in my part of the ballet', and in an undated later letter declared, 'I am much more pleased with my part, which I have largely redone, and the whole thing is starting to flow as it never did before' (quoted in MCBFE, pp. 96–7). See also Letter 894 n. 3.

The reference to 'shades of Gloriana' concerns the abandoned scheme for Coleman's production of the opera to be staged at La Scala in 1953: see Letter 731 n. 4.

6 See Letter 884 n. 4.

7 Britten told Ronald Duncan (14 March 1957):

Things have been unconscionably complicated – Festival matters have gone utterly mad (it's the time of year when things happen), & this E.O.G situation has gone from bad to worse & has taken a fearful lot of handling – oh, how I loathe changes – but this one is certainly for the best, I know . . . the job's been to persuade Basil D.

887 To Ronald Duncan

4 CRABBE STREET, ALDEBURGH, SUFFOLK

Feb. 3rd, 1957

My dearest Ronnie,

I still feel very guilty about not having written to you, & about having had to tell you over that cold, heartless machine, the telephone, about my composition change of plans. It is only one of many things I've not done these last weeks, but a symptom of the low state I've been in. Anyhow, please forgive me.

But I find this change of ideas a recurrent thing in my life, I'm afraid. I get terribly worked up about a thing, then cool off, & then, if the idea was originally a good one, come back with renewed vigour to it. The work has gone on boiling in the back of the old mind, & usually to good effect. Grimes was like this (I delayed over a year on starting the music after Slater[1] had finished the first draft of the libretto) – so was the Spring Symphony, & the Turn of the Screw. I'm sure St Peter is a good idea, but I'm equally sure that I'm not in the right frame of mind to do it well now. It must be maddening for you, all keyed up about it, to be put off like this – but please don't despair, because it'll happen in the end, I know![2]

I do so sympathise with you over the Daily Mail business; I can't see you happy in that world, although you may decide to bear it for a short while.[3] The thing is that I can't help feeling that journalism needn't necessarily be a bad thing, if the journalist (or editor) has constructive ideas/feelings, a missionary spirit; but at the moment they are the dustmen, no the plumbers, no worse, the sewage collectors – no, I can't think of anything low enough – of humanity, & it is an indignity to have anything to do with them. I'll ring you when I get to London, & let's have a good talk.

Much love, & to Rose Marie,

BEN

1 Montagu Slater (1902–1956), British poet, playwright, editor and literary critic, prominent in left-wing circles in the 1930s and after. He collaborated first with Britten in a number of film and theatre projects and was later to become the librettist of *Peter Grimes*. See also Letter 98 n. 1.

2 The libretto remained unset.

3 Duncan had presumably taken a regular position with the *Daily Mail*.

888 To James Fisher[1]
[*Carbon copy*]

[4 Crabbe Street, Aldeburgh, Suffolk]
8th February, 1957

Dear James Fisher,

I am so sorry not to have answered your letter of December 17th before this, and I realise that you must be getting very impatient at my silence.[2] The truth is that since that date I have been very much involved with my Ballet at Covent Garden, and have since that occasion been in Aldeburgh resting under doctor's orders. This has also meant, as you will have guessed, that Imogen Holst and I have not had a chance of writing the "inspiration document" which you and Mr. Foges[3] asked for. But all the same we have had several long talks about the proposed book, and we have come to several conclusions which we would like to set before you. We are both extremely keen to do the book with you; we have clear ideas of what we would like to include in the book, but the time factor even for your "inspiration document" remains the first problem. My illness months have severely dislocated my programme, and although we can have discussions in the near future, it is extremely unlikely that we can show you anything on paper until the end of the summer. This may seem impossibly delayed to you, in which case we shall be disappointed but will quite understand if you decide to look elsewhere for your authors.

The other conclusion we have come to is to do with the visual side of the book; it is clear that this aspect is as important as the reading matter, therefore the collaboration between the artist and writers should be as close as possible. In the past I have always worked in opera, ballet, straight stage and film with artists in whom I have complete confidence; in fact I have usually played a large part in the selection of such an artist. We feel that in the present case the procedure must be the same. You can take it that we understand the nature of these illustrations, that they must be direct, vivid and simple, suitable for the young people for whom the books are intended. One person whom we have in mind is Ceri Richards,[4] whom I gather worked for many years in an advertising firm, is an artist whom we both admire enormously, and happens to be a first-class amateur musician; he also happens to be extremely nice, and easy to work with.

Imogen Holst and I are most interested to know what your reactions to these points will be.

With best wishes,
Yours sincerely,
[BENJAMIN BRITTEN]

1 British broadcaster, writer, naturalist and ornithologist (1912–1970), who was the editor of the 'Wonderful World' series of books published by Rathbone Books, which included Fisher's own *Adventure of the Sea* and Julian Huxley's *The Story of Evolution*. The series was intended to provide popular general knowledge for teenagers. Fisher had lectured at the 1954 Aldeburgh Festival on 'Nature Protection', on which occasion he had stayed as Britten's guest at Crag House. He had been encouraged by Lord Harewood to contact Britten about contributing a volume to the 'Wonderful World' series. Fisher had appeared alongside Harewood as a panellist on the popular BBC radio programme *The Brains Trust*. See also the obituary in *The Times* (28 September 1970).

2 Fisher had first approached Britten by letter on 27 September 1956; by the time of his next letter (17 December 1956), it is clear that he, Britten and Imogen Holst had met to discuss the project: Britten's and Holst's children's book about music, which appeared in 1958 as *The Story of Music*, with specially commissioned collages by Ceri Richards (see n. 4 below). Although the book appeared under the joint authorship of Britten and Holst, it was in fact mainly written by the latter, who submitted her drafts for Britten's approval. Manuscript and typescript drafts of the book survive at BPL; it was republished in 1968 as *The Wonderful World of Music*.

The teenage Roger Duncan acted as a 'guinea-pig' reader of the book's early drafts, Britten writing to him on 2 February 1958 to say, 'We [Holst and Britten] are both terribly grateful for your help on that old book. You were really useful over it.' On the book's publication later in 1958, Britten sent the boy a copy:

Here is my first copy of Imo's & my dotty book – a small 'thank-you' for your considerable help & criticism on it! Actually I don't think it is as dotty as all that, in fact

I think it's come out pretty well, altho' in one or two places the colour is a bit on the 'technicolour' brightness side. But there are some pretty impressive pictures, don't you think? Anyhow I hope you like it.

3 Wolf Foges, Managing Director of Rathbone Books. The 'inspiration document' was a 2000-word outline of the book, which Fisher had requested in his letter to Britten and Holst of 17 December 1956.

4 British artist and stage designer (1903–1971), who was probably introduced to Britten by John Piper, as he and Richards had been friends since the 1930s. Richards's involvement with Britten and his circle resulted in his designing the costumes and sets for the EOG productions of Lennox Berkeley's *Ruth* (1956) and the costumes and animal masks for Britten's *Noye's Fludde* (1958). (Seven of Richards's designs for *Ruth* and over sixty for *Noye's Fludde* survive at BPL.) In addition there were exhibitions at the 1967 and 1972 Aldeburgh Festivals (the latter a memorial exhibition shared with his wife, Frances) and his designing of the cover of the Aldeburgh Festival Programme Book in 1971, his final contact with the composer (the original design is at BPL). At his memorial service in December 1971 at St James's, Piccadilly, London, Britten accompanied Pears in songs from Schubert's *Die Winterreise*, a cycle much loved by Richards.

In 1957–58 Richards provided a sequence of seven collages to illustrate Britten's and Holst's *The Story of Music*, one of which – *The Little Concerto* – is at BPL. Richards's collages headed each chapter (*The Little Concerto* appears before the chapter entitled 'Composer; Performer; Listener') and another was used on the jacket. He was probably also responsible for the selection of other illustrations (for example, by Picasso) used in the volume. Other Richards works at BPL are a coloured lithograph entitled *Poissons d'or* and *Clair de lune*, which is part of a sequence based on Debussy's movement from his *Suite bergamasque*. See also Paul Banks and Philip Reed, *Painting and Music*, exhibition catalogue, pp. 10 and 19–20, and Mel Gooding, *Ceri Richards*.

889 To Norman Del Mar
[*Typed*]

4 CRABBE STREET, ALDEBURGH
27th February, 1957

My dear Norman,

I was very pleased to get your letter, and to know that there was an idea to do a piece of mine at the Royal Philharmonic. I am afraid that there is absolutely no chance of any of the concertos that you mention being ready next season; I have them in mind, but I am refusing to let myself be committed to any dates for their performance.[1] The only first performance that it might be possible to give you would be that of the Ballet Suite;[2] I am not quite sure myself what the arrangements are to date, although one or two possibilities have been mentioned[3] – the person who knows is Anthony Gishford of Boosey & Hawkes. As I am just going away, do you think you could possibly telephone him, and ask him what the position is – if you think it is something that would interest the R.P.S. I should, of course, be very pleased if something could be arranged.

Excuse haste.

Much love,
Yours ever,
BEN

1 Del Mar had written to Britten on 16 February at the request of the Royal Philharmonic Society, on whose committee he served:

> They were discussing the programmes for next season and wishing that they could have some new piece of yours to introduce by way of first performance as this would provide the best possible cachet to the season. I said, I hope not unwisely, that I knew you once had had a group of concertos in mind, but that I didn't know whether you were waiting for a suitable opportunity to proceed, or whether you had shelved the ideas for the time being. The Concerto for String Quartet and Orch. in particular impressed them as a most exciting project [...] I have myself been tremendously tantalized at the prospect of such a work ever since you told me of your interest in writing it during the rehearsals of the 'Beggar' [*The Beggar's Opera*] at the People's Palace [in October 1948] [...]

The Concerto for String Quartet and Orchestra, surely intended for the members of the Amadeus String Quartet, was never written.

2 At this time Britten was considering the preparation of a suite from *The Prince of the Pagodas*. In his letter to Britten (16 February 1957), Del Mar had commented: 'The Ballet is magnificent & I am waiting eagerly for the appearance of a Concert Suite!' Britten wrote to Paul Sacher (11 March 1957):

> The suite from the new Ballet is not ready yet, I am afraid, but as soon as it is you can be sure we will let you see it. But it is being a most tremendous task to extract twenty minutes out of a work lasting nearly two hours!

Britten's suite remained unachieved; moreover, he was less than enthusiastic when approached by others, Del Mar included, who wished to make their own suites from the ballet. In 1963 Del Mar compiled his own *Prelude and Dances from 'The Prince of the Pagodas'*, which draws on music from Acts I and III only, thereby excluding any reference to the Pagoda Land music from Act II, which uses additional percussion instruments. Del Mar performed his suite at the 1974 Aldeburgh Festival, and in the last year of his life Britten finally approved the publication of Del Mar's suite. See also Richard Alston, *Norman Del Mar*, pp. 21–2.

3 Apart from Del Mar's and Sacher's interest in the *Pagodas* suite, the BBC

was also involved in negotiations. A letter from Maurice Johnstone (Head of Music Programmes) to Anthony Gishford (4 February 1957) reveals that Britten hoped that the BBC Symphony Orchestra conducted by Rudolf Schwarz might give the first performance of the suite, possibly at the Proms. This was ruled out by Johnstone:

> First because we cannot include Rudolf Schwarz among Prom conductors, and secondly because it does not seem that Ben could conduct the work himself [. . .] Ben has told me that the Suite would be as light-weight in character as *Casse-Noisette* [Tchaikovsky's *Nutcracker* suite], and our feeling is that on a rare occasion when we can represent Ben's music at one of our symphony concerts [. . .] we should play one of his more substantial works such as the *Spring Symphony* or *Sinfonia da Requiem*.

In his letter Johnstone goes on to offer a studio performance of the suite under Schwarz's direction but recognizes that Britten may prefer a public first performance.

Schwarz and the City of Birmingham Symphony Orchestra gave the first performance of the *Pas de Six from 'The Prince of the Pagodas'*, in the Town Hall, Birmingham, on 26 September 1957. It was the only section from the ballet that Britten himself authorized for separate performance.

890 To Peter Pears

4 CRABBE STREET, ALDEBURGH, SUFFOLK
March 16th 1957

My darling,

I do hope you had a nice trip across from Wolfsgarten – that Julian looked where he was going for most of the time, anyhow. I am so glad you enjoyed the time at Wolfsg., & that they enjoyed you so much. I bet it sounded ravishing in the big room.[1] Now I suppose you are in Munich, & preparing for the Passions.[2] I do hope they go well, & that Richter isn't too Brahmsy for you – or Bach![3] I'll be thinking of you.

We've applied for extra petrol – & got it![4] – so now Jeremy [Cullum] can drive you back in the Morris after the Birmingham concert,[5] which'll be much quicker than going via London. We must get you back quick because there have been 45 entries for the Blake competition[6] so far, & we'll have a lot of work to do! There are actually other reasons for wanting you back quick, but we won't go into those now, & probably you can guess what they are . . . !

Not much news – Edith has wired 'yes' about the Blake, which is a relief.[7] She says she's writing about Day Lewis.[8] Nothing yet about Marjorie Thomas[9] or Denis Dowling,[10] but I'm agitating.

It was nice having Maurice[11] for 2 days; he is a dear, & a jolly good 'cellist now – played a Bach Suite really well – but he's ever such a teensy bit boring, he do go on so about his loves, & his problems, etc. etc. – I forget to listen, occasionally. To-day I've got Barbara [Britten] & Vlado H.[12] coming; that'll be less intense, I daresay! Poor Mary is depressed about the Red House-Studio[13] problems, but I daresay we'll solve them.

Much, much love – I'm very devoted – all my thoughts are in Munich – see you soon, I pray –

B.

Do you want to do a concert with me in Canterbury on July 8th (Festival)[14] – I'm not mad keen, because it's a work period – but shall I suggest Julian Bream?

1 Pears and Bream had given a private concert at Wolfsgarten on 14 March. Pears wrote to Britten on 18 March 1957:

> Peg & Lu [Hesse] were in very good form – they had invited about 40 people to hear us [. . .] including my oboist from Detmold, and a young tenor admirer of mine. It was a v. sweet occasion – Julian played beautifully & it sounded prima in that room. Altogether lovely.

2 Pears stayed in Munich first at the Hotel Eden Wolf and, from 19 March, with his friend Leslie Sayers of the British Council. He had been engaged to sing the Evangelist in Bach's *St John Passion* at the St Lukaskirche, Munich, on 21 March, in a performance with the Munich Bach Choir conducted by Karl Richter. The other soloists were Horst Günther (Christus), Lotte Schädle (soprano), Beatrice Krebs (contralto), Robert Price (tenor) and Kieth Engen (bass).

3 An undated letter Pears sent Britten from the 1955 Ansbach Festival (Letter 836) suggests what the tenor considered to be the stylistic limitations of Richter's Bach (though he was later to modify his views):

> The line seems to be straight & narrow Bach with no room to expand – an occasional, very, ornament played pokerfaced to show we know about them. Plenty of lively down-beats but precious little living rhythm.

4 The Suez crisis of 1956 resulted in severe fuel shortages and petrol rationing was introduced in the UK. At that time approximately 80 per cent of Western Europe's oil was transported via the Suez Canal.

5 An entry in Pears's pocket engagement diary suggests that the Birmingham concert was a BBC Midland broadcast of Vaughan Williams's song-cycle *On Wenlock Edge* on 23 March 1957.

6 To celebrate the bicentenary of the birth of William Blake (1757–1827), the Aldeburgh Festival held a competition for the best new setting of one of his poems for voice and piano by a composer under the age of thirty. According

to the 1957 Aldeburgh Festival Programme Book, more than fifty manuscripts were submitted, and the four songs chosen for the final short-list were performed at a concert entitled 'Young Composers and Performers' given at the Jubilee Hall on 21 June, by Josephine Nendick (soprano) and Cornelius Cardew (piano). One of the other 'young performers' was the twenty-three-year-old clarinettist Harrison Birtwistle. The short-list comprised Cardew's 'Why cannot the ear be closed to its own destruction?', Michael Nuttall's 'A Cradle Song', Alexander Goehr's 'Narration' and Malcolm Williamson's 'The Fly'. According to the Programme Book, the winner was to be announced immediately following the performance of the fourth song; the annotated copy of the Programme Book at BPL indicates that no single award was made and that the four young composers received equal sums of prize money.

According to his biographers Anthony Meredith and Paul Harris, in *Malcolm Williamson: A Mischievous Muse*, p. 83, Williamson had entered the competition only to please Pears and 'was naturally disappointed when Britten and Pears evaded decision-making and awarded the finalists £6 5s 0d each'. Goehr later recalled (quoted in Meredith and Harris) that the occasion was:

> Like a public school prize-giving! We were all called up, one after the other, to receive our miserable prize! I was fairly rebellious at that time and refused to get up and be patted on the head like a schoolboy! Eventually, however, Malcolm, who was sitting next to me, gave me such a shove that I simply had to go!

It is evident from this letter that Pears was one of the competition judges, with Britten and probably Imogen Holst (the other Artistic Director of the Festival). Surviving at BPL are Britten's handwritten comments on the entries, the vast majority of which are dismissive of the composers' submissions. (Britten's comments are inscribed on a list drawn up by Pears.) Of the finalists, Goehr's and Cardew's entries are described by Britten as '12 tone'; Nuttall's entry he regarded as 'simple, rather naïve, not eventful but complete in expression, dullish vocal line, but singable', while Williamson, whose work Britten was beginning to get to know at this time, is praised as a 'real composer', whose setting was 'a good idea, dull middle section, but well-shaped'. See also JBBC, pp. 262–4.

7 Sitwell had agreed to take part in a poetry and music recital at the Aldeburgh Festival (18 June 1957) to mark Blake's bicentenary. According to the Programme Book, the recital included 'readings from the Prophetic Books of William Blake [...] and organ music by J. S. Bach'. Her fellow performers were Cecil Day Lewis and Ralph Downes (organ).

8 Cecil Day Lewis (1904–1972), British poet and writer, who succeeded John Masefield as Poet Laureate in 1968. He had been associated with Auden, Spender and MacNeice during the 1930s. Day Lewis was to publish an edition of *The Collected Poems of Wilfred Owen*, which included a memoir of Owen by Edmund Blunden, in 1963.

9   British mezzo-soprano, whose career during more than two decades following the Second World War embraced both opera and concert singing. She was often heard in Handel's *Messiah*, which she recorded with Beecham, and as the Angel in Elgar's *The Dream of Gerontius*, which she recorded with Sargent. She later taught at the Royal Academy of Music. She did not participate in the 1957 Aldeburgh Festival.

10 New Zealand baritone (1910–1996), who sang with the English Opera Group, 1947–48, and who was a member of Sadler's Wells Opera (later English National Opera), from 1939 until 1984. See also Letter 592, n. 9. Dowling did not participate in the 1957 Aldeburgh Festival.

11 Maurice Gendron (1920–1990), French cellist and conductor whom Britten had met in Paris in March 1945 and with whom he and Pears gave recitals in December 1945 at the Wigmore Hall, London (see Letter 499 nn. 3 and 4). Gendron was to appear at the 1960 and 1963 Aldeburgh Festivals. See also Letter 499 n. 1 and Philip Reed's CD liner notes to the BBC Legends CD of Britten, Menuhin and Gendron performing piano trios by Mozart, Beethoven and Bridge at the 1963 Aldeburgh Festival.

12 Vlado Habunek (1906–1994), Croatian theatre and opera director, who had directed Britten's *The Rape of Lucretia* in 1952 and whose association with Britten's music was to continue when he directed *A Midsummer Night's Dream* in Zagreb in 1962, and *Curlew River* in the United States in the late 1960s. He was a contributor to PPT.

13 The first reference in the correspondence to the exchange of houses that Britten and Mary Potter were to effect later in the year, when Britten moved to the Red House, a mile or so inland, and Mary Potter from the Red House to Crag House on the Aldeburgh sea front. Since her divorce from Stephen Potter in 1955, and with both her sons now grown up, Mary Potter had found the Red House too large and expensive to manage; with their increasing celebrity, Britten and Pears had found the location of Crag House afforded them little privacy, so the exchange suited both parties. (Mary Potter's son, Julian, had first suggested the exchange.) But Crag House was also a substantial property and it would appear that from the outset Britten intended to build some kind of studio-cum-domestic dwelling for Mrs Potter in the grounds of the Red House, for which he would levy a modest rent. The nature of the specific problems referred to in this letter to Pears remains unclear, but it was not until September 1963 that Red Studio, with its purpose-built north-facing studio room, was ready for occupation. (The projected expenditure on the studio was certainly much greater than either Britten or Pears had originally anticipated.) See also Julian Potter, 'Biographical Note', in *Mary Potter: 1900–1981, A Selective Retrospective*, exhibition catalogue, pp. 32–3, and the same author's *Mary Potter: A Life of Painting*, pp. 102 and 109–10.

14 It would appear that neither Britten nor Pears took up the invitation to perform at the Canterbury Festival.

891 To Anthony Gishford
[*Typed*]

4 CRABBE STREET, ALDEBURGH
19th March, 1957

My dear Tony,

John Andrewes[1] has inserted in the piano score of the Ballet John Cranko's stage directions, and I have just seen them for the first time. I propose to write to John Cranko about them, because I feel they are far too detailed and precise.[2] In other words they seem to approach choreographic instructions rather than state the basic details of the story, which to my mind is what stage directions should do. For instance, in the Court scene at the beginning of Act III there is a direction "Belle Epine walks on the Courtiers like a human staircase". I feel that that is a detail of choreography, and not an essence of the story. Things like "The Dwarf is drunk" seem to be right, but the details of how he is drunk seem to me up to the choreographer. Other things I am worried about in his directions are, where in his Covent Garden production he has gone against our original scenario (such as the Court leaving the stage during Belle Rose's dance in Act I); I propose to return to our original ideas, which seem to me better dramatically, although I still understand John's reasons for changing them because of the special conditions at Covent Garden.

Now, why I am bothering you with all this is to find out what the arrangement with him actually is. We pay him, I presume, for his general idea which started me off writing the ballet, and guided me during its creation.[3] Actually I don't feel that he will mind very much if we return to the original version. Incidentally, in the published score of Swan Lake there is a fairly full synopsis at the beginning, and then only the briefest instructions over the music.[4] [*Handwritten:*] That is what I think we should do in this case. [*Typed:*] Before I write to him perhaps you or Dr. Roth have comments to make.

I have had the enclosed letter from the Board of Trade Choir. As you will see it is to do with a concert version of "Peter Grimes". This would obviously have to be very carefully worked out, and certainly I have not got the time to do it. Concert versions of operas are very tricky affairs, and sometimes demand severe rewriting. Knowing nothing of Mr. Farncombe,[5] I find it difficult to agree. On the other hand I have no-one else to suggest, unless Ken Straker[6] has some suggestion. Actually perhaps you can discuss with him about the suitability of the whole idea; personally I have grave doubts since the work seems to me too operatic by nature to stand amateur choral interpretation in the concert hall.

I am here all this week, and in London for a few days next week, and hope to see you then.

Yours ever,
BEN

[*Handwritten*:] P.S. A young friend of mine here, one of the Cranbrook cousins (Sam[7] – of the Children's opera!) is just out of the army, & is jobless. He wants to go to Canada, perhaps as farmer or forester – & doesn't know how to set about finding out. Do you happen to know (or does Campbell)[8] where he should go to – Canada House, or some appointments bureau? Sorry to bother, but he's a nice young chap.

Thank you so much for being so good about Basil D.[9]

1 John Andrewes (b. 1915), British music publisher, and a member of staff at Boosey & Hawkes with responsibilities for editorial and promotional activities. He was closely involved in 1958 in the production of the instrumental parts of *Noye's Fludde*, and was one of the few staff at Boosey & Hawkes to impress Britten. When the composer left Boosey & Hawkes in 1964 for the newly created music publishing wing of Faber and Faber (later Faber Music), Britten tried unsuccessfully to persuade Andrewes to join the venture. A photograph of Andrewes with Nicholas Maw and his then wife appears in Helen Wallace, *Boosey & Hawkes: The Publishing Story*, p. 118.

2 Britten's letter to Cranko has not survived. Cranko wrote to Britten on 3 May from Milan, where he was rehearsing for the Italian premiere of *Pagodas* at La Scala:

> As to the printed score, of course do what you think best. I wasn't sure if what I had written was any help anyway muddling rather than clarifying the whole thing.

Gishford and Roth were also in agreement with Britten. Britten told Princess Margaret of Hesse and the Rhine (20 March 1957):

> I am getting the score of the ballet ready for publication, & there are endless semiquavers to check, & stage-directions to consider; I shall be awfully glad to be finished for good with the wretched thing.

3 According to a letter from Gishford to Britten dated 21 March 1957, the arrangement with Cranko allowed him, as author of the scenario, to receive 7½ per cent of the net performing fees on stage performances (Britten received 67½ per cent), and 6⅔ per cent of the net performance fees for television and radio broadcasts and films (Britten received 60 per cent). Cranko, unlike the librettists of Britten's operas, received no royalties in respect of sheet music sales or performances of the music in the concert hall.

4 *Swan Lake* and Tchaikovsky's other ballet scores were among Britten's close

companions during the composition of *The Prince of the Pagodas*, and furnished Britten with models on which he could base his own dances. See also vol. 3, Letter IX n. 1 (p. 74).

5 Charles Farncombe (1919–2006), British conductor and founder (with E. J. Dent) of the Handel Opera Society, of which he was Musical Director for thirty years from 1955. He played a leading role in the re-establishment of Handel's operas on the London stage, a generation after their rediscovery in Germany. Farncombe was later Music Director of the Drottningholm Court Theatre, Sweden (1970–79). Vaughan Williams had encouraged Farncombe's aptitude for training amateur choirs, and during the 1950s Farncombe was Director of the Board of Trade Choir, a group comprised of civil servants who worked in that government department. See also obituaries in *The Times* (2 August 2006) and by Anthony Hicks, *Guardian* (19 August 2006).

6 A member of staff at Boosey & Hawkes. Straker and Gishford agreed with Britten about the Board of Trade Choir's proposal.

7 Samuel Gathorne-Hardy (b. 1936): see Letter 576 n. 4.

8 Sir Campbell Stuart (1885–1972), Canadian newspaper manager, and Gishford's partner. During the First World War, Stuart had first served as military secretary to Lord Northcliffe at the British War Mission in New York and subsequently in London. On demobilization Stuart was offered the managing directorship of *The Times* and managing editorship of the *Daily Mail*, and he served as an active director of *The Times* until 1960. He also filled a succession of roles in Empire and Commonwealth communications from 1923 to 1945, and post-war served on various committees and trusts, including the Canadian History Society and the Pilgrims (Chairman, 1948–58). Stuart shared his seventeenth-century house in Highgate, north London, with Gishford. See also Stuart's autobiography *Opportunity Knocks*, the obituary in *The Times* (15 September 1972) and the entry by William Haley, revised by Robert Brown, in *The Oxford Dictionary of National Biography*.

Stuart's Canadian origins self-evidently recommended him to Britten as someone from whom he could seek advice on behalf of Samuel Gathorne-Hardy. Gishford recommended that Gathorne-Hardy make an appointment with one of the counsellors at Canada House.

9 Britten wrote to Basil Douglas (20 March 1957):

As I can't get to London before you go off on your holiday at the end of the week, I thought I'd write you a line wishing you a really lovely time. Go off, forget all about Groupy & Festivally problems, & come back strong. Remember you have many good friends (Peter & me included) who wish you so very well, & who will really do everything they can to help straighten out the future – if you want help, that is! – so don't worry over much, will you?

Perhaps Gishford, who was a director of the English Opera Group, had seen Douglas as Britten evidently was unable to do so, and calmed Douglas's anxieties about taking holiday leave at this critical juncture.

892 To Anthony Gishford
[Typed]

4 CRABBE STREET, ALDEBURGH
8th April 1957

My dear Tony,

I enclose the letter and documents which you were going to be very kind and forward to Whitney Straight[1] for me. I am sorry to trouble you like this, but I am sure a little note of introduction to him (I don't know him, although I do know his Mother extremely well) will carry a great deal of weight.

I was relieved that Ernst [Roth] is going to Milan tomorrow. I do hope he will be able to clear up some of the wretched muddle about the Ballet there.[2]

You asked for the various curious honours that I have received in the last few years. I have searched, and the rather incomplete results of my searching are as follows:

1. Award from MUSIC CRITICS CIRCLE (New York) for Choral Music October 1950 – January 1952: THE SPRING SYMPHONY.

2. Freedom of the Borough of Lowestoft 1953 (that you know about)[3]

3. Accademia Nazionale Cherubini (Music, Letters, Figurative Arts). "Accademico Effettivo Corrispondente" (???!) 1955

4. Member of Royal Flemish Society of Science, Art and Belles Lettres, 1952[4]

5. Mus. Doc. Belfast (that you know about)[5]

6. Associate of Royal Academy of Belgium (Music Section 1955)

7. Catholic Stage Guild of Dublin "Award for his work for Music", 1950. (A perfectly hideous statuette of a deformed St. Cecilia)

8. The Royal Swedish Academy of Music. "Som räknar för en Skyldighet, att ihagkomma, och för en vinst, att tillagna Sig (and a lot more in the same style) Tonsättare Benjamin Britten" 1953[6] – I have lost the original letter, which was in a more civilised tongue. All I have is the above sentence on a large certificate and a drawing of a bit of a suit I am supposed to wear as Tonsättare. Perhaps you can get someone to translate.

9. Honorary Member of the American Academy of Arts and Letters and do [i.e. ditto] of the National Institute of Arts and Letters, New York 1957[7]

10. I am also something of the Accademia Nazionale di Santa Cecilia (Rome) but I cannot find the letter, nor can I remember.[8] Perhaps the B & H representative in Milan could tactfully find out. (I should also myself rather like to know.)

I hope this rather crazy list will amuse you even if it is no use.

Yours ever,
BEN

[*Handwritten*:] P.S. Afraid I can't possibly get up for Spring Symph: next Monday,[9] because if I am to get to Vienna in time I <u>must</u> leave that afternoon.[10] Will you give Sw:[11] my regrets & best wishes, please?

1 Anglo-American businessman (1912–1979), the eldest son of Dorothy Elmhirst (see Letter 849 n. 3) and her first husband, Willard Straight. Following a successful though brief career as a Grand Prix racing driver, and war service in the RAF, Straight became Managing Director of the British Overseas Airways Corporation (BOAC) in 1947. He was later Deputy Chairman of Rolls-Royce. Gishford knew Straight through the Pilgrims, an organization dedicated to fostering Anglo-North American relations. Britten was probably approaching Straight for corporate support for the Aldeburgh Festival or the English Opera Group.

2 This concerned the hope of the Intendant of La Scala, Ghiringhelli, that Britten would himself conduct the Italian premiere of *The Prince of the Pagodas*, and expressed Britten's anxieties about the musical standards of the ballet company at La Scala. Roth was to write to Britten from Milan (9 April 1957) to confirm that La Scala's permanent ballet conductor, Luciano Rosada, would conduct the performances. At the time of Roth's letter, the first performance was planned for 27 May; this was, however, brought forward to 9 May, presumably because Britten, who was already in Italy on holiday (see Letter 894 nn. 2 and 3), would be able to attend the final rehearsals and first night.

Cranko wrote to the composer from Milan (undated letter) shortly after arriving for rehearsals:

Musically, I hope it will be all right, they seem to have that side much more under control here, and to understand the music much more easily. The rehearsal pianist gets it right first time and that side is never a drag as it was in London. The conductor, whose name I'm ashamed to say I cannot remember, is sympatico, although how good he is is another question. They ask me lots of musical questions which I cannot possibly answer and are rather anxious to know when you are coming.

One thing would be most useful [...] to get John Andrewes to send the new coda for the *pas de six* and the cuts in Svetlana's solo which are not marked [...]

Altogether I am feeling [...] excited about the second chance which this affords me to get my part right.

Cranko wrote again to Britten on 3 April 1957:

The direction here appears very vague indeed and although Rosada is a kind of resident conductor they have made no arrangements about getting anybody specially for the ballet, furthermore Ghiringhelli fondly imagines that you are going to just take up the baton when you arrive and do it yourself. They think that everybody is so overjoyed to work for the Scala they needn't bother to inform them [...]

I find the dancers very nice to work with, and although they often lack technique they have a quality which is very sympatico. The new coda [in the *pas de six*, Act III] is a great success and the seven-eight *pas de deux*, which is now a *pas de trois* [Act III], is very good (even if I do say it meself). Altogether the choreography is flowing and I realize now just how unmusical a lot of it was [at Covent Garden].

Also Booseys have sent us the weirdest set of cuts which none of us can understand. I think they must be for [the Decca] recording or something [...]

Anyway I am very happy with myself and the dancers.

Apprehensive about conductors and the state of the cuts.

Downright panicky about the sets and costumes.

And feeling slightly hostile to Ghiringhelli and Benois [who was in charge of the scenic department at La Scala].

3 *Recte*: 1951; see Letter 675.

4 *Recte*: an honorary member of the Académie Royale des Sciences, des Lettres, et des Beaux-Arts, Brussels, 1955.

5 Britten was subsequently to receive honorary degrees (Doctor of Music) from the Universities of Cambridge (1959), Nottingham (1961), Hull (1962; for Britten's 'Speech on Receiving Honorary Degree at Hull University', see PKBM, pp. 214–16), Oxford (1962), Manchester (1964), London (1964; see PFL, plate 311), Leicester (1965), East Anglia (1966), Wales (1975) and Warwick (1975). He was also an Honorary Fellow of Magdalene College, Cambridge (1966), and an Honorary Member of Worcester College, Oxford (1964).

6 The Svenska Musicaliska Academiens, Vangar. The quoted Swedish citation is incomplete and slightly mistranscribed in Britten's letter. It translates as: 'who regarded as a duty, to remember, and with profit to dedicate [...] composer Benjamin Britten' (translation by John Mosesson).

7 See Letter 898.

8 Britten was an honorary member.

9 A performance on 15 April 1957 at the Royal Festival Hall, London, with Jennifer Vyvyan (soprano), Pamela Bowden (contralto), William Herbert (tenor), the London Philharmonic Choir, the boys' choir of Alleyn's School and the London Philharmonic Orchestra, conducted by Hans Swarowsky (see n. 11 below). The other work in the programme was a long-standing passion of Britten's: Mahler's *Das Lied von der Erde*.

10 Britten departed on 15 April for Europe, travelling to Wolfsgarten where he stayed with the Hesses. Pears, who was already in Europe working, joined him there after singing in Bach's *St Matthew Passion* in Vienna on the 19th, and the party of four travelled on together by car, with Pears and Britten giving recitals in Vienna (Mozartsaal, 23 April) and Graz (24 April), before going on to Venice and a touring holiday of Italy.

11 Hans Swarowsky (1899–1975), Austrian conductor, who studied composition with Schoenberg and Webern, and conducting with Weingartner and Richard Strauss. Unable to conduct in Germany from 1936 until 1945, because of the political situation, he worked in opera administration as well as occasionally conducting abroad. Post-war he held appointments with the Vienna Symphony Orchestra, the Graz Opera and the Vienna Staatsoper, and succeeded Karl Rankl as Musical Director and Principal Conductor of the Scottish National Orchestra, 1957–59. He was particularly associated with the music of Mahler, the composers of the Second Viennese School and Richard Strauss.

893 To Imogen Holst

4 CRABBE STREET, ALDEBURGH, SUFFOLK
April 13th (12th) 1957

A rather tactless present – is there anything you would rather <u>less</u> have than this beastly Ballet which has confused, obscured, & nearly wrecked two years of your life??[1] But, dear Imo, there may be (here & there) the odd semiquaver which is worth just a little, & if it is any comfort to you, that has been made possible by your selfless encouragement, devotion & tireless work. I can't begin to say thank-you, only just . . . thank God it is over & done with (all except those . . . metronome-marks).[2]

With love, thanks, & many happy returns of the first half-century: may we be together on your 100th birthday (but I promise you NO BALLET for that).

BEN

1 As a fiftieth-birthday present for Imogen Holst (her birthday was 12 April, hence the somewhat idiosyncratic dating of this letter), Britten gave her the composition draft of *The Prince of the Pagodas*. She was also the co-dedicatee of the ballet (with Dame Ninette de Valois). Holst presented the *Pagodas* draft to BPL in 1983.

2 It was Britten's custom to leave the entering of metronome marks into a score until after the work had been performed several times and thus had had an opportunity to settle down. It was usually his music assistant's responsibility to calculate the metronome markings.

894 To E. M. Forster
From Benjamin Britten, the Prince and Princess of Hesse
and the Rhine and Peter Pears
[*Postcard*: S. Gimignano, Italy]

[8 May 1957]

Dear Morgan,

   We thought of you so much coming thro' here to-day especially as we came via Poggibonsi – but alas no "Lucia"[1] anywhere to hear, no opera anywhere at all in fact. We are having 2 weeks' driving around Venice–Ravenna–Perugia–Sienna[2] ending with the ballet in Milan tomorrow. Hope you are well.

Much love,
BEN

Sideways through Italy was nearly as much fun as sideways thro' Suffolk with you.

Best wishes,
MARGARET & LUDWIG OF H.

We are all a little dizzy with so much heady beauty – but I expect Milan will cool us right off.[3]

Much love from
PETER

1 Donizetti's opera *Lucia di Lammermoor* (1835), after Walter Scott, which features in Forster's novel *Where Angels Fear to Tread* (1905), set in Tuscany (where Poggibonsi is a town to the east of San Gimignano). Britten mentioned the passage in 'Some Notes on Forster and Music', his contribution to Oliver Stallybrass (ed.), *Aspects of E. M. Forster: Essays and Recollections written for his Ninetieth Birthday 1st January 1969*, pp. 81–6 (reprinted in PKBM, pp. 316–20):

The purpose of the big musical episode in *Where Angels Fear to Tread* is to dent deeper Philip Herriton's defences by confronting him with Gino at his gayest and most ingenuous. The scene, *Lucia di Lammermoor* at the Monteriano opera house, is long and gloriously funny: the fat lady of the railway journey 'who had never, never before . . .' turning up as the prima donna; Harriet trying to stop an Italian audience from talking, and trying to follow the plot; the triumph of the Mad Scene with the clothes-horse of flowers; and the cries of 'Let the divine creature continue'. But, as always with Forster (as with Mozart, too), under the comedy lies seriousness, passion, and warmth: the warmth of the Italians loving their tunes, being relaxed and gay together, and not being afraid of showing their feelings – not 'pretending', like Sawston.

Calling to mind *Albert Herring* (which is dedicated to Forster), one could add Britten's name to those of Forster and Mozart for whom 'seriousness, passion and warmth' lurk beneath the comedy.

2 Britten and Pears were on holiday with the Hesses in Italy from 26 April until 7 May. Britten wrote to Mary Potter (2 May 1957):

> It is the most incredible country – every village a gem, & such a school of painters which never ends. Just the list of places we've been to reads [like] a poem – Udine, Venice, Torcello, Ferrara, Ravenna (Mosaics!) [...]
>
> The Hesses are with us, in fact are driving us everywhere, which is nice & fun, because their stamina is about the same as ours – rather an important point – because one gets damnably tired – almost as bad as tennis.

3 After the Hesses returned home to Germany, Britten wrote to Princess Margaret of Hesse and Rhine (14 May 1957) about the Italian premiere of *Pagodas* and his and Pears's journey home:

> Milan was a sad, sad contrast. After that ghastly rehearsal, we worked & threatened, pleaded & bullied – to an interminable accompaniment of "si, si, caro Maestro", & nothing at all being done. I got extra rehearsals put in (to practically no avail), the orchestra took against the conductor, & I had to cajole individual members to try & get some improvement. The first public rehearsal was pretty awful – David Blair had to dance without an orchestral rehearsal before it, & was miserable, & every time the scenery fell down (or one of the dancers even) or there was a particularly vile blob in the orchestra, there were murmurs of "bella, bella!" from all the management who bothered to turn up – incidentally we never saw any of them, & they took no notice of our existence at all. The fact is they don't take ballet seriously, even in that essentially non-serious institution. So our fury against the Italians in general, & the Scala in particular, grew & grew. Imagine our chagrin then when it went well on the first night ('what was all the fuss about'?), & in spite of no farewells, our hotel bill was discovered to have been paid! It would have been so much easier to have gone on hating! But for Johnny [Cranko] & the boys & girls, it was most rewarding to be so successful after all, & smiles were seen on the faces of the tigers for the first time...
>
> We had a lovely train journey to Basel with the Pipers, then took a car into France to see the Léger church [in Audincourt] (wonderful) & the Corbusier too (pretty chi-chi) near Belfort [at Ronchamp] – a lovely trip. Then caught the night-train & day-boat into the midst of Festival problems!

895 To Elizabeth Mayer

4 CRABBE STREET, ALDEBURGH, SUFFOLK
July 2nd 1957

My dearest Elizabeth,

I feel awful not to have written to you before, but the Festival & all the preparations are a gigantic task, & many things one should & wants to do get left undone.

Thank you for your note of this morning. Our plans for Canada & Stratford are as follows:

We arrive in Toronto (& I suppose Stratford soon after) on Aug. 15th.

The performances (8 of the Turn of the S. & 3 recitals by PP & me) take place between 20th & Sept. 6th.[1] We catch (as the plan is at the moment) the boat from Montreal on 10th. It would be heavenly if you could get up to Ontario, because honestly that seems to be the only chance of seeing you. We can't delay our departure I'm afraid (& we're neither of us good at flying nowadays!!), & there are no free days to speak of … We are staying in a small flat, where I don't think there'll be room for you. But I'm sure we can look after accommodation for you somehow. Will you let us know? I shall be around here until July 28th when I go to Ansbach to hear the end of the Bach Festwoche (Peter doing B minor Mass and Matthew Passion etc), then on with him for two little concerts with Yehudi Menuhin at his home in Gstaad.[2]

Our Festival here was really lovely; it was so sad you couldn't come, but we quite understood & hope for next year. I'll get a Programme book sent to you, so I won't bore you with details now. The weather was lovely, not too hot. Princess Mary (George H's mother) came & loved what she heard – the house party was the Harewoods & Peg & Lu of Hesse, & my sister Barbara, & the Menuhins while they could be here. He was an angel, & very nice to work with, & he adores his concerts,[3] & wants to come next year.

Peter was made a C.B.E. just before his birthday[4] – not that it moved him very much (you can imagine), but it delighted his friends & admirers, & also puts heart into those few who try & do serious things without show off & senseless glamour & publicity. I think it's amazing that authority should have recognised him so early – but then, surprising & nice things do happen! He's deep in income tax figures at the moment, but sends lots of deepest love & joins me in hoping & praying somehow we can be together in August.

Much love,
BEN

1 The English Opera Group presented seven performances of *The Turn of the Screw* at the Stratford (Ontario) Festival between 20 August and 6 September, one of the performances being broadcast by CBC; four of the performances were conducted by the composer, two (3 and 4 September) by Charles Mackerras. The cast was the original one which had given the opera's premiere in Venice, except that in Canada Judith Pierce sang Mrs Grose and Miles was played by Michael Hartnett, David Hemmings's voice by this time having broken. The orchestra was not that of the EOG but a group of Canadian musicians whom Mackerras rehearsed prior to Britten's arrival.

Pears and Britten gave recitals at the Festival Concert Hall, Stratford, Ontario, on 24 August (Purcell, Schubert, Britten's *Michelangelo Sonnets* and folksong arrangements), 27 and 31 August (no programmes for these survive at BPL); they also gave a broadcast recital for CBC on 2 September 1957.

2 Pears was engaged for concerts at the annual Ansbach Bach Festival, which in 1957 included performances of the *St Matthew Passion* (24 July), B minor Mass (28 July) and *St John Passion* (31 July) under Karl Richter's direction. Britten joined Pears in Ansbach on 29 July, in time to attend performances of the First, Third and Fourth Brandenburg Concertos, the E major Violin Concerto with Menuhin (on the 30th), and the *St John Passion*.

Britten and Pears participated in two concerts at Gstaad with Menuhin and the cellist Maurice Gendron, on 4 and 6 August.

3 At the 1957 Aldeburgh Festival, Menuhin's concerts comprised a recital with Britten at Blythburgh Church on 16 June (Bach, Bartók, Schubert and Grieg), and as soloist in an orchestral concert in the Jubilee Hall on the 18th (Vivaldi: *Four Seasons*; Mozart: 'Haffner' Serenade (K. 250)), with the Aldeburgh Festival Orchestra conducted by Britten. The performance of Schubert's Fantasie in C (D. 934) from the recital was released on CD by BBC Legends in 2001. See also the CD liner note for this recording by Tully Potter, 'An Enduring Musical Bond'.

4 Pears was created a Commander of the British Empire (CBE) in the Queen's 1957 Birthday Honours List, which was announced on 13 June. Pears wrote to Mary Behrend on 25 June 1957: 'My pat on the back was timed very nicely to coincide with the Festival, wasn't it?' He was to be knighted (KBE) in 1978.

896 To Francis Poulenc

4 CRABBE STREET, ALDEBURGH, SUFFOLK

July 2nd 1957

My dear Francis,

Were you serious when you told our friend Maurice Gendron you would like to come to Aldeburgh next year & do 'Mamelles' on two pianos with me at the Festival?[1] We would try to do it as well as we can – with John Cranko (you remember the young choreographer?) doing the translation & production. He adores the work, & is most charming & gifted. As you remember there is no room for an orchestra in the Jubilee Hall, but I am sure you & I can make up for that with our 20 nimble fingers! We could fix the piano arrangement ourselves, couldn't we? (& would you like percussion too?), or have you another suggestion? We would like to do two performances (June 13th & 16th) & you can come as late to rehearsals as you like, or as early! Would you be an angel & let me have some idea if you really would like to do it?

I hear that the 'Dialogues' has started in Paris.[2] I do hope that it is as successful & good as it was at the Scala. I should love to get over & see it, but for the moment I cannot leave as I am beginning to do some writing – our Festival being over for this year.[3]

Much love, my dear Francis, & may we hope to see you here with us for a really worthy performance of your lovely opera next June!

BEN

1 Poulenc's opera-bouffe *Les Mamelles de Tirésias* (composed 1944), after Apollinaire's play, was given by the English Opera Group at the 1958 Aldeburgh Festival (13 and 16 June) in a production directed by John Cranko and designed by Osbert Lancaster, with Pears as the Husband and Jennifer Vyvyan as Thérèse/Tirésias; Charles Mackerras conducted. The performances were sung in an English translation by Cranko, Colin Graham and Pears. As Britten suggests later in this letter to Poulenc, the opera was performed in an arrangement for two pianos (no percussion was in the event used). Surviving at BPL as part of the EOG Archive is Britten's copy of the vocal score, which he has annotated in pencil to correspond to the second piano part (see p. 530).

Britten's interest in *Tirésias* was stimulated by the 1953 Columbia recording of the opera, conducted by André Clutyens with Denise Duval in the title role, which Poulenc gave him during his visit to Aldeburgh in June 1956 (the copy survives at BPL, inscribed from Poulenc to Britten). Britten wrote to him on 12 July 1956, following Poulenc's appearance at that year's Aldeburgh Festival:

May I say also that I have had tremendous pleasure from the record of "Les Mamelles". Last night after a tremendous day of work, feeling very depressed and exhausted, I played it through, and it made me laugh aloud, and also touched me (a rare combination). I am impatient now to see the score, or at least a libretto.

A year passed before Britten approached Poulenc about the possibility of including *Tirésias* in the EOG's repertory. Poulenc replied (in French) on 1 August 1957 to Britten's proposal of 2 July, having been prompted by a further letter from Britten on 27 July 1957:

Apologies for my dreadful silence but as soon as Paris was finished [see n. 3 below] I had to go to Cologne for the German *Carmélites* [which opened on 14 July 1957]. YES, YES, YES, with joy, for *Les Mamelles*, both of them. I want Peter as the husband (there is a tenor version). I shall try to make a brilliant transcription!!!!

(English translation from Sidney Buckland (ed. and trans.), *Francis Poulenc: 'Echo and Source': Selected Correspondence 1913–1963*, p. 248; original French text in Myriam Chimènes (ed.), *Francis Poulenc: Correspondance 1910–1963*, p. 876.)

Poulenc, however, was forced to cancel his visit to the 1958 Aldeburgh Festival owing to illness, and his place was taken by EOG répétiteur Viola Tunnard. He wrote to Britten on the day of the performance (Buckland, p. 253; Chimènes, p. 895):

Britten's copy of the vocal score of Poulenc's *Les Mamelles de Tirésias*, annotated by Britten to correspond to the second piano part

By an odd stroke of fortune, your premiere, like that of my *Stabat* [*Mater*] in '51, is taking place on the day of the feast of St Anthony, my favourite saint. May he not take offence at the 'Balloon-breasts' of Thérèse-Tirésias! I think of you constantly with *wild regret*. I am much better (I am sleeping a little again) [...]

Do not forget to send me photos. I want to see Peter in a dress. I am sure that, thanks to you, dear Ben, the music will be marvellous.

I was looking forward to this performance so much, and I want to thank you with all my heart for holding it all together and for having so kindly understood that my defection was as melancholy as it was involuntary.

I embrace you as well as Peter.

Britten duly sent Poulenc the much anticipated photographs of the production (the accompanying letter has not survived), which Poulenc acknowledged, in French (here translated by PR), on 25 September 1958:

> I have just received the marvellous photos of *Tirésias*. It increases my regret still further but perhaps we have avoided a drama as . . . I have fallen in love with Peter with a moustache!!!!

For more on the Britten–Poulenc friendship, including their exchange of correspondence and occasional collaborations, see Philip Reed, 'Poulenc, Britten, Aldeburgh: a Chronicle' in Sidney Buckland and Myriam Chimènes (eds.), *Francis Poulenc: Music, Art, Literature*, pp. 348–62.

2 The French premiere production of Poulenc's opera *Dialogues des Carmélites*, after the play by Georges Bernanos, which opened at the Paris Opéra on 21 June 1957. The world premiere of *Dialogues des Carmélites* had taken place at La Scala, Milan, on 26 January 1957.

3 Britten may have seen *Carmélites* when it was given at Covent Garden in January 1958: his pocket engagement diary has an entry 'Carmelites' on 24 January. There is an entry – 'Poulenc' – across 13/14 January (the opera opened on the 16th).

897 To William Plomer

4 CRABBE STREET, ALDEBURGH, SUFFOLK
July 10th 1957

My dearest William,

I was so very happy to get your letter. We so often think & talk about you, & missed you sadly at the Festival this year. Yes, it went very well – lovely large audiences, heavenly weather (Princess Mary came & enjoyed herself hugely, & was as a result sweet & relaxed) – & some really nice concerts. A nice addition to the family party was Yehudi Menuhin, who was an angel & played angelicly. But, as I said, we missed you. Perhaps next year . . .

What good news about Dr. Gruber![1] I long to get to know him, & am impatient that I shall have to wait till this spring. Obviously you are pleased with him – to judge by the tone of your letter – I am so glad.

I have had a frustrating year, as far as writing is concerned, with much travelling, organising with dreary meetings, & concerts. But after a dreadful visit to Canada (where we are for most of August), & one to Berlin[2] – I have October, November, & December free, & I hope to do some serious work then, at last. I have been trying the last 24 hours, to write a National Anthem for Malay [sic], a curious, & I'm afraid rather unsuccessful job.[3]

I don't know anything about David Engela,[4] but I'd love to meet him, if it can be arranged sometime . . . I'm afraid it looks like waiting till the autumn, because I shall be away so much till then.

The 'Sumidagawa' doesn't come into any <u>immediate</u> plans, I've rather put it to the back of my mind; but anytime <u>you</u> feel you'd like to talk about it, it can be brought forward again. It is something I'm deeply interested in, & determined to do sometime. Isn't it a curiously moving & disturbing story? I wonder which translation you've got.[5]

I oughtn't really to have started a new page, because I'm due up to Mary's to play tennis with Peter, her, Laurens & Ingaret(!) [van der Post]. Laurens gave a nice little talk & showed some of his films at the Fest.[6] – but I've seen very little of him recently.

Much love, dear Dr. G., to you & Charles. I'm sorry he's troubled with this lumbago . . . but bathing is no great penance, even in Aldeburgh, in this weather. It's even been hot here.

Peter, off as usual on his travels tomorrow, Holland, Germany, Switzerland, & then Canada with me, joins me in sending you both, much love.

BEN

1 In a letter of 5 July 1957, Plomer had told Britten that he had recently completed a volume of 'memoirs and ruminations . . . provisionally called *Are You Doctor Gruber?*' This book was published by Jonathan Cape in March 1958 as *At Home: Memoirs*, Plomer's original title having been rejected by the publisher. Peter F. Alexander identifies Dr Gruber as an alter ego adopted by Plomer and originating from an incident shortly before the Second World War when a refugee German couple greeted Plomer in the street with the words, 'Ach! Sind Sie wirklich Doktor Gruber?' (See Alexander, *William Plomer*, p. 156.)

2 As well as taking part in three performances of *The Turn of the Screw* at the Berlin Festival at the beginning of October 1957, Pears and Britten were to give a recital in Berlin on 30 September (Haydn, Schubert, Wolf, Britten's *Winter Words* and folksong arrangements).

3 The Chief Minister of the newly independent Malaysia had approached Boosey & Hawkes on 19 June 1957 with the suggestion that either Britten or Walton might be interested in composing a national anthem; he asked that it include a 'slight oriental strain'. As a Boosey & Hawkes composer (Walton was published by Oxford University Press), Britten agreed to accept the commission and completed his first version on 10 July. (He wrote to Yehudi Menuhin on the same day: 'I am struggling to write the Malayan National Anthem – a frightful job.') Britten's anthem was duly scored for military band by Norman Richardson and dispatched to Malaysia.

On 25 July Britten received via Leslie Boosey a letter from the Chief Minister and tape recordings of Malaysian folk songs; the Minister suggested that Britten might include one of the indigenous melodies in a revised version of the anthem. The composer wrote to Anthony Gishford (25 July) with his reaction:

Leslie Boosey sent me the tape from Malay this morning, and also the letter from the Chief Minister of Malay. I am afraid the former is not really very helpful – in fact it is one of the oddest noises I have ever heard (but you had better not tell them this!). The second folk song they sent is a really awful piece of mock Western light music, certainly not more than one generation Malayan, I am sure. The first one is, I am sure, more characteristic, but played in such a lugubrious way (and with such a ghastly Western piano accompaniment) that all I can do is to just recognise the phrase of the music the Chief Minister sent in his letter. However this morning, very much at the eleventh hour, I have managed to extend the middle part of my anthem so as to quote – I think quite clearly – this phrase. Could you please get this new version scored for military band, and get it sent off as quickly as possible with the gentle hint that this is my last effort to satisfy them. Actually it really ought to satisfy them because it makes a nice little piece (incidentally my tune was in the same scale as their first folk song – quite a coincidence!).

I also send back the original military band transcription with several suggestions which you could perhaps pass on to the arranger.

1) I have changed the third and fourth horn chords in several places.
2) My feeling is that the little introductory bar should always be scored the same way (possibly adding flutes each time it appears <u>softly</u>).
3) I am afraid the drum part (temple blocks) may appear to them as it stands to be a rather cheeky parody of Eastern music; I have written an alternative one in pencil on the first page, which can, of course, be played on any suitable percussion instrument the arranger suggests.
4) I think it would be tactful if the last eight bars could be scored fully although marked <u>soft</u>, so that if they wish they can end loudly.

By the way, would you please apologise to the Chief Minister for my not being able to send the sketches of the other tunes I wrote? They are too incomplete, and I have not got time to work them up. Besides, I do not think them nearly as good or suitable. [...]

P.S. I think it would be tactful to send off my original MS instead of a copy. What do you think?

Boosey forwarded a subsequent letter from the Chief Minister to Britten while the composer was on tour in Canada, which the composer acknowledged on 10 September. The minister's letter evidently rejected Britten's anthem. Britten told Boosey:

Like you I was not surprised but infuriated. I think their decision is really a sensible one because I was too much in the dark over the whole matter to be able to please them, but I cannot think they have been very gracious over the matter. However, your reply was restrained and dignified as I think it ought to have been, and I am glad you resisted the temptation of returning the cheque as you at one time contemplated. But you must let me know what out of pocket expenses the firm had over the matter, and I will of course refund them. Don't you think we should ask for the return of the manuscript – after all it might come in handy for some other Eastern nation.

The manuscript was returned a few days later. Britten wrote to Boosey (17 September 1957):

What a very surprising but rather typically Eastern reaction to your letter from Kuala Lumpur. If I ever go to that very humid part of the world again, I shall certainly go and see Tunku Abdul [Rahman, the first Prime Minister of Malaysia] as he suggests, whose second letter was much more attractive than his first.

Britten received the agreed fee of 50 guineas (£52.50) plus a further payment of 50 guineas. See also MCBFE, pp. 85–9, which includes a facsimile of Britten's manuscript.

To mark the fiftieth anniversary of Malaysian independence, Britten's anthem was first performed as a *Sketch for Malaya* in an orchestration by Tazul Tajuddin, at the Cadogan Hall, London, on 14 November 2007.

4 Dawid Engela (1931–1967), South African broadcaster, composer and musicologist, who in 1957 was working in the Afrikaans Division of the BBC World Service while also studying composition at the Royal College of Music with Herbert Howells.

5 Plomer had written to Britten on 5 July 1957:

Somebody brought me a book of Nō plays from Japan the other day and I have been re-reading *Sumidagawa*. Have you thought of it at all again?

This exchange of correspondence reveals that the possibility of adapting the Nō play for the Western stage had already been discussed. Plomer drew Britten's attention to a recent scholarly translation of the play, but the two men did not begin work on the libretto in earnest until the summer of 1958, when they used as a basis the English translation Plomer has already recommended.

6 Van der Post gave a lecture at the Aldeburgh Festival on 19 June entitled 'Stone Age Dance and Music' which focused on 'the almost vanished stone age men of Southern Africa'.

898 To Peter Pears

4 CRABBE STREET, ALDEBURGH, SUFFOLK

July 18th 1957

My darling old thing,

Lovely to get your letter & to hear news at last. It seems an age since you went away, & not always knowing where you are is a bit horrid. How sickening about the weather at Wolfsgarten; that kind of thing is so upsetting both for Peg & Lu, & you two as well.[1] The rain here has been colossal too, cloud-burst after cloud-burst. Poor old Roger's [Duncan] week-end was a bit washed out – the Saturday was lovely, we went & bathed at Covehithe,[2] & then played tennis – but the Sunday was ghastly. He was very sweet, & affectionate, but worried about his exams I think – felt sick (familiar feeling – – ??!!) going back & all. Otherwise things have been madly hectic – crises in every direction, & one hasn't had a moment to think of work (except that I've completed the Dido edition for printing, at last).[3] The Opera School[4] was thoroughly on the rocks, but was salvaged at the very last moment by the Arts Council, Covent Garden (!), the Elmhirsts, & the E.O.G. Association (our suggestion, very much backed up by Stephen [Reiss]). The Canadian visit is intolerably boring still – the E.O.G. situation maddening. But they'll all be over soon. I've got the Screw cast coming for the week-end, but had to invite Jimmie Lawrie too, to talk over all these things, which will complicate matters a bit.[5]

The Red House has been a nuisance a bit too, Stephen [Potter] has behaved very poorly towards Mary, & into the bargain written really spoiled-child letters. But Isador's [Caplan] being good, & I hope by the week-end that a valuation will be made, & then Leslie P. [Periton] is coming down next Tuesday to discuss it all with me (& Mary too).[6]

I spent 2 days in London. Heard Ab. & Isaac at Decca (really _wonderful_ record).[7] Then went to the 'Chairs'[8] at the Court, which I agree _is_ very interesting & moving. Extraordinary performance by that girl.[9] Devine[10] is pleased at the idea of coming here, I gather.

Spent the morning on Grimes with Kubelik, & then my Palace lunch[11] . . . Rather boring, because so formal, but nice people there (v. nice ex. Minister – Edward Boyle,[12] friend of George's – Freya Stark[13] – Group-Captain Cheshire[14] (anti-atomic pilot)) about 6 altogether – but alas little time or opportunity to talk to them. The Queen[15] is a real dear I think, & awfully easy to talk to! Philip[16] I find difficult, I think resents us a bit vis a vis Peg & Lu [Hesse]. Then the American Embassy for the 'Citation'.[17] A nice ambassador, badly arranged reception, rather silly people invited (Leslie & Ethel Boo[sey] – David Webster etc.) – but Marion [Harewood] came along & held my hand. I've got a nice large certificate, but at last something to wear in my button-hole, a little knobbly thing – very swell! Then home with Stephen [Reiss] & Jeremy [Cullum], in pelting rain – stopping at Harlow for a meal in Maurice Ash's[18] restaurant – not bad, but v. expensive.

Robert Ponsonby[19] has been down today. He's really rather a dear, very keen, but got so few ideas. I think he'd really rather like us to run Edinburgh for him! But nice to have a sympathetic person in that position. He's just gone, & I'm going to have a bathe then Francis Bennett[20] (here for a _few_ days) comes in for a drink, & then to Mary's for dinner – so you see, even the stay at homes have busy lives!

Sorry about Baden muddle,²¹ but at least you'll have a day off. I do hope that Ansbach goes well & pleasantly. Take it easy, my darling – don't worry. Give my love to Julian. I'm <u>delighted</u> that Schemelli²² begins to go well, & by hook or (Harwich) crook I'll be there to hear you on the Monday.

Much much love (all of it) –
Your devoted
B.

Sorry I opened Iris'²³ letter – but didn't recognise the writing, especially as she addressed it to <u>Craig</u> House!!

1 Pears and Julian Bream had taken part in what was planned as an open-air concert at the Hesses' home at Wolfsgarten on 15 July 1957. Pears described the event in a letter to Britten (16 July):

> The whole day had been showery & thundery but it looked as if it wd. hold off in the evening. Concert at 6: shower at 5.30: chairs etc put out after shower: players begin with Mozart Horn 5tet. O.K.: Julian & I begin: at once the largest Turbo jet slowly drifts over, destroying "Amarilli" [Caccini's 'Amarilli mia bella', from *La nuove musiche* (1602)]; we gallantly continue, quite hopeless: then Thank God the rain returns & we go indoors [. . .] When you have an adorable Saal like this, why bother about the courtyard? & we all settled happily to make real music, without thunder or bombers.

2 Covehithe is situated on the coast between Lowestoft and Southwold; like Dunwich, it is a Suffolk town that has almost vanished owing to centuries of coastal erosion. Covehithe's ruined church was the subject of a celebrated watercolour by John Sell Cotman.

3 The edition of Purcell's *Dido and Aeneas*, which Britten co-edited with Imogen Holst, first performed in 1951: see Letter 698 n. 3.

4 The National Opera School (originally named Opera Studio), an institution for operatic training, founded in 1948 by Joan Cross and Anne Wood. The nature of the crisis in July 1957 remains unclear: it was probably connected with securing adequate funding. The National Opera School closed in 1963, following the foundation of the London Opera Centre.

5 Britten wrote to Pears on 22 July 1957:

> I must say I've just staggered thro' one of the most strenuous, complicated & in many ways frustrating week-ends of my life – & feel pretty whacked. I can't, & won't bore you by trying, to describe it all. But what was going to be a simple week-end rehearsing the Screw [prior to the tour to Canada] was complicated by i) having to have J. Lawrie too (on account of the Opera School crisis which thank God is now solved, but Jimmie wanted to discuss it, & the E.O.G. too, & could only manage <u>this</u> week-end) ii) [the architect H. T.] Cadbury-Brown, with nice plans for the Stu<u>dio</u> [for Mary Potter: see Letter 890 n. 13], & wanted to discuss them <u>on</u> the plot – naturally – but they are <u>fearfully</u> expensive, & may be prohibitive <u>iii</u>) Michael

Hartnett [playing Miles in *The Turn of the Screw*], having infinite complications with Mother, London digs (tears & homesickness too!), worries about Canada, finally leading up to a bed-wetting, poor kid – & being so good too in the rehearsals iv) Basil C.[Coleman] really digging his heels in about those bloody blocks [i.e. rostra for staging] for Canada, and Television [see Letter 899] – so long letters have had to be written...o, etc. etc. & with weather ghastly, & you know picnics to entertain the chaps getting washed out. Miss Hudson was a brick of course, but the dogs hated it, especially the thunder. Today we've had James Fisher down, but that was painless & we got on well. Tomorrow Leslie Periton. I'm thinking of moving to North Scotland so as to be able to work a bit...!

6 In a letter to Roger Duncan (21 July 1957), Britten writes:

We are having awful trouble over the Red House, but somehow I am determined to get it, – tho' I don't want to be quite ruined. The problem is at the moment arisen over the agreement on the price – Stephen P. is asking half as much again as the price the valuers are putting on it!!

7 A recording of *Canticle II: 'Abraham and Isaac'* made by Norma Procter (contralto), Pears and Britten for Decca on 25 February 1957, but not released until 2001 (*Benjamin Britten: The Rarities*). The recording was originally planned by Decca to be part of a release of all three Britten Canticles written by that date; but there was a delay in recording *Canticle III*, which involved horn-player Dennis Brain who was bound by an exclusive contract to HMV. While negotiations were underway, Brain was killed in a car crash later in 1957. The project temporarily foundered, and was not advanced until 1961 when Britten invited Barry Tuckwell, a horn-player whose virtuosity matched Brain's, to join him and Pears for *Canticle III*. By this time he had also decided to re-record *Canticle II* with John Hahessy, a boy alto, with whom he also recorded five songs from *Friday Afternoons*, 'The Birds' and 'Corpus Christi Carol'. Quoted by Kenneth Chalmers (liner note to CD recording of *Benjamin Britten: The Rarities*), Norma Procter recalls:

Whilst we were waiting, unbeknown to me, Ben became interested in a young Irish chorister – John Hahessy – [...] in Liverpool, as Peter and I were in a taxi *en route* for a rehearsal [...] he then broke the news to me that they had already recorded *Abraham and Isaac* ('Abe and Ike') with young John, but our/my recording would still be released later. This was [...] a great disappointment for me – I so loved that work.

8 Eugene Ionesco's *Les Chaises* (1952), performed in Donald Watson's translation from the French at the Royal Court Theatre, London, in the summer of 1957 in a production by Tony Richardson, with George Devine (Old Man), Joan Plowright (Old Woman) and Richard Pasco (Orator). According to *The Times* (15 May 1957), this was the first play by the Romanian-French writer to be staged in London, and was somewhat controversial. In his biography of Devine, *The Theatres of George Devine*, p. 204, Irving Wardle writes:

It was [. . .] with Ionesco that [Devine's] French work began in 1957 when he and Plowright appeared as the ancient couple in *The Chairs*, and here, for once, he escaped the run of authority roles. For Devine, no less than for the partner half his age, it was a complete disappearance into character, and also an occasion when counting the house could be turned to advantage. Amid the walkouts and cries of 'Surrealist rubbish', the two decrepit figures treated the actual public as an extension of their invisible throng of stage visitors: issuing garrulous instructions to the house and responding to abuse by asking each other, 'What did he say, dear?' and other quavering ad libs which, for all the public knew, might have been in the text. Plowright says she had never seen him happier. 'When people went out shouting and grumbling into Sloane Square, George would watch through his window and smoke his pipe and think, "That's what I'm here for." He would never look out of his window when they were all gliding out into their Daimlers after a Restoration revival.'

9 Joan Plowright (b. 1929), British actress, who was a member of the English Stage Company during its celebrated seasons in the mid-1950s at the Royal Court Theatre, and subsequently of the National Theatre. In 1961 she married Sir Laurence (later Lord) Olivier. She was created a DBE in 2004. Writing of her performance in *The Chairs*, the theatre critic of *The Times* (15 May 1957) considered 'young Miss Joan Plowright excels as the old lady, being exactly right in her elderly ecstasies, her sudden lapses into wanly reflective silence, her affectionate pride in her husband's cleverness'.

10 George Devine (1910–1966), British actor and theatre director, who founded the London Theatre Studio (1936–39) with Michel Saint-Denis, the Director of the Compagnie des Quinze. Following war service, Devine rejoined Saint-Denis at the Old Vic Centre (1945–52), a training, touring and experimental offshoot of the Old Vic Company, which produced a remarkable crop of young actors, directors and designers. Following the Centre's closure in 1952, Devine turned to freelance directing, including Shakespeare repertory at Stratford-upon-Avon (the 'Japanese' *King Lear* designed by Isamu Noguchi, with John Gielgud, in 1955) and opera (the premieres of Walton's *Troilus and Cressida* at Covent Garden and Berkeley's *Nelson* at Sadler's Wells, both 1954). In 1956 he was appointed Artistic Director of the newly formed English Stage Company. Beginning with John Osborne's seminal *Look Back in Anger*, the ESC spearheaded new work by hitherto unknown writers such as John Arden and Arnold Wesker that challenged prevailing dramatic conventions and asserted the theatre's role as a vehicle for expressing radical opinion. See also Irving Wardle, *The Theatres of George Devine*.

The English Stage Company presented an 'Evening' (as it was described in the Programme Book) at the 1958 Aldeburgh Festival, on 21 June, when they performed two plays by Keith Johnstone: *Brixham Regatta* (directed by William Gaskill) and *For Children* (directed by Ann Jellicoe), both of which were devised 'to be performed without decor'. The manner of presentation at Aldeburgh was similar to the ESC's series of Sunday evening try-out performances for their house writers given at the Royal Court Theatre.

11 Britten attended a lunch given by the Queen and the Duke of Edinburgh at Buckingham Palace on 17 July 1957. Britten described the occasion to Roger Duncan (21 July 1957):

> I had my hectic social day in London – & I survived all right! The lunch at Buckingham Palace wasn't bad, although I was pretty nervous to start off. Quite small, about 6 or 7 besides the Queen & D. of Ed. I couldn't quite see the point of it, although there were some very interesting people there. The trouble as far as I was concerned was that although the <u>names</u> of the people there (Group-Captain Cheshire, Sir Ed. Boyle, Freya Stark etc.) were familiar, not reading newspapers enough, I couldn't remember or didn't know <u>exactly</u> what they did, & didn't really have enough opportunity to find out during <u>lunch</u> (or cheek enough to ask them!). The Queen was extremely sweet, talked to her a lot; she was very interested in Aldeburgh, had heard how good it was, & we discussed Wimbledon too, & how awful it was being booked up so far ahead. The D. of Ed. I don't find easy. I think he resents us a bit, the fact that we are such friends of his cousins the Hesses – & also a bit suspicious of this art business too. But the fact they gave this little lunch party showed they were doing their best in that direction.

Britten's attitude towards the Duke of Edinburgh altered when they both found themselves guests of the Hesses at Wolfsgarten in March 1958. He told Roger Duncan (12 March 1958):

> The last days we were there Philip, Duke of Edinb. was there – he is a cousin of Lu (the Prince of H.), & great friends of theirs – & it was nice to get to know him. He really is very intelligent, & more interested in our sorts of things than he usually seems. We played & sang to him one evening, & apparently he liked it a lot (or tolerated it!).

12 Sir Edward (later Lord) Boyle (1923–1981), British Conservative politician, MP for Handsworth, Birmingham, 1950–70, who resigned as Economic Secretary to the Treasury at the time of the Suez crisis in 1956. His later ministerial appointments included Minister of Education, 1962–64, and Minister of State at the Department of Education and Science, 1964. He served as Pro-Chancellor of the University of Sussex, 1965–70, and was Vice-Chancellor of the University of Leeds, 1970–81. Boyle was a regular concert and opera-goer, and worked on, though never completed, a biography of Fauré.

13 French-born British writer and traveller (1893?–1993), who had a particular affinity with the countries of the Middle East. She published volumes of travel writing and autobiography, as well as eight volumes of her letters at her own expense.

14 Leonard Cheshire (1917–1992), British Air Force officer and charity founder, who was a member of Bomber Command during the Second World War. He was the founder of the Cheshire Foundation Homes for the Sick, the activities of which were to expand to the Third World, notably India. In 1959

he married Sue Ryder, whose own post-war charitable work among Polish refugees in Warsaw was well known, and together they lived in Cavendish, Suffolk.

15 HM Queen Elizabeth II (b. 1926), who succeeded her father, King George VI, as sovereign in February 1952. The Queen supported Britten and Pears and the Aldeburgh Festival by opening Snape Maltings in 1967 and again in 1970 after the hall's destruction by fire in 1969 (after which she telephoned Britten personally with a message of sympathy). She commissioned from the composer his *Birthday Hansel* for tenor and harp to celebrate the Queen Mother's seventy-fifth birthday in 1975. While it remains true that music has never been one of the Queen's principal enthusiasms, the small collection of personal letters from her to Britten at BPL suggests an interest greater than required by the obligations of her position. In 1965 she appointed Britten a member of the Order of Merit (OM), an honour in her personal gift. See also HCBB, pp. 463–4.

16 HRH Prince Philip, Duke of Edinburgh (b. 1921), the Queen's consort. Prince Philip was to visit the Aldeburgh Festival in 1962 when he opened the Festival Club, and was to return in 1967 and 1970 when he accompanied the Queen. In 1961, he invited Britten to compose his *Jubilate Deo in C* for St George's Chapel, Windsor.

17 At a ceremony held at the US Embassy in London on 17 July 1957, Britten was given honorary membership of the American Academy of Arts and Letters.

18 Maurice Ash (1917–2003), British farmer, writer, and civic and environmental activist, who had been a contemporary of Britten's at Gresham's, and who, in 1947, married Leonard and Dorothy Elmhirst's daughter, Ruth. The Ashes lived and farmed near Bishop's Stortford, Essex, during the 1950s, when Ash also founded the Harlow Arts Trust and established a top-class restaurant near by, which, according to Roger Berthoud, 'proved too far ahead of its time to last long'. See also obituaries by Roger Berthoud, *Independent* (28 January 2003); in *The Times* (6 February 2003), and by Richard Boston, *Guardian* (13 February 2003).

19 British music administrator (b. 1926), who studied at Trinity College, Oxford, where he was organ scholar (1948–50), before joining the staff at Glyndebourne (1951–55). He succeeded Ian Hunter as Artistic Director of the Edinburgh Festival (1955–60), worked for the Independent Television Authority (1962–64), and was General Administrator of the Scottish National Orchestra (1964–72). In 1972 Ponsonby succeeded William Glock as Controller, Music at the BBC, a position he held until 1985.

20 Edwin Keppel (Francis) Bennett (1887–1958), British academic, who had first met Forster before the First World War. Bennett had gone to Cambridge on a scholarship and later became a Fellow of Gonville and Caius College.

He wrote several books under the *nom de plume* of Francis Keppel, and was to become a close friend of E. M. Forster in the latter's old age.

21 Pears informed Britten in a letter of 16 July 1957 that his and Bream's planned recital in Baden-Baden had been cancelled.

22 At this period Pears and Bream were programming 'Geistliche Lieder' from the *Musikalisches Gesang-Buch* by Georg Christian Schemelli (c. 1676–1762). For example, at the 1958 Aldeburgh Festival they performed four sacred songs as well as a 'Praeludium' for lute solo. In his letter of 16 July 1957 to Britten, Pears reported that Bream was 'playing v. well & charming everyone by being his natural self. The big lute Schemelli went very well in Holland – I was awfully pleased.'

Britten was enthusiastic about the recital partnership between Pears and Bream and was proud of the success of their concerts together. He told Pears in a later letter (undated, but probably 22 July 1957): 'I must say I am fired to write some guitar songs for you both.' These songs proved to be the *Songs from the Chinese* to texts by Chinese poets in translations by Arthur Waley, composed in the autumn of 1957: see Letter 910 n. 4.

23 Iris Holland Rogers (d. 1982), a friend of Pears and a gifted linguist; see also Letter 169 n. 6, CHPP, pp. 70–71, and CHPP, plate 4 (which is incorrectly captioned: for Harley Place read Charlotte Street).

899   To Basil Coleman
[*Carbon copy*]

4 CRABBE STREET, ALDEBURGH, SUFFOLK
22nd July, 1957

My dear Basil,

I am afraid you must be feeling we are very difficult; the trouble is, at this distance with all of us so hectically busy in so many different directions, the elaborate discussions which should have taken place before making radical changes in a production like this could not occur. I have been all along frankly dismayed at the idea of no scenery – I had been led to believe that the compromise screen-scenery plan by John Piper and Colin Graham[1] could be used on this stage; then, just before I left on a long Continental tour, it was broken to me that after all that was not possible. I protested, vainly. Then the furniture. After discussion with John and Myfanwy [Piper], doing our best to see your point of view, agreement was reached that at least the furniture must be realistic. Still no compromise from your side. Now I am sure that a production <u>could</u> be done with nothing but black screens and black blocks, but it would have to be worked on together with everyone, obviously including performers, right from the start (and preferably not for "The Turn of the Screw" which was conceived, as you know, quite differently!) Besides, are we not coming 3,000 miles to do the original English Opera Group production? All this is to explain why we are apparently being so intransigent.

Anyhow, Colin has been here this weekend, and we have been having very useful rehearsals with some of the cast. We have also had the opportunity to discuss your letter[2] in great detail, and make the following comments. It is quite clear that some furniture moving has got to take place in full view of the audience. The stage must be clear for exterior scenes; for instance, how otherwise can one make quite sure that the audience realises after the piano playing scene that Flora is by the lake, or at any rate outside the house? Has everything been done to minimise the spill from the orchestral lights? What about gauze erections? What about blue bulbs in the music stands (as they have in Munich), or at any rate blue gelatines? But even if a certain spill is inevitable, I would much rather that the audience accepted the idea of stage hands (suitably clad, obviously) being visible moving pieces of furniture than the impression being given that Miles was sleeping on a tomb, playing the piano on a desk, or that it all took place in a sort of gloomy nowhere – neither indoors nor out. Anyhow, I enclose the list of suggestions which Colin and I together (with telephonic communications to the Pipers) have worked out as the last possible compromise.

<u>Television production</u>. I am still uncompromisingly against cutting the work at all. "Billy Budd" on N.B.C. was a quite different case; it was a longer and much more episodic work.[3] "The Turn of the Screw" is as concise and musically knit as a work can be. Of course, I understand the difficulty of finding visual images for the interludes; that is why I think Basil D. [Douglas] has suggested that you yourself, knowing the work so well, should be in charge of such a production. But even you may feel the overwhelming difficulty of these long interludes, in which case the solution is not to televise the opera rather than to cut them. The music is nonsense without them; in fact it would be better to do it as a play. I was appalled at the idea of not including Olive Dyer in the cast for this. Not only would I hate to hurt her feelings since she is such a splendid and loyal trouper, but in a company of this small size all travelling and working together in the closest collaboration, it might well be fatal to have one disgruntled (or even only depressed) member. And imagine how much confidence it would take away from her performance – playing the part of a younger sister with a boy younger than her own daughter – to have it rubbed in again that her looks were not suitable. I am sorry, but I feel adamant about these two points, and so clearly we must drop the television plan.[4]

[BEN]

1 British (subsequently naturalized American) opera director and librettist (1931–2007), whose close collaboration with Britten resulted in his directing the premieres of *Noye's Fludde* (which he also designed), *Curlew River*, *The Burning Fiery Furnace* and *The Prodigal Son* (all in St Bartholomew's Church, Orford, between 1958 and 1968); *Owen Wingrave* (BBC Television, 1971; Royal Opera House, 1973); *Death in Venice* (Snape Maltings, 1973) and the revised version of *Paul Bunyan* (Snape Maltings, 1976). In addition, he wrote the libretto and directed the first performance of *The Golden Vanity* (Snape Maltings, 1967), Britten's vaudeville for the Vienna Boys' Choir, and directed the 1969 English Opera Group production of *Idomeneo*, which Britten conducted. Graham undertook important stagings of most of Britten's other operas, including *Gloriana* (Sadler's Wells, 1966) and *The Turn of the Screw* (Snape Maltings, 1972, conducted by the composer).

After training at RADA, Graham began his career as a stage manager with the English Opera Group, playing a key role in the first production of *The Turn of the Screw* in 1954 in Venice, where his recent mastery of Italian was put to good use smoothing over communication difficulties with the stage hands of La Fenice. His involvement in *Noye's Fludde* confirmed Britten's confidence in him, and with the absence in Canada of Basil Coleman, the company's principal director, Graham was given increased responsibility, not only for revivals but also for his own productions. Although he remained committed to Aldeburgh (he became an Artistic Director of the Festival in 1968), the EOG and its successor, the short-lived English Music Theatre (1975–80), Graham expanded his activities elsewhere, directing for the Sadler's Wells Opera Company (later English National Opera) productions of operas by Janáček, Prokofiev's *War and Peace* and the first performances of Iain Hamilton's *The Royal Hunt of the Sun* and *Anna Karenina*. (His libretto of Tolstoy's *Anna Karenina* (1967/68) remained one of Britten's unachieved projects.) Graham was Director of Productions at English National Opera from 1978 until 1984. During his long career in opera he directed over fifty premieres.

In 1977 he established what would prove to be an important connection with the Opera Theatre of St Louis, which he developed following the collapse of English Music Theatre in 1980 after the withdrawal of Arts Council funding; he became Artistic Director of the St Louis company in 1985. In the mid-1980s he cancelled his professional engagements in order to study theology for two years, and in 1987 became a minister ordained by the New Covenant Church. He subsequently resumed his career as a director in St Louis and elsewhere in the United States and, occasionally, Europe (including a revival of *Death in Venice* at the Royal Opera House in 1992).

See also Colin Graham, 'Staging first productions 3', in DHOBB, pp. 44–58; Graham's contribution to PPT, p. 39; Donald Mitchell's interview with Graham (London, 3 March 1992; transcript at BPL); a recorded conversation between Graham and Keith Grant about the EOG and EMT (London, 1988; transcript at BPL); and obituaries in *The Times* and *Daily Telegraph* (9 April

2007); by Vivien Schweitzer, *New York Times* (9 April 2007); by Alan Blyth, *Guardian* (10 April 2007); by Elizabeth Forbes, *Independent* (11 April 2007), and by Steuart Bedford, Keith Grant and Rodney Milnes, *Opera* (June 2007), pp. 664–8.

2   Coleman had written to Britten earlier in the year to share his ideas for an adaptation of his EOG production of *The Turn of the Screw* appropriate for the special circumstances of the theatre at Stratford, Ontario. In particular, Coleman was concerned about the scene changes during the orchestral interludes and the difficulty of achieving a suitable level of darkness at Stratford which would render the changes invisible to the audience. (He had been told by a friend that the scene changes had been distracting during the 1956 run of *The Turn of the Screw* at the Scala Theatre in London because the stage hands were unfortunately visible.) He therefore proposed a more radical adaptation of his original staging by dispensing with some of the furniture, leaving a few items on stage throughout the performance. As Britten's letter to Coleman made clear, this proposal was unacceptable to the composer.

3   The NBC-TV production of 'Scenes from *Billy Budd*' was televised live on 18 October 1952 from the Center Theatre, New York, as the opening broadcast of NBC's fourth season of televised operas. The restrictions of the series format meant that no televised opera broadcast could be longer than ninety minutes, hence the need to make an abridged version of *Billy Budd*. The cast included Theodor Uppman in the title role, Andrew McKinley as Vere and Leon Lishner as Claggart, conducted by Peter Adler. See also BBMCPR, pp. 152–3, and Quantance Eaton, 'Billy's Bow', *Opera News* (31 March 1979), p. 28.

4   This plan for a television production of *The Turn of the Screw* was dropped, but an Associated Rediffusion film of the opera, directed by Peter Morley, was made in 1959 and broadcast on Christmas Day (Act I) and 28 December 1959 (Act II); it featured two members of the original cast (Jennifer Vyvyan and Arda Mandikian), with the EOG Orchestra conducted by Charles Mackerras. The 1959 film used Piper's original set and costume designs, realized for television by Michael Yates. For this film version the variations were illustrated by specially created Piper designs, which were filmed in close-up before cutting back to the life-size set. After attending a preview screening of the film, Britten told Pears (14 December 1959):

TV of Screw was awfully good, scenically rather than musically, actually. Peter Morley is really quite a chap (the producer) & John has done some spiffing new designs.

900 To Friedrich Krebs[1]
[*Carbon copy*]

[4 Crabbe Street, Aldeburgh, Suffolk]
26th July, 1957

Dear Mr. Krebs,

Thank you for your letter.[2] I am so glad you are enjoying playing my Six Metamorphoses, and I look forward to hearing your forthcoming performance on the radio.

I will endeavour to answer your questions, but please forgive me if the answers are brief because I am just about to go away.

1) You are quite right about the Pipe of Pan. I have no very clear pictorial image for the repeated A sharps, except perhaps that they show hesitation. I am sorry they are ponderous on your oboe; the original oboist (Joy Boughton[3]) was able on hers to make them very light and short.

2) The soft C major arpeggios in Phaeton could perhaps suggest a similar movement to the beginning, but at a distance – perhaps even an echo – but something anyhow to give a sense of space.

3) You were quite right, Niobe's lamentation becomes granite in the last four bars.

4) In Bacchus, as before, I find it difficult to give a precise indication of any particular bit, but perhaps it will help you to think of "the shouting out of boys" as being the più vivo, and the "tattling tongues" as the C major con moto passage.

5) Narcissus should not be too slow, but it must be very peaceful.

6) Arethusa is pictured here entirely as being become a fountain, although there are pools of stillness (the trills).

In case it is useful to you I append a list of rough metronome marks.[4]
Thank you very much for your kind remarks about the work itself.

With best wishes,
Yours sincerely,
[BENJAMIN BRITTEN]

1 A prominent freelance German oboist, Krebs was at this time a student in Cologne and may well have been known to Pears from the tenor's many engagements in West Germany during this period.

2 Krebs's letter has not survived at BPL but, as Britten's reply indicates, it evidently concerned performance issues relating to Britten's *Six Metamorphoses after Ovid* for solo oboe. Krebs gave several performances of

Metamorphoses in the 1950s and 1960s, as well as a broadcast for WDR Köln.

3 British oboist (1913–1963), daughter of the composer Rutland Boughton (see Diary for 10 September 1931, n. 7). She was a member of the EOG Orchestra during the late 1940s and 1950s and was the dedicatee of *Six Metamorphoses after Ovid*, the first performance of which she gave on 14 June 1951 at the Meare, Thorpeness, as part of the Aldeburgh Festival. According to Sarah Francis:

> Ben wanted Joy to play the *Six Metamorphoses after Ovid* standing on a raft, but she felt unsafe, so a compromise was reached and she stood on an island. Ben was very disappointed, but Joy was right to be suspicious of that raft. On a later occasion it broke away from its mooring and drifted off down the Meare carrying the choir and the madrigals with it. Joy did play the piece standing on a barge two years later.

See Sarah Francis, 'Joy Boughton: A Portrait', *Double Reed News* 26 (February 1994), pp. 4–7; George Caird, 'Benjamin Britten and his *Metamorphoses*', *Double Reed News* 76 (autumn 2006), pp. 18–22, and Caird's essay and CD, *Britten 'Six Metamorphoses after Ovid': Anatomy of a Masterpiece*, which includes transcriptions and a performance of Britten's composition draft and sketches, as well the first broadcast performance from 1952 by Joy Boughton.

4 A copy of the list of metronome marks does not survive at BPL. According to George Caird, the metronome markings did not appear in the published score of the *Six Metamorphoses after Ovid* until Boosey & Hawkes reprinted the piece in 1968 ('Benjamin Britten and his *Metamorphoses*').

901 To Roger Duncan

CANADIAN PACIFIC EMPRESS OF BRITAIN
August 14th 1957

[...]

Sorry this is only one of these dreary air-mail letter things but anyhow there is not much news so far. I expect by now you are back at Meade.[1] I'm afraid the weather at Aldeburgh must have been pretty stinking those last days, but I hope you all managed to find something to do, & didn't go murdering each other for boredom![2] I am sorry I was only there for such a short time with you, but better that than nothing, & anyhow I hope there'll be a chance of seeing you before you go back to school. I expect Jeremy [Cullum] told you details of our trip across England – how the first part was fun & quick, & then how everything slowed up – ghastly traffic through the potteries,[3] cloudburst in Warrington.[4] However he drove very well & we only arrived ten minutes late. Usual battery of press men when we arrived, & as usual we were feeling tired & cross & not in the mood for being interviewed & photographed. We then settled in to this journey which has been fearfully dull, & rather uncomfortable. We are all travelling Tourist (3rd class) because that's all the E.O.G. can afford & we thought we ought to stick together. I don't mind the lack of luxury, but what is boring is the cramped cabins & hoards of people in all the public rooms. However we have managed by staying in bed lots of the day – reading & writing (I've done quite a bit of work) & then in between rain-storms dashing on to the deck for a quick walk round & perhaps a game of deck-tennis with Michael [Hartnett] (the boy who is playing Miles) – which of all games is my least favourite. However the last days we have made friends with the Captain, been up on the bridge which is fearfully interesting – watched thro' the Radar, seen quite a few icebergs, & today a school of whales! We are now approaching Quebec & then tomorrow we disembark at Montreal fly to Toronto, train to Stratford & then I'll write to you again. [...] enjoy your holiday.

See you soon,
[...] BEN [...]

1 Duncan's family home at Meade Farm, Welcombe, near Bideford, North Devon.

2 Roger Duncan, his sister Briony and a friend stayed for a week at Britten's home in Aldeburgh during the school summer holidays, looked after by Miss Hudson, the composer's housekeeper; Britten was away for most of the week, except for a brief visit of twenty-four hours. Duncan thanked Britten (undated letter, probably 11 August 1957) for letting them use the house, telling him, 'Miss Hudson has been terribly sweet to us and very kind giving us all my favourite puddings.'

3 A common name for the region of the Midlands centred on the city of Stoke-on-Trent, Staffordshire, which from the time of the Industrial Revolution was the centre for the manufacture of pottery in the UK.

4 A large town in Cheshire, and an important crossing point over the River Mersey.

902 To Princess Margaret of Hesse and the Rhine
From Peter Pears

94 Hibernia St, Stratford, Ont. [Canada]
[20 August 1957]

Dearest Peg –
Tuesday A.M.

These last days have been spent in endless rehearsals with only time over for eating & sleeping. Today we await with trepidation tonight's first performance.[1]

We have to struggle against heavy odds. The theatre is no theatre, the stage has no curtain & no top, there is no orchestra pit. It is far far worse than Aldeburgh. The platform-stage is a mile wide, & 3 yards deep. The audience surrounds us up to a semicircle. The floor of the Hall is flat so that some seats will have their vision obscured by the harp, others will peer round Ben or the double-bass. Those at the outsides will only receive such crumbs as the singers deign to throw them. The acoustic is quite good, so is the orchestra. The musical side will be fair, one hopes. But to look at, it is deadly; only tall black screens, some black steps for the tower, and an occasional table (occasionally) & an occasional piano & tomb. Oh for John P. & his gauzes! Ben's score will have to carry everything.

One relief is that "Flora" has entirely recovered! Naturally; as soon as her under-study had been flown out at vast expense! She is quite well again; incredible, that three days ago she was very very mad.[2]

We are staying in the ground floor of an 1890 villa, which belongs to a music teacher (fem.) now on holiday in Europe. Her stalwart Salvation Army lassie Mabel looks after us. I blotted my copy book the first night by leaving whiskey stains on the French Polish of the Dining-room table, but Mabel can take it – (but prefers to let it alone!). The rooms are as neat & as clean can be; one stands one's glass on a coaster on a doyley on a mat on a lace table cloth on a blanket on the table. There are many ceramic horrors behind glass. Thorvaldsen's "Eros & Psyche"[3] is much in evidence, but there is no television – and it is really as quiet as the grave.

Friday. [23 August 1957]

Well, the first night is over – long over now. And it wasn't too bad. There were one or two near disasters, & some scenery was moved in brilliant daylight owing to cues being missed, but the performance was reasonably representative. Afterwards, we went on to a reception at the Festive Club, & met huge numbers of mostly quite boring & bewildered people, who had no idea of opera or Henry James or Benj. Britten. Some people adored it & some obviously hated it. But we are trying hard not to let the Festival get away with thinking that this concert hall stage is perfect for opera. They want to imagine that it's wonderful and that opera can be done "in the round" just as well as Shakespeare.

Last night we went to see 'Hamlet'[4] in their new theatre, opened last month, costing $1½ million. This is the shape: not unlike the original Elizabethan shape. No footlights, no scenery: only permanent built set (in this case, very ugly & dull). Advantage is that you get a remarkable feeling of nearness & intimacy, & three dimensional reality. Disadvantages: that because actors have to address all parts of the house, you miss a great deal of their words when they face another part of the audience. Important too that one should have a beautiful permanent set. Theatre "in the round" is very much the vogue, this side of the Atlantic. It is cheap relatively; no scenery: you could do it in a large hall, in the middle of the floor. But the look of it tends to be dreary, & it is obviously only suitable for certain styles. Now they would like to think that Opera "in the Round" is a possible & desirable scheme. They won't face the musical problems or rise airily above them: however we are being very downright against such ideas, and quash them when presented with them.

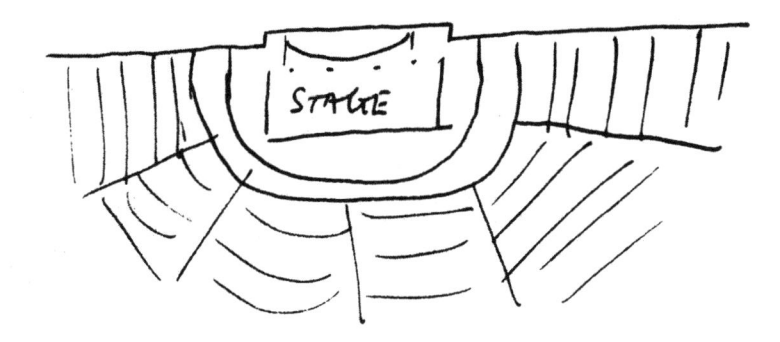

Wednesday was a day almost wholly devoted to the dear Press... one interview after another.[5] The Canadian music critics seem to be even less educated than their English colleagues. Ben was asked "What is the difference between the Rape of Lucretia (done here last year) & the Turn of the Screw?" I ask you!! Ben's answer was a good one. "The notes are the same, but they are in a different order."

In the evening there was a concert given by the Canadian Broadcasting Symph. Orch., which included Ben's Sinfonia da Requiem.[6] As Erwin Stein would say, it was bad of course, but it could have been worse. The players are really rather good, but no ensemble or discipline to speak of.

One of the nicest things for us is that our old friend Elizabeth Mayer has come up from New York for 10 days, & we spend most of our time with her. She was wonderful to us before & at the beginning of the war, & it is a great joy to see her again. In our darker moments, we say that it is the only reason we came here. She is enjoying "The Screw" terrifically, & being with us.

I must send this off – otherwise I shall keep it indefinitely & merely add from time to time.

It was lovely to have your letter. Delighted to hear of Chonia's safe "accouchement" – was it psychological to start with & then began actual, do you think?[7] Triumph of mind over matter? Exciting about the Lute.[8] Julian [Bream] will be thrilled.

We are both longing to be back in the Old Continent! Very sweet kind people here – BUT.

Much love to you all. We are off for the weekend to the Lakes.[9] It is pouring, has been for 36 hours & may well go on for another 36.

Ugh!

Ughox
BENPET[10]

1 Britten described the rehearsals and first performances of *The Turn of the Screw* in a letter to Roger Duncan postmarked 26 August 1957:

We have had to work like mad things to get the Opera onto this mad stage, like a concert hall, without scenery or curtains, & all of us with the feeling that the situation was impossible, that it wasn't worth the effort. We had also to rehearse their orchestra, not bad, but not as good as ours, & with some pretty bad players (the bell-player went mad in the Churchyard scene & pretty well wrecked everything, in the last performance). However our own singers do very well (Michael, you remember, is really very good), & I think some of the audience enjoy it. Life otherwise is hectic too, loads of parties & interviews with critics(!) – all considered very important in America; you can imagine how I enjoy it.

In a letter of 24 August, Basil Douglas told Maureen Garnham (quoted in Garnham, *As I Saw It*, p. 106):

We've had two performances, the first good, and the second not half bad but bad enough to warrant another orchestral rehearsal before the broadcast at hideous cost (about $300 – don't tell our players!). They are good players, but they don't really know the work yet, and memory is fallible in a work of this kind; there were disasters last night, which no one noticed but drove Ben into a frenzy. I go about with a brandy bottle which makes the players laugh [...]

2 In an earlier letter to Princess Margaret of Hesse and the Rhine (11 August 1957) Pears explained:

Our "Flora" [Olive Dyer] has had a total mental collapse. Poor little thing – after so many years of playing little girl parts, she is now a little girl and needs a governess all the time. She has suddenly got persecution mania, thinks the other singers are plotting against her, she hears people talking all night outside the door. Poor Arda [Mandikian] who shares a cabin with her hasn't slept a wink. We shall have to send for her understudy who doesn't know the part [...]

Maureen Garnham relates this episode in *As I Saw It*, p. 105:

Olive Dyer had had a nervous collapse and had convinced herself that her husband and daughter, who were travelling in Holland, had met with a terrible accident [...] Olive was in perpetual floods of tears, and in no condition to perform.

Garnham had to arrange for Dyer's understudy, Shirley Blasdale, to fly out to Canada immediately, at which point Dyer made a swift recovery:

There is no cure for an opera singer's illness to equal the sight of an understudy present and ready to perform. As soon as Shirley arrived, Olive made a speedy recovery – helped, indeed, by having been able to get news of her husband and daughter and discover that all was well.

3 The Danish sculptor and collector Bertel Thorvaldsen (1768/1770?–1844), whose *Eros and Psyche* dates from 1823.

4 A production directed by Michael Langham and designed by Desmond Heeley (who had created the costumes for *The Prince of the Pagodas* at Covent Garden), with Christopher Plummer as Hamlet. The production played in the newly opened Stratford Festival Theatre, a building that revolutionized modern theatre architecture by reinventing the Elizabethan thrust stage and inspired more than a dozen major theatres elsewhere the world. The Stratford (Ontario) Shakespeare Festival was founded in 1953.

5 A recording of Tom Patterson's CBC interview with Britten (broadcast 23 August 1957) survives at BPL.

6 The performance was given in the Festival Concert Hall, Ontario, on 21 August 1957, conducted by Thomas Mayer. The other works in the programme included Purcell's Chacony for strings, Walton's Violin Concerto (with Betty-Jean Hagen as soloist) and Stravinsky's *Firebird* suite.

7 Princess Margaret's dog Chonia had given birth to a litter of puppies; possibly this pregnancy had followed a phantom pregnancy, a condition to which some breeds of dog are prone.

8 This reference remains unclear: perhaps Princess Margaret had commissioned a new lute for Julian Bream.

9 See Letter 903.

10 The collective nickname Britten and Pears used when writing to the Hesses. The Hesses' equivalent was 'Lupeg'; Pears also called them 'Pegwig'.

903 To Princess Margaret of Hesse and the Rhine
From Peter Pears

94 Hibernia [Street], Stratford, Ont. [Canada]
Thursday [29 August 1957]

Dearest Peg –

The keeping up of the promised Chronicle has proved more difficult than I envisaged. Apart from my incurable laziness, which keeps me from the lighter joys of postcard writing even, a total lack of anything to tell you of interest persists. Stratford is the most ordinary little provincial town; the people are amiable and dull; the performances have gone all right; my hayfever has been a bore; Ben's tummy is unreliable; we have got round the licence law and are drinking lots of Scotch; we have been entertained very warmly & nicely & rather boringly; we took ourselves off for a week-end to a Lake 400 miles (?) wide to bathe; Ben complained that it wasn't salt & was too warm, but the Inn where we stayed was kinda cute, and gave us lots of lovely food, & we had Scotch out of tooth mugs up in our bedroom, which made us nostalgic for Karachi and die Hessen.

The Concert hall, where we perform "the Screw", has on finer evenings developed a new snag. Immediately adjoining the back of the stage is a Sports Club, where Bowls is much in favour just now, and my Cadenzas at the end of the first Act are punctuated by howls of dismay and shouts of triumph – "Miles" I sing. "Hurrah" yell the Bowlers. "Mi-i-i-i-les" – "Booh! booh!" from the Bowlers. Very confusing for our audience.

Ben has had a very happy long dream about going through sort-of-fire and water trials, with all the while Clytie hugging him round the neck. He was quite a new man in the morning. Last night, on the other hand, after beef stew and cheese at midnight, I dreamt about cutting down a rival tenor from the gallows, half-dead. I didn't quite make out who it was or perhaps I would have left him.

Friday [30 August 1957]

Last night we went to "Twelfth Night"[1] & were shown round the new theatre. Oh for the half of the money which went into the building of all this concrete & steel – it's not yet properly finished but in many ways enormously impressive and a wonderful centre for "Theatre culture" in this country. They need a lot of work on the actors who are still raw and unclever at speech, but I dare say experience will bring that, if they can persuade Tyrone Guthrie[2] to stay on & work with them, which I expect he will.

As far as the weather is concerned, we might be in the Cotswolds in November – wisps of fog are climbing round the windows, the chestnut trees are turning brown & dripping persistently onto the sidewalk, ferns droop, mosquitoes are coming out from behind closets in which one's shoes will quickly turn green, reporters call & take a photograph & sit for half an hour and go away, the air is saturated with gloom. One will soon perhaps get up enough strength to walk across to the cupboard where Mabel keeps the Scotch.

Only Ten days more!

Much love to you all –
PETER OXOXO

1 A production of Shakespeare's comedy directed by Tyrone Guthrie and designed by Tanya Moiseiwitsch.

2 Tyrone Guthrie (1900–1971), Anglo-Irish director and theatre designer. A Director of the English Opera Group since 1947, he had directed the first Covent Garden production of *Peter Grimes* and the 1948 EOG production of Britten's realization of *The Beggar's Opera*. See also Letter 416 n. 6. He was Artistic Director of the Stratford Shakespeare Festival in its inaugural season in 1953 and again in 1955. It was he and Tanya Moisewitsch who had specified the architectural relationship between the stage and the audience.

904 To Princess Margaret of Hesse and the Rhine
From Peter Pears

94 Hibernia [Street, Stratford, Ontario, Canada]
September 4th [1957]. Wednesday.

Dearest Peg,

Here beginneth the 1st verse of the last ch. of the Eposhle to the Hesshns.

Since I last wrote, we have been whizzed around a small part of this enormous province of Ontario (which is half as big again as Texas). In fact if the Americans want size they'd better come to Canada. It seems to me that, materially, Canada is the country of the future. Poor old Uncle Sam is quite played out – only he's interested too. It's largely U.S. money which is building a pipe line to convey Natural Gas from Alberta 3000 miles down to Detroit & Toronto! and of course we have three lines of defence in the snows against the Russians which only Americans are allowed to penetrate. It's quite like home: one might be in East Suffolk.[1]

We were driven off on Sunday morning up 250 miles into the Muskoka lakes; on the way we took a wrong turning and had driven 40 miles before we realised we were off our track. So vast – so empty, and yet they calculate there will be 700,000 unemployed in Toronto this winter!

This weekend was Labour day weekend[2] which meant that the roads were covered with highly coloured metal roadsters, bumper to bumper, for miles on end. We were therefore 2½ hours late for lunch which displeased our lunch-proud hosts. The cottage by Lake Muskoka which we were visiting had belonged for years to Campbell McInnes,[3] a famous baritone of years ago, ex-husband of Angela Thirkell.[4] Does the name ring a bell? (a Camp-bell? perhaps!). Ben & I had visited him in this same cottage in 1939 for 24 hours & I had had a lesson.[5] He was, I believe, very remarkable, though I never heard him sing. He did a great deal for Toronto music & his name is very much alive still, though he died in 1945. Anyway, the visit was full of associations and echoes. Our hosts overfed us grossly in the Transatlantic style on stuffed chickens & sweet corn & relishes & peach pie & old-fashioneds, & meatloaf (farm style) & squash & pickles & wine jelly

& so-on. And the rain teemed & the landscape got more & more blurred & thunder got nearer & nearer, & the Canadian Pacific trains moaned through the night on their way to Vancouver, and one switched on the light & mixed oneself a strong Eno's,[6] & tried to get back to sleep.

The next day cleared a bit & we drove around the very lovely belaked & wooded country. The leafs are beginning to turn & occasionally you come across a quite crimson branch on a yellow tree. The silver birches are incredibly beautiful, so young & slim & clean.

In the evening we had promised to record a half hour of songs for the C.B.C., so we drove off at 5. But the thunder roared & the rain fell upon us in solid streams, & there were a million people going the same way, & we got later & later & fetched up 1 hour late at the Radio after a long drive in the dark against bright car-lights on a wet road: Ben's favourite conditions before a concert. However, they had waited for us & it went all right.

Stayed the night in Toronto with dear Basil Coleman, whom it has been a great joy to see again, & who seems happy enough doing Television Production. Then I came on here for last night's performance (to a very small audience) conducted by Chas. McKerras,[7] while Ben stayed in Toronto.

I've heard in Toronto of Dennis Brain's death – which is a tragedy & a hopeless loss to British music – oh these damned accidents.

Neither of us can wait to get back to England, away from this very kind, hospitable, beautiful, rich, boring country. We fly on Saturday.

Much love to you all, & thank you v. much, for letter & photos of Boni II[8] & Clytie & Jove which we have devoured.

PETER OXOXO

1 A reference to the many US airbases in Suffolk; the closest to Aldeburgh was a few miles inland at Bentwaters.

2 The annual Labour Day public holiday, celebrated in Canada and the US on the first weekend in September.

3 Campbell McInnes (1873/74–1945), British baritone, who studied in London and Paris and, following his debut in 1899, quickly established himself as a leading concert singer and a familiar participant in English festivals, beginning with Leeds in 1910 (where he sang in the premiere of Vaughan Williams's *A Sea Symphony*) and Worcester in 1911 (premiere of the same composer's *Five Mystical Songs*). In 1919 McInnes settled in Toronto, where for the next twenty-five years he worked as a singer and teacher.

4 British novelist (1890–1961) of high-Tory sensibilities who was popular in the 1930s. She was the eldest child of the classical scholar and Oxford Professor of Poetry John William Mackail and the grand-daughter of Edward

Burne-Jones; she and McInnes married in 1911 (despite McInnes's homosexuality), and they divorced in 1917 amid a torrent of publicity. Their second son, Colin (1914–1976), was also a novelist.

5 See Letters 190 and 221.

6 A proprietary brand of liver salts taken as relief from indigestion.

7 Charles Mackerras (b. 1925), Australian conductor, who studied at the New South Wales Conservatorium, Sydney; in 1945 he joined the Sydney Symphony Orchestra as principal oboist, also occasionally conducting the orchestra. Two years later he settled in Europe and became a conducting pupil of Václav Talich in Prague, where he developed a special enthusiasm for Slavonic music, that of Janáček in particular, whose operas he introduced to the UK at Sadler's Wells in the 1950s and 1960s. Other composers with whom he has a special affinity are Handel and Mozart. His many appointments include First Conductor at the Hamburg Staatsoper, 1966–69; Music Director of Sadler's Wells Opera (later English National Opera), 1970–77, and of Welsh National Opera, 1987–92. He was knighted in 1979, made a Companion of the Order of Australia in 1998 and a Companion of Honour in 2003, and in 2005 was the first recipient of the Queen's Medal for Music. See also Nancy Phelan, *Charles Mackerras: a Musicians' Musician*.

Mackerras's association with Britten began in the mid-1950s when he conducted EOG productions of Blow's *Venus and Adonis*, Holst's *Sāvitri*, and *Let's Make an Opera* at the 1956 Aldeburgh Festival. He returned to Aldeburgh the following year for Lennox Berkeley's *Ruth* (Mackerras had conducted the premiere in October 1956), Buxtehude's *The Last Judgement*, an orchestral concert (shared with Imogen Holst) in which he conducted a performance of Stravinsky's *In Memoriam Dylan Thomas* with Pears as soloist, and a further orchestral concert of music by Purcell, Dowland, Haydn, Elgar, Henze, Villa-Lobos and Britten (*Courtly Dances from 'Gloriana'*). In 1958, in addition to conducting a 'wind concert' of music by Mozart, Stravinsky and Handel (*Royal Fireworks*), and Poulenc's *Les Mamelles de Tirésias*, Mackerras was entrusted with the first performance of Britten's *Noye's Fludde*.

During rehearsals for the latter, his hitherto excellent relationship with Britten came under stress. Along with other members of the English Opera Group, Mackerras had occasionally joked in private about Britten's and Pears's homosexuality and particularly about the number of boys involved in the new children's opera. As Mackerras explained to Humphrey Carpenter (HCBB, pp. 384–5) in 1991,

I always felt uncomfortable in Ben and Peter's presence, because you couldn't ever quite say what you thought. You always had to couch everything in slightly false terms not to offend them. But the fact that people laughed at homosexuality didn't mean that we didn't all worship Britten as a musician, and even as a person.

Word of Mackerras's indiscretion reached Britten via John Cranko (according to Mackerras), and the young conductor now received

> a horrible letter from Peter, saying 'You've ruined the pleasure of Noye's Fludde.' I was told to go to the Red House, and when I got there Ben said to me, 'Because I like to be with boys, and because I appreciate young people, am I therefore a lecher?' – he actually said that to me. And I couldn't explain to him that on the one hand we worshipped him, and on the other hand we were amused by this. I must say, though, that he was extraordinarily restrained, extraordinarily calm. It was I who was white with nerves!

Mackerras was not dismissed as conductor of *Noye's Fludde*. He recalled that following the interview with Britten,

> We were very, very polite to each other, and I know he was trying hard to be nice, and I was trying hard to make up, of course. But after that I didn't get employed by Aldeburgh for some time.

In fact, Mackerras returned to the Aldeburgh Festival the next year, conducting *The Rape of Lucretia*, and it was this occasion which proved to be his last appearance there until 1973 when he conducted Handel's *Messiah* at Easter. For a further account of the interview between Britten and Mackerras, see JBBC, pp. 236–8.

Despite this rupture in their personal relationship, Mackerras continued his association with the composer and his music: for example, in 1959 he conducted the Associated Rediffusion broadcast of *The Turn of the Screw*, and in 1966 the BBC Television production of *Billy Budd*, as well as frequently conducting Britten's operas at home and abroad, often in new productions. In 1993, he conducted the premiere recording of *Gloriana*.

8 Princess Margaret's pet bullfinch.

905 To Elizabeth Mayer

Stratford [Ontario, Canada]
[postmarked 6 September 1957]

My dearest Elizabeth,

Since you left we have been counting the days till we could leave for England – not that there have not been some nice things about the time here, but it has mostly felt frustrating & a waste of time. The opera has gone better – orchestra better – but it still looks ghastly. The concerts were nice, Peter more pleased with himself, & receptions nice too. But we have missed you sadly. It was lovely that you managed to come up to see us, & now we must think forward to next year! I am interested to see what 'Young Apollo'¹ is like, but I don't expect a master-piece! Could you give it to Basil D. [Douglas] to bring back, do you think? I wonder what else you have got, but don't bother to send any more unless we decide it's necessary.² This is only a scribbled note in the midst of packing & 1001 other things one must do on the last day here.

We are absolutely shattered by Dennis Brain's death – what have we done to deserve these blows to our poor old music – Kathleen Ferrier, Noel Mewton-Wood, & now him? And such a sweet person too.

Well, my dear Elizabeth – our fondest love to you, & yours.

It was lovely to see you.

BEN

Hope you & Muki [Elizabeth Mayer's granddaughter] enjoy the Ballet.³

1 *Young Apollo*, for piano, string quartet and string orchestra, composed 23 July–2 August 1939, commissioned by the Canadian Broadcasting Corporation and first performed (a CBC broadcast) on 27 August 1939 by Britten (piano) and the CBC String Orchestra, conducted by Alexander Chuhaldin (the dedicatee). Following a further broadcast with the composer as soloist (CBS, New York) on 20 December 1939, the work was withdrawn. *Young Apollo* was not revived until after Britten's death, when it was given at the 1979 Aldeburgh Festival, on 20 June, by Michael Roll (piano) and the English Chamber Orchestra, conducted by Steuart Bedford. It was published by Faber Music in 1982. See also Letter 192 n. 2 and, for an examination of the connection between *Young Apollo* and Wulff Scherchen, JBBC, pp. 99–104, where John Bridcut suggests personal rather than musical reasons for Britten's withdrawal of *Young Apollo*.

2 Several of Britten's manuscripts, including *Young Apollo*, were left behind in the US in Mrs Mayer's care when Britten sailed back to the UK in March 1942. These included the composition drafts of the Violin Concerto, *Les Illuminations* and the First String Quartet. See Letter 370 n. 3.

Mrs Mayer had come across the manuscript of *Young Apollo* when going through her collection of Britten material – 'a whole archive of papers and photos and clippings about B.B.', as she told Britten in a letter of 28 August 1957. In the same letter she remarks, 'You could at least let Mrs Adaskin(?) know about its existence here.' Naomi Adaskin contributed 'Evenings with Benjamin Britten' to the Canadian magazine *May Fair* (December 1957), an article that discussed her husband John Adaskin's friendship with Britten in 1939. Adaskin, chief producer in charge of musical programmes for the CBC, had in 1939 invited Britten and Pears to give several broadcast recitals, and was responsible for commissioning *Young Apollo*. In her article Mrs Adaskin recalled the party she and her husband gave at their sparsely furnished apartment after the first performance of *Young Apollo*:

The guests, including Ben Britten, cheerfully sat on the floor. Also the hostess couldn't cook, her interests at that time being solely a career as a pianist ... so we chose the easiest food to prepare. Fortunately, King George VI and Queen Elizabeth had just been entertained by the Roosevelts and introduced to the American hot-dog... thus we followed royal precedent and served Benjamin Britten his first hot-dog, too.

After the hot-dogs we had more music... the Delius Sonata for cello and piano, played by Britten, pianist, and John Adaskin, cellist. Then Mrs John Adaskin and Benjamin Britten played a few piano duets, and he was a delightful ensemble player ... sensitive, rhythmically subtle and easy both to follow and to lead.

The Adaskins met Britten again when he and Pears toured North America in 1949; it was on this occasion that Mrs Adaskin enquired about *Young Apollo*, remarking on its absence from any list of his compositions. Britten explained that he had not seen the score or parts since 1939; the Adaskins therefore set to work to find the (apparently) lost material, searching at the CBC Library and in Chulhaldin's collection. The Adaskins (and, in 1949, the composer) had no knowledge that the manuscript was in the safe-keeping of Elizabeth Mayer.

3 In September 1957, the Royal Ballet gave a four-week season at the Metropolitan Opera, New York, including among their repertory *The Prince of the Pagodas*. According to Zoë Anderson (*The Royal Ballet: 75 Years*, p. 135), *Pagodas* 'did no better [at the box office] in New York than it had in London'. Mrs Mayer had sent Britten a postcard (postmarked 1 November 1957):

I thought Cranko's ideas could have been better knitted, but the music was lovely and throughout consistent and *so* danceable. Audience enthusiastic – critics as usual, stupid.

906 To Prince Ludwig of Hesse and the Rhine
[*Typed, with handwritten insertions*]

4 CRABBE STREET, ALDEBURGH
25th September, 1957

[*Handwritten:*] My dear Lu

– Please forgive typewritten note, but rather in a hurry – & I thought you might like to show some of it to Sellner.[1]

[*Typed:*] I ought to have written to you ages ago about the Dido translation[2] – please forgive me, but it has taken a certain time for us to recover from Canada and the journey, and since then I have had a spate of work.

It is excellent news that you have completed the sketch of the translation.[3] Now where do we go from here? Neither Imo [Holst] nor I can come to Wolfsgarten at the moment, much as we should like it. Do you think it would be possible or make any sense to send us your sketch, and we together with Erwin [Stein] could look at it and make any suggestions that occurred to us about its fitting with the notes? We could then send it to you for your reactions. Of course, if you could come here it would be heavenly, and you could stay with me as long as you liked, but I hesitate to suggest this knowing how fearfully busy you are, and how much of your time we have already taken up. I am seeing Boosey & Hawkes in London this week, and shall get then a clearer idea of when the translation is needed; perhaps I might even ring you up from Berlin next week to give you these further details, and learn your reactions to the above suggestions.

About "The Turn of the Screw" in Darmstadt, I believe you are seeing Sellner this week. Stupidly I do not know his full name, so I cannot write to him direct, but anyhow I would rather at this moment communicate with him through you since I have had no dealings with him direct, and anyhow you can put the matters more clearly to him – always presuming you have the time. It is good news there are chances of getting a good boy for Miles. I am sure it will not be too difficult once the theatre realises that the boy need not be an experienced actor (most boys can act, anyhow). I am, however, worried about Flora; perhaps I am prejudiced by the fact that we have a little grown woman to do it, and very well she does it too; but, as you know, we scoured this country to find a girl, and came to the conclusion that little girls just cannot sing, or at any rate can only sing well enough to manage the first gay childish scenes. It is essential that she must be able to sing the last Lake scene: that as I see it is the crux of the opera as far as she is concerned. It is better that she should look ninety and a dwarf and be able to spit this scene out (see Henry James)[4] than to fluff this moment. I suggest the conductor may understand this point more than the producer.

About the date of the first performance, I cannot leave here before the 28th November. That will of course not give me much time to attend rehearsals if December 1st is to be the date. Perhaps you could ask Sellner about this also.

[*Handwritten*:] Would you please thank Peg for her letter. I loved it, but didn't like hearing about Diana M.'s[5] last visit – what a problem she is. I hope you are both otherwise well & all your enormous activities are flourishing. I am having to tear myself away again – but only, thank God, a week this time, & then – – no more for ages! No definite news yet about the Red House but things look promising, in spite of the Bank Rate![6]

    Much love, & from Peter (he's much better now) to you both,
                             BEN

1 Gustav Rudolf Sellner (1905–1990), German director and opera administrator, who served as Intendant of the Darmstadt Landestheater, 1951–60, and subsequently at the Deutsches Oper, Berlin, 1961–72, where he was noted for his promotion of contemporary opera including works by Henze (*Der junge Lord*, *The Bassarids*). Beginning in the late 1940s at Kiel and

Essen, Sellner developed a style of operatic production in which set design was reduced to its abstract formal components, a practice he continued at Darmstadt.

Sellner directed a production of *The Turn of the Screw* in the Orangeriehaus of the Landestheater Darmstadt on 20 December 1957, the first to be given in Prince Ludwig's German translation. The performance was attended by Britten, the Hesses and Erwin and Sophie Stein. The production was designed by Franz Mertz (sets) and Elli Büttner (costumes), with George Maran (Quint), Ursula Lippmann (Governess), Dorothea von Stein (Miss Jessel), Martha Geister (Mrs Grose), Willi Hauser (Prologue), Reinhold Bill (Miles) and Irene Gut (Flora); Hans Zanotelli conducted.

In a letter of 2 December 1957 to the Hesses Britten wrote:

All being well we (Erwin, Sophie & I) hope to arrive the afternoon of 16th (2.15, is it, at Frankfurt?) Hope all goes well in rehearsals – let me know if advice is needed!

I hope the enclosed few sentences will do what they want for the programmes at Darmstadt.

Britten's 'few sentences' were published in a German translation in *Das neue Forum* 8 (1957), a programme magazine published by the Landestheater, as well as reproduced in facsimile:

Among my works 'The Turn of the Screw' is one of my most favourite. I am therefore happy that the first German production (& independent of the English Opera Group, for which the work was written) will take place in Darmstadt. I have the highest opinion of the Landestheater & its splendid Director, & I look forward to the first performance with great excitement.

Benjamin Britten, <u>Aldeburgh, Suffolk</u>

The same issue of *Das neue Forum* included articles by Stein, 'Die Musik zu "The Turn of the Screw"', and by Prince Ludwig, 'Bemerkungen des Übersetzers' ('Translator's Note').

In an interview with Donald Mitchell (3 March 1992), Colin Graham recalled:

Britten had intended *Curlew River* to be directed by Sellner [...] that was supposed to happen in 1960 but *A Midsummer Night's Dream* had supplanted it [in Britten's composition schedule] because an opera was suddenly needed for the Jubilee Hall – by the time he got back to *Curlew River* [in 1963/64] he'd gone off the idea of Sellner.

2 Prince Ludwig's German translation of Nahum Tate's libretto for Purcell's *Dido and Aeneas* (realized and edited by Britten and Imogen Holst) was published by Boosey & Hawkes in 1960.

3 Prince Ludwig had been working more recently on his German translation of Myfanwy Piper's libretto for *The Turn of the Screw*.

4 The scene to which Britten refers forms chapter xx of James's novella (pp. 213–14, Lustig edition):

To see her, without a convulsion of her small pink face, not even feign to glance in the direction of the prodigy I announced, but only, instead of that, turn at me an expression of hard still gravity, an expression absolutely new and unprecedented and that appeared to read and accuse and judge me – this was a stroke that somehow converted the little girl herself into a figure portentous [. . .] I had said shortly before to Mrs Grose that she was not at these times a child, but an old, old, woman [. . .] as she [Flora] stood there holding tight to our friend's [Mrs Grose's] dress, her incomparable childish beauty had suddenly failed, had quite vanished. I've said it already – she was literally, she was hideously hard; she had turned common and almost ugly.

It is clear from photographs of this production at BPL that Britten's advice prevailed and Flora was played by a woman rather than by a girl.

5 Diana Menuhin (née Gould; 1912–2003), British ballerina and actress, second wife of Yehudi Menuhin; they married in 1947. She wrote a memoir of her life with the violinist entitled *Fiddler's Moll: Life with Yehudi*. In her *Dictionary of National Biography* entry for Diana Menuhin, Jane Pritchard notes that while 'she could be unforgiving and had a sharp tongue and acerbic wit', she also possessed 'a gift for friendship'. Diana Menuhin would sometimes refer to herself in deprecating tones as 'the awfully frank and frankfully awful Diana'. See also obituaries in *The Times* (28 January 2003), *Daily Telegraph* (29 January 2003), by Nadine Meisner, *Independent* (1 February 2003), and by Humphrey Burton, *Guardian* (7 February 2003).

6 The interest rate on loans set by the Bank of England, which affected the level of mortgage repayments.

907 To Basil Coleman

4 CRABBE STREET, ALDEBURGH, SUFFOLK
October 16th 1957

My dear Basil,

It was lovely to hear from you. I had been hoping to write you a note all these weeks, but things have been difficult since we got back across the ocean. We had an easy flight, but both of us had a very low 2 weeks on arrival – Peter was extremely tired, & took a long time to shake off his depression. And I was thrown out by the change of locality & time; so only after we had had independent drives around the most lovely bits of England – I met Roger [Duncan] down in Dorset & had with him a nice exploration together of the West Country – did we get back to form & work. Berlin went well – lovely to be on a stage again! – although not too easy a one for Colin [Graham], who had a struggle with old equipment, a poor staff, & inadequate orchestral pit. But, as I said, in spite of 'Flu rearing its ugly head, it went well, & they loved & really understood us.

Peter succumbed to flu on return, & is only just up – but a poor way to spend the first two weeks of his only Summer holiday! But he's up now, & tomorrow we go off to London together, & we will have a few days driving around together over the week-end. I am getting down to the new opera, Noah,[1] that I told you about, so that's nice for me.

I am very glad you think after all that you may do Let's Make [an Opera].[2] I feel under your direction it ought to go very nicely in Toronto. Boyd[3] is certainly a good choice, if he'll do it seriously, but there should be a local chap as well, I should have thought. There are always the records to learn off![4] I don't think the version [of the play] that the Group used recently is anyone's copyright specially – it is only another curtailed version. But I'm getting Colin to send you the cut copy, & think it may be useful, but of course don't feel yourself bound by it.

No time for a long letter, my dear. It was lovely to see you in Canada, & easily compensated for the rather uncomfortable experiences! I hope the visit was worth-while, tho' sometimes I doubt it. I am glad you saw Elizabeth Mayer again, in New York. Do try & see her again another time; I'm sure she'd love it. Give Mell[5] my love. I do hope all goes well in your life – from every angle. Let us know news from time to time. Things in the Group stagger on. Basil [Douglas] was very good in Berlin but it's a pretty awful situation.[6] Stephen [Reiss] is being calm & splendid. Morgan [Forster] is here for the week-end. Billy's [Burrell] child was christened on Sunday – sweet ceremony. Peter sends much love to you both – so do I

(please excuse rush:)

BEN

1 Britten's setting of the Chester miracle play, *Noye's Fludde*, composed between 27 October 1957 and March 1958; the composition draft of the opera, the first work Britten completed at the Red House, is dated 18 December 1957 (see p. 585). Pears wrote to Princess Margaret of Hesse and the Rhine on 11 August 1957 that during the voyage to Canada, 'Ben has done some new Folk Song arrangements and we have been planning his new M-operality(!).' The opera, which includes audience hymns, as did *Saint Nicolas* ten years earlier, was first performed during the 1958 Aldeburgh Festival on 18 June at Orford Church, in a production directed by Colin Graham, with costume designs by Ceri Richards, and conducted by Charles Mackerras.

Britten's setting originated in a commission from Associated Rediffusion Ltd, the London-based commercial television company (hence the reference to 'endless meetings with the television people' in Letter 910), whose Head of Schools Broadcasting, Boris Ford, had initiated the project. Associated Rediffusion was responsible for the UK's first regular schools' programmes, which had begun in May 1957. Ford wrote to Britten on 10 April 1957 with a detailed proposal:

I. NOAH'S FLOOD. 13

Yf through amendment thy mercye
  Woulde fall to mankinde,
Have donne, you men and wemen alle,
Hye you, leste this watter fall,
That iich beaste were in sialle,   155
  And into the shippe broughte;
Of cleane beastes seven shalbe,
Of uncleane two, this God bade me;
The fludde is nye, you maye well see,
  Therefore tarye you naughte.   160

*Then Noye shall goe into the Arcke with all his familye, his
wife excepte, and the Arcke must be borded round about,
and one the bordes all the beastes and foules painted.*

SEM. Sir, heare are lions, leopardies, in,
  Horses, mates, oxen, and swyne;
Goote and caulfe, sheepe and kine   165
  Heare sitten thou maye see.

CAM. Camelles, asses, man maye fynde,
  Bucke and doo, harte and hinde,
And beastes of all maner kinde
  Here be, as thinketh me.

JAFFETT. Take heare cattes, dogges too, 170
  Atter and foxe, fullimartes alsoe;
Hares hoppinge gaylie can goe,
  Heare have coule for to eate.

NOYES WIFFE. And heare are beares, woulfes sette,
  Apes, oules, marmosette,
Weyscolles, squirelles, and firrette,   175
  Heare the eaten ther meate.

SEMES WIFFE. Heare are beastes in this howse,
  Heare cattes make yt crousse,
Heare a rotten, heare a mousse,
  That standeth nighe togeither.   180

16 CHESTER PLAYS.

SEM. In faith, mother, yett you shalle,
  Whether thou wylte or [noughte].
NOYE. Welckome, wiffe, into this botte. 245
NOYES WIFFE. Have thou that for thy note!
NOYE. Ha, ha! marye, this is hotte!
  It is good for to be still.
Ha! children, me thinkes my botte reneves,
Our tarryinge heare highlye me greves,   250
Over the lande the watter spreades;
  God doe as he will.
A! greate God, that arte so good,
That worckes not thy will is wood.
Nowe all this worlde is one a flude,   255
  As I see well in sighte.
This wyndowe I will shutte anon,
And into my chamber I will gone,
Tell this watter, so greate one,
  Be slacked through thy mighte.   260

*Then shall Noye shutte the wyndowe of the Arcke, and for a
littill space be silent, and afterwards lookinge rounde
aboute shall saye:*

[Now* 40 dayes are fullie gone
Send a raven I will anone
If ought-were earth, tree or stone,
  Be drye in any place.
And if this foule come not againe   265
It is a signe, soth to sayne,
That drye it is on hill or playne,
  And God hath done some grace.

Tunc dimittet corvum et capiens columbam in manibus dicat.

Ah, Lord, wherever this raven be,
Somewhere is drye, well I see;   270

* The following 47 lines occur only in MS. Harl. 2124.

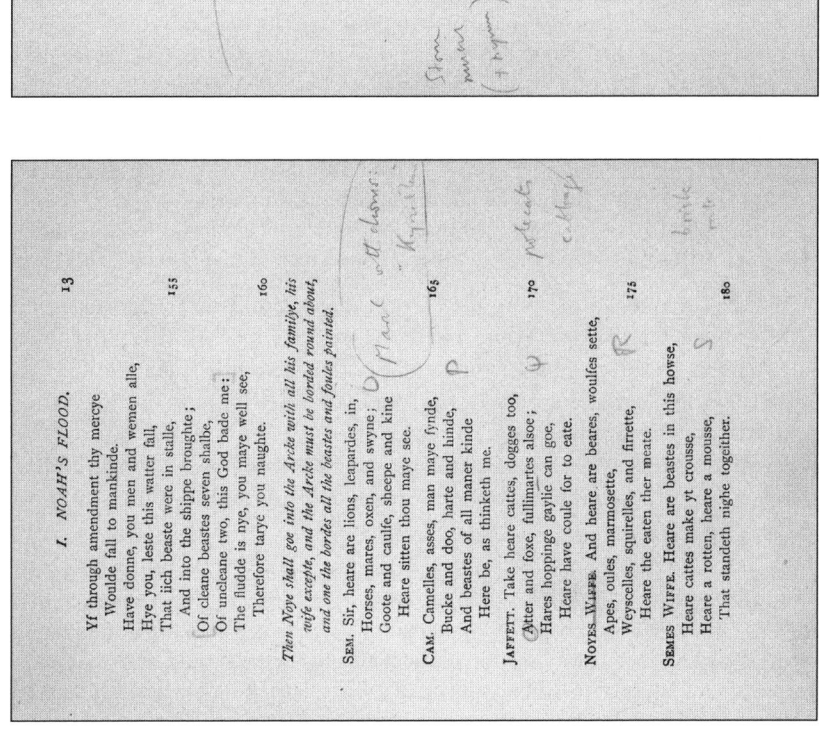

Britten's copy of the Chester miracle play *Noah's Flood*. Page 13 (left) shows the entrance of the animals into the Ark, which Britten has annotated: 'March with chorus: "Kyrie eleison"'. On p. 16 (right) Britten has indicated, 'Storm music (& hymn)'.

What I have thought of is that one of our series of ten half-hour programmes in the Christmas term should consist of yourself composing and rehearsing, week by week, a Christmas charade. The purpose of the series would be to provide children with an intimate piece of musical education, by giving them some conception of what composing music amounts to and thus watching a piece of music take shape and in some degree growing with it.

As I see it, the series would introduce yourself in your 'natural habitat' at work on this Christmas charade, and each week you would try it out with us, think back over the material already composed and think ahead somewhat, and also every now and then gather together a few children to rehearse the music already composed. And so, gradually building it up week by week we would end on the last programme of the series with the children actually performing or playing the charade.

We would have issued in advance to teachers in classrooms notes on this series and perhaps even the music itself, so that they could also rehearse with their own classes week by week and have their own final performance after seeing our final televised performance.

Britten responded on 15 April:

It is a most interesting idea of yours that I should collaborate over a series of programmes for Schools, and something which, under different circumstances, I should love to have done. Unfortunately I am frantically busy travelling this year, and will have very little time for writing, and my plans for that are more than complete. Besides, I feel that with "Let's Make an Opera" I have rather done this idea before, and although I firmly intend to write another Opera for Children one day, it would be boring to make it follow the same plan as that piece. However, if you have time which coincided with my being in London (for instance the last week of May) perhaps we could meet and have a talk about other possibilities.

Incidentally I was very impressed that Commercial Television is tackling something so worthwhile as your present scheme. Good luck to it!

Britten's proposed meeting for further discussion was postponed until 11 July, when he, Imogen Holst and Ford met in London. It is clear from Ford's letter to the composer the next day that it was at this meeting that Britten agreed to write an opera for Associated Rediffusion's schools programmes for the summer term of 1958.

In an interview with Donald Mitchell (8 November 1989), Ford recalled that his original idea was for a series of weekly programmes that would

show medieval Chester week by week, writing its script, getting together a cast and allocating [the roles] out to the guilds, producing them, etc., till the final programme would be a performance of whichever play. We'd got some distance thinking this out when I had a stroke of imagination: 'Why don't we see if Britten might be interested to do a Britten version of the play, and then we could have the two in parallel, with Chester making its thing and Britten making his modern play in Aldeburgh, and we could cut back and forth week by week; Britten would be collecting his cast, rehearsing his children, since I'd seen there would be children in it.'

While the subject matter contradicts the documentation above, the proposed manner of presentation across the series is similar, and it seems possible that the idea of using a miracle play emerged during the weeks between Britten's letter rejecting Ford's 'Christmas charade' proposal and the meeting on 11 July. In the same interview, Ford recalled Britten telling him that 'he had indeed for some months or a year vaguely been thinking of doing something with the miracle plays', and that they fixed on the Chester version of the story of Noah.

According to Ford, he and his script editor (Martin Worth) travelled to Aldeburgh to discuss the proposal with the composer (Ford remembered also meeting Pears and Julian Bream, who happened to be staying there, on this occasion), and their driving around to look at possible churches where Britten's version could be performed. Ford mentioned that Blythburgh Church was chosen, though Orford Church was in fact the venue for the first performance, chiefly because its lack of fixed pews made it a more flexible performing space than most other churches in East Suffolk. For this reason the same venue was used for the premieres of the Church Parables in the 1960s.

Contractual negotiations between Boosey & Hawkes and Associated Rediffusion were set in motion, but when the first estimate of the costs was calculated, Associated Rediffusion considered that Britten's publishers were asking too inflated a price and the project was cancelled. When Ford informed Stephen Reiss at the Aldeburgh Festival of this decision, a new proposal was made: Britten instructed Anthony Gishford that Boosey & Hawkes must reduce its terms 'very considerably' (Ford to T. M. Brownrigg, General Manager of Associated Rediffusion, 18 November 1957), in an attempt to bring the costs within the available budget. In his 1989 interview, Ford recalled the commission had been approved by the executives at Associated Rediffusion and he was authorized to offer Britten a commissioning fee of £200, a figure that embarrassed Ford 'but he [Britten] said he didn't mind about that'.

Britten attended meetings at Associated Rediffusion's London headquarters on 18 October 1957 to discuss 'Noah' (noted in the composer's pocket engagement diary), and there was an 'ITV [Independent Television] meeting here [i.e. Aldeburgh]', on 6 November 1957. Less than a month later, however, Ford himself was dismissed from Associated Rediffusion, apparently for administrative shortcomings and inexperience, his employers citing (according to Ford's letter to Brownrigg, 18 November 1957) his handling of the 'Benjamin Britten Opera' as an example of his failings. In this letter, a copy of which he sent to Britten, Ford answers the charges levelled against him; his letter also discloses further aspects of the project, notably that when Associated Rediffusion was about to withdraw from the project for financial reasons, a second independent commercial television company, ATV, under the chairmanship of Lew Grade, was approached to bridge the financial shortfall. In his letter to Brownrigg (18 November 1957), Ford writes,

Mr Lew Grade rang me up and told me that the project was now on. I asked when the contract would be signed, and he said that he was assuming responsibility for signing the contract [...] he added that Benjamin Britten should be told to start work on this opera at once.

In 1989 Ford recollected that when Associated Rediffusion lost interest in the project,

I went round to Norman Collins, who was the deputy head of ATV, who lived on the next floor to us, and said, 'Look, this is absolutely outrageous of Associated Rediffusion. At least wouldn't you like to give the performance?' And so the first performance of *Noye's Fludde* was broadcast on a Sunday morning by ATV – what they broadcast was actually a rehearsal.

A further cause for grumbling by Associated Rediffusion was an article that appeared in the *TV Times* (25 October 1957) by Paul Sheridan, who had approached Ford for a story about the Britten opera; Ford had refused his request but 'agreed to check the facts he had already collected', insisting that 'no story must appear until the contract had been signed' (Ford to Brownrigg, 18 November 1957). Sheridan's article not only broke the news of the opera's existence, but also reveals ATV's involvement in the project:

The opera will be first transmitted 'live' by Associated Television [ATV] on a Sunday early in the New Year and tele-recordings will be made by Associated Rediffusion and put out over the following two weeks in the school programmes.

It remains unclear if the broadcast on 22 June 1958 (directed for television by Quentin Lawrence) – the first of a Britten opera to be shown on British television – actually was live or was pre-recorded.

Britten did not in fact complete the full score until March 1958.

Following his dismissal, Ford met Britten on 5 December 1957; as a result of this meeting, Britten wrote to the conductor John Barbirolli, at that time a music adviser to Associated Rediffusion, on 13 December:

As you know, I expect, the head of School Broadcasting of the Associated Rediffusion, Boris Ford, has been rather summarily dismissed. One of the reasons given for his dismissal was that he would pursue the idea that I write a children's opera for the School Broadcasting programme in spite of the fact that you were "totally against it". I have only heard this second hand, so there may easily be some mistake, which frankly I should naturally prefer! But if not, I should be extremely interested in your reasons, since as I said above I am so inexperienced in this world [of commercial television]. I should have thought that whatever people have to say against my music, it could scarcely be denied that my music for young people ("Let's Make an Opera!", "Saint Nicolas", "The Ceremony of Carols") has been at least useful. But I am sure you can clarify the odd situation.

Barbirolli responded immediately to the composer's letter: there had indeed been a mistake and it was untrue that Barbirolli had opposed *Noye's Fludde*. Britten wrote to him on 14 January 1958: 'you can't imagine how relieved I was [...] and to know that my supposition over this curious Associated Rediffusion was correct'.

The saga continued with Ford writing to the composer on 15 January 1958 with further information about the involvement of Grade's ATV in the project and the role of Associated Rediffusion's Controller of Programmes in the affair:

As far as I could discover, the agreement between A-R and ATV to acquire the rights jointly was settled smoothly enough; but unfortunately Macmillan, A-R's Controller of Programmes, failed to inform his Board and also failed to notify Barbirolli, and in the event both raised queries. I don't believe they were particularly serious queries, but none the less Macmillan decided to avoid further worry by simply cancelling the project altogether. At the same time he was also 'simply cancelling' me, and so I was unable to do anything effective except protest [...] I am indeed sorry to have involved you in this matter, and the Educational Advisory Committee were also outraged.

Britten replied to Ford on 22 January 1958:

Of course we were all very disappointed that the A.R. project did not materialise; even if another television company takes the opera it clearly cannot have the same kind of plan as we worked out together, and that is a great pity. But sorry as we are for ourselves, we are twice as sorry for you who have clearly been treated disgracefully. It is extraordinary how a spot of culture can scare these big business people into the most odd behaviour.

Incidentally, I wrote a note to Barbirolli briefly informing him that his lack of enthusiasm was one of the reasons for your dismissal. He naturally wrote back a highly indignant letter asking for chapter and verse, and I immediately sent him the relevant passage from your "apologia" which Stephen Reiss had lent me. I hope you do not mind my doing this, since he is aware that A.R.'s account of his opinions is libellously inaccurate.

In 1960 Ford was invited to appear before the Pilkington Committee on Broadcasting by Richard Hoggart, one of the members of the committee. As part of his evidence, Ford laid out the story surrounding *Noye's Fludde*. In response to a memorandum from Ford, Britten wrote on 19 December 1960:

"Noye's Fludde." As far as we [Britten and Stephen Reiss] can remember, I had written two-thirds of the opera when the withdrawal took place [...] Actually, the irony of the situation is that I.T.V. is showing considerable keenness to broadcast operas of mine, and I have no contacts whatsoever with B.B.C. television!

Despite its withdrawal from *Noye's Fludde*, Associated Rediffusion continued its association with Britten: not only was it responsible for the highly successful broadcast of *The Turn of the Screw* in 1959, but during 1961/62 Peter Morley, Director of Television, was keen to commission from Britten a 'Christmas project'.

2 Coleman was to direct a production of *Let's Make an Opera* at the Crest Theatre, Toronto, which opened on 18 December 1957, conducted by David Ouchterlony. The play was evidently adapted to suit local conditions: for example, the programme indicates that 'the play is set in a Church Hall in Toronto'.

3 Boyd Neel (1905–1981), British conductor, who founded the Boyd Neel Orchestra in 1933. Britten composed the *Variations on a Theme of Frank Bridge* and Prelude and Fugue, for eighteen-part string orchestra, for this ensemble. See also Letter 562 n. 12.

4 Britten's Decca recording of *The Little Sweep*, made in 1955.

5 Coleman's partner.

6 Maureen Garnham describes the English Opera Group's visit to the Berlin Festival for three performances of *The Turn of the Screw* (2, 4 and 5 October 1957) in *As I Saw It*, pp. 107–8. These were Douglas's last performances as General Manager of the EOG. See also Letter 908.

908 To Basil Douglas[1]
[*Typed file copy*]

[4 Crabbe Street, Aldeburgh, Suffolk]
20th October, 1957

My dear Basil,

Of course we all hate breaking bad news (if we didn't we wouldn't be friends – if you take my meaning), and I for one would do a lot to avoid doing it. But when it really matters I can really "summon the courage", and have done repeatedly in the E.O.G.'s last few years – as you honestly know. Of course there have been many, many occasions when you have had to do the dirty work – that is, alas, the General Manager's job, and was not done out of the kindness of your heart "to lessen the hurts to other people". In this case I certainly would have broken the news myself about not requiring your services at Aldeburgh next year, if there had been anything to break. When in January or February we had our talk at St. George's Terrace, it was my sincere wish that you could go on being employed by both the Festival and the Group. We all wished it. But slowly through the Spring and Summer, and part of this Autumn, it has looked to Stephen more and more difficult – for a variety of reasons chapter and verse of which can be given you (if you will listen) – and he is the one who must decide this. As it happened, after our return from Berlin, being so impressed with the way you had handled so many situations, we (S. and I) had a long talk to examine once again the position carefully to see whether the services of your office could not be used; and I know that that was his intention, in visiting you last Wednesday to discuss this (if only, again, if you had listened). But your attitude to him has botched all that, and that brings me to the main point of my letter.

Of course, as an old friend, you have every right to take up your pen and fling ink at me, and if our friendship is warm enough it will stand the strain, and won't matter – much. But if you are going to succeed as an agency, you <u>must</u> be more careful in what you say or write to your business acquaintances, whether they are Stephen, Emmie Tillett,[2] or Decca. Do come off your high, righteously indignant, horse, and try and understand other people's points of view – even if it is only for political reasons. Your job will be to manage people, artists, managers, publishers and even composers, and you can't say or write the things that you do (right as you often feel yourself to be, I know) without jeopardising your future, which all of your friends hope will be a happy and successful one. Do get it out of your head that any of us are treating you badly – that the Group has let you down. You must have realised since the time you nobly left the B.B.C. and came to us, that the job could close at any moment. Besides you remember that twice you have considered leaving us – once, I can't help saying, when Peter and I were at the beginning (Istanbul) of a five months' tour abroad, which wasn't for us the happiest time to do it. But, you have absolutely full right to do it, and we didn't complain. The Group has given you nearly a year's notice and rewarded you handsomely. And, for goodness sake, stop telling people that the Group is suspending operations, or ceasing, or whatever you say or let be understood. I am bored stiff and embarrassed by having to correct that impression. Surely the truth is just as palatable, and certainly understandable?

All right, then – bash away at me, who will, I hope, be always your friend – but for heaven's sake be gentle with your potential business colleagues.[3]

Yours ever,
BEN

1   This letter was a response to a frank letter from Douglas to Britten of 17 October 1957, quoted in Maureen Garnham, *As I Saw It*, pp. 111–12, which was provoked by the news that Douglas would not be working on a freelance basis for the English Opera Group or the Aldeburgh Festival:

My dear Ben,
    I believe that you and Peter are still fond of me, as I am of you, and that you would not willingly do me a hurt. I also understand two other things – one, that hurts have sometimes to be done for political reasons; and two, that you in particular are curiously incapable of breaking bad news, and can thus (unintentionally) aggravate the hurt.
    These two things I have learnt from the last seven years, as well as a great many other things for which I'm very grateful; and I'm glad to say that quite often I have been able to lessen the hurts to other people by breaking the news myself. I couldn't break my own bad news, however, and it was one of the bitterest aspects of the Opera Group debacle that I had to hear about it from an outsider. You seemed able to discuss it with everyone else in the Group but me, and naturally the news got around.

That's nearly done with, however, and I think that the three of us managed to get through the Stratford and Berlin festivals fairly well. We talked very little about me, only once about your new opera [*Noye's Fludde*], and of the EOG not at all. There was no unpleasantness.

But couldn't you, between you, have summoned the courage to tell me that you wouldn't require my services at Aldeburgh next year? Why did I have to hear it from Stephen [Reiss]?

Stephen seemed surprised that I did not know, and said that he has been intending 'for a long time' to do the booking [of the EOG Orchestra] himself in future. Which does not altogether explain his request in July for a quotation of our fee for next year, or the various talks we have had with him during which nothing was said to prevent us from assuming, as we did in fact assume, that we were to be involved in the next Festival. It is also possible, to be fair, that Stephen said nothing which might be called a commitment; but the atmosphere of an engagement was there, and it should have been dispelled much earlier.

You and I have hardly mentioned Aldeburgh, but you Ben have not forgotten, I hope, that when you last came to dinner here (was it in February?) you tried to console me by expressing your intention that there would be part-time work for me and Maureen [Garnham] next year, both for the Group and for the Festival. You said you were sorry that it might not involve more than £500 for us, but it would be something. I was too miserable to care very much at the time, but Martyn [Webster, Douglas's partner] does remember your saying that, and Maureen remembers my telling her next morning; in fact, she dates the birth of this agency idea [Basil Douglas Ltd] from that day, but of that I can't be sure. I do remember your saying that, and I only wish that you had told me more that evening; it might have prevented the next disastrous talk we had.

Let me say at once that whatever you said or did not say that night, you had every right to change your mind; the circumstances of the Festival and of the Group may have made it unavoidable in any case, for all I know. I don't question it for a moment. But why was I not told before, and above all, why did neither of *you* tell me?

In the event, it may all be for the best. I realize that in any case we shall inevitably see much less of each other from now on, and if we are to remain friends, as I sincerely hope we shall, it will be better if I can be as independent of you both as possible.

But my life is empty enough at the moment without that additional turn of the old screw.

My love to you both,
BASIL

Garnham recalls (*As I Saw It*, p. 110) that:

It was [...] a very nasty shock, sometime in October [16 October 1957], to receive a visit from Stephen Reiss, who announced baldly that the Festival could not afford to employ us, and therefore he was going to do the orchestral booking himself, and indeed had been so intending for a long time. I am not certain whether he said he was sorry. I saw Basil's face tighten with a cold anger I knew masked deep hurt. He did not precisely order Stephen out of the office, but Stephen was left in no doubt of Basil's feelings, and departed quickly, looking disconcerted [...]

I am sure that this decision emanated from Stephen [...] I am also convinced that the real reason was not the money but that Stephen did not want Basil around –

possibly because Basil's greater experience and his popularity with the players made Stephen nervous, possibly because he just wanted to have control of everything. I do not think that Ben, left to himself, would have retracted his offer for the sake of such a comparatively small proportion of the Festival's budget, but of course he would have gone along with Stephen's wishes, for the usual reason – that Stephen and not Basil was the person Ben needed at that moment.

2 Artists' agent (1897–1982), Managing Director of Ibbs & Tillett, the agency acting for Britten and Pears at this time.

3 The exchange of correspondence continued with a further letter from Douglas on 25 October 1957 (quoted in Garnham, pp. 115–16):

Dear Ben,
 I'm sorry that you decided to bark back at me, instead of answering the important part of my letter. Please understand this – I do *not* feel that the Group is treating me unfairly – quite the contrary. And I do *not* feel that everyone is against me. It's you and Peter I'm getting at, as you know very well, and no one else. If you had been more open with me you might have saved yourselves a lot of trouble and me a nervous breakdown. That was the point you omitted to answer.
 Well, you've come out with a few other things. What you say about being tactful with business colleagues is very sensible. From the context I conclude that I've offended Stephen, Decca, and Emmie Tillett. I can't expect you to be more explicit than that, but perhaps I can find out by other means what it is all about. I may be able to put it right.
 But why on earth shouldn't I say that the Group is suspending operations temporarily? Is it not true? If there has been a change of policy since that Board Meeting, when it was assumed that the Group would probably do nothing until the spring of 1959, then it would have been wiser to tell me. I don't find that so sensible.
 I have nothing to add that calls for a reply. These letters have been horrid to write and to read, but they have cleared the air a little – perhaps enough. In any case, you have much more important things to think about.

Love,
BASIL

Britten responded on 27 October:

Dear Basil,
 You are right, I'm sure, to say we should stop this correspondence – which I did my best to stop becoming "horrid" – but I must say one thing. Please stop "getting at" Peter and me, and try and realise we do not wish you ill; and have tried to do everything possible to help you. You have good friends in us, unless, of course, you are determined to call us enemies. The situation is in your own hands.

Yours ever,
BEN

After Douglas's departure from the EOG, relations between him and Britten and Pears were professionally cordial but no longer as close as they had been previously. Douglas's artists' agency managed the 1958 EOG fund-raising Opera Ball and, the following year, the memorial concert for Erwin Stein. The agency also managed Imogen Holst's Purcell Singers as well as occasionally providing artists for the Aldeburgh Festival. Douglas attended the latter annually until 1970, as well as all of Britten's and Pears's London recitals. In his interview with Donald Mitchell (16 November 1987), Douglas recalled that after leaving the EOG he 'would occasionally meet Peter and talk to him and he was always very friendly and nice; but I didn't meet Ben at all really after that. I think he was feeling guilty.' See also HCBB, pp. 376–7.

909 To Olive Zorian
[*Typed file copy*]

[4 Crabbe Street, Aldeburgh, Suffolk]
20th October, 1957

My dear Olive,

I wonder if you are back from your Amsterdam visit. I hope it has been a great success, and that working with Szymon [Goldberg] has been as lovely and profitable as you hoped it would be.

I hate to have to greet you with disappointing news, but I feel I cannot delay any longer writing to you about a matter which has been on my mind for sometime now. I have been seriously worried both from your and from our points of view about your leading of the E.O.G. orchestra and the Festival one too. In spite of our mutual pacts about self denigration (!), I feel that your confidence has not grown but even lessened, and that I am afraid has rather diminished your power as leader – and I am quite sure has made you quite unhappy, very often. It is no slur at all on your playing, because I am still a great admirer of it, and above all your taste and style (if, of course, you are happy in the job), but I think the last years have not allowed you to be at your best. I think actually that it is a man's job – the Festival particularly (altho' in the future of the E.O.G., last minute, rather under-rehearsed shows will be equally straining) needs a physically strong and confident person to help me through the difficult and worrying situations – not only me but Imogen and the kind of director [i.e. conductor] that we have here. So I am afraid, my dear, that we are having to think of asking someone else to take over that (thankless!) position.[1] I hate having to write like this – you have had so much trouble and disappointment these last years. But when the blow has receded I am sure you will be happier; and also to show that we love and admire you as much as ever, we want to encourage the quartet quite terrifically – then, with the people who admire and trust you, you will really be at your best. Do let me come in January and hear you – and then, if we and you are all happy at the way things are developing you would come and do a concert at the Festival next year?[2] We would love that.

Much love,
[BEN]

1 Britten invited the British violinist Emanuel (Manny) Hurwitz to be Zorian's replacement. Hurwitz (1919–2006) had studied at the Royal Academy of Music and received coaching from Bronislaw Huberman. His first contact with Britten was immediately after the war, when Hurwitz led the orchestra for the first performance of *The Rape of Lucretia* at Glyndebourne, in 1946. (Hurwitz later recalled (quoted in HCBB, p. 238) that 'during the breaks, the singers would eat with the Christies, but the orchestra were treated like servants and sent round to the kitchen quarters for sandwiches'.) He was leader of the Goldsbrough (later English) Chamber Orchestra from 1948 until 1968, and of the New Philharmonia from 1969 until 1971. As a chamber musician, he was first violinist of the Hurwitz String Quartet, 1946–52, the Melos Ensemble, 1956–72, Britten's preferred ensemble for the chamber orchestra in *War Requiem*, and the Aeolian Quartet, 1970–81, recording with the last the complete quartets of Haydn. Among Hurwitz's numerous connections with Britten and Aldeburgh, chiefly as leader of the ECO, were performances and the Decca recording of Bach's Brandenburg Concertos conducted by Britten; with Vishnevskaya, Rostropovich and Britten, Hurwitz took part in the UK premiere of Shostakovich's *Seven Blok Romances* at the 1968 Aldeburgh Festival (a performance first released on CD by Decca in 2000).

In an interview with Humphrey Carpenter (quoted in HCBB, p. 250), Hurwitz recalled Britten as

a quite wonderful conductor in the greatest sense of the word. He was a conductor who made the orchestra feel they wanted to play for him. His stick technique was unassuming, but so were Weingartner's and Richard Strauss's [...] Ben had a small beat, and if it went a foot high, that meant *forte*. An incredible difference from Beecham, who enjoyed doing things that looked like sword-fighting – and we had to decide which of his ninety-three movements was the actual beat! Twenty years ago, I wrote in the *Radio Times*: 'When you work for Ben, everything is an occasion.' There was no routine about it; you were making music in the highest sense.

Hurwitz also remarked (quoted in HCBB, p. 416):

If somebody had, say, made faces at a first performance of Ben's when he was conducting them at the age of twenty-five, he'd remember. He wasn't at all a vindictive man, but he felt nervous, off-balance, if he knew someone didn't like his music.

See also obituaries by Anne Inglis, *Guardian* (20 November 2006) and Margaret Campbell, *Independent* (21 November 2006), and Riki Gerardy, *Talks with Emanuel Hurwitz: 82 Years With the Violin.*

2 Zorian did indeed play again at the Aldeburgh Festival in 1958 with her string quartet, and in 1961 and 1962 as a member of the Julian Bream Consort.

910 To Erwin Stein
[*Typed*]

[4 Crabbe Street, Aldeburgh, Suffolk]
13th November, 1957

[*Handwritten:*] Dearest Erwin

Please forgive typewritten note, but what with the move, the work and endless meetings with the television people about Noah life is hectic.[1]

I was delighted with your sweet letter, but please don't think I was cross with anyone particular about the Ballet proofs. I was only just cross in the abstract to have to go back to that beastly work, of which at the moment I am heartily sick. The maddening thing is that after we have all spent hours reading it there will quite clearly remain dozens of mistakes. I frankly don't know what we can do, but I am clear that at the moment I don't want any more to do with it! But I must not be silly, and your nice remarks about it make me feel that the work was not just a waste of a year's work.

I am so delighted you enjoyed Herring[2] so much. It was clearly a real achievement on Joan's part. I was sad I could not get to the performance, but the rehearsal I went to was most enjoyable. If they could manage to sing it, that particular work gains enormously by having young fresh performers.

You will be getting a letter from a boy now up at Cambridge called Jonathan Harvey. I have kept an eye on him for about three years, and in many ways I feel he is the most gifted of all the children I have tried to help. He has a music scholarship to St. John's, but is worried that he cannot get serious instruction in composition up at the University. I have recommended that he should come to you every week or fortnight (whichever you can manage). I do hope you can fit him in. He is a very nice person, and I am sure worthwhile – he comes from an interesting and musical family.

I am very worried about finding time for Ferencsik;[3] I dare not suggest he comes here at the moment – if he did he might easily get rolled up in a carpet and moved to Red House! I shall be in London on December 9th and 10th; will he by any chance still be there? In which case I could easily manage some time. Could you give him my greetings please, and say I hope this will be possible.

It looks as if I shall be going to Wolfsgarten on December 15th or 16th by boat from Harwich. But why, if you and Sophie can go earlier, do you not fly the previous week, (Peg [Hesse] says she can have you)? We could then come back by boat together.

[*Handwritten*:] Much love to you both
from Peter & from
BEN

[*Handwritten*:] Julian Bream has been staying (not in the house because there's no room left furnished!) in Aldeburgh for 2 days & worked with me at the new Guitar songs (6 of them!)[4] & I'm quite pleased with them. They make a lovely noise.

1 Britten and Pears were about to move house, from 4 Crabbe Street to the Red House. Britten told his sister Barbara (11 November 1957):

So sorry not to have written before – but what with work, Festivals, Groups, & moving house on top of everything, life is that hectic. I'm afraid we shall literally be in moving-vans on 21st–23rd, when you suggested coming here [. . .] We are very excited about life at the Red House, & have countless plans for it. Peter (in the middle of his Summer(!) holiday) is highly occupied & enjoying himself, moving this & that, & fixing curtains, carpets etc. etc.

2 Presumably a performance of *Albert Herring* presented by the National Opera Studio, directed by Joan Cross.

3 János Ferencsik (1907–1984), Hungarian conductor whose career was exclusively based in Budapest apart from brief periods as music assistant at the Bayreuth Festival, 1930–31, and guest conductor at the Vienna Staatsoper, 1948–50, 1964. He held a succession of conducting posts at the Budapest Opera from 1931 until his death, and was appointed Chief Conductor of the Hungarian National Philharmonic Orchestra in 1953. Ferencsik made his UK debut in April 1957 with the London Philharmonic Orchestra.

4 *Songs from the Chinese*, for high voice and guitar, six settings of texts by Chinese poets, translated by Arthur Waley, which were first performed by Pears and Bream on 17 June 1958 at Great Glemham House, Suffolk, as part of the Aldeburgh Festival. The songs bear the dedication 'To Peg and Lu [Hesse], from Ben, Peter and Julian'. In his review of the 1958 Aldeburgh Festival, 'An Ideal Setting for a Festival', *Yorkshire Post* (21 June 1958), Ernest Bradbury considered that the *Songs from the Chinese* showed 'all Britten's flair for appreciating the inside character of a poem and for understanding the technical possibilities of unfamiliar instruments'.

Britten's composition draft of 'The Herd-Boy' (text by Lu Yu, translated by Arthur Waley) from *Songs from the Chinese*

911 To Elizabeth Mayer

4 CRABBE STREET, ALDEBURGH, SUFFOLK
Nov. 14th 1957

My dearest Elizabeth,

It was lovely to get your letter, & the postcard coda following closely behind! I am sorry not to have written before, but things have been pretty frightful for a long time now – so much to do & to think about – but in many ways they have been nice too. I have at last got back to work, & have enjoyed myself hugely! After the long break, all the summer's travelling, & then Berlin (& of course Stratford!), things were rather pent-up inside, & they've come tumbling out . . . a complete book of folk-song arrangements,[1] six guitar songs for Peter & Julian Bream, and at least half a new children's opera – Noe & the Arke! – which will happen at the Festival here next year, & on television. Peter has had his summer(!) holiday this last month or so, but poor dear, started it with a really horrid dose of 'flu. It got him down really badly, & I'm afraid he didn't enjoy much of the enforced rest. But he's much better now, & has been enjoying planning the great move . . . we go up the hill to the Potters' house, Red House, next week!! Mary & we swap houses. It should be lovely, but of course it will take time to get straight & comfortable. The move is endlessly complicated, & there'll be lots to do when we get in, I, for instance, am having a studio built,[2] & we are knocking walls down, redecorating; etc., etc.; but, it is such a sweet place, such a lovely garden, and so quiet after this house, which has become more & more public these last years. I long for you to see it – perhaps, next year?

Berlin went really extremely well – we managed to fight off the 'flu germs until the very last, & the performances were really excellent. How I wish you had seen it there instead of Stratford! The Berliners, maddening in so many ways, did really see what it was all about, & there was a most warm reaction.

I am so glad you liked the 'Prince of Pagodas'. I had heard it went well in New York. Johnny Cranko was here in Aldeburgh for the week-end – he is doing a Poulenc opera & a Monteverdi (Ballo del Ingrate!) for the Festival next year.[3] Did you meet him when he was in New York? – an enchanting creature.

The Opera Group is in the process of moving down to Aldeburgh & we anticipate, in its new and rather relaxed life, will be less of a bother & tie than heretofore. Poor old Basil [Douglas] has taken it very hard; but quite honestly, we think, very unreasonably. However it may be useful for him to have a 'whipping boy' although uncomfortable for the people chosen, in this case, us! But he so loved being with you in New York. How kind you were to all of them.

I haven't had a moment to write to Michael [Mayer]. I expect he'll get in touch with us if he needs anything – but as soon as we get settled, I promise to write to him.

I'm here for a month or two, working away – except for a dash to London, to conduct a Dennis Brain memorial concert[4] (what a ghastly, senseless, tragedy), & a few days in Germany for the first German performance of the Turn of the Screw – so, "Red House, Aldeburgh", for next letter, please!

Much love, & from Peter too, my dear,
BEN

Please give my love to Alma M-W[5] when you see her, & tell her how I loved her letter. I'll write to her again soon, but writing in German is such an effort!

1 Volume 4 of Britten's Folk Song Arrangements, Moore's *Irish Melodies*, for high voice and piano. The arrangements were mostly undertaken in the autumn of 1957, though at least two songs from the total of ten – 'How sweet the answer' and 'The minstrel boy' – were certainly finished by April of that year, as Pears and Britten included them in a recital in Vienna on the 23 April. See also Philip Reed, 'Britten's Folk Song Arrangements: Documentation', CD liner notes for *Benjamin Britten: The Folk Songs* (Collins Classics, 1995), and MCCCBB, pp. 300–301.

Volume 4 was published in 1960 with a dedication to Anthony Gishford. Britten prefaced the publication with the following explanatory note:

> All the texts of these songs are from Thomas Moore's *Irish Melodies*, published between 1808 and 1834 – in one case from the slightly later *National Melodies*. In most instances I have also taken the tunes from the same sources (music arranged by Sir John Stevenson); however, in a few cases I have preferred to go back to Bunting's *Ancient Music of Ireland*, which had in the first place inspired Tom Moore to write his lyrics.

2 Britten's studio at the Red House occupied the first floor of an outbuilding (subsequently named Red Cottage) in the grounds. Its south-facing aspect overlooked the garden. See also PFL, plates 286 and 305–6.

3 Monteverdi's *Il ballo delle ingrate* (realized by Raymond Leppard) and Poulenc's *Les Mamelles de Tirésias* were performed at the 1958 Aldeburgh Festival as a double-bill, directed by Cranko, on 13 and 16 June.

4 According to Britten's diary, this concert took place on 10 December 1957 in Chelsea Town Hall. For this occasion Britten suggested omitting the solo horn's Epilogue from the *Serenade*: the silence following the final Keats setting would make its own eloquent memorial to Brain.

5 Alma Mahler-Werfel, née Schindler (1879–1964), Gustav Mahler's widow;

Britten and Pears had met her in New York in 1942 and again in California in the autumn of 1949 while on tour. In 1958 Britten was to dedicate his final orchestral song-cycle, the *Nocturne*, to her. See also Letter 397 n. 5.

Alma Mahler-Werfel had written from New York on 8 October 1957:

Dear friend Ben,
Thank you for *your nice letter*! Seit wir uns nicht gesehen haben, war ich *immer Ihr bewundernder* Freund und habe Ihr Bild *immer* vor mir stehen! –
Ich was den ganzen Sommer *sehr krank* – bin noch *jetzt nicht* gesund!
Wann kommen Sie nach Amerika? Ich lebe jetzt *ganz* hier – denn ich bin dem *langweiligen Bev. Hills seit langem* entlaufen!

All my wishes for you,
love and kisses,
ALMA MAHLER

[Translation (by Marion Thorpe):

Since we have not seen each other, I was *always* your *admiring* friend and your picture *always* stands in front of me! –
I was *very ill* for the whole summer – and am still *not* well!
When are you coming to America? I now live here *permanently* – as I ran from *boring Bev. Hills long ago*!]

This was followed by a telegram on Britten's birthday, 22 November 1957:

DEAREST FRIEND I AM THINKING OF YOU ON YOUR BIRTHDAY WITH VERY FOND WISHES FOR YOUR LIFE AND YOUR WORK ALWAYS YOURS ALMA MAHLER

While there is a small collection of correspondence at BPL from Alma Mahler-Werfel to Britten, none of the composer's letters to her appears to have survived.

912 To Owen Brannigan[1]
[*Carbon copy*]

The Red House, Aldeburgh, Suffolk
7th December, 1957

My dear Owen,

You may have heard that I am writing an operatic version of one of the Chester Mystery Plays, "Noah's Deluge" for the Aldeburgh Festival combined with television for next year (actually the discussions are still a bit complicated with the television people, and although it is practically certain, nothing has yet been signed – the Festival performances are, however, fixed). It is not a very long affair (less than an hour). I am writing it for two grown-ups and six professional children,[2] and literally hundreds of local school children in the choruses. We are doing two or three performances in a very beautiful local church (Orford), very much in the naive mediaeval style.

Noah, as you can imagine, is a very big part and really carries the whole thing. There is no one I can think of who would do this better than yourself. Would you consider doing it for us? The actual dates of performance are slightly variable at the moment, but they would certainly be the second half of the week June 16th–22nd, with rehearsals two or three weeks before.

If you are interested, and may I say how very much I hope you are, Colin Graham[3] who I think you know, and who has the mammoth task of producing the opera, will get in touch with you and discuss practical arrangements. He will also tell you about a possible television introduction to the work, and repetition a week or so later.

With very best wishes,
Yours sincerely,
[BEN]

1 British bass (1908–1973), who had already created two major Britten roles – Swallow (*Peter Grimes*, 1945) and Collatinus (*The Rape of Lucretia*, 1946) – and who was to be the first Noye and later Bottom (*A Midsummer Night's Dream*, 1960). See also Letter 517 n. 8.

2 The opera is cast for two adult singers (Noye and Mrs Noye) and six children (Noye's sons, Sem, Ham and Jaffett, and their wives). In addition, there is a speaking part for the Voice of God.

3 Graham wrote about the first production of *Noye's Fludde* in his 'Staging first productions 3', in DHOBB, pp. 44–6:

It was during this period of extensive rehearsal and touring [of *The Turn of the Screw*] that I got to know Benjamin Britten and, on the ship taking us all to the Stratford Festival in Ontario, he told me that he would like me to direct *Noye's Fludde*.

Noye's Fludde is taken from the Chester Miracle Plays, a copy of which was given to Britten by Eric Crozier. The opera was conceived primarily to entertain and exploit the talents of the wealth of young musicians in East Anglia; it was only natural that Britten's personal commitment to the area in which he lived should also find him creating suitable musical opportunities. Some of the forces required by the opera are now legendary: the handbells from Leiston Modern School, which heralded the appearance of the rainbow; the percussion group from Woolverstone Hall, with its set of slung mugs for the raindrops which start and end the storm; the recorders from Framlingham College which vie with the wind; the bugles from the Royal Hospital School, Holbrook, which play the Animals in and out of the Ark and end the opera so poignantly. And the Animals themselves, of course, who were auditioned (coincidentally in the presence of Aaron Copland) from schools right across the County of Suffolk.

The large orchestra (originally 150 players) includes strings, allowing for three grades of proficiency, and the whole lot, with the professional stiffening of a piano duet, string quintet, recorder and one percussion player, were massed around the font of Orford Church while the opera was played out on a stage erected at the end of the nave. The Aldeburgh Festival always depended on the use of local churches – in fact made a virtue of it – and the white simplicity of the twelfth-century Church of St Bartholomew was ideally suited to this event. The jagged church tower, struck by lightning early in the 1800s (since rebuilt), has often watched a motley and sizeable crew struggling, in various stages of costume, across the old town square to the church below; the cast of *Noye's Fludde* were the first, the monks of the three Church Parables followed after.

The preparations for the first performance, given as part of the 1958 Aldeburgh Festival, were complicated and hilarious. The choirs (eighty Animals) and orchestra rehearsed in their separate groups all over East Anglia for some months before the concerted final rehearsals, to which they were ferried along the country roads in a fleet of charabancs. They were aided by a 'demo' record made with the composer at the piano, and with all the roles sung by him, Peter Pears, Imogen Holst, the composer's two sisters, and myself – a collector's item! [A copy survives at BPL.] John Schlesinger [later a feature-film director] used the opportunity of *Noye* to make one of his early documentaries for BBC Television's *Monitor* programe.

For the first production, the principal solo roles of Sem, Ham, Jaffett and their wives were given to boys and girls chosen from wide-held auditions; these supported the more experienced performances of Owen Brannigan as Noye and Gladys Parr (and later, Sheila Rex) as his drunken wife. Mrs Noye's gossips were to have come from a Suffolk school, but at the last minute the headmistress got wind of the innocently dissolute parts they were to play and had them withdrawn. Mrs Noye was Gladys Parr's last role before retirement, Owen Brannigan made Noye one of his most enduring and endearing characterizations, while Jaffett was sung by Michael Crawford, then a very recently broken-voiced young tenor.

The Chester plays were originally played on floats or carts at fairs, and Britten was anxious to retain their basic naivety (though the music is far from naive). Trevor Anthony, the Welsh bass, was chosen (rather than a straight actor) to speak the Voice of God and, to achieve a similarly unsophisticated effect, it was decided that I should do the set. The ark was basically a combination of painted screens set by the Property Men around a flight of steps (Mount Ararat); they represented a galleon complete with waves and a cabin for Mr Noye in which the Raven and Dove sheltered. The design was taken from a medieval primitive painting of an ark in full sail. A palm tree was chopped down to use as the mast, from which the rigging slapped in the storm while Mrs Noye and a monkey were violently sick over the side.

At the climax of the storm the hymn 'Eternal Father strong to save' was sung by cast and audience; it was one of Britten's masterstrokes, having additional significance on the storm-bound fishing coasts of East Anglia. This and the other two hymns provided much of the basic musical material.

One of the most ingenious features of the opera is that it can be performed by almost any group of musicians, using local resources as available. The same goes for the staging: Ceri Richards, the eminent Welsh painter, designed the original costumes for the principals and the set of masks and heads worn by the Animals over their school uniform, but many later productions have been as successful with simpler means. There is room even for a certain amount of extemporization in the orchestration: James Blades, the percussionist, rejoiced in helping Woolverstone Hall devise outlandish percussion instruments to be played alongside the slung mugs and the wind machine.

If I have written at some length about *Noye's Fludde*, it is because it represented my first, and most responsible, work for Britten who, many felt, was taking some risk with a virtually untried director.

Graham was also occasionally responsible for adaptations of, or additions to, the libretto: for example, when Britten required an extra verse for the song when Noye and his family are building the ark, Graham provided it (see his interview with Donald Mitchell, 3 March 1992). See also JBBC, pp. 228–40.

913 To Edith Sitwell

<del>4 CRABBE STREET, ALDEBURGH, SUFFOLK</del>
Red House
December 14th 1957

My dearest Edith,

I feel dreadful that I have neglected you so these last months. But I know you understand that writing is difficult for me, especially with so much work on hand – actually in the last two months I've done loads of work, including a new children's opera – a charming 14th century Mystery Play – on Noe and his Fludd! Peter & I to crown it all have moved house, as the enclosed little Christmas card shows you[1] – even a more difficult and ghastly operation than usual, because we and a friend of ours swapped houses, making any initial preparations (& there are plenty to be done!) impossible till one's in. You can imagine the final bars of the opera are punctuated by hammer-blows! However, we are now about half in, & can already see that it is going to be lovely. A little further from the sea, but with a splendid garden, & it is a beautiful old house. I long to show it to you.

Actually, I was delaying writing to you for another reason, which now has evaporated, & whenever I think of it my blood boils afresh. It is this: after Dennis Brain's tragic death we were wondering how best to pay tribute to his wonderful gifts; & it was suggested that we should issue a memorial record, & what lovelier or more suitable than the one that was taken of your readings here last year, with the incidental pieces of music, played by him with Peter & me (including 'Still Falls the Rain').[2] This was all recorded by the BBC Transcription,[3] & could be released commercially (by Decca, who do the Festival records) as long as we all gave up our royalties, & the money to go to his widow – which was why I was going to write to you. And do you know, the other company, to whom Dennis had been contracted,[4] has threatened to stop it, & is <u>succeeding</u> – they have, I gather, no legal right, & you can imagine how much musical or moral right! It is really ghastly, considering that Dennis can no more record for anyone, & also to deprive the public of that wonderful evening etc. etc. Sorry to write at such length, but I wanted to get it off my chest, & I thought you would sympathise! To what lengths will greed, & "business acumen" go?

How sweet of you to think of sending us the new 'English Eccentrics'. I look forward to reading the lovely book again in its new form.[5]

It was sad that we couldn't come to see you as we'd hoped. But I finally didn't take a Summer holiday, on our return from Canada & Germany, & Peter's summer holiday (spent in October–November!) was mostly in bed – knocked out flat by a fantastic year of work. However he's better now, & singing away all over the world.

But I hope we shall coincide here before you go off to the U.S.A. – but it doesn't look good, since we shall both be in Germany mid-February to mid-March. Another disappointment.

Peter joins me in sending you, & Osbert [Sitwell], best Christmas love. I do hope he's feeling better.

Yours affectionately,
BEN

1 Britten's and Pears's Christmas card for 1957 was a woodblock illustration of the Red House, designed by Mary Potter as a gift; see p. 582.

2 *The Heart of the Matter*: see p. 460. The idea of a Dennis Brain memorial record first appears in Britten's correspondence in a letter to Frank Lee of Decca on 14 October 1957. Britten wrote to Lee on 23 October 1957 after having had an opportunity to listen to the BBC Transcription Service recording of the 1956 Aldeburgh Festival concert:

It seems to me that it would make a wonderful memorial, and I am most anxious that we should go ahead with the idea. It will have to be cut slightly since it will be too long as it stands for one LP [. . .] Actually, from the same year they have a wonderful record of Dennis playing an Adagio and Allegro by Schumann to my accompaniment (lasting about five minutes). It has been suggested that we could perhaps cut a little bit more of the poetry reading [by Edith Sitwell] so as to include this extraordinary piece of playing as a little extra at the end of the record [. . .]

I have looked at my contract with the B.B.C. Transcription Service, and there is no mention of any recording rights, nor does [there] seem to be any contract with the Aldeburgh Festival itself (although Stephen Reiss is writing to you about this himself). But I think it is understood by everyone concerned that these records are never issued commercially. I presume, therefore, that permission must be obtained from all the participants including the Aldeburgh Festival and the B.B.C. I know there will be no difficulty about this, but would you like me to write personally to Dame Edith? Leslie Periton is in touch with Dennis's executors, and could approach them for you if you wished.

Edith Sitwell responded to Britten's letter on 22 January 1958, apologizing for the delay because of illness. She was as incensed as Britten about HMV's attitude and proposed that she and Britten 'make the hell of a row about it'. However, the recording as proposed was not released at that time, and in fact it was not until 1999 that the performance of *Canticle III* from the 1956 Aldeburgh Festival concert was issued by BBC Legends, as part of the 'Britten the Performer' series.

The performance of Schumann's Adagio and Allegro in A flat, Op. 70, was given by Brain and Britten in the Jubilee Hall, Aldeburgh, on 21 June 1956. It was released on CD as one of the BBC Legends series in 2006.

3 The BBC Transcription Service, at that time the commercial arm of BBC Radio, was responsible for packaging and selling domestic recordings to broadcasting companies around the world. For many years concerts promoted by the Aldeburgh Festival were broadcast live and/or recorded by both BBC Radio 3 and the Transcription Service.

4 HMV, with whom Brain had an exclusive contract and for whom he made several celebrated recordings, notably of the four Mozart horn concertos with the Philharmonia Orchestra conducted by Herbert von Karajan.

5 Sitwell's *English Eccentrics*, first published in May 1933, was republished in a new and enlarged edition in 1958. Sitwell had written to Britten on 27 November 1957:

I have asked my American publisher to send you the new edition of my 'The English Eccentrics', and also one to Peter.

I believe I *did* give you both the previous edition, but this one has new chapters, one being about the – to me – strange fact that the original of 'The Ancient Mariner' was one of the pirates who rescued Robinson Crusoe; and also one about the noise-stricken home life of the Carlyles.

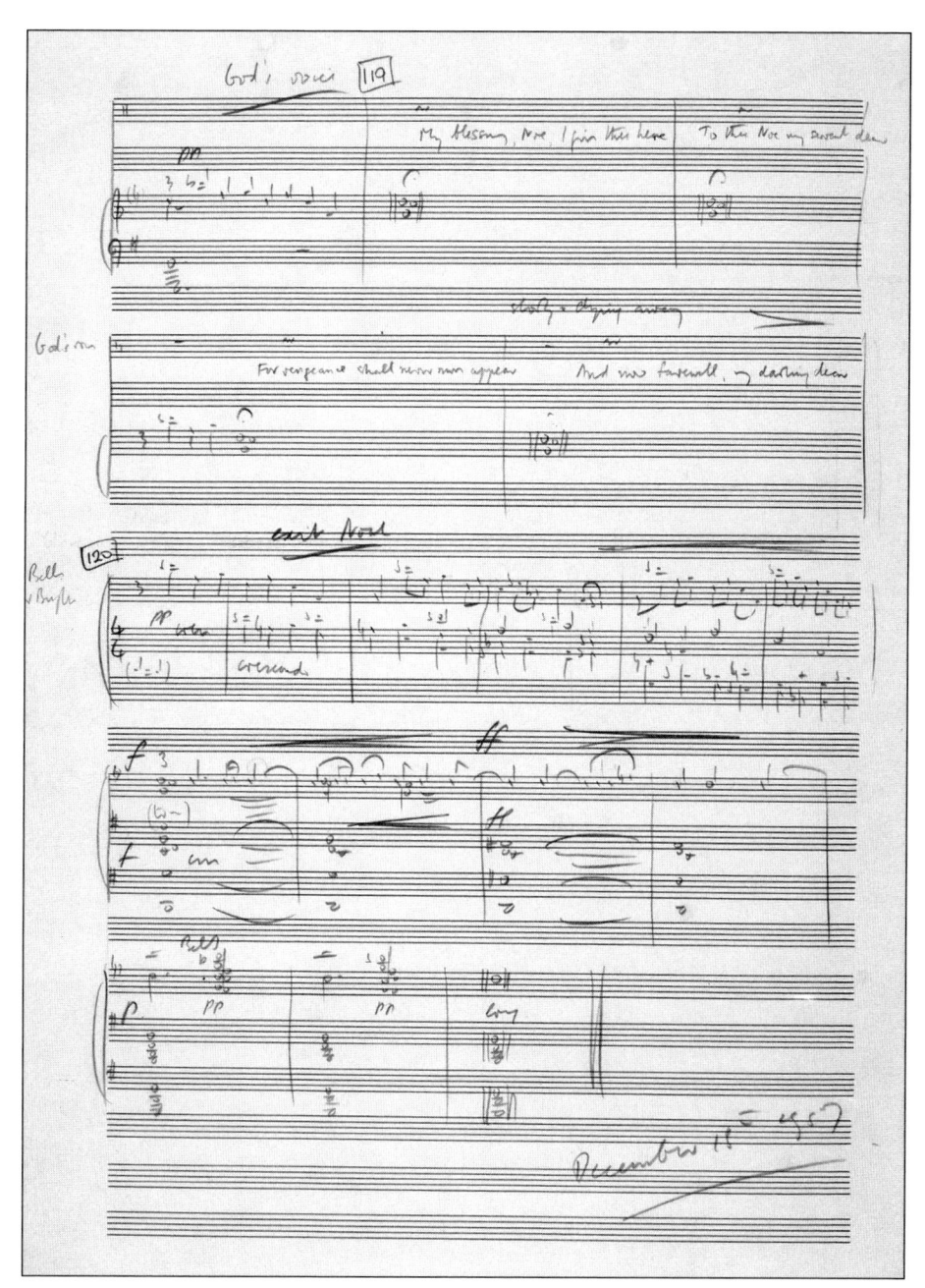

The final page of Britten's composition draft of *Noye's Fludde*, dated 'December 18th 1957'

BIBLIOGRAPHY

Alexander, Peter F., *William Plomer*, Oxford: Oxford University Press, 1990
Alston, Richard, *Norman Del Mar*, London: Thames Publishing, 2000
Amis, John, *Amiscellany*, London: Faber and Faber, 1985
Anderson, Zoë, *The Royal Ballet: 75 Years*, London: Faber and Faber, 2006
Ansermet, Ernest, *Les fondements de la musique dans la conscience humaine*, Neuchâtel: La Baconnière, 1961
Arbeau, Thoinot, *Orchésographie, et tracte en forme de dialogue, par lequel toutes personnes peuvent facilement apprendre & practiquer l'honneste exercise des dances* [1588], translated by C. W. Beaumont London: C. W. Beaumont, 1925

Banks, Paul (ed.), *Britten's 'Gloriana': Essays and Sources*, Aldeburgh Studies in Music vol. 1, Woodbridge: The Boydell Press/The Britten–Pears Library, 1993 (PBBG)
– (comp. and ed.), *Benjamin Britten: A Catalogue of the Published Works*, Aldeburgh: The Britten–Pears Library for The Britten Estate, 1999 (PBCPW)
Banks, Paul, and Philip Reed, *Painting and Music*, exhibition catalogue, Aldeburgh: The Britten–Pears Library, 1993
Banks, Paul, and Rosamund Strode, '*Gloriana*: A List of Sources', in PBBG, pp. 95–170
Behrend, George, *An Unexpected Life*, Findochty: George Behrend, 2007
Benesh, Rudolf, and Joan Benesh, *An Introduction to Benesh Dance Notation*, London: Black, 1956
Blades, James, *Orchestral Percussion Technique*, London: Oxford University Press, 1961; 2nd edn, 1973
– *Drum Roll: A Professional Adventure from the Circus to the Concert Hall*, London: Faber and Faber, 1977
– *Percussion Instruments and Their History* with a foreword by Benjamin Britten, London: Faber and Faber, 1970; rev. 4th edn, 1992
– *These I Have Met . . .: Reminiscences*, London: Thames Publishing, 1998
Bliss, Arthur, *As I Remember*, London: Thames, 1990
Blyth, Alan, *Remembering Britten*, London: Hutchinson, 1981
– 'Reputations: Peter Pears', *Gramophone* (January 2005), pp. 30–33
Bradbury, Ernest, 'An Ideal Setting for a Festival', *Yorkshire Post* (21 June 1958)
Bridcut, John, *Britten's Children*, London: Faber and Faber, 2006 (JBBC)
Brett, Philip, 'Eros and Orientalism in Britten's Operas', in Philip Brett, Elizabeth Wood and Gary Thomas (eds.), *Queering the Pitch: The New Gay and Lesbian Musicology*
Brett, Philip, Elizabeth Wood and Gary Thomas (eds.), *Queering the Pitch: The New Gay and Lesbian Musicology*, New York and London: Routledge and Kegan Paul, 1994
Britten, Benjamin, 'Three Premieres', in Neville Cardus (ed.), *Kathleen Ferrier 1912–1953: A Memoir*, London: Hamish Hamilton, 1954, pp. 54–61; also PKBM, pp. 123–7
– 'Dennis Brain 1921–1957', *Tempo* 46 (winter 1957), pp. 55–6; also PKBM, pp. 158–60

- 'Speech on Receiving Honorary Degree at Hull University' [1962]; PKBM, pp. 214–16
- 'Britten Looking Back', *Sunday Telegraph*, 17 November 1963; also PKBM, pp. 250–53
- 'Some Notes on Forster and Music', in Oliver Stallybrass (ed.), *Aspects of E. M. Forster: Essays and Recollections written for his Ninetieth Birthday 1st January 1969*; also PKBM, pp. 316–20

Britten, Benjamin, and Imogen Holst, *The Story of Music*, London: Rathbone Books, 1958; republished as *The Wonderful World of Music*, London: Macdonald, 1968

Buckland, Sidney (ed.), *Francis Poulenc: Echo and Source: Selected Correspondence 1915–1963*, London: Gollancz, 1991

Buckland, Sidney, and Myriam Chimènes (eds.), *Francis Poulenc: Music, Art and Literature*, Aldershot: Ashgate, 1999

Busch, Fritz, *Pages From a Musician's Life*, trans. Marjorie Strachey, London: Hogarth Press, 1953

Butt, John, *Bach: Mass in B minor*, Cambridge: Cambridge University Press, 1991

Caird, George, 'Benjamin Britten and his *Metamorphoses*', *Double Reed News* 76 (autumn 2006), pp. 18–22
- *Britten 'Six Metamorphoses after Ovid': Anatomy of a Masterpiece*, London: Oboe Classics, 2007

Caldwell, Virgina, 'Profile: The Princess of Hesse and the Rhine', *Aldeburgh Soundings* (autumn 1986)
- 'Profile: Jeremy Cullum', *Aldeburgh Soundings* 10 (February 1998)

Campion, Paul, *Ferrier: A Career Recorded*, 2nd edn, London: Thames Publishing, 2005

Cardus, Neville (ed.), *Kathleen Ferrier 1912–1953: A Memoir*, London: Hamish Hamilton, 1954

Carpenter, Humphrey, *W. H. Auden: A Biography*, London: Allen & Unwin, 1981
- *Benjamin Britten*, London: Faber and Faber, 1992 (HCBB)

Chalmers, Kenneth, liner note to CD recording of *Benjamin Britten: The Rarities*, Decca 468 811-2

Chimènes, Myriam (ed.), *Francis Poulenc: Correspondance 1910–1963*, Paris: Fayard, 1994

Clayton, Sylvia, *Edward Piper*, Newton Abbott: David Charles in association with the Catto Gallery, 1991

Coast, John, *Dancing Out of Bali*, London: Faber and Faber, 1954

Coleman, Basil, 'Staging First Productions 2', in DHOBB, pp. 34–43

Conway, Helen, *Sir John Pritchard: His Life in Music*, London: André Deutsch, 1993

Cook, William (ed.), *Goodbye Again: The Definitive Peter Cook and Dudley Moore*, London: Century, 2004

Cooke, Mervyn, 'Britten and the Shō', *Musical Times* 129 (1988), pp. 231–3
- *Britten and the Far East: Asian Influences in the Music of Benjamin Britten*, Aldeburgh Studies in Music vol. 4, Woodbridge: The Boydell Press/The Britten–Pears Library, 1993 (MCBFE)
- *Benjamin Britten: 'War Requiem'*, Cambridge: Cambridge University Press, 1996 (WRMC)
- (ed.), *The Cambridge Companion to Benjamin Britten*, Cambridge: Cambridge University Press, 1999 (MCCCBB)

Cooke, Mervyn, and Philip Reed, *Benjamin Britten: 'Billy Budd'*, Cambridge: Cambridge University Press, 1993 (BBMCPR)

Covarrubias, Miguel, *Island of Bali*, New York: Alfred A. Knopf Inc., 1937

Cox, Peter, *The Arts at Dartington, 1940–1983*, Dartington: Peter Cox, 2005

Cranko, John, 'Making a Ballet', *The Sunday Times*, 13 and 20 January 1957

Cunningham, Valentine, 'Filthy Britten', *Guardian* (5 January 2002)

Dickinson, Peter, *The Music of Lennox Berkeley*, 2nd, rev. edn, Woodbridge: The Boydell Press, 2003

Drogheda, Lord, *Double Harness*, London: Weidenfeld & Nicolson, 1976

Duncan, Ronald, *Working with Britten: A Personal Memoir*, Welcombe: The Rebel Press, 1981 (RDWB)
Dunnert, Roderic, 'A Close and Intense Collaboration', programme book for Welsh National Opera production of *The Turn of the Screw* (2000)
Drummond, John, *Tainted by Experience: A Life in the Arts*, London: Faber and Faber, 2000

Eaton, Quantance, 'Billy's Bow', *Opera News* (31 March 1979)
Enright, D. J., *Memoirs of a Mendicant Professor*, London: Chatto and Windus, 1969
Evans, John, 'The Sketches: Chronology and Analysis', in PHTS, pp. 63–70
– liner note to CD recording of *The Heart of the Matter*, EMI 5 7436 2, 1987

Fifield, Christopher (ed.), *Letters and Diaries of Kathleen Ferrier*, Woodbridge: The Boydell Press, 2003
Fischer-Dieskau, Dietrich, *Echoes of a Lifetime*, translated by Ruth Hein, London: Macmillan, 1989
Forster, E. M., *The Hill of Devi*, London: Edward Arnold, 1953
Francis, Sarah, 'Joy Boughton: A Portrait', *Double Reed News* 26 (February 1994), pp. 4–7
Franks, A. H., *Svetlana Beriosova; A Biography*, London: Burke, 1958

Garnham, Maureen, *As I Saw It: Basil Douglas, Benjamin Britten and the English Opera Group, 1959–1957*, London: St George's Publications, 1998
Gendre, Claude, '*Dialogues des Carmélites*: the historical background, literary destiny and genesis of the opera', in Buckland and Chimènes (eds.), *Francis Poulenc: Music, Art and Literature*, pp. 274–319
Gerardy, Riki, *Talks with Emanuel Hurwitz: 82 Years with the Violin*, London: Zelia, 2006
Gishford, Anthony (ed.), *Tribute to Benjamin Britten on His Fiftieth Birthday*, London: Faber and Faber, 1963 (TBB)
Glendinning, Victoria, *Edith Sitwell: A Lion Among Unicorns*, Oxford: Oxford University Press, 1983
Goddard, Scott, 'Fanfare for Britten', *Collins Young Elizabethan*, June 1953, pp. 19–21
Gooding, Mel, *Ceri Richards*, Moffat: Cameron and Hollis, 2002
Greene, Richard (ed.), *Selected Letters of Edith Sitwell*, London: Virago Press, 1997
Griffiths, Paul, *New Sounds, New Personalities*, London: Faber and Faber, 1985
Graham, Colin, 'Staging First Productions 3', in DHOBB, pp. 44–58
Grogan, Christopher (ed.), *Imogen Holst: A Life in Music*, Woodbridge: The Boydell Press/The Holst Foundation/The Britten–Pears Library, 2007
Groome, Francis Hindes, *Two Suffolk Friends*, London: William Blackwood & Sons, 1895

Haley, William, rev. Robert Brown, 'Sir Campbell Stuart', *The Oxford Dictionary of National Biography*, www.oxforddnb.com
Handford, Basil, *Lancing College: History and Memoirs*, Chichester: Phillimore, 1986
Happé, Peter (ed.), *English Mystery Plays*, Harmondsworth: Penguin, 1975
Harewood, Lord, 'Foreword', Aldeburgh Festival Programme Book 1954
– *The Tongs and the Bones*, London: Weidenfeld and Nicolson, 1981
Harman, Claire (ed.), *The Diaries of Sylvia Townsend Warner*, London: Virago, 1995
Hayes, Malcolm (ed.), *The Selected Letters of William Walton*, London: Faber and Faber, 2002
Headington, Christopher, *Peter Pears: A Biography*, London: Faber and Faber, 1992 (CHPP)
Hemmings, David, *Blow-Up and Other Exaggerations*, London: Robson Books, 2004
Herbert, David (ed.), *The Operas of Benjamin Britten*, London: Hamish Hamilton, 1979 (DHOBB)
Hesse, Prince Ludwig of, *Ausflug Ost 1956*, Darmstadt: Eduard Roether, 1956 (LHAO)
– 'Bemerkungen des Übersetzers', *Das neue Forum* 8 (1957)
Hesse, Princess Margaret of, *Dear Friends 1956–1986*, compiled by Edward Mace, private publication, 1988

Hewison, Robert, '"Happy were He": Benjamin Britten and the *Gloriana* Story', in PBBG, pp. 1–16
Holst, Imogen, 'Britten and the Young', in DMHK, pp. 276–86
– 'Working for Benjamin Britten', *Musical Times* 118 (March 1977), pp. 202–6
– 'Working for Benjamin Britten (I)', in CPBC, pp. 46–50
– 'Aldeburgh Diary 1952–54', in Christopher Grogan (ed.), *Imogen Holst: A Life in Music*, 129–91 (IHD)
Howard, Patricia (ed.), *Benjamin Britten: 'The Turn of the Screw'*, Cambridge: Cambridge University Press, 1985 (PHTS)
Hughes, Davina, 'A Boy Finds Opera is Grand', *Illustrated* (9 October 1954), pp. 23–4
Huntley, John, *British Film Music*, London: Skelton Robinson, 1948

Isaacs, Leonard, *Five Lives in One: Selected Memoirs*, Nova Scotia: Hubbards, 1998

Jackson, Holbrooke (ed.), *The Complete Nonsense of Edward Lear*, London: Faber and Faber, 1947
James, Henry, *The Turn of the Screw and Other Stories*, edited with an introduction and notes by T. J. Lustig, Oxford: Oxford University Press, 1998
Jeffries, Richard, *Bevis: The Story of a Boy* [1882], with an introduction by C. Henry Warren, London: Eyre & Spottiswoode, 1948
Jenkins, Alan, *Stephen Potter: Inventor of Gamesmanship*, London: Weidenfeld & Nicholson, 1980
John, Nicholas (ed.), *Peter Grimes/Gloriana*, ENO Opera Guide No. 24, London: John Calder, 1983
John Piper: Catalogue of a Retrospective Exhibition of his Work, London: Tate Gallery, 1983
Jones, J. D. F., *Storyteller: The Many Lives of Laurens Van der Post*, London: Scribner, 2002
Jones, Vivien, 'Henry James's *The Turn of the Screw*' in PHTS, pp. 1–22

Kavanagh, Julie, *Secret Muses: The Life of Sir Frederick Ashton*, London: Faber and Faber, 1996
Keller, Hans, 'The Musical Character', in DMHK, pp. 319–51
– '*Peter Grimes*: The Story; The Music not Excluded', in DMHK, pp. 111–24
Kemp, Ian, *Tippett: The Composer and his Music*, London: Eulenburg, 1984
Kennedy, Benjamin Hall, *The Shorter Latin Primer*, new and rev. edn by J. W. Bartrum, London: Longmans Green, 1948
Kennedy, Michael, *Britten*, London: Dent (Master Musicians series), 1981; rev. pbk edn, 1993 (MKBMM)
– *Portrait of Walton*, Oxford: Oxford University Press, 1989; rev. pbk edn, 1998
Kenyon, Nicholas, *The BBC Symphony Orchestra: The First Fifty Years 1930–1980*, London: BBC, 1981
Kildea, Paul (ed.), *Britten on Music*, Oxford: Oxford University Press, 2002 (PKBM)
– *Selling Britten: Music and the Market Place*, Oxford: Oxford University Press, 2002 (PKSB)
Kögler, Horst, et al., *John Cranko und das Stuttgarter Ballett*, Pfulligen: Neske, 1978
Komparu, Kunio, *The Noh Theater: Principles and Perspectives*, Tokyo and New York: Weatherhill/Tankosha, 1983
Krips, Harriet, *Ohne Liebe kann man keine Musik machen: Erinnerungen*, Vienna: Böhlau Verlag, 1994

Lebrecht, Norman, *Covent Garden – The Untold Story: Dispatches from the English Culture War, 1945–2001*, London: Pocket Books, 2001
Lees-Milne, James, *Fourteen Friends*, London: John Murray, 1996
Lehmann, John, and Derek Parker (eds.), *Edith Sitwell: Selected Letters*, London: Macmillan, 1970
Lucas, John, *Reggie: The Life of Reginald Goodall*, London: Julia MacRae Books, 1993

Mackay, Jane, *The Turn of the Screw: Visual Responses to Britten's Opera*, with commentary by Andrew Plant, London: Sounding Art Press, 2007
McPhee, Colin, *Music in Bali: A Study in Form and Instrumental Organization in Balinese Orchestral Music*, New Haven: Yale University Press, 1966; rp New York: The Da Capo Press, 1976
Malcolm, George, 'Dido and Aeneas', in DMHK, pp. 186–97
– 'The Purcell Realizations', in DMHK, pp. 74–82
– 'Boys' Voices', in TBB, pp. 100–103
Malloy, Antonia, 'Britten's Major Set-Back? Aspects of the First Critical Response to *Gloriana*', in PBBG, pp. 49–65
– '*Gloriana*: A Bibliography', in PBBG, pp. 171–81
Malloy-Chirgwin, Antonia, '*Gloriana*: Britten's "slighted child"', in MCCCBB, pp. 113–28
Man of Our Time, A, exhibition catalogue (Michael Tippett), London: Schott & Co., 1977
Mangan, Richard (ed.), *Gielgud's Letters*, London: Weidenfeld & Nicolson, 2004
Mary Potter: 1900–1981 – A Selective Retrospective, exhibition catalogue, Newtown: Oriel 31, 1989
Matthews, David, 'A Note on Cuts', in the preliminary matter to the published study score of *The Prince of the Pagodas*, London: Boosey & Hawkes Music Publishers, 1989
Mayer, Tony, 'L'affaire *Gloriana*', Opera 4/8 (August 1953), pp. 456–60
– *La Vie anglaise*, Paris, 1960
Menuhin, Diana, *Fiddler's Moll: Life with Yehudi*, London: Weidenfeld and Nicholson, 1984
Meredith, Anthony, and Paul Harris, *Malcolm Williamson: A Mischievous Muse*, London: Omnibus Press, 2007
Mitchell, Donald, 'The Musical Atmosphere', in DMHK, pp. 9–58
– 'Britten's Revisionary Practice: Practical and Creative', *Tempo* 66–7 (autumn/winter 1963), pp. 15–22, reprinted in DMCN, pp. 397–406
– 'An Afterword on Britten's *Pagodas*: The Balinese Sources', *Tempo* 152 (March 1985), pp. 7–11
– (ed.), *Benjamin Britten: 'Death in Venice'*, Cambridge: Cambridge University Press, 1987 (DMDV)
– 'The Paradox of *Gloriana*: Simple and Difficult', in PBBG, pp. 67–75
– *Cradles of the New: Writings on Music 1951–1991*, selected by Christopher Palmer, edited by Mervyn Cooke, London: Faber and Faber, 1995 (DMCN)
– 'Fit for a Queen?', liner notes to recording of *Gloriana*, Argo 440 213-2, 1993, pp. 14–18
Mitchell, Donald, and John Evans, *Pictures from a Life: Benjamin Britten 1913–1976*, London: Faber and Faber, 1978 (PFL)
Mitchell, Donald, and Hans Keller (eds.), *Benjamin Britten: A Commentary on his Works from a Group of Specialists*, Rockliff: London, 1952 (DMHK)
Mitchell, Donald, and Philip Reed (eds.), *Letters from a Life: Selected Letters and Diaries of Benjamin Britten*, vol. 1: 1923–39; vol. 2: 1939–45, London: Faber and Faber, 1991
Mitchell, Donald, Philip Reed and Mervyn Cooke (eds.), *Letters from a Life: Selected Letters of Benjamin Britten*, vol. 3: 1946–51, London: Faber and Faber, 2004
Mullins, Charlotte, *A Festival on the River: The Story of the Southbank Centre*, London: Penguin, 2007

Neale, J. E., *Queen Elizabeth*, London: Jonathan Cape, 1950
– *Elizabeth I and Her Parliaments, 1584–1601*, London: Jonathan Cape, 1950; 1957 impression
Neunzig, H. A., *Dietrich Fischer-Dieskau: eine Biographie*, Stuttgart, 1995; English translation, London: Duckworth, 1998
Nissel, Muriel, *Married to the Amadeus: Life with a String Quartet*, London: Giles de la Mare Publishers, 1998
Noel, Conrad, *Life of Jesus*, London: Dent, 1937
Northen, Michael, 'Designs for the Theatre', in *John Piper: Catalogue of a Retrospective Exhibition of his Work*, London: Tate Gallery, 1983

Oldham, Arthur, *Living with Voices: An Autobiography*, London: Thames Publishing, 2000
Owen, Wilfred, *The Collected Poems of Wilfred Owen*, edited by Cecil Day Lewis, with a memoir by Edmund Blunden, London: Chatto & Windus, 1963

Parsons, Charles H., *A Benjamin Britten Discography*, Lewiston: E. Mellen Press, 1990
Palmer, Christopher (ed.), *The Britten Companion*, London: Faber and Faber, 1984 (CPBC)
Palmer, Tony, *Julian Bream: A Life on the Road*, London: Macdonald, 1982
Percival, John, *Theatre in My Blood*, London: The Herbert Press, 1983
Pettit, Stephen, *Dennis Brain: A Biography*, London: Robert Hale, 1976
Phelan, Nancy, *Charles Mackerras: A Musicians' Musician*, London: Gollancz, 1987
Piguet, Jean-Claude, and Jacques Burdet (eds.), *Ernest Ansermet–Frank Martin, Correspondance 1934–68*, Neuchâtel: La Baconnière, 1976
Piper, Myfanwy, 'Portrait of a Choreographer', *Tempo* 32 (summer 1954), pp. 14–23
– 'Writing for Britten', in DHOBB, pp. 8–21
Plant, Andrew, *Rumours and Visions*, exhibition catalogue, Aldeburgh: The Britten–Pears Library, 2004
Plomer, William, *Museum Pieces*, London: Jonathan Cape, 1952
– 'Notes on the Libretto of *Gloriana*', *Tempo* 28 (summer 1953), pp. 5–7
– 'Let's crab an opera', *London Magazine* 3/7 (October 1964), pp. 101–4
Pollard, Alfred (ed.), *English Miracle Plays, Moralities and Interludes: Specimens of the Pre-Elizabethan Drama*, 8th edn, rev., Oxford: Clarendon Press, 1927
Potter, Julian, 'Biographical Note', *Mary Potter: 1900–1981, A Selective Retrospective*, exhibition catalogue, Newtown: Oriel 31, 1989, pp. 32–3
– *Mary Potter: A Life of Painting*, Aldershot: Scolar Press, 1998
– *Stephen Potter at the BBC: 'Features' in War and Peace*, Orford: Orford Books, 2004
Potter, Tully, 'An Enduring Musical Bond', CD liner note for BBC Legends (BBCL 4083-2), 2001
Pritchard, Jane, 'Diana Menuhin', *The Oxford Dictionary of National Biography*, www.oxforddnb.com

Reed, Philip, *The Incidental Music of Benjamin Britten: A Study and Catalogue of His Music for Film, Theatre and Radio*, PhD dissertation, University of East Anglia, 1988 (PRIM)
– 'A Cantata for Broadcasting: Britten's *The Company of Heaven*', *Musical Times* 130 (June 1989), pp. 324–31
– 'The 1960 revisions: a two-act *Billy Budd*' in BBMCPR, pp. 74–84
– 'The Creative Evolution of *Gloriana*', in PBBG, pp. 17–47
– 'Introductory Note' to Benjamin Britten, 'Three Songs from *The Heart of the Matter*', London: Boosey & Hawkes, 1994
– (ed.), *The Travel Diaries of Peter Pears 1936–1978*, Aldeburgh Studies in Music vol. 2, Woodbridge: The Boydell Press/The Britten–Pears Library, 1995; rev. rp, 1999 (PRPP)
– 'Britten's Folk Song Arrangements: Documentation', CD liner notes for *Benjamin Britten: The Folk Songs*, Collins Classics (70392), 1995
– 'Poulenc, Britten, Aldeburgh: a Chronicle' in Sidney Buckland and Myriam Chimènes (eds.), *Francis Poulenc: Music, Art, Literature*, pp. 348–62
– (ed.), *On Mahler and Britten: Essays in Honour of Donald Mitchell on His Seventieth Birthday*, Aldeburgh Studies in Music vol. 3, Woodbridge: The Boydell Press/The Britten–Pears Library, 1995 (PROMB)
– 'An Historic Partnership', CD liner note, BBC Legends 1969 recording of *War Requiem*, BBCL 4046-2, 2000
– Liner note to BBC Legends CD of Britten, Menuhin and Gendron playing piano trios by Mozart, Beethoven and Bridge at the 1963 Aldeburgh Festival, BBC Legends, BBCL 4134-2, 2003
Reiss, Stephen, *Aelbert Cuyp*, London: Zwemmer, 1975

Roscow, Gregory (ed.), *Bliss on Music: Selected Writings of Arthur Bliss, 1920–75*, Oxford: Oxford University Press, 1991
Roseberry, Eric, '"Abraham and Isaac" Revisited: Reflections on a Theme and its Inversion', in PROMB, pp. 253–66
– 'Old songs in new contexts: Britten as arranger', in MCCCBB, pp. 292–305
Rosza, Suzanne, *The Amadeus: Forty Years in Pictures and Words*, private publication, 1988
Roth, Ernst, *The Business of Music: Reflections of a Music Publisher*, London: Cassell, 1969

Sanders, Alan (ed.), *Walter Legge: Words and Music*, London: Duckworth, 1998
Scarfe, Norman, *Suffolk: A Shell Guide*, London: Faber and Faber, 1960
Schmidgall, Gary, 'The Natural: Theodor Uppmann is Billy Budd', *Opera News*, 28 March 1992
Schuttenhelm, Thomas (ed.), *Selected Letters of Michael Tippett*, London: Faber and Faber, 2005
Searle, Muriel V., *John Ireland: The Man and his Music*, Tunbridge Wells: Midas Books, 1979
Sitwell, Edith, *Taken Care Of: An Autbiography*, London: Hutchinson, 1965
Sitwells and the Arts of the 1920s and 1930s, The, exhibition catalogue, London: National Portrait Gallery, 1994
Snowman, Daniel, *The Amadeus Quartet: The Men and the Music*, London: Robson Books, 1981
– *The Hitler Emigrés: The Cultural Impact on Britain of Refugees from Nazism*, London: Chatto & Windus, 2002
Sorrell, Neil, *A Guide to the Gamelan*, London: Faber and Faber, 1990
Staging History, catalogue for the exhibition held at the Britten–Pears Library, June 2001, Aldeburgh: The Britten–Pears Library, 2001
Stallybrass, Oliver (ed.), *Aspects of E. M. Forster: Essays and Recollections written for his Ninetieth Birthday 1st January 1969*, London: Edward Arnold, 1969
Stein, Erwin, *Orpheus in New Guises*, trans. Hans Keller, London: Rockcliff, 1953
– 'Die Musik zu "The Turn of the Screw"', *Das neue Forum* 8 (1957)
Stephenson, Lesley, with Don Weed, *Symphony of Dreams: The Conductor and Patron Paul Sacher*, Zurich: Ruffer & Rub, 2002
Stock, Noel, *The Life of Ezra Pound*, Harmondsworth: Penguin, 1974
Strachey, Lytton, *Elizabeth & Essex, A Tragic History*, London: Chatto & Windus, 1928
Stray, Christopher, 'A Preference for Naughty Boys in Apple Trees', in *Ad Familiares* 20 (spring 2001), pp. 6–7
– 'Sexy Ghosts and Gay Grammarians: Kennedy's Latin Primer in Britten's *Turn of the Screw*', in *Paradigm* 2/6 (August 2003), pp. 9–13
Strode, Rosamund, 'Working for Britten(II)', in CPBC, pp. 51–61
– 'Reverberations' in PPT, pp. 89–90
– 'A *Death in Venice* Chronicle', in DMDV, pp. 26–44
Sutcliffe, Tom, 'Haunting Parallels Between Art and Life', programme for *The Turn of the Screw*, Welsh National Opera, 2000
Stuart, Sir Campbell, *Opportunity Knocks*, London: Collins, 1952

Tappolet, Claude (ed.), *Ernest Ansermet: Correspondances avec des composituers Européens (1916–1966)*, vol. 1, Geneva: Georg Editeur, 1994
Tausky, Vilem, *Vilem Tausky Tells His Story*, London: Stainer and Bell, 1979
Thorpe, Marion (ed.), *Peter Pears: A Tribute on his 75th Birthday*, London: Faber Music/The Britten Estate, 1985 (PPT)
Tooley, John, *In House: Covent Garden – 50 Years of Opera and Ballet*, London: Faber and Faber, 2000
Turn of the Screw, The, programme, Welsh National Opera, 2000

Vaughan, David, *Frederick Ashton and His Ballets*, London: A. & C. Black, 1977

Walker, Patrick, and Valerie Potter, *Aldeburgh Music Club 1952–2002*, Saxmundham: Aldeburgh Music Club, 2001
Wallace, Helen, *Boosey & Hawkes: The Publishing Story*, London: Boosey & Hawkes Music Publishers, 2007
Walton, Susana, *William Walton: Behind the Façade*, Oxford: Oxford University Press, 1988
Wardle, Irving, *The Theatres of George Devine*, London: Eyre Methuen, 1979
White, Eric Walter, *Benjamin Britten: A Sketch of His Life and Works*, new edn, rev. and enlarged, London: Boosey & Hawkes, 1954
– *A Tarot Deal and other poems*, Lowestoft: Scorpion Press, 1962
– *Benjamin Britten: His Life and Operas*, 2nd edn, edited by John Evans, London: Faber and Faber, 1983 (EWW)
Whittall, Arnold, *Jonathan Harvey*, London: Faber and Faber, 1999
Whitton, Kenneth S., *Dietrich Fischer-Dieskau Mastersinger: A Documentary Study*, London: Wolff, 1981
Willans, Geoffrey, and Ronald Searle, *Molesworth*, with an introduction by Philip Hensher, London: Penguin Classics, 2000
Wiebe, Heather, '"New and England": Britten, *Gloriana* and the "New Elizabethans"', *Cambridge Opera Journal* 17/2 (2005), pp. 141–72
Woods, Robin, *Robin Woods: An Autobiography*, London: SCM Press, 1986

Young, Michael, *The Elmhirsts of Dartington: The Creation of an Utopian Community*, London: Routledge & Kegan Paul, 1982

Zander, Benjamin, 'If it doesn't flow, I can't dance to it', www.benjaminzander.com/journal, accessed 2007
Zoete, Beryl de, and Walter Spies, *Dance and Drama in Bali*, London: Faber and Faber, 1938; 2nd edn, Oxford: Oxford University Press, 1973

TELEVISION AND RADIO BROADCASTS

Blow the Wind Southerly, a documentary film on Kathleen Ferrier, written, narrated and directed by John Drummond, BBC Television (*Omnibus*), 6 October 1968
Britten's Children, a documentary film by John Bridcut, BBC Television/Mentorn, 2004
The Instrument of His Soul, a BBC radio feature on Peter Pears, produced by John Evans
Kathleen Ferrier: An Ordinary Diva, a documentary film on Kathleen Ferrier, directed by Suzanne Phillips, Forget About Film and TV for BBC Wales, 2003
Scenes from 'Billy Budd', NBC Television, 1952
Voice is a Person, A, a radio documentary on Kathleen Ferrier, 4 October 1978

DISCOGRAPHY

WORKS BY BRITTEN

Benjamin Britten: The Folk Songs, Collins Classics 70392, 1995
Benjamin Britten: The Rarities, Decca 468 811-2, 2001
Billy Budd (off-air recording of first performance), VAIA 1034-3, 1993
A Boy was Born, Decca, LXT 5416, 1957
Canticle III [1956], BBC 'Britten as Performer', BBCB 8014-2, 1999
A Ceremony of Carols, Decca, LXT 2981, 1954
Four Sea Interludes from 'Peter Grimes': Decca, LXT 2886, 1954
Gloriana, Argo, 440 213-2, 1993

The Little Sweep, Decca, LXT 5163, 1955
Peter Grimes: Decca, LXT-5521/3, 1959; Philips, 6769 014, 1978
Prelude and Fugue on a Theme of Vittoria, Aeolian Skinner Organ Co. 6, 1954; MGM E-3064, 1954
Rejoice in the Lamb, Decca, LXT 5416, 1957
Saint Nicolas, Decca, LXT 5060, 1955
Sinfonia da Requiem, Decca, LXT 2981, 1953
The Turn of the Screw, Decca, LXT 5038/9, 1955
Variations on an Elizabethan Theme, Decca, LXT 2798, 1953
The Young Person's Guide to the Orchestra, Decca, LXT 2886, 1954
War Requiem [1969], BBC Legends, BBCL 4046-2, 2000
The World of the Spirit, Chandos, CHAN 9487, 1996

PERFORMANCES BY BRITTEN AND/OR PEARS, IN WORKS BY OTHER COMPOSERS

Bach: Brandenburg Concertos, Decca, SET 410-11, 1969
Bach: Three Cantatas, Teldec SAWD 9904-B, 1960
Elizabethan Lute Songs by Dowland, Ford, Morley and Rosseter, Decca, LW5243, 1956
English Song Recital, Decca, ECS545, 1956
Handel: *Acis and Galatea*, L'Oiseau-lyre, SOL60011/2, 1960
Haydn: Symphony No. 45 and Symphony No. 55, Decca, LXT 5312; reissued in 'Britten at Aldeburgh' series, Decca, 458 869-2, 2000
Martin: *Sechs Monologe aus Jedermann*, Pearl, GEM 0227, 2005
Mozart: Piano Concerto in A major, K. 414, Decca, LW 5294; reissued in 'Britten at Aldeburgh' series, Decca, 458 869-2, 2000
Mozart, Beethoven and Bridge: Piano Trios [1963], BBC Legends BBCL 4134-2, 2003
Puccini: *Turandot*, Decca, SET 561, 1973
Purcell: Chacony in G minor, Z. 730, Decca, SXL 6405, 1969
Schubert: Fantasie in C (D. 934) [1957], BBC Legends, BBCL 4083-2, 2001
Schumann: Adagio and Allegro in A flat, Op. 70 [1956], BBC Legends, BBCL 4192-2, 2006
Shostakovich: *Seven Blok Romances* [1968], 'Britten at Aldeburgh' series, Decca, 466 823-2, 2000
Tippett: *The Heart's Assurance* [1952], Argo, DA34, 1962
Walton: *Façade*, Decca, LXT 2977, 1954

PERFORMANCES BY ARTISTS OTHER THAN BRITTEN OR PEARS

Blades, James: *Blades on Percussion (All About Music* series), ABK 13
Ferrier, Kathleen: *Kathleen Ferrier: The Singer and the Person*, introduced by Peter Pears, BBC Artium REGL 368, 1979
Gender wayang selendero, Parlophobe MO 105
Ghosh, Pannalal: *Yaman* and *Shri (ragas)*, EALP 1252
Haydn: Horn Concerto in D major (H. VIID:3) [1957], BBC Legends, BBCL 4066-2, 2001
Poulenc: *Les Mamelles de Tirésias*, Columbia, FCX 230, 1954
Uppmann, Theodor: *Art of Theodor Uppmann, The*, VAI Audio, VIAI 1181, 1999

INTERVIEWS

The tapes of the following interviews, and in some cases transcripts, are available at BPL. Recordings are audio only unless otherwise indicated.

Britten, Benjamin, with Tom Patterson, CBC, broadcast 23 August 1957
Coleman, Basil, with Donald Mitchell, Aldeburgh, 29 October 2000; with William Kerley, London, May/June 2004
Cullum, Jeremy, with Donald Mitchell, Horham, 20 August 1998

Douglas, Basil, with Donald Mitchell, London, 16 November 1987
Ford, Boris, with Donald Mitchell, London, 8 November 1989
Graham, Colin, with Keith Grant, London, 1988; with Donald Mitchell, London,
   3 March 1992
Harewood, The Earl of, with Donald Mitchell, Harewood House, Leeds, 2006 (video)
Holst, Imogen, with Donald Mitchell, Aldeburgh, 22 June 1977
Mitchell, Donald, with Humphrey Carpenter, for HCBB
Piper, Myfanwy, with Elizabeth Sweeting, September 1986
Reiss, Stephen, with Donald Mitchell, Aldeburgh, 18 July 1998
Rogerson, Paul, with Donald Mitchell, London, 27 July 2005
Schweitzer (née Welford), Sally, with Donald Mitchell and Philip Reed, London, 21 July 2005
Tooley, John, with Michael Oliver, London, 9 January 1992

REVIEWS AND MEDIA COVERAGE OF BRITTEN AND HIS WORKS

Goddard, Scott, 'Fanfare for Britten', *Collins Young Elizabethan*, June 1953, pp. 19–21
Tracey, Edmund, interview with BB, *Sadler's Wells Magazine*, autumn 1966, pp. 5–7

Billy Budd   The Earl of Harewood, 'Foreign Diary', *Opera* 2/6 (May 1952; 'Britten issue'),
   pp. 268, 307; Willi Schuh, *Schweitzerische Musikzeitung*, 1 January 1952; John Waterhouse,
   review, *Birmingham Post*, 17 December 1951

Canticle II: 'Abraham and Isaac'   [Colin Mason], *Manchester Guardian*, 26 January 1952;
   Nottingham Guardian (and *Nottingham Journal*; edited version of the same review),
   22 January 1952; *The Times*, 5 February 1952; John Waterhouse, *Birmingham Post*,
   23 January 1952

Canticle III: 'Still Falls the Rain'   Desmond Shawe-Taylor, *New Statesman and Nation*,
   12 February 1955; *The Times*, 29 January 1955

Gloriana   Beverly Baxter, *Evening Standard*, 9 June 1953; Beverly Baxter, 'The One Sour
   Note of the Coronation', *Maclean's*, 1 September 1953; Stephen Baylis, '*Gloriana* brings a
   night of Coronation glory', *Daily Mail*, 9 June 1953; Richard Capell, *Daily Telegraph*, 9 and
   13 June 1953; Martin Cooper, *Spectator*, 12 and 19 June 1953; *Daily Express*, 'Bow for
   Britten', 12 June 1953; *Daily Telegraph*, 'The Queen goes to see new Britten opera', 9 June
   1953; *Le Figaro*, 10 June 1953; Scott Goddard, *News Chronicle*, 9 June 1953; Philip Hope-
   Wallace, *Manchester Guardian Weekly*, 11 June 1953; *Le Monde*, 10 June 1953; Ernest
   Newman, *The Sunday Times*, 14 June 1953; Joseph Newman, *New York Herald Tribune*,
   14 June 1953; Desmond Shawe-Taylor, *New Statesman and Nation*, 13 June 1953; James
   Thomas, *News Chronicle*, 'But the glitter was cold', 9 June 1953; *The Times*, 9 June 1953;
   Die Welt, 10 June 1953; Stephen Williams, *New York Times*, 9 and 14 June 1953

The Prince of the Pagodas   Felix Aprahamian, *The Sunday Times*, 6 January 1957; Cyril
   Beaumont, *The Sunday Times*, 6 January 1957; Martin Cooper, *Daily Telegraph*, 2 January
   1957; John Cranko, 'Making a Ballet – 1/2', *The Sunday Times*, 13/20 January 1957; Peter
   Heyworth, *Observer*, 6 January 1957; 'London Ballet Critic', *Manchester Guardian Weekly*,
   5 January 1957; Donald Mitchell, *Musical Times*, February 1957; *The Times*, 2 January 1957

Seven Sonnets of Michaelangelo   M. Kaindl-Hönig, *Salzburg Nachtrichten*, 3 March 1952

The Turn of the Screw   Felix Aprahamian, *The Sunday Times*, 19 September 1954; Eric Blom,
   Observer, 10 October 1954; Martin Cooper, *Daily Telegraph*, 15 September 1954; Riccardo
   Malipiero, *Il popolo*, 15 September 1954; Colin Mason, *Manchester Guardian*, 15 September
   1954; Ernest Newman, 'Some Don'ts for Librettists', *The Sunday Times*, 10 October 1954;
   Desmond Shawe-Taylor, *New Statesman and Nation*, 16 October 1954; Virgil Thomson,
   New York Herald Tribune, 26 September 1954; *The Times*, 16 September 1954

Winter Words   Ernest Bradbury, *Yorkshire Post*, 9 October 1953; Colin Mason, *Manchester Guardian Weekly*, 15 October 1953; *The Times*, 9 October 1953

OBITUARIES

Adams, David   *The Times*, 14 November 2000
Ash, Maurice   Roger Berthoud, *Independent*, 28 January 2003; Richard Boston, *Guardian*, 13 February 2003; *The Times*, 6 February 2003
Beriosova, Svetlana   Mary Clarke, Guardian, 12 November 1998; Clement Crisp, *Financial Times*, 12 November 1998; Nadine Mesiner, *Independent*, 13 November 1998; *The Times*, 13 November 1998
Blades, James   Graham Melville-Mason, *Independent*, 24 May 1999; *The Times*, 25 May 1999
Brain, Dennis   Benjamin Britten, *Tempo* 46 (winter 1957); Walter Legge, *Gramophone*, November 1957
Brainin, Norbert   Christopher Driver and Anne Inglis, *Guardian*, 11 April 2005; Philip Reed, *Guardian*, 19 May 2005
Dalberg, Frederick   *The Times*, 9 May 1988
Dolmetsch, Carl   *Daily Telegraph*, 15 July 1997; Shelagh Godwin, *Independent*, 14 July 1997
Farncombe, Charles   Anthony Hicks, *Guardian*, 19 August 2006; *The Times*, 2 August 2006
Fisher, James   *The Times*, 28 September 1970
Geddes, Pytt   *Daily Telegraph*, 21 March 2006
Gellhorn, Peter   Martin Anderson, *Independent*, 21 February 2004; John Calder and George Benjamin, *Guardian*, 16 February 2004; *Daily Telegraph*, 26 February 2004
Goldberg, Szymon   Margaret Campbell, *Independent*, 23 July 1993
Graham, Colin   Steuart Bedford, Keith Grant and Rodney Milnes, *Opera*, June 2007, pp. 664–8; Alan Blyth, *Guardian*, 10 April 2007; *Daily Telegraph*, 9 April 2007; Elizabeth Forbes, *Independent*, 11 April 2007; Vivien Schweitzer, *New York Times*, 9 April 2007; *The Times*, 9 April 2007
Hamburger, Paul   Leo Black, with Roger Vignoles, *Independent*, 21 April 2004; *Daily Telegraph*, 29 April 2004; Donald Mitchell, with Thomas Hemsley, *Guardian*, 29 April 2004; *The Times*, 22 April 2004
Hemmings, David   *Daily Telegraph*, 5 December 2003; Philip French, *Observer Review*, 7 December 2003; Tim Pulleine, *Guardian*, 5 December 2003; Philip Reed, *Guardian*, 11 December 2003; *The Times*, 5 December 2003; Tom Vallance, *Independent*, 5 December 2003
Hesse and the Rhine, Prince Ludwig of,   *The Times*, 1 June 1968
Hesse and the Rhine, Princess Margaret of   *Daily Telegraph*, 1 February 1997; Edward Mace, *Guardian*, 7 February 1997; Philip Mansel, *Independent*, 30 January 1997; *The Times*, 31 January 1997
Hurwitz, Emanuel   Margaret Campbell, *Independent*, 21 November 2006; Anne Inglis, *Guardian*, 20 November 2006
Leigh, Adèle   *Daily Telegraph*, 26 May 2004; *Guardian*, 18 June 2004; *The Times*, 29 May 2004
Malcolm, George   *Daily Telegraph*, 14 October 1997; *The Times*, 15 October 1997
Mayer, Tony   John Calder, *Independent*, 6 November 1997
Menuhin, Diana   Humphrey Burton, *Guardian*, 7 February 2003; *Daily Telegraph*, 29 January 2003; Nadine Meisner, *Independent*, 1 February 2003; *The Times*, 28 January 2003
Piper, Edward   Sylvia Clayton, *Guardian*, 14 May 1990; Reg Singh and Fay Weldon, *Independent*, 14 May 1990
Reiss, Stephen   Alan Blyth, *Opera*, February 2000, pp. 181–2; Ian Collins, *Guardian*, 14 October 1999; Elizabeth Forbes and Ian Collins, *Independent*, 19 October 1999; *The Times*, 13 October 1999

Rozsa, Suzanne   *Daily Telegraph*, 18 November 2005; Anne Inglis, *Guardian*, 17 November 2005

Sacher, Paul   Sibylle Ehrismann, *Guardian*, 27 May 1999; *Independent*, 27 May 1999; *Musical Times*, autumn 1999; *The Times*, 27 May 1999

Stuart, Campbell   *The Times*, 15 September 1972

Tausky, Vilem   Meirion Bowen, *Guardian*, 19 March 2004; *Daily Telegraph*, 18 March 2004; Graham Melville-Mason, *Independent*, 20 March 2004; *The Times*, 18 March 2004

Uppmann, Theodor   Alan Blyth, *Guardian*, 22 March 2005, and *Opera*, May 2005; *Daily Telegraph*, 19 March 2005; Elizabeth Forbes, *Independent*, 22 March 2005; Anthony Tommasini, *New York Times*, 19 March 2005; *The Times*, 23 March 2005

Valois, Ninette de   Peter Brinson, *Independent*, 9 March 2001; Mary Clarke and James Monahan, *Daily Telegraph*, 9 March 2001; *Guardian*, 9 March 2001

Woods, Robin   Michael De-la-Noy, *Guardian*, 23 October 1997; *The Times*, 24 October 1997; Alan Webster, *Independent*, 23 October 1997

Zander, Walter   Sir James Craig, *Independent*, 18 April 1993

Zorian, Olive   *The Times*, 18 May 1965

INDEXES

Compiled by Jill Burrows

As in the earlier volumes in this series, the index has been divided into three: an Index of Britten's Works, an Index of Other Composers and a General Index. As both Britten and Pears are constant presences on virtually every page, it has not proved useful or desirable to reference every element of their lives in their individual entries in the General Index, although a number of personality traits and recurring aspects of their lives are listed there. The reader might find it easier to trace an event or performance through one of the Works indexes or through an organization or a venue in the General Index.

Where a reference is to a plate or an illustration in the text and/or its caption, the entry appears in *italic* type. **Bold** type is used to show the recipient of a numbered letter and underlining indicates a major biographical annotation.

Abbreviations used in the indexes are as follows:

AF   Aldeburgh Festival
BB   Benjamin Britten
IOC Index of Other Composers
PP   Peter Pears

INDEX OF BRITTEN'S WORKS

Abelard and Heloise (unrealized opera or cantata project): 397
Albert Herring, Op. 39, 322, 500, 525; BB on, 574; casts and companies, 35, 39, 66, 88, 130–31, 478; composition, 4; dedication, 525; libretto, 1, 64; and PP, 142, 478; performances and productions, 8, 353: Glyndebourne (1947), 38–9, 257; AF (1953; 1957), 19, 132, 163, 177, 477–8, 493; Wiesbaden Festival (1953), 18, 88, 132, 142; National Opera Studio (1957), 574; Milan (1979–80), 369; publication, 38; reception and reviews, 88
Alpine Suite (1955): composition, 102, 211, 288, 374; dedication, 374; performance, 375
Am Stram Gram (theatre music; 1954), 215; composition, 172, 216; performance, 172, 216; reception and reviews, 216
Anna Karenina (unrealized project): 543
Antiphon, Op. 56b: composition, 433; performances, 434

Ballad of Little Musgrave and Lady Barnard, The, (1943): performances, 459
Beggar's Opera, The (Gay realization), Op. 43, 322; casts and companies, 35, 66–7, 553; and PP, 165–6; performances, 8, 166, 251, 500, 513, 553
Billy Budd, Op. 50, 322; analysis, 24–5, 275–6; 'Billy in the Darbies' (as concert item), 45; broadcast, 45; casts and companies, 21, 32–3, 39, 56, 138, 544; composition, 4–6, 12; dedication, 43; design, 41; extracts as concert items, 45; libretto, 1, 41, 44, 64; manuscript, 112; original version (four acts), 53, 56–7; play-throughs, 265; and PP, 28, 41, 66, 117–18, 497; productions and performances: Covent Garden (1951), 5, 8, 33, 44, 45, 52, 68; UK tour and Covent Garden (1952), 17, 36, 38, 41–2, 50, 56–7; Wiesbaden (1952; German-language premiere), 17, 41, 44, 52–6, 118; Paris (1952), 17, 63–4, 65, 66–7, 118, 275; NBC-TV ('Scenes from Billy Budd'; 1952), 18, 45, 542, 544; Cologne (1966), 118; BBC Television (1966), 556; Chicago (1970), 44; Hamburg (1972), 118; New York (1978), 118; reception and reviews, 31, 36, 53–4, 64, 66–7, 154–5, 161–3, 276; revised version (1960) two acts), 53, 57; and La Scala, Milan, 55; Vere's Epilogue (as concert item), 28
'Birds, The' (1934): recording, 537

Birthday Hansel, A, Op. 92: commission, 202, 540; composition, 202
Boy was Born, A, Op. 3: 'Corpus Christi Carol', 537; performances, 341, 352–3, 502; recording, 354, 493, 537; revisions, 288, 341, 354
Burning Fiery Furnace, The, Op. 77: bells, use of, 385; casts and companies, 543; composition, 375; dedication, 116; and Far Eastern musics, 405–6; and Gagaku theatre, 420; and Kabuki theatre, 420; libretto, 29; and Nō theatre, 417, 420; performances: Orford Church (AF; 1966), 543; translation, 201

Cabaret Songs, 320: 'Calypso', 320, 324, 325; 'Funeral Blues', 320, 324; 'Tell me the truth about love', 324–5, 334; performances, 320, 334–5; reception and reviews, 334; revision, 324, 325
Cantata Misericorium, Op. 69: analysis, 86; performances, 311, 441, 464; reception and reviews, 311; soloists, 463–4
Canticle I: 'My beloved is mine', Op. 40: analysis, 24; composition, 4
Canticle II: 'Abraham and Isaac', Op. 51: analysis, 24–5, 28, 294–5; BB on, 5, 23–4, 472; broadcast, 35; composition, 4–6, 17, 23; manuscript, 25; performances, 17, 24, 35–6, 287; and PP, 17, 21, 35, 37, 287, 493, 53; proposed string-orchestra version (unrealized), 28; publication, 36; reception and reviews, 35–6, 37; recording, 24, 28, 194, 493, 535, 537; soloists, 17, 21; staging, 472; text, 5, 23–4, 26–7; unauthorized orchestration, 28
Canticle III: 'Still Falls the Rain – The Raids, 1940, Night and Dawn', Op. 55: analysis, 294–5, 318; BB on, 6, 289, 316; composition, 4, 6, 287, 289, 291; manuscript, 292–3; and PP, 291, 294–5, 319; performances, 291, 294–5, 327, 454, 583; reception and reviews, 294–5, 316, 318; recording, 537, 583, 584; text, 289, 291, 294–5, 316; see also The Heart of the Matter
Ceremony of Carols, A, Op. 28: BB on, 566; composition, 196; performances, 73–4, 235; recording, 74, 73, 177, 179, 181
Charm of Lullabies, A, Op. 41: dedication, 67
'Children and Sir Nameless, The' (Hardy setting, 1953): 5n, 185
children's opera (Greek mythology theme; unrealized project): 2, 298–9, 302, 312–13

Church Parables, 29, 366; librettos, 2; Nō influence, 49–50, 416–17; percussion writing, 398; performances, 565, 581: Edinburgh Festival (1968), 416; City of London Festival (1968), 416; *see also* *The Burning Fiery Furnace*, *Curlew River* and *The Prodigal Son*

Company of Heaven, The (radio music; 1937): concert version, 315; performances, 315; publication, 315; scores, 315

Concerto for String Quartet and Orchestra (unrealized project): 513

Curlew River, Op. 71: bells, use of, 385; casts and companies, 543, 560; composition, 50, 299, 560; and Far Eastern musics, 414, 416; and Gagaku theatre, 420, 456; genesis, 3, 49–50, 299, 313, 532, 534; libretto, 29, 50, 166, 299, 416, 420, 534; and Nō theatre, 3, 414, 416–20; performances: Orford Church (AF; 1964), 543, 560; US (late 1960s), 517; translation, 201

Dark Valley, The (radio drama incidental music; 1940): 196

'Deaf Woman's Courtship, The' (folk-song arrangement, 1950s): performances, 24; and PP, 24

Death in Venice, Op. 88: casts and companies, 38, 45, 543; choreography, 38; composition, 201; and Far Eastern musics, 387, 397–8, 406; libretto, 2, 88; performances and productions; Snape Maltings (AF; 1973), 38, 543; Royal Opera House, Covent Garden (1992), 543

Five Flower Songs, Op. 47: 'Marsh Flowers', 385, 391; composition, 383; dedication, 383; performances, 383, 385, 391

Folk Song Arrangements: composition, 450, 494, 562, 577–8; performances, 46, 296, 348–9, 379, 406–7, 427, 433, 448, 528, 532, 578; and PP, 433, 448, 532, 578; reception and reviews, 411–12; recordings, 194, 578; vol. 1: British Isles: 'The Salley Gardens', 412; 'Oliver Cromwell', 412; vol. 2: France, 348–9; orchestral versions, 198; vol. 3: British Isles: 'The Miller of Dee', 412; vol. 4: Moore's *Irish Melodies*, 494, 577–8; 'How sweet the answer', 578; 'The minstrel boy', 578; vol. 6: England, for high voice and guitar: 'I Will Give My Love an Apple', 433, 450; 'The Soldier and the Sailor', 433, 450; 'The Shooting of His Dear', 433, 450, 451; *and see also* 'Deaf Woman's Courtship, The'

Four Sea Interludes from 'Peter Grimes', Op. 33a: recording, 440

Friday Afternoons, Op. 7: recording, 537

Gloriana, Op. 53, 323: BB on, 147, 165, 177, 196–7, 204, 214, 216–18, 228; broadcast(s), 147; casts and companies, 12, 21, 56, 61, 87–8, 90–1, 93, 126, 137–40, 189, 543; *Choral Dances from 'Gloriana'*, 168, 172, 202–3; choreography and dance element, 38, 90–1, 93–4, 118–19, 122–3, 189; composition, 1, 4, 13, 18, 36, 58, 88, 90–6, 99–100, 103–4, 106, 111–12, 120, 125, 130, 133–7, 179, 183, 299; and Coronation, 58–9, 62, 90–1, 107, 136, 139, 143–7, 148–9, 150–52; *Courtly Dances* (arr. Bream), 203; *Courtly Dances from 'Gloriana'*, 168, 200, 555; dedication, 58; extracts as concert items, 163, 166, 168, 203; fanfares, 144–5; *Five Courtly Dances from 'Gloriana'* for school orchestra (arr. Stone), 203; genesis, 17, 58, 62–3; libretto, 1–2, 18, 29, 49, 59, 62–3, 67, 74, 76, 78, 80–83, 84–5, 86–7, 90, 92, 95, 99–100, 103–4, 110–11, 117–19, 122–3, 128–30, 151, 155, 157, 160, 164–5, 173–4, 179, 188, 299; Lute Songs, *plate 14*; 12, 76, 78, 80, 84–5, 86, 129, 153, 157, 163, 168, 203; opus number, 58; and PP, *plates 10, 12, 14*; 12, 19, 62–4, 78–9, 91, 95, 112–13, 142–3, 150, 152, 155, 157–8, 163–4, 177, 202, 216–18; play-throughs, 98, 126, 129, 142–3; performances: Covent Garden (1953), *plates 9–16*; 2, 8–10, 19, 68, 87–8, 90–91, 93, 97, 118–19, 122, 126, 129, 138–40, 143–7, 148–9, 150–65, 177, 180, 280; tour to Southern Rhodesia (1953), 137–8; Covent Garden revival and tour (1954), 103, 138–9, 166, 168, 172, 188, 214, 216–18, 239; Cincinnati (1956), 433, 449–50, 455; Royal Festival Hall (concert; 1963), 168; Sadler's Wells (1966), 168, 219, 543; English National Opera (1984), 168; Opera North (1993), 168; and the press, 63, 142, 151–2; publication, 80, 112, 135, 145–6, 167, 168, 173, 200, 202–3; reception and reviews, 12, 138, 147, 150, 152–66, 177, 196–7, 200, 214, 218, 228, 276, 280–81, 449–50, 455; recordings, 168, 556; revisions, 166, 168, 172–3, 217–19; and La Scala, Milan, 55, 94, 203, 507, 509; scenario, 78, 79; *Second Lute Song of the Earl of Essex* (arr. I. Holst), 203; source material and research, 62–3, 78, 86, 93, 95, 111–12; *Symphonic Suite: 'Gloriana'*, Op. 53a, 171–2, 182, 200, 202–3, 238–9, 309, 312, 351

Golden Vanity, The, Op. 78: casts and companies, 543; libretto, 543; productions: Snape Maltings (AF; 1967), 543

Heart of the Matter, The (1956): performances, 356, 433, 459, 460; and PP, 433, 583; recordings, 454, 583; structure, 294, 453–4; choral arrangement of 'We are the darkness in the heat of the day' (arr. I. Holst), 454; shortened version (Pears), 454; *see also Three Songs from 'The Heart of the Matter'*

Holy Sonnets of John Donne, The, Op. 35: composition, 4; performances, 43, 459

Hymn to St Cecilia, Op. 27: dedication, 43

Hymn to St Peter, Op. 56a: composition, 288; performance, 341

'If it's ever spring again' (Hardy setting, 1953): 5n, 185

Illuminations, Les, Op. 18, 485; as ballet music, 39; manuscript, 557; performances, 39, 46, 412; and PP, 39, 412; reception and reviews, 36

Jubilate Deo in C (1961): composition, 540

King Lear (unrealized project): 44, 463

Lachrymae, Op. 48: composition, 6; performances, 46, 294; reception and reviews, 294

Lear, Edward: children's opera based on nonsense verse (unrealized project): 312–13

Let's Make an Opera: BB on, 47–8, 562, 564, 566; and EOG, 21, 30; casts and companies, 30, 95, 555, 567; performances and productions, 500: Lyric Theatre, Hammersmith (1951–52), 32–3,

INDEX OF BRITTEN'S WORKS

52, 95; High Wycombe Grammar School (1952), 32–3; Wimbledon Theatre (1952), 49–50; Taw and Torridge Festival (1953), 166; UK tour and London performances (1955), 338, 371–2; Ankara (1955), 369; Budapest (1956), 472; AF (1956), 555; Toronto (1957), 562, 567; play script, 64; reception and reviews, 52; *and see Little Sweep, The Lines on the Map* (radio incidental music; 1938): 101

Little Sweep, The, Op. 45; 'The Coaching Song', 48, 50; companion work for performance, 298; and Gathorne-Hardy family, 189, 519; libretto, 1, 64; performances, 8; recording, 221, 288, 568; *and see Let's Make an Opera*

Malaysian national anthem (abortive commission; 1957): 386, 493, 532–4; *see also Sketch for Malaya*
Mass (unrealized project for Leeds Festival): 493, 496, 498–500
Matinées Musicales, Op. 24: as ballet music, 39
Mea Culpa (unrealized project): 337
Midsummer Night's Dream, A, Op. 64: analysis, 86; *bel canto* parody, 219; casts and companies, 94, 138, 355, 517, 580; composition, 247, 560; dedication, 247; libretto, 2n; performances and productions: AF (1960), 38, 220, 247, 474, 560; Zagreb (1962), 517; and recorders, 211
Missa Brevis in D, Op. 63: dedication, 220; first performance, 72
Mont Juic, Op. 12 (with L. Berkeley): composition, 72

Night Mail (film music; 1936): 361
Nocturnal after John Dowland, Op. 70: composition, 6n; dedication, 450; structure, 6n
Nocturne, Op. 60: analysis, 86; composition, 499; dedication, 579; performances, 366, 457, 499; and PP, 499; texts, 454; translation, 201
Noye's Fludde, Op. 59: analysis, 24; bells, use of, 385; casts and companies, 223, 543, 555–6, 579–82; commission, 493; composition, 1, 494, 562, 577, 579, 582; dedication, 269; design, 512, 581; genesis and development, 562, 564–7, 580–82; libretto, 23, 563, 582; manuscript, 585; and PP, 581; productions: AF (1958), 519, 543, 555–6, 570, 577, 579–81; and recorders, 211; television broadcast (ATV; 1958), 566–7, 574, 577, 579–80; television documentary (BBC *Monitor*), 581; translation, 201

'Old friends are best' (revue song; 1955): composition, 288, 320, 334; performance, 288, 320, 334
On the Frontier (theatre music; 1938): 196
organ concerto (unrealized project): 198
Owen Wingrave, Op. 85: casts and companies, 543; genesis, 300; libretto, 2, 88; productions: BBC Television (1971), 300, 543; Royal Opera House, Covent Garden (1973), 543

Paul Bunyan, Op. 17: casts and companies, 543; libretto, 1; productions: Snape Maltings (AF; 1976), 543
Peter Grimes, Op. 33, 179, 281, 322; analysis, 249; BB on, 189; bells, use of, 385; casts and companies, 39, 88, 94, 138, 182, 187, 189, 192, 248, 326, 552, 580; composition, 4, 7, 509; extracts as concert items and mooted concert version, 239, 518–19; as influential work, 94; libretto, 1, 336, 509–10; and PP, 171, 178, 189–92, 239, 245, 497; productions: 8; Sadler's Wells (1945), 64; Covent Garden (1953, and revivals), 41, 45, 94, 138–9, 171, 178, 187–92, 197, 214, 498, 535, 553; Brussels (1954), 245; Netherlands Opera (1955), 326–7; Zagreb (1955), 353, 357, 360; Amsterdam (1956), 438; reception and reviews, 7, 154–5, 197, 278, 281, 326–7; recordings, 438–40; *see also Four Sea Interludes from 'Peter Grimes'*

Phaedra, Op. 93: composition, 28; dedication, 28; performances, 28
Phantasy, Op. 2: analysis, 21
Piano Concerto, Op. 13: dedication, 72
Plymouth Town (1931): composition, 3n
Prelude and Fugue, Op. 29: composition, 568
Prelude and Fugue on a Theme of Vittoria (1946): recordings, 438–9
Prince of the Pagodas, The, Op. 57: BB on, 496, 507, 518; casts and companies, 91, 311, 440–41, 508, 551; composition, 1, 3–4, 14, 260, 264, 288, 303, 332–4, 360, 391, 430, 433–6, 441, *442–3*, 444, 449–50, 454, 456, 458–9, 461, 465–6, 468, 470–71, 473, 487–8; dedication, 123, 524; and Far Eastern musics, 14, 307, 318, 333, 389, 391–2, 397–8, 430, 483, 485–6; genesis and scenario, 3, 257–8, 259, 260, 271, 486–7; manuscript, *442–3*, 461, 524; orchestration, 466; performances, 350, 474; Royal Opera House, Covent Garden (1957–60; 1989), *plates 49–52*; 8, 13n, 14, 264, 311, 332–3, 434–5, 438, 440, 444, 458, 467–8, 470–71, 473, 475–9, *480–81, 482–9*, 493, 507–8, 510, 518, 523, 551; Milan (1957), 475, 493, 507, 509, 519, 521–3, 525–6; New York (1957), 475, 557–8, 577; Munich (1958), 474; Stuttgart (1960, 1968), 474–5; Leningrad (1971–72), 475; AF (1988), 475; and PP, 13n, 477; and press, 171; publication, 518, 574; reception and reviews, 475, 482–6, 489, 507, 509; recordings, 475, 479, 493, 496–7, 523; revisions and cuts, 475, 493, 497, 523; royalties, 518–20; suites and concert extracts, 475, 512–14: *Pas de Six from 'The Prince of the Pagodas'*, 514; *Preludes and Dances from 'The Prince of the Pagodas'* (Norman Del Mar), 513; Suite for concert performance (Donald Mitchell and Mervyn Cooke), 475
Prodigal Son, The, Op. 81: casts and companies, 543; composition, 102, 375; libretto, 29; and Nō theatre, 417; performance: Orford Church (AF; 1968), 543

Rape of Lucretia, The, Op. 37, 322; casts and companies, 21–3, 35, 44, 66, 88, 131, 182, 192, 218, 247, 441, 517, 573, 580; composition, 22; libretto, 1, 43, 175, 336; performances and productions, 8, 350, 357, 371, 500: Glyndebourne (1946), 21, 64, 257, 573; AF (1954), 190; Geneva (1954), 245–6; Stratford, Ontario (1956), 549; Dubrovnik (1959), 360; AF (1959), 556; on tour, 254; and PP, 245–6; publication, 38; reception and reviews, 157, 276; translation, 43
Rejoice in the Lamb, Op. 30: arrangement/orchestration by Imogen Holst, 12, 17, 73; commission, 89; performances, 17, 73, *89*; reception and reviews, 31; recording, 331; text, 31

Rocking Horse Winner, The (radio drama incidental music; 1941): 196

Saint Nicolas, Op. 42: BB on, 566; performances, 166, 221, 288, 319, 328, 337, 472; and PP, 166, 221, 288, 472; recording, 221, 288, 310; soloists, 221; structure, 337, 562; text, 64
St Peter (unrealized oratorio project): 287, 334, 336–7, 433, 435–6, 438, 461, 473, 493, 509–10
Scherzo (1954): composition, 211; dedication, 211; publication, 211
Sechs Hölderlin-Fragmente, Op. 61: dedication, 201
Serenade, Op. 31: BB on, 5; and Dennis Brain, 68; composition, 5; performances, 68, 113, 312, 314, 349, 578; and PP, 5, 68, 113, 117, 314; soloists, 68; subject-matter, 5; text, 578
Seven Sonnets of Michelangelo, Op. 22: performances, 43, 46, 172, 348–9, 406–7, 411, 527; reception and reviews, 43, 411; recording, 172
Simple Symphony, Op. 4: 485
Sinfonia da Requiem, Op. 20, 514; and Japan, 407, 412; performances, 197, 412, 457, 549; recording, 171, 177, 181
Sinfonietta, Op. 1, 321: performance, 349
Six Metamorphoses after Ovid, Op. 49: BB on, 545; broadcast, 546; composition, 546; dedication, 546; performances, 545–6; publication, 546; soloists, 545–6; source material, 299
Sketch for Malaya (1957): 534
Soirées Musicales, Op. 9: as ballet music, 39
Songs from the Chinese, Op. 58: 'The Herd-Boy', 576; composition, 450, 494, 541, 575, 577; dedication, 201, 575; manuscript, 575; performances, 575; and PP, 575, 577; reception and reviews, 575; texts, 575
Songs and Proverbs of William Blake, Op. 74: dedication, 464; performances, 464, 522; soloists, 463–4
Spring Symphony, Op. 44, 321, 514; award for, 521; composition, 509; performances, 197, 498, 523; soloists, 21, 23, 523
String Quartet No. 1, Op. 25: manuscript, 557
String Quartet No. 2, Op. 36: dedication, 197–8; performances, 310
String Quartet No. 3, Op. 94: dedication, 116; performances, 193
Symphony for Cello and Orchestra, Op. 68: performances, 366

Tale of Mr Tod, The (unrealized project): 2, 48, 62, 298
This Way to the Tomb (theatre music; 1945): 175
Three Songs from 'The Heart of the Matter' (1956): composition, 433
Timpani Piece for Jimmy (1955), 362–5; composition, 341, 361; performance, 361; recording, 361
Tit for Tat (1931/1968): publication, 227; texts, 227
Turn of the Screw, The, Op. 54: 12-note 'Screw' theme, 231, 233, 244, 275–6, 282; analysis, 44, 275, 295, 318, 484; auditions, 171–2, 220–21, 222, 223; BB on, 218, 248, 256, 284, 289, 300–301, 314, 316, 559; bells, use of, 385; broadcasts, 8, 268, 272, 338, 542; casts and companies, 12, 21, 131, 138, 224, 226, 247, 252–4, 266, 272, 310, 319, 354, 535–6, 542–4, 558–60; character list, 205; commission, 62, 87, 137, 139, 177; composition, 1, 4, 6, 62, 137, 139, 172, 177, 182, 199, 214, 218, 223–4, 225, 230, 231, 232, 235–7, 240–44, 248, 250–52, 254, 256–8, 261, 262–3, 264–7, 509; and Far Eastern musics, 279, 389; film proposal, 88; introduction (Wigmore Hall, 1954), 272; Latin text, 10, 207, 208, 209; libretto, 1–2, 10, 88, 171, 174, 179, 188–9, 192, 199, 205–9, 216–17, 219–21, 230, 232–3, 235–7, 240–44, 248–9, 250, 251–2, 256–7, 261, 264–5, 272, 274–7, 279–80, 282–3, 300–301, 471, 558; 'Malo' song, 206–7, 223–4, 225, 226, 23; play-throughs, 2, 243, 256, 265; and PP, plates 17, 18, 20, 24, 25; 209, 240, 261, 266, 272, 274, 277, 279, 283–4, 532, 548–9; productions, 350, 353, 371, 440, 580; La Fenice, Venice (1954), plates 17, 19–25; 8, 87–8, 139, 172, 177, 226, 247, 252, 266, 272, 273, 296, 333; Sadler's Wells (1954), 266, 272, 280–84, 287, 296, 300; European tour (1955), 288, 318–19, 328; AF (1955), 288, 316, 319; Paris (1956), 371, 433, 459; Scala Theatre, London (1956), 39, 338, 434; Stratford, Ontario (1957), plate 18; 494, 496, 527, 535–6, 541–2, 544, 548–50, 552, 556; Berlin Festival (1957), 494, 532; Darmstadt (1957), 494, 559–60; Berlin Festival (1957), 561, 568, 577; Associated Rediffusion Television (1959), 544, 556, 567; Snape Maltings (AF; 1972), 543; Welsh National Opera (2000), 223; Prologue, 236, 238, 261, 262–3, 264–56; publication, 360–61; reception and reviews, 8, 125, 207, 268, 272, 274, 275–84, 296, 299–301, 319; recording, 221, 287, 296, 298, 310; rehearsal period (Aldeburgh), 172, 223–4, 251, 266–8; rights, 244; title, 188, 214, 220, 230, 232–3, 243; translation, 201, 471, 494, 558–60
Tyco the Vegan (unrealized project): 2, 17, 29, 36, 42, 46–50, 51, 52, 58, 62, 298

Variation on an Elizabethan Theme (1953): composition, 18, 106; and *Gloriana*, 106; performance, 19, 46, 104, 106, 115; recording, 106, 132, 163; *see also* Berkeley et al., *Variations on an Elizabethan Theme* (10C)
Variations on a Theme of Frank Bridge, Op. 10, 485; as ballet music, 38–9; composition, 568; performances, 351, 457
Violin Concerto, Op. 15: dedication, 38; manuscript, 557; performances, 68, 109–10; recording, 110; revisions, 109–10, 306–7; soloists, 109–10

War Requiem, Op. 66: analysis, 28; composition, 4, 337, 499; recording, 55; soloists and forces, 463, 573; texts, 464; translation, 201, 464
Wealden Trio, A: The Song of the Women (1930/1967): dedication, 331
Wedding Anthem, A (Amo Ergo Sum), Op. 46: dedication, 43
Winter Words, Op. 52: 'At Day-close in November', 186; 'Midnight on the Great Western', 184, 186, 228; 'Wagtail and Baby', 4, 18, 182, 184; 'The Little Old Table', 182, 184; 'The Choirmaster's Burial', 186; 'Proud Songsters', 182, 184, 185; 'At the Railway Station, Upway', 182–4, 186; 'Before Life and After', 183, 186, 228; analysis, 186; BB on, 6n, 177, 183–4, 204, 290; broadcast, 171, 182, 188; composition, 4–6, 18, 58, 171, 177, 182–5; dedication, 182; opus number, 58; order, 184; performances, 5n, 171, 182, 183, 186, 204, 228, 229, 261, 294, 305, 348–50, 379, 427, 532; and PP, 172, 182, 184,

228, 261, 296, 532; reception and reviews, 6n, 186, 204, 228, 350; recording, 171–2, 188; texts, 72, 177, *184*, 186; *see also* 'The Children and Sir Nameless', *and* 'If it's ever spring again'
World of the Spirit, The (radio music; 1938): publication, 315; recording, 315; scores, 315

Young Apollo, Op. 16: BB on, 556; commission, 557; composition, 557; dedication, 557; manuscript, 557–8; performances and broadcasts, 557; publication, 557
Young Person's Guide to the Orchestra, The, Op. 34, 322, 485; as ballet music, 39, 308; and Far Eastern musics, 389; performances, 412; recording, 440; text, 64

'Youth with the Red-Gold Hair, The' (incomplete Sitwell setting): 454

PURCELL REALIZATIONS

Chacony in G minor: performances, 348, 351–2, 551; publication 350, 352; recording, 352
Dido and Aeneas (with Imogen Holst): casts and companies, 39, 67; performances, 8; publication, 535–6, 560; translation, 558, 560
Suite of Songs from Orpheus Britannicus; performances, 46, 312, 349, 352; publication, 350, 352
'When Night her purple veil' (attrib. Purcell): performances, 464

INDEX OF OTHER COMPOSERS

Adam, Adolphe: *Giselle*, 483
Addison, John: *Divertimento* for brass, 115; *Serenade* for wind and harp, 115
Arne, Thomas: songs, 46
Arnold, Malcolm: Guitar Concerto, Op. 67, 506; *Rinaldo and Armida* (ballet music), 308; Second String Quartet, Op. 118, 506; Sinfonietta No. 1, Op. 48, 504, 506
Auric, Georges: *Caesar and Cleopatra* (film music), 108; *and see* Honegger et al., *La guirlande de Campra*

Bach, Johann Sebastian: *Art of Fugue* (arr. Isaacs), 115; B minor Mass, 466, 494, 496–7, 527–8; Brandenburg Concerto No. 1, 528; Brandenburg Concerto No. 3, 528; Brandenburg Concerto No. 4, 528; Brandenburg Concertos, 573; Cantata No. 55, 131; Cantata No. 56, 467; Cantata No. 110, 466; Cantata No. 140, 467; Cantata No. 145, 143; Cantata No. 160, 125; Cantata No. 171, 466; Cantata No. 189, 125; cantatas, 29, 181, 330–31, 464; cello suites, 515; *Christmas Oratorio*, 476; organ music, 516; *St John Passion*, 172, 190, 494, 514–15, 528; *St Matthew Passion*, 341, 424, 426–7, 467, 524, 527–8; Violin Concerto in E major, 528
Bartók, Béla: *Duke Bluebeard's Castle*, 113; Sonata for two pianos and percussion, 114–15, 290; string quartets, 310
Beethoven, Ludwig van: *An die ferne Geliebte*, 134, 166; piano trio, 517; songs, 125
Bellini, Vincenzo: *Norma*, 93–4
Benjamin, Arthur: *Jamaican Rumba*, 320, 324
Berg, Alban: *Lulu*, 200, 204; *Wozzeck*, 277–8
Berkeley, Lennox: *A Dinner Engagement*, 8n, 141, 172, 190, 193, 254–6, 338, 371, 373; *Mont Juic* (with BB), 72; *Nelson*, 109, 124, 126–7, 127, 129, 254, 256; *Ruth*, 512, 538, 555; songs, 288; *Songs of the Half-light*, 449; *Stabat Mater*, 89, 163; *Variations on a Hymn-tune of Orlando Gibbons*, Op. 35, 71–2, 115
Berkeley, Lennox, et al.: *Variations on an Elizabethan Theme*, 18, 19, 104–7, 114, 132, 163, 304–5
Berkeley, Michael: *Wessex Graves*, 72
Berlioz, Hector: arias, 213; *Les Troyens* (*The Trojans*), 457
Bizet, Georges: arias and ensembles, 213

Bliss, Arthur: Piano Concerto, 290; Piano Sonata, 290
Bloch, Ernest: string quartet(s), 310
Blow, John: songs, 254; *Venus and Adonis*, 353, 355, 371, 555
Boughton, Rutland: *The Immortal Hour*, 283
Brahms, Johannes: songs, 414, 464
Bridge, Frank: Piano Trio No. 2 (1929), 179, 517; songs, 288, 348
Buxtehude, Dietrich: *The Last Judgement*, 555
Byrd, William: 'Sellinger's Round' (keyboard version), 105–6

Caccini, Giulio: 'Amarilli mia bella' (*La nuove musiche*), 536
Cardew, Cornelius: 'Why cannot the ear be closed to its own destruction?', 516
Copland, Aaron: folk-song arrangements, 125, 134; *Quiet City*, 506

Dalayrac, Nicolas: arias and ensembles, 213
Debussy, Claude: arias, 213; *Pelléas et Mélisande*, 44; 'Poissons d'or', 134; 'Reflets dans l'eau', 134; *Suite bergamasque*, 512
Delius, Frederick: Sonata for cello and piano, 558
Dohnányi, Ernö: Suite in F sharp minor, 94
Donizetti, Gaetano: *Lucia di Lammermoor*, 218–19, 525
Dowland, John: 'Come, heavy sleep', 6; 'Flow my tears', 6; 'If my complaints could passions move', 6; songs, 45, 254, 406–7, 497; 'Two Pieces' for orchestra, 45

Eastwood, Thomas: 'At Baia', 506; *Christopher Sly*, 505; String Trio, 505
Elgar, Edward: *The Dream of Gerontius*, 517

Farnaby, Giles: 'Tower Hill', 211
Finzi, Gerald: Hardy settings, 184
Ford, Thomas: songs, 497
Fricker, Peter Racine: Concertante No. 1 for cor anglais and strings, 504–6

Gay, John, and John Christopher Pepusch: *The Beggar's Opera*, 35, 66–7, 165–6, 251; *see* realization by BB (Index of Britten's Works)

INDEX OF OTHER COMPOSERS

German, Edward: *Merrie England*, 86, 150, 154–5
Gluck, Christoph Willibald von: *Alceste*, 157; *Iphigénie en Tauride*, 98; *Orfeo ed Euridice*, 139, 193
Goehr, Alexander: 'Narration', 516
Gounod, Charles: arias and ensembles, 213
Grétry, André: arias and ensembles, 213
Grieg, Edvard: songs, 125, 134
Gruber, Franz: *O du fröhlicher!*, 202

Hamilton, Ian: *Anna Karenina*, 543; *The Royal Hunt of the Sun*, 543
Handel, George Frideric: *Acis and Galatea*, 219; choral music, 319; *Messiah*, 22, 113, 517, 556; *Music for the Royal Fireworks*, 555; *Samson*, 433, 459; songs, 46, 296; 'Where'er you walk', 221
Haydn, Joseph: concertos, 433, 459; Horn Concerto No. 2 in D, 309, 504, 506; Notturno No. 2 in C, 436; Notturno No. 4 in F, 437; *The Seven Last Words from the Cross*, 37; songs and canzonets, 348, 379, 427, 532; string quartets, 573; symphonies, 433, 459; Symphony No. 45, 132; Symphony No. 55, 132
Henze, Hans Werner: *The Bassarids*, 559; *Elegy for Young Lovers*, 140, 463; *Der junge Lord*, 559; *Kammermusik 1958*, 449
Hindemith, Paul: *Ludus Tonalis*, 290
Holst, Gustav: Double Concerto, 309; *Fugal Concerto*, 114–15; *The Planets*, 355, 361, 366; *Sāvitri*, 8, 247, 353, 355, 371, 555; songs, 288; *The Wandering Scholar*, 8, 30
Honegger, Arthur, et al.: *La guirlande de Campra*, 106

Ireland, John: *The Forgotten Rite*, 267; *London Overture*, 267; Piano Concerto, 267; *These Things Shall Be*, 267

Janáček, Leoš: Concertino, 506; *From the House of the Dead*, 141; *Jenůfa*, 457; operas, 543

Lesur, Daniel: *see* Honegger et al., *La guirlande de Campra*

McPhee, Colin: *Balinese Ceremonial Music*, 388–90, 392; *Tabuh-tabuhan*, 397
Mahler, Gustav: *Das Lied von der Erde*, 22–3, 193, 523
Manuel, Roland: *see* Honegger et al., *La guirlande de Campra*
Martin, Frank: Concerto for seven wind instruments, timpani and strings, 309; *Inter Arma Caritas*, 311; *Sechs Monologe aus Jedermann*, 311; *Der Sturm*, 311, 444; *Le Vin herbé*, 311
Massenet, Jules: arias and ensembles, 213
Messager, André: *Fortunio*, 213; *Isoline*, 213; *Véronique*, 213
Messiaen, Olivier: *Sept haïkaï*, 456; *Turangalîla-symphonie*, 456
Milhaud, Darius: *La Création du monde*, 436–8
Monteverdi, Claudio: *Il ballo delle ingrate*, 577–8; *Il combattimento di Tancredi e Clorinda*, 220
Morley, Thomas: canzonets and songs, 23, 194, 497
Mozart, Wolfgang Amadeus: arias and songs, 28, 125, 131, 261; chamber music, 433, 459; concertos, 433, 459; Concerto in E flat for two pianos (K. 365), 348, 459; *Così fan tutte*, 44–5; *Don Giovanni*, 44–5, 256–7; Horn Concerto in E (K. 494a) (fragment), 504–6; horn concertos, 584; Horn Quintet in E flat (K. 407), 536; *Idomeneo*, 46, 543; Masonic Cantata (K. 619), 134; *Le nozze di Figaro*, 138–9; operas, 45–6, 98, 181; Piano Concerto in A major, (K. 414), 132; piano trio, 517; Quintet in E flat (K. 452), 166; Serenade in C minor (K. 388), 437; Serenade in D (K. 250) (Haffner), 428; symphonies, 433, 459; Symphony No. 33 in B flat, 506; violin concertos, 310; *Die Zauberflöte (The Magic Flute)*, 44, 218, 332–3, 357, 457, 478, 496
Musorgsky (Mussorgsky), Modest: *Boris Godunov*, 158, 281; 'The Seminarist', 209

Nuttall, Michael: 'A Cradle Song', 516

Oldham, Arthur: *Bonne-Bouche*, 57; *The Commandment of Love*, 89; *Love in a Village*, 91, 94, 254–6; songs, 288; *and see* Berkeley, Lennox, et al., *Variations on an Elizabethan Theme*

Pérotin: *Beata viscera*, 320
Poulenc, Francis: *6 Improvisations*, 212; *Aubade: concerto choréographique*, 437–8; Cello Sonata, 213; Concerto for Two Pianos, 108, 287, 307; *Dialogues des Carmélites*, 131, 218, 258, 369, 457, 528–9, 531; Flute Sonata, 213; *Les Mamelles de Tirésias*, 94, 213, 528–9, 530, 530–31, 555, 577–8; songs, 213; *Stabat Mater*, 530; *and see* Honegger et al., *La guirlande de Campra*
Prokofiev, Sergey: *War and Peace*, 543
Puccini, Giacomo: *La Bohème*, 138–9; *Madama Butterfly*, 44; *Tosca*, 414; *Turandot*, 219
Purcell, Henry: Chacony in G minor, 46, 349–52, 551; choral music, 319, 354; 'Corydon and Mopsa', 194; *Dido and Aeneas*, 8, 39, 168, 220, 247, 304, 535–6, 558, 560; songs, 46, 254, 296, 349–50, 352, 406–7, 527; *Timon of Athens*, 210; 'When Night her purple veil' (attrib. Purcell), 464; *see also* Index of Britten's Works: Purcell Realizations

Rainier, Priaulx: *Cycle for Declamation*, 115, 348–9
Ravel, Maurice: arias, 213; *L'Enfant et les sortilèges*, 278
Reimann, Aribert: *Lear*, 463
Rimky-Korsakov, Nikolay: *Le Coq d'or (The Golden Cockerel)*, 483
Rosseter, Philip: songs, 254, 497

Sammartini, Giuseppe: cello sonata, 69
Sauguet, Henri: *see* Honegger et al., *La guirlande de Campra*
Schemelli, Georg Christian: *Geistliche Lieder*, 536, 541; *Musikalisches Gesang-Buch*, 541; *Praeludium*, 541
Schubert, Franz: 'Der Hirt auf dem Felsen', 166; Fantasie in C (D. 934), 528; Impromptu in A flat, 134; Impromptu in G flat, 134; *Lieder*, 23, 43, 46, 254, 296, 348, 379, 406–7, 427, 464, 527, 532; 'Nacht und Träume', 228; *Die schöne Müllerin*, 40, 288, 318, 381, 384, 387; 'Sprach der Liebe', 228; String Quintet in C major, 384; Symphony No. 5 in B flat, 309; 'Trout' Quintet, 319; *Die Winterreise*, 462–4, 512
Schumann, Robert: Adagio and Allegro, in A flat,

INDEX OF OTHER COMPOSERS

Op. 70, 584; Andante and Variations, for two pianos, 348; *Dichterliebe*, 381, 384, 407; *Lieder*, 348, 427; *Szenen aus Goethes 'Faust'*, 464
Searle, Humphrey: *Aubade*, 309, 312; *Put Away the Flute*, 312; *and see* Berkeley, Lennox, et al., *Variations on an Elizabethan Theme*
Shostakovich, Dmitri: *Seven Blok Romances*, 573
Skalkottas, Nikos: *Six Sketches* for string orchestra, 309
Slade, Julian: *Salad Days*, 320
Strauss, Johann, II: *Die Fledermaus*, 44; *Der Zigeunerbaron*, 350
Strauss, Richard: *Ariadne auf Naxos*, 45; *Die Frau ohne Schatten*, 55; *Der Rosenkavalier*, 55, 139
Stravinsky, Igor: Cantata, 192; *Capriccio*, 290; Concerto in E flat ('Dumbarton Oaks'), 506; Concerto for Piano and Wind Instruments, 290; *Duo Concertant*, 310; *Firebird* suite, 551; *In Memoriam Dylan Thomas*, 555; *The Rake's Progress*, 8, 131; *The Soldier's Tale*, 125
Sullivan, Arthur: *The Mikado*, 427; *The Yeoman of the Guard*, 304

Tailleferre, Germaine: *Le petit navire*, 213; *and see* Honegger et al., *La guirlande de Campra*
Tchaikovsky, Piotr Ilyich: *Eugene Onegin*, 44, 98; *The Nutcracker* (*Casse-Noisette*) (ballet and suite), 482, 514; Piano Concerto No. 1, 54; *Pique Dame* (*The Queen of Spades*), 123; *The Sleeping Beauty*, 482–4; songs and arias, etc., 28, 261; *Swan Lake*, 483, 489, 518–19
Telemann, Georg Phillipp: Suite in F, for two horns and strings, 506
Thomson, Virgil: *Four Saints in Three Acts*, 66
Tippett, Michael: *Boyhood's End*, 108, 134, 287, 303–4; *Divertimento on 'Sellinger's Round'*, 107, 304–5, 309; *The Heart's Assurance*, 108, 125, 134, 291; *King Priam*, 140; *The Midsummer Marriage*, 108, 139–40, 218, 287, 304–6; Piano Sonata No. 1, 290; *Songs for Achilles*, 449; String Quartet No. 2, 310; String Quartet No. 3, 310; Symphony No. 2, 108; *and see* Berkeley, Lennox, et al., *Variations on an Elizabethan Theme*

Vaughan Williams, Ralph: *Five Mystical Songs*, 554; folk-song arrangements, 125, 134; *On Wenlock Edge*, 515; *A Sea Symphony*, 554
Verdi, Giuseppe: *Aida*, 138, 155, 445; arias, etc., 28, 261; *Un ballo in maschera*, 93–4, 140, 369; *Falstaff*, 1; *Messa di Requiem*, 4n; operas, 45–6; *Otello*, 1; *La traviata*, 98
Vivaldi, Antonio: *The Four Seasons*, 528

Wagner, Richard: *Die Meistersinger von Nürnberg*, 44, 349–51, 457, 496–7, 508; *Das Rheingold*, 497; *Tristan und Isolde*, 55
Walton, William: *Anon in Love*, 449; *Façade*, 192, 254, 255, 289, 327–8, 338; *Hamlet* (film music), 469; *Henry V* (film music), 469; March: *Orb and Sceptre*, 107; National Anthem, arrangement of, 145, 151–2; *Richard III* (film music), 469; Te Deum, 107; *Troilus and Cressida*, 56, 66, 98, 107, 287, 291, 305, 307, 313, 538; Violin Concerto, 551; *and see* Berkeley, Lennox, et al., *Variations on an Elizabethan Theme*
Warlock, Peter: folk-song arrangements, 125, 134
Weelkes, Thomas: choral music, 354
Wellesz, Egon: *Incognita*, 248
Wilbye, John: 'Happy, O Happy He', 79; 'Sweet Honey-sucking Bees', 413
Williams, Grace: folk-song arrangements, 125, 134
Williamson, Malcolm: 'The Fly', 516; Piano Sonata, 502
Wolf, Hugo: songs, 532

GENERAL INDEX

Abbey Theatre, Dublin, *see* Dublin: Abbey Theatre
Abraham and Isaac (Chester miracle play), 24
Académie Royale des Sciences, des Lettres, et des Beaux-Arts, Brussels, 521, 523
Academy of St Martin in the Fields, 220
Accademia Nazionale Cherubini, 521
Accademia Nazionale di Santa Cecilia, 522
Actors' Studio, New York, 469
Ad Familiares (periodical), 207
Adam, Adolphe: *see* 10C
Adams, David, 351, 352
Adaskin, John, 557–8
Adaskin, Naomi, 557–8
Addison, John, 114, 115; *and see* 10C
Adeney, Richard, 498
Adler, Peter, 544
Aeolian Quartet, 573
Afghanistan, 381
Agra, 370, 373, 376, 380, 382; Red Fort, 377, 379–80; Taj Mahal, 370, 373, 376, 378, 380–82
Airs on a Shoestring (revue), 320–23
Aix-en-Provence, 66, 74, 81; Cour de l'Hôtel de Ville, 46, 76, 77
Aix-en-Provence Festival, 76, 77, 106; PP–BB recital, 42, 46, 66, 77, 81
Ajunta, 424
Akbar the Great, 378, 380–81
Alberta, 553
Alde, River, 247
Aldeburgh: East Suffolk Hotel, 193, 239; floods (1953), 53; Jubilee Hall, 177, 180, 239, 247, 255, 400, 468, 477–8, 505, 516, 528, 560, 584; Moot Hall, 193, 239; public tennis courts, *plate 26*; Wentworth Hotel, 24, 438, 468
Aldeburgh Baptist Chapel, 30, 164
Aldeburgh Carnival and Regatta, 175–6, 268
Aldeburgh-Deutsch, 202
Aldeburgh Festival, 8, 97, 101, 109–10, 198, 220, 228, 289, 307, 371, 500, 505, 539–40, 581, 584; 1948: 352, 478; 1951: 13, 89, 177, 220, 546; 1952: 12–13, 17, 24, 41, 49, 67, 72–4, 311, 449; 1953: 19, 104, 106–7, *107*, 114–15, 125, 132, 163, 166, 177; 1954: 8n, 172, 181, 192, 212–13, 238, 247–8, 258, 511; 1955: 107, 181, 218, 239, 288, 304, 309, 316, 328, 337, 352, 375, 391; 1956: 126, 132, 348, 355–6, 399, 433, 436–8, 447, 453–4, 459, 461, 505, 529, 555, 583–4; 1957: 464, 477, 493, 504, 506, 516–17, 526–8, 531–2, 534, 555; 1958: 94, 108, 113, 115, 375, 464, 528–9, 538, 541, 555–6, 562, 568, 570–71, 573, 575, 577–8, 580–81; 1959: 464; 1960: 94, 126, 220, 474, 517, 560; 1961: 573; 1962: 115, 53; 1963: 179, 464, 517; 1965: 375, 464; 1967: 145, 512; 1968: 573; 1969: 46, 247; 1970: 46, 247; 1972: 464, 512; 1973: 46, 556; 1974: 513; 1975: 45; 1976: 28; 1979: 557; 1983: 221; 1994: 246; 1998: 220; finances and fund-raising, 197, 201, 227, 305, 468, 522; management and officers, 13, 29, 42, 43, 64, 131, 178, 239, 246, 385, 391, 399–400, 429, 462, 465, 500–503, 507, 509, 543, 565, 569–72; *see also* Hesse Memorial Lecture *and* Hesse Students Scheme
Aldeburgh Festival Calendar (1954), 190, *191*, 192
Aldeburgh Festival Choir, 72–4
Aldeburgh Festival Chorus, 288
Aldeburgh Festival Club, 247, 540
Aldeburgh Festival Council, 247, 465
Aldeburgh Festival Friends, 130, 131, 373
Aldeburgh Festival Orchestra, 19, 72–3, 288, 528, 572
Aldeburgh Festival Programme Books, 74, 142, 180–81, 202, 212, 220, 247, 512, 516, 527
Aldeburgh Festival Theatre (unrealized project), 180–81, 195, 197, 247, *253*, 314, 399–400, 468, 501–2
Aldeburgh Foundation, 201
Aldeburgh Music Club, 70, 101, 210–11, 373, 375, 382, 384
Aldeburgh October Britten Festival (1994), 213
Aldeburgh Parish Church, 72–3, 181, 288, 319, 433
Aldeburgh Soundings (periodical), 180, 202
Aldeburgh Town Council, 247
Alexander, John, 450
Alexander, Peter F., 48, 60, 62, 81, 86, 104, 143, 147, 165, 174, 175, 239, 298–9, 313, 420, 532
Alford, Violet, 3n
All Hallows (school), Somerset, 330, 347, 395, 411
Alleyn's School boys' choir, 523
All-India Radio, 375, 397, 427
Alston, Richard, 310, 513
Alwyn, Kenneth, 479
Amadé, Raymond, 213
Amadeus String Quartet, 115, 190, 192, 310, 319, 372, 433, 459, 502, 513
Amadeus Scholarship Fund, 311
Ambassadors Theatre, London, 375

America, United States, of, 39, 136–7, 495–6, 517, 554, 558, 583; government of, 49, 474; *see also* US Embassy, London, *and individual locations*
American Academy of Arts and Letters, 522, 540
Amis, John, 120, 310, 323
Amityville, Long Island, 192, 495
Amsterdam, 132, 136, 341, 343–5, 572; American Hotel, 345; Concertgebouw, 348, 440, 475; *Peter Grimes*, 326–7, 438, 440; PP–BB recitals/concerts, 296, 345, 347; *The Turn of the Screw*, 328
Anderson, Martin, 141
Anderson, Zoë, 558
Andrewes, John, 518, 519, 522
Andy Pandy (BBC Television), 30
Ankara, 341, 353, 367–70, 373, 376; PP–BB recital, 370
Ankara Radio, 370
Ansbach Bachwoche (Bach Festival), 266, 328, 330, 494, 528; and PP, 266, 328, 330, 371, 462–3, 465–7, 494, 515, 527–8, 536
Ansermet, Ernest, 246, 311, 440, **441**, 444, 456, 458; *Les fondements de la musique dans la conscience humaine*, 444
Ansermet, Mme, 246, 441
Anthony, Trevor, 127, 581
Antigone (ballet), 508
Antonioni, Michelangelo, 227
Antwerp: PP–BB recital, 305
Apocrypha, 336–78
Apollinaire, Guillaume: *Les Mamelles de Tirésias*, 529
Aprahamian, Felix, 277, 484
Arbeau, Thoinot, 95–6; *Orchésographie*, 95–6
Archibald, William, 232; *The Innocents*, 232
Arden, John, 538
Arion (story), 299, 302
Arne, Thomas: *see* 10C
Arnhem: *The Turn of the Screw*, 328
Arnold, Malcolm, 308, 506; *and see* 10C
Art of Theodor Uppman, The (CD recording), 45
Arts Council, 154, 195, 501, 503, 507, 535, 543; officers, 82, 97
Arup Associates (architects), 247
Asahi Shimbun (newspaper, Tokyo), 411
Ash, Maurice, 535, 540
Ash, Ruth, 540
Ashbridge, Bryan, 484
Ashkenazy, Vladimir, 475
Ashley, Edwina, *see* Mountbatten of Burma, Lady Edwina,
Ashton, Frederick, 37, 38–9, 90, 93, 122–3, 256, 308, 483, 508; and *Albert Herring*, 38; and *Death in Venice*, 38
Ashton, Roy, 478
Aspen, Colorado, 126
Associated Rediffusion (television company), 493, 544, 556, 562, 564–7
Associated Television, *see* ATV
Association of Art Circles of Indonesia, 445
Atatürk, Kemal, 367–8, 369
Athens, 132, 248
Athens Conservatory, 248
Atlantis Verlag (publishing house), 244
Atlee, Clement, 427
ATV (Associated Television), 565–7
Auckland, University of, 332
Auden, W. H. (Wystan Hugh), 1, 8n, 66, 163–4, 164, 192, 302, 516; at Aldeburgh, 19, 164, 177; and *Cabaret Songs*, 320, 334–5; *The Dark Valley*, 196; 'The Hero in Modern Poetry', 164; 'The Musée des Beaux Arts', 302; *On the Frontier* (with Christopher Isherwood), 196
Audincourt, 526
Aulnoy, Madame d', 260, 484; *Serpentin Vert* (*The Green Serpent*), 260, 484
Auric, Georges, 106, 108, 213; *and see* 10C
Aurunjabad, 424
Auschwitz (concentration camp), 457
Australia, 332, 393
Austria, 17, 78, 346, 350, 425; *see also individual locations*
Avignon, France, 77
AXIS (periodical), 88
Azaria, Victor, 216

Bach, Johann Christian, 126
Bach, Johann Sebastian, 29, 126, 181, 261, 329–32, 459, 464, 476, 498, 514, 516, 528; Gesellschaft Edition, 498; *and see* 10C
Backhouse, Rhoda, 382, 384
Baden-Baden, 474, 536, 541; PP–BB recital, 474
Badings, Henk, 126
Baily, Leslie, 58
Baines, Francis, 319
Baker, Emma, 450
Baker, Janet, 28, 116; and *Phaedra*, 28
Baksic (Yugoslavian conductor; spelling uncertain), 357
Balcon, Michael, 88
Bali, *plates 30–32*; 333, 342, 379, 385, 387, 390, 392, 395–6, 399–403, 405, 407, 420, 429; *see also individual locations*
Bali: cremation rite, 385, 389
Bali: shadow plays, 385, 390, 392
Balinese dance, 385–7, 390, 395, 402
Balinese music, 14, 388–9, 391, 395, 402, 416
Balinese painting, 386
Ballet Club, 256
Ballet Rambert, 501–3
Ballets Jooss, 475
Ballets de Paris, 39
Ballets Russes, 475
Balliol College, Oxford, 246
Bandung, 342, 388, 392
Banff Centre, Calgary, 115
Bang (Nellie Hudson's cat), *plate 5*
Bangkok, 342, 403, 407, 409–11, 420
Bank of England, 561
Banks, Paul, 106, 512
Bantry Bay, Count Cork, 136
Barber (doctor), 176, 188
Barbara of Prussia, Princess, 199, 202, 266–7
Barbirolli, John, 566–7
Barclay's Bank, Aldeburgh, 178
Bardgett, Herbert, 498
Bärenreiter (music publisher), 436
Barnstaple, 165–6, 256, 435; *The Beggar's Opera*, 166
Barnstaple: Queen's Hall, 256, 261
barong (Balinese mythical creature), 405
Barrington, Christopher (Kit), 344, 347, 405
Bartók, Béla, 114–15, 125, 278, 310, 352, 448, 528; *and see* 10C
Barton, Francis, 235
Basel, 526

GENERAL INDEX

Basil, Wassily de, 289
Basil Douglas Ltd, 570–72
Bath: *Let's Make an Opera*, 372; Theatre Royal, 372
Bavaria, 465
Bavaria, Franz, Duke of, 199, 202
Bavarian Radio Symphony Orchestra, 457
Bavarian Staatsoper, 463
Bawan, Timir, 375
Baxter, Beverly, 154–5
Bayliss, Stephen, 151
Bayreuth Festival, 463, 575
Bayswater, London, 39, 126
BBC (British Broadcasting Corporation), 256, 309, 311, 361, 436–7, 513–14, 584; personnel, 72, 101, 115–16, 540, 569; *and see individual programmes and services*
BBC Artium (record label), 22
BBC Chorus, 141, 315, 498
BBC Concert Orchestra, 141
BBC Features Department, 101
BBC Home Service, 120, 497
BBC Legends (record label), 504, 517, 584; 'Britten the Performer' series, 584
BBC Midland Chorus, 203
BBC Midland Home Service, 515; *Canticle II*, 35; *Choral Dances from 'Gloriana'*, 172, 203
BBC National Programme: *The Company of Heaven*, 315; *The World of the Spirit*, 315
BBC Philharmonic Orchestra, 315
BBC Promenade Concerts, 267, 514; *Les Illuminations*, 39
BBC Radio 3, 116, 454, 584; *The Heart of the Matter*, 454
BBC Radio 4, 324
BBC Scottish Symphony Orchestra, 220
BBC Sound Archive, 504
BBC Symphony Orchestra, 140, 457, 499, 514
BBC Television, 21, 30, 371–2, 567, 581; *Billy Budd*, 556; *Owen Wingrave*, 543
BBC Third Programme, 101, 115, 238, 497; *Billy Budd*, 45, 57; *Canticle II*, 35; *Gloriana*, 147; *The Rape of Lucretia*, 22; *The Turn of the Screw*, 8, 172, 272, 280, 338; *Variations on an Elizabethan Theme*, 19, 106; *Winter Words*, 182, 188
BBC Transcription Service, 454, 583–4; *The Heart of the Matter*, 454, 583
BBC Wales, 22
BBC World Service, 534
BBC2 Television: *Idomeneo*, 46
BEA (British European Airways), 132
Bean T. C. (Royal Festival Hall), 198–9
Beard, Kenneth, 434
Beaton, Cecil, 10n, 39, 144, 174
Beaumont, C. W., 96
Beaumont, Cyril, 484
Beauty and the Beast (ballet), 260
Beauvais, 459
Beaverbrook, Lord, 10n
Bedford, David, 35, 37
Bedford, Lesley, 5, 35, 35
Bedford, Steuart, 35, 45, 544, 557
Beecham, Adrian, 193
Beecham, Thomas, 110, 517
Beethoven, Ludwig van, 125, 517; *and see* IOC
Begh, Idris, 428
Behrend, George, 71, 198, 228–9, 228, **452**; *An Unexpected Life*, 198, 228

Behrend, John Louis (Bow), 197, 228, 452
Behrend, Mary, 6n, 64, 66, 96, 124, 135, **197**, 197, **227–8**, 291, 528
Beinum, Eduard van, 440
Beirut, 341, 370, 376, 425
Belfast, University of, 521
Belfort, 526
Belgium, 37, 266, 298; PP–BB recitals, 287, 296, 305, 313
Belgrade, 341, 356–7, 359–61, 367; Hotel Moscow, 357, 361; PP–BB recital, 358
Bell, George, Bishop of Chichester, 353, 356
Bellini, Vincenzo: *see* IOC
Belsen (concentration camp), 110, 457
Benesh, Joan, 461
Benesh, Rudolf, 461; *An Introduction to Benesh Dance Notation*, 461
Bengal, Bay of, 422
Benjamin, Arthur, 320, 324; *and see* IOC
Benjamin, George, 141
Bennett, Alan, 323
Bennett, Edwin Keppel (Francis), 535, 540–41
Bennett, Richard Rodney, 211
Benny (Danish boy singer), 181
Benois (scenic department, La Scala), 523
Bentwaters, RAF, 554
Berg, Alban, 282, 308, 463; *and see* IOC
Beriosova, Svetlana, *plate 51*; 91, 308, 477, 482–4, 507, 508, 522
Berkeley, Freda, 72
Berkeley, Lennox, 8, 17, 18, **71–2**, 72, **104–5**, 109, **162–3**, 210–11, **254–5**, 288, 371, 373, 449; *and see* IOC
Berkeley, Michael, 72, 106, 108; *and see* IOC
Berlin, 33, 115, 117–18, 125, 462, 467, 505, 531, 559, 561, 568; political situation, 30–31; PP–BB recitals, 466, 532; *The Turn of the Screw*, 561–2, 568, 577
Berlin (West): Deutsches Oper, 351, 559
Berlin Festival, 494, 568, 570
Berlin Philharmonic Orchestra, 125
Berlioz, Hector, 158, 213; *and see* IOC
Bernadic, Drago, 357
Bernanos, Georges: *Dialogues des Carmélites*, 531
Bernard, James, 211
Bernstein, Leonard, 352
Berthoud, Roger, 540
Bertini, Gary, 118
Betjeman, John, 195, 239
Beyond the Fringe (revue), 323
Bideford, 165–6, 547; PP recital, 124; *Saint Nicolas*, 166
Bill, Reinhold, 560
Billows, Lionel, 427
Birmingham: Alexandra Theatre, 372; Town Hall, 36, 117, 514; *Billy Budd*, 17, 38, 41, 52–3, 56–7; *Canticle II*, 17, 24, 35, 36; *Gloriana*, 218; *Let's Make an Opera*, 372; *Serenade*, 117; *Symphonic Suite: 'Gloriana'*, 172, 202, 238; PP and/or BB performances, 305–7, 514
Birmingham, University of, 31, 159
Birmingham Post (newspaper), 31, 36
Birmingham Town Hall, 172
Birtwistle, Harrison, 516
Bishop's Stortford, 540
Bizet, Georges, 213; *and see* IOC
Blacher, Boris, 505
Black, Leo, 116

Blackburn Museum: Ferrier Collection, 36
Blackwell, Jessie, 114, 378, 381
Blackwell, John, 114, 378, 381
Blades (?restaurant/hotel/club), 307–8
Blades, James, 115, 226, 361, 361–2, **398**, 581
Blair, David, *plates 49, 51*; 482–4, 507, 508, 526
Blake, William, 516; Aldeburgh Festival song competition (1957), 493, 514–16; bicentenary (1957), 516
Blasdale, Shirley, 550–51
Blickling Hall, Norfolk, 371, 373
Bliss, Arthur, 290–91, 309, 311, 312; *and see* IOC
Bloch, Ernest, 310; *and see* IOC
Blom, Eric, 158, 281–2
Blow, John, 254; *and see* IOC
Blow the Wind Southerly (BBC TV film), 21–23
Blow-Up (film), 227
Blunden, Edmund, 516
Blyth, Alan, 23, 29, 45, 247, 331, 544
Blythburgh Church, 247, 528, 565
BOAC, 427, 522
Board of Trade Choir, 518, 520
Böhm, Karl, 350, 351
Boito, Arrigo, 2
Bolero (ballet), 308
Boleyn, Anne, 373
Bomangee, Lady, 377, 379
Bombay, 341–2, 370, 373, 376–7, 379, 382, 393, 421–2, 424–5; Apollo Bunder, 379; Regal Theatre, 379; Taj Mahal Hotel, 379; PP–BB recitals, 377, 379, 393, 396
Bomber Command, RAF, 539
Bonaparte, Napoleon, 92
Bonhoeffer, Dietrich, 356
Boni II (Princess Margaret of Hesse and the Rhine's pet bullfinch), 554, 556
Bonington, Richard Parkes, 245, 247; *Crypt of a Church*, 247
Bonne-Bouche (ballet), 56–7
Boosey, Ethel, 129, 535
Boosey, Leslie, 98, 129, 303, 306, 359, 532–5
Boosey & Hawkes, 11, 28, 52, 54–5, 82, 90, 116, 135, 194, 211, 214, 234, 244, 303, 306–8, 352, 439, 458, 467, 513, 522–3, 532, 546, 559–60, 565; hire department, 350; personnel, 31, 43, 203, 519–20
Borkh, Inge, 450
Borneo, 385, 392, 399
Bösendorfer pianos, 380
Bosphorus, River, 353, 360, 367, 370
Boston (USA), 359
Boston, Richard, 540
Boston Symphony Orchestra, 369
Boughton, Joy, 115, 125, 545, 546
Boughton, Rutland, 546; *and see* IOC
Boulez, Pierre, 141
Boult, Adrian, 219
Bournemouth: St Peter's Hall, 125; PP recital, 124–5
Bow Street, London, 151
Bowden, Pamela, 523
Bowen, Meirion, 141
Bowesman, Dermot, 234–5, 235
Bowesman, Joy, **234–5**
Boyd Neel Orchestra, 568
Boyle, Edward, 535, 539
Boys, Henry, **37–8**, 38, 49, 125, 137
Bradbury, Ernest, 186, 575
Bradshaw, William, 115

Brahms, Caryl, 160
Brahms, Johannes, 414, 464; *and see* IOC
Brain, Alfred, 505
Brain, Aubrey, 506
Brain, Dennis, *plate 44*; 287, 295, 309, 312, 433, 494, **504**, 505–6, 554, 557, 578; and *Canticle III*, 287, 289, 295, 319, 537, 583–4; and *Serenade*, 68, 295, 314; *see also* Dennis Brain Chamber Orchestra, Dennis Brain Wind Ensemble, *and* Dennis Brain Wind Quintet
Brain, Leonard, 504, 505
Brainin, Norbert, 115, 193, 310
Brains Trust, The (BBC radio series), 511
Brannigan, Owen, **579–80**, 580, 581
Bream, Julian, 6n, 78, 203, 246, 449–50, 506, 514, 549, 551, 565, 575, 577; in duo partnership with PP, *plate 47*; 78, 96, 349, 433, 448–50, 496, 515, 536, 541, 575; *see also* Julian Bream Consort
Brenan, Gamel, 336
Brenan, Gerald, 336
Bridcut, John, 10, 223–4, 226, 269–70, 557
Bridge, Ethel, 28
Bridge, Frank, 204, 288, 321, 348, 517; *and see* IOC
Briggs, Sir Harold, 387
Brighton, 165, 336
Brinson, Peter, 123
Bristol: *Canticle II*, 17, 24, 35
Bristol Old Vic, 87, 90
British Council, 445–6; Fine Arts Committee, 446; personnel, 132, 135, 411; offices in: Delhi, 379; Madras, 427, 428; Munich, 515; Tokyo, 342, 411, 413, 419; Vienna, 346, 349, 351; Zagreb, 356–8
British European Airways, *see* BEA
British Friends of the Hebrew University in Jerusalem, 34
British Overseas Airways Corporation, *see* BOAC
British War Mission, New York, 520

BRITTEN, BENJAMIN
plates 1–4, 8, 9, 23–31, 33, 34, 36, 37, 39–41, 45, 46, 48, 54, 57; as administrator, 29; Aldeburgh as base for work and discussion (*see also* Crag House, Aldeburgh, and Red House, Aldeburgh), 47, 63, 76, 78, 87, 90, 92, 98, 136, 150, 223–4, 298, 333, 356, 434, 575; and Aldeburgh Festival, 72–3, 118, 436–7; anti-militarism, 58–9; and arts funding, 445–7, 501–3; on audience participation, 47, 50; birthdays, 41, 100, 103, 190, 193, 200, 354, 357, 473–4; cars and driving for pleasure, 76, 173, 176, 178–9, 271; as chamber musician, 433, 459; Christmas celebrations, 41, 82, 111, 199, 302–3, 378, 381–2, 476, 583; as concert-planner, 309, 436–7, 504–6; as conductor, *plate 46*; 7, 17, 18, 19, 39, 41–2, 45–6, 57, 64, 74, 98, 110, 137–8, 142, 166, 172, 178, 221, 272, 276, 318–19, 346, 433–4, 440, 458–9, 464, 475, 477–9, 487–8, 493–4, 527–8, 532, 543, 573; as continuo player, 459; critical approach to, 119–22, 161; criticism and analysis, reaction to, 82, 119–22, 165, 204; diaries, 30, 50, 57, 59, 61, 86, 90, 92, 94, 113–14, 119, 132, 176, 188, 264, 328, 330, 343, 347, 350, 355, 360, 369, 406–7, 411, 427, 435, 468, 471, 478, 496, 531, 565, 578; drinks, taste in, 103, 349, 377, 552; on education, 32; Executors of, 28, 31, 343; and female admirers, 37, 39, 439–40, 461; on Kathleen Ferrier, 22–3, 194; and film music, 472; finances, 118, 166, 175, 343, 355; food, tastes in, 182, 302, 395–6, 398;

GENERAL INDEX

godchildren, 109; gongs, use of, 399; gravestone, 227; at Gresham's School, 421, 448, 540; guests, 33, 68–9, 71, 82, 100, 103, 130, 142, 176; health, 104, 111, 175, 179–80, 196, 302–4, 312–13, 346, 349, 394, 400, 403, 487, 551: streptoccuccus infection (1940), 196; sprained ankle (1952), 69; bursitis (1952–54), 12, 45, 115, 138–9, 166, 172, 178, 182, 187, 189–90, 192, 194, 198–200, 228, 230, 232, 239; gallstones (1956), 400; exhaustion (1957), 500, 507, 510; depression (1975), 202; on his own music, 6, 204, 316; *see also entries in* Index of Britten's Works; holidays and working periods abroad: Paris (1945), 213; Austria (1952), 17, 41–3, 77–8; France (1952), 18, 74–8; Ireland (1953), 18, 133, 135–7; Zermatt (1955), 102, 305, 313, 373–4; world tour (1955–56), *plates 29–31, 33, 34, 36, 37*; 1, 7, 11, 14, 260, 318, 333, 341–430, 441, 445, 454–5; Schloss Tarasp (1956), 14, 434; Italy (1957), 493, 522–6; Venice (1968), 102; homes: *see entries for* Chester Gate (No. 5), London; Crag House, Aldeburgh; Marlborough Place (No. 59), London; Melbury Road (No. 22), London; Old Mill, Snape; Red House, Aldeburgh; honours and awards, 9, 18, 162–3, 521–3, 540; innocence, lost, theme of, 49; as interviewee, 36, 459, 551; Japan, attitude towards, 400, 404, 407–8, 410, 412; leisure activities: bird-watching, brass-rubbing, 69, 173, 175–6; indoor games, 69; letters, recipient of, **114**; librettos, contributions to, 217; and literature for boys, 30; as mentor, 33–4, 178, 234–5, 447–8, 574; metronome marks, 524, 545–6; pacifism, 10, 175, 318, 469; as pianist, *plates 37, 41*; 7, 116, 132, 142, 163, 239, 272, 287, 307, 311, 433, 459, 464, 502, 528, 557–8, 584; and political ideas, 10, 58–9, 67; and the press, 509–10, 546, 549; press, letters to, 58–9, 445–6; on recital partnership with PP: 97, 495, *and see locations, venues and promoting organizations*; and recorded music, 359, 389–91, 402, 419–20, 455–6, 562; and recorded speech, 22, 23; as recorder-player, 209–10, 245; relationships with adolescent boys, 12, 68–71, 224, 269–71, 379; religious views, 69–71; satire, subject of, 61–2, 321–3; sexuality, 10, 68, 143–4, 180, 209, 224, 269, 324, 465, 469–70, 555–6; sporting activities: badminton, 130; cricket, 67, 176, 178, 449; deck tennis, 547; sailing, 176; skiing, 17, 41, 43, 47–8, 102, 287, 305, 313, 336, 374; swimming, 173, 175–6, 266, 269, 449, 532, 534, 552; table-tennis, 234; tennis, *plates 26–28*; 67, 173, 175–6, 266, 326–7, 467, 526, 532, 535; walking, 189; stage fright, 345, 348; as student, 38, 267; temper, 140; typing, 187–9, 192; and United States, 39, 42–3, 47, 495, 549, 557–8, 579; as violaplayer, 10, 211; Will of, 28, 31, 343; writings: 'Britten Looking Back', 204; 'Dennis Brain 1921–1957', 295, 505; Foreword to James Blades, *Percussion Instruments and their History*, 366; 'Some Notes on Forster and Music', 525; 'Speech on Receiving Honorary Degree at Hull University', 523; *The Story of Music* (with Imogen Holst), 510–12; 'Three Premieres', 22, 194

Britten, Charlotte Elizabeth (Beth), *see* Welford, Beth
Britten, (Edith) Barbara (BB's sister), 24, 42, 46, 124, 180, 190, 199, 515, 527, 575, 581
Britten, Florence (BB's aunt), 243

Britten (née Hockey), Edith Rhoda (BB's mother), 196
Britten, Robert Harry Marsh (BB's brother), 180, 243
Britten Estate Ltd, 116, 331
Britten–Pears Foundation, 72, 116, 331, 343
Britten–Pears Library, 125, 207; EOG Collection, 478; exhibitions, 512
Britten–Pears School for Advanced Musical Studies, Snape, 197; personnel, 45, 67, 401
Britten's Children (TV documentary film), 30, 224
Brno Opera, 141, 457
Brodsky, Horace, 101
Broecheler, Caspar, 327
Brosa, Antonio, 110
Brown, Robert, 520
Browning, Robert, 221
Brownrigg, T. M., 565
Brucksaler: PP–BB recital, 474
Brueghel, Pieter, 302; *The Fall of Icarus*, 302
Brussels, 296; *Peter Grimes*, 245; PP–BB recital, 305
Brussels: Astoria Hotel, 246
Brussels: Théâtre de la Monnaie, 38, 140
Bryanston School, Dorset, 74
Bryanston Summer School of Music, 73–4
Buckingham, May, 187, 189
Buckingham, Robert (Bob), 187, 189
Buckingham Palace, 58, 145, 163, 393, 494, 535, 539
Buckland, Sidney, 258, 529, 531
Budapest, 352, 473, 575; *Let's Make an Opera*, 472
Budapest Opera, 575
Bugaku (subgenre of traditional Japanese court music), 455
Bulawayo, Southern Rhodesia, 138
Bulawayo: Theatre Royal, 138
Bulganin, Nikolai Aleksandrovich, 374, 376
Bunraku puppet theatre, 416
Bunting, Edward: *Ancient Music of Ireland*, 578
Bunyan, John: *The Pilgrim's Progress*, 38
Burdet, Jacques, 311
Burford: PP recital, 124
Burghclere, 228
Burmah-Shell (company), 378, 381
Burne, Gary, 484
Burne-Jones, Edward, 554–5
Burnside, Iain, 454
Burra, Edmund, 39
Burrell, Barbara, 130, 187
Burrell, Billy, 67, 69, 71, 121, 130, 187, 562
Burton, Humphrey, 561
Bus Stop (film), 469
Busch, Adolf, 198
Busch, Fritz, 140, 197, 198; *Pages from a Musician's Life (Aus dem Leben eines Musikers)*, 197–8
Bush House, London (BBC studios), 47
Business Art Galleries, 246
Busoni, Ferruccio, 198
Butt, James, 211
Butt, John, 498
Büttner, Elli, 560
Buxtehude, Dietrich, 73; *and see* IOC
Byrd, William, 104; *and see* IOC

Cable Ship (film), 196
Caccini, Giulio: *see* IOC
Cadbury-Brown, H. T., 536
Cadogan Hall, London, 534

Caesar and Cleopatra (film), 108
Caine, Michael, 227, 373
Caird, George, 546
Calcutta, Grand Hotel, 396; 375, 380–82, 385, 393, 396–7
Calder, John, 141, 213
Caldwell (doctor), 188
Caldwell, Virginia, 180, 202
Calgary, University of, 115
California, 44, 579
Callas, Maria, 94
Calverley, Lord (George Duff; 1st Baron), 86–7
Camargo Society, 3n
Cambridge, 187, 189, 379; Arts Theatre, 372; *Let's Make an Opera*, 372
Cambridge, University of, 270, 523; *see also individual colleges*
Cambridge Opera Journal, 11n, 159
Camden Theatre, London, 437
Camelot (musical film), 227
Campbell, Margaret, 126, 573
Campion, Paul, 22
Canada, 8, 115, 249, 508, 519, 526, 531–3, 535–7, 543, 550, 553–4, 558, 562, 583; *see also individual locations*
Canada House, London, 519
Canadian Broadcasting Corporation, *see* CBC
Canadian History Society, 520
Cantelo, April, 132, 315
Canterbury Cathedral, 356; choir, 331
Canterbury Festival, 515, 518
Capell, Richard, 153
Caplan, Isador, 343, 461, 503, 535
Capote, Truman, 232
Caracas, 438
Cardew, Cornelius, 516; *and see* IOC
Cardiff: *Billy Budd*, 57; *Gloriana*, 218
Cardus, Neville, 22, 193
Carl Rosa Opera Company, 141
Carleton College, Minnesota, 31
Carlyle, Thomas, 584
Carolan, John, 315
Carpaccio, Vittore, 228; *Annunciation*, 228
Carpenter, Humphrey, 73, 88, 164, 224, 555, 573
Carter, Alan, 473, 475
Case, John Carol, 497
Catholic Stage Guild of Dublin, 521
Catley, Gwen, 130
Cavelti, Elsa, 311
Cavendish, 540
CBC (Canadian Broadcasting Corporation), 508, 527, 551, 554; PP–BB recitals, 528, 554, 557; *Young Apollo*, 557
CBC Library, 558
CBC String Orchestra, 557
CBC Symphony Orchestra, 549
CBS, New York, 557
CBSO, *see* City of Birmingham Symphony Orchestra
Cecil, Sir Robert, 78, 86
celempung (Javanese zither), 388
Center Theatre, New York, 544
Ceylon, *see* Sri Lanka
Chair, Somerset Struben de, 373
Chair, Thelma de, 372–3
Chalmers, Kenneth, 537
Champs-Elysées, Théâtre des, Paris, *see* Paris:

Théâtre des Champs-Elysées
Chappell, William (Billy), 254–5, 256
Charge of the Light Brigade, The (film), 227
Charles, Prince of Wales, 175
Charles I, King, 202
Charlotte Street, London, 541
Chartres, France, 77
Chelsea School of Art, London, 246, 256
Chelsea Town Hall, 578; *Serenade*, 578
Cheltenham, 37, 371
Cheltenham Festival, 30, 72
Cheltenham Open Competitive Music Festival, 505
Chenka (game), 69
Cheshire, Leonard, 535, 539–40
Cheshire Foundation Homes for the Sick, 539
Chester Gate (No. 5), 18, 114–15, 145, 177, 190, 223, 267, 269, 298, 337, 420, 497
Chester miracle plays, 5, 23–4, 26–7, 563, 564–5, 579, 581
Chiang Kai-Shek, 420
Chicago: Arts Club, 164; *Billy Budd*, 44; French Folksong Arrangements, 198; *Variations on a Theme of Frank Bridge*, 351
Chicago Symphony Orchestra, 457
Chichester, 356
Chichester Festival Theatre, 71
Chilcott, Barbara, 508
Chimènes, Myriam, 258, 529, 531
China, 403–4, 406, 455
Chinese opera, 385
Cholmondeley, Sybil, 173, 174
Chonia (Princess Margaret of Hesse and the Rhine's dog), 549, 551
Christie, John, 256, 257
Christie family, 573
Christie's (auction house), 305
Chuhaldin, Alexander, 557–8
Churchill, Winston, 209, 374, 376, 427
Churriana, near Malaga, 336–7
Cincinnati: Music Hall, 433, 450; *Gloriana*, 433, 450, 455
Cincinnati May Festival, 433, 450, 455
Cincinnati Symphony Orchestra, 450
City of Birmingham Symphony Orchestra (CBSO), 117, 202, 457, 514
City of London Festival, 416
Clark, Kenneth (Kay), 97, 239
Clarke, Mary, 123, 508
Clayton, Jack, 232
Clayton, Sylvia, 221
Clodd, Edward, 142
Close, Reginald, 419–20
Clough, Prunella, 190, 192
Clutyens, André, 529
Clytie (I; miniature dachshund belonging to John Cranko), 462, 463
Clytie (II; BB's and PP's miniature dachshund), *plates 4, 56*; 220, 221, 330, 336, 344, 352, 361, 382, 405 463, 467, 476, 552, 554
Clytie (III; miniature dachshund belonging to Alison Pritt), 468
Coast, John, 389
Cochran, C. B., 256
Cocteau, Jean, 213, 486
Çokorde Gde Agung, 390
Cold War, 49
Coleman, Basil, 1–2, 11, 21, 21, 28, 41, **87–8**, **90–91**,

GENERAL INDEX

248–9, 266, 269, **313–14**, 347, 502, **506–8**, **541–2**, 543, 554, **561–2**; as interviewee, 249; and *Billy Budd*, 41, 56; and *Gloriana*, 21, 87–8, 90, 93, 118–19, 135–6, 151–2, 158, 216, 509; and *Let's Make an Opera*, 567; and *The Turn of the Screw*, plates 10, 23, 25; 21, 172, 209, 223, 261, 274, 277, 279, 284, 537, 541–2, 544
Coleman, C. J. R., 341
Coleridge, Samuel Taylor: 'The Ancient Mariner', 584
Collegium Musicum, 304
Collins, Anthony, 328
Collins, Cecil, 383
Collins, Ian, 247
Collins, Norman, 566
Collins Young Elizabethan (periodical), 161
Cologne, 465, 529, 545; *Billy Budd*, 118; PP–BB recital, 474
Cologne: Dom Hotel, 465
Cologne Opera, 140
Colombo, 411, 422–3, 426; PP–BB recitals, 422–3, 426–7
Columbia, 529
Company des Quinze, 538
Conati, Marcello, 2n
Connell, Howard, 472
Constance, Lake, 496
Conway, Helen, 139–40, 145
Cook, Peter, 323–4
Cook, William, 324
Cooke, Arnold, 210
Cooke, Mervyn, 33, 414, 475, 497
Coombs Parish Church, 320
Cooper, Martin, 155–6, 161, 276–7, 482–3
Copenhagen 73–4, 78, 122, 373; Hotel d'Angleterre, 181; Tivoli Gardens, 73, 75; PP–BB recital, 18, 75
Copenhagen Boys' Choir, 17, 73, 177, 181
Copland, Aaron, 125, 134, 352, 506, 580; *and see* IOC
Copyright Bill, 447
Corbusier, Le, 526
Cornwall, 408
Coronation celebrations (1953), 10, 17, 18, *20*, 38, 58–9, 90–91, 106–7, 136, 151, 154, 158–9, *162*, 177; televising of, 50
Cortot, Alfred, 15
Cosman, Milein, 83
Cotman, John Sell, 536
Couraud Choir, 190, 192, 212
Covarrubias, Miguel, 386
Covehithe, 535–6
Covent Garden Opera Company, 9, 57, 457; *Billy Budd*, 17, 41, 65; *and see* (subsequently) Royal Opera House, Covent Garden, London
Covent Garden Orchestra, 434, 493
Coventry, 187, 189
Coventry Cathedral, 500
Coventry Cathedral Festival, 499–500
Cox, Peter, 384
Crabbe, George, 172, 190, 193, 238–9, 322, 391; *The Borough*, 239; 'Marsh Flowers', 391; bicentenary, 172, 190, 193, 238–9
Crabbe Street (No. 4), Aldeburgh, *see* Crag House, Aldeburgh
Crag House, Aldeburgh, *plate 3*; 33, 69, 78, 103, 124, 126, 179, 210, 223, 337, 439, 494, 511, 517, 575
Craig, Sir James, 34

Cranbrook, Fidelity, Countess of, 130, 131, 181, 239, 449, 462, 465
Cranbrook, John (Jock) Gathorne-Hardy, 4th Earl of, 238, 239, 449
Cranko, John, *plate 50*; 38, 94, 257–8, **332**, 333, 355, 462, 508, 528–9, 556, 577–8; 'The Green Serpent', 259, 260; as choreographer, 57, 305; as dog breeder, 221, 462; and *Gloriana*, 38, 91, 93–4, 103, 122–3, 138, 142, 152–3; and *A Midsummer Night's Dream*, 94, 355, 474; and *Peter Grimes*, 139, 189, 192; and *The Prince of the Pagodas*, 3, 94, 257–8, 259, 260, 271, 332–3, 435, 465, 467, 474–5, 477, 479, 482–4, 486–8, 507, 509, 518–20, 522–2, 526, 558
Cranmore, 408
Crawford, Michael, 223, 581
Crimean War, 367, 369
Crisp, Clement, 508
Critics' Circle, 31
Cross, Joan, 88–9, 197, 248, **252–4**, 323, 536; concert and recital performances, 28, 166, 192, 261; and *Albert Herring*, 90, 478, 574–5; and *Gloriana*, plates 10–12, 14–16; 18, 19, 87, 90–91, 113, 138, 140, 142–3, 150–52, 156–8, 164, 177–8, 216; and *Peter Grimes*, 88, 178, 239; and *The Rape of Lucretia*, 88; and *The Turn of the Screw*, *plate 19*; 90, 252–4, 272, 274, 277, 279, 284, 314, 319
Crozier, Eric, 1, 23, **64**, 64, 88, 478, 580; *Billy Budd* (libretto), 44
Cubism, 102
Cullum, Jeremy, *plate 6*; 176, 178–80, 216, 219, 241–2, 343–4, 347, 352, 371, 385, 400, 462, 465, 476, 514, 535, 546; as interviewee, 179–80; letters written on behalf of BB, 233–4
Cullum, Sylvia, 179
Cullum, Tommy, 178
Cultural Freedom, Congress of (Paris, 1952), 64
Cunningham, Valentine, 207, 209
Curcio, Maria, *plate 3*; 348, 459
Currant, Miss (*Women's Journal*), 461
Curtis Institute, Philadelphia, 44, 352
Curwen Prints, 246
Cuyp, Aelbert, 246
Cydrax, 67, 71
Cyprus, 425, 446
Czech Philharmonic Orchestra, 457
Czechoslovakia, 457

da Costa, Eric, 381
Dachau (concentration camp), 202
Daily Express (newspaper), 152, 334
Daily Herald (newspaper), 138
Daily Mail (newspaper), 151, 509–10, 520
Daily Telegraph (newspaper), 45, 116, 123, 139, 141, 151–3, 202, 210, 220, 227, 276, 291, 310–11, 401, 482–3, 543, 561
Dalayrac, Nicolas, 213; *and see* IOC
Dalberg, Frederick, 53, 56
Dan, Vishnu, 375
Danco, Suzanne, 450
Dancy, John, 220, 221
Danish State Radio Symphony Orchestra, 181
Darmstadt, 54, 200–201; *The Turn of the Screw*, 471, 494, 559–60
Darmstadt: Landestheater, 471, 494, 559–60
Dartington Hall, 12, 13n, 73, 193, 331, 383, 475; *Five Flower Songs*, 383
Dartington Hall Trust, 383

Davis, Donald, 508
Davis, Murray, 508
Day Lewis, Cecil, 514, 516
Debussy, Claude, 213, 441; *and see* IOC
Decca Records, 110, 131–2, 219, 328, 464, 569, 571, 573, 583; 'Aldeburgh Festival' series, 177, 583; BB recordings, 106, 172, 221, 287–8, 296, 308, 354, 438–40, 475, 493, 496, 523, 535, 537, 568; 'Britten at Aldeburgh' series, 132; PP–BB recital of English song, 288
Decca Recording Studios, 296
Dehn, Paul, 255
Del Mar, Norman, 137, 141, 163, 166, **309**, 310, **512–13**
De-la-Noy, Michael, 421
Delhi, 341, 368, 370, 373, 377–82, 393, 396, 445; Constantia Hall, 380; Gymkhana Club, 379; Tughlaqabad, 381; PP–BB broadcast recital, 377, 379
Delibes, Léo, 123, 485
Delius, Frederick: *see* IOC
Denmark, 73, 177, 181, 188, 192
Dennis Brain Chamber Orchestra, 504
Dennis Brain Wind Ensemble, 505
Dennis Brain Wind Quintet, 319, 505
Denpasar, 342, 385–6, 389, 391–2
Denpasar: Bali Hotel, 385
Dent, E. J., 520
Desert Island Discs (BBC radio series), 324
Destination Moon (film), 48
Detmold, 515
Detroit, 553
Deutsches Symphonie-Orchester Berlin, 475
Devereux, Robert, Earl of Essex, *see* Essex, Earl of
Devine, George, 256, 535, 537–8, **538–9**
Devon, 433, 435
Dewas Senior (Indian State), 188
Diaghilev, Sergey, 123, 475
Diamand, Maria, *see* Curcio, Maria
Diamand, Peter, 344, 347–8, 438–9
Dickinson, Peter, 255
Disney, Walt, 472; *see also* Walt Disney British Films
Dix, Mr (schoolteacher at All Hallows), 408, 411
Doctor, Jenny, 207
Dohnányi, Ernö, 94; *and see* IOC
Doig, Desmond, 397
Dolin, Anton, 123, 308
Dolmetsch, Arnold, 210
Dolmetsch, Carl, **209–10**, 210, 320
Dolmetsch recorders, 209–11, 246
Donaueschingen: PP concert, 296
Donizetti, Gaetano: *see* IOC
Dorchester, 228, 229, 410; PP–BB recital, 228, 229
Dorset, 561; *see also individual locations*
Double Reed News (periodical), 546
Douglas, Basil, *plate 42*; 30, 190, 209, 248, 319, **370–72**, 385, 438, 453, 478, 506, 519–20, 556, **568–9**, 570–72, 577; and EOG, 8, 21, 28, 30, 48, 87, 91, 226, 252, 255, 280, 314, 353, 373, 399, 494, 500, 502–3, 507, 509, 521, 542, 550, 562, 568–70, 577; *see also Basil Douglas Ltd*
Dowland, John, 6, 45, 254, 406, 497, 555; *and see* IOC
Dowling, Denis, 514, 517
Downes, Herbert, 294
Downes, Ralph, 72, **198**, 198, 199, 516
Doyle, Desmond, 484
Drake, Alfred, 45

Drake, Francis, 154
Drama Critics, Society of, 31
Dresden, 352
Dresden: Staatsoper, 198
Driver, Christopher, 193
Drogheda, Garrett, Earl of, 150
Drottningholm Court Theatre, Sweden, 520
Drummond, John, 22
Dublin, 136; Abbey Theatre, 123; Gaiety Theatre, 94
Dubrovnik, 357, 359–60, 371
Duff, George, *see* Calverley, Lord
Duff, Lesley, *see* Bedford, Lesley
Duke of York's Theatre, London, 288, 334
Dukes, Ashley, 49
Dumka Trio, 310
Duncan, Briony, 269–70, 368, 547
Duncan, Roger, *plates 53, 54*; 10n, 11–12, 68, 102, 161, **268–9**, 269–71, 314, 318, **326**, 327, 329–30, 336, **344–7**, 347, 349, 357–9, **367–8**, **376–9**, **393–6**, **402–5**, **407–10**, 411, 417, **421–6**, 435, **448–9**, 450, 452, 459, 461, 471, 497, 508, 511, 534, 537, 539, **546–7**, 550, 561
Duncan, Ronald, *plate 26*; 1–2, 11, 39, 44, 49, 63, 66, 125, 165, **175**, 175, 193–4, 269–70, 287, **320**, **324**, 325, 329, **334**, 335, 337, 349, 359, 368, 374, 405, 433, **435**, 436, 438, 440, **461**, **470**, 493, 497, 505, 509, **509–10**; *Christopher Sly* (libretto), 505; *The Death of Satan*, 324–6; *Don Juan*, 325; *Mea Culpa*, 337; *The Rape of Lucretia* (libretto), 175, 336; *St Peter*, 287, 334, 336–7, 433, 435–6, 438, 461, 473, 493, 509–10; *This Way to the Tomb*, 175
Duncan, Rose-Marie, 269, 287, 347, 368, 374, 433, 435–6, 440, 461, 497, 510
Dundee, 127, 130, 132
Dundee: Royal British Hotel, 131
Dunlop, R. O., 446
Dunmow, Essex, 143, 384
Dunne, Veronica, 137, **139**
Dunnert, Roderic, 223
Dunwich, 536
Durey, Louis, 213
Dussek [Dušek], František, 281
Dusseldorf, 341, 343, 345, 348, 473; Robert Schumann-saal, 348; PP–BB recitals, 348–9, 474
Dutt, Mrs (radio producer, Delhi), 380
Duval, Denise, 213, 529
Dyer, Olive, *plate 19*; 130, **131**, 272, 274, 277, 279, 284, 542, 548, 550–51

East Anglia, University of, 331, 523
East China Sea, 405
East Coast floods (1953), 18, 70, 124, 177
East India Company, 404
Eastbridge, 452
Eastwood, Thomas, 504, **505**; *and see* IOC
Eaton, Quantance, 544
Ebert, Carl, 198, 257
Eddison, Robert, 87, 90
Edinburgh, 130, 132–4, 137, 471, 505; Freemasons' Hall: PP recital, 131
Edinburgh Festival, 22, 110, 139, 194, 348, 416, 535, 540
Education and Science, Department of, 539
Edward Arnold (publishing house), 188
Edwards, Leslie, 483
Egypt, 474
Ehrismann, Sibylle, 305

GENERAL INDEX 617

Eichstadt, 474
Eisenhower, Dwight D., 474
Eisteddford, International, 328
Elephanta caves, 377
Elephanta Island, 379
Elgar, Edward, 555; *and see* 10c
Elizabeth, The Queen Mother, Queen, 81, 134, 135, 201–2, 540, 557
Elizabeth I, Queen, 43, 78, 86, 146, 159, 373
Elizabeth II, Queen, 2, 9, 17, 43, 58–9, 90, 145, 159, 202, 247, 420, 494, 535, 539, 540; Coronation, 2, 10–11, 17, 18, 38, 58–9, 90, 136, 154, 158–9, *162*; and *Gloriana*, 18, 58–9, 90, 107, 143, 145, 150–52, 159, 177; Honours Lists, 18, 113, 163, 493, 528, 540
Elkin, R. S., 447
Ellis, Osian, 72
Ellis, Vivian, 447
Ellora, 425
Elmhirst, Dorothy, 382, 383, 521–2, 535, 540
Elmhirst, Leonard, 382, 383–4, 535, 540
Elmhirst, Ruth, *see* Ash, Ruth
Elmhirst, Susanna, 384
Elsasser, Richard, 439
Elwes, John (formerly John Hahessy), 28, 537
EMI (recording company), 110
Emil und die Detektive (film), 30
Engela, Dawid, 531, 534
Engen, Kieth, 515
English, Gerald, 338
English Chamber Orchestra (formerly Goldsbrough Orchestra), 45, 220, 310, 352, 557, 573
English Music Theatre, 543
English Opera Group (EOG), 8, 176, 228, 344; *Albert Herring*, 8, 18, 132, 163, 353; *The Beggar's Opera*, 8, 553; *Il combattimento di Tancredi e Clorinda*, 220; *Dido and Aeneas*, 8, 39, 220, 247; *A Dinner Engagement*, 254–5, 338; *Façade*, 254, 338; *Idomeneo*, 543; *Let's Make an Opera/The Little Sweep*, 8, 30, 48, 338, 371, 555, 562; *Love in a Village*, 91, 94, 254–5; *Les Mamelles de Tirésias*, 94, 108, 529; *Nelson*, 109, 126; *Noye's Fludde*, 223, 512; *The Rape of Lucretia*, 8, 247, 371; *Ruth*, 512, 555; *Sāvitri*, 247, 353, 371, 555; *The Turn of the Screw*, 8, 87–8, 139, 224, 226, 244, 251–2, 272, 274, 276–7, 282, 314, 318, 338, 353–4, 371, 433–4, 459, 494, 496, 527, 535, 542, 544, 568; *Venus and Adonis*, 353, 371, 555; (*see also* Index of Britten's Works *and* 10c); administrative amalgamation with Aldeburgh Festival, 500–503, 507, 509, 577; Archive, 529; commissions, 72, 255; concerts and recitals, 21, 28, 163, 192, 254, 255, 327; finances and fund-raising, 30, 35, 197, 251–2, 314, 355, 371–3, 383, 473, 500–502, 507, 522, 571; management, board and personnel, 8, 12, 21, 28–30, 35, 42, 64, 87, 90, 97–8, 116, 141, 224, 226, 246, 249, 309, 314, 343, 353, 361, 371–3, 385, 429, 445, 494, 500–502, 507, 509, 517, 521, 535, 553, 568–72; and Glyndebourne Festival Opera, 357, 357; and National Opera School, 197; Opera Ball (1958), 571; opera film project, 88; and Royal Opera House, Covent Garden, 98; and Sadler's Wells, 297; and Taw and Torridge Festival, 165, 256, 261; European tour (1955), 318; London season (1955), 338; UK tour (1955), 371; Paris (1956), 433, 459; tour to Stratford, Ontario (1957), 8, 47, 373, 494, 495–6, 506, 535, 544, 547, 570, 577; Berlin Festival (1957), 568, 570, 577; *see also* EOG Orchestra *and* EOG Chamber Orchestra
English National Opera (ENO), 517, 543, 555; *Gloriana*, 168
English Stage Company (ESC), 175–6, 538
Enigma Variations (ballet), 508
Eno's (indigestion medicine), 554–5
Enright, D. J., 413
EOG, *see* English Opera Group
EOG Association, 503, 535
EOG Chamber Orchestra, 163
EOG Ensemble, 328
EOG Orchestra, 166, 254, 307, 310, 328, 502, 544, 546, 570, 572
ENO, *see* English National Opera,
Erdmann, Charles, 76, 81–2, 83 96, 99–100, 103–4, 111, 135, 142, 165, 173, 239, 298, 312, 455, 532
ESC, *see* English Stage Company
Essen, 560
Essex, Earl of, 58, 59, 78
'Eternal Father, strong to save' (hymn), 581
Eton College, Berkshire, 32, 34
Evans, Geraint, 44, 116, 192, 497
Evans, John, 78, 83, 150, 264–5, 449, 454
Evans, Nancy, 21, 23, 64, 66–7, 126, 166, **477–8**, *478*
Evening Standard (newspaper), 10n, 154–5
Evening Star (newspaper, Karachi), 428

Faber and Faber (publishing house), 164, 326, 519
Faber Music, 55, 116, 315, 519, 557
Fairfax, Bryan, 168
Fanfare for Europe (1972), 246
Farnaby, Giles, *see* 10c
Farncombe, Charles, 518, 520
Farron, Julia, 482–4
Fass, Marjorie, 375
Fatehpur Sikri, 378, 380
Fauré, Gabriel, 539
Fawley Bottom Farmhouse, Oxfordshire, 243
Federick, Bill, 290
Fenice, Teatro La, Venice, *see* Venice: Teatro La Fenice
Ferencsik, János, 574, 575
Ferguson, Howard, 447
Ferrara, 526
Ferrier, Kathleen, *plate 45*; 21–3, 24, 112–13, 134–5, 139, 192–4, 557; and *Canticle II: 'Abraham and Isaac'*, 17, 23–4, 35–7; and 'The Deaf Woman's Courtship', 24; and *The Rape of Lucretia*, 21–3; and *Spring Symphony*, 21, 23
Festival Piano Quartet, 126
Feuermann, Emanuel, 125
Fifield, Christopher, 36
Figaro, Le (newspaper), 66, 155
Fille mal gardée, La (ballet), 508
Financial Times (newspaper), 508
Finzi, Gerald, 184; *and see* 10c
Firbank, Ronald: *Vainglory*, 174
Fischer-Dieskau, Dietrich, 201, 330, 462–4, 465–7
Fisher, James, **510–11**, 511, 512, 537; *Adventure of the Sea*, 511; 'Nature Protection' (lecture), 511
Fisher, Sylvia, 192
FitzGerald, Edward, 100
Flanders, Michael, 11, 320; *And Then We Wrote* (gramophone record, with Donald Swann), 320–23; 'A Guide to Britten' (song, with Donald Swann), 11, 320–23

Fleming, Ian, 308
Flesch, Carl, 125
Fletcher Buildings, Covent Garden, 151
Florence, 316; Uffizi Gallery, 319; *The Turn of the Screw*, 288, 318–19
Flowerpot Men, The (BBC Television), 30
Foges, Wolf, 510, 512
Folies-Bergères, 483
Folkes, Martin, 78
Folkestone, Kent, 66, 76
Fonteyn, Margot, 508
Forbes, Elizabeth, 45, 247, 544
Ford, Boris, 562, 564–7
Ford, Thomas, 497; *and see* IOC
Foreign Office, 10, 133, 445
Forget About Film and TV, 22
Formosa, *see* Taiwan
Forster, E. M. (Edward Morgan), 1, 41–2, 44, 112–13, 118, 142, **187**, 190, 193, 238–9, 384, 387, **525**, 540–41, 562; *Billy Budd* (libretto), 41, 44, 64; *The Hill of Devi*, 187–8; *A Passage to India*, 188, 387; *Where Angels Fear to Tread*, 525
Forsyth, Bruce, 139
Foss, Hubert, 384
Foss, Lukas, 352
Fournier, Pierre, 212, 213
Framlingham, Suffolk, 176, 182
Framlingham Church, 247
Framlingham College, 207, 580
France, 18, 66, 74, 78, 471, 474, 493, 526; *see also individual locations*
France, South of: PP–BB recitals, 18
Francis, John, 115, 125
Francis, Sarah, 546
Frankfurt, 206, 387, 425, 427, 466, 473–4, 476, 560
Franks, A. H., 508
Fransel (Yugoslavian tenor), 357
French, Philip, 227
French Embassy, London, 213
Fricker, Peter Racine, 447, 504, 505; *and see* IOC
Friends' Ambulance Unit, 320
Fujiyama, 408
Fuller, Erwin, 54
Fuller, Frederick, 245, 246, 349
Fuller, Patricia, 245–6, 349
Furtwängler, Wilhelm, 125

Gagaku (traditional Japanese court music and dance), 318, 342, 414, 420, 455
Gage, Sir Berkeley, 410, 420; *It's Been a Marvellous Party*, 420
Gaiety Theatre, Dublin, *see* Dublin: Gaiety Theatre
gambang (Balinese bamboo xylophone), 390, 397
gamelan music, *plate 32*; 14, 307, 318, 333, 342, 385, 388–9, 397, 402–3, 405–6; *see also individual instruments and works*
Gandhi, Indira, 374, 376, 377, 382
gangsa (Balinese metallophone), 397
Garbo, Greta, 328
Gargellen, Austria, *plate 8*; 39, 43–4, 46
Garnham, Maureen, 8, 39, 131, 226–7, 229, 247, 310, 328, 338, 355, 366, 372–3, 437, 459, 502, 550, 568–71
Garrick Club, London, 228
Gascoigne, Lady, 420
Gaskill, William, 538
Gathorne-Hardy, Samuel, 519, 520
Gathorne-Hardy family, 187, 189

Gaudier-Brzeska, Henri, 100–101; *Boy's Head*, 101; *Children with Kite and Duck*, 101; drawings, 101; portrait of Horace Brodsky, 101; *Torso*, 101
Gay, John, 166, 322; *see also* IOC
Geddes, 1st Lord, 331
Geddes, David, 329, 331, 400–401, 404, 406, 410
Geddes, Margaret Campbell, *see* Hesse and the Rhine, Princess Margaret of,
Geddes, Gerda Meyer (Pytt), 329, 331, 400, **401**, 404, 406, 410
geisha performance, 413
Geister, Martha, 560
Gellhorn, Peter, 57, 137, 141
Gencer, Leyla, 369
gender wayang selendero (Balinese shadow-play ensemble), 390
Gendre, Claude, 258
Gendron, Maurice, 179, 514, 517, 528
Geneva, 341, 369, 441, 444; Théâtre de la Cour St-Pierre, 245, 349; *Death in Venice*, 45; PP–BB recitals/concerts, 305, 343, 346, 349; *The Rape of Lucretia*, 245
George V, King, 117
George VI, King, 17, 35, 58, 540, 557
Geraldo and his Orchestra, 139
Gerardy, Riki, 573
German Embassy, London, 201
Germany, 81, 199, 239, 327, 348, 425, 474, 476, 495, 500, 520, 526, 578, 583; in Nazi era, 33, 141, 197, 201–2, 356, 524; political situation, 81, 524; PP and/or BB recitals and concerts, 178, 434, 436, 474, 532, 545; *see also individual locations*
Gerrards Cross, 32–3
Ghiringhelli (Intendant, La Scala), 522–3
Ghosh, Pannalal, 375
Gibbs, Philip, 58
Gibson, John, 426
Gielgud, John, 138, 144, 538
Gifford, Charles, 399, 400
Gilbert, William, 427; *and see* IOC (Sullivan, Arthur)
Gimpel, Bronslaw, 109, 110
Gishford, Anthony, 11, 30–31, 31, 94, 103, 117, 168, 195–6, **214**, 233, 302–3, 306, 308, 318, **350–51**, 359–60, 370, 438–9, 446, 450, **458**, 459, 465, 470–71, **472**, **473**, 507, 513–14, **518–19**, 520–21, 521–2, 522, 533, 565, 578
Giulini, Carlo Maria, 55; and *War Requiem*, 55
Glasgow, 112–13, 130; St Andrew's Hall, 131; *Billy Budd*, 57; PP concert, 131
Glasgow, University of, 448
Glasgow Choral Union, 113
Glemham, Great, Suffolk, 238–9
Glendinning, Victoria, 328, 469
Glock, William, 74, 540
Gluck, Christoph Willibald von: *see* IOC
Glyndebourne Festival Opera, 116, 140–41, 143, 198, 478, 540; *Albert Herring*, 38–9, 257; *The Rape of Lucretia*, 21, 22, 182, 257, 441, 573
Goble recorders, 245–6
Goddard, Scott, 154, 161
Godwin, Shelagh, 210
Goehr, Alexander, 516; *and see* IOC
Goehr, Walter, 309, 497–8
Goldbeck, Frederick, 113
Goldberg, Szymon, 124, 125, 348, 572
Goldsbrough Orchestra (later English Chamber

Orchestra), 498, 573
Goldscheider, Ludwig: *Michelangelo Drawings*, 28
Goldsmith, Oliver, 90; *She Stoops to Conquer*, 90
Gone with the Wind (film), 469
Gonville and Caius College, Cambridge, 540
Goodall, Reginald, 45, 138, 168, 172, 182, 189, 192, 214, 218, 228
Gooding, Mel, 512
Goossens, Joan, 366
Gould, Diana, *see* Menuhin, Diana
Gounod, Charles, 213; *and see* IOC
GPO Film Unit, 196, 361
Grade, Lew, 565–7
Graf, Herbert, 351
Graham, Colin, 209, 270, 529, 543–4, 560, 562; *Anna Karenina* (libretto), 2n, 543; *The Golden Vanity* (libretto), 543; and *Curlew River*, 418, 543; and *Noye's Fludde*, 543, 562, 580–82; and *The Turn of the Screw*, 224, 280, 541, 543, 561, 580
Graham, Martha, 396–7, 445, 447
Gramercy Park, No. 1, New York City, 495–6
Gramophone (periodical), 295, 450
Grant, Alexander, 308
Grant, Keith, 543–4
Graz: PP–BB recital, 493, 524
Graz Opera, 524
Great Bealings, Suffolk, 195
Great Glemham House, Suffolk, 193, 238–9, 575
Great Lakes, 550, 552
Great Malvern, 243
Great Malvern Priory, 243
Greece, 10, 131–3, 135–6, 248, 425; political situation, 10, 132–3, 136, 248; royal family, 134–5
Greek National Opera, 248
Green Table, The (ballet), 475
Greene, Kenneth, 327
Greene, Richard, 316
Grenfell, Joyce, 101, 320
Gresham's School, 226, 246, 421, 540
Grétry, André, 213; *and see* IOC
Grieg, Edvard, 125, 134, 528; *and see* IOC
Griffiths, Paul, 448
Grogan, Christopher, 13, 29, 74, 112, 331, 384
Groome, Francis Hindes, 100; *Two Suffolk Friends*, 100
Groome, Robert Hindes, 100
Grosvenor Chapel, South Audley Street, London, 341, 354
Group Theatre, 88
Gruber, Franz, *see* IOC
Gschwend, August, 44, 54
Gstaad, 527–8
Guardian, 45, 116, 123, 139, 141, 193, 202, 207, 221, 227, 247, 305, 310, 421, 428, 508, 520, 540, 544, 561, 573; *see also Manchester Guardian*
Guildhall School of Music and Drama, London, 116, 310
Günther, Horst, 515
Gunung Agung (Balinese volcano), 387
Gut, Irene, 560
Guthrie, Tyrone, 192, 552, 553
Gyde, Humphrey, 108–9

Habunek, Vlado, 356–7, 515, 517
Häfliger, Ernst, 467
Hagen, Betty-Jean, 551
Hague, The: *The Turn of the Screw*, 328

Hahessy, John, *see* Elwes, John
Hale, Binnie, 334
Haley, William, 520
Hallé Orchestra, 68, 138
Hamburg, 466; *Billy Budd*, 118
Hamburg Chamber Orchestra, 46, 77
Hamburg Staatsoper, 555
Hamburger, Paul, 114, 115, 121, 310
Hamilton, Ian: *see* IOC
Hamlet (film), 469–70
Handel, George Frideric, 296, 319, 555; *and see* IOC
Handel Opera Society, 520
Handford, Basil, 221
Handsworth, 539
Haputale, 436
Hardy, Thomas, 4–5, 72, 142, 178, 182, 186, 228, 229; *Collected Poems*, 5, *184*, 185; *Jude the Obscure*, 182; poetry, 178, 182; *The Return of the Native*, 184; 'Wagtail and Baby', 18
Harewood, George Lascelles, 7th Earl of, *plates 7, 8*; 9–10, 17, 18, 43, 49, 62, 17, 18, 38, 52–3, 83, 134, 177, 200, 321, 351, 356–7, 359, 369, 435, 457, 459, 465, 478, 498–9, 511, 527, 535; and Aldeburgh Festival, 180; collection of recordings, 22, 311; and EOG, 98; and English Stage Company, 176; family holidays with BB and PP, 10, 17, 18, 41–4, 58, 76, 78, 133, 135–6; and *Gloriana*, 58, 63, 78, 83, 86, 90, 93, 107, 137, 140, 147, 150; as host to BB and PP, 18, 96, 113, 117, 123, 143, 329; as interviewee, 43; and Leeds Triennial Festival, 498–9; lineage, *59*; as music critic, 53–5; as presenter, 28, 166, 213, 261, 272; and *The Turn of the Screw*, 189, 280
Harewood, Marion, Countess of, *plate 8*; 10, 17, 18, 41–3, 47, 52, 76, 83, 133, 136, 143, 177, 188, 200, 359, 459, 465, 527, 535, 579; as pianist, 33; tribute to Princess Margaret of Hesse and the Rhine, 202
Harewood House, Yorkshire, 42, 113, 119, 199, 306, 327–9; *Winter Words*, 178, 182–3
Harlaxton Manor, Lincolnshire (monastery), 70
Harley Place, London, 541
Harley Street, London, 14, 130
Harlow, 535
Harlow Arts Trust, 540
Harman, Claire, 228
Harper, Heather, 116, 497
Harris, Joan, 475
Harris, Paul, 430, 516
Harrow School, 345, 349, 395, 405, 422, 450, 452, 461, 508
Hartley, L. P., 446
Hartnett, Michael, 354, 527, 536–7, 547
Harwich, 326, 344, 428, 536, 574
Harvey, Jonathan, *447*, 448
Harvey, Trevor, 315, 315
Haselden (caricaturist), 246
Hasketon, Suffolk, 46, 245
Hassall, Christopher, 66, 107
Hatfield House, 83, 86–7, 92
Hauser, Willi, 560
Hawes, Martin, 397
Hawkes, Ralph, 352
Haydn, Joseph, 126, 348, 427, 433, 436–7, 459, 532, 555; *and see* IOC
Hayes, Malcolm, 66, 107, 291
Head, Michael, 32–3
Headington, Christopher, 43, 54, 201
Heckel, Erich, 495–6

Heeley, Desmond, 482, 484, 486, 551
Hein, Ruth, 464
Hemmenhofen, 496
Hemmings, David, *plates 56, 57*; 12, 221–7; *Blow-Up and Other Exaggerations*, 12n, 223; and *Saint Nicolas*, 288; and *The Turn of the Screw*, *plates 19, 20, 22, 23*; 12, 172, 221, 222, 223–4, 225, 226–7, 272, 274, 277, 279, 281, 284, 296, 301, 314, 318, 326, 354, 372, 527
Hemsley, Thomas, 116, 126, 163
Hendon Technical College, 120
Henley-on-Thames, 118–19, 124
Henry V (film), 469
Henry VIII, King, 373
Hensher, Philip, 161
Henze, Hans Werner, 201, 449, 463, 555; tribute to Princess Margaret of Hesse and the Rhine, 202; *and see* IOC
Hepworth, Barbara, 305
Herbage, Julian, 120
Herbert, George, 433
Herbert, William, 523
Herodotus, 302
Heron, Patrick, 246
Hesse and the Rhine, Prince George of, 201
Hesse and the Rhine, Prince Ludwig (Lu) of, 4, 9, 17, 54, 76, 142, 199, 200–202, 266, 284, 301, 424–5, 436, 462, 467, 470, 527, 535–6, 539, 551, **558–9**; *Ausflug Ost 1956*, 201, 386–8, 390–91, 396, 398–401, 405–6, 413, 418–19, 426–7, 429; and Far East trip (1956), *plates 30, 35*; 201, 341, 385, 387, 394, 397, 400, 403, 411, 416, 418, 422, 426–7, 429, 456; as host to BB and/or PP, 199, 329, 433, 466, 470, 515, 524, 534, 539; and Italian holiday (1957), 201, 493, 524–6; and Yugoslavian trip (1959), 360; as translator, 201, 464, 471, 494, 558, 560; *see also* Tarasp, Schloss, *and* Wolfsgarten, Schloss
Hesse and the Rhine, Princess Margaret (Peg) of, 9, 17, 54, 76, 111, 142, 199, 200–202, 218, 232, 243, 266, **272**, 284, 301, 329, 406, 424–6, **429**, 436, 462, 465, 467, 474, 515, 519, 527, 534–5, 536, 539, **547–50**, 551, **551–2**, **553–4**, 556, 559–60, 562, 575; *Dear Friends 1956–1986*, 202; and Far East trip (1956), *plate 30*; 201, 341, 384–5, 387, 391, 394, 396–7, 400–401, 403–4, 406, 410, 412–16, 420, 426–7, 429, 456; and Italian holiday (1957), 201, 493, 522, 524–6; *see also* Tarasp, Schloss, *and* Wolfsgarten, Schloss
Hesse family, 201
Hesse Memorial Lecture (Aldeburgh Festival), 201
Hesse Students Scheme (Aldeburgh Festival), 201
Hewetson, Christopher, 344, 347, 405
Heyworth, Peter, 485
Hickox, Richard, 315
Hicks, Anthony, 520
Higgs (doctor), 187
High Wycombe Grammar School: *Let's Make an Opera* (1952), 32
Highgate, 520
Hildalgo, Elvira de, 248
Hill, Miss (Jakarta), 406
Hill, Rose, 320
Hilversum: PP–BB broadcast recital, 296
Himalayas, 382, 394
Hindemith, Paul, 125; *and see* IOC
Histories of Lot and Abraham (Chester miracle play), 23, 26–7

HMV (record company), 537, 584–5
Hogarth Press (publishing house), 198
Hoggart, Richard, 567
Holland, *see* Netherlands, The
Holland Festival, 8, 348, 438–9; *The Turn of the Screw*, 288, 328
Hollywood, culture of, 49
Holst, Gustav, 12, 29, 184, 211, 288, 356, 384; *and see* IOC
Holst, Imogen, *plates, 3, 39–42*; 12–14, 29, **72–3**, **111–12**, **352–4**, 356, **361**, **382**, **384–5**, **399–400**, 496, 508, **524** ; and Aldeburgh Festival, 12–13, 72–3, 88, 356, 433, 516, 572; and Aldeburgh Music Club, 210–11; as arranger and music editor, 13n, 17, 73, 106, 203, 355, 454; as BB's confidante and friend, 9n, 10, 13–14, 97–8, 100, 111–12, 123, 136, 140, 143–4, 344, 374, 422, 524; as BB's music assistant, 12–14, 18, 21, 28–9, 95–6, 111–12, 137, 168, 182–4, 188, 200, 203, 223, 265, 320, 466, 470–71, 508, 524, 558, 564, 581; at Bryanston, 73–4; as choir trainer, 13n, 73; as concert planner, 114; as conductor, 29, 210–11, 319, 341, 354, 383, 391, 555; at Dartington, 12–13, 73, 331, 383; diary, 5, 13, 29, 68–70, 79, 82, 87, 94–6, 98, 102–3, 106, 111–12, 121, 123, 125, 129–30, 132, 136, 140, 145, 168, 182–3, 210–11, 290, 337–8; as editor, 39, 211, 536; in interview, 13, 29, 476–7; and PP, 29, 330, 477; and Purcell Singers, 73, 341, 571; as teacher, 32–3; as writer, 9n, 121, 493, 510–12
Holst, Isobel, 143, 354, 382, 384, 385
Holt, Anne, 462
Holt, Oliver, 114, 357, 462
Honegger, Arthur, 106, 108, 213; *see also* IOC
Hong Kong, 147, 342, 400–404, 406–8, 410–11; PP–BB concerts and recitals, 400, 404, 406
Hong Kong: Empire Theatre (Cinema), 406
Hong Kong: Victoria Peak, 331, 404, 406
Hong Kong airport, 410
Hong Kong Radio, 406
Hook of Holland, 77, 326, 344, 425, 536
Hope, Vida, 334–5
Hope-Wallace, Philip, 146, 155
Horham, Suffolk, 179
Houghton, Norfolk, 81, 173–4
Housman, Laurence, 58
'How' series (BBC radio), 101
How to Listen to the Radio (BBC radio feature), 101
Howard, Patricia, 301
Howells, Herbert, 534
Howes, Frank, 6, 272, 274
Huberman, Bronislaw, 573
Huddersfield, 39, 440
Huddersfield Choral Society, 498
Hudson, Elizabeth (Nellie), *plate 5*; 41, 43, 69–70, 102, 104, 125, 145, 352, 361, 382, 462, 467, 476, 537, 547
Hughes, Davina, 227
Hull: PP–BB recital, 47
Hull, University of, 523
Hungarian National Philharmonic Orchestra, 575
Hungary: during Second World War, 202; 1956 uprising, 473–4
Hunter, Ian, 540
Huntley, John, 108
Hürlimann, Bettina, 349
Hürlimann, Martin, 349
Hurwitz, Emanuel (Manny), 573

Hurwitz String Quartet, 573
Hussey, Reverend Walter, *89*, 196
Huxley, Julian, 511; *The Story of Evolution*, 511
Huysmans, Madame (Belgium), 37, 38

Ibbs & Tillett, 112–13, 430, 571
Ibsen, Henrik, 281
Icarus (myth), 299, 302
IJzerdraat, Bernard (Penny), 385–8, 389, 391–2, 399, 403, 405
Ilfracombe: Holy Trinity Church, 261; PP–BB recital, 261
Illuminations (ballet), 39
Illustrated (periodical), 227
Imperial Household Agency, Tokyo, *see* Tokyo: Kunaicho-Gakubu
Independent (newspaper), 34, 45, 116, 123, 126, 141, 202, 210, 213, 221, 227, 247, 305, 366, 421, 508, 540, 544, 561, 573
Independent Television Authority, 540; *see also* ITV
India, 7, 341–2, 347, 353, 361, 370, 372–4, 376–7, 379, 382, 384, 387, 400, 410, 423, 425, 427, 429, 447, 539; *see also individual locations*
Indian dance, 375, 382, 384, 424
Indian drumming, 375, 424
Indian music, 368, 374–5, 377, 381–2, 384
Indonesia, 7, 384, 393, 396, 403; *see also individual locations*
Indonesian dance, 388
Indonesian music, 388
Indonesian National Party, 406
Inglis, Anne, 193, 310, 573
Ingoldstadt: PP–BB recital, 474
Ingram, Michael, *see* Crawford, Michael
Innocents, The (film), 232
Instone, Anna, 120
Instrument of his Soul, The (BBC radio documentary), 449
International Red Cross, 201
Ionesco, Eugene, 537–8; *Les Chaises* (*The Chairs*), 535, 537–8
Ipswich, 134, 195
IRA (Irish Republican Army), 427
Iran, 425
Iraq, 425
IRCAM (Institut de Récherche et Co-ordination Acoustique-Musique), Paris, 448
Ireland, 18, 133, 135–7
Ireland, John, **267**, 267, 268; *and see* IOC
Irish Republican Army, *see* IRA
Irvine, J. Thorburn, 161
Irving, Robert, 478
Isaacs, Leonard, 114, 115
Isaacs, Susanna, *see* Elmhirst, Susanna
Isherwood, Christopher, 185; *see also* Auden, W. H.
Israel, 474
Istanbul, 341, 348, 351, 356–7, 366–7, 369–70, 373, 376, 569; Santa Sophia, 353–4, 360–61, 367–8; PP–BB recital, 370
Istanbul Conservatory, 370
Istanbul Philharmonic Orchestra, 370
Italy, 140, 316, 369, 493, 522, 524, 526; *see also individual locations*
ITV (Independent Television), 565, 567
Ives, Burl, 157
Izmir, 248

Jadhav, Clubwala, 429
Jakarta, 401, 403, 406, 445
James, Henry, 76, 113, 174, 192, 274–7, 279–82, 300–301, 548; *Owen Wingrave*, 2, 300; *The Turn of the Screw*, 2, 76, 88, 139, 166, 189, 192, 205, 230, 232–3, 236–8, 240–41, 256, 272, 274–7, 279–82, 300–301, 559–61
James, William, 274
Janáček, Leoš, 172, 555; centenary, 172; *and see* IOC
Japan, *plates 33–38*; 7, 313, 331, 342, 374, 379, 400, 404, 407–9, 411, 416, 455; in Second World War, 125, 407; *see also individual locations*
Japanese Broadcasting Authority, *see* NHK
Japanese Old Instrument Company, 414, 455
Jardine Matheson Hong Kong (company), 331, 401, 404, 406
Java, 125, 342, 384–6, 388, 392–3, 394, 396–7, 400, 403–4; *see also individual locations*
Javanese music and dance, 400–401
Jeffries, Richard, 30; *Bevis: The Story of a Boy*, 30
Jellicoe, Ann, 538
Jenkins, Alan, 101
Jeppesen, Knud Christian, 73
Jerusalem, 369
Jesus College, Cambridge, 147
ji-utai (chorus in Nō theatre), 417
Jochum, Eugen, 476
joged (Balinese dance), 387, 397
John, Augustus, 248
John, Gwen, 245, 248; *The Messenger*, 248
John, Nicholas, 78, 140, 150
John Lehmann Ltd (publishing house), 83; *see also* Lehmann, John
John Murray (publishing house), 239; *see also* Murray, John, and Murray, Sir John
Johnstone, Keith, 538; *Brixham Regatta*, 538; *For Children*, 538
Johnstone, Maurice, 514
Jolly, Father, 69–70
Jonathan Cape (publishing house), 298–9, 455, 532
Jones, J. D. F., 175
Jones, Rowland, 166
Jonson, Ben, 61
Jooss, Kurt, 473, 475
Jooss–Leeder School of Dance, 475
Journal of the Society for Research in Asiatic Music, 414
Jove (miniature dachshund), *plate 4*; 476, 554
Jubilee Hall, Aldeburgh, *see* Aldeburgh: Jubilee Hall
Jugoslavia, *see* Yugoslavia
Julian Bream Consort, 203, 310, 573
Justin (Royal Opera House), 56

Kabuki theatre, 409, 416, 420
Kaindl-Hönig, M. (music critic), 43
Kallin, Anna, 305
Kandy, 423, 426
Kangen (subgenre of traditional Japanese court music), 455
Kapi Radja (gamelan piece), 389, 397
Karachi, 341, 367, 370, 376, 425, 552
Karachi: Palace Hotel, 370
Karajan, Herbert von, 351, 584
Kästner, Erich, 30; *Emil und die Detektive*, 30
Katchenjunga, 394
Kathleen Ferrier: An Ordinary Diva (TV documentary), 22

Kathleen Ferrier: The Singer and the Person (LP recording), 22
Kathleen Ferrier Cancer Fund, 14
katjapi-players (Balinese musicians), 392
Katsua, 413
Katsua: Detached Villa, 413
Katzin, Olga ('Sagittarius'), 10, 61; 'The Elizabethans', 61–2
Kavanagh, Julie, 39
Keats, John, 578
kecak (Balinese monkey dance), 390
Keighley: PP concert, 312
Keller, Hans, 9n, 18, 46, 114, 116, **119–20**, 204, 448, 497; as translator, 116; *see also* Mitchell, Donald
kendang (gamelan drums), 397–8
Kennedy, Benjamin Hall: *The Shorter Latin Primer*, 207, *208*, 209
Kennedy, Michael, 106, 145, 291, 469–70
Kensington High Street, London, 47
Kenyon, Nicholas, 457
Keppel, Francis, *see* Bennett, Edwin Keppel (Francis)
Kerley, William, 21, 508
Kerr, Deborah, 232
Kerr, Muriel, 56–7
Kertész, István, 118
Ketèlbey, Albert, 380
Keys, Robert, 33, 93, 95, 127
Khrushchev, Nikita, 376
Kiel, 559
Kihl, Richard, 69, 207, *208*
Kildea, Paul, 252
King's Lynn, 163, 173–4; PP and PP–BB recitals, *105*, 174, 327–8
King's Lynn Festival, 174
Kingsland Central School, 33
Kirby, James, 117
Kirov Ballet, 475
Kishinami, Yukiko, 411
Kiyotsugu, Kan'ami, 416
Klee, Paul, 486
Kletzki, Paul, 68
Klungkung, 387
Klungkung: Bale Kambang, 387
Klungkung: Kerta Gosa, 387
Knokke: *The Turn of the Screw*, 328
Knussen, Oliver, 475, 497
Koeman, Greet, 327
Kögler, Horst, 94
Köhler-Helffrich, Heinrich, 44, 54
kokata (child performer in Nō theatre), 417
Köln, *see* Cologne
Komparu, Kunio, 416–17
Korea, 455
Kotelawala, John, 423, 426
ko-tsuzumi (Japanese drum), *plate 35*
Krannhals, Alexander, 327
Kraus, Otakar, 28, 216, 218
Krebs, Beatrice, 515
Krebs, Friedrich, **545**, 545
Krips, Harriet, 45
Krips, Josef, 42, 45, 433, 450
Kuala Lumpur, 534
Kubelík, Rafael, 131, 311, 333, 456, *457*, 458, 497, 535
Kunst, Jaap, 396
Kurosawa, Hiroshi (Peter), 411, 413–14, 417, 455–6
Kurosawa, Kei-ichi, *plates 33, 36*; 210, 411, 413–14, 436

Kurosawa, Teijiro, 411
Kuta, 385, 405
Kyoto, 408–9, 413–14, 455; Imperial Palace, 413; Nijo Palace, 413; textile museum, 413; Tsuraya teahouse, 413

Labour Day (Canada and US), 553–4
Lady and the Fool, The (ballet), 508
Lancaster, Osbert, 57, 529
Lancing College, Sussex, 32, 34, 37, 142–3, 220–21, 320; *A Boy was Born*, 352–4; PP–BB recital, 37, 221; *Saint Nicolas*, 221
Landgraf, Ludwig, *see* Hesse and the Rhine, Prince Ludwig of
Landmark Trust, 92
Langdon, Michael, 166
Langham, Michael, 551
Langridge, Philip, 116
Lannigan, John, 138
Lascelles, Alan (Tommy), 10, 58
Lascelles, David, 42, 47, 109, 117, 177, 182
Lascelles, James, 177, *182*, 200
Lawrence, Quentin, 566
Lawrie, James, **500–501**, 502, 507, 535–6
Lawson, Catherine, 126–7
Leach, Bernard, 383
League for Democracy in Greece, 132–3
Lear, Edward, 312, 313; *Girgenti*, 313; *Grant's Castle*, 313; nonsense verse, 313; *Parnassus*, 313; *Ravenna*, 313
Lebanon, 376, 425; *see also individual locations*
Lebrecht, Norman, 98, 457
Lee, Frank, 132, 181, 354, 438, 440, 583
Lee, Noel, 115
Leeder, Sigurd, 475
Leeds, 188, 498–500, 554; Town Hall, 499; PP–BB recital, 47, 178; *Winter Words*, 178, 182, *183*
Leeds, University of, 539
Leeds Centenary Festival, 499
Leeds Triennial Music Festival, 178, 182, 188, 493, 498–500
Lees-Milne, James, 29
Lefébure, Yvonne, 113
Lefort, Bernard, 213
Léger, Fernand, 526
Legge, Walter, 295
legong (Balinese dance), 390–91, 405
Lehmann, John, 83
Leicester, University of, 523
Leif (Danish treble), 181
Leigh, Adèle, 137, 138, 152
Leigh, Vivien, 468, 469–70
Leipzig: Thomaskirche, 331
Leiston Modern School, 580
Leningrad (St Petersburg): *The Prince of the Pagodas*, 475
Lensky, Margaret, 478
Leppard, Raymond, 224, 578
Lesur, Daniel, 106; *and see* 10c
Lewes, Sussex, 257
Lewis, Anthony, 159–60
Liebl, Karl, 44, 54
Life (periodical), 469
Linden, Anya, 484
Lines on the Map (radio series), 101
Lippmann, Ursula, 560
Lipton's tea plantation, 426

GENERAL INDEX

lira da braccio, 437
lira organizzata, 436–7
Lishner, Leon, 544
Lister, Laurie, 320–21
Litton Cheney, 219
Litvin, Natasha, 112, 113
Liverpool, 537; *Canticle II*, 17, 24, 35
Liverpool Street railway station, London, 92
Ljubljana, 341, 356–8; Hotel Slon, 357; PP–BB recital, 358
Llangollen, 328
London, University of, 523
London Airport, 450
London Magazine (periodical), 147
London Opera Centre, 141, 536; *see also* National Opera School
London Philharmonic Choir, 523
London Philharmonic Orchestra (LPO), 68, 140, 523, 575
London Polish Quartet, 310
London Sinfonietta, 475, 497
London Symphony Orchestra, 246, 361
London Symphony Orchestra: Wind Ensemble, 166, 186
London Theatre Studio, 538
London theatres, *see* individual venues
Long Acre, Covent Garden, 151
Long Island Home, 43
Long Melford, 29
Lord Chamberlain, office of, 143, 283
Lords Cricket Ground, 461
Lot, Lawrence, 56, 57
Lovett, Martin, 193, 310
Low, David, 11
Lowe, John, 203
Lowestoft, 521, 536
LPO, *see* London Philharmonic Orchestra
LSO, *see* London Symphony Orchestra
Lübeck, 246
Lucas, Major Sir Jocelyn Morton, 373
Lucas, John, 138
Ludwig, Prince, of Hesse and the Rhine, *see* Hesse and the Rhine, Prince Ludwig of
Lumsden, Norman, 163, 478
Lympe, 459
Lyric Theatre, Hammersmith, 501–3
Let's Make an Opera, 32–3, 52, 95

Mabel (Stratford, Ontario), 548, 552
MacAlpine, Bill, 411
Macau, 342, 400–401, 404; PP–BB recital, 407
Macau: Music Circle, 407
Macau: Pedro V Theatre, 407
McCready, Michael, 114–15, 176
MacDonald, Malcolm, 424, 427
MacDonald, Ramsay, 427
Mace, Edward, 202
Machov, Sasa, 39
McInnes, Campbell, 553, 554, 555
McInnes, Colin, 555
Mackail, John William, 554
Mackay, Jane, 207, 209
Mackenzie, Sir Compton, 133
Mackerras, Charles, 94, 168, 527, 529, 544, 554, 555–6, 562
Mackie, Neil, 454
McKinley, Andrew, 544

Maclean's (periodical; Canada), 155
Macmillan (Associated Rediffusion executive), 567
Macmillan, Harold, 324
MacMillan, Kenneth, 475, 485, 508
Macmillan (publishing house), 289
MacNeice, Louis, 516
McPhee, Colin, 385, 388–91 396–7, 416; *and see* IOC
Madras, 342, 382, 424, 427, 429, 445; orphanage, 429; PP–BB recitals, 342, 424, 427; Raj Bhavan, 424
Magdalene College, Cambridge, 523
Magito, Suria, 49
Mahabalipuram, 424
Mahler, Gustav, 457, 524, 578; centenary (1960), 457; *and see* IOC
Mahler-Werfel, Alma, 578, 578–9
Malaya, 385, 394, 493; *see also individual locations*
Malaya: State of Emergency (1948–60), 387, 394
Malayan Peoples' Anti-Japanese Army, 387
Malaysia, 387, 531–2, 534; national anthem, 387
Malcolm, George, 115, 121, 125, 219, 219–20, 221, 223
Malipiero, Gian Francesco, 278
Malipiero, Riccardo, 278
Malloy, Antonia, 219
Malvern, *see* Great Malvern
Man, Isle of: and internment, 34, 115
Manchester: *Billy Budd*, 57; *Canticle II*, 17, 24, 35; *Gloriana*, 218; PP–BB recitals, 289
Manchester, University of, 523
Manchester Guardian (newspaper), 11, 36, 274–6, 447; *see also Guardian* (newspaper)
Manchester Guardian Weekly, 6n, 146, 155, 186, 483
Manchuria, 455
mandi (Indonesian bath), 396
Mandikian, Arda, *plates 18, 21*; 126, 163, 192, 226, 245, 247–8, 272, 274, 277, 284, 371, 544, 550
Mangan, Richard, 138
Manhattan School of Music, 45
Manitoba, University of, 115
Mannes College, New York, 45
Mansel, Philip, 202
Manuel, Roland, 106; *and see* IOC
Maran, George, 560
Marchant, Bill, 345
Marcks, Gerhard, 348
Mare, Walter de la, 227
Margaret, Princess, 134, 135
Margaret, Princess, of Hesse and the Rhine, *see* Hesse and the Rhine, Princess Margaret of
Maribor, 341, 356–8; PP–BB recital, 358
Markes, Charles, 268
Markevitch, Igor, 309, 309, 456
Marlborough Place (No. 59), London, 115
Marmora, Sea of, 367
Martello Tower, Aldeburgh, 91–2
Martin, Frank, 310, 311; *and see* IOC
Martlett Court, Covent Garden, 151
Marx, Joseph, 351
Mary, Princess, the Princess Royal, 9, 58, 117, 143, 329, 478, 527, 531
Mary, Queen, 136
Marylebone Cricket Club, *see* MCC
Mas, 389
Masefield, John, 516
Masefield, Nancy, 239
Mason, Colin, 6n, 36, 186, 274–6
Mason, Sir Paul, 345, 348

Massenet, Jules, 213; *and see* IOC
Matare, Ewald, 348
Matthews, Colin, 13n
Matthews, David, 497
Matthews, Thomas, 65, 68
Maud, Humphrey, 68, 69
Maw, Nicholas, 72, 210, 519
Maxwell-Fyffe, Sir David, 10, 143, 209
Mayer, Beata, *see* Sauerlander, Beata
Mayer, Christopher, 42, 47, 495
Mayer, Elizabeth, 2, 5n, *40–42*, 43, 46, 124, 147, 164, 166, **176–8**, **189–92**, 291, **495–6**, 499, **526–7**, 549, **556–7**, 558, 562, **577–8**; as translator, 43
Mayer, Michael, 42, 47, 190, 578
Mayer, Thérèse, 216
Mayer, Thomas, 551
Mayer, Tony, 76, 78, 212, 213, *215*, **216**; *La vie Anglaise*, 213
Mayer, Ulrica, 47
Mayer, William, 41–2, 43, 176–8, 190, 192, 495–6
Mayer family, 176
Mayerl, Billy, 447
May Fair (periodical; Canada), 557
MCC (Marylebone Cricket Club), 425, 427, 461
Meade Farm, Welcombe, 546–7
Mechanical-Copyright Protection Society, 447
Medak, Lotte, 319
Medan, 403
Medea (myth), 302
Medici, Mario, 2n
Mehta, Zubin, 219
Meisner, Nadine, 561
Melbury Road (No. 22a), 42, 47, 57, 113–14, 177
Mell (partner of Basil Coleman), 562, 568
Melos Ensemble, 361, 573
Melville, Alan, 322
Melville-Mason, Graham, 141, 366
Ménerbes, 76
Menotti, Gian Carlo, 279
Menton, 66, 77; Riviera Palace Hotel, 77; concert conducted by BB, 18, 46, 77; PP–BB recital, 42, 66
Menton, Festival de Musique de, 46
Menuhin, Diana, 109, 559, 561; *Fiddler's Moll: Life with Yehudi*, 561
Menuhin, Yehudi, **109**, 109–10, 179, 457, 462, 464–6, 517, 527–8, 531–2, 561; and Violin Concerto, 109–10
Mercury Theatre, London, 49
Meredith, Anthony, 430, 516
Merrick, Frank, 115
Mersey, River, 547
Mertz, Franz, 560
Mesiner, Nadine, 508
Messager, André: *see* IOC
Messel, Oliver, 145–6, *146*
Messiaen, Olivier, 141, 448, 456; *and see* IOC
Metropolitan Opera, New York, 44, 558
Mewton-Wood, Mrs, 291
Mewton-Wood, Noel, *plate 43*; 62, 115, 134, 287, 289–90, 291, 294, *317*, 318, 557; as accompanist for PP, 62, 96, 105, 125, 131, 133–4
Mexico, 329
Middlesex County Cricket Club, 461
Milan, 260, 522, 526; La Scala, 55, 94, 203, 350, 369, 475, 493, 509, 519, 522–3, 526, 529, 531; Piccola Scala, 369; *Billy Budd*, 55; *The Prince of the Pagodas*, 475, 493, 507, 509, 519, 521–2, 525–6

Milhaud, Darius, 213; *and see* IOC
Miller, Arthur, 469
Miller, Jonathan, 323
Milnes, Rodney, 544
Milngavie: PP recital, 131, 134
Mitchell, Donald, 7, 9n, 18, 46, 102, 114–16, 116, **119–20**, 143, 159, 181, 204, 246–7, 265, 296, 307, 315, 331, 389, 496; *Benjamin Britten: A Commentary on His Works from a Group of Specialists* (with Hans Keller), 9n, 18, 83, 115–17, 119–22; as critic, 485; eulogy for Jeremy Cullum, 179; interviews, 13, 29, 43, 46, 68, 179–80, 247, 249, 476–7, 543, 560, 564–5, 572, 582; as music editor, 315, 475
Mitchell, G. F. (Trinity College, Dublin), 136
Mitchell, Kathleen, 110, 116; 'Edinburgh Diary 1968', 110
Mitford, Nancy, 66
Mitropoulos, Dimitri, 109
Moisewitsch, Tanya, 552–3
Monahan, James, 123
Monde, Le (newspaper), 66, 155
Monitor (BBC Television series), 581
Monnaie, Théâtre de la, Brussels, *see* Brussels: Théâtre de la Monnaie
Monroe, Marilyn, 468, 469
Montecatisir, 444
Monteux, Pierre, 44
Monte Carlo, 77
Montegufoni, Castello di, 316, 319
Monteriano, 525
Monteverdi, Claudio: *see* IOC
Montmartre, Paris, 66
Montreal, 527, 547
Mookerjee, Sir Birendra Nath, 382, 383
Mookerjee, Lady Ranu, 382–3
Moor, Edward: *Bealing Bells*, 194–5
Moore, Dudley, 323–4; 'Little Miss Britten', 323–4
Moore, Gerald, 36
Moore, Henry, 383, 396, 429
Moore, Thomas, 578; *Irish Melodies*, 578; *National Melodies*, 578
Moreton House, 166
Morison, Elsie, 130, 131
Morley, Peter, 544, 567
Morley, Thomas, 497; *and see* IOC
Morley College, London, 147, 304, 475
Morocco, 133
Moscow, 445
Mosesson, 523
Motet de Genève, 305
Motokiyo, Zeami, 416
Motomasa, Jūrō, 416; *Sumidagawa*, 3, 49, 342, 409, 416–19, *419*, 420, 455, 532, 534
Mountbatten of Burma, Lady Edwina, 424, 427
Mountbatten of Burma, Lord Louis, 424, 427
Mozart, Wolfgang Amadeus, 28, 42, 45–6, 98, 125–6, 131, 181, 261, 333, 346, 433, 459, 463, 517, 525, 555; *and see* IOC
Mullaghmore, 427
Mullins, Charlotte, 198
München, *see* Munich
Munich, 330, 366, 434, 465, 467, 470, 473, 476, 514, 542; Hotel Eden Wolf, 515; Jahreszeiten Hotel, 465; St Lucaskirche, 515; PP and/or BB performances, 474, 514–15; *The Turn of the Screw*, 288, 318

GENERAL INDEX

Munich Bach Choir, 331, 515
Munich Bach Orchestra, 331
Munich Ballet, 473, 475
Muromachi (Japanese historical period), 416
Murray, John, 239
Murray, Sir John (Jock), 238, 239
Music Critics Circle, New York, 521
Music & Letters (periodical), 121
Music Magazine (BBC radio series), 120
Music Magazine (Hong Kong Radio series), 406
Music Survey (periodical), 9n, 115–16
Musical Times (periodical), 29, 305, 307, 315, 485
Muskoka, Lake, 553
Musorgsky [Mussorgsky], Modest, 209; *and see* IOC
Muti, Riccardo, 369

Nagy, Imre, 473–4
Nara, 413–14, 455–6
Nasser, Gamal Abdel, 474
National Gallery, London, 97, 246
National Institute of Arts and Letters, New York, 522
National Opera School (formerly Opera Studio; later London Opera Centre), 195–6, 249, 535–6, 575
National Portrait Gallery, London, 78, 289
National Theatre, London, 538
NBC Symphony Orchestra, 447
NBC Television: *Scenes from 'Billy Budd'*, 18, 45, 542, 544
Neale, J. E.: *Elizabeth I and Her Parliaments, 1584–1601*, 63; *Queen Elizabeth*, 62–3
Neel, Boyd, 50, 562, 568; *see also* Boyd Neel Orchestra
Nehru, Jawaharlal, 370, 372, 373, 377, 382, 423, 427
Netherlands, 188, 298, 326, 344–5, 392–3, 396, 425, 550; PP and/or BB recitals/concerts, 287, 296, 347, 532; *The Rape of Lucretia*, 22; *see also individual locations*
Netherlands Chamber Orchestra, 126
Netherlands Opera, 326; *Peter Grimes*, 326
Nendick, Josephine, 516
Nepalese dance, 397
Nettleship, Ursula, 147, 498
neue Forum, Das (programme magazine; Darmstadt), 560
Neue Zürcher Zeitung (newspaper), 31
Neunzig, H. A., 464
Neville-Smith, Esther, 143, 190, 193, 320
Neville-Smith, Jennifer, 190, 193
New Covenant Church, 543
New Elizabethan Age, concept of, 59, 62, 81, 159, 161
New Philharmonia, 573
New South Wales Conservatorium, Sydney, 555
New Statesman and Nation, 6, 10, 61–2, 156–7, 282–4, 294, 301, 328
New York, 109, 352, 475, 549, 562, 579; *Billy Budd*, 18, 118; *The Prince of the Pagodas*, 475, 577
New York City Opera, 44
New York Herald Tribune (newspaper), 158, 278–80
New York Philharmonic Orchestra, 109
New York Times (newspaper), 45, 155, 192, 544
New Zealand, 332
Newbury, 435
Newman, Ernest, 121, 157, 280–81
Newman, Joseph, 158

Newmark, John, 36
News Chronicle (newspaper), 152, 154, 458
Newton, John, 429
NHK (Nippon Hoso Kyokai), 342, 407, 411–12, 455; PP–BB recital, *plates 37, 38*; 411–12
NHK Orchestra, 412
Nicholas (BB's godson), 109
Nicholson, Ben, 383
Nicholson, Winifred, 383
Nightingale, Florence, 367, 369
Night Mail (film), 361
Nilsson, Raymond, 163
Nippon Hoso Kyokai, *see* NHK
Nissel, Muriel, 311
Nissel, Sigmund, 115, 193, 310
Nō theatre, 3, 49–50, 313, 318, 342, 409, 416–17, 429, 441, 455, 534
Noel, Conrad: *Life of Jesus*, 338
Noguchi, Isamu, 538
nōkan (Japanese bamboo flute), 417
nōmen (mask in Nō theatre), 417
North Atlantic Council, 348
Northcliffe, Lord, 520
Northen, Michael, 257, 333, 502
Northern Sinfonia, 457
Norwich, 233, 246; St Andrew's Hall, 314; St Peter Mancroft, 341; choir of, 341; Theatre Royal, 372; *Hymn to St Peter*, 341; *Let's Make an Opera*, 372; *Saint Nicolas*, 328; *Serenade*, 314
Norwich Philharmonic Society, 314, 328
Nottingham: Albert Hall, 35; *Canticle II*, 17, 24, 35; PP–BB recitals, 188
Nottingham, University of, 348, 523
Nottingham Guardian (newspaper), 36
Nottingham Journal (newspaper), 36
Nowakowski, Marian, 113
Nureyev, Rudolf, 508
Nuttall, Michael: *see* IOC

Observer (newspaper), 10n, 158, 227, 281–2, 485
Oeuvre du XXième Siècle festival, 64
Old Mill, Snape, 72, 326–7
Old Vic Centre, 538
Old Vic Company, 538
Oldham, Arthur, 8, 18, 39, 57, 90, 91, 106, 211, 288; *and see* IOC
Oliver, Michael, 3n, 487
Olivier, Laurence, 468, 469–70, 482, 538
Omnibus (BBC TV series), 21
Ontario, 527, 553; *see also individual locations*
Ootacamund, 375
Opera (periodical), 44, 45, 53, 55, 213, 247, 497, 544
Opera News (periodical), 45, 544
Opera North: *Gloriana*, 168
Opera Studio (later National Opera School), 196–7
Orange, France, 66
Oranienburg (concentration camp), 202
Orford: St Bartholomew's Church, 247, 543, 562, 565, 579–81
Ormandy, Eugène, 181–2
Orme Square (No. 2), 124, 143
Orr, Robin, 211
Osborne, John, 325, 538; *Look Back in Anger*, 325–6, 538
Ostend, 201, 330
ō-tsuzumi (Japanese drum), *plate 35*
Ottawa, 314

Ouchterlony, David, 567
Oundle School, 34; PP–BB recital, 34
Ovid, 299, 302; *Metamorphoses*, 299, 302
Owen, Wilfred, 28, 464, 516; 'The Parable of the Old Man and the Young', 28
Oxford, 95, 320; Playhouse, 372; *Let's Make an Opera*, 372
Oxford, University of, 523; *and see individual colleges*
Oxford Dictionary of National Biography, The, 520, 561
Oxford University Opera Club, 248
Oxford University Press, 315, 384, 532
Oxfordshire, 433

Pacific Ocean, 329, 331, 402, 405
Paddington station, 439
Pakistan, 341, 367, 370, 427–8; *see also individual locations*
Palembang, 341, 388
Palmer, Tony, 450
Pan-American (airline), 422, 425
Pandy, Mr (Balinese art dealer), 386
Parade (ballet), 486
Paradigm (periodical), 209
Parham, Suffolk, 239
Parikian, Manoug, 306, 307
Paris, 64, 66–7, 115, 192, 212–13, 256–7, 369, 371, 517, 528–9, 554; Théâtre des Champs-Elysées, 17, 64, 433, 459; *Billy Budd*, 17, 64, 65, 66–7, 118; *The Turn of the Screw*, 226, 433, 459
Paris, Festival of (1956), 433, 459, 500
Paris Opéra, 531
Parknasilla, County Kerry, 136
Parr, Gladys, 478, 581
Parsons, Charles H., 439
Parsons, William, 478
Pascal, Gabriel, 108
Pasco, Richard, 537
Patterson, Tom, 551
Pavlova, Anna Pavlovna, 380
Peabody Buildings, Covent Garden, 151
Pearl, River, 404
Pears, Jessie, *see* Blackwell, Jessie
Pears, Peter, *plates* 3, 8, 10, 12, 14, 17, 18, 20, 24–26, 29, 30, 34–36, 38, 39, 45, 47; 23, **112, 117, 124–5, 130–31, 133–4, 245, 329–30, 462, 464–5, 466–7, 476, 514–15, 534–6**; and Aldeburgh Festival, 72, 181, 239, 437, 516; as administrator, 29; as art collector, 100–101, 247–8; as bassoonist, 211; education, 34; finances, 221, 527; food, taste in, 398; honours and awards, 9n, 493, 527–8; and humour, 125; as keyboard-player, 210–11; as music editor, 352; as narrator, reader and presenter, 22, 23, 254, 255, 328, 454; as recorder-player, 210; sexuality, 10, 224, 324, 555–6; social contacts and relationships, 38, 41, 42, 48, 53, 76, 82, 83, 99–100, 103, 165, 173, 187, 189, 200, 218, 228, 257–8, 267, 269, 271, 272, 290, 303, 319–20, 329, 351, 368, 395, 400, 416, 418, 429, 436, 455, 470–71, 473, 525, 547–54, 562, 575, 578–9; suggestions and support for BB's compositions, 48, 184, 477; as teacher, 331; as translator, 529; travel diary, 343, 369, 375, 379–81, 383–4, 396–8, 411, 414, 421; and Wagner, 497, 508; and Walton's *Troilus and Cressida*, 287, 291; works written for, 72; and young people, 33, 69; *for association with works written by BB, see* Index of Britten's Works; *for details of daily personal and professional life, see entries for* Britten, Benjamin; *for performances, see concert-promoting organizations and locations in this* General Index, *and for performances of works by composers other than BB, see* IOC

Pears, Susan (Sue), 429, 430
Pearson, John, 289
Pease, James, 497
Pecht St Gallen, Hotel, 114
Peers, Donald, 11
Peliatan, 389
Peliatan gamelan, 389, 391
Pemungkah (Balinese shadow-play music), 392
Peng, Chin, 387
Penny Plain (revue), 320
People's Palace, London, 513
Percival, John, 57, 91, 192, 260, 474
Pergolesi, Giovanni Battista, 73
Periton, Leslie, 21, 28, **343**, 452, 535, 537, 584
Periton, Muriel, 343
Pérotin: *see* IOC
Persia, *see* Iran
Perugia, 525
Petipa, Marius, 486
Petri, Egon, 115
Pettit, Stephen, 295
Phaethon (myth), 298–9, 302
Phelan, Nancy, 555
Philharmonia Orchestra, 505, 584
Philip, Prince, Duke of Edinburgh, 18, 143, 147, 151–2, 201, 494, 535, 539, 540
Philips (recording company), 392, 438–40
Phillips, Suzanne, 22
Philomusica of London, 115, 220
Phipps, Jack, 430
Phipps, Sue, *see* Pears, Susan (Sue)
Phoenix Productions, 246
Picasso, Pablo, 102, 512
Picture Post, 9
Pierce, Judith, 527
Piguet, Jean-Claude, 311
Pilgrims (trust), 520, 522
Pilkington Committee on Broadcasting, 567
Pineapple Poll (ballet), 94, 508
Piper, Clarissa, *plate* 24
Piper, Edward, *plate* 24; 220, 221, 236
Piper, John, *plate* 24; 44, 82–3, 88, 182, 190, 192, 206, 221, 227, 239, 243, 257, 319, 323, 328, 433, 435–6, 493, 496, 502–3, 507, 509, 512, 526; *Clymping*, 227; *Portland Foreshore*, 227; and *Gloriana*, 81, 87, 90–91, 103–4, 118, 124, 135–6, 145–6, 153–4, 164, 167, 177; and *The Prince of the Pagodas*, 258, 271, 332, 482–4, 486, 507; and *The Rape of Lucretia*, 44; and *The Turn of the Screw*, 2, 87, 209, 243, 249, 275, 277, 279, 284, 541–2, 544, 548
Piper, Myfanwy, *plates* 23, 24; 3, 11, 87, 88, 90, 94, 118, 124, 182, **205–6, 216–17, 219, 220–21**, 221, 227, **230, 233–4, 235–6, 236–7, 240–41, 241, 242, 242–3, 251–2, 256–7, 261**, 433, 435–6, 493, 507, 509, 526; and EOG, 30; as interviewee, 88; and *Death in Venice* (libretto), 88; and *Owen Wingrave* (libretto), 88; and *The Turn of the Screw* (libretto), 1–2, 88, 166, 174, 188–9, 199, 205–9, 216–17, 248–9 219–20, 222, 223, 230, 232, 235–8, 240–42, 248–9, 250, 251, 256, 261, 264, 274–7, 279–80, 282–3, 300–301, 541–2, 560

GENERAL INDEX

Piper, Suzanna, 109
Pirandello, Luigi, 275; *Six Characters in Search of an Author*, 275
Plant, Andrew, 48, 207, 209
Plomer, James, 147
Plomer, William, *plate 7*; 2, 11, 29, **47–8**, **50–52**, **57–8**, **60**, **63**, **74**, **83**, **92**, **95**, 99, **100**, **103**, **110–11**, 114, **118**, **126**, **128**, **135**, **142**, **165**, **173–4**, 175, 182, 187–9, 193, **217–18**, 221, **238–9**, **298**, **301–2**, **312**, 320, 328, 336, **454–5**, 456, 478, **531–2**, 534; *At Home: Memoirs*, 531–2; 'Let's crab an opera', 147; *Museum Pieces*, 83, 86; 'Old friends are best', 288, 320, 334, 336; 'The Quest for Clodd', 142; *A Shot in the Park* (Ballads), 239; Aldeburgh, visits to, 18, 21, 28, 67, 82, 130, 134, 188–9, 193, 239; health, 86, 95–6, 99–100, 103–4, 110, 299; as lecturer, 78; as poet, 121; and children's opera (Greek subject), 2, 287, 298–9; and Church Parables, 3, 29, 416, 420, 534; and *Gloriana* (libretto), 1–2, 29, 60, 62–4, 67, 74, 76, 78, 80–83, *84–5*, 90–96, 99–100, 103–4, 110–11, 117–19, 122, 126, 128–30, 134, 136, 142, 147, 151–5, 157, 160, 164–6, 173–4, 177, 188, 202–3, 217–18; and *The Tale of Mr Tod*, 2, 48, 62, 86, 298; and *Tyco the Vegan*, 2, 17, 29, 36, 42, 46–50, *51*, 52, 58, 298
Plomer family, 312–13
Plomley, Roy, 324
Plompton Rocks, Yorkshire, 113
Plowright, Joan, 535, 537–8, 538
Plummer, Christopher, 551
Poggibonsi, 525
Poil de Carotte (film), 30
Pollard, Alfred, 23, 26–7
Polonnaruwa, 423–4, 429
Ponsonby, Robert, 535, 540
Pont du Gard, France, 77
Poona, 375, 377, 382; Khala caves, 377, 382
popolo, Il (newspaper), 278
Poppen, Irmgard, 464
Portland Bill, Dorset, 221
Potter, Beatrix: *The Tale of Mr Tod*, 2, 48, 298
Potter, Julian, *plate 40*; 101–2, 192, 211, 517
Potter, Mary, *plates 28*, *40*; 69, 78, 100, 101–2, 103, 125, 175, 190, 192, 211, 287, 352–3, 356, *359–61*, **373–4**, 382, 449–50, 476, 508, 515, 517, 526, 532, 535–6, 577; lithograph, Aldeburgh Festival Calendar (1954), *191*; portraits, 101–2, 449–50; woodblock illustration of Red House, *582*, 583
Potter, Stephen, *plate 28*; 100, 101, 103, 125, 130, 131, 175, 190, 211, 449, 517, 535, 537; *The Theory and Practice of Gamesmanship*, 101
Potter, Tully, 528
Potter, Valerie, 211, 384
Potteries, 546–7
Poulenc, Francis, *plate 48*; 11, 106, 108, 190, **212**, 213, **257–8**, 281, 437–8, **528–9**, *530*, 530–31; as lecturer, 212–13; as pianist, 213, 287, 307, 433, 437–8, 528; *and see* IOC
Pound, Ezra, 49
Powell, Ray, 482–3
Prague, 457, 555
'Praise, my soul, the King of Heaven' (hymn tune), 421
Prakasa, Sri, 424, 427
Price, Robert, 515
Primrose, William, 126
Prince and the Showgirl, The (film), 469

Prince's Theatre, London, 39
Pritchard, John, 19, 140, 143, 305; and *Gloriana*, *plate 9*; 19, 94, 137–8, 140, 152, 154, 158, 228
Pritt, Alison, 467–8
Pritt, Lyn, 468
Procter, Norma, 493, 537
Prokofiev, Sergey, 4; *and see* IOC
Provence, France, 66
Pryce-Jones, Alan, 256
Puccini, Giacomo, 55
Pugin, Augustus, 421
Pulleine, Tim, 227
Punch (magazine), 334
Punch Revue (1955), 288, 320, 334–6
Purcell, Henry, 37, 46, 254, 296, 308, 319, 321, 354, 406, 527, 555; *and see* IOC *and* Index of Britten's Works (Purcell Realizations)
Purcell Singers, 73, 330–31, 341, 354, 493, 502, 571

Qantas (airline), 422
Quarterly Review (periodical), 239
Quebec, 547; *see also* individual locations
Queen Mother, *see* Elizabeth, The Queen Mother, Queen
Queen's Medal for Music, 555

RADA (Royal Academy of Dramatic Art), 543
Radio Indonesia, 392
Radio Italia: *The Turn of the Screw*, 8, 172, 272
Radio Times (periodical), 573
Radley College, Oxfordshire, 32, 34
RAF Central Band, 505
Rahman, Tunku Abdul, 534
Rainier, Priaulx, 115; *and see* IOC
Raleigh, Sir Walter, 78
Rambert, Marie, 256, 502
Ramin, Günther, 467
Rampal, Jean-Pierre, 212, 213
Randell, Sheila, 33
Rank (film company), 361
Rankl, Karl, 9, 46, 97, 113, 130, 131, 134, 457, 524
Ransome, Arthur, 30; 'Sailing in East Anglia' (AF lecture), 30; *Swallows and Amazons* (series), 30
Ratcliffe (doctor), 188
Rathbone Books, 493, 511–12; 'Wonderful World' series, 511
Rattigan, Terence, 469; *The Prince and the Showgirl*, 469
Ravel, Maurice, 213, 441, 485; *and see* IOC
Ravenna, 525–6
Rawsthorne, Alan, 106, 108
RCM, *see* Royal College of Music
RCM Magazine, 331
Read, Sir Herbert, 446
Reading, 435
rebab (Balinese string instrument), 398
Rechid, Djemac, *see* Rey, Cemal Reşit
Red Cottage, Aldeburgh, 577–8
Red Cross, *see* International Red Cross
Red House, Aldeburgh, *plates 27, 28*; 101–2, 125, 452, 494, 515, 517, 535, 537, 556, 559, 562, 574–5, 577–8, 582, 582–3
Red Studio, Aldeburgh, 515, 517, 536
Reed, Philip, 55, 193, 227, 315, 331, 454, 512, 517, 531, 578; interviews, 46
Regent's Park, London, 177, 190, 223
Reimann, Aribert, 463; *and see* IOC

Reiner, Fritz, 349, 351, 352
Reinking, Wilhelm, 44
Reiss, Beth, 246
Reiss, Delia, 246
Reiss, Richard, 246
Reiss, Stephen, 245, 246–7, 535; and Aldeburgh Festival/English Opera Group, 385, 391, 399, 465, 478, 501, 503, 507, 562, 565, 567–71, 584; as interviewee, 247
rejang (Balinese dance), 386
Renard, Jules, 30; *Poil de Carotte*, 30
Rendham, Suffolk, 239
Renishaw Hall, Derbyshire, 289, 290, 327, 329
Renton, Edward, 50
Repton (school), 448
Reşit Rey, Cemal, *see* Rey, Cemal Reşit
Rêve de Léonor, Le (ballet), 39
Rex, Sheila, 581
Rey, Cemal Reşit, 368, 369–70
Rhine, River, 345
Rhodes, Harold W., 160
Rhodes Centenary celebrations, 138
Rhyl: *Canticle II*, 17, 35
Rich, John, 322
Richard III (film), 469
Richards, Ceri, 511, 512; *Clair de lune*, 512; *Poissons d'or*, 512; *The Little Concerto*, 512; and *Noye's Fludde*, 562, 581
Richards, Frances, 512
Richardson, Norman, 532
Richardson, Tony, 537
Richter, Karl, 329, 330, 331, 466–7, 514–15, 528
Richter, Sviatoslav, 464
Riley, H. T.: *Dictionary of Latin Quotations*, 207
Rimsky-Korsakov, Nikolay: *see* 10C
Rinaldo and Armida (ballet), 308
rindik (Balinese xylophone), 387, 397
Rishton, Martin, 78
Ritchie, Margaret (Mabel), 130, 131, 132
RLPO, *see* Royal Liverpool Philharmonic Orchestra
Roberton, Matthew, 109
Roberts, R. M., 160
Robertson, Alec, 500
Robindra (Indian dancer), 375
Robinson (British Council representative, Delhi), 379
Rockliff (publishing house), 120, 200
Rogers, Iris Holland, 536, 541
Rogerson, Haydn, 68
Rogerson, Mamie, 68–70
Rogerson, Paul, *plates 3*, 55; 12, 65, **67**, 68–71, 337
Roland-Manuel, *see* Manuel, Roland
Roll, Michael, 557
Rolls-Royce (company), 522
Rome, 132, 445
Romeo and Juliet (ballet), 508
Ronchamp, 526
Rooke, Peggy, 314
Roosevelt, Eleanor, 557
Roosevelt, Franklin D., 557
Rosada, Luciano, 522–3
Roscow, Gregory, 291
Roseberry, Eric, 28
Rosenthal, Harold, 497
Ross Castle, Killarney, County Kerry, 136
Rosseter, Philip, 254, 497; *and see* 10C

Rostropovich, Mstislav, 202, 573
Roth, Ernst, 55, 135, 200, 203, 303, 350, 352, 471, 473, 518–19, 521–2; *The Business of Music: Reflections of a Music Publisher*, 55, 203
Rothenbühler, Kurt, 458–9
Rotterdam, 188; PP–BB recital, 296; *The Turn of the Screw*, 328
Roubert, Lucien, 258
Roussin, André, 172, 216; *Am Stram Gram*, 172, 216
Row, Biddy, 382, 384
Rowley, Alec, 380
Royal Academy of Belgium, 521
Royal Academy of Dramatic Art, London, *see* RADA
Royal Academy of Music, London, 517, 573
Royal Air Force, *see* RAF
Royal Albert Hall, London: *War Requiem*, 55
Royal Ballet (formerly Sadler's Wells Ballet), 489, 558; management and personnel, 57
Royal College of Music, London (RCM), 116, 267, 321, 324, 534; former students, 38, 115, 310, 331, 449
Royal Court Theatre, London, 221, 320, 325, 371–2, 501–2, 535, 537–9
Royal Festival Hall, London, *plate 48*; 162, 168, 192, 287, 307, 327, 523; organ, 198–9
Royal Flemish Society of Science, Art and Belles Lettres, *see* Académie Royale des Sciences, des Lettres, et des Beaux-Arts, Brussels
Royal Hospital School, Holbrook, 580
Royal Liverpool Philharmonic Orchestra (RLPO), 140
Royal National Theatre, London, *see* National Theatre, London
Royal Opera House, Covent Garden, London, 9, 39, 94, 123, 144–7, 148–9, 193, 287, 291, 304–5, 308, 333, 346, 369, 409, 461, 496–7, 508, 510, 531, 535, 538; *Billy Budd*, 5, 8, 17, 36, 38, 41, 44–5, 52, 57, 65; *Gloriana*, *plates 9–16*; 8, 19, 60, 63, 123–4, 129, 137–9, 144–6, 146, 147, 148–9, 150–60, 168, 172, 177, 180, 214; *Owen Wingrave*, 543; *Peter Grimes*, 45, 139, 178, 187, 189, 192, 197, 214, 439–40, 553; *The Prince of the Pagodas*, 8, 13n, 14, 264, 271, 311, 332–3, 434–5, 441, 444, 458, 467, 470, 475, 477, 480–81, 482–7, 493, 507, 518, 523, 551; administration, 45, 57, 131; BB invited to become Musical Director, 9, 46, 97–8, 131; company of, 56, 139–401
Royal Philharmonic Orchestra (RPO), 143, 348, 505, 512
Royal Philharmonic Society, 513
Royal Swedish Academy of Music, *see* Svenska Musicliska Academiens, Vangar
Rozsa, Suzanne (Susi), 309, 310–11
RPO, *see* Royal Philharmonic Orchestra
Rubbra, Edmund, 106
Rubinstein, Ida, 256
Rudney, Jeremy, 109
Russia, Soviet, *see* USSR
Rustington, Sussex, 165, 174
Ryder, Sue, 540
ryokan (Japanese inn), 414–16

Sabata, Victor de, 55, 94
Sacher, Maja, 436
Sacher, Paul, 192, 304, 305, 353, 356, 433, **436**, 437–8, 456, 513

GENERAL INDEX

Sackville-West, Edward, **296**, 296
Sackville-West, Vita, 296
Sadler's Wells Ballet (subsequently Royal Ballet), 3, 39, 56–7, 93–4, 138, 189, 256–8, 260, 308, 475, 508; and *Gloriana*, 38, 90–91, 97, 118, 122–3, 219; and *The Prince of the Pagodas*, 434, 479, 483, 486, 493
Sadler's Wells Ballet School, 123, 475
Sadler's Wells Opera, 106, 109, 141, 168, 327, 517, 543, 555; *Gloriana*, 543
Sadler's Wells Theatre, 256, 266, 272, 280–82, 287, 538
saih gender wayang (Balinese pentatonic tuning), 390
St Andrew's Cathedral, Singapore, 406, 410, 421–2
St Cecilia Orchestra, 315
St George's Chapel, Windsor, 420, 540
St George's Terrace, London, 568
St James's Church, Piccadilly, 512
St John's College, Cambridge, 447–8, 574
St Louis, Opera Theatre of, 543
St Matthew's Church, Northampton, 89, 196
St Michael's College, Tenbury Wells, 434; choir, 434
St Paul's Cathedral Choir School, 178
St Petersburg, *see* Leningrad
St Vincent's nursing home, London, 97
Saint-Denis, Michel, 538
Salisbury, 435
Salisbury, Lady, 86–7
Salisbury, Lord (5th Marquis), 83, 86–7
Salzburg, 77, 349–50, 357; Mozarteum, 43, 46, 346, 349; PP–BB recitals, 17, 18, 41–3, 46, 77, 341, 346, 349–50
Salzburg Nachrichten (newspaper), 43
Sammartini, Giuseppe: *see* IOC
Samurai (Japanese warrior class), 416
San Francisco, 44, 369
San Francisco Opera, 140
San Gimignano, 525
sanghyang dedari (Balinese dance), 390
Sanur, 342, 385–6
Sargent, John Singer, 174
Sargent, Malcolm, 267, 287, 381, 517
Sassoon, Siegfried, 174
Satake, Tōzaburō, 414, 455
Satie, Erik, 213
Sauerlander, Beata, 42, 47, 176, 193
Sauguet, Henri, 106; *and see* IOC
Saunders, Neil, 301
Saxby, Joseph, 210
Saxmundham, 92, 112
Sayers, Leslie, 515
Scala, La, Milan, *see* Milan: La Scala
Scala Theatre, London, 334, 338, 500, 507, 544
Scandinavia, 266, 298, 371, 373; *see also individual locations*
Scarborough, 377
Scarfe, Norman, 452
Schädel, Lotte, 515
Schemelli, Georg Christian: *see* IOC
Scherchen, Wulff, 557
Schidlof, Peter, 193, 310
Schindler, Alma, *see* Mahler-Werfel, Alma
Schiøtz, Aksel, 182
Schlesinger, John, 581
Schleswig-Holstein, 246
Schlieffen, Captain Ernst-Albrecht von, 267
Schlieffen, Countess Sigrid von, 266, 267

Schmidgall, Gary, 45
Schoenberg, Arnold, 260, 308, 312, 385, 524
Scholes, Percy, 321
Schott (music publisher), 304
Schubert, Franz, 23, 43, 46, 110, 126, 254, 296, 348, 406, 427, 464, 527–8, 532; *and see* IOC
Schuh, Willi, 31
Schumann, Robert, 427, 459; *and see* IOC,
Schuttenhelm, Thomas, 108, 304–5
Schütz, Heinrich, 36
Schwarz, Rudolf, 117, 202, 456, 457–8, 499, 514
Schweitzer, Sally, *plate 3*; 46, 190, 193, 269; as interviewee, 46
Schweitzer, Vivien, 544
Schweizerische Musikzeitung (newspaper; Zurich), 31
Schwetzingen: PP–BB recital, 318; *The Turn of the Screw*, 288, 318
Scott, J. W. Robertson, 58
Scott, Walter, 525
Scottish National Orchestra, 113, 131, 524, 540
Scutari, 367
Sea Change (ballet), 94
Searle, Humphrey, 18, 106, 309, 312; *and see* IOC
Searle, Muriel V., 268
Searle, Ronald, 161; *and see* Willian, Geoffrey
Secombe, Harry, 139
Second Viennese School, 448, 524
Seefehlner, Egon, 350, 351
Seefried, Irmgard, 351
Seine, River, 459
seka (Balinese music clubs), 386
Sellers, Elizabeth, 160
'Sellinger's Round', 105–6
Sellner, Gustav Rudolf, 558–9, **559–60**
Sellström, Miss A. (concert agent), 465
Semarang, 342, 388, 398; gong factory, 342, 398–9
Shadow, The (ballet), 94
Shakespeare, William, 62, 154, 538, 548; *Hamlet*, 469, 548, 551; *Henry V*, 469; *King Lear*, 44, 260, 463, 538; *Measure for Measure*, 90; *Richard II*, 138; *Richard III*, 469; *The Taming of the Shrew*, 505; *The Tempest*, 87; *Twelfth Night*, 314, 552
shakuhachi (Japanese bamboo flute), 414
shamisen (Japanese string instrument), 413
Shanghai, 401
Shankar, Ravi, 375–6
Shankar, Uday, 375
Sharp, Frederick, 261
Shaw, George Bernard, 108; *Caesar and Cleopatra*, 108
Shaw, Sidney, 349
Shawe-Taylor, Desmond, 6, 156–7, 282–4, 294, **300**, 301
Sheffield, 68; *Serenade*, 68
Shell County Guides (book series), 221
Sherborne School, Dorset, 32, 34
Sheridan, Paul, 566
shite (protagonist in Nō theatre), 417–18
shō (Japanese wind instrument), *plate 33*; 414, 415, 455–6
Shostakovich, Dmitri: *see* IOC
Shramm, Friedrich, 327
Shri (*raga*), 375
Sicily, 133
Sidney, Sir Philip, 78
Sienna, 525

Siginja, 423
'Silly Symphonies' (Disney cartoon series), 472
Simkie (Indian dancer), 375
Simon, Enid, 73–4, 181
Sinclair, Monica, *plates 15, 16*; 152
Singalese dance, 423, 426
Singapore, 341–2, 382, 385, 387–8, 393–7, 403, 406–7, 411, 420–22; Hotel Cathay, 395; Victoria Memorial Hall, 394; State of Emergency, 387; PP–BB recitals, 384, 394, 422; *see also individual locations*
Singh, Reg, 221
Singher, Martial, 198
siter (Javanese zither), 388
Sitwell, Edith, 6, 11, 86, 254, 255, **289**, 289, 290–91, 295, **316**, 318–19, **327**, 328–9, 353, 356, 433, **453**, 454, 459, **468–9**, 469, 514, 516, **582–3**, 584; *English Eccentrics*, 583–4; *Façade*, 254, 255, 289, 328; 'Still Falls the Rain', 6, 287, 289, 291, 294–5, 316, 318; *Taken Care Of*, 469; 'The Two Loves', 453–4; 'The Youth with the Red-Gold Hair', 454
Sitwell, Sir George, 319
Sitwell, Osbert, 289, 289, 290, 316, 319, 327, 329, 468, 583
Six, Les, 212
Sizewell Hall School, 207
Skalkottas, Nikos: *see* IOC
Skipton: PP–BB recital, 47
Slade, Julian, 320, 324; *and see* IOC
Slade School of Fine Art, London, 101
Slater, Montagu, 1, 509, 510; *Peter Grimes* (libretto), 509–10
Sloane Square, London, 538
Slough, 34
Smart, Christopher, 31
Smith, Kenneth, 450
Smyrna, 248
Snape Maltings Concert Hall and complex, 145, 197, 227, 247, 315, 400, 540; fire and rebuilding, 247, 400, 540; *Death in Venice*, 543; *The Golden Vanity*, 543; *Paul Bunyan*, 543; *The Turn of the Screw*, 543
Snow, Peter, 308
Snow White and the Seven Dwarfs (film), 472
Snowman, Daniel, 34, 311
Söderström, Elisabeth, 116
Solo, 403
Solti, Georg, 257
Somerville, Peggy, 246
Sorrell, Neil, 388
Southend: EOG concert, 21
Southend-on-Sea Music Club, 28
Southern California, University of, 44
Southern Rhodesia (later Zimbabwe), 137–8
Southwell Minster, 472
Southwell Minster Grammar School, 472
Southwold, 536
Soviet Union, government of, 49
Spectator (periodical), 155–6, 161, 328
Spenser, Edmund, 62
Spencer, Stanley, 197
Spender, Natasha, *see* Litvin, Natasha
Spender, Stephen, 112, 113, 516
Spies, Walter, 385, 387, 390–91
Spink, Charles, 315
Split, 360, 371
Sri Lanka (formerly Ceylon), 342, 374, 379, 400, 411, 421, 423, 426; Mount Lavinia Hotel, 422; *see also individual locations*
Stallybrass, Oliver, 525
Stamp, Terence, 227
Stanford University, 44
Stark, Freya, 535, 539
Statham, Heathcote, 314, 328
Stein, Dorothea von, 560
Stein, Erwin, *plates 7, 25*; 11, 43, 78, 96, 98, 115, 129, 178, 182, **199–200**, 202, 204, 303, **306–7**, 307–8, 310, 320, 324, 357, 370, 388, 448, 465, 467, 471, 498, 505, 549, 558, 560, **574–5**; *Orpheus in New Guises*, 199; memorial concert, 571
Stein, Marion, *see* Harewood, Marion, Countess of
Stein, Sophie, *plate 25*; 42, 47, 66, 177–8, 199–200, 307–8, 357, 388, 465, 467, 560, 574
Steinberg, Saul, 486
Steinway pianos, 349
Stephenson, Lesley, 305
Stern, Georg, 44, 54
Sternefeldt, Daniel, 245
Stevenson, Sir John, 578
Stignani, Ebe, 94
Stock, Noel, 49
Stockholm, 298, 373
PP–BB recital and concert, 296
Stoke-in-Trent, 547
Stokes, Richard, 387
Stokowski, Leopold, 427
Stone, David, 203
Stone, Janet, 220–21, 348–9, 410
Stone, Reynolds, 220–21, 227, 239, 348
Stonehenge, 381
Stopes, Marie C., 160
Strachey, Lytton, 153, 155–7; *Elizabeth & Essex, A Tragic History*, 59, 153, 156
Strachey, Marjorie, 198
Strafford House, Aldeburgh, 142
Straight, Dorothy, *see* Elmhirst, Dorothy
Straight, Whitney, 521, 522
Straight, Willard, 522
Straits Times (newspaper, Singapore), 406
Straker, Ken, 518, 520
Strasberg, Lee, 469
Stratford, Ontario, 8, 47, 494, 495, 506, 526–7, 544, 547–51; Festival Concert Hall, 527, 548, 551–2; Festival Theatre, 548–9, 549, 551; PP–BB recitals and concerts, 556; *The Turn of the Screw, plate 18*; 8, 547–51, 577, 580
Stratford (Ontario) Shakespeare Festival, 527, 548–9, 551, 553, 570
Stratford-upon-Avon, 538
Strauss II, Johann: *see* IOC
Strauss, Richard, 55, 198, 352, 524, 573; *and see* IOC
Stravinsky, Igor, 4, 126, 352, 441, 485, 555; *and see* IOC
Stray, Christopher, 207, 209
Strode, Rosamund, 13n, 125, 145, 220, 330, 331, 354, 383
Stuart, Sir Campbell, 519, 520
Stucley, Sir Hugh, 166
Stuttgart, 94, 341, 343, 345, 474; PP–BB recital, 349, 474
Stuttgart Chamber Orchestra, 445
Suez Canal, 474, 515
Suez crisis (1956), 474, 515, 539
Sukarno, Achmed, 403, 406

GENERAL INDEX

suling (Javanese wind instrument), 388, 398
Sullivan, Arthur, 94, 427; *and see* IOC
Sumatra, 341, 388, 403
Sumidagawa, see Motomasa, Jūrō
Sunday Times, The (newspaper), 3n, 66, 121, 157, 277, 280–81, 301, 484, 486
Surabaya, 400–401, 403; PP–BB recital, 401
Surakarta, 400–401
Sussex, 140
Sussex, University of, 116, 539
Sussex Gardens, Bayswater, 440
Susskind, Walter, 137, 141
Sutcliffe, Tom, 226
Sutherland, Joan, 216, 218–19, 333, 459, 497
Svenska Musicaliska Academiens, 521, 523
Swann, Donald, 11, 320, 320; *see also* Flanders, Michael
Swarowsky, Hans, 522–3, 524
Sweden: PP–BB recitals, 287, 296
Sweeting, Elizabeth, 29, 41, 43, 73, 88, 124–5, 179, 181, 246, 391
Switzerland, 14, 112–14, 245, 319, 343, 346, 352–3, 360, 427, 457, 466, 469–70; BB concert, 304; PP and/or BB concerts and recitals, 287, 305, 313, 532; *see also individual locations*
Sydney Symphony Orchestra, 555
Sylvia (ballet), 483
Symphony of the Air, 445, 447

Tabuh Telu (Balinese melody), 392
Tagore, Rabindranath, 383
t'ai chi ch'uan, 401
Tailleferre, Germaine, 106, 213; *and see* IOC
Taiwan, 404
Tajuddin, Tazul, 534
Talich, Václav, 555
Tamililingan (gamelan piece), 389, 392
Tandawa Nrittya (dance), 375
T'ang dynasty, 455
Tappolet, Claude, 441
Tarasp, Schloss, Switzerland, 266–7, 360, 434, 466, 470, 496
Tate, Nahum, 560; *Dido and Aeneas* (libretto), 560
Tate Gallery, London, 257, 333
Tausky, Vilem, 137, 141, 254–6, 328; *Vilem Tausky Tells His Story*, 141
Taw and Torridge Festival, 19, 150, 163, 165, 172, 175, 254, 256, 261, 269, 325, 337, 435, 470
Tchaikovsky, Piotr Ilyich, 4, 28, 261, 485, 488, 519; *and see* IOC
tea ceremony (Japan), 413–14
Telemann, Georg Phillipp, 126, 459; *and see* IOC
Tempo (periodical), 214, 216, 265, 389, 505
Tenganan, *plate 31*
Teyte, Maggie, 44
Thailand, 420; *see also individual locations*
Thatcher, Margaret, 175
Thaxted, Essex, 211
Theatre Royal Drury Lane, London, 409
Theberton Hall, Suffolk, 452
Thirkell, Angela, 553, 554–5
Thomas, Marjorie, 514, 517
Thomas, Nancy, 113
Thomson, Virgil, 278–80, 301; *see also* IOC
Thorndike, Sybil, 58
Thorpe, Marion, *see* Harewood, Marion
Thorpeness, 353

Thorpeness: Meare, 375, 546
Thorvaldsen, Bertel, 548, 551; *Eros and Psyche*, 548, 551
Tibetan dance, 397
Till, Barry, **771**, 771
Tillett, Emmie, 569, 571
Time and Talents Club, 379
Times, The (newspaper), 6, 37, 45, 56, 116, 139, 141, 152, 159, 186, 202, 216, 218, 220, 227, 247, 272, 274, 291, 294, 305, 308, 310–11, 320, 323, 334, 352, 366, 421, 446–7, 458, 482, 508, 511, 520, 537–8, 540, 543, 561; letters to the editor, 10, 58, 159–60, **445–6**
Tinker, Christopher, 13n
Tippett, Michael, 18, 106, 108, 176, **303–4**, 305, 310, 449, 470; *and see* IOC
Tito, Josip Broz, 10, 353, **359**
Todas, 375
Todd, Philip, 330, 331–2
Tōgaku (subgenre of traditional Japanese court music), 455–6
Tokyo, *plates 33, 34, 37, 38*; 3, 337, 404, 407–9, 411, 414, 420, 445; Haneda airport, 407, 411, 455; Hotel Imperial, 411; Kunaicho-Gakubu (Imperial Household Agency), 342, 414, 455–6; Suidōbashi Nō Theatre, 417; PP–BB concerts and recitals, 408, 411
Tokyo Madrigal Singers, *plate 36*; 342, 411, 413–14
Tokyo Polyphonic Orchestra, 411
Tolstoy, Leo: *Anna Karenina*, 2n, 543
Tommasini, Anthony, 45
Tooley, John, 3n, 457, 487–9
Torcello, 526
Toronto, 314, 526, 547, 553–4, 562; Crest Theatre, 314, 506, 508, 567; *Let's Make an Opera*, 567
Toscanini, Arturo, 447
Totnes, 383
Townsman (periodical), 49
Toynbee Hall, London, 141, 172, 216
Tranchell, Peter, 121
Traynor, Leo, 414
Treasury, 60, 539
Trianti, Alexandra, 248
Trieste, 369
Trinity College, Cambridge, 411, 540
Trinity College, Dublin, 136
trois coups, les, 262, 264
trompong (Balinese instrument), 398
Truro Cathedral, Cornwall, 178
Tuckwell, Barry, 454, 502, 537
Tunnard, Viola, 150, 529
Tureck, Rosalind, 330, 332
Turkey, 341, 345, 347, 361, 366–8, 370; *see also individual locations*
Turkish music, 368
Turner, Walter, 290
Tuscany, 525
Tuxon (Danish conductor), 181
TV Times (periodical), 566
Tynan, Kathleen, 10n
Tynan, Kenneth, 10n

Ubud, *plate 30*; 342, 385–7, 389–91, 393, 396, 406
Udine, 526
Umetani Group (Kanze School), 417
Umewaka, Takehisa, 417
United Nations, 31, 246

United States of America, *see* America, United States of
United Steamship Company, Copenhagen, 78
Universal Edition, Vienna, 204
University College Hospital, London, 172, 230
Uppingham School, Rutland, 34
Uppman, Theodor (Ted), 18, 44–5; and *Billy Budd*, 18, 41, 53, 56, 544; and *Death in Venice*, 45; and *Gloriana*, 450
US Embassy, London, 535, 540
USSR, 473–4

Vallance, Tom, 227
Valois, Ninette de, 14, 123, **391**, 475, 508; and *Gloriana*, 91, 122; and *The Prince of the Pagodas*, 3, 333, 391, 435, 438, 477, 479, 487, 524
Van der Post, Ingaret, 174–5, 532
Van der Post, Sir Laurens, 174, 175, 532, 534; 'Stone Age Dance and Music' (AF lecture), 534
Vancouver, 271, 554
Variations on a Theme of Purcell (ballet), 39, 308
Vaudeville Theatre, London, 324
Vaughan, David, 39, 308
Vaughan Williams, Ralph, 115, 125, 134, 160, 447, 520; *and see* IOC
Venice, 87, 269, 271–2, 284, 366, 524–6; St Mark's Square, 226; Teatro La Fenice, 8, 172, 264, 272, 273, 274, 276, 280, 296, 543; *The Turn of the Screw*, plates 17, 19–25; 137, 172, 178, 218, 226, 251, 264, 266, 272, 273, 280, 282, 527, 543
Venice Biennale Festival, 62, 139, 178, 252, 272, 277
Venice International Festival of Contemporary Music, 139, 272, 274
Verdi, Giuseppe, 1, 28, 42, 45–6, 55, 261; *and see* IOC
Verlaine, Paul: 'Colloque sentimental', 283
Vezelay, 77
Vickers, Jon, 440
Vic-Wells Ballet, 256
Victoria, Queen, 427
Victoria and Albert Museum, London: *Canticle II*, 24, 35; PP recital, 125; PP–BB recital, 40
Vienna, 115, 310, 312, 346, 350–51, 367, 450, 522, 524; British Embassy, 346; Konzerthaus, 43, 350–51; Mozartsaal, 524; Palais Pallavicini, 43; Redoutensaal, 350; Staatsoper, 7, 140, 346, 351, 444, 463, 524, 575; PP–BB recitals/concerts, 7, 17, 41, 43, 341, 346, 349–50, 493, 524, 578
Vienna Boys' Choir, 543
Vignoles, Roger, 116, 454
Villa-Lobos, Heitor, 555
Virgin Classics (recording company), 475, 497
Vishnevskaya, Galina, 573
Voice is a Person, A (BBC radio documentary), 22
Vroons, Frans, 327
Vyvyan, Jennifer, plates 17, 19, 21–23; 113, 137, 137–8, 152, 226, 248, 272, 274, 277, 284, 523, 529, 544

Wachstein, Beata, *see* Sauerlander, Beata
Wachstein, Margaret Anne (Muki), 47, 190, 557
Wachstein, Max, 47, 193
Wachstein, Monica Elizabeth Marie, 47
Wade, Philip, 381
Wagner, Richard, 56, 86; *and see* IOC
waki (deuteragonist in Nō theatre), 417
waki-tsure (second or third performer in Nō theatre), 417
Wales (film), 472

Wales, University of, 523
Waley, Arthur, 494, 541, 575
Walker, Patrick, 211, 384
Wallace, Helen, 203, 303, 352, 519
Walt Disney British Films, 472
Walter, Bruno, 22, 44, 193, 351
Walthamstow Assembly Hall, 496
Walthamstow Town Hall, 440
Walton, Susana, 290–91
Walton, William, 18, 66, 98, 106, 107, 144–5, 291, 449, 469–70, 506, 532; *and see* IOC
Ward, David, 498
Wardle, Irving, 537–8
Warlock, Peter, 125, 134; *and see* IOC
Warner, Sylvia Townsend, 228
Warren, C. Henry, 30
Warrington, 546
Warsaw, 125, 540
Warsaw Pact, 473
Warwick, University of, 523
Warwickshire, 104
Watch with Mother (BBC Television series), 30
Waterhouse, John, 30, 31, 36
Watkins, Richard, 454
Watson, Donald, 537
Watts, Helen, 116, 497
Waugh, Evelyn, 328
wayang kulit (Balinese shadow play), 390
WDR Köln (radio station), 546
Weaver, William, 2n
Webern, Anton, 312, 524
Webster, Alan, 421
Webster, David, plate 52; 9, 11, **56**, 56–7, **93**, **97**, **122**, 136–7, 145–6, **271**, **456**, 535; and *Billy Budd*, 45, 56; and *Gloriana*, 60, 63, 87, 90–91, 93, 97, 122–4, 138, 142, 144–6, 214; and *Peter Grimes*, 438, 440; and *The Prince of the Pagodas*, 271, 333, 438, 441, 444, 458, 465, 467, 470, **478–9**; and Royal Opera House, Covent Garden, 98, 144–5, 487
Webster, Martyn, 372, 570
Weed, Don, 305
Weelkes, Thomas, 354; *and see* IOC
Weil, Terence, 125–6
Weill, Kurt, 198
Weingartner, Felix, 524, 573
Weldon, Fay, 221
Welford, Beth (BB's sister), 42, 46, 100, 175–6, 180–82, 190, 242–3, 247, 326, 353, 374, 581
Welford, Christopher (Kit), 46
Welford, Elizabeth Ellen Rosemary (Roguey), plate 3; 46, 190, 193, 269
Welford, Sarah Charlotte, *see* Schweitzer, Sally
Welford, (Thomas) Sebastian, plate 3; 46, 109, 236, 269
Wellesz, Egon: *see* IOC
Wellingborough (school), 243
Welsh National Opera (WNO), 141, 555; *Gloriana*, 168; *The Turn of the Screw*, 223, 226
Welt, Die (newspaper), 155
Wehrmacht, 201
Wesker, Arnold, 538
West (as political and cultural entity), 367
West, Christopher, 305, 333
Westdeutscher Konzert (agency), 466
Westminster Abbey, London, 19, 22, 23
Westminster Cathedral, London, 72, 219–20
Westminster Cathedral Choir, 72, 220

GENERAL INDEX

Weymar (Director, Ansbach Bachwoche), 467
Whinyates, Seymour, 132, 134, 135, 446
White, Eric Walter, 7–8, 48, **82**, 82, 83, 163, **163**, 172, **194–5**, 216, **244**, **299–300**, 349; *Benjamin Britten: His Life and Operas*, 83; *Benjamin Britten: A Sketch of His Life and Works*, 82–3, 172, 194–7, 244, 349; *Men in the Moon*, 48; *A Tarot Deal and other poems*, 195; and Arts Council, 82, 195
Whitney, William Collins, 383
Whitred, Gladys, 21, 30, 163
Whittall, Arnold, 448
Whitton, Kenneth S., 464
Whitty, Dame May, 196
Who's Who, 86
Wiebe, Heather, 11n, 159
Wiesbaden, 87; Hessisches Staatstheater, 132; Staatsoper, 53; *Albert Herring*, 18, 132, 142; *Billy Budd*, 17, 41, 44, 52–6, 118
Wigmore Hall, London, 109, 126–7, *127*, 193, 212, 272, 281, 287, 291, 294, 433, 450, 454, 517
Wilbye, John, *see* 10C
Willan, Geoffrey (with Ronald Searle): *Whizz for Atoms*, 161
Willett, Noreen, 330
Williams, Grace, 125, 134; *and see* 10C
Williams, Stephen, 155
Williamson, Malcolm, 430, 502; *and see* 10C,
Wimbledon Theatre: *Let's Make an Opera*, 48, 50
Winchester (school), 221
Windsbach, 467
Windsor, 377
Wirth, Dr Joseph, 31
Witte, Erich, 497
Wittelsbach family, 202
WNO, *see* Welsh National Opera
Wöldike, Mogens, 73, 181
Wolf, Hugo, 532; *and see* 10C
Wolfsgarten, Schloss, 17, 54, 199–201, 205, 267, 329, 342, 391, 400, 411, 413, 428, 436, 465, 474, 514–15, 524, 534, 536, 539, 558, 574
Women's Journal (periodical), 461
Wood, Anne, 21, 29–30, 163, 197, 502, 536
Woodbridge, Suffolk, 46, 195, 247
Woodgate, Leslie, 72
Woods, Reverend Robin, 410, 420–21
Woodward, Robert, 221
Woolverstone Hall (school), 580–81

Worcester, 554
Worcester College, Oxford, 523
Worth, Irene, 328
Worth, Martin, 565
Wright, Basil, 196
Wright, Frank Lloyd, 411
Wupperthal, 348–9, 473; Stadthalle, 345, 349; PP–BB recitals, 345, 348–9, 474
Wurmser, Leo, 504
Württemberg State Theatres, 474
Wyatt, Woodrow, 160
Wyck, Wilfred Van, 71
Wyton, Andrew, 439

Yaman (raga), 375
Yates, Michael, 544
Yeats, W. B. (William Butler): 'The Second Coming', 209, 274, 277
York, 255–6; Theatre Royal, 255; *The Rape of Lucretia*, 254
York Festival, 438
York Minster, 336–7
Yorkshire, 18
Yorkshire Post (newspaper), 186, 575
Young, Michael, 383–4
Yugoslavia (former), 10, 329, 341, 347, 350, 352–3, 356–60, 368, 370, 425; *see also individual locations*

Zagreb, 341, 353, 356–7, 360, 517; Hotel Palace, 357; *Peter Grimes*, 353, 357, 360; PP–BB recital, 358
Zander, Benjamin, 32–3, 34
Zander, Gretl, **32**, 32, 33–6
Zander, Walter, 32, 33–4; *Is This The Way?*, 34
Zanotelli, Hans, 560
Zermatt, 102, 287, 336, 373–4
Zimbabwe, *see* Southern Rhodesia
Zionism, 34
Zoete, Beryl de, 387, 390–91
Zorian, Olive, 248, 309, 310, 494, **572**, 573
Zorian String Quartet, 310, 572–3
Zosel, Josef, 44
Zurich, 44, 132, 296, 304, 341, 360; PP–BB concert, 305, 343, 346, 349
Zurich: Tonhalle, 305
Zwemmer (publishing house), 246